THE SIEG

JONATHAN KEATES

PIMLICO

Published by Pimlico 2006

2 4 6 8 10 9 7 5 3 1

First published in Great Britain in 2005 by
Chatto & Windus

Pimlico edition 2006

Pimlico
Random House, 20 Vauxhall Bridge Road,
London SW1V 2SA

Random House Australia (Pty) Limited
20 Alfred Street, Milsons Point, Sydney,
New South Wales 2061, Australia

Random House New Zealand Limited
18 Poland Road, Glenfield,
Auckland 10, New Zealand

Random House South Africa (Pty) Limited
Isle of Houghton, Corner of Boundary Road & Carse O'Gowrie,
Houghton 2198, South Africa

Random House UK Limited Reg. No. 954009

A CIP catalogue record for this book is available from the British Library

ISBN 9780712673693 (from Jan 2007)
ISBN 0712673695

Papers used by Random House UK Ltd are natural, recyclable products
made from wood grown in sustainable forests. The manufacturing processes
conform to the environmental regulations of the country of origin

Printed and bound in Great Britain by Bookmarque Ltd, Croydon, Surrey

CONTENTS

LIST OF ILLUSTRATIONS

Plate section I

Plate section II

LIST OF MAPS

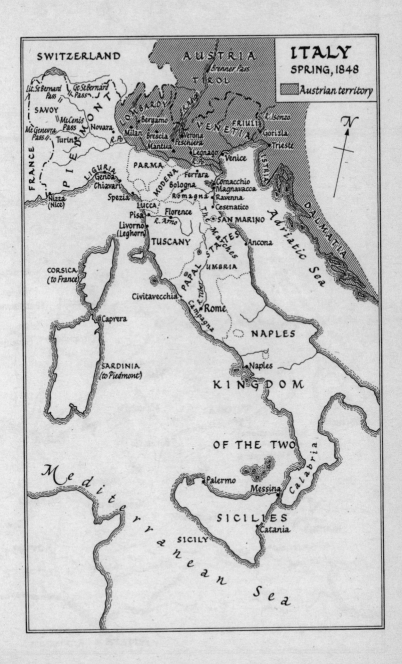

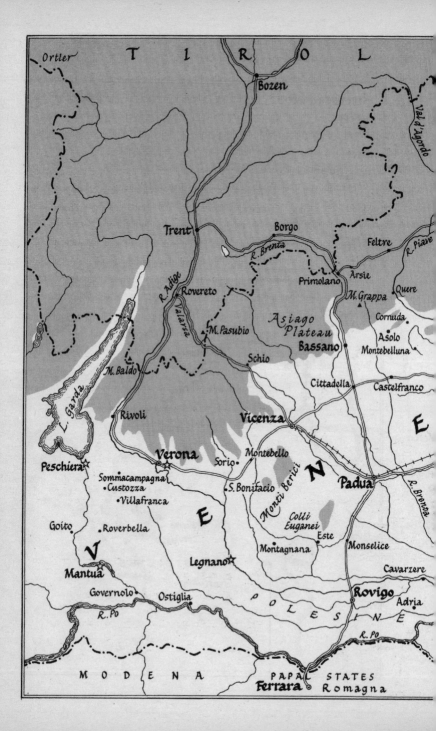

Cortina

Carnia

R. Tagliamento

Osoppo

Belluno

Val Zaldo

Cadore

Julian

R. Isonzo

M. Nero

Caporetto

Cividale

Udine

Plava

Vittorio
Veneto

Pordenone

F R I U L I

Codroipo

Gorizia

Sacile

R. Tagliamento

Palmanova

Visco

R. Isonzo

Carso

Conegliano

R. Livenza

R. Tagliamento

Aquileia

Treviso

R. Piave

R. Sile

Trieste

FT MARGHERA

Mestre

Burano

Porto di Lido

I S T R I A

Fusina

Venice

Malamocco

Porto di Malamocco

A D R I A T I C

Pellestrina

Porto di Chioggia

S E A

Laguna

Conche

Chioggia

FORT BRONDOLO

Bocche del Po

VENETIA 1848

Land over 200 metres (656 feet)

+++++ Railway   ═══ Main roads

⊙**Padua** Provincial capitals   ☆ Forts

| 0 | 10 | 20 | 30 miles |

| 0 | 10 | 20 | 30 | 40 | 50 km |

N

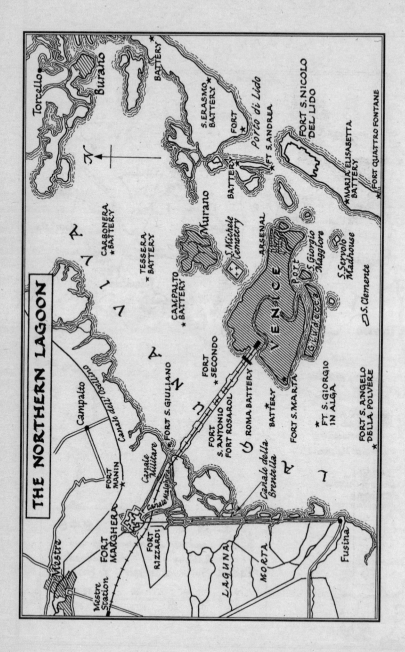

THE NORTHERN LAGOON

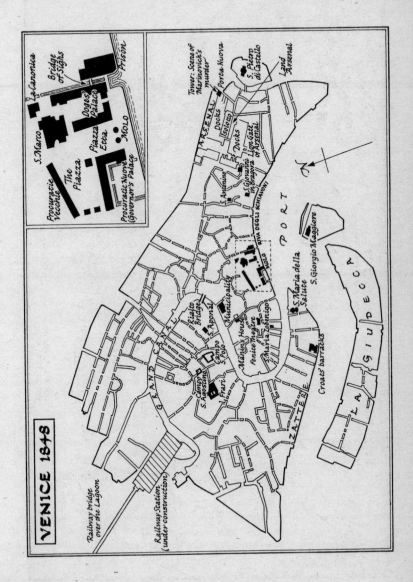

VENICE 1848

Inset:
S. Marco
La Canonica
Bridge of Sighs
Procuratie Vecchie
The Piazza
Doge's Palace
Piazza Etta
Procuratie Nuove (Governor's Palace)
MOLO
Prison

Main map:
Railway bridge over the Lagoon
Railway Station (under construction)
GRAND CANAL
Campo S. Agostino
I Frari
Campo S. Polo
Rialto Bridge
S. Aponal
Manin's House
Fenice Theatre
S. Maria Zobenigo
Municipality
MOLO
RIVA DEGLI SCHIAVONI
S. Giovanni in Bragora
Lion Gate of Arsenal
Docks
S. Antonino
Soloto
ARSENAL
Docks
Tower: Scene of Marinovich's murder
Porta Nuova
S. Pietro di Castello
Land Arsenal
PORT
S. Maria della Salute
Croats' barracks
ZATTERE
S. Giorgio Maggiore
LA GIUDECCA

To Venice, for all she has given me

HISTORICAL NOTE

Until its invasion in 1796 by a French army under Napoleon Bonaparte, Italy consisted of a number of independent states. In 1805 Napoleon as Emperor proclaimed himself King of Italy, with his stepson Eugène de Beauharnais ruling as Viceroy. After his defeat at Waterloo in 1815, the Congress of Vienna, staged by the victorious alliance led by Britain, Austria and Russia, restored the rulers of eight out of the ten Italian states occupied by the French. As for the other two, the territory of the Genoese republic was awarded to the King of Piedmont, while Venice was returned to Austria, to which it had originally been presented by Napoleon in 1797. With each restoration the status quo ante was emphatically reasserted, and Austria, to whose imperial family most of the sovereigns were related by marriage, became the dominant power in Italy.

For many Italians, however, their experience of French imperial control had brought a taste of progressive administration and meritocratic career opportunities, the memory of which was hard to shake off. This, together with a sense of Italy's former glory and prosperity during the Middle Ages and the Renaissance, helped to encourage ideas of what it might become as a unified nation. The newly reinstated sovereigns found their despotic governments challenged both by those in search of greater political freedom and by others for whom their very prerogatives as independent rulers were called into question. For an increasing number of Italians during the 1820s and 1830s, Italy was not merely a geographical expression, as Austria's chancellor Clemens von Metternich persistently declared it to be. It was *la patria*, the motherland, an ideal with the potential for becoming a reality. Interestingly, the word 'Risorgimento' applied by historians to the political activism that such dreams inspired means 'resurgence'. It suggests that the medieval and Renaissance visions of an Italy free of alien domination and in charge of her own destiny were alive once more and bright with promise.

They certainly helped to inspire the revolutions taking place in various parts of Italy during 1820–21 and 1831, but the Risorgimento was at no stage a coherent movement equipped with a programme and a manifesto. Those involved in the uprisings, or sympathetic to their aims, reflected every shade of political opinion from liberal Catholic monarchists to anti-clerical republicans and socialists. When in 1848 the whole of Italy exploded in revolt, the impetus in many cases was checked or dissipated by the failure of the revolutionaries to make a common cause or to fulfil their grandiloquent patriotic pledges of mutual support. Also lacking, alas, was the military expertise needed to combat the armies Austria sent to deal with the emergency. This enduring sense of political confusion characterised the whole episode to the extent that any kind of muddle or mess thereafter could be described as 'un vero quarantotto', 'a right forty-eight'.

It is in this historical context that the events described in this book took place.

~

WHO DIES FOR
THE MOTHERLAND?

IN THE *SESTIERE* OF CASTELLO, easternmost of Venice's seven districts, along the Riva degli Schiavoni, past the grand hotels, Danieli, Savoia Iolanda, Londra Palace, the immense equestrian statue of King Victor Emmanuel II, the vaporetto stop and the ferry station for the Lido, past the sellers of necklaces, caricatures, clockwork toys, souvenir hats, plastic gondolas and bad paintings, the ice-cream parlours with their vats of sludgy granita and flavour selections – Mirtillo, Amaretto, Stracciatella, Pistacchio, Limone, Yogurt, Menta – beyond the church of the Pieta, its ceiling frescoed by Tiepolo and its classical façade completed as late as 1906, a little lane named, like several others of its kind, Calle del Dose, leads you up into the Campo San Giovanni in Bragora.

Nobody knows what a *bragora* is or was. Perhaps the name derives from the dialect word *bragola*, meaning a market square, or the term *bragolare*, used to refer to the fishing business. The Gothic church of San Giovanni itself is among Venice's oldest, with three aisles and a wood-beamed ceiling. Cima da Conegliano painted the lyrical 'Baptism Of Christ' above the high altar, and in the font the composer Antonio Vivaldi was baptised 'being supposed close to death' in 1678.

Outside in the mournful campo, apart from an ironmonger's shop and a big palazzo divided into holiday rental flats, there are a few unpromising trees, a *vera da pozzo* or decorated well-head, often spray-painted with graffiti, and a rusting bench on which housewives en route to the shops in Salizzada San Antonin pause to let their children kick a football about over the pale flagstones. Even the robust, confident voices of these little Venetians cannot purge the place of its sadness, the legacy, as it might seem, of a story connected with the small grey house standing at its north-west corner. For, as a marble plaque between the shuttered, iron-balconied windows tells us, this was once the home of Attilio and Emilio Bandiera, among the bravest, most famous and most foolish martyrs in the cause of Italian political liberty.

Nine years divided the brothers from one another in age. They were the sons of Baron Francesco Bandiera, a vice-admiral in the Austrian imperial navy, commanding the Levant squadron in the war conducted on behalf of the Turkish sultan in 1840 against the rebel Pasha of Egypt Mehmet Ali. Admiral Bandiera was a *schwarzgelber*, the name given in Austria to subjects unquestioningly faithful to the imperial black-and-yellow (*schwarz/gelb*) flag. 'Having grown grey under the discipline of arms,' Attilio once described his father, 'he respects nothing but an oath of loyalty sworn once and once only. He strives to make himself useful to his motherland by fulfilling all the duties appropriate to his profession.' Bandiera's sons, despite following him into the navy, learned early enough to question these ideals.

In a city which had started increasingly to live on its memories of vanished glory, Venice's great maritime traditions were particularly cherished among pupils and staff at the Imperial Naval Academy (now the Collegio Navale Morosini) on the island of Sant'Elena. Among its teachers was the historian and savant Emilio Tipaldo, a Greek from the Ionian Islands, then a British crown dependency but formerly part of the Venetian empire. Like many of his fellow islanders, Tipaldo was committed both to the cause of Greek independence and to the liberation of Italy, and his lessons were full of reminders as to the valiant feats of Italians on sea and land. 'In fiery words,' recalled one of his pupils, 'he recounted to us the greatness of Rome, the glories of the motherland during the middle ages, the chronicles of the Venetian Republic, and of heroic actions by Italians in Spain during the memorable campaigns of Napoleon Bonaparte.'

The effect of Tipaldo's teaching on Emilio Bandiera was predictably inspiring, clinched as it was by reading forbidden texts by Italian patriotic poets and novelists. Attilio Bandiera, having passed through the school with honour, was now a lieutenant in the Austrian fleet, staffed almost entirely by Italian-speaking officers from ports along either side of the Adriatic. Among the various crews, a nostalgia for the days when Venice was unchallenged ruler of the Adriatic bred a corresponding hatred of the alien power they now served. 'Italy was our mother,' wrote a former officer, 'and a spurt of rage, of generous indignation, shook us whenever we recalled that a people which had given civilisation to the world now groaned in chains.'

Serving alongside their father in the war against Mehmet Ali, his two sons had shown their own courage and enterprise, but experience of battle convinced them that their manhood could be put to better use in liberating Italy than in following the Austrian flag. While the allied fleets lay at anchor off Beirut, the young men began developing plans for a secret society, devoted to some drastic project which should spark off revolutions throughout the various Italian states. Like others of its kind in Italy during this period, their society had its own articles of affiliation, rules of conduct and initiation ritual. Its name was 'L'Esperia', and its members, dedicated to physical fitness, moral purity and mental agility, were expected to contribute 5 per cent of their annual income to a central fund. Each initiate was pledged 'to the service of human progress' and to 'every principle and obligation L'Esperia prescribes for the achievement of Italy's wished-for regeneration'. Self-sacrifice was central to this commitment. 'If, from the dawning of the great day of liberty,' the oath continued with sombre prolixity, 'I should ever refuse, at any moment, to shed my blood for my beloved country, may I even then, having stooped so low, become useful, however indirectly, to this sacred cause, by falling beneath the stroke of the hand that is dearest to me, thereby providing a terrible example of the revenge that hand may provoke.' The initiate was then kissed by the head of the society as a final token of acceptance.

For two years the Bandiera brothers worked hard to build up membership of L'Esperia and develop contacts with the growing number of Italian exile cells establishing themselves throughout Europe. Despite the difference in age, Attilio and Emilio were mutually devoted and neither was prepared to make plans which should not involve the other. Their closest associate was Domenico Moro, lieutenant on the corvette *Leipzig*, a fellow Venetian noted for his extraordinary handsomeness and nobility of bearing. He provided the essential link for L'Esperia with the man all Europe regarded as the most committed, energetic and visionary of all the Italian revolutionaries.

The Christlike figure of Giuseppe Mazzini inspired awe and love in almost everyone who met him. An exile living in London since 1836, he had built up a constituency of British admirers including Charles Dickens, Robert Browning, Alfred Tennyson and the Whig political leader Lord John Russell. His integrity and earnestness, calculated to appeal to the Victorians, were tempered with genuine charm and affability. 'Whatever I may think of his practical insight and skill in worldly affairs,' remarked Thomas Carlyle, hardly noted for a liberal outlook, 'I can with great freedom testify to all men that he, if ever I have seen one such, is a man of genius and virtue, a man of sterling veracity, humanity and nobleness of mind.'

Mazzini's judgement of the likely outcome of successive revolutionary enterprises had not always been sound, especially as regarded the political or emotional cost to the families of those involved. When Domenico Moro visited him in London in 1842, he seems to have offered only the vaguest support for the society's newest scheme for a patriotic mutiny within the Austrian fleet. In connection with this, the Bandieras also contacted Italian exiles in Malta, led by the Modenese revolutionary Nicola Fabrizi, a wiser head than Mazzini's when it came to practical issues. Though Fabrizi assessed the risks as being negotiable, however likely, the uprising, scheduled for 31 July 1844, never got beyond the planning stage. The Austrian authorities, increasingly alert to the presence of subversion, had planted an informer within L'Esperia, but the three ringleaders, Attilio and Emilio Bandiera and Domenico Moro, were apprised of their danger just in time. The tip-off seems to have come from the captains of the very ships they meant to seize, all of whom, despite fundamental loyalty to the crown, had patriotic leanings, as well as a comradely desire to save Admiral Bandiera from being compromised through his sons' treachery. Circumstances extracted Emilio from danger when he was recalled to Venice on official business before news of the conspiracy had time to spread. Attilio meanwhile managed to jump ship at Smyrna, fleeing to Malta with the help of a forged passport obtained from Spanish refugees.

While the Austrian government now ordered a close watch to be set on the Bandieras in their comings and goings across the Mediterranean, they somehow managed to maintain contact with Giuseppe Mazzini. Their political views were nevertheless beginning to diverge significantly from his consistently espoused republicanism, as they edged closer to ideas of united Italy under a constitutional monarch. Doubtless this would have been advanced in their favour at the tribunal at which they were now ordered to present themselves within ninety days. Their response was appropriately scornful. 'Our choice is between betraying the motherland and humanity, or else turning our backs on a foreign oppressor. The laws, to which it is presumed we are still subject, are decrees written in blood, which like everyone else touched with justice and humanity we utterly abhor.' Emilio Bandiera was in any case courting danger by his return to Venice. He had been summoned there as adjutant to his commanding officer, Admiral Amilcare Paolucci delle Roncole. Before leaving for his country villa at the beginning of April, Paolucci, still not suspecting Emilio's involvement in the plot, left orders that he was to open and deal with all official correspondence. Among the letters the young adjutant examined was one from the government in Vienna ordering his immediate arrest.

Emilio reckoned he had two days, from opening the warrant on 4 April 1844, to make good his escape. Putting a story about that he had been invited to a ball in Trieste, he hurried to the house at San Giovanni in Bragora to take leave of the family. Evidently they were unaware of the conspiracy, and his agitated manner mystified Attilio's wife Maria Graziani. 'When he shook my hand, his own seemed positively frozen. His leavetaking was like a last farewell. I asked him what the matter was and observed that it seemed as if he were departing for forty-eight days rather than forty-eight hours. He made no answer, and to similar remarks merely rejoined, "It's nothing, nothing at all."' Having reached Trieste the following day, Emilio furnished himself with false papers and a heavy disguise before taking the first ship to Corfu.

Since 1815 the Ionian Islands had been a British crown protectorate, administered by a governor with a legislative council partly formed from the local aristocracy. Romantic philhellenism had made the archipelago a halfway house for volunteers from all over Europe en route to join the struggle for Greek independence from the Ottoman empire. Once this had been achieved, the British, to the chagrin of Austria and her Italian satellite states, continued to allow the islands to be used as a haven for political refugees. Spying, information-gathering and the interception of letters might be practised by the consular staff of the various nations represented in Corfu and the other ports, but the government itself, while maintaining a watch on all exiles and dissidents, declined to turn most of them away.

Emilio Bandiera arrived in Corfu on 6 April, and was soon joined by his brother Attilio and their friend Domenico Moro, who, like him, had fled to Malta after the failure of the naval mutiny scheme. The three now began discussing a more ambitious project, initially for landing men and weapons on the desolate coast of the Maremma, the south-western region of the Grand Duchy of Tuscany. Soon enough, however, their thoughts turned to the even more rugged and lawless terrain of Calabria, southern-most mainland province of the Kingdom of Naples (also known at this period as the Kingdom of the Two Sicilies). Here the political situation had remained volatile after the French, occupying the area during the Napoleonic war, abolished feudalism. Local barons were succeeded by a new class of bourgeois landowner, replacing small peasant holdings with extensive sheep and cattle ranches. Estates were managed by bullying and corrupt agents, agriculture declined amid ignorance and inertia, brigands grew more shameless, while law-abiding inhabitants became sullenly resigned to bad government stifling local enterprise. A few of them had begun to cherish hopes and ambitions for better times, not just in the Kingdom of Naples, but throughout Italy, but their attempts at revolution were mostly half-hearted. The only serious insurrection, staged in the city of Cosenza in March, 1844, had been ruthlessly suppressed and six of its ringleaders shot.

The Bandiera brothers ought to have taken warning from the fact that almost no one among Cosenza's ordinary citizens had chosen to join the original parade through the streets, intended to spark off a general uprising. Instead they chose to see the episode as proof that a popular revolt was simply waiting for enterprising spirits to light the touchpaper. Others were less certain. Writing from Malta, Nicola Fabrizi urged caution, but a more powerful advocate was Baroness Anna Bandiera, mother of the two fugitives, shaken as she was by her sons' treachery to the black-and-yellow flag. Like her husband, she came from a naval family, Bosnian Croats named Marsich who had shown equal loyalty to the Venetian Republic and the Austrian Emperor. A certain grimness of demeanour made her a difficult wife for the admiral to live with, and her sons were evidently more afraid of her than of their father. Life was in any case a good deal tougher for the Baroness and her family at San Giovanni in Bragora since the arrest warrants for Attilio and Emilio had been issued. Her daughter-in-law Maria, though seriously ill after a miscarriage, had been interrogated by persistent Austrian police, who also questioned her doctors. As a further harassment, the Emperor's uncle Archduke Rainer, Viceroy of the province of Lombardy Venetia, sent a personal message to Baroness Bandiera offering a pardon for Emilio if he were prepared to give himself up. Attilio, seen as a bad influence on his younger brother, was to be treated more severely at first, but could expect clemency in due course. Responding to emotional blackmail, the anguished mother decided to leave for Corfu, in hopes of making her sons understand what suffering their idealism had brought upon the family.

Once on the island, she failed for several days to contact them, until Emilio sent a message agreeing to meet her at night, alone. The encounter was agonising for them both. 'I lack the strength to confront you in your wretchedness,' Emilio had written earlier. Now he was scarcely able to face the distraught woman who denounced him as 'a scapegrace, a criminal, an assassin'. Abandoning any further attempt at persuasion, the Baroness returned to her lodgings to find a long letter from Attilio awaiting her. Its initial tone of indignation softened towards the close. 'Farewell, most beloved mother, forgive me for all the suffering I am fated to cause you. Give me your most powerful blessing; preserve me in your memory, but do whatever is possible to face the situation with a stout heart. Reflect that everyone on earth must be tormented by misfortune, and that it is the duty of us all to bear it worthily.' She herself had brought with her a tortured letter from his ailing wife, who never shared or understood his Italian patriotism, imploring him to end the family's wretchedness. To this the Baroness added her own reproaches. 'What kind of foolishness is yours,' she wrote to Attilio, 'on a mere frenzied impulse to cast aside your parents, your wife, your rank, name and family, for the sake of nothing at all? You must be madmen, both of you!'

Once she had left Corfu, gloomily resigned to her sons' decision, the Bandieras and their associates began consolidating a plan of operation for the Calabrian venture. Again Nicola Fabrizi attempted to dissuade them – 'the whole operation simply looks like crazy despair' – but their minds were made up. With nineteen companions and a local guide, they would leave for Calabria, raising revolt among towns and villages with the help of two proclamations, one to the region's inhabitants, the other to the people of Italy, each one vigorous in its denunciation of the various sovereign rulers. On 11 July 1844, the night of the expedition's planned embarkation, Emilio wrote a final letter to his mother. 'The Italian revolution has begun, and we are swift to take part in it. Make no mistake, God will protect us. You and I will see one another again. Two ways to your loving embrace were open to me, one through the infamy of seeking the Emperor's pardon, the other via that generous object of driving the Austrians out of Italy. The latter course is dangerous, yet we shall follow it, calling upon God our Protector. Give my love to Grandmamma, Aunt Adriana and those others I dare not name. Forgive and love your Emilio.'

The fighters gathered for the cause came from very different backgrounds. Nicola Ricciotti of Frosinone, official commander of the enterprise, had spent nine years in a Neapolitan gaol for his part in the abortive 1821 revolt against King Ferdinand I. Anacarsi Nardi, the exiled son of Modenese patriots, worked as a land agent for a Corfiote noble family. Like him, Giuseppe Miller of Forli was a member of Mazzini's 'Giovine Italia' society, escaping to the island after imprisonment in the grim Papal fortress of San Leo. Others were of humbler origin, like the stonemason Domenico Lupatelli from Perugia, the barber Giacomo Rocca of Lugo, his fellow townsman Francesco Berti, employed in the making of *pietra dura* (stone marquetry) and the Riminese coachbuilder Giovanni Venerucci. Several, such as Giuseppe Tesei and Tommaso Masoli, were barely out of their teens and had little experience of dissident activity, let alone the staging of a full-scale rebellion.

With good reason, the volunteers had begun to suspect that details of their mission were being leaked to Austrian and Bourbon* intelligence-gatherers, and that the British in Corfu were poised to interfere with their embarkation. The initial idea of sailing on the night of the 11th was set aside, and the expedition waited another day before slipping down the coast in small boats to a spot six miles out of Corfu town, where a brigantine lay at anchor, captained by an Apulian named Mauro Caputi. The voyage should then have taken only a day and a half, but the winds were against them, and not until 1.30 in the morning of 16 June did they come ashore in the marshy Neto estuary on Calabria's eastern coast. Caputi did not linger once his passengers were landed. He was later suspected of colluding with the Bourbon government to lure the Bandieras into a possible trap, since no effort was made to intercept his ship once it left the Ionian Islands, though a Neapolitan vessel was known to be patrolling the waters nearby.

Whatever the truth, the expedition was jubilant on disembarking. The two brothers, with Domenico Moro beside them, sank to their knees and kissed the sand, crying 'You have given us life and we shall spend it for you!' The band of patriots, twenty-one strong, now mustered in the special uniform Giuseppe Miller had designed: a blue cotton blouse with scarlet cuffs and collar and a black cap sporting the Italian tricolour cockade. They carried no provisions with them, in a naive assumption that they could live off the country once the expedition set out. There was no definite plan of campaign, except to march westwards across country to Cosenza, where they counted on the patriotic spirit which the abortive uprising two months earlier had mysteriously failed to arouse.

At least, before leaving Corfu, they had managed to acquire a local guide, a man named Giuseppe Meluso whom Miller had met at a little tavern he kept on the island. Known as 'La Nivara', 'the Snow-Woman', after his mother's business selling ice and impacted snow from underground stores, he had fled his native town of San Giovanni in Fiore on suspicion of murder. Available evidence does not support Mazzini's idea that Meluso was deliberately hired to mislead the expedition. Miller seems to have convinced him of the justice of their cause, and though events separated him from the rebels he subsequently became a willing martyr to his newly-acquired belief in a united republican Italy.

Despite the remoteness of the Neto estuary, the landing in the small hours had not gone unnoticed. A local proprietor, Don Filippo Albani, learning that a party of strangers was advancing into the country, sent

---

* 'Bourbon', the name of the reigning dynasty in the Kingdom of Naples, is used by historians as a term of convenience to refer to all aspects of the regime.

his steward Girolamo Calojero to alert the guardians of his various farms. At Poerio there was an amicable encounter between the Bandieras and Calojero, who resisted the temptation to turn them over to the law, but declined their request for food and transport. Fatally as it turned out, the men did not move on at once, preferring to rest in the olive groves throughout a day whose blinding heat had taken them completely by surprise. That night one of their own number betrayed them.

The Judas Iscariot in this story was Pietro De Boccheciampe, a thirty-year-old Corsican, who had kept apart from the others during the voyage from Corfu, pleading seasickness. When the Bandieras found he had slipped away from their encampment under cover of darkness, they assumed he had gone to seek shelter in a nearby farm. He had in fact set out to cover the five miles southwards to the town of Cotrone, where at dawn he slipped in unobserved by customs inspectors at the main gate. Presenting himself at the police station, Boccheciampe told his story to the deputy intendant Antonio Bonafede, who subjected him to a thorough interrogation before sending a precise account of the expedition's plans and identifying marks to his opposite number at Catanzaro, nearest large town to the south. Weighing up the evidence later, Bonafede tended to believe that Boccheciampe's betrayal was a delaying tactic arranged with his companions, keen to secure the powder magazine inside Cotrone's massive sixteenth-century fortress. The fact that he now requested secure custody in this very same stronghold for fear of the Bandieras' reprisals suggests, however, that he was simply turning king's evidence, as opposed to staging a double bluff.

Bonafede lost no time in summoning reinforcements from as far off as Naples, while mustering a mounted posse to scour the country for rebels. To the annoyance of Cotrone's nobility, he hastily commandeered all available carriages to bring back the expected prisoners, ordering garrisons in outlying villages to search the area as narrowly as possible. Pietro De Boccheciampe meanwhile, too important a witness to be left cowering in the fort, was sent to Catanzaro for further examination, before being brought to Naples to confront King Ferdinand II's detested police chief Francesco Saverio Del Carretto. Their comrade's disappearance continued to mystify the Bandieras as their party moved onwards up the Neto valley towards the mountain range of La Sila. Not a soul had stirred to help them among the scattered farms and hamlets they passed, and it soon became obvious that the revolutionary animus they counted upon to provide followers and material assistance was nonexistent in the region, sparsely populated and suspicious of strangers. Word of their passing had now reached the local gendarmerie, and a troop of these suddenly found themselves face to face with the rebels in a cornfield near the village of Belvedere. Both sides opened fire, but when their commander was killed the soldiers lost their nerve and ran away. It was an advantage the patriots failed to pursue, retreating in a disorderly straggle towards the outskirts of San Giovanni in Fiore, perched in the Sila foothills, where they hoped to find proper refreshment and decent beds.

Once again an elementary misjudgement ruined their calculations. At a hamlet name Stragola they halted, footsore, thirsty and all too conscious of the lack of organisation bedevilling their enterprise. There was talk by now of returning to the estuary in the hope that Caputi and his ship were still there, or else of crossing to the western coast of this Calabrian toe of Italy to escape on the first available vessel. For the time being the inn at Stragola looked inviting enough, and the men sat down, some taking off their boots, and prepared to rest for an hour or so. What they failed to notice was the building's vulnerable position, commanding no view along the road and completely exposed to surprise attack.

Suddenly, out of nowhere as it seemed, the place was surrounded by militia, now bent on showing fight and reinforced by an enraged mob of peasants. The patriots had no time even to pick up their weapons. When Giuseppe Miller and Francesco Tesei flung themselves on their knees, hailing the gendarmes as fellow Italians, they were promptly and brutally cut down. Others managed to flee across the surrounding fields, but most were taken prisoner and immediately robbed by the peasantry of their small arms, watches and jewellery. Attilio Bandiera had a locket containing his wife's portrait tugged from his neck. All the rebels save 'La Nivara', who knew the country well enough to evade capture, were eventually rounded up and taken to Cosenza. The bodies of Miller and Tesei, stripped naked, lay abandoned to rot by the roadside.

According to the laws of the Kingdom of the Two Sicilies, the Bandieras and their associates were to be charged on five counts. Most serious was that of conspiracy to overturn the government and incite King Ferdinand's Calabrian subjects to revolt. A second charge proposed them guilty of secret disembarkation under a rebel flag. Besides these they were accused of resisting public authority in the discharge of its duties, causing the deaths of its agents, infringing sanitary regulations by landing without quarantine clearance and introducing prohibited books and papers. The outcome of the impending trial, conducted by a special military commission, may have looked like a foregone conclusion, but in a case as significant as this, with its implicit warning to those tempted to follow the Bandieras' example, justice must be seen to have been done. Major Filippo Flores, the tribunal's president, therefore nominated four of Cosenza's leading lawyers to defend the accused. Three of these advocates were suspected liberals and all declared their reluctance to take part in what seemed destined to become an elaborate show trial. Their proposed line of defence was to demonstrate that the rebels, dogged by unfavourable circumstances, could hardly have expected to carry out their coup successfully. Flores responded to this with a brusque 'Do you wish me to waste my time?', and the trial swiftly turned into a series of ruthless cross-examinations of the accused, with no further advocacy allowed on their behalf.

At first not everything went the government's way. Emilio's truculent, hair-splitting answers to the judges earned him considerable admiration. 'What is your name?' asked Flores. 'Emilio Bandiera.' 'Are you a baron?' 'I'm not interested in that.' 'Where do you come from?' 'Italy.' 'But where were you born?' 'Venice.' 'How did you get to Cosenza?' 'On a mule among a bunch of robbers.' 'I wasn't asking about that.' 'Well explain yourself better.' 'What did you come to do in Calabria?', and so on, to Flores's evident irritation. Domenico Moro, whose good looks and dignified manner deeply stirred those present, claimed immunity from prosecution as the subject of a foreign government, an example followed by the Bandieras and by Nicola Ricciotti. Several others protested complete ignorance of the two revolutionary proclamations, denying any intention of overthrowing the Bourbon monarchy. Attilio Bandiera even told the examining magistrate shortly after his arrest that their appearance in Calabria was merely a gesture of support for the new Italian constitutional monarchy they believed King Ferdinand was about to initiate.

The accused now seemed curiously eager to avoid patriotic martyrdom, yet the citizens of Cosenza, far from censuring the Bandieras for cowardice, took the young men to their hearts. Visitors arrived at the prison each day with baskets of fruit, bottles of wine, and bouquets and morale-boosting letters, several containing requests from ladies for locks of the men's hair. Even the gaolers treated them with respect, while the prison governor attempted to intervene discreetly on their behalf with the tribunal. To the government in Naples the situation grew more embarrassing as the trial continued, and it became imperative that sentences should be determined and carried out as swiftly as possible if the groundswell of popular feeling was not to turn into sullen discontent or open rioting.

The judges, though the verdict was hardly in doubt, failed nevertheless to agree on the scale of penalties. After a whole night of dispute, they returned to court, on 24 July, with the decision that twelve of the rebels should be executed within twenty-four hours, according to what Neapolitan law termed 'the third degree of public example', which involved the accused marching barefoot, dressed in black and with their heads covered. When this was read out by judge Raffaele Piccolo, Nicola Ricciotti immediately shouted, 'You coward!', and the court was adjourned amid the protests of his companions. At length the judges, aware of potential damage to the reputation of the legal system, let alone of the Bourbon regime itself, returned with the announcement that the death sentences had been reduced from twelve to nine. Pardons were given to some of the youngest rebels on grounds of ignorance or unhelpful influences. The artist Giuseppe Pacchione and several others were given terms of imprisonment, with the likelihood of commutation through royal clemency.

It was the nine men picked for execution by a firing squad the next morning whose fate now gripped the Cosentines' imagination. Priests ministering to the prisoners had protested to the court against the fetters and manacles with which they were loaded and these were immediately struck off. On their last night in gaol, while Pacchione hurriedly sketched their portraits, they were visited by Father Beniamino De Rose, a liberal priest, accompanied by the Dominican friar Rosario Stumpo, who heard their confessions. When Stumpo offered to confess Anacarsi Nardi, however, he was met with a courteous rebuff. 'Reverend friar, I thank you for the care you have taken over my soul, but I beg you to spare me the sermon on belief in God. All of us know and follow the religion of Jesus Christ like you, or, if you'll permit me, somewhat better than you and your Saint Dominic – since charity and love, symbols of that religion, are what led us to this cruel destiny. Whereas you, knowing nothing of these things, make religion serve vile and ignoble purposes. But be as certain of this as you are of dying, that tomorrow, despite the terrible anathemas of Pope Gregory,* we shall be up there,' – Nardi nodded towards heaven – 'but we shan't find Saint Dominic beside us.' After the priests left, a plate of maccheroni was brought to the condemned as a final meal. The builder Domenico Lupatelli joked savagely that if they couldn't digest it properly, tomorrow's bullets would act as a purge.

As dawn broke on 25 July, a huge, silent crowd gathered along the sides of the Vallone del Rovito, a valley between low hills outside the city, normally used for the bleaching of laundry and now selected as a place of execution. The nine men, Attilio and Emilio Bandiera, Domenico Moro, Nicola Ricciotti, Anacarsi Nardi, Francesco Berti, Giacomo Rocca, Domenico Lupatelli and Giovanni Venerucci, marched towards death in a state of exalted defiance. Entering the valley they launched into a chorus

---

* The Venetian monk Bartolomeo Capellari, elected pope as Gregory XVI in 1831 and noted for his reactionary views. In the letter on Mazzini quoted earlier, Thomas Carlyle refers to 'that imbecile old chimaera of a pope'.

from *Donna Caritea*, an opera written nearly twenty years earlier by Saverio Mercadante, whose words had an almost unbearably poignant relevance:

> Chi per la Patria muor,
>   Vissuto è assai;
> La fronda del allor
>   Non langue mai.
> Piuttosto che languir
>   Sotto i tiranni
> Meglio è morir
>   Sul fior degli anni.

'Who dies for the motherland has lived long enough. The laurel crown will never fade. Rather than languish under tyranny, it is better to die in the flower of our years.'

It was not the first time the valley had witnessed such a scene. A few months earlier the leaders of the abortive 15 March uprising had faced a firing squad here, and presumably most of those watching then were present now. Several witnesses noted a surly resentment, more powerful through its silence, directed at the guard accompanying the condemned men. Some at least must have been impressed by the care the prisoners took over their appearance, 'as if they were about to accomplish an act of religious solemnity'. One of them was heard to bid the soldiers, 'Spare our faces, for they were made in God's image.' When the trumpet sounded the signal to take aim, the squad at first refused to fire, and it was up to one of the patriots, Nicola Ricciotti, to call out, 'Obey your orders!' Even so, the first round only grazed or wounded its targets. 'Viva l'Italia!' they cried as the soldiers loaded and fired once more. This time seven fell dead, but Lupatelli the stonemason, who had joked about a purge of balls, was alive enough to exclaim, 'Fire again!', and when Attilio Bandiera lifted up his manacled hands to show he was not yet dead, the officer commanding gave the order for both men to be finished off.

Afterwards Father De Rose, aided by the local society known as the Compagnia della Buona Morte,* arranged burial for all nine bodies in Cosenza's church of Sant'Agostino. Beside each he placed a bottle

---

* Its principal purpose was to bring comfort and assistance to those under sentence of death. The Bandieras and Domenico Moro must have recalled the existence, in their native Venice under the old Republic, of a similar organisation, known as La Scuola dei Picai, whose members, wearing black hoods, had accompanied processions to the scaffold.

containing a slip of paper for identification. In 1848 a Bourbon officer sent to suppress rioting in the town ordered the remains to be dug up and thrown into the River Neto. Instead the clergy concealed all the bones in a remote corner of the church, whence, in 1866, they were disinterred and taken to Venice for an honourable funeral. Their memorial at Cosenza was designed by Giuseppe Pacchione, perhaps as an atonement for telling the tribunal that he only joined the expedition under Giuseppe Miller's influence and never seriously understood the issues involved.

Another survivor might well have thought it better to enter the valley of death beside his comrades. During interrogation in Naples, Pietro De Boccheciampe had told the minister Del Carretto, among other things, that Nicola Ricciotti had been despatched expressly to Corfu by Mazzini and that the expedition, on landing, was convinced that at least 600 Calabrian rebels awaited them in the mountains. Sent back to Cosenza for trial, he was kept apart from his comrades for fear of reprisals. A cosmetic five-year sentence for carrying offensive weapons was soon cancelled and the Corsican was set free. His betrayal of his comrades may not have led directly to their capture, but it undoubtedly helped, and Boccheciampe soon realised that he could go nowhere without his reputation preceding him. For a time he took refuge in Albania, where he wrote a long letter to Mazzini seeking to prove his innocence. When the apologia remained unanswered, he plucked up the courage to return to Corfu, where the ultimate humiliation awaited him. His fiancée Maria Sarandopoulo, having learned of his treachery, banished him with the words 'A Greek girl cannot embrace a traitor. I carry with me the blessings of my dead parents, you bear the eternal curse of God.'

Maria's crushing verdict reflects the impact of the Bandiera affair on liberal opinion throughout Europe. In an official report on the episode, Don Antonio Bonafede, deputy intendant at Cotrone, tried to warn King Ferdinand and his ministers as candidly as possible of the likely political fallout. The rebels' heroic demeanour in front of the firing squad had seriously harmed the government's image throughout the southern provinces, and worse could only follow. In a subsequent memoir, published clandestinely at Naples in 1848, Bonafede refers to the expedition, interestingly enough, as 'gli Italiani', 'the Italians', as though naming members of some alien nation. The Bourbon monarch's sole reaction was to distribute over 150 medals of different kinds, with Queen Maria Cristina going in person to San Giovanni in Fiore to hand out awards to loyal townsfolk.

For all those prepared to blame Ferdinand personally for the Bandieras' death, many acknowledged the pointlessness of the expedition, its lack of any coherent plan or ideology and its failure to establish links with local revolutionary cells. Such ineptitude should have made it simply another embarrassment in the catalogue of bungled attempts at initiating an Italian revolution, whether by Mazzini and his followers or by independent patriot groups. Cosenza, what is more, hardly ranked as a place of much importance. The uprising in the town on 15 March made no lasting impression on revolutionaries outside the kingdom, and it may well have seemed to the King and Del Carretto that the Bandieras too would be swiftly forgotten.

Bonafede was right in perceiving this as a serious miscalculation. True, the cause of Italian unity was scarcely short of martyrs. In Piedmont, Modena, Rome and Sicily brave men had died for the cause. Yet the very rashness of the Bandieras gave the doomed expedition of 1844 an imperishable glamour. The members of the expedition were mostly young, and even as their fate swiftly metamorphosed itself into legend they also became beautiful – easier, doubtless, for Domenico Moro, so captivatingly handsome, than for Attilio Bandiera, whom illness had made bald by his midtwenties. Though Italians, hard-headed and temperamentally unromantic, generally see no particular attraction in failure, the courage of the patriots in their last hours seized hold of popular imagination. They themselves, what was more, seem to have grasped the iconic significance of their own foolhardy adventure, almost as if ending up in front of a firing squad had been its ultimate intention. 'They wished to die,' Mazzini later declared, 'for they had perceived the great cause which hinders us from being free – the want of harmony between thought and action.'

Poetry seized avidly on their heroism and victimhood. In his London exile the Neapolitan bard Gabriele Rossetti, father of those two great Italo-Victorians Dante Gabriel and Christina Georgina, devised a dignified parody of the Passiontide hymn 'Stabat Mater Dolorosa', imagining the Bandieras' mother grieving at their tomb like the Virgin Mary over the crucified Christ. In Paris, where the French Catholic hierarchy forbade the large Italian refugee community to hold a memorial mass for the martyrs, Louise Colet, best known to us as mistress and muse of Gustave Flaubert, poured forth her outrage at the execution in a poignant elegy. It was left to the young writer of what would become Italy's national hymn, the Genoese poet Goffredo Mameli,* to express the collective shame felt by Italians in the light of the Bandieras' noble example. 'At the sacred tomb of the martyred brothers,' he wrote, 'my genius could not lift up the voice of a mere slave.

---

* Mameli died aged only twenty-two, during the siege of Rome in 1849, from gangrene resulting from a botched leg amputation. In his final delirium he was heard declaiming extensive snatches of poetry. His 'Fratelli d'Italia' remains the national anthem.

Such brave men deserve none but the hymns of those equally brave. Only when we have risen ourselves shall we be worthy to commemorate you.'

Had they been betrayed to the Bourbon government even before setting out for Calabria? In March 1844 the aged architect of the system which kept Italian despotism in place, Austria's chancellor Prince Clemens von Metternich, confided to his wife Melanie his disquiet at the news of the Bandieras' escape to Corfu. When at length they were captured, she noted in her diary that the British authorities on the island had made no attempt to intercept the expedition. 'Poor Clemens makes what efforts he can, and naturally wears himself out a great deal in the process.' Melanie's doubts were not wholly justified. Mazzini, the man the Metternichs saw as the Bandieras' evil genius, believed that interception by British post office agents acting as spies had been crucial in ensuring that the Austrian and Neapolitan governments knew that insurgency of some sort was being planned in Corfu with Calabria as its object, though actual details of timing and personnel might not necessarily have been disclosed. An official statement from the Foreign Office in London declared that 'representations had been made to the British Government from high sources' regarding Mazzini's designs for an Italian revolution. 'Such insurrection, should it assume a formidable aspect, would, from peculiar political circumstances, disturb the peace of Europe.' The government had passed on the necessary details to Austria, 'but the information so communicated was not of a nature to compromise, and did not compromise, the safety of any individual within the reach of that foreign power'.

The questionmark over British involvement in the expedition's failure enhanced the Bandieras' image as martyrs to a system of tyranny supported by international reactionary consensus. For those who survived them, this odour of patriotic sanctity offered no obvious consolation. Covered in shame as the father of traitors to his flag, Vice-Admiral Bandiera left Venice to live quietly on a farm at Carpenedo, near the mainland town of Mestre. Doubtless the Austrian government assumed, or at least hoped, that outside his family circle memories of Attilio, Emilio and their comrades as participants in just another failed insurrection would fade quickly enough. By Italians, however, they were not forgotten. By no special irony it was not in Calabria but in Venice, where the brothers were born, that their memory would help to ignite revolution on a scale the pair of them could scarcely have dreamed possible.

CHAPTER I

∽

THE PEACE OF THE TOMB

FOR NEARLY FORTY YEARS THE city in which the Bandiera brothers grew to manhood had been part of the Austrian empire. By the Treaty of Campoformio, signed on 17 October 1797 by plenipotentiaries of Emperor Francis I and General Napoleon Bonaparte, the existence of the Venetian Republic as an independent political state was extinguished for ever and her territories divided between the two powers. While France seized the Ionian Islands as a useful strategic base in the central Mediterranean to see off possible threats from Russia, Turkey and Great Britain, Austria was more than content with the prize of fertile lands and handsome cities north of the Po and with the chance to extend her naval capability by taking control of the ports along the Dalmatian coast.

Actually concluded not at Campoformio, the Friulan village whose name it bears, but at the rococo villa of Passariano some few miles to the south, the treaty was the most sordid of political compromises. Venice herself, it scarcely needs saying, was allowed no part in the framing of the final document and secured little in the way of immediate practical advantage. The ancient structures of Venetian government under a doge and a Senate drawn from a limited caste of patrician families, with its system of dependent committees, had been dismantled five months earlier in the extraordinary events of the second week of May, which saw the Serene Republic* voting itself out of existence in a panic induced by the

---

* The state of Venice was officially styled 'La Serenissima Repubblica' – 'The Most Serene Republic'. For reasons of economy and (occasionally) euphony I have dropped the 'Most' throughout this book.

apparently unstoppable advance of Bonaparte's army through the Austrian province of Lombardy. His intention of violating Venice's nominal neutrality was plain. Warnings from the French government's envoys turned to menaces as to what the Republic must expect, should she fail to comply with their demands for free passage of troops, for the unimpeded movement of French shipping through her waters and the expulsion of royalist émigrés. By April 1797 Napoleon, having seized the key Venetian forts of Osoppo and Palmanova, was confidently proclaiming himself a latterday Attila, poised to complete what the Hunnish conqueror had failed to achieve centuries earlier in this very region, when fugitives from nearby Roman cities had fled for safety to the islands of the lagoon. Furious that the Republic had rejected an earlier offer of French alliance, Bonaparte now resolved to humiliate her completely, via a series of demands with which, in theory at least, she would be reluctant or frankly unwilling to comply. Accepting them would have meant indignity for the state and, by implication, for the disenfranchised majority of ordinary citizens, whose pride in Venice's unique system of government and loyalty to the badge of St Mark's lion with the open book between his paws seemed unshakable.

Just how frail Venice was when faced with a major international crisis became clear when the Grand Council of the Republic met in their great chamber within the Doge's Palace on 12 May 1797 to vote on the French demands. The 547 members of the council were not enough to constitute a quorum, but the emergency demanded that they hasten to some sort of vote. What sealed their deliberations was a burst of gunfire from outside the palace. Since few, if any, of those gathered in the Sala del Maggior Consiglio, under Tintoretto's enormous 'Last Judgement' adorning its east wall, had ever heard a military fusillade, the reaction among the senators was a general panic. It was in vain for anybody to point out that the noise came from a platoon of Dalmatian infantry about to leave the city, where they had been standing guard in the Piazzetta and expressing their loyalty to the Republic in a farewell salute. Voting 512 to thirty, with five abstentions, in favour of accepting Bonaparte's demands, the terrified patricians struggled out of their robes of office, whose various brocade and velvet panels, sleeve lengths and braidings had indicated their positions in the state's complex hierarchy, and flung them aside before making a speedy exit from the different side doors of the palace rather than face the huge crowd milling anxiously around its two main entrances. The Doge himself, Lodovico Manin, whose resignation to the turn of events Venetians have always been inclined to attribute to the fact that his family was a very recent addition to the nobility, retired to an antechamber to set aside his *corno dogale*, the horn-shaped cap of office which since the early Middle Ages had symbolised the Doge's function as the Republic's elected figurehead. As his servant paused in untying the white linen coif traditionally worn beneath it, Manin said: 'Take it off, it will never be wanted again.'

The Grand Council made no attempt to reassemble. Its undignified final session, while not putting an end there and then to the Venetian state's autonomous existence, was seen as essentially embodying the collapse of a political order long viewed throughout the rest of Europe as effete and decadent. In the Republic's *terraferma* domains the various towns and cities, Brescia, Bergamo, Udine, Bassano and others, jostled one another in their eagerness to cast off the old allegiance to La Serenissima and embrace the promises of equality and self-determination held out by the invading French. As for Venice itself and its immediately surrounding mainland area known as the *dogado*, a provisional municipality composed of leading figures from various social echelons now assumed such control as it was allowed under Napoleon's occupation force. For the rest of the summer and autumn this local government remained uneasily in place, a suddenly Jacobinised community of 'citizens', 'citizenesses', pigtails, striped pantaloons, Phrygian bonnets and liberty trees.

Napoleon had other ideas for Venice. Despite initial enthusiasm from the mainland communities, there was an increasing sense throughout the Veneto that the French were overstaying their welcome. Certain country districts began to witness menacing stand-offs between the soldiers and local peasantry. Bonaparte himself, what was more, had been watching with concern the triumphal progress through southern Germany of another French force, led by his rival Lazare Hoche, who seemed poised to reap the glory of an ultimate invasion of Austrian heartlands culminating in the seizure of Vienna. The logical solution to this problem had seemed at first to be a straightforward peace settlement with the Habsburg emperor, drawn up in its earliest form in April 1797 and at that point including an arrangement whereby Venice would receive the northern territory of the Papal States, around Bologna and Ferrara, known as the Legations, in exchange for ceding an ample portion of its mainland territories to Austria. Subsequent events, including an attack on the French warship *Libérateur d'Italie* by the Venetian captain Domenico Pizzamano and the so-called 'Pasque Veronesi' ('Veronese Easter Days'), in which the citizens of Verona revolted against the occupying French, set Napoleon firmly against any further notion of trying to conciliate, let alone preserve, the Serene Republic. By October a new and far more drastic settlement had been agreed, and the Treaty of Campoformio, whose signing took place at ex-Doge Lodovico Manin's family villa (he was not present on the occasion), removed from the Venetians their last illusions of freedom.

The Austrians did not immediately take possession of Venice, but when the first imperial officials arrived on 18 January 1798 their presence was welcomed by the nobility and bourgeoisie as a desirable alternative to that of the high-handed, democratising Directoire. In its earliest form this *Venezia austriaca* lasted scarcely more than eight years, and the occupying power made comparatively little impact during this period. In 1805 war broke out afresh between Austria and France. Napoleon's sequence of crushing victories at Jena, Ulm, Wagram and Austerlitz forced Emperor Francis I to conclude a humiliating peace the following year. Among its terms was the absorption of Habsburg lands in Lombardy and Veneto into the so-called Kingdom of Italy, ruled from Milan as part of Bonaparte's empire by his stepson Eugène de Beauharnais.

This 'Napoleonic parenthesis', as historians term it, brought significant changes to the quality of life within Venice itself and, still more notably, to the city's physical character. In Piazza San Marco, for example, the elegant sixteenth-century church of San Geminiano was pulled down to make room for a wing containing a ceremonial staircase and a suite of grand reception rooms, designed to join together the arcaded Procuratie on either side. Effective in itself, this Ala Napoleonica, the work of the Modenese court architect Giuseppe Maria Soli, is as good an emblem as any of the modernising spirit of Napoleon's empire, with its Gallic fondness for imposing order and system even on an urban profile as resistant as Venice's to straight lines. A similarly drastic adjustment took place in the traditionally impoverished northern reaches of the Castello district, beyond the Arsenal, where a long boulevard, nowadays called Via Garibaldi but originally styled Via Eugenia, was opened across the quarter along the bed of a former canal.

Perhaps the most devastating alteration was brought about through the suppression of monastic communities and the destruction of churches. At the Republic's fall in 1797, Venice contained almost three times as many religious institutions of various kinds as it does today. The Venetians, whatever their well-founded reputation for hedonism and their irrepressible passion for novelty and entertainment, were notably devout, and the state, despite its long history of quarrels with the papacy, encouraged lavish celebration of holy days and patronal festivals throughout the calendar. In 1806, when the Napoleonic government took control, thirty-four monasteries were dissolved and nine churches were demolished or converted to other uses. In addition, more than 300 of the charitable institutions known as *scuole*, most of them attached to churches, were dismantled, though not before being pillaged of their various treasures. By 1810 a further twenty-six monasteries and fifteen churches had gone the same way. The many works of art which they contained were either dispatched to Paris, to join the bronze horses of St Mark and Paolo Veronese's great 'Wedding Feast at Cana', most prized articles of loot from the Venetian treasurehouse, or used to adorn the various viceregal residences and fill the rooms of the new Brera Gallery in Milan.

The French eventually withdrew from Venice in 1814, following a blockade by combined Austrian and British forces, which, lasting nearly a year, had reduced the citizens almost to starvation. Once an armistice was signed, there was little cheer for those who still clung to a faint hope of regaining some sort of independence, whether for the city alone or even for the Veneto as a whole. The Congress of Vienna confirmed the true extent of Austria's long-cherished Italian ambitions by endorsing Habsburg sovereignty over all Venetian lands acquired via the Treaty of Campoformio. For the next fifty-one years, apart from a single brief interval which forms the subject of this book, Austria both ruled directly over an extensive area of Italy and used her influence to dominate the sovereign states making up the rest of the peninsula's political map from the Alps to Sicily.

The traditional legitimist argument is that successive Habsburg emperors during this period, Francis I, Ferdinand II and Franz Josef, together with their satellite rulers in the duchies of Tuscany, Parma, Modena and Lucca, were simply maintaining peace and order via the exercise of lawful authority in virtue of a divinely conferred status. Against such an idealised concept, it needs to be pointed out that, with the exception of the Duke of Modena,* none of these sovereigns had any legitimate claim to their Italian lands beyond what had been given them via the dynastic and territorial horse-trading of international peace negotiations following major wars during the eighteenth and early nineteenth centuries. In Naples the French Bourbons had acquired their kingdom in the wake of the War of the Spanish Succession (1702–13), while the Habsburgs had been compensated with the city of Milan and its surrounding domains. A cadet branch of the Bourbons gained, at more

---

* Modena had passed to the Habsburgs through the marriage in 1771 of Beatrice d'Este to Archduke Ferdinand. She was the sole heir of Francesco III, last of the Estense dukes who had ruled the state since its creation in 1598. On assuming control of the duchy in 1814, her son Archduke Franz styled himself 'Francesco IV'.

or less the same time, the Duchy of Parma, while Mantua, wrested from its feckless, opera-mad Gonzaga duke by the Austrians in 1707, was quickly absorbed into their imperial province of Lombardy. Tuscany became a Habsburg appanage by international agreement rather than direct inheritance, and even the popes might be said to have had no legitimate claim to territory whose possession was validated solely by the fraudulent 'Donation of Constantine'.

To the consternation of many in Italy, the Congress of Vienna not merely endorsed these earlier settlements, but tightened Austria's grip, by awarding Parma to Napoleon's ex-empress Marie Louise, herself a Habsburg princess, and by compensating its Bourbon rulers with a new duchy created from the former republic of Lucca. While the ancient maritime republic of Genoa and its territories were annexed by the King of Piedmont, Austrian forces moved swiftly through the other Italian states to wipe out potential disaffection. Watching in disgust, Vincenzo Monti, Italy's leading poet of the age, wrote an angry sonnet on the Congress, calling the victorious allies 'the desolators of the earth' and declaring 'your proclamation of peace buries the rights of man deep underground. You have clipped the wings of freedom. If this is peace, what then must war be?'

Austria's emperor Francis I (who had been Francis II until he renounced his Holy Roman imperial title in 1806) cared nothing whatever for the wings of freedom. He had no scruples in accepting Venice and her surrounding provinces as a restoration of what his defeated son-in-law Napoleon had awarded him seventeen years earlier at Campoformio. The cynical Francis would doubtless have been flattered to note the poet Monti's abject homage to the Habsburg regime once it was established in the new provinces of Lombardy and Venetia. Without the personal glamour surrounding his fellow sovereign Tsar Alexander I of Russia, or the iconic status as military leader distinguishing Prussia's King Frederick William III (both of whom he envied and resented), Francis displayed an absorbing combination of natural shrewdness, low self-esteem, lack of imagination, a certain measure of indolence and a complete conviction in his divinely conferred status.

Idleness did not mean that the Emperor was not, at the same time, a thoroughly conscientious monarch. Unlike his grandmother Maria Theresa or his uncle Joseph II, Francis possessed no cultural interests. His idea of amusement was confined to such simple pleasures as making toffee in saucepans on top of the tiled stoves which heated his palaces, or else, if Stendhal's scurrilous gossip is to be believed, painting eyes in the bottoms of ladies' chamberpots. He showed little enthusiasm for travel, declining to visit England with the other allied sovereigns in the summer of 1814 and making relatively few tours of his own extensive dominions. His concern instead was with maintaining consistency and equilibrium within the imperial administration through exercising an absolutism which should be seen to work towards the general good of his subjects, however humble their status. Like many another ruler of his kind, he was temperamentally suspicious of all who might be thought to know too much, whether as a result of experience, education or mere curiosity. Such autocrats invariably feel more comfortable in the society of so-called ordinary people, whose artless directness is readily accepted as rough-hewn wisdom, to be valued above that of scholars or politicians as much because unlettered simplicity of utterance makes it less threatening as because these humble folk can be relied upon to assume that their master, in the end, knows best. So it was with Francis. Far from denying his subjects a hearing, he was only too pleased to receive them in audience and, unlike other contemporary monarchs, made a point of spending a part of each day listening patiently to what were often the most banal and trivial of requests. Conservatives, of whom Austria has always had more than its fair share, commended such a dutiful, hands-on fatherliness. The diplomat Joseph von Hübner, in a memoir written fifty years after Francis's death, recalled him admiringly as 'full of good sense and that bonhomie which constitutes one of the essential qualities of an Austrian; affable, familiar and dignified at the same time, joining with his simple tastes the morals of a bourgeois paterfamilias, yet remembering when necessary that he was a son of the Caesars'. For Hübner, Francis's continued accessibility to the poorest of his people was the secret of his greatness as a ruler.

Taken for granted here is the fact that none of these petitioners brought with them anything so inconvenient as a plea for greater liberties of expression and association, let alone for a voice in the councils of the realm. There was only one voice, in any case, which the Emperor was ever likely to heed. It belonged to the man regarded, rightly or wrongly, as Europe's most influential statesman during the years immediately following Napoleon's fall, a figure either revered as the prudent architect of good order and firm government among nations still reeling from the notional trauma of Bonaparte, or detested as the apostle of tyranny, repression and obscurantism, chief creator of what Giuseppe Mazzini would later refer to in a memorable phrase as 'the peace of the tomb'.

When the Austrian forces entered Venice in 1814, Prince Clemens Wenceslas Lothar von Metternich-Winneburg-Beilstein was fifty-nine years old and enjoying the extended climacteric of his power as Chancellor of the Empire. Versatile, opinionated and loquacious to an extent which rendered him either fascinating or insufferable, he had preserved the good looks and abundant personal charm which made him so attractive to women, including three wives and a series of mistresses. Unrivalled experience as a diplomat and politician provided him with one valuable reserve of practical wisdom, while another was furnished from his acute psychological assessments of everyone he met, in terms of motive, ambition or personal weakness. Unsurprisingly, Metternich was vain about what he considered a superior grasp on the world's essential realities. Byron might have libelled him as 'power's foremost parasite', and Palmerston was later to pronounce it 'a great blessing for Europe that his orb should set in the night of private life', but this was the man who could confidently declare of Napoleon, 'He found in me a calm which must have infuriated someone in the habit of speculating on the passions', who believed he had got the exact measure of the famously enigmatic Tsar Alexander I and who saw the British foreign secretary Lord Castlereagh as 'devoted to me heart and soul, not only from a personal attachment but also from conviction'. Metternich's sense of himself as an international political magus, whose judgement must always be confirmed by the outcome of events and by the predictable reaction of those taking part in them, hardened soon enough into an invincible self-assurance precluding the slightest shadows of doubt or any impulse towards introspection.

If Emperor Francis trusted Metternich, it was not just because he needed to do so as somebody stolidly aware of his own limitations and lack of curiosity or foresight. The Chancellor never betrayed the least suggestion of an indecorous contempt or impatience towards his sovereign, praising instead Francis's candour, energy, strict moral principles and unswerving resolution. In his turn the Emperor admired Metternich's constancy to the dynastic principle, his belief in absolute rule as the sole guarantee of political stability and social harmony, and his dedication to the role of bulwark between order and anarchy, whose presence beside the throne all other monarchs and princes must envy.

Metternich always denied that he had ever been responsible for creating anything like the so-called conservative governmental 'system' which contemporaries soon came to attribute to him, though he referred to it on more than one occasion with the kind of satisfaction which suggested that he was fully aware of himself as its principal architect. The essence of Austrian rule in the newly formed 'kingdom' of Lombardy-Venetia, as its inhabitants soon discovered after 1814, was an overwhelming centralisation, concentrating power and decision-making on Vienna rather than on an executive appointed from among the Emperor's Italian subjects.

Under Napoleon's Kingdom of Italy, genuine efforts had been made to train an administrative class drawn from the more liberal elements within the local aristocracies and the bourgeoisie. On entering Lombardy in 1814 at the head of an Austrian army, Field Marshal Heinrich de Bellegarde began a wholesale dismantling of the more obviously representative or even mildly democratic features distinguishing the Napoleonic administration. Away went the Senate, the Council of State and the electoral colleges, with a variety of vague promises offered instead as to the Austrian emperor's 'paternal care', 'solicitude' and 'benevolent disposition', not to speak of the 'satisfying and stable form' of the new government as a guarantee of 'the future felicity of his subjects'.

A year later an imperial letter-patent and a further proclamation from Bellegarde raised hopes that the new province might be accorded at least some measure of administrative autonomy. The so-called Kingdom of Lombardy-Venetia was to be ruled by a viceroy drawn from among members of the Emperor's numerous family. Metternich, it seems, was considering a measure of independence for territories whose annexation, he claimed, had been forced on a reluctant Austria at the Congress of Vienna. Francis, on the other hand, showed himself unwilling to offer any special treatment for his new Italian lands. Like other provinces of the empire, they were to be governed with the sovereign's fiat and veto as ultimate sanctions with respect to all decrees, privileges and penalties.

The popular image of Austrian rule in Venice and the Veneto, after Italy's unification was completed in 1870, was that of an unremitting tyranny, deaf to reason or petition and abusive of fundamental claims to justice among the citizens whose free movement, choices, decisions and opinions it sought to control. In fact, during the 1820s at least, Francis I's Italian subjects were not merely resigned to the reality of his rule, but accepted it as a desirable alternative to those of the sovereigns whose states shared their frontiers. When a series of revolutions broke out in areas of northern Italy during 1831, there was no significant attempt at initiating similar uprisings in Lombardy-Venetia. Whatever discontent might be felt among the nobility and professional classes in urban areas, the members of other social groupings, small tradesmen, those involved in local industries and the rural labouring class, all seem to have felt that the Habsburg government (whatever its incidental disadvantages) was at any rate conscientious, relatively lacking in corruption and at some pains to protect the ordinary citizen under the rule of law.

The various town councillors, bureaucrats and police officers charged with maintaining civic order were encouraged to take pride in their official positions. Twelve basic classes of public employee were distinguished by the different kinds of braid and frogging on their dark-green coats donned for ceremonial occasions. To qualify for service at the humblest level, it was necessary to be an Austrian citizen, with a proven record of good moral conduct, no political misemeanours, sufficient means and at least four years' schooling. The police could, and frequently did, block official appointments with a bewildering array of objections. Potential council members were vetoed not merely for such peccadilloes as 'suspect relationship with chambermaids', but for having acquired a reputation as a ladies' man, for excessive talkativeness or for overmuch interest in financial speculation. As one Austrian commentator noted in a private memorandum, 'Under the aegis of the police here, one is born, one lives and dies. It may be said that in Italy no social relationship exists that is not subject to its direct interference.'

As for the letter of the law itself, this was enshrined within a penal code whose Italian version was published in Milan in 1815. Beginning with fines and confiscations, the degrees of punishment embraced the removal of civil rights and licences and several different forms of detention, including two types of imprisonment: first-grade without chains, second-grade with fetters, one hot meal a day, labour assigned to the prisoner and no visitors allowed. A sentence of banishment could involve the culprit being forced to quit his home town, removal to another imperial province or outright exile from Austrian territory. The most explicitly humiliating penalty in the whole judicial system was corporal punishment, limited to twenty-five strokes and given to men with a stick and to women and children with a wand. A deliberate class distinction governed this form of sentence, which was generally awarded to domestic servants, artisans and day-labourers as a preferable alternative to a spell in gaol, which would materially affect either their employers or their families. This and other punishments were assigned according to six categories – transgressions against public safety and decency, damage to private property and offences against the life, honour or good esteem of individual citizens.

A wide range of activities was specifically targeted by single articles in the code. Anybody caught, for example, defacing or even verbally 'insulting' a public notice or government order was condemned to a period of arrest ranging from twenty-four hours to a week, or to a *bastinado* of up to twenty-five strokes. Innkeepers and hoteliers were bound to notify the police of all their patrons, and failure to do so could lead to a fine. The law struck at those who threw stones at street-lamps, people who gave bogus names and addresses, women bearing children out of wedlock who had failed to notify a midwife, careless drivers, negligent doctors, insufficient watchfulness over children in dangerous places, architectural ignorance resulting in the collapse of buildings, the dropping of objects out of windows into the street, smoking in barns where straw and hay were stored, attempted suicide and unauthorised bathing or skating.

What Francis and Metternich feared most of all was the mushrooming throughout Italy, in the years after 1815, of the secret revolutionary societies generically referred to by historians as the Carbonari or Carboneria, after the most famous of them all. In 1821, after an abortive Carbonarist uprising in Lombardy, the ringleaders, including the distinguished poet and dramatist Silvio Pellico, were sent to Venice for trial. Though the government was determined to make an example of them, not least via the solemn public proclamation in Piazza San Marco of the rigorous sentences handed down, and though its harshness occasioned considerable resentment, Venetians were reluctant to follow the example of the Carbonari by forming their own secret societies within the city itself. Elsewhere, a confederacy such as the Bandiera brothers' 'Esperia' figured as merely another among the hundreds whose brief period of activity generally ended in police raids, imprisonment and exile. Article 37 of the Austrian penal code made membership of such societies a major offence, and much effort was expended by the police force, with its extensive network of spies and informers, on identifying and infiltrating any association that seemed likely to encourage even the most mildly critical view of the regime. Hence Freemasonry, which had famously thrived in Austria during the reign of the Emperor's uncle Joseph II and included in its ranks several of Vienna's most distinguished cultural figures, was now vigorously proscribed, both for its potential in promoting liberal ideas and as the original model for all secret societies that had sprung up ever since. In Venice alone, five masonic lodges were identified and suppressed almost as soon as the city's new rulers had taken over in 1814.

A glance at the Venetian police archives during this period reveals a positive obsession with secret societies, their names becoming more exotic with the years. Agents in 1816 submitted details of the Philadelphians, the Deciders, the Illuminati, the Guelph Cavaliers and the Oratory Priests; by 1822 unsettling information was arriving as to the Reunited Spectres of the Tomb, the American Hunters, the Sons of Mars and the Friends of Science. In connection with such clandestine activity, a famous name now and then cropped up. In 1819 Prince Colonna di Sciarra, chief of the papal police at Bologna, wrote to his opposite number in Venice that a certain Lord Byron was about to take up residence there. 'He is more than usually well-versed in polite letters,' wrote Colonna, 'and is taken for a fine poet in his own country.' An informer had further revealed that 'he is well-known for his scandalous domestic life, an insatiable appetite for pleasure and an interest in the fair sex'.* Other celebrities were likewise fingered over the years for their political affiliations, known or suspected. In 1821 the composer Gioacchino Rossini was listed as 'strongly infected with revolutionary principles', while the painter Horace Vernet, on his way to assume the directorship of the French Academy in Rome, was apparently 'well known for his dangerous political ideas'. When Alexandre Dumas, creator of *The Three Musketeers* and *The Count of Monte Cristo*, was refused a visa to enter the Two Sicilies in 1835, the Austrian minister in Naples speedily alerted Count Spaur, civil governor of Venice. Dumas was, he admitted, 'without doubt a man of genius, but one who has dedicated himself unrestrainedly to the bad taste currently prevailing in France . . . what is more, a republican and boastful with it'.

Had anyone in Venice wished to purchase Dumas's works at one of the city's bookshops, they would not have been able to do so without arousing suspicion from the police. From the earliest years of Austrian rule in Italy, press censorship was a major grievance even among more moderate elements in society and a continuing source of amazement to foreign travellers. As well as managing the news content of the relatively few newspapers and magazines allowed a general circulation, the Foreign Office and Ministry of Police in Vienna kept a watchful eye on all foreign publications, banning the majority as the instruments of a pernicious liberalism from whose influence loyal subjects needed constant protection. Now and then the situation might improve, as Metternich's view of the international political climate grew temporarily more sanguine, but almost as soon a fresh wave of prohibitions or price increases on foreign newspapers would begin, dashing hopes of a more permanent relaxation.

At the heart of such an outlook lay a fear of the potency of the printed word in stimulating independent thought and liberating the citizen from passive acquiescence to established authority. The mere act of reading, in the early nineteenth-century Habsburg empire, was a bold one, given the continual disadvantages placed in the reader's way by the police. The contemporary writer Johann von Mailath, himself the victim of Metternich's interference while trying to compile a history of Hungary, referred to official censorship as the state's 'Chinese wall', and so indeed it was. Once prepared for possible publication, a book was to be submitted

---

* Byron's compositions 'are almost all modelled on the new Romantic system', the same source observes, but helpfully points out that the term 'Romantic' should not be confused with the recently-identified secret society known as 'Roma Antica'.

in manuscript to the Revision Office, which then forwarded it to the Police Ministry. At the end of this process, which might take as long as two years, the work in question was assigned to one of four Latin-designated categories. *Admittitur* meant that it was deemed harmless; *transeat* that it was allowed, but could only be sold under particular circumstances and was not to be translated into other languages; the *erga schedam* label meant that, though the tendency of the book was dangerous, it might be issued to persons of known good character; but if the word *damnatur* were applied, then the offending work was forbidden entirely.

The most seemingly innocuous of literary productions fell victim to such obsessive interference. An essay on the art of tying cravats, for example, was forbidden because one of the fashionable knots dem-onstrated was called '*a la Riego*', after the martyred hero of the Spanish constitutionalist revolt of 1820. A treatise on silk-weaving was censored because it presumed to evaluate the quality of silks from various centres of production in Lombardy-Venetia and produce a comparative judge-ment. The German dramatist Gottfried von Lessing's play *Emilia Galotti* was banned because its most badly behaved character was a duke, and the regulation decreed that nobody above the rank of baron should be unfavourably represented on a public stage. Even Italian classics, such as the Renaissance epics of Ariosto and Tasso, the sonnets of Petrarch and the poems of Boccaccio, were subject to serious emendation and expur-gation. It goes without saying that all theatrical presentations were anxiously monitored by the police, who held the relevant impresario responsible for submitting the text well in advance, so that any hint of subversion or offence against decorum could be swiftly excised.

Foreign authors were deemed especially suspect. A list of *erga schedam* or *damnatur* volumes found on sale at a Venetian bookshop in 1841 includes the novels of Balzac, George Sand and Eugène Sue, together with plays and poems by Victor Hugo, Lamartine and Musset. The works of Jeremy Bentham and Chateaubriand are simply proscribed, as are Stendhal's diffuse pseudo-guidebook *Promenades dans Rome* and the much-admired history of the Italian republics by Joseph Simond de Sismondi. Even the apparently harmless seafaring yarns of Captain Marryat are included on the list, presumably because it was known that he had stood on several occasions as a Member of Parliament on the radical fringe of the Whig party, Metternich's traditional foes in England.

Another English writer among the damned was the historian Henry Hallam. Metternich had always been doubtful of allowing unrestrained access to historiography, whatever its provenance or antiquity, ranking it, along with philosophy, as 'the most dangerous of public enemies'. In

Italy, which could boast a tradition of fine historical writing stretching back to the Renaissance and the Middle Ages, almost all major works in this field were either heavily censored or prohibited altogether, and even Roman writers like Sallust and Tacitus were looked at askance for the shrewdness of their observations on the timeless theme of 'greatness going off'. History was emphatically not among the disciplines encouraged when the Austrians reorganised the education system in their Italian provinces. 'Those who devoted themselves to such a study,' noted Johann von Mailath, 'were seen as dangerous or mad, and in either case useless to society. The government, more especially the police, mistrusted history, from a fear that its teaching must encourage ideas of liberty and the spirit of rebellion . . . It was believed that in obliterating the past it would be easier to manipulate the present.' The whole thrust of the educational programme was in any case heavily utilitarian, offering encouragement, in the form of grants, scholarships, prizes and medals, to the various branches of science, engineering and mathematics.

To Austria's credit it should be said that its schools were much the best among the Italian states. Obliged to attend primary classes from the age of six, pupils of either sex were expected, besides acquiring basic literacy and mathematical skills, to learn 'gratitude to parents and love of those arts to which they might be disposed to apply themselves', besides 'love of the sovereign and the fatherland, obedience to the laws, respect for magistrates and due acknowledgement of those who provide them with free education and strive to ennoble their souls'. In the second year the politicisation of the curriculum grew more obvious, with the introduction of a secular catechism entitled 'Duties of Subjects towards their Sovereign'. Its questions and answers included such no-nonsense exchanges as 'How should subjects behave towards their Sovereign? Subjects should behave towards their Sovereign as faithful servants towards their master'; 'Why should subjects behave as servants? Subjects should behave as servants because the Sovereign is their master and has absolute power over their property and their lives'; 'How can subjects make payment of taxes easier? By working diligently and living frugally.'

Throughout the schools, from the village primary to the six-year *ginnasio* or high school of the larger towns, teaching was based exclusively on textbooks sent from Vienna, often poorly translated from the German and littered with misprints. Though education was nominally secular, the clergy supervised teachers at all levels, and headmasters of the so-called *scuole maggiori*, which added Latin to the primary curriculum, had to be in holy orders. Candidates for teaching posts had to sign a declaration of loyalty to the Emperor, which included a promise never to join a secret society. Even after screening for their political and religious views, their behaviour, reputation and professional capacity, teachers remained a focus of constant vigilance from the police. Headmasters were expected to report annually on their staff, while agents recorded terse notes for the police files – 'Grandis, Austrian in his profession but a republican at heart'; 'Giuliani, perhaps not very Austrian but exceedingly prudent'; 'Mabil, lover of independence, not at all content with the present government, perhaps because preferred by the former, suspected freemason'; 'Brera, in favour of whatever government pays best'; 'Piloni, Austrian with all his heart'.

Both the teachers and the police who spied on them were merely units in a complex bureaucratic government system regulated by directives from Vienna, barely accountable to ordinary citizens save through direct appeals to the Emperor in person, and notoriously slow to stir. Its official figurehead in Italy was Francis's younger brother, Archduke Rainer. Based in Milan, the Viceroy was a worthy but uninspiring man, whose good intentions on behalf of Lombardy-Venetia were easily forgotten in preference to a more easily assimilated image of him as a smug stool pigeon of the regime, piously wringing his hands and always ready with promises, but reluctant to challenge established attitudes or upset routines. Below Rainer were the governors of the two provinces, appointed from among the German, Bohemian and Hungarian aristocratic caste, whose *schwarzgelber* loyalty to the Crown was to prove the Habsburg dynasty's salvation in the darkest hours of the revolution when it eventually came. The two provinces over which these functionaries presided were in turn split into districts and communes, with mayors and local councils. Power at every level was carefully limited. The only attempt at establishing anything like a genuinely representative body was the institution of so-called 'congregations', whose members were selected personally by the Emperor from a heavily vetted list of local landowners and leading citizens. The congregations themselves wielded no real executive force, forbidden as they were to discuss financial issues and able to make representations to central government only in the humblest possible terms.

It soon became obvious to Emperor Francis's Italian subjects that whatever the stabilising influence of Austrian rule under the law, its administrative wheels ground with an exasperating sluggishness. All decisions and requests had to be referred to relevant ministries and a practical response might take anything up to five years. Sympathy and encouragement from intermediate echelons within Italy itself were not a foregone conclusion, since so many of the higher positions within the Habsburg bureaucracy were filled by non-Italians, reflecting a suspicion on the part of Francis and Metternich as to the volatile loyalty of native inhabitants corrupted by more than a decade of French rule. Heavily represented as it was within the army, the police and even, in certain cases, the clergy, such 'German' influence pervaded the law courts to the extent that even those judges purporting to be Italian by birth hailed more often than not from the South Tyrol – yet further proof, it was felt, of the Emperor's deeply grounded mistrust of Italians as regulators of their own affairs.

A stronger cause of popular resentment was a widespread realisation that the two Italian provinces were essentially a fiscal milch-cow for the empire as its economy plunged ever further into debt. The bad impression created by the Austrian army on its arrival in 1814, with its draconian conscription methods and callous requisitioning of foodstuffs from even the poorest peasant communities, was not greatly improved over subsequent decades. Many village households learned to dread the moment when the males of the family were called up for a military service that might last for as long as eight years. Fresh taxes, meanwhile, continued to erode the hard-won savings of everybody from landowners large or small to the most wretched of farmworkers and itinerant labourers. Besides the traditional tithes yielded to the clergy, there was the heavy duty to be paid on salt as a state monopoly, the constant imposition of a stamp tax on the multitude of forms and certificates which bureaucracy required for official transactions, and the poll tax – '*il Filippo*' as it was called from the days when a similar levy was raised in Lombardy under the Spanish kings – exacted from every male citizen between the ages of fourteen and sixty. Add to this the rents payable to local landlords and it was a wonder that the average peasant, in what was still largely an agricultural economy, managed to reach the end of each year in a state approaching solvency.

Even in the poorest areas, such as the Polesine region around the city of Rovigo in the Po delta, where many people lived in miserable cabins of straw and reeds and families were routinely racked by the nutritional disease known as pellagra, life was tolerable only as long as the harvests were good. In the years immediately following Austria's assumption of control, however, the good faith and efficiency of the imperial regime were severely tested by a series of those El Niño-related famines that blighted Europe during the early nineteenth century, revealing the hopeless inflexibility of central governments when faced with the challenges posed by starvation, epidemics and resultant rural unrest.

By 1815 the Veneto was already crippled by serious unemployment and in several towns traditional industries such as silk-weaving and canvas-making had ground to a standstill for lack of materials. At Verona ugly scenes in markets and shops threatened to turn into major riots as food supplies ran short. At Padua more than 10 per cent of the population was soon reckoned to be living below the poverty line, while in Udine and its surrounding districts a mass exodus of the workforce began to other parts of Europe or to America. Pellagra ravaged the villages, in several of which the inhabitants were reduced to chewing grass and wisps of hay, picking berries and even eating animal manure. The people of Bassano, it was reported, were living off lupin seeds and boiled vegetable peelings. Both in the mountains and on the plains the staple resources of local agriculture had already been eroded by the recent political instability. Foraging French, Austrian and Russian troops had wrecked the vineyards around Verona and Mantua, and in the Polesine a newly introduced policy of enclosure undermined the age-old pastoral economy based on grazing cattle in the open grasslands along the Po and its tributaries.

At first the government in Vienna, like its London counterpart during the Irish potato famine of 1845–6, refused to take these problems seriously, but by the beginning of 1816 they were forced to note reports of wholesale migration to the towns by starving peasants clamouring for relief. In the provinces of Venice, Treviso and Padua, hopes of a good harvest were dashed by alternating droughts and heavy flooding, which did as much harm to roads and drainage ditches as to the fields themselves. As winter came on, hundreds began dying of hunger, and in several cities typhus epidemics thinned out the population still further.

Belatedly facing its responsibilities, the administration now did its best to calm potential unrest, facilitating the free movement of goods, offering subsidies in the worst-hit areas, promoting public-works programmes for the unemployed and ladling out that dismal constant of agricultural hardship, the 'economic soup', made of boiled bones and vegetables. There was no attempt, on the other hand, to lift or at least reduce the hated 'Filippo' or to seize the opportunity such a crisis presented of adjusting tariffs that restricted local entrepreneurs, particularly in the silk-weaving industry which dominated Lombardy-Venetia. That notorious Chinese wall fencing the empire against political subversion and the spread of cancerous liberalism was equally firm in its encirclement of the two provinces as a consumer market for Austrian goods, cutting out foreign competition.

Venice itself suffered grievously from this economic short-sightedness. For more than ten centuries its very existence as a city had been based on commercial enterprise. Even in its final years as capital of the Republic, when the economy had ceased to be seriously competitive with those of other European states, the port remained a busy one, its enormous Arsenal still employing thousands of workers in ship-building, and living standards were generally higher for even the humblest sectors of the population than they were in most other Italian cities. After the long blockade of 1813–14 had been lifted and the Austrians took over in earnest, they might have been expected to exploit Venice's potential as a centre for Mediterranean trade, a worthy rival to such Italian ports as Genoa, Naples and Leghorn. Instead, for the next fifteen years, the government seemed resolutely inclined to turn its back on the city, as if explicitly intending to humble its pride as 'La Bella Dominante', whose doges had symbolically married the Adriatic each year by casting a ring into the waves on Ascension Day. Though the Arsenal shipyards were not altogether idle, the Emperor, convinced that he needed no more than a small navy, sold off the battleships left behind by the French to the King of Denmark. Traditional industries such as glass-blowing and the weaving of fine textiles drastically declined, over one-third of Venice's inhabitants lived below the poverty line or resorted to begging, and the inevitable result was a haemorrhaging of the population. In 1799 census figures stood at around 136,000. By 1812 these had dropped to 125,000, and ten years later the once-vital, bustling metropolis contained barely 100,000 souls.

How could this not happen when Austria seemed so determined to promote the advantages of Venice's nearest Adriatic competitor, the port of Trieste? The Triestines had been favoured with trading privileges since the early eighteenth century and there was a loyal Austrophile constituency among the city's merchants, though many of them were Italian in language and culture. Their fortunes seemed assured, what was more, by the presence of the headquarters of Austrian Lloyd, a steamship line running vessels to all the ports of Greece, Egypt and the Levant, which became one of the most successful business enterprises in the Habsburg empire. Though Venice would have seemed an ideal choice for such a base, the government pointedly chose its rival, seeing off any possible Venetian competitors with the guarantee of a monopoly.

If Emperor Francis, paying his first visit to Venice in December 1815, was satisfied with the warmth of his welcome, Prince Metternich, who accompanied him, was probably aware that the Venetians' enthusiasm owed less to unadulterated loyalty than to the hope that he might favour fresh economic initiatives towards rescuing the city from total decay. Metternich, at least, understood what needed to be done in the way of reducing harbour duties on shipping, but was nevertheless unimpressed by the place itself. 'Venice,' he told his mother, 'resembles one vast ruin', while remarking elsewhere that it seemed like a grandiose palace whose owner had been forced through poverty to live in a hut alongside it. Such an image of unstoppable decline easily seized hold of foreign visitors and incoming residents during the peaceful tourist invasion of Europe beginning after Napoleon's downfall. To the English Romantic poets, Venice became an irresistible symbol of the nemesis that follows hubris in the fatal trajectory of human affairs. As early as 1797, William Wordsworth (who had not yet set foot in the city) composed a head-shaking sonnet on the apparent demise of 'the eldest child of Liberty' who 'once . . . did hold the gorgeous East in fee.' Shelley, obsessed with the denial of political freedom callously sanctioned by the Congress of Vienna's absolutist settlement, moralised gloomily in 'Lines written among the Euganean Hills' (1818) on the 'conquest-branded brow' of the 'Sun-girt City', whose palaces and churches were:

> Sepulchres, where human forms,
> Like pollution-nourished worms,
> To the corpse of greatness cling,
> Murdered, and now mouldering.

Byron, taking up residence on the Grand Canal in 1817 amid pet dogs and monkeys, encapsulated the classic expression of Romantic melancholy at the prospect of an unpeopled Venice and her now-pointless monumental magnificence. The second of two new cantos added to *Childe Harold's Pilgrimage* opens with an evocation of the city as essentially a massive illusion, a repository of dreams and memories, while the 'Ode on Venice', written in 1819, lamented that:

> Even the Lion all subdued appears,
> And the harsh sound of the barbarian drum
> With dull and daily dissonance, repeats
> The echo of thy tyrant's voice along
> The soft waves, once all musical to song.

Increasingly the image of Venice in early nineteenth-century Europe was defined by its degraded status as the former capital of an ancient sovereign power whose wealth and splendour had vanished with the same dramatic suddenness as its independent statehood. The urban infrastructure may have been improved through the creation of new streets by means of earthing in and paving over numerous canals and by the building of many more bridges, but between 1815 and 1840 the Austrians had no scruples in continuing the policy begun by the French of demolishing churches and monasteries or assigning them to other uses. The church of Santa Marina, for example, in the Castello district, was destroyed and the saint's incorrupt body transferred to Santa Maria Formosa in the adjacent campo. Immediately behind Piazza San Marco's newly built Ala Napoleonica, Santa Maria dell'Ascensione was torn down to allow enlargement of the next-door hotel, Albergo della Luna. Across the city and the lagoon islands, only the names of streets and squares survive to remind us of the vanished parishes – San Basegio, San Stin, San Provolo, La Celestia, Sant'Angelo and the orphanage church of the Incurabili, which in the eighteenth century had boasted a world-famous orchestra. On the island of Murano alone, almost a dozen ecclesiastical buildings of various kinds were swept away.

Once the churches themselves were gone and their attached convents and *scuole* given over to secular use, what was to happen to the art treasures so many of them contained? Here, as elsewhere, the Austrian official attitude was strikingly ambivalent. Many of the altarpieces, sculptures and other works looted by Napoleon's commissioners had been restored to the city after 1815. The return of the four antique bronze horses to their rightful position on the façade of St Mark's basilica was rightly viewed as an event charged with immense propaganda value for the Venetians. The government, to its credit, made much of the occasion, though it is tempting to wonder whether the files of white-coated infantry, three deep, lining either side of the Piazzetta were there as a warning to potential demonstrators rather than simply for ceremonial purposes. The Austrians looked favourably, what was more, on the initiatives of Count Leopoldo Cicognara, the enterprising Ferrarese president of the Accademia delle Belle Arti, originally founded in the eighteenth century to provide a life-drawing class for painters and now promoted, alongside its gallery, as one of the leading Italian art schools. With his charm, professional expertise and good social standing, Cicognara did whatever he could to ensure the preservation of Venice's surviving art-works during a period in which it must have seemed as if nothing was safe from the depredations of foreign dealers or the envious eyes of the imperial government itself. For all the looted patrimony they returned to the city, the Austrians continued periodically to remove paintings to Vienna. In 1838, for example, the Akademie der Bildenden Kunste received no fewer than sixty-seven canvases and panels, including works by Veronese, Carpaccio and Alvise Vivarini. As for the 1,500 pictures assembled in the Doge's Palace the previous year, taken from various dismantled religious foundations, many of these were distributed among churches elsewhere in the Veneto, but some eventually found their way into galleries a considerable distance away. Even the surviving fabric of Venice itself was not entirely safe. Though a grandiose project intended to turn the Riva degli Schiavoni into a massive hotel-and-shopping complex never got beyond the architect's drawing board, other areas were hardly so fortunate. The dispossessed church of San Gerolamo in the Cannaregio district was transformed into a flour mill, while the Doge's Palace was given over to government offices, its painted halls crammed with files and documents. Several other palazzi were turned over to similar practical uses. On the Grand Canal, the Gritti and Giustiniani-Morosini became hotels; the Farsetti, formerly home to a highly regarded art academy, became the seat of Venice's town council; and a Grimani palace at San Luca housed the Post Office, before its installation in the old Fondaco dei Tedeschi near the Rialto Bridge. Wealthy expatriates buying palaces from the more drastically impoverished of Venetian noble families had few qualms in adjusting them to modern taste and convenience without regard for the historical integrity of their architecture and décor.

An influx of foreign visitors was nothing new. Venice had always needed admirers, but after 1815 the city became still more attractive to tourists and resident incomers, whether for its cheapness or its deeply layered historicity. Those curious as to the Venetian past scarcely bothered to enquire whether modern historians, busy turning over the now readily accessible archives of the Serene Republic, were concerned with representing it at all fairly. It suited late Romantic Europe's morbid obsession with the shame and misery of former ages that Venice under the doges should figure as the ultimate incarnation of tyrannical oppression and the rule of fear. Out of the pages of works such as *Histoire de la république de Venise*, which Stendhal's cousin Pierre Daru, Napoleon's ex-Minister for War, published in 1819, James Fenimore Cooper's novel *The Bravo* or Edward Smedley's popular *Sketches from Venetian History* (both issued in 1831) arose what Italian historians have since called '*la leggenda nera*', 'the Black Legend' of the Republic as a state whose callous pursuit of material wealth and disdain for human rights had at length drawn down a righteous punishment from heaven. Behind Wordsworth's hand-wringing over 'the extinction of the Venetian Republic' lay, if not consciously, a certain frisson of told-you-so smugness. The same idea that La Serenissima somehow had it coming to her and merited neither pity nor regret inspired Byron's eminently effective closet-dramas of medieval Venice, *Marino Faliero* and *The Two Foscari*, both of them later transformed into operas by Donizetti and Verdi.

The Black Legend could be contradicted easily enough, as Daru discovered when his book was ferociously picked over for inaccuracies by the antiquarian Domenico Tiepolo. It was useful, however, not just to poets, composers and painters, but to politicians and propagandists besides. The imperial regime could counter any insidious nostalgia for vanished glories with an image of the old Venetian government as even more deeply mired than its Habsburg successor in secretiveness, obfuscation and obsessive surveillance of ordinary citizens. Not all foreign observers were content to echo the Briton J. D. Sinclair's remark, in 1829, that 'the people here know they are slaves; but although their chains gall them to the quick, they have neither the moral nor the physical force to break their fetters and throw off the yoke'. W. H. Stiles, America's chargé d'affaires at Vienna, believed instead that with Austrian annexation 'the change to Venice could not but have been a desirable one', while a Tory journalist in the London *Quarterly Review* praised the Austrian government as 'working soberly, steadily and unostentatiously for the public good' and suggested that the benign takeover in 1815 had actually rescued the city from destruction by its own inhabitants.

The fact nevertheless remains that, as Tiepolo and subsequent critics of *la leggenda nera* pointed out, the majority of Venetians had lived happily and prosperously under their supposedly pitiless, unprincipled oligarchs for nearly a thousand years, and that apart from two or three isolated incidents no significant attempt had been offered during this entire period towards subverting the status quo. In addition it was difficult not to feel, as the 1820s drew on, that there was something calculated in Austria's continuing neglect of Lombardy-Venetia except as the food-bank of the empire, whose inhabitants effectively subsidised other areas of the realm by paying one-third of the imperial revenue when they constituted only one-seventh of the total population within Habsburg domains. Surveying the two newly acquired territories in 1814 on Metternich's orders, a former ambassador, Johann von Wessenberg, indicated the chief priority of Austrian rule as being 'to exploit the Italian provinces to the monarch's best advantage'. As the state lurched from one financial crisis to another, the tax surplus from Lombardy-Venetia became essential to an economic continuum, and the introduction of fresh dues and levies was a dismal constant of new legislation throughout the 1830s and 1840s.

Fruitful though the mainland might be, the imminent ruin of Venice itself as a commercial centre at length became obvious even to the bureaucrats of Vienna. In 1830 the government at last conceded free-port status to the city, placing trade in the lagoon beyond the Lombardo-Venetian customs barriers. In order not to create problems for local manufacturing, tariff duties were lifted from all products exported to the *terraferma*, though the enterprises concerned had to be already up and running and no encouragement was offered to fresh initiatives. Yet even if there was no likelihood of mercantile supremacy being wrested from Trieste, the city embarked on a modest but perceptible recovery. To the existing export of foodstuffs – flour, rice, barley, cheese and wines – as well as glass, canvas, timber, hides, hats, candles, vitriol and chalk, Venice now added an increased trade in silk to England and France from the factories of Schio, Thiene and Asolo. Beet-sugar refineries were set up within the city limits, together with felt-making workshops using English steam engineering. By 1838 Venice had become the third-busiest Italian port after Genoa and Leghorn, rivalled elsewhere in the Mediterranean only by Constantinople and Marseilles.

The Emperor Francis I did not live to witness more than the initial phase of this regeneration. Early in 1835, during a particularly cold February, he was struck down with pneumonia and on 2 March he died, at the age of sixty-seven. Though not exactly beloved in Vienna itself, he was respected for the stability he had seemed to ensure by remaining so accessible to people of all ranks and conditions, as well as for his plodding dedication to duty. His legitimate successor, on the other hand, was not calculated to inspire confidence. The Archduke Ferdinand was the Emperor's son by his third wife, Maria Ludovica of Modena, whose discontent with her husband began early, culminating in a scandalous liaison with one of her brothers-in-law.* A grotesquely enlarged forehead and vacant blue eyes made Ferdinand, in appearance at least, the very incarnation of inbred royal idiocy. As an epileptic in an age which knew nothing of the causes of such a condition or its appropriate therapy, he had been denied a proper upbringing and was thought retarded simply because there was no awareness of his need for specialised teaching. Ferdinand's reputation as an imbecile was nevertheless unjustified. Evidence suggests that he had serious artistic leanings and that he was by no means ineducable if assisted by a patient and sympathetic tutor. The often-repeated canard that his character was summed up in the single remark 'I'm the Emperor and I want my dumplings' is simply not borne out by closer scrutiny of his admittedly unfortunate career.

The trouble was that Ferdinand's sheltered upbringing had made him abnormally shy, while his father had been insufficiently concerned to school him in the management of ministers, courtiers and the more ambitious members of the imperial family. If those who met him face to face or observed his behaviour in public tended to write him off as the classic

---

* It was through his discreet suppression of any possible scandal arising from this affair that Metternich originally made himself indispensable to the Emperor.

product of royal genetic imbalance, his intellectual pursuits, which included the creation of an extensive private library and an interest in history, numismatics and engineering, suggested that he was not the fool they took him for. The shrewd Emperor Francis had been confident enough in Ferdinand's ability to rule. Just before his death, the old man had written a memorandum summarising the basic principles he desired his heir to maintain. 'Do not alter the fundamental structure of the state,' he wrote, 'change nothing, have the same trust in Prince Metternich, my most loyal servant and friend, that I had in him over many years. Honour established rights, for then you will be able to insist firmly on the reverence due to you as a monarch. Make no decisions about people or public issues without having consulted Prince Metternich first of all.'

Metternich was indeed there to be consulted, at the age of sixty-two still very much alive and conscious of what was due to him as the acknowledged doyen of European statesmen and pilot of the Habsburg empire's conservative course. Francis's death, however, had removed from the Chancellor a stalwart working partner for whom Ferdinand was no suitable replacement. Metternich, invincibly vain as he was, may have seemed indestructible, to himself as to others, but the rivals he had managed to hold at bay during the former reign now started to close in. An attempt at seeing off the most serious challenger, Finance Minister Count Franz Kolowrat-Liebsteinsky, by means of constitutional changes confining him to a purely advisory role in a council of ministers, seemed at first to have paid off, but the Chancellor had not reckoned on Kolowrat's opportunism in gathering support among the various branches of the imperial family. A court faction, led by the liberally inclined Archduke Johann, saw to it that Metternich's scheme should be sufficiently neutered as to give him no greater influence than Kolowrat on the management of affairs, within a council of regency whose task was to govern in Ferdinand's name.

The new Emperor, besides being acknowledged as sovereign in Vienna and Prague, was also expected formally to accept the Iron Crown of Lombardy, symbol of his rule over the Italian provinces and a hallowed relic of the Longobard kings who had reigned from Pavia and Milan in the centuries before Charlemagne. Lavish festivities were planned with the probable object of fanning loyal sentiment among subjects least inclined to profess it, and after his coronation in Milan Cathedral on 10 September 1838, Ferdinand set out on a tour of the neighbouring cities, arriving in Venice on 5 October. A cortège of gondolas accompanied the imperial barge down the Grand Canal to the sound of church bells and the cheers of a generally well-disposed crowd watching from boats and landing stages. Metternich was at the Emperor's side, together with his ever-watchful wife Melanie, who confided effusively to her diary that the whole event had produced 'a magical impression. The richly decorated gondolas and the other vessels, adorned with splendid draperies and flags glittering with silver and gold, rowed by their gondoliers in the most varied costumes, both original and bizarre, combined to create a truly fairytale spectacle . . . Everyone was happy and contented; joy appeared in every face, it was all marvellously beautiful.' There were regattas, triumphal arches on Murano, a foundation-stone laid at Malamocco, gala performances at La Fenice, all enhanced, rather to the Princess's surprise, by a prevailing air of bonhomie and good behaviour among the common people. Ferdinand's innocent determination to enjoy himself charmed the Venetians, especially when he insisted on dismissing the customary entourage of courtiers and police while he toured the canals or attended mass. Even Metternich himself was courteously received by those with no particular reason to approve of him.

The city which extended such a welcome was in rather better shape economically than it had been on the Chancellor's last visit some twenty years earlier. Its population had embarked on a brisk increase. Though there was never any likelihood that Venice would regain the prosperity enjoyed under the doges, a new confidence was discernible among merchants, bankers and shopkeepers, as inhabitants of something more than a ghost town nurturing the melodramatic fancies and cheap moralising of tourist visitors. This newly enriched Venetian bourgeoisie had largely taken the place of the old aristocracy as the most significant social echelon. A chamber of commerce was augmented in 1840 when a group of businessmen founded the Società Veneta Commerciale, a joint-stock company based on capital of fifteen million Austrian lire. Uneven though its progress was, the venture reflected fresh optimism as to Venice's revival as a creditable competitor with other Mediterranean ports. The number of ships in the lagoon, meanwhile, increased by 100 per cent between 1836 and 1844, many of them carrying the goods produced in the factories springing up in the Cannaregio and Giudecca districts. Several enterprises were set on foot by businessmen from outside Italy. The German mill owner Friedrich Oexle was joined by his fellow countryman Friedrich Bertuch, owner of a successful silk warehouse, and by Scots cloth merchants Thomas Holm and Alexander Malcolm.

In all the salons, theatres and learned societies of Venice in the 1840s, men like these, together with lawyers and doctors, many of whom came from within the Jewish community emancipated by Napoleon, now rubbed shoulders with members of the patrician class that had formed the governing oligarchy of the old Republic. The names of these displaced grandees – Mocenigo, Gradenigo, Morosini, Foscarini, Loredan, Savorgnan, Zen, Sten, Tron – had been inscribed in the *Libro d'Oro*, that very same Golden Book which Napoleon ordered to be burned in token of the state's destruction. Their powers were not restored in 1815, and though many nobles were prepared to accept the title of count from Emperor Francis in exchange for a fixed sum of money, several proudly chose to decline the proffered honour. Such scorn was reinforced by a certain feeling among the Venetian nobility that their time had come and gone. With the gradual dispersal of palaces and heirlooms and the sale, on the mainland, of the great estates whose farms and rents had sustained a patrician lifestyle, came the extinction of branch after branch of the Golden Book's most illustrious clans. The names of Venetian streets and canals, a *ramo*, a *rio*, a *sottoportego* or a *salizzada*, are often all that remains of these descendants of doges, admirals and senators, whose movable inheritance is now scattered among the art collections of Europe and the USA.

In their heyday the patrician households had supported hundreds of servants and gondoliers. The latter could, of course, still find work when a palace changed hands, and the canals and the lagoon were still busy with craft of all kinds, needing occasional repairs at the *squero*, or boat-yard, a much commoner sight within Venice than it is today. Elsewhere the city's labouring population looked for work in the ship-building yards of the Arsenal, a shadow of its former self, but still employing more than 1,000 hands, or otherwise found jobs as waiters, maids, cooks and porters among the various cafés and hotels. In the *sestieri* of Cannaregio, San Niccolò and Giudecca lived much of this hungry, ill-clad and (despite Austrian legal requirements) largely uneducated workforce, an urban peas-antry many of whom could scarcely depend on stable jobs earning a regular wage. Certain trades inevitably attracted those dwelling in partic-ular parishes. Makers of glass beads congregated around San Francesco della Vigna, butchers at San Geremia and San Marcuola and fishermen at Angelo Raffaele, and though Murano's glass-blowers were no longer forbidden, as they had been before 1797, to leave the island, many of them still lived in its parish of San Pietro Martire. For dwellers in all these quarters, however, long spells of idleness were unavoidable. Venice had never possessed a class of professional loafers along the lines of the Neapolitan *lazzaroni*, but the town had more than its fair share of beggars, many eking out their mendicant earnings by hawking foodstuffs, matches and trinkets through the streets.

What visitors invariably noticed among even the poorest Venetians, lounging in the sunshine on the Riva degli Schiavoni, hanging out ragged clothes to dry in some poky courtyard off the Barberia delle Tole or haggling fiercely in the markets around San Giacomo di Rialto, was their unquenchable verve, energy and independence of spirit, coupled with extraordinary graces of feeling and expression underlying even the most raucous exchanges in their singsong dialect. If the muse of Carlo Goldoni, whose eighteenth-century comedies had celebrated the vivacity and variety of Venetian street life, was still very much alive, so too was a profoundly rooted sense of pride among these people in their unique inheritance as 'the children of St Mark', who had never been slaves to a foreign conqueror until now and were not among the Habsburg emperor's most loyal subjects. A passionate, undivided allegiance on the part of so many Venetians to their city and what it represented was something never properly noted or understood by the Austrians until too late.

On its simplest level, Austria's role as an occupying power could easily be assessed by any traveller who set foot in Piazza San Marco. Its porticoes were lined, then as now, with shops and cafés, the latter inviting obvious distinctions among their clientele. While the noisy, smoke-filled Caffè Quadri, on the square's sunnier western side, became the resort of white-tunicked officers from the imperial army, the Caffè Florian, in the Procuratie Nuove immediately opposite, was altogether a more courteous and civilised establishment, favoured by Venetians whose politics, if at this stage not openly declared, tended towards the patriotic. No wonder Florian declined to display the German word *Kaffeehaus*, which identified Quadri as pro-Austrian, a character given further emphasis by a sign that read 'Military Café'. The French author of the most comprehensive guidebook to Venice in the 1840s, Jules Lecomte, commended Florian for everything from the availability of foreign newspapers (whose readers were routinely reported to the police) and the excellent fork suppers, to the politeness of the waiters and the fact that women could enter 'without the least inconvenience'. Quadri too offered good food and the best of the European press, and in summer it was hard to choose between either for the quality of their sorbets, yet 'both inside and outside, the Café Florian retains a physiognomy more aristocratic and exotic than any other'.

The pages of Lecomte's *Venise, description littéraire, historique et artistique*, first published in 1845, reveal a place whose intrinsic fascination as an art city was balanced by the allure and variety of its shops and hotels. The availability of acceptable inns and lodgings had much improved under Austrian rule, helped of course by the number of patrician palaces ripe for conversion. Venerable establishments like the Cavalletto and the Luna were joined, after 1815, by such handsomely appointed hotels as the

Europa, occupying a former Palazzo Giustiniani, and its neighbour on the Grand Canal the Albergo d'Italia (now the Hotel Bauer Grünwald). 'In winter,' says Lecomte of the Italia, 'all the rooms are furnished with carpets, something by no means common in Italy.' Most sought-after of them all was the Albergo Reale del Leone Bianco, better known from the name of its enterprising proprietor Giuseppe Danieli, which has stuck to it ever since. Danieli's hotel, originally in a building near the Rialto bridge, reopened in 1822 amid the far grander surroundings of the fifteenth-century Gothic Palazzo Mocenigo, on Riva degli Schiavoni close to the Doge's Palace. Here Charles Dickens stayed in 1843, mesmerised by the sheer outlandishness of Venice as a construct, its devastating stillness and thrilling extremes of light and shadow (Franz Liszt, visiting the city on an Italian concert tour, had spoken perceptively of its 'silent noises'). Honoré de Balzac was a guest in 1837, sufficiently inspired to make Venice the setting for his novel *Massimila Doni*, but the Albergo Danieli's most enduring link with French Romanticism had been forged three years earlier by the novelist George Sand, arriving with her lover Alfred de Musset somewhat reluctantly in tow. Both were at once excited by the *mise-en-scène*, Musset composing several effective little poems based on Venetian popular song, and Sand writing some of the more eloquent pages of the delightful *Lettres d'un voyageur*. The love affair, however, had already threatened a crisis before they arrived. Bored by now with Sand's daily workaholic routine, Musset, indolent and sottish, went in search of entertainment, leaving her fretting at the hotel. Around them spread the inimical Venetian winter, with its freezing fogs and rheumatic damps. Musset promptly fell ill, and Sand, though prepared to mother the invalid, saw no reason not to fall in love with the handsome young doctor, Pietro Pagello, whom she summoned to the bedside. Packing Musset back to Paris (there was still life in their liaison), she lingered on to enjoy Pagello's attentions and the onset of a particularly agreeable spring.

Sand's delight in the city around her, reflected in the second of the *Lettres d'un voyageur*, typified the sensitive tourist's response to the paradox inescapably presented by Habsburg Venice. 'How can anyone stop me,' she wrote, 'from sleeping peacefully when I see Venice, so decayed, so oppressed and so impoverished, refusing to allow time or mankind to mar her beauty and serenity? It would take years of slavery to brutalise entirely this happy-go-lucky, frivolous disposition. Life is still so simple in Venice!' Or so at any rate it seemed for the fishermen curled up under their coats asleep on the marble steps, the housewives shopping in markets crammed with fruit and vegetables from the island gardens of the lagoon, the boating parties on the canals with their snatches of song and laughter, or the virtuoso banter of tradesmen, street hawkers and gondoliers. Even the moon appeared to shine more brightly than in Paris.

Ten years afterwards Jules Lecomte was more than ready to agree. By now the moonbeams were assisted by gas lighting, introduced to Venice on 19 August 1843 with a magnificent *festa popolare* featuring three different bands in Piazza San Marco. On the Piazza's night-time pleasures the guide-book grew positively ecstatic. 'The moon, like a torch closed within an alabaster globe, moves across the heavenly vault sprinkled with stars, serving in some degree as a lamp to illuminate this saloon. In the middle of the square the excellent band of one of the garrison regiments has placed its music desks and offers a concert of numbers from the operas of the fecund Donizetti, the dramatic Mercadante and even of Ferrari himself, a young Venetian composer. Often this orchestra begins with the bounding melody of a waltz or of some provocative galop, so that it seems as if everyone is ready to fling themselves across the smooth stones forming the pavement of this gigantic space.' Lecomte admired the democratic atmosphere prevailing among the crowd. 'The Countess spreads herself across three chairs to taste an ice cream at Florian or Suttil while not far off her dressmaker is taking the air beside a husband smoking a black cigar.' Under the arcades of the Procuratie Nuove, sheltering the offices of steamer lines and law firms, the throng was truly international, featuring, besides sizeable numbers of French, Germans and English, a sprinkling of Turks, Armenians, Greeks and Egyptians. Perhaps among all these strollers was that anonymous foreigner whom the youthful and prodigiously gifted Friulan writer Ippolito Nievo satirised in his poem 'Il touriste' as the archetype of the ignorant day-tripper 'doing' Venice:

Hotfoot from Marseilles, guidebook in his pocket,
Falling plump into the Piazza comes the illustrious ultramontane.
He snubs Saint Mark, throws a sidelong look at the Doge's Palace,
Buys a pair of gloves and sprawls in Florian's.
He takes a dab at the newspaper to see how his shares are doing
Before paying for his tea and a cigar.
Back on board the boat he tucks into a beefsteak.
Venice? He might as well be at Mecca for all the difference it makes.

If such a traveller chose to stay on, he could take note of the subtle suggestions in Lecomte's guidebook as to what was on offer in and around the piazza after most of the city had gone to bed. Without identifying the presence of prostitution and homosexual cruising in so many words, the Frenchman paints an ageless picture of the way in which the square empties itself late at night, leaving only 'those whom Venice has taken to its bosom, who return again and again to enjoy its pleasures' amid the nocturnal stillness. What the modern phrase identifies as 'sex tourism' had been a Venetian speciality since the Middle Ages, and in 1797 the number of working girls was estimated at 20,000 – one-seventh of the total population, an obvious exaggeration, but one that bears witness to their significant presence. Under the Austrians, according to a jaundiced English observer, they were as profitable a source of revenue as they had been in the days when the Republic devoted its tax on prostitution to the building of battleships. 'The tender-hearted and accommodating portion of the fair sex are charged a stipulated sum before they are allowed to carry on their meretricious profession. Being classed, by the present well-ordered and religious government, in the list of regular traders, of course they are in duty bound to contribute their fair proportion to the exigencies of the state.'

More respectable amusement was provided by the Venetian theatres. Five of these had survived the Republic's fall, including the San Benedetto (where today's Cinema Rossini stands), the Apollo at San Luca (now Teatro Goldoni) and the Malibran, which had begun life in the seventeenth century as an opera house belonging to the Grimani family of San Giovanni Grisostomo. Following an unsuccessful spell as Teatro Emeronittio (literally 'day-and-night') it was taken over by the impresario Giuseppe Gallo, who rescued it by persuading the legendary diva Maria Malibran, visiting Venice in 1835, to give a pair of benefit concerts, which more than fulfilled their objective, and to bestow her name on the theatre.

Stateliest of all was the Gran Teatro della Fenice. Built in 1791–2 to a radical design by the learned Venetian architect Giannantonio Selva, it witnessed triumphant first nights from Rossini, Meyerbeer and Bellini before the destruction of its interior by fire on the night of 13 December 1836. Winners of the rebuilding competition were the brothers Giambattista and Tommaso Meduna, the former a brilliantly eclectic though often ruthless restorer of Venetian palaces and churches, the latter a talented engineer. Around them they gathered a team of painters and sculptors from the Accademia delle Belle Arti, and at a cost of 600,000 Austrian lire the phoenix proved true to its name. Though the opera with which it reopened on 26 December 1837, Giuseppe Lillo's *Rosmunda in Ravenna*, was speedily forgotten, the state-of-the-art theatre was soon to see the premières of Donizetti's *Belisario*, *Pia de'Tolomei* and *Maria di Rudenz*, while during the 1840s the young Giuseppe Verdi scored triumphs here with his *Ernani* and *Attila*.

Like all Italian theatres of the period, La Fenice provided an inevitable focus for social activity throughout the winter months, when a crowded opera house must always have been warmer than a draughty palazzo. During the carnival season a grand ball was given, with supper served in the first-floor rooms known as the Sale Apollinee. In 1846, according to the indefatigable Venetian journalist Tommaso Locatelli, the ball, on the Monday before Ash Wednesday, 'surpassed in luxury and variety all those of past years: the participants could not tear themselves away from such a place of enchantments, and at nine in the morning no fewer than sixty-five indefatigable couples derided the sun's rays and challenged the stamina of the band'. Dancing on a professional level had become a speciality of La Fenice's seasons. Carlotta Grisi, later famous as the first Giselle, made a dramatic Venetian debut in 1833, in the *ballabili* of Rossini's *William Tell*; the Viennese ballerina Fanny Elssler won over the Italian patriots with her thrilling acount of Esmeralda in a ballet based on Victor Hugo's *The Hunchback of Notre Dame*; and Marie Taglioni, having taken Paris and London by storm in *La Sylphide*, repeated her triumph at La Fenice in 1843.

Like her fellow dancers, Taglioni arrived in Venice by gondola. For the first forty years of the nineteenth century the city remained what it had always been since its foundation on the Rialto mudbanks in the early Middle Ages, a collection of densely inhabited offshore islands in an Adriatic lagoon. The boat journey from Fusina, on one of the three mouths of the Riva Brenta, merely served to enhance the visitor's aware-ness of entering on a unique experience, to which words like 'dream' and 'vision', however used by Byron and Dickens, seemed the most hackneyed of verbal equivalents. For another English writer, the young John Ruskin, that earliest waterborne contact was to furnish what remains, in its mixture of reverence and physical excitement, one of the most miraculous accounts ever composed of an intelligent traveller's first engagement with the place: the single massive paragraph, covering two pages in many editions, which forms the opening of Part II of *The Stones of Venice*.

Ruskin's awed yet ecstatic celebration is also a threnody. It is scarcely ironic that the man who, above all others, influenced the way in which the modern world has evaluated the achievements of medieval and Renaissance art in Venice should have so detested the idea of the place as a living city, whose leading inhabitants, whatever their aesthetic sensi-tivities, were keen to ensure its economic survival as part of Europe's second-largest empire. Ruskin was horrified as much by the presence of factories amid the sacred fanes bedecked with the glories of the divine 'Tintoret' and 'Giambellino' as by the apparent indifference of contemporary Venetians in Piazza San Marco to the basilica itself. 'You will not see an eye lifted to it, not a countenance brightened by it,' he wrote. 'Up to the very recesses of the porches, the meanest tradesmen of the city push their counters; nay, the foundations of its pillars are themselves the seats – not "of them that sell doves" for sacrifice, but of the vendors of toys and caricatures.' We can hardly wonder at his horror, on returning to Venice in 1845, at discovering that the gondola ride from Fusina had been superseded by that ultimate symbol of resistless nineteenth-century progress, the railway.

A project for joining Venice to the mainland by a rail link that should stretch at least as far as Milan had been mooted as early as 1826, but it was another nine years (and only a few months after Ruskin made his first exultant landfall on the Rialto) before anyone of influence, either in the Venetian Chamber of Commerce or the Austrian government, began to take it seriously. The general scheme had the blessing of Prince Metternich, whose absorbing interest in new technology made him aware of the long-term benefits to Austria of an invention that Pope Gregory XVI had recently banned from the States of the Church as a diabolical agent of progress. For the Venice – Milan railway a commission, including several prominent Venetian businessmen, was set up to determine, among other things, the exact route of the track across the imperial provinces. The choice lay between a direct line over the Veneto-Lombard plain, via Verona, Brescia and Treviglio, and a more circuitous journey veering north from Brescia to take in the towns of Bergamo and Monza before curving down towards Milan.

For more than seven years this single issue remained a strong enough bone of contention to obstruct real progress on the project. Spirited Venetian propagandists, encouraging speculation from strictly local concerns within the Italian provinces, finally secured the Treviglio route, but at the cost of the railway's commercial independence. Imperial decrees issued on 19 December 1841 and 3 January 1842 confirmed the government's determination, prompted by the Finance Minister Karl von Kübeck, to take an active part in the construction and running of all lines within the realm, declaring them state railways. The first stretch of what was to be officially christened the Linea Ferdinandea, running from the fortress of Marghera, via Mestre and Dolo, as far as Padua, was opened on 12 December 1842, with three locomotives ordered the previous year from the Manchester firm of Sharp & Roberts, each pulling two goods wagons, four first- and two second-class carriages, with a single third-class coach cramming in seventy-two passengers.

To begin with, the Ferdinandea was bitterly opposed by Venetian boatmen and gondoliers, especially when a fleet of oared omnibuses was launched, taking railway passengers to a series of stops along the Grand Canal, whose prices undercut those for gondola rides over similar distances. The rowers of the *traghetti*, traditional ferries across the canal, far more numerous than the handful operating nowadays, added their protests, fearful lest the new craft, with their six oarsmen and curtained passenger cabin, should do them out of business. Despite genuine attempts to conciliate the gondoliers, several of whom had made efforts at sabotage, the omnibuses were there to stay, inevitable harbingers of the steam vessels whose name, *vaporetto*, is still given to the motorised ACTV buses plying the main waterways of Venice.

With the building of a viaduct, completed in 1846 to designs by Tommaso Meduna and Luigi Duodo, and the creation of a railway terminus on the site of the former church of Santa Lucia (the relics of the patron saint of oculists having been transferred to a shrine in San Geremia), the union of Venice with the mainland was complete. There was an inescapable symbolism in the presence of this handsome railway bridge with its white limestone piers and arches. If only in the most practical sense, it bound the city to a place that existed, for a growing number of Venetians, if not yet as a political actuality, then at least as an attainable ideal. It was the place Metternich on various occasions famously dismissed as a geographical expression, and whose name had been on the lips of the Bandiera brothers and Domenico Moro as they fell dead before their Bourbon executioners. It was somewhere called Italy.

~

CHAPTER 2.

A LITTLE MAN IN SPECTACLES

'WHO DOES NOT KNOW WHAT Italy is?' wrote the historian Francesco Guicciardini in 1530. 'A province queen over all the others by virtue of her fortunate position, her temperate climate, the number and skill of men dedicated to every honourable undertaking, the profusion of those things which are useful to mankind and the magnificence of so many noble cities, as the abode of religion and the former glory of the Roman empire, and for a multitude of reasons besides.' More than a century later, the poet Vincenzo da Filicaja, a Florentine like Guicciardini, sounded a more depressing note in the first poem of a sonnet sequence. 'Italy, Italy, if only you were less fair or at least more powerful, you to whom Fate has given the unhappy gift of beauty which has brought you a dowry of infinite misery, its sorrows traced upon your brow!' These two ideas of Italy – on the one hand a sovereign among nations, principal seat of Holy Mother Church, heir to ancient Rome and naturally endowed with inexhaustible resources of beauty and human ingenuity, and on the other a land cursed with an enchantment that leaves her prey to ceaseless invasions – were by no means dead when Venice found itself joined to the mainland by Meduna and Duodo's viaduct in 1846. Italy always meant more to its native inhabitants than that mere 'geographical expression' Metternich so smugly declared it to be. With the incorporation of former Italian kingdoms and duchies into the newly designated states forming part of Napoleon's empire after 1805, awareness of a common heritage among Italians grew more pronounced. The rapid evolution, under Bonaparte's satraps and procon-suls, of a bourgeois administrative class was accompanied by opportuni-ties for a meritocratic military career, designed to expand the horizons of young officers through academic training and foreign travel, even if only as far as death in a Russian snowdrift. The men who sought these new career paths were those keenest to engage in the broadening dialogue around the idea of Italians as a single nation, united by bonds stronger than that of the literary language they already shared.

Restoration of the old sovereign powers after 1814 strengthened rather than dissipated a gathering awareness of national identity. The secret societies active in the aborted revolutions of 1820–21 drew on ideas of nationhood fostered by the reading of classic texts such as Dante's *Divine Comedy* and the works of Machiavelli, writings which, implicitly or explicitly, appealed to a sense of what Italy might become by contrasting this with what she currently was. By no very singular irony, one of the very first works to appear from the pen of Giuseppe Mazzini was an essay entitled 'Dante's Love of His Country', submitted to the liberal Florentine review *Antologia* in 1827, though the editor Gian Pietro Vieusseux chose not to publish it.

Mazzini became the dominant ideologue of the Italian 1830s, founding his own secret society, 'La Giovine Italia', with its eponymous journal. The society's activities, even though they failed to bring about any positive change in the prevailing climate of reaction, had at least the negative merit of consciousness-raising among a generation of young patriots frustrated by an instinctive suspicion, on the part of Austria and her satellites, of anything that smacked too much of originality, either in initiative or expression. Out of this dissident Mazzinian sub-culture sprang the Bandieras' 'Esperia' cell within the ranks of the Habsburg fleet. The impetus behind their expedition needs to be placed in the wider context of a hope, inspired by Mazzini, that Italy might pioneer its own liberation without aid from a foreign power.

What Italy was, or might yet be, started to engross Italians more than bungled opportunities for militant action ending in exile, imprisonment or execution. This new hunger for ideas caused patriotic readers in 1843 to seize avidly on the turgid and eccentric pages of *Del primato morale e civile degli italiani, On the Moral and Civil Pre-eminence of the Italians*, by the Piedmontese court chaplain turned radical exile Vincenzo Gioberti. The work proposed a confederation of Italian states under the leadership of the Pope, and its appeal was to that particular conservative establishment, temporal and spiritual, which had ostentatiously kept its distance from the Mazzinians, mistrustful of their dangerous egalitarianism. Hard on Gioberti's heels came another Piedmontese, Cesare Balbo, whose *Delle speranze d'Italia* (*What Italy Can Look Forward to*) engaged more directly with the need to remove Austria from Italy altogether, perhaps by compensating her with the Balkan provinces of the Ottoman empire, cynically viewed as up for grabs since the triumph of the Greek independence movement. Like Gioberti, Balbo was essentially a Catholic reactionary, his political programme that of a constitutional monarchy operating through bicameral government, a system inspired less by liberal impulses than by fears of rampant Jacobinism.

Venice had so far contributed nothing whatever towards evolving similar concepts of a resurgent Italy freed from Austrian domination and recovering a greatness of spirit lost since the Renaissance. With the rise of *la leggenda nera*, pervasive and pernicious, there came an idea of the Venetians as a contemptible slave race, grovelling to the Habsburgs and unworthy of serious attention from patriots. It was accepted wisdom among many Italian liberals that Venice was a city of triflers whose inhabitants were more likely to dawdle in cafés and theatres than devote their energies to the cause of national unity. As the Paduan patriot Carlo Leoni observed, 'What people could possibly be more frivolous, inept and effeminate than the Venetians?' A particularly dim view of Venice's revolutionary potential was taken in its neighbour province of Lombardy, where the Milanese continued to preen themselves on the cultural vitality that had turned their city into one of the capitals of the European Enlightenment and later into a hotbed of subversion during events leading to the baffled revolutions of 1821. When the Lombard princess Cristina Belgiojoso Trivulzio, one of the best known outside Italy of all polemicists for the patriotic cause, came to publish her perceptive (if factually inaccurate) account of the events of 1848 in the Parisian *Revue des Deux Mondes*, she could scarcely avoid recalling the unfavourable perspective surrounding Venice and the Venetians in the eyes of most Italian revolutionaries during the 1820s and 1830s. Venice, it was widely believed, had fallen too easily for Austria's weasel-worded pledges of freedom and mildness in the wake of Bonaparte's tyranny. As the old Republic had allowed the common people no sort of share in the government, they were ready victims for Austrian oppression, and there were few among the middle classes, let alone the decayed patricians, with either the talent or the means to challenge the status quo. Not unjustly, Belgiojoso questioned Venice's curious failure to contribute to the vigorous debate on Italy's future now being carried on, despite all the vigilance and harshness of state censorship, under the very noses of Austria and her client sovereigns. 'While the clandestine press,' she pointed out, 'was working unceasingly to diffuse patriotic and nationalist sentiment throughout Italy, Venice alone stayed silent. As far as I can tell, neither in 1846 nor in 1847 did a single work inspired by these new ideas issue from her presses, to swell the tide of political publications swamping the rest of the penin-sula at that period.' Up to a point she was correct. The railway promoters' patriotic sympathies, for example, had remained secondary (for the time being) to their preoccupation with advancing the prosperity of major commercial centres with potential outlets to foreign trade from as far off as America and the Far East. Such polemic as there was – including a vigorous newspaper campaign – had never been openly channelled into the larger Italian national discourse.

Yet this did not mean that influential opinion-formers in Venice were not sensitive to the changing times. In 1846, the very year when the railway viaduct opened, a dramatic alteration overtook the apparently quiescent political atmosphere in the surrounding region. Poor harvests across the Austrian empire the previous year, part of a calamitous Europe-wide El Niño effect, were now starting to depress what had seemed to be an improving economic climate. The price of maize flour, the basic food staple of north Italian peasant communities, rose with terrifying suddenness during the early spring, while bread riots broke out in the villages of the Veneto plain, and the spectre of the never-to-be-forgotten famine of 1816–17 began troubling those in authority, fearful as they already were of the knock-on impact of a commercial crisis rapidly grip-ping European markets. As tensions increased with summer's onset, police reports from everywhere between the alpine foothills and the Po valley warned of smouldering unrest. In Udine women rallied in the market square to attack the houses of prosperous merchants. An ugly crowd at Chioggia told the mayor, 'We're hungry and we want our polenta.' In Verona the custom usually followed by wealthier citizens on Good Friday of scattering sugared almonds among the poor was tactfully replaced with the distribution of loaves. As with the shortages thirty years earlier, the government failed to act quickly enough, whether in preventing specu-lators from buying up maize in bulk for export to other famine-hit areas of Europe – Ireland being the most notorious – or by freezing prices, reducing taxation and initiating work-schemes for the growing numbers of unemployed. By the spring of 1847 Austria could no longer count on the general goodwill of her Italian subjects. Metternich (his hand, however shaky, still on the tiller) was perturbed by a tide of political events threat-ening to upset altogether the internal stability on whose maintenance, for the past three decades, he so prided himself.

On 1 June 1846, after a reign of fifteen years, Pope Gregory XVI died in the Quirinal Palace in Rome at the age of eighty-one. A monk of the Camaldolese order, who had to be consecrated Bishop of Rome before he ascended the throne of St Peter, Gregory, like his immediate predecessors, was an intransigent conservative, dedicated to preserving theocracy from the inroads of the modern world following the papacy's traumatic experiences at the hands of Napoleon Bonaparte. 'The times,' wrote one observer in the Vatican, 'were unfavourable to him, and those fears with which he was burdened made him perpetually doubtful and wavering in the government of the state.' To the most devout Catholics, his attitude was no worse than could be expected of a deeply unworldly man for whom the power and authority of his office as God's Vicar mattered more than anything else on earth. For others, including Metternich, he was merely an embarrassment, allowing his position as spiritual leader and sovereign ruler to become discredited through the mismanagement, corruption and cruelty exercised by those in authority under him. With its ramshackle administrative framework, its oppression of heretics and Jews, its army of spies and informers reinforced by gangs of thugs known as 'centurions', its heavily rigged judicial procedures and its dungeons substantially unaltered since the Middle Ages, the papal government in the early 1840s presented distinctly unfavourable comparisons with even the most reactionary regimes elsewhere in Italy. An anonymous cardinal put it succinctly and devastatingly enough when, on Gregory's demise, he remarked, 'This holy man has left us without a farthing in the bank, without credit, without men of any ability, without an army, and with our public morality wholly corrupted.'

The election for Gregory's successor was a contest between the conservative Luigi Lambruschini, Secretary of State from 1836, and the favourite of Italian liberal Catholics, Giovanni Maria Mastai Ferretti, Bishop of Imola. Winning by twenty-six votes, Mastai Ferretti took the name of Pius IX. He was an aristocrat, sensitive, idealistic and a good deal better educated than some of his immediate papal forerunners. His immediate proclamation of an amnesty for political prisoners, his recall of exiles, his reform of governmental machinery, concessions of partial freedom of speech and relaxation of censorship all seemed to suggest the arrival of a numinous figure whose example might at last shame fellow Italian rulers into offering fundamental civic and political freedoms to their subject populations. The new Pope's portrait figured as a holy icon in framed engravings, embroidered on banners, printed on handkerchiefs and stamped in metal up and down Italy, while his name 'Pio Nono', 'Pius IX', became synonymous with the cause (however vaguely defined) of liberating Italians from alien tyranny.

Such popularity, without example in the entire history of the papacy, was a matter for serious concern in Vienna. Metternich had not approved either of Gregory XVI or his equally reactionary predecessor Leo XII, and at the time of the 1846 conclave had told his ambassador to Rome, Count Lützow, that Austria wanted a pope with moderate principles and 'a conciliating and impartial character'. Loyalty to Vienna was taken for granted. Now, with the sudden upsurge of enthusiasm for Pius, Metternich doubtless regretted that he had not chosen to interfere more directly in the election. His irrepressible vanity may also have been piqued by the adulation – almost a glamour – surrounding somebody whose role was meant to be that of a complaisant domestic chaplain to the legitimist household of European crowned heads. Austrian military force had significantly intervened during the Italian revolutions of 1821 and 1831, and now Metternich decided that once again strong-arm tactics were needed. According to an earlier treaty, Austrian troops were permitted to occupy the papal fortress at Ferrara. On 17 July 1847, in response to gathering political unrest in the region, they were ordered to take control of the entire town. Pius lodged a stern protest with the Habsburg government and refused to allow an Austrian army to march across the Papal States when, early the following year, disorder spread to the Kingdom of the Two Sicilies. Both acts served to increase his standing as a leader of truly national significance, the first in Italy to have openly defied Metternich's customary high-handedness. For the time being Italian hopes of political change seemed to find their most palpable embodiment in this shy, modest and unquestionably devout pontiff, who responded with apparent surprise – almost alarm – to the popular fervour.

His election had taken place against a background of mounting unease both within the Italian states and throughout the Habsburg empire, where events had begun to suggest that Metternich was starting to lose his grip on public affairs. An abortive revolt in Galicia led to Austrian occupation of the free city of Krakow, with its surrounding territory, and thence to their outright annexation. International protests, led by Britain's energetic Foreign Secretary Lord Palmerston, were less effective in deflecting the Chancellor's resolve in the autumn of 1846 than they proved the following year, when Metternich undertook a misguided intervention in the internal politics of neighbouring Switzerland so as to protect a breakaway grouping of reactionary Catholic cantons. Like the assault on Krakow's liberties, guaranteed as these had been by the Congress of Vienna, this kind of sabre-rattling was viewed, even by more conservative Austrian elements, as distinctly ill-advised. When events forced Metternich into unaccustomed backtracking and compromise, the whole business was seen as an unmistakable indicator of his slackening influence on the conduct of international affairs.

He had guessed that Austria, as the bulwark of traditional order and stability, must be ready to face a radical challenge within her borders, suspecting that this would come from Italy first of all. The Bandiera brothers' ill-fated adventure was an augury of a restlessness which declared itself in a variety of different forms throughout the Italian peninsula during the mid-1840s, and which Austria and her satellites had no practical means of containing. A revolt in the papal city of Rimini in 1845, breaking out during a game of *pallone** between two local teams, was quashed after only two days with what seemed a wholly disproportionate heavy-handedness, involving scores of arrests and prison sentences, giving a menacing profile to the operations of the 'centurion' law-and-order gangs. When the roving Piedmontese political networker Massimo d'Azeglio, destined to play a leading role in the forthcoming struggle, published his essay on the affair, *Degli ultimi casi di Romagna*, later that year, the book's sustained criticism of Gregory XVI's government, combined with a vein of common sense and moderation emphatically distancing its views from those of Mazzini and his followers, lent it a special resonance within the context of unfolding events. The phrase of d'Azeglio's which particularly captured the Italian patriots' imagination was 'a conspiracy in open daylight' – the notion that a movement for national unity no longer had to be conducted as a cloak-and-dagger operation, but through alerting public opinion to the possibility of moderate political change. Censorship was useless in seeking to suppress d'Azeglio's tract. Everybody read it who officially ought not to have, and its ideas, like those of Gioberti and Balbo, became central to the growing debate on the nature and practicability of Italian patriotic aspirations.

Once it seemed as if Pope Pius, on his election, were ready to address the problems highlighted by d'Azeglio, some among the Italian sovereigns realised the expediency of carrying out progressive reforms, on however limited a scale. In Tuscany Grand Duke Leopold, a cousin of Emperor Ferdinand whose well-meaning paternalism had earned him much popularity, granted press freedom, reformation of the penal code and a promise of improvements in the running of the government. Even though he personally mistrusted his son-in-law King Charles Albert of Piedmont, the Grand Duke was prepared to enter alongside him into the customs union that Pius proposed between the three of them in August 1847. The officiousness and corruption of officials at the various frontiers between Italian states forms a leitmotif in the voluminous travel literature of the period, so that the idea of some form of harmonisation in dues and revenues between three of the larger states with common borders

* Pallone is a ball game mixing elements of basketball and fives.

must have seemed a thrilling indication of greater closeness. Though what was concluded a few months later turned out to be merely a draft agreement, the symbolic value of the gesture was considerable. Did not the document, after all, speak of the three sovereigns as 'being at all times desirous to contribute, by their mutual accord, to the increase of the dignity and prosperity of Italy, and being convinced that the real and substantial basis of Italian union lies in the fusion of the material interests of the populations which form their states'?

By now the sense that Italians, whatever their nominal allegiances, were fulfilling the ancient Chinese curse of living in interesting times filled everybody with a vaguely defined excitement and foreboding. The summer months of 1847 raised the tension, especially in central Italy. Rome itself seemed in danger of a confrontation between the mob (whose reluctant hero Pius had become), led by its charismatic boss, the Mazzinian carter Angelo Brunetti (known as Ciceruacchio), and a group of reactionary clerics gathered around the pro-Austrian Cardinal Luigi Lambruschini. Sporadic rioting was reported in areas of Romagna and the Marche, and it was partly in response to this that the Austrian high command had decided on its ill-judged show of force at Ferrara. Pius's concession of a civic guard throughout the Roman states, to be formed from able-bodied citizens between the ages of twenty-one and sixty, was viewed in this context as the ultimate provocation. As the Austrian ambassador Lützow warned Metternich, 'The catastrophe is announced as imminent with a cynical impudence, as if it were merely the staging of a new opera.'

It was at this juncture that the British government, increasingly attentive to developments in Italy, decided to send its own fact-finding envoy to the peninsula in the person of the Lord Privy Seal, Gilbert Elliot, 2nd Earl of Minto. Though he owed his government position to nepotism, as father-in-law of the Prime Minister Lord John Russell, Minto was an experienced diplomat with a sound enough grasp of Italian affairs and was determined to carry out his mission as thoroughly as possible. Yet its precise nature, during nine months spent first at Turin, then in Florence, Rome and Naples, would never be properly clarified. Some would see him as a mediator between conservative and liberal elements in the various states, others as a promoter of British-style constitutional democracy. Pius IX's ministers initially welcomed Minto's presence in Rome as lending influence to their reforms, but at home Prince Albert was more keen to emphasize Minto's role in upholding the right of Italian governments to conduct their affairs without Austrian intervention. 'The conduct of Austria,' wrote the Prince to Russell, 'can only be explained in one way: that it is one of the convultions [sic] of a dying man. Her system is rotten, and conscious of her own disease and weakness she struggles in despair.' Russell himself, as he had told Queen Victoria some days earlier, saw the purpose of Minto's journey, backed as it was by the appearance off the Tuscan coast of the British Mediterranean fleet under Admiral Hyde Parker, as a direct warning to the Austrians to refrain from any further show of force in Italy.

The Tory opposition gathered around the former Foreign Secretary Lord Aberdeen, professed disciple of Metternich, shared the imperial Chancellor's view of the Minto mission as an unwarranted interference, set on foot by Austria's *bête noire* Lord Palmerston, Aberdeen's successor. Another Metternich pupil, the rising star of conservatism Benjamin Disraeli, would later deride the initiative as 'a very peculiar and roving mission to teach politics in the country in which Machiavelli was born'. Though Minto's tour had no direct impact on Austria's Italian province, it must have been obvious nevertheless that some challenge to the regime was imminent, given the new political climate that Pius's reforms were helping to create. On 10 March 1847 a petition was addressed to the Emperor by leading citizens of Venice asking for their city, rather than the rival port of Trieste, to be made the entrepôt for imports from the East, with the help of a railway link across the Dolomites to Innsbruck. Experience should have taught them that the request would be rejected out of hand, or made subject to the kind of bureaucratic dawdling designed to kill off the project by deliberating it in Vienna. But what mattered to both sides, as events would soon reveal, was the temerity of merely submitting the document in the first place.

Just how important was the theme of Venice's commercial survival became obvious a few months later when the leading European apostle of free trade, the English Member of Parliament Richard Cobden, arrived in the city at the close of what he referred to as 'a private agitating tour through the Continent'. That typical phenomenon of 1840s public protest, the political banquet, now made its mark on Italian life. Cobden had already been the guest of honour on similar occasions in Rome, Florence and Milan (where he had received an anonymous letter asking him not to propose the Emperor of Austria's health). Venice now obliged with the most elaborate feast of all, on 22 June in a garden on the Giudecca. The eighty guests, led by the Mayor Count Giovanni Correr, sported ears of corn in their buttonholes to symbolise the MP's triumphant campaign against Britain's protectionist Corn Laws. In vain had the authorities given orders for two military bands to assist at the dinner and start playing as soon as anybody looked likely to propose a toast or make a speech. As with the entrepôt petition, the gesture mattered as much as the words. Cobden greatly enjoyed Venice, especially his trip up the Grand Canal. 'The music and the gay liveries of some of our boatmen soon attracted a great number of gondolas; the sound and sight also brought everybody into their balconies; as we returned, the moon, which had risen, gave a fresh charm to the picturesque scene, which was sufficiently romantic to excite poetical emotions even in the mind of a political economist.' There was little the Austrians could do to dampen the effect of Cobden's visit, and the regimental bands had clearly failed to drown the after-dinner speakers.

Words and the way Italians used them at this ticklish moment assumed a heightened significance when in September Venice hosted the ninth of the scientific congresses held up and down Italy since 1839. Ostensibly these gatherings were a chance for savants in various fields to pool their knowledge and discuss the latest developments in science, medicine, technology and social reform. In fact, as everyone knew, they afforded an ideal opportunity for the transmission of progressive opinions and patriotic politics, and their implicit demonstrations of Italian unity were unmistakable to the various governments under whose nervous scrutiny they were permitted to take place. The Austrians, initially reluctant, at length allowed the Venice congress to go ahead as a sop to liberal agitators.

A Venetian September is noted as a particularly agreeable month, with the edge taken off the summer heat but the weather staying fine, and the city was well prepared to welcome the 800 learned representatives from all over Italy who assembled for the inaugural session in the Sala del Maggior Consiglio of the Doge's Palace. To mark the occasion the Venetian organisers presented each of the delegates with what must surely rank as the most handsome commemorative publication ever produced, a worthy ancestor of those superb *omaggio* volumes nowadays distributed by Italian banks to their more profitable customers. The three immense tomes of *Venezia e le sue lagune*, with their gold-tooled red morocco binding, are essentially a massive propaganda blast on behalf of Venice in all its aspects. Volume I, the largest at more than 1,000 pages, a collection of historical studies, reverberates with the pride of the children of St Mark in their goodly heritage and is haughtily dismissive of *la leggenda nera*, the image of the Serene Republic as a tyrannical oligarchy ruling through fear and secrecy. The second volume is divided into two parts, one on scientific aspects of the city and the lagoon,* including a section on public health and population statistics, the other an extensive guide to the city and its monuments.

---

* The ornithological section of *Venezie e le sue lagune* is outstanding, and includes local dialect names for all the birds mentioned, with details of their diets, songs and nesting habits.

Throughout *Venezia e le sue lagune*, in its various sections, the anti-Austrian bias is clearly discernible. Not for nothing do we notice in the city guide that, save in one instance, the engraved views of the great buildings and open spaces such as Piazza San Marco, Campo San Stefano or the Rialto Bridge fail to feature among the scale-giving foreground figures a single example of that constant of contemporary Venetian street life, the white-tunicked soldier, whether from a Croat or Bohemian regiment or else an Italian conscript. Even an apparently innocent remark made in the previous century by the architect Tommaso Temanza is plainly quoted for its kernel of patriotic sentiment. 'We look poorly on certain foreigners who, armed with little in the way of penetration, use every effort to emphasise certain defects of us Venetians, not appreciating that like little pustules on the surface of a large body, these are signs of inner health and strength.'

An implicit warning could be read here by all those inclined to see Venice as a spent force, living on a diet of memories and resentments. In this same spirit of confident renewal, the Venetians made the scientific congress into an event of national significance, whose proceedings were imbued from beginning to end with a robust spirit of Italian patriotism. The talismanic name of Pio Nono was frequently invoked, even if attachment to it of the exclamation 'Viva!' was officially a criminal act within the Austrian provinces. The railway question was once again on the table, and this, like every other topic for discussion, was politicised with the kind of liberal slant which the hour and the participants seemed to demand. As for agriculture, its potential for such exploitation was obvious. For years the nickname *patate*, potatoes, had been applied in northern Italy to the Austrian troops whose staple food they were. At the scientific congress the delegates had a field day with sneering references to potatoes, their disastrous failure as a crop in the various parts of Europe where the blight had recently struck, their disagreeable taste, their complete unsuitability for growing in Italian soil, and so on. As one of the government spies reported, 'You can well imagine that witticisms abounded, and if I had to accuse anyone, I should have had to accuse the whole room.'* According to the same source, the popular

---

* The same mole supplied a disgruntled account of the lunch given to delegates: 'Thin soup, with an equally meagre omelette, a miserably tough morsel of beef, boiled meat with sauce made of goodness knows what, pieces of roast pigeon so blackened and hard that it was said they came straight out of the Piazza, an egg pudding worse than any served in the poorest trattoria, no salami of any sort, no cheese, vegetables or condiments save a small plate of butter, all followed by fruit better left untouched and a dish of little plums and biscuits'.

local poet Giovanni Prati was heard remarking to a friend, 'In our country only the Germans really like potatoes. I wish they would go and eat them in holy peace in their own countries and not dirty our fields with this disgusting vegetable. I am beginning to hope they will soon be gone.'

Prati was only one of several noted Italian writers attending the conference. From Milan came the learned Andrea Maffei, who had recently supplied Giuseppe Verdi with the libretto for *I masnadieri*; Verona sent Aleardo Aleardi, one of the most successful and prolific poets of the Risorgimento era, who was to play an important diplomatic role in the coming revolution. Music was represented by Saverio Mercadante – his *Donna Caritea* had given the Bandiera rebels their last defiant marching song. The venerable University of Pavia, a Lombard city long identified by Austria as a potential trouble-spot, sent its young rector, the *abbate* Pertile, while from Tuscany the keen reformers Cosimo Ridolfi and Raffaele Lambruschini had journeyed to Venice as delegates of the Grosseto Agricultural Society. They were treated to a wide variety of papers, on electromagnetics, astronomy and telegraphy, on central heating, water pollution, sub-aqueous illumination, physiology and phrenology, on land use and drainage, archaeology and numismatics, on philology, cartography, epidemics, medical mapping of urban communities, and on the flora of Australia.

Among the more fervently committed delegates was the Milanese journalist Cesare Cantù, whose speech on the likely benefits to be conferred by the railway was perhaps the most inflammatory of the whole conference. Starting with an obligatory invocation to Pius IX, he made conscious reference to the new invention as a potential agent of political change and described the Alps as 'a barrier created for us by Nature but created in vain'. The police spies noted 'the shower of frenetic applause' greeting Cantù's closing words. 'This part of Italy,' he declared, 'must unite its destinies and interests with those of its immediate neighbours, among whom so much radiance has recently blazed. Any kind of inertia at such a moment would be cowardice.'

Cantù had not made himself popular, on the other hand, by certain slighting remarks on Venice herself. The city, he observed, had risen through its conquest of others and was now weakened in turn as the victim of a conqueror. This sneer did not go unnoticed. One of his listeners, a little man in thick spectacles, sporting the kind of chin-fringe beard fashionable among local patriots, rose to deliver a withering riposte. 'It is ungenerous to insult the fallen Lion in such bitter terms,' he shot back. 'Inexcusable, what is more, when these words are both pointless and untrue. To admonish modern Venetians as to the misuse of their historic conquests is superfluous, inopportune and ridiculous. Yet it may not be altogether useless to remind the Venetians of today in the severest terms that no vice is more harmful to a people than cowardice. With this defect a people cannot live in dignity or be pitied for its misfortune, maintain its dignity or recover it once lost.' Here was an angry rallying call from a speaker who undoubtedly meant business. Cantù, like the other delegates – let alone the Austrian informers and the civil governor Lajos Count Palffy von Erdödy, for whom the congress's sessions provided several *mauvais quarts d'heure* – were left in no doubt as to its implications.

The man who picked up with such enthusiasm the glove Cantù had scornfully thrown down was already famous among patriotic Venetians as one of the so-called 'Italian' party in the railway project of the early 1840s. Italy, immemorially obsessed with beauty, *bella figura*, line, form and surface, likes its champions (in whatever field) to look the part. This could never be said of Daniele Manin. To his stunted growth, partial baldness and the curiously batrachian aspect conveyed by a pair of spectacles giving him a certain resemblance to his musical contemporary and fellow Austrian subject Franz Schubert, he added several character traits which, in his own judgement at least, must have made him unfit to be a leader of men. Continuing bouts of illness, mostly related to his stomach and bowels, rendered him easily depressed and inactive, and he saw himself as fundamentally an idler, hampered still further by a general sense of physical weakness which made life 'an effort and a penance'. Some special stimulus, he believed, was always necessary to snap him out of lingering slothfulness. 'When exaltation is lacking,' he confessed, 'I feel myself below average; I feel incapable of doing what ordinary men do with ease.'

Manin was born on 13 May 1804 in Ramo Astori, a little lane just beyond Campo Sant'Agostin, a few streets away from the great Franciscan basilica of Santa Maria Gloriosa dei Frari. His father's parents were Jews, who had changed their name on being received into the Catholic Church in 1759. Samuele Medina and his wife Alegra Moravia were sponsored at their conversion by a brother of Ludovico Manin, eventually to become the last Doge of Venice. It was his surname they assumed, according to the customary practice symbolic of a change of social identity and of renouncing the Jewishness associated, according to Catholic teaching, with those responsible for Christ's death.

The Jews of Venice had been confined within their ghetto – itself a word of Venetian origin – since the Middle Ages. Released by the enlightened dispensation of French law under Napoleon's empire, they retained many of their new civil liberties when the Austrians returned, since the Habsburgs during the previous century had already taken significant steps towards improving the status of non-Catholics within their domains. Jews were permitted to own land and houses and to enter state employment, though the higher administrative echelons, such as the judiciary and membership of provincial congregations, were barred to them, and they were forbidden to set up in practice as notaries or apothecaries (the latter prohibition owing something to an atavistic terror that Christians might be in danger of poisoning). They were not allowed to witness Christian wills or to give evidence that should prejudice a judge in favour of fellow Jews. Marriage contracts within the community, what was more, became legal only if sanctioned by Gentile authority. Though Francis I, in a Sovereign Resolution promulgated in 1820, had declared his intention of reducing these restrictions 'according to the level of civilisation Jews may be about to reach' and had ordered that Jewish children be allowed to attend state schools in the ordinary way, the attitude of the government, the police and the clergy was generally mistrustful, based on apparently indestructible ideas of a hatred (dating from the Crucifixion itself) directed by Jews towards Christians. It seems to have occurred to nobody to consider that even in Italy, where pogroms against Jews since the Middle Ages had been comparatively few compared to those in other areas of Europe, Christians had done little to earn respect or gratitude from their Jewish neighbours. A petition signed by distinguished Jews of Lombardy-Venetia, aimed at securing improved civil rights and presented to Johann Baptist von Spaur, civil governor of Venice, in May 1840, was rejected on several hoarily anti-Semitic pretexts – Jews, being naturally more skilful in business operations than Christians, were as likely as not to cheat them; good Catholics would be offended by the presence of Jewish witnesses to a solemn final testament made by a true believer; the presence of a Jew in an exalted official capacity at the religious functions associated with public festivities was inappropriate in view of his inherited guilt for the death of Jesus Christ; et cetera. It comes as no surprise therefore to find most, if not all, of the prominent Jewish citizens of Venice during the 1840s offering tacit support to the cause of Italian liberty, with its promises of full – or at any rate increased – emancipation for the community.

There were never more than two and a half thousand Jews in a Venice whose population now stood at around 120,000. While many continued to live in poverty within the ancient confines of the ghetto in the *sestiere* of Cannaregio, others, in the wake of the French occupation, now formed a highly influential grouping of entrepreneurs, bankers, insurance agents, art dealers and physicians, mingling socially with Gentiles and using their wealth to promote the city's prosperity, especially in the light of its rivalry with Trieste. A Jewish identity was never suppressed, but an obvious gulf existed, in terms of assimilation, between these families, a sort of bourgeois aristocracy, and their poorer counterparts, with many of whom they were connected by earlier marriage ties, in the squalid alleys around Campo del Ghetto Nuovo.

Catholicism for the newly baptised Manins was more of a social passport than a profound spiritual experience. Their son Pietro married a Christian Gentile, Anna Bellotto, but the three daughters of the marriage were given names – Arpalice, Ildegarda and Ernesta – which have the air of being deliberately chosen so as to avoid any religious connotation, while that of the only son Daniele was strangely apt in recalling the biblical child prophet of the Jewish captivity. According to one family friend, the association of Daniel with virtuous resistance to the oppressive Babylonians implied a veiled protest against foreign servitude. Pietro's faith, as befitted an age of rationalism and revolution, was in that generic republicanism embraced by many Italian democrats after the French invasion of 1797, and his stout political principles undoubtedly influenced the children. Theirs was a happy and united family, one in which the girls as well as their brother were encouraged to read widely and value independence of thought and expression. For Daniele, however, study and intellectual exercise were a consuming passion, sharpened rather than diminished by lingering ill health and given further direction by a Jewish cultural inheritance of textual exegesis, respect for the institution of the law, and forensic argument as to its points and potential interpretations.

While still only a boy, he had set up, along with his sisters, a little reading room for their friends in the house by the Ponte dei Baratteri, not far from St Mark's, to which they had recently moved. After beginning his own written commentary on the New Testament, Daniele translated from the Greek the apocryphal 'Book of Enoch', known in Italian as *Degli egregori*. By now, aged sixteen, he had determined to follow his father into the legal profession, and four years later he produced an Italian version, with accompanying notes, of the French jurist Jean-Baptiste Pothier's edition of the 'Pandects' of Justinian, that classic compendium of Roman law upon which most European judicial systems rest. Reading widely in several languages, including English, German and Hebrew, he developed a talent for focusing on essentials and a view of the world some might have considered too cynical and hard-nosed, but which was firmly based on a lawyer's need for concrete evidence and a refusal to be fobbed off with official excuses and obstructive manoeuvring. An English phrenologist Dr Castle, who in 1846 examined Manin's head according to its various bumps, commented that 'his philosophical creed is that of *explained facts*; his mind tending somewhat to scepticism with regard to subjects on which he has not *convincing proofs*! This is one of the reasons why Mr Manin is not of a religious character.'

Bookish as he appeared, the young Manin was also a keen gymnast and gained further exercise from his pastime of amateur woodwork and cabinet-making, fashioning small articles on a lathe or a carpentry bench, something he continued as a therapeutic relaxation throughout his life in Venice. Such activities were additional safeguards against what he saw as his beset-ting sin of indolence. 'I love to rest, I love sleeping and the comfort of a feather bed,' he wrote. 'I've spent more than half my life idling away my time in a warm bed.' This was obviously untrue, as his family and friends could easily testify. Much sleep was lost during his late teens, in any case, when he fell passionately in love with Carolina Fossati, who was literally the girl next door. Her parents, minor nobility from Friuli, had liberal leanings and her brother was a colonel in Napoleon's army, but they looked askance at her *tendresse* towards the son of a Jewish lawyer with little in the way of financial prospects. After Daniele and Carolina kissed one another while left alone on a sofa, and were afterwards surprised by her mother in an early-morning tryst on the balcony, Count Fossati gave orders to seal up the connecting door between their two houses, and seventeen-year-old Daniele was only prevented from committing suicide by an indul-gent letter from his father, absent on business at the time.

Genuine and enduring attachment came two years later, when Manin, having recovered from the galling news that Carolina had accepted a husband chosen for her by her parents, was admitted to the salon of Giustina Renier Michiel. Daughter of the last doge but one, Giustina Michiel was among a group of patrician women who kept the spirit of Venetian inde-pendence alive during the years immediately following Austrian annexa-tion, welcoming artists, writers, visiting celebrities and the best of the city's rising generation to her salon. When Manin paid his first visit, his weak eyesight made him fancy that all the young women present must be divinely beautiful. 'At first, having left my spectacles in my pocket, all I could see of those girls was the mere fleshly oval crowned with hair, where the face must be, and my imagination helped my feeble eyes in delineating angelic features . . . once I'd taken out my glasses and settled them on my nose, ah, what misfortune! All those demigoddesses lost their attractions, defects were suddenly perceptible everywhere, and the illusion vanished.'

Perhaps not entirely, for among the company was Teresa Perissinotti, daughter of a respected advocate, with whom Manin's acquaintance deepened quickly into love. Teresa was as well educated as his three sisters. Her letters reveal a resourceful, articulate, strong-willed woman, whose devotion never faltered during the testing months that led to their engagement. Her family, like Carolina Fossati's, was reluctant to welcome Daniele as a suitor and whisked Teresa off to their country house near the hill town of Feltre, where she remained for nearly six months, fending off the amorous attentions of a half-mad local priest and keeping up an ardent correspondence with her suitor. Realising that separation was merely strengthening the bond between the lovers, her father eventually gave his consent, and the pair were married in the church of Santa Maria del Giglio on 8 September 1825, setting up house in a rented apartment overlooking Campo San Paternian.

Of their two children (a son, Giorgio, and a daughter, Emilia), it was the latter, born prematurely, who gave them most cause for concern. Soon after her third birthday she collapsed in the first of the epileptic fits that recurred with alarming frequency throughout her short life. Almost every one of Teresa's surviving letters thereafter, and of Manin's when writing from home, contains some mention of Emilia's ill health, though seldom specifying epilepsy in particular. The condition was inadequately understood at the time, and for several years her frightened parents tried to keep all knowledge of it from their child. Various therapies were tried, including magnetism, the fashionable nineteenth-century panacea, but without success. While Giorgio became his mother's favourite, Emilia, intellectually precocious and winning in her ways, was her father's adored companion, mastering mathematics, reading avidly among classical texts and Italian authors and writing better German and English than Daniele himself.

Manin soon acquired a reputation as one of Venice's ablest lawyers, yet he was not resigned, whatever his acknowledged idleness, to quiet obscurity as a family man with a name for probity and efficiency within his profession. From his father he had acquired a passionate loyalty to his native city, viewing her destiny as intrinsically connected to the larger cause of Italian independence. In his scale of priorities, Venice would always come before Italy – a fact that later drew sharp criticism from his political opponents and undoubtedly affected his posthumous standing among heroes of the Risorgimento – but he never saw the struggle for liberation from imperial Austria as a purely isolated issue. When still a boy he had watched the leaders of the abortive Milanese uprising in 1821, brought for trial in Venice, being led away to eventual imprisonment in a distant corner of the empire. Ten years later Manin himself was briefly involved in plotting a revolutionary uprising with three of his childhood friends. One of them, Antonio Zanetti, was a nephew of Leopoldo Cicognara, President of the Accademia, who, though apparently sympathetic, had declined to join them on grounds of old age. The four knocked together a little printing press and cranked out a few seditious posters, but the police never managed to nail them. As Manin became more concerned with Venetian civic affairs, he began trying to galvanise local initiative so as to raise the city's profile and bolster the self-respect of his fellow townsfolk. He was a founder member of the trading company set up to further Venetian enterprise after the opening of the free port, and was among the leading citizens who welcomed Cobden at the celebratory banquet on the Giudecca. Most admired of all by the more progressive elements in the business community was his fervent commitment to securing the Treviglio route for the projected railway. At every stage he played a crucial role, making decisive interventions at shareholders' meetings, firing off polemic articles in the *Gazzetta privilegiata di Venezia* and campaigning tirelessly for the support of influential figures in Venice and Milan. The outcome may not have been quite the triumph Manin anticipated – though the Treviglio line was finally adopted, the Ferdinandea became state-owned rather than remaining under exclusively Italian management – but he was now an acknowledged champion of Venice's best interests, firmly identified with liberal interests and patriotic causes.

A figure such as this was bound to be interesting to the police. Manin had been fingered by Austrian intelligence agents from as early as 1834, when his name appears in a list of those likely to contribute to the newly founded *Gazzetta privilegiata di Venezia* and known as possessing 'unsound' political views. By the mid-1840s he was clearly the object of careful and continuous scrutiny by spies and informers. A letter from Teresa Manin to a friend, dated 2 June 1846, indicates that the family was beginning to feel the pressure of this surveillance. A few days earlier, in the small hours of the morning, Daniele's office had been broken open, its various desk drawers pulled out and their contents examined, though only money had actually been removed. The police claimed that they had arrested a suspect, but the Manins were mistrustful of this speedy reaction, and of certain details which made the episode look scarcely like an orthodox burglary. 'We don't wish the innocent to suffer on our account, either directly or indirectly,' wrote Teresa. 'We are tired of interrogations, officials, special visits, theories offered to no purpose, tired of them all.'

The close of the scientific congress on 29 September 1847 left Manin exposed in full view of the government as a dangerous champion, both of improvements to the political status quo within the Austrian provinces, and of Italian unity, however nebulous its current form in the minds of its adherents. By now the momentum for change among the various sovereign states had gathered speed. Spasmodic gestures of revolt were being offered in the Two Sicilies, whose king, Ferdinand II, seemed inclined to conciliate liberals with changes to the taxation system and an uncommon willingness to listen to the advocates of wholesale reform. In Tuscany, Grand Duke Leopold conceded a consultative assembly and, in the teeth of Metternich's warnings, allowed a civic guard to be formed. Piedmont's King Charles Albert undertook a shake-up of the judiciary, the police and local government, while openly declaring himself in favour of something called 'the liberation of Italy'. Pope Pius IX had also begun overhauling the administration of his states, preparing to grant a consultative assembly and a reorganised council of ministers, which should include secular members as well as the customary cardinals. So rattled was Austria by apparently trustworthy allies trimming their sails to the revolutionary wind that Metternich desperately started putting out feelers for a defensive alliance with Parma and Modena, currently the only two states whose rulers were soundly reactionary, and sent the elderly diplomat and ex-cavalry general Count Karl von Ficquelmont on a fact-finding mission to Milan, a right-wing equivalent of the Italian tour Lord Minto was making at more or less the same time.

Armed with no special powers, Ficquelmont could only wring his hands over the chaos poised to overwhelm Lombardy-Venetia and over the inability of the Viceroy, Archduke Rainer, to do much beyond stalling with promises of reform on the one hand and misapplied demonstrations of brute force on the other. The two provinces, Ficquelmont reasoned, were united solely by their residual loyalty to the Emperor. Once this was allowed to fall away, nothing could keep them from deciding their respective destinies as part of an independent Italy. While police attacked demonstrators in the streets of Milan and Lombard aristocrats made common cause with the bourgeoisie in sullen resistance to Ficquelmont's effort to get at the truth of the situation, the baffled Rainer and his wife, a sister of the King of Piedmont who emphatically failed to share his patriotic change of heart, withdrew to their villa on Lake Como. Even there the insolent liberals rowed out on the lake by night to sing hymns in praise of Pio Nono and covered the walls around the property with graffiti honouring the pontiff and threatening death to the Austrians.

In Venice, on the other hand, Daniele Manin was meditating a subtler form of civil disobedience. The cue for his so-called *lotta legale*, or legal struggle, had come from Cobden and the free-trade agitation in England, but on 19 December 1847 it received a fillip from a source closer to home. A lawyer from Bergamo, Giovanni Battista Nazari, his city's representative on the Lombard provincial congregation, submitted a request to the government for a commission of inquiry into the disturbed state of affairs in Austrian Italy, their possible causes and cure. There was nothing remotely subversive in Nazari's action, legalised in any case by a privilege conceded to congregation members in 1815. The petition, with its references to 'faithful subjects', 'sovereign clemency' and the author's sense of duty to his emperor, was a model of decorum, even if it made daring mention of 'bad institutions' and the mutual mistrust of governors and governed, presuming to claim on behalf of the congregations a 'moral independence' that must render them ideal interpreters of the general discontent. The Viceroy's response was predictably ambiguous. Promising to consider Nazari's request with due care, he nevertheless ordered the police to conduct a thorough investigation of the Bergamasc deputy. A further set of more specific demands, asking for legal reforms, amendment of the salt tax and a reduction in the period of military conscription, was allowed to go forward to Vienna, doubtless in the knowledge that the imperial ministers would reject it out of hand.

Nazari's initiative gave a clear signal to Manin. A few days before Christmas 1847, he presented to the central congregation of the Veneto a document far more strongly worded than its Lombard counterpart, calling on the deputies to break their obsequious silence and act in a manner worthy of their position, daring to acquaint the government, for the first time in thirty-two years, with the feelings and desires of the people. Manin was not a congregation member, but his 'instance', as this type of petition was known, received immediate support from many who were, and its contents were widely discussed throughout Venice and the surrounding province. Summoned to explain himself to the city's police superintendent, Baron Karl Call zu Rosenberg Kulmbach, Manin was told that changes were indeed possible, but that as a leading citizen he must do his best to prevent disorder. Manin warned Call that unless reform was swift and substantial, the government would reveal itself as contemptuous of the legally expressed wishes of the people via their elected representatives. A letter he sent on 8 January 1848 to the civil governor Count Palffy made such menaces still clearer. It was time, he declared, that abuses of power should cease, that every violation of the law by superior authority should be answered with protests, not just from those who had suffered directly but from everyone else, in clear indication of the implicit harm done to the community as a whole.

Such classic little-man-versus-big-government bravery was inspiring to others who shared Manin's opinions. As 1848 began, two leading Jewish businessmen, Isacco Pesaro Maurogonato (a key figure in the great Venetian insurance firm of Assicurazioni Generali) and Cesare della Vida (owner of a major shipping company) came to ask him, on behalf of their co-religionists, whether he might include in his reform programme a plea for the total emancipation of Jews in the Austrian dominions. The Venetian chamber of commerce meanwhile was encouraged to submit its own demands to Vienna, including the abolition of remaining port duties, the building of a railway line to Innsbruck and the completion of the dredging and repair work at Malamocco, on the entrance to the lagoon, which had dragged on for almost twenty years. As with Nazari's instance, there was absolutely no guarantee that anyone in Vienna would deign to listen to the merchants. Even though they forbore to mention such key issues as the chamber being allowed total freedom from central government intervention, their requests and the sheer audacity of making them inexorably mirrored the changing times.

Most resonant of all the demonstrations of support for Manin's *lotta legale* came from a body which the authorities had every reason to view with the utmost suspicion. The Ateneo Veneto was then – as it remains – the city's most distinguished cultural institution, formed from an amalgamation of several learned societies and installed in the former Scuola di San Gerolamo on Campo San Fantin, close to the Fenice theatre. Among the Ateneo's most eminent and active members was that phenomenal figure of nineteenth-century Italian culture, the writer Niccolò Tommaseo. Born in 1802 in the Dalmatian port of Sebenico (modern Sibenik) to a family of minor patricians originally from Italy, Tommaseo was educated, like Daniele Manin, at Padua University, but soon abandoned a legal career for that of a poet, journalist and translator. He made contacts with writers like Alessandro Manzoni, author of the classic novel *I promessi sposi*, and the melancholy poet Giacomo Leopardi, whom he considered 'cold, arrogant and mediocre',* while working in Florence for the influential literary magazine *Antologia*, preparing a dictionary of synonyms, making a study of folksong in various languages and embarking on a monumental commentary on Dante's *La divina commedia*. There was nothing, it seemed, to which 'the Dalmatian' could not turn his hand. During a seven-year exile in France, Tommaseo produced two novels and a volume of verse, and after his return to Italy in 1840, when he settled in Venice, he translated the psalms, busied himself with two further dictionaries, one of aesthetics and the other of the Italian language,

---

* Leopardi himself referred to Tommaseo as 'a Dalmatian ass'.

published four folksong collections and continued to pour out critical essays, literary studies and polemic articles.

Of all the leaders of the Venetian revolution, Niccolò Tommaseo emerges as the most high-minded and the least likeable. In his time he was a major literary figure, though today, apart from a handful of finely wrought poems, his immense oeuvre remains monumentally unread, even by the small number of Italians interested in the literary culture of their momentous *ottocento*. From his personal papers, including a voluminous correspondence and a long memoir of the revolution written in a characteristically dense, mannered prose style, he appears tough, resilient and uncompromising, but hopelessly intolerant of others' failure to match his exalted idealism, tinged with the Catholic socialist beliefs he had absorbed while living in Paris. Scornful, peevish and condescending to humour only when it served to wither his opponents, Tommaseo reminds us of no one so much as that modern embodiment of dissident gloom and general contempt for human inadequacy in the face of great political challenges, Aleksandr Solzhenitsyn. The events of 1848–9 are nevertheless unthinkable without the inspiration afforded the Venetians by Tommaseo's dour tenacity, single-mindedness and absolute determination to speak as he found, regardless of personal consequences.

Speaking out got the writer into trouble on the present occasion, as he had known it must. The subject of his address to the Ateneo Veneto on 30 December 1847 was the apparently innocuous one of the current state of Italian literature. What in fact Tommaseo gave his audience was an extended plea for reform of the press censorship laws. Conceding that the original legislation compared favourably with that of other Italian states, he nevertheless presumed to remind the government (addressing the Emperor in person, as it were) that the relevant statue of 1815 had allowed writers to examine and comment on possible defects in the Austrian legal code. This guarantee was not now being honoured, and the speaker himself had been fined for certain comments made in a recently published work on education, not properly cleared with the censor.

The tone of the whole speech, delivered to a packed hall, was threatening rather than polite. 'The honour of the nation,' warned Tommaseo, 'requires acts of civil courage, whereby public opinion is allowed plainly to declare itself. Time is pressing and our rulers know it. If the uprising planned by the Bandiera brothers aroused so much fear and suspicion, think of what is happening now, when the altar no longer rules the throne, when Italy has become a focus of concern for the great powers of Europe and for the conscience of the human race. She must either learn to know her own rights or else, after an agony as long as it is accursed, perish utterly.' As the discourse swelled into a demand for greater autonomy and the right of every citizen to express his wishes for this in print, the Ateneo's Vice-President, the poet Luigi Carrer, whom Tommaseo wrongly suspected of pro-Austrian sentiments tried to interrupt. But the President, Count Ludovico Manin, checked him at once, realising both the occasion's momentousness and the plain fact that the speaker, once in full flow, was simply unstoppable.

Thunderous applause greeted Tommaseo's address, emboldening him to collect signatures for a petition and to send a copy to the relevant minister in Vienna, Karl von Kübeck. The fact that the *Gazzetta privilegiata di Venezia*, in its next issue, carefully failed to report the speech's most significant observations merely heightened its importance in view of the anticipated stand-off between the government and an increasingly disaffected Venetian bourgeoisie, headed by Daniele Manin. He could never have counted himself among Tommaseo's friends. Comparatively few could claim that privilege. The Dalmatian had never forgiven Manin for failing to promote an initial request for censorship reform left in his care during the scientific congress. As leaders of popular protest, the two men were radically dissimilar – one a sceptical pragmatist preoccupied with the facts as they stood and ruthless in pursuit of his goals, the other an ideologue poised on the edge of fanaticism, implacable and driven by a conviction never likely to be tempered by the changing realities of a given situation. Even if Manin shared Tommaseo's reluctance to forgive, he never fully realised that the offence he had caused was permanent, and he continued to admire and trust the other man completely. 'If I am a clever fellow,' he once joked, 'he is a saint.' By no special irony, the two were now about to find themselves yoked inextricably together as heroes of a drama whose outlines and denouement neither could have guessed at or believed possible.

Tommaseo's speech to the gathering in the Scuola di San Gerolamo undoubtedly helped to empower Manin's next, even bolder initiative, a two-pronged assault on the appointed representatives of the regime. In a letter to governor Palffy he wrote, as if deliberately defiant, 'It is not to be wondered at that the country, having waited quietly and in vain for thirty-three years, should now show itself impatient and dissident.' On the same day, 8 January 1848, he dispatched a second instance to the central congregation, demanding what was in essence a form of devolution for Lombardy-Venetia. The two provinces were to be liberated from central government altogether, with total control of the armed forces, fiscal policy, agriculture, customs exactions and the emancipation of religious minorities. The property qualification for membership of the congregations was to be abolished forthwith. Police powers were to be curtailed, press censorship must be swept away and a civic guard established, that ultimate symbol of local autonomy in the European revolutions of 1848.

By now the authorities were watching every move made by Manin and Tommaseo and preparing for the appropriate moment to strike. In a confidential report justifying speedy action against the dissidents, police chief Call declared Manin guilty of disturbing the state's internal tranquillity through his readiness to circulate the two instances in print rather than submitting them through the proper channels. This impudent lawyer, however talented and worthy of respect within his own profession, was noted for his high-handedness, irritability, tendency to litigious nitpicking and vast conceit. 'He makes every effort, in discussion, to place the interests of these provinces before those of the government.' As for Tommaseo, was he not 'a rebel against every kind of subordination, insolently scornful of all those who fail to share his false political doctrines'?

The subversive Dalmatian, as Call was about to discover, had been busy since New Year in a further attempt at exposing the regime's obscurantism and incompetence. During late autumn rumours of Venetian discontents had started percolating among the cities of the Veneto. The normally placid atmosphere in these communities, troubled already by news of what was happening elsewhere in Italy, began to shift more noticeably towards nervous, sullen impatience as to which side would give way first. In the town of Treviso, on 23 November 1847, the Teatro Onigo had presented Verdi's opera *I Lombardi alla Prima Crociata*. The work was scarcely new, having received its première at La Scala Milan in 1842, but Verdi was the ascendant star among Italian composers, and theatre managers needed to feature him in their programmes. *I Lombardi*, what was more, contained one of his most popular choruses, 'O Signore dal tetto natio', an obvious attempt to capitalise on the success of the well-loved 'Va pensiero sull'ali dorate' from *Nabucco*, a piece that has since become a kind of unofficial Italian national anthem.

Many members of the Treviso audience would already have known 'O Signore dal tetto natio', and printed libretti were always available at opera performances. Thus when the chorus of crusaders and pilgrims sang its third line, 'Siam corsi all'invito d'un pio', 'We have hastened to answer the bidding of a pious man', the theatre echoed to loud cheers for the 'pio' of the hour, Pio Nono, that tutelary saint and demiurge of awakening Italy. In successive performances the chorus was applauded to the rafters, tricolour bouquets of red, white and green were thrown to the dancers in the ballet, and on 5 December the whole affair erupted into a political demonstration. Diners at a trattoria after the show went off with the theatre musicians, bawling the chorus through the streets. Finding the impresario enjoying a drink in the Caffè degli Specchi, they toasted and serenaded him before escorting him home with further impromptu Verdian selections. The police, far from trying to quash this surge of patriotism, contented themselves with issuing a notice forbidding 'any sort of allusion, direct or indirect, either to the person of the reigning Pontiff or to the political commotions of the day'. This audible clatter of stable doors being locked after the horses had bolted grew noisier in a flurry of frightened reports from informers all over the district – a certain Signora Ravagnin Moretti of Asolo had given a political dinner whose guests included two priests; 'Bengal lights' were seen burning at Montebelluna and Cornuda; while in Treviso itself soldiers were openly insulted in the streets and a local member of the provincial congregation named Agostini was mobbed for his known *austriacante* sympathies.

Unlike the music-loving Giuseppe Mazzini, whose enthusiasm led him to compose a whole essay on the beauties of Donizetti's *Anna Bolena*, Tommaseo had no special penchant for opera, but the Treviso affair seemed to him a singular augury of a new revolutionary mood in the provinces. Writing to his Florentine friend the veteran publisher Gian Pietro Vieusseux, he told him gleefully how 'the police commissioner, an Italian, gathered together those most responsible and begged them not to applaud. "Tonight," he said, "you are saluting an adjective: tomorrow it will be the noun itself. You'll cry 'Long live Pius IX!', then 'Long live Italy!' and after that, 'Death!'"' When Tommaseo heard that the Bishop of Treviso, at a hint from the government, had weighed in with an exhortation to obedience from all good Catholics, the opportunity to capitalise on his ground-breaking Ateneo address was irresistible. The speech itself, together with certain other relevant writings, was due to be published in Florence by the firm of Le Monnier, so an open letter to the Bishop would act as an appropriate chaser to this revolutionary cocktail. Its lines seethed with the kind of triumphant scorn representing the writer at his steely best. 'You, a priest and an Italian, having spoken to the people recommending submission, ought now to address the Emperor, counselling justice and warning him of the danger in which he stands. You have rendered unto Caesar a good deal more than that which is Caesar's: give whatever they deserve to honour and humanity.' Tommaseo reminded the Bishop that the privilege of his sacred office, as a priest appointed by the Church rather than the government, and receiving his stipend not from the imperial treasury but from 'the earnings of the miserable populace', allowed him to speak on their behalf and to remind the Austrians of their broken promises made in 1815. 'The pastor who, silent and inert, sees his flock scattered, will bear the name of hireling at the Day of Judgement: the priest who does not act as a responsible citizen is a living blasphemy.'

The broken promises themselves provided Tommaseo with headings for his next assault on official complacency, a series of demands rather more moderate than Manin's, but tending towards the same implicit accusations of neglect, mismanagement and dishonesty in Austria's dealings with its Italian subjects. Putting their differences aside, the two men were now in regular consultation, and the police could scarcely avoid seeing the pair as potential disturbers of public order. Tommaseo, an indefatigable force once the pen was in his hand, had dashed off his own polemic in favour of Jewish emancipation, at the request of Isacco Pesaro Maurogonato. To the furious Baron Call, the Ateneo Veneto now seemed a very Pandora's box of potential subversion, and he rapped its presiding officers sharply over the knuckles for having ever permitted the offending address to be given.

To those on either side, the pace of events elsewhere allowed little time for further feints or finessing. In Milan, during early January, an extraordinary gesture of mass civil disobedience had involved patriotic citizens in an anti-smoking campaign, designed as a protest against the state tobacco monopoly. Soldiers arrogantly puffing cigars were jeered at and pelted with stones, whereupon they attacked the unarmed crowd with swords and bayonets, wounding sixty-four people including a woman and a four-year-old girl. In Rome meanwhile, the newly formed consultative assembly prepared the Papal States for what seemed an inevitable war with Austria, by inviting experienced officers from Piedmont to reorganise the ramshackle armed forces. It was in Sicily, however, that the revolution began in earnest, on 12 January 1848. Everybody in the capital, Palermo, knew when it was due to take place, since a defiant proclamation had been issued two days earlier. The date chosen was significant: it was the birthday of His Majesty King Ferdinand II of the Two Sicilies. After a confused burst of fighting during the official parade in the sovereign's honour, the army failed to seize the initiative against the rebels, and within a few days the movement in favour of a separate constitution had gathered such force that the King had to face the possibility of withdrawing troops from the island altogether.

After two weeks of fighting, the garrison of 11,000 men was indeed ordered to the mainland and Ferdinand promised a constitution, not just for Sicily but for the whole kingdom. As each day brought further news of such events, Austria grew more unnerved by the surge of liberalism.

Metternich felt his grip starting to weaken as other sovereigns besides Ferdinand began seeking accommodation with their restless subjects. All the Austrians could do, it appeared, was offer a show of force within their own imperial provinces, which should frighten ordinary citizens into proper obedience. Even before the Sicilian uprising, the Milanese had been taught a lesson by the military's savage reaction during the anti-smoking riot. Now it was Venice's turn. Neither Palffy nor Call was prepared to hold off any longer in the face of what seemed like a concerted campaign of defiance by Daniele Manin and Niccolò Tommaseo. Early on the morning of 18 January 1848 both men were arrested and taken to Venice's central police station, near the church of San Lorenzo.

CHAPTER 3

❦

22 MARCH 1848

I N THEIR HOUSE IN CAMPO San Paternian the Manins acknowledged
the arrival of the police without any obvious surprise. Teresa offered
the two officers, Corner and Marconi, a cup of coffee, which they
accepted before announcing that it was their duty to make a thorough
search. No doubt she recalled the supposed 'burglary' of two years previously. On the present occasion Manin was able to object that such action
was in breach of his legal rights, even if the police could argue that they
were merely following Baron Call's orders and that their prisoner had
little choice in the matter. Nevertheless he told them to go ahead with
the inspection, unaware that his faithful clerk, in a moment of absent-
mindedness, had left a sheaf of copies of Tommaseo's letter to the Bishop
of Treviso on one of the desks. The officers also found a Tuscan patriotic song, 'La fiorentina e il suo tesoro', whose presence in the house was
sufficiently damning evidence in itself. Manin must therefore accompany
them to San Lorenzo, in a closed gondola, the floating Black Maria in
which suspected criminals were customarily conveyed along the canals.
At the police station (which remains Venice's central *questura* to this day)
his pockets were turned out and their contents removed. He was made
to present a deposition and sign it, following which he was taken once
more to the closed gondola and carried to the gaol next to the Doge's
Palace on the Riva degli Schiavoni. Though nothing had been said as to
the destination, Manin, in the shuttered darkness, knew the Venetian
canals so intimately that he could guess from the turns of the boat and
the gondolier's warning 'Oè!' and 'Stalì!', as well as from a sudden rattle
of Austrian rifles from the Ponte della Paglia, that prison was where he
was headed.

Before leaving San Lorenzo he had been allowed to send a note to Teresa, which read, 'All is well; these gentlemen are entirely civil, but the formalities take time. You had better be patient.' The family – not just Teresa, Emilia and Giorgio, but Daniele's three sisters, duly informed of the arrest – had little idea of how much patience would actually be needed. From the report prepared by Baron Call for an impending tribunal it becomes clear that the police chief had long meditated the prosecution of Manin and Tommaseo on a charge of 'disturbing the domestic tranquillity of the State' and that the 'rigorous perquisition' of their private papers had yielded what the Baron deemed the necessary evidence. He had no reason to doubt that the tribunal, whatever the laboriousness of its proceedings, would produce the desired judgement. Both agitators could then be silenced with an extended prison sentence, served somewhere out of the Italian provinces, such as the Moravian fortress of Spielberg, near Brno, where the leaders of the Milanese Carbonarist uprising of 1821 had notoriously been doomed to languish.

Hence the first police interrogation was somewhat more than a simple formality. Its focus was on the correspondence appropriated during that morning's visit by Corner and Marconi. Manin had to answer a whole string of questions as to the nature of individual letters, the identity of particular correspondents and the extent of his acquaintance with them. There were copies of his instance to the Central Congregation, of Tommaseo's address to Baron Kübeck and of a memorandum sent to the merchant Leone Pincherle on the subject of steam navigation on the Po. There were miscellaneous letters from fellow lawyers; a pair from Giacinto Mompiani of Brescia, 'that venerable old man', who had worked alongside Manin on a commission appointed by the scientific congress to enquire into the nature of public charitable institutions in Lombardy-Venetia; and a letter from a young doctor, Giacomo Nani Mocenigo, consulted as to available treatments for Emilia's epilepsy. In all, the police had seized some sixty documents, whether because their contents looked promisingly suspicious or because their various authors had been fingered as politically unsound.

That same morning of 18 January 1848, Niccolò Tommaseo had been getting dressed when the officers arrived to arrest him. They would later acknowledge that 'during the whole period of his stay in Venice his political conduct, to speak truly, has not demonstrated anything worthy of censure', even if 'by taking part in the current agitation he has begun to reveal himself as one of the [movement's] principal champions'. Tommaseo was not going to leave the house without a protest. Summoning his landlady, Signora Clementini, he loudly ordered her to inform Manin that the police had forcibly entered his lodging and to urge him to spread the news of this arbitrary proceeding throughout Venice. At the police station itself he adopted a similarly defiant attitude, refusing to countersign the list made of his confiscated letters, and submitting a written remonstrance typical of him in both its courage and its unrelenting verbosity, accusing the officers of acting illegally in seizing his papers and of violating his personal freedom. Demanding an apology, he concluded, 'I shall protest, not merely for my own sake, but in the name of all those who have been, or may yet be, injured by the arbitrary power of the police; so that by my example I may confirm the necessity of a new law, designed to impose limits on a department which, in the eyes of all, has been discredited, even if the intelligence and consideration shown by its officials should serve to soften its odiousness.' Otherwise his preliminary examination followed the same course as Manin's, but it seems to have left him feeling more vulnerable. There were no loving wife and children to whom he could turn, and this haughty, unbending, generally charmless figure had made few real friends in Venice. No wonder he sought relief, while waiting in the police station, by writing a poem to his lifelong idol Pope Pius IX.

When the tribunal assembled three days later, the accused could at least expect a fair hearing from their examining magistrate, Dr Benevenuto Zennari, and his two assessors, Napoleone Albrizzi and Agostino Silvestri. According to Austrian law, no defending counsel was allowed, so Manin was free to make what use he could of his legal experience in fencing with the interrogation. Zennari, noted for his integrity and thoroughness, allowed him to speak at considerable length as to why he had sought to 'trouble public tranquillity' with his instances and letters. The substance of Manin's address is a fascinating mixture of disingenuousness with indications of more complex personal motives inducing him to challenge the government with its failure to deliver on the promises made in 1815. He praised the empire's 'excellent constituent laws embracing the essence of progressive improvements, allowing our civilisation to move forward', claiming that the reforms recently undertaken in their respective states by the Pope, the Grand Duke of Tuscany and the King of Piedmont were merely those already conceded to his own subjects by Francis I thirty years earlier, when Lombardy and Venetia became part of the Habsburg empire. 'We should be wrong to envy our neighbours, since our legal condition is equal to, indeed better than, their own. We should be committing the sin of ingratitude towards our government by not recognising benefits already granted.' He praised the institution of the congregations, 'intended to serve every need, every desire, every prayer of the people', and the censorship laws 'conceived in a spirit of liberalism without parallel anywhere else'.

For these very motives of devotion to the government and the throne, claimed Manin, he had chosen to act. What was more, the menace of dangerous revolutionary movements operating elsewhere in Italy, 'wherever the seeds of discontent and a restless desire for novelty flourished', had inspired him to move swiftly, so that the Emperor and his ministers, warned in time, should be able, through prudent concessions, to stave off bloodshed and anarchy. Once Benedetto Nazari had presented his proposal from Bergamo, it had seemed only fitting that Venetia should stand alongside Lombardy in undertaking such a laudable initiative. Manin was able to point out, in detailing the successive phases of his *lotta legale*, Call's own observation (made in his hearing) that if the Emperor conceded to the nation's fairly expressed desires, this would constitute justice rather than mere sovereign clemency. The instances, furthermore, had received the blessing of various congregation members, concerned that the current problems to which Manin's documents referred should find a peaceful solution.

Since the accused, managing to wind up his address at last, was quite understandably tired, the judge, needing time for consideration, adjourned the court till tomorrow morning. A copy of the proceedings, it was noted, would be brought to the prisoner in his cell for signature. Zennari now faced an interesting dilemma. Either Manin was, according to his claims, motivated by disinterested devotion to the public good and loyalty to the Emperor, or the whole apologia was an artfully woven tissue of bogus humility and fraudulent altruism, designed to persuade the court of his innocent conviction that he had simply been acting according to his conscience as a faithful Austrian subject. Had he in any case broken the law? Reading the address from a distance of 150 years, it is difficult not to admire its shameless exercise of barrister's rhetoric, its continuous insistence on the rectitude and punctilio underlying every phase of Manin's campaign, and the subtlety with which the speaker balances external political pressures against his own instincts as an ordinary member of civil society under a government purporting to be just and well intentioned towards its subjects.

Certain of the apprehensions Manin adduced as motives were wholly genuine. Violent revolution was deeply repugnant to him, and so was any political upheaval likely to foment popular disorder, endangering the sort of bourgeois securities, based on capital, property and status, which he had taken for granted as a well-educated professional practitioner within an evolved urban community. Fears of this kind were to influence

Manin's acts and decisions throughout every stage of the spectacular scenario about to develop around him. There is no reason to doubt that, from this aspect at least, he was entirely straightforward in protesting a sincere intent in his original presentation of the instances.

At the tribunal's second morning session, Zennari began to probe more deeply in search of Manin's real motives. With whom had he discussed his views on the nature of the legal code, and why, once news arrived of the reforms due to be granted in other Italian states, had he persisted in making these opinions known, when it must have been obvious that by doing so he was stirring up discontent? Zennari wanted names, especially among the delegates to the scientific congress and members of the congregations, but Manin now pleaded that peculiar species of focused amnesia which always comes in handy on such occasions. He couldn't remember exactly who was present in the Doge's Palace on such-and-such an evening during the congress, his recollection was confused as to the person or persons he had directed to examine the censorship laws, and he wasn't sure whether the details of Nazari's instance had been sent to him through the post or delivered by hand. Similar fencing occurred when various letters were placed in front of him for comment on their contents and addresses. When Count Nani's name was mentioned, Manin, remembering Emilia's sufferings, burst into tears, but quickly pulled himself together and told the court how the doctor had suggested a course of animal magnetism as a possible cure for epilepsy. In fact, he said, 'the magnetic agent merely increased the poor girl's agony and I was forced to abandon it', after which Nani had left Venice and nothing further was heard from him until the present letter arrived.

Zennari, whatever his scruples, was not going to let the matter slip. Nani's letter was full of praise for Manin's actions and contained 'a declaration of patriotic feeling'. Had it come through the post in the normal way? Yes, but Manin had thrown away the envelope. What exactly did Nani mean by 'being ready to put everything at your disposal and awaiting your orders'? Somewhat nettled by now, Manin loftily answered, 'Whatever it may mean, I cannot assume responsibility for explaining and justifying others' opinions and expressions.' That, it seemed, would have to suffice, but Zennari continued picking through the correspondence, rather more minutely than the police at San Lorenzo had done. Manin's association with Tommaseo was obviously of special concern, but here the prisoner was better prepared, ready to praise his fellow detainee for his intelligence, kindness and nobility of soul, yet careful to point out that the two had not been in consultation before the instances were presented. 'Tommaseo's dominant fear, often expressed to me, was that disturbances might arise from agitators ready to take advantage of the uncertain situation, placing themselves at the head of the movement with irreparably disastrous consequences. Hence he saw it as imperative for us to follow the strict path of legality, moderation and a practical outcome, as well as observing a scrupulous probity in the process.'

Moderation and practicality were not uppermost in Tommaseo's list of priorities, as Manin would soon discover, but Zennari was more interested in trying to establish who else might have been present at the two men's various meetings, presumably to identify a possible network of sedition among Venice's leading citizens. On this note the tribunal resumed the following day. The session, however, was brief. After a few further questions as to letters and documents, Manin was allowed to explain his protest, in the instance of 8 January, against taxpayers' money being spent on Austrian support for reactionary movements in Portugal, Spain and Switzerland, when it ought to be devoted to the specific needs of Lombardy-Venetia. He was then returned to his cell to await the court's deliberations.

Niccolò Tommaseo meanwhile, though deemed a somewhat less dangerous disturber of public tranquillity, was seen as equally at fault for having dared to circulate copies of his various writings and speeches in the cause of free expression and changes to the law. His appearances in front of the court (with the same assessors, but a different judge) took a shorter time than Manin's, but allowed him a display of that scornful intransigence which was to characterise his behaviour throughout the coming revolution. Asked if he knew the lawyer Giuseppe Calvi of Padua, arrested in the same trawl which had netted the Venetian suspects, he answered no, and when invited to consider a possible reason for Calvi's arrest, he burst out: 'I cannot know, since I am not aware of having done or spoken or thought anything contrary to the laws of this country, or those of God and humanity, which could possibly be worthy of criminal investigation! On the contrary, I have viewed with sorrow the onset of discord and disorder. My one intention has been to direct the thoughts and desires of the Italians towards those paths of legality and loyalty which must lead to a real improvement in their condition.' He had circulated copies of his address to the Ateneo and his letter to Baron Kübeck in complete good faith that their spirit and purpose would be taken seriously as part of a contribution, however humble, towards the public good.

Tommaseo's declared altruism was of no significance to police commissioner Call, who had already made up his mind – and accordingly sought to influence those of the judges – on the motives in the case, supposing one actually existed. Having personally warned Manin some weeks earlier that his *lotta legale* risked overturning the established order, Call saw the tribunal as a good excuse to make an example of those who dared to demand what the government in its wisdom could never concede without 'sad effects on the public spirit'. The overriding tone, in his charge to the court prior to the arrests, was one of peremptory impatience, as if a guilty verdict were a foregone conclusion.

The judges were not so sure. Further hearings were adjourned for a fortnight, a fatal delay where the Austrian authorities were concerned. It gave Manin time to write to Teresa, asking her to send in to the prison a number of home comforts, such as a feather pillow, a blanket, a towel, two handkerchiefs, a tin bowl in which to make soup, two plates, glasses, napkins, cutlery, a foot-warmer and some fur slippers. The winter was a bitter one and Teresa grew understandably alarmed for her husband's health, never at its best in the foggy damp of a Venetian January. She was well aware, nevertheless, that any appeal to the police on purely compassionate grounds was unlikely to receive a sympathetic hearing. Call could easily argue that Manin, lodged in a large room on the corner of the building overlooking the Ponte della Paglia, had so far been accorded better treatment than any prisoner had a right to expect.

Not for nothing was Teresa Manin the wife of one lawyer and the daughter of another. Her approach, in a letter to the police chief, was crisply legalistic. She pointed out that her husband had not been arrested on a criminal charge, and that the tribunal, prior to the seizure of his papers, had made no effort to examine the case and prepare evidence beforehand. The preliminary investigation had so far failed to prove him guilty, and the arrest had not followed the due process laid down by the existing penal code. Instead, Manin should have received a caution preventing him from either destroying material which might assist in uncovering the truth or from seeking to escape altogether from the reach of justice. Since he had attempted neither of these things, what was the point of keeping him locked up? Only after she had reminded Call of the relevant statutes, with numbers and dates, did Teresa add a personal note. 'I beg for justice more fervently because of my husband's delicate constitution. So tender is the love he has for his children, one of whom is continually ill, that the isolation to which he has been condemned must necessarily be a pernicious influence on his health.'

On the same day, 27 January, Teresa sent a further plea, directed to the tribunal and putting more or less the same legal questions as those expressed in her letter to Call. Another went to the office of civil governor Palffy, demanding to know why a licence had been withheld which would allow a reprint of Manin's essay on Venetian jurisprudence, originally written for the scientific congress's *Venezia e le sue lagune* volumes. Since imprisonment effectively prevented him from earning money in the ordinary way, republication of the essay would have brought the family some much-needed income. After twenty days' silence, the grudging concession of a licence arrived from Palffy's office, with the attached provision that the printed copies should not be advertised either through posters or in the newspaper. As for the request to Call, this was answered by his junior, Herr Strobach, with a flat negative. Teresa's inclusion of a list of nearly a hundred signatures in support of her petition probably did more harm than good, since it included the names of several dangerous 'progressives' known to the police, such as the lawyers Gian Francesco Avesani and Giovanni Giuriati, a number of Jewish business leaders who had associated themselves firmly with Manin in the railway scheme, and at least a dozen members of the old Golden Book nobility whose loyalty to the government was decidedly questionable. It is perhaps worth pointing out that none of these – and indeed nobody else – had petitioned for the release of Niccolò Tommaseo.

It would not be long before the Manin family and their friends realised how much the changing political situation was on their side rather than the government's. During January and February of 1848, a wave of patriotic demonstrations swept across Italy. In Naples, King Ferdinand, shaken by the Sicilian revolt, hastened to grant a constitution, followed swiftly by Charles Albert's concession to his subjects in Piedmont of what was more guardedly termed a 'statute', and Grand Duke Leopold's promises to the Tuscans of imminent press freedom and administrative reforms. At the beginning of February the Pope was induced to concede what would turn out to be the last of his major government reforms, later issuing a *motu proprio*, which seemed, in the words 'Oh Lord God, bless Italy!', to bestow the ultimate sanction on Italian liberal initiatives at a moment when some sort of armed conflict looked more or less unavoidable. For the time being it did not matter to most of those reading the document that Pius's chief concern was the inviolability of the Catholic Church as embodied by his temporal sovereignty. The Faith, he declared, would always protect Italy so long as the Holy See remained untouched. The *motu proprio* had sealed his position as high priest of Italian national movements, whether or not he wished to assume such a status, and 'Viva Pio Nono!' would be a mantra repeated long after the pontiff's credit with revolutionary leaders had run out.

In the Veneto, during these months, the Austrians faced an increasingly sullen, fractious populace, angry at the latest increases in stamp duty and estate tax, not to speak of the continuing high price of food in the wake of recent poor harvests. Even in Verona, with its top-heavy Austrian military presence and many of the guns on its massive fortifications trained inwards on the citizens rather than outwards against a notional enemy, signs of discontent were noted by the police. Much bad feeling had been caused by the government's rejection of an instance, following Manin's example, in favour of reforms. What was more, news of the ruthless clampdown following the Milan tobacco boycott created a bad enough impression for a number of Veronese to attempt their own anti-smoking demonstration. Patriotism had other means than this of making its presence felt. Ladies attending the city's smartest balls that season became less and less willing to dance with anyone sporting an Austrian uniform, and none was more ostentatious in her refusals than Countess Maria Teresa Alighieri Gozzadini. With a heritage of national sympathies (her mother Anna had been friendly with several of the Carbonari leaders) she was suspected, with good reason, of smuggling prohibited books into the city and distributing them to dissident acquaintances. Among garrison officers attending any party at which Gozzadini was a guest, it became a favourite practical joke to persuade some greenhorn lieutenant to ask her for a waltz, and then watch her turn contemptuously on her heel, leaving the young man thoroughly discomposed.

A far more serious manifestation of anti-government feeling occurred in Padua, where the students of the ancient university had seized enthusiastically on the idea of the tobacco boycott. At the end of January news had arrived in the city of the Austrians' harsh repression of a rally in the Lombard town of Pavia, a still more venerable university town. As a show of solidarity, the Paduans announced a funeral mass for the victims, to take place in the basilica of Sant'Antonio, known as the Santo. Feeling ran high against the Austrian garrison commander, General Constant D'Aspre, and a Hungarian military band was greeted with derisive whistles while giving a concert in one of the city's piazzas. When a throng of more than a thousand students joined a funeral procession for a recently dead classmate, this was viewed as a deliberate act of provocation, made worse by the mourners' hostile obstruction of D'Aspre's carriage, which drove straight into the cortège. His cavalry escort, infuriated by the young men's impudence, made such menacing gestures that afterwards several students applied to the university rector for a guarantee of their safety.

On the following afternoon, 8 February, the streets around the central university building, known as the Bo,* and the handsomely appointed neo-classical Caffè Pedrocchi were thronged with people

---

* From the inn Il Bue (The Ox) which formerly occupied the site.

awaiting a violent confrontation and doubtless in many cases wanting it to happen. The Austrians did not disappoint them. At a pre-arranged signal, parties of troops converged on the crowd, pushing their way towards the café and lashing out with sabres and bayonets at those inside. Shots were fired in the streets and at least one student died of fright. Another, named Giovanni Anghinoni, was killed in the scuffle while trying to escape from a side window of the Pedrocchi. His murderer, to the horror of several witnesses, had ostentatiously failed to wipe his bayonet by the next morning. General D'Aspre, a hardened military mastiff and deep-dyed *schwarzgelber*, was impenitent, following up the outrage by ordering multiple arrests and expulsions, suspending two professors from the university and clapping a local newspaper editor named Stefani in irons for having dared to report the episode exactly as witnessed.

In Venice, news of the Padua incident merely served to exacerbate the bad feeling already created by the arrest of Manin and Tommaseo. Many citizens donned mourning, either for Anghinoni or as a symbolic protest in favour of the detainees. Tricolour scarves and ribbons began to be fearlessly sported, Pio Nono medallions were distributed and men laid aside their top-hats to wear the bandit-style wide-awakes known, ostensibly for their southern-peasant look, but with an obvious genuflection towards the martyred Bandieras, as '*alla Calabrese*'. Cigar-smoking was out of the question for patriots, who took up clay pipes instead. A graffito appeared on the walls to this effect, reading 'Chi fuma per la via/E tedesco o spia', 'Whoever smokes in the street/Is a German or a spy'. For the wounded in the Milanese tobacco riot, two noblewomen, Countess Giustinian and Marchesa Bentivoglio d'Aragona, organised a collection among the patrician families. Such politically targeted benevolence was illegal, and they were eventually betrayed to the police by the *austriacante* Countess Morosini Gatterburg. The officers investigating Marchesa Bentivoglio found her at breakfast, reading through some documents beside a roaring stove. Asked for the list of those who had pledged donations, she coolly answered, 'Do you think I am stupid enough to keep that by me? If I had it here, I would throw it in the fire along with these other papers', and promptly threw the bundle – containing the list – into the stove.

Even Venetian cuisine now took on a patriotic Italian slant. The favourite local dish of *polenta colle seppie* (polenta with cuttlefish) was spurned for its 'Austrian' black and yellow colours. Gastronomes true to the motherland favoured *risi e bisi* (rice with peas) followed by bottled strawberries – white, green and red, the perfect tricolour meal. Music-lovers too could make their protest gestures. Previously the evening strollers in the piazza had listened contentedly enough to the marches and waltzes played by the bands of the various garrison regiments stationed in Venice. Now, as soon as the bandmaster raised his baton, the civilian throng hurriedly swept out of the square, leaving only the soldiers to listen amid empty café tables and colonnades.

Another name for the fashionable Calabrese hats was 'all'Ernani', after the eponymous hero of Victor Hugo's play and Giuseppe Verdi's opera, which had received its première at Teatro La Fenice in 1843 and was still hugely popular. Alessandro Guiccioli, grandson of Byron's 'last attachment' Teresa, remembered years afterwards how, during his youth in 1840s Venice, the streets had echoed to the second-act chorus 'Si ridesti il Leon di Castiglia'. 'Among the very earliest memories of my childhood is this melody, which I heard in the streets, sung repeatedly in chorus by innumerable voices. Despite its wretched verses it became the hymn of the Risorgimento and of brotherhood among the Italians.' Though other anthems by different composers became popular with Italian patriots, Verdi was undoubtedly the biggest name in the Fenice's programme. His *Attila*, its libretto by the Venetian theatre-poet Francesco Maria Piave littered with patriotic nudges, was a great success in 1846, but none of his works was better loved by the theatre's regular audience in the winter of 1847–8 than *Macbeth*, originally composed for Florence two years earlier. In this opera Piave had managed to slip a patriotic allusion past the censors in the shape of the chorus 'Patria oppressa!' and Macduff's cabaletta 'La patria tradita' in the same scene, with its ensuing choral reprise. The words of both numbers, adapted from Shakespeare's 'Alas, poor country!', harp on the sufferings of the motherland and the willingness of exiles to die for it. There had already been noisy demonstrations during a performance of the opera at La Fenice on 31 December 1847, when, according to a police informer, an encore of 'La patria tradita' was demanded.

The same report noted the suspect enthusiasm of patrician families in the various boxes: 'two daughters of the nobleman Soranzo in box no. 32, first tier', 'the usual occupants of no. 7, same row, Gritti', 'the husband of Countess Valmarana was noted for his noisy and continued calls for a repeat, as were a great many others, whether in the boxes or in the stalls'. To make matters worse, the soprano taking the role of 'La Lady', as Italians call Lady Macbeth, had ostentatiously refused to pick up the bouquets of yellow flowers tied with black ribbons tossed onto the stage as if by *austriacante* admirers, though obviously thrown by patriots who had arranged the gesture with her beforehand. Bunches in red and white were of course seized at once and ardently pressed against the white robe she wore for the sleepwalking scene in the last act.

When *Macbeth* was given further revivals in the early days of February 1848, the patience of the police ran out. Operas at La Fenice were always performed with a ballet attached, and that season's star ballerina was the internationally admired Fanny Cerrito, praised by the French poet Théophile Gautier for her dainty feet, graceful arms and well-rounded bust.* With her came her husband, the choreographer Arthur Saint-Léon, who later created *Coppelia*. In his ballets Cerrito now eclipsed the earlier Italian triumphs of Fanny Elssler, darling of the Austrian officers and for that very reason hissed off the stage by the Milanese at her most recent visit to La Scala. On 6 February, Cerrito was due to repeat her current success in Saint-Léon's *La Vivandière*, which featured at its climax a brilliant 'Siciliana' exhibiting all her famed nimbleness of footwork. A Neapolitan by birth, she had numerous patriot friends, and at London theatres, where she was known as 'Cherry-Toe', the claque that made sure of her regular ovations seems to have consisted exclusively of Italian political exiles. This particular evening the Fenice audience cheered louder than ever when the dancer bounded onstage in a costume trimmed with red, white and green, rattling a tambourine beribboned with the same colours. The resulting uproar was quite enough for the authorities, who, after making the statutory arrests, ordered the theatre to be closed until further notice.

A sardonic observer of the whole event was the British consul-general Clinton Dawkins, former private secretary to Lord Aberdeen, whose intransigently pro-Austrian stance he shared. He would remain *en poste* throughout the forthcoming revolution and siege, unaltered in his scorn for Manin's initiative, though grudgingly respectful of his personal integrity. His dispatches provided a significant dissenting voice at a time when so many foreign observers in Italy were sympathetic towards the Italian patriots. Dawkins was never convinced that ordinary Venetians genuinely supported the revolutionary cause, nursing the typical conservative belief in the existence of a silent majority which would openly endorse the regime, were it not for the machinations and terrorist tactics of a small number of troublemakers. On 18 January he had written to London that 'there is hardly a Venetian house into which an Austrian is admitted. This determination has been come to very unwillingly by many, but they act under a system of intimidation that is carried on to a degree

---

* The British politician William Ewart Gladstone, seeing Cerrito perform in Paris in 1850, declared, 'She is a wonderful work of art, a statue made alive.'

scarcely credible. Persons supposed to have a leaning towards the Government are held up to publick execration, and their names written upon the walls, as Traitors to their Country.'

Dawkins had no quarrel with Austrian intransigence in the face of political upheaval, an approach strongly supported by conservative elements in the army and the court. The commander-in-chief of the army in Italy, Field Marshal Radetzky, was heard to use the term '*Krakowieren*' with reference to what was necessary for the rebel Italians, alluding to the brutal suppression of the Polish revolt in Krakow two years earlier. His formula, a brutally simple one, was 'three days of blood, ten years of peace'. Such an intransigent reaction received strong support from conservative elements in the Austrian army and at the imperial court in Vienna. Metternich, who grasped the real extent of the dangers ahead in Italy, was ignored, and the results of Count von Ficquelmont's fact-finding mission to Milan, which the Chancellor himself had instigated, were not taken seriously until too late. It looked as though Austria, far from merely toughing out the gathering storm, was determined to confront it head-on, in a mood of bellicose vindictiveness designed to bring the Italians abjectly to heel. This attitude, as much as any more ambivalent long-term view of Italian politics, explained the government's reluctance to release Manin and Tommaseo, whatever the final decision on the issue of disturbing public order.

It was nearly a month before the interrogation of the prisoners was resumed. Zennari's questioning of Manin was more minutely detailed than before, both as to the contents of individual letters and his dealings with suspect acquaintances (Dr Nani Mocenigo's name surfaced once more), but two days later he was given the chance to explain his conduct at length. He spoke of the causes, as he understood these, of current popular discontent, including the oppressiveness of the police state and the unwelcome role of the clergy in recommending blind submission to authority rather than favouring any movement towards social change. As before, he emphasised violent revolution as the menace which had decided him, in his position as a responsible citizen, to go ahead with his petition. He stressed the need for people to see that their representatives in the provincial congregations were acting in their best interests, and deplored the lethargic official response to the earlier of his two appeals. He praised Call's 'most courteous manner, enlightened and perspicacious mind and indications of moderately liberal ideas' at their meeting on 5 January. He referred continually to the promises seemingly indicated by the proclamations of 1815, and elaborated on original requests for franchise reform, for the right of Italian conscripts to serve in their native provinces rather than elsewhere within the empire, for Lombardy-Venetia to join the recently instituted custom union among Italian states, and for a general revision of the laws in order to adapt them to changing conditions. Finally, while acknowledging that his tone in presenting these requests might have seemed lacking in the appropriate decorum, Manin appealed to the court's good sense in judging whether or not he had acted in the best interests of the empire and its people. 'I believe,' he declared, 'that the strongest bulwark of a throne is the devotion shown by its subjects, and that such devotion is not won at the point of a bayonet. To those under government I have said "Stay calm, seek for reforms and hope that the Sovereign may concede them." To the rulers I have said "Concede". This tribunal may try me and sentence me, but it has no power over the conscience which has absolved and justified me.'

A note of desperation now began creeping into Call's attempts at influencing the court against the two prisoners. Tommaseo's hearings had gone especially badly for Zennari and his assessors, if only because the accused had skilfully managed to obstruct, deflect or blunt the edges of most of their questions and the overall interrogation was tediously unproductive. Finding no evidence of his adherence (or Manin's) to a secret society, Call started probing Tommaseo's links with noted liberals such as the Florentine publisher Vieusseux and the Milanese political journalist Cristina Belgiojoso, before fielding Giacomo Nani Mocenigo as a debauched wastrel, whose father was known to the police and who had recently appeared at a patriotic rally in Florence waving what purported to be the flag of Lombardy-Venetia symbolically draped in a black veil, while he himself sported a tricolour buttonhole and cockade.

The police chief's reaction can easily be imagined when, on 9 March, Zennari returned a verdict of 'Not Proven'. On the basis of evidence received, none of those arrested or mentioned in the trial records could be conscientiously referred to a higher court, and some – though by no means all – of their confiscated letters and documents were to be returned to them. The judge's summing-up, submitted to Call, was exemplary in its thoroughness, yet at the same time very little reading between the lines was needed to see where Zennari's doubts were leading him. Five lengthy paragraphs discussed the jurisprudential semantics of words such as 'might' and 'should' in terms of the penal code, or considered the true nature of '*avversione*', which in legal Italian possessed a stronger sense than the English 'aversion'. What exactly had Manin meant by the word '*Governo*'? Zennari believed it referred, not to the Austrian government as a whole, but to the provincial administration, in which case the instance had justified its author's impatience in the light of changing times and circumstances. 'It is not our duty,' he concluded, in a paragraph admirably tempering firmness with tact, 'to examine either the suitability of Manin's demands or whether the congregation is bound to fulfil them. However His Majesty may decide on the matter, it must appear disrespectful in us to anticipate his wise resolutions by our judgements.' Only the actual manner adopted by the accused in making their protests lay within the judge's brief, and even here Zennari was not convinced that any serious attempts at subverting authority had seriously been intended. Tommaseo, it was true, had taken a somewhat acerbic tone in his appeal on behalf of Jewish civil rights and the letter to the Bishop of Treviso, but this was no more than the Dalmatian's habitual style. The fact that he had chosen to live in Venice after the Emperor's amnesty in 1838 allowed him to return from exile suggested that he was well enough disposed towards the government.

Had Zennari been moved by Manin's resolute defence of the *lotta legale*, and was he indeed broadly sympathetic to its aims as they emerged from the successive interrogations? Call and Governor Palffy may have thought so. A Not Proven judgement, if made public, would instantly raise the stakes in the campaign for legal reform, not to speak of bolstering resolve among more extreme revolutionary elements. Releasing Manin, Tommaseo and others arrested in the January police trawl would not only be an acknowledgement of weakness and judicial blundering, but risked making the accused yet more heroic. The continuing presence of those crowds patrolling the Riva degli Schiavoni, with their mourning weeds, Calabrese bonnets and clay pipes, doubtless confirmed the Austrians' decision to ignore Zennari's verdict and detain the prisoners indefinitely. Something else had happened in any case, before the judge presented it, which now seemed to make an implacable show of force more necessary than ever.

For some months European governments had watched with concern the worsening political situation in France. The constitutional monarchy of Louis-Philippe, brought to the throne by the revolution of July 1830, had succeeded in pleasing nobody throughout the next eighteen years. A series of bungled foreign-policy decisions had left the nation embarrassed or humiliated internationally. Rapid industrialisation, in response to Prime Minister Guizot's encouraging 'Enrichissez-vous!', while it filled the speculators' pockets, succeeded in antagonising compassionate Catholics with its callous treatment of the workforce and exploitation of child labour. Demands grew louder for extension of the franchise, increased press freedom (one Paris prison had cells set aside for frequent visits by offending newspaper editors) and proper management of government finances. The notoriously pear-shaped Louis-Philippe himself, together with his homely-looking family, possessed none of the glamour and *physique du rôle* that France requires of its political leaders, and the King had alienated conservatives, who already saw him as a parvenu usurper, by his failure to espouse a suitably *ultra* shade of Catholicism and by the cost-cutting drabness of his court at the Tuileries. By 1847 most of France was bored, disillusioned or angry enough to contemplate a serious upheaval. As the political theorist Alexis de Tocqueville warned, revolution had broken out in 1789 because 'the class that was then the governing class had become, through its indifference, its selfishness and its vices, incapable and unworthy of governing the country'. He urged Guizot's ministry to 'change the spirit of the government, or else that very same spirit will lead you to the abyss'.

On 22 February 1848 the ministers who should have heeded de Tocqueville's words found the abyss opening with unwelcome rapidity. That day the first of several demonstrations took place in Paris upholding the right to oppose the government by means of popular assemblies and banquets. Within forty-eight hours Guizot resigned, but when soldiers fired on a crowd gathered outside the Foreign Ministry, the city was swiftly transformed, by means of barricades, into a potential battleground. With comparable speed, the troops, ordered by Louis-Philippe not to shoot save under exceptional circumstances, simply melted away or joined the insurgents. The King lost his nerve, and instead of showing himself to the people as a conciliatory gesture, signed an act of abdication in favour of his son, the dim, unpopular Duc de Nemours. The fate of the monarchy was sealed later that afternoon when the poet-politician Alphonse de Lamartine urged the proclamation of a republic on the assembled Chamber of Deputies.

Lamartine's speech, followed by the King's escape to England with the help of the British consul at Le Havre and a set of false whiskers, marked the beginning of one of the most turbulent moments in the history of France. News of these events convulsed Europe. Tsar Nicholas I of Russia, not given to theatrical gestures, was sufficiently appalled to exclaim to his courtiers, 'Gentlemen, saddle your horses, France is a republic!' Metternich, however, believed that neither he nor, in the long run, Austria itself was in any particular danger from the crisis. If the Viennese were slow to react to the bulletins as they arrived from Paris, it was because no one initially seemed quite sure what a first move should entail. The instability of the situation registered itself in a run on the banks, a rise in food prices and a recruiting drive by the secret police, but not until the second week of March did the students of Vienna University gather to petition Emperor Ferdinand in favour of abolishing press censorship and reviewing the limitations on teaching and the curriculum. When these requests were returned with a polite indication that they would be examined in due course, the enraged students marched on the Landhaus, the meeting place of Lower Austria's provincial congregation, now assembled for an emergency meeting. Fuelled by news from Budapest that the leading Hungarian activist Lajos Kossuth had called for a constitutional monarchy, the demonstrators began demanding Metternich's dismissal. The scenes in Paris replicated themselves in Vienna. Troops were brought up, the mood grew ugly, civil blood was shed, the Landhaus itself was sacked. Melanie Metternich, having earlier dismissed the revolutionaries with the comment that 'all they need is a sausage stall to make them happy', now feared for her husband's life as he went to the Hofburg, the royal palace, to advise the imperial family on a suitably resolute stance to take. Prompted by a mixture of personal apprehension and boredom induced by the old man's by now almost pathological long-windedness, the assembled archdukes hastened, at his invitation, to absolve him of his oath of fealty. At nine o'clock that evening, 13 March, Metternich resigned and set off, accompanied by Melanie, on a nightmarish zigzag across German states in various stages of political meltdown towards exile in England, whose current Chartist agitations were mild in comparison.

News of the Chancellor's fall was greeted with jubilation throughout Italy, and nowhere more gleefully than in Venice. No amount of censorship could have blacked out affairs in France altogether, and the city, from the salons of the nobility to the gondoliers of the *traghetti*, had been following the Paris revolution with mounting excitement over successive weeks. On 10 March there had been a patriotic rally in Piazza San Marco, to which the authorities, it was noted, had shown no inclination to react. Graffiti in praise of Manin and Tommaseo now appeared everywhere, in open defiance of the law. The pitch had been raised still further by Alphonse de Lamartine's ringing manifesto, distributed to the European powers through the new French republic's consular agents, declaring the provisions of the Congress of Vienna in 1815 to be at an end. 'If the hour of reconstruction seemed to us to have been decreed by Providence for any nationality whatsoever,' he proclaimed, 'if the independent states of Italy were invaded, if anyone were to impose limits and obstacles on their interior transformation or contested their right to make alliances so as to consolidate an Italian motherland, the French Republic would consider it her right to arm herself so as to protect such legitimate impulses towards nationhood.' Whether this actually meant that France was prepared to play a central role in the new context of Italian politics was a more ambiguous issue than at first appeared, but in

this heady moment of seeming fraternity between European liberal movements nobody bothered, or especially wanted, to read between Lamartine's
lines.

Even before the revolution in France, Count Ferdinand Zichy, Venice's
military governor and Metternich's uncle by marriage, had tried to warn
his commander-in-chief, Field Marshal Radetzky, that the city seemed to
be on the brink of a serious upheaval. The recent bad harvests and price
increases had been accompanied by worsening unemployment, and the
workers at the Arsenal were earning a wage which 'not even to the slightest
degree keeps pace with the rising inflation'. More troops were needed at
once, and to add to Zichy's worries, the naval officers – keeping faith, as
it were, with their dead comrades, the Bandiera brothers – were listening
all too readily to political agitators. Civil servants were growing casual in
the execution of their duties and joining the disaffected element among
the citizens either through inclination or fear. The tidings from Paris only
made matters worse, but both Radetzky in Milan and the government
in Vienna chose, throughout February, to ignore Zichy's repeated pleas
for reinforcements.

By mid-March, with Metternich gone and Radetzky seeking to hold
down the lid on a Milan seething with insurrection, it was too late to
expect any substantial back-up. While Zichy and the naval commander
in Venice, Admiral Martini, fretfully awaited instructions from Vienna,
the civil governor Count Lajos Palffy was somewhat more calm. With
the loyalty and firmness typical of his caste, he had continued to maintain the structures of order and legality within the city as though nothing
had happened, even if the detention of Manin and Tommaseo seemed
by its very nature to indicate a political emergency. The truth was that
in this instant, in Metternich's absence and with the Emperor apparently
resigned to conceding every demand made by the Viennese revolutionaries, there was no one either authorised or competent to transmit the
relevant orders. When on 16 March rumours of events in Vienna started
circulating in Venice, the question for Palffy rapidly turned from business as usual to whether or not he could contain the citizens any longer
without a show of force. As a crowd began to fill the Piazza under the
very windows of the Governor's residence in the Procuratie Nuove, his
wife chose this inopportune moment to go out for a walk along the colonnade beneath, accompanied by the aged Duke of Ragusa. Better known
to history as Marshal Marmont, he had earned his title and military
honours from Napoleon, but was notorious for having been the first to
desert his master in 1814. Onlookers catching sight of the pair set up a
chorus of whistles and abuse, driving the terrified Countess Palffy back

into the palace while Marmont fled as fast as he could and quitted Venice the same day.

The citizens now seized the initiative. It was time not just to demand, but to secure, the release of Manin and Tommaseo. A big demonstration on their behalf, planned to take place on the 16th was postponed until the following afternoon. On the morning of the 17th the Lloyd Line steamer arriving from Trieste with the post from Vienna brought details of Metternich's resignation, together with the news that the Emperor had agreed to grant his subjects a constitution. The Italian provinces were to be given, if not exactly home rule, then many of the privileges associated with it, including employment of Italians in upper echelons of the government and armed forces, the creation of a civic guard and a guarantee of full civil rights for all. The bringer of the glad tidings, a French businessman named Alban Gatte, brandished, as proof of veracity, a charred fragment of a picture frame once surrounding Metternich's portrait, set on fire the previous night by an angry Triestine mob.

An excited crowd had assembled on the Riva to await the news Gatte called down to the boatmen clustered around the steamer. Almost as soon as they reached the shore there was a surge towards the Piazza, and the cry went up, 'Release Manin and Tommaseo!' A hastily mustered deputation, led by Manin's friend the liberal notary Giuseppe Giuriati, brushed past the astonished guards on the palace staircase to confront Palffy and his wife at its head. The pair were accompanied by Zichy, generally thought of as being well disposed towards Italians, if only because his mistress was a Milanese ballerina and he was known to be fond of art and music. His responsibility now was to give Palffy suitable military support, but apart from a Croat battalion stationed at San Francesco della Vigna, the rest of the soldiers near at hand were Italian conscripts, and the remaining non-Italian troops were in barracks on the other side of the Grand Canal. After some hesitation, Palffy agreed to address the crowd in the square below. A scene unimaginable a few hours earlier now took place, as His Imperial Majesty's official representative havered and bargained with the citizens over the issue of the prisoners' release. His first objection, that such an act was not within his official powers, met with derision. An offer to send to Vienna for authorisation was still more angrily brushed aside. Finally his hearers' patience snapped, and a group of young men, led by Manin's son Giorgio, set off for the prison to free the detainees by force.

Given their status as potential if not proven enemies of the state, Manin and Tommaseo had continued to receive more than adequate treatment during their incarceration. Manin, allowed to read the newspapers, including several from France, was *au courant* with political events and had decided that, given the illegality of Austria's proceedings against him, a compromise within the existing framework of government was no longer possible. Venice must secure her total independence, but in a form that ruled out any likely upsurge of that lawlessness which was always his deepest fear. The new administration would take shape as a true republic, not the oligarchy of aristocratic committees that had constituted the Serenissima of old, but a representative authority with an elected assembly at its heart. Tommaseo meanwhile, grateful for the stove that his friend Carlo Leoni of Padua had prompted the prison governor to install in his cell, had sought refuge, as so often, in his Catholic faith, completing his translation of the Greek New Testament and Pope Leo I's homilies, and dreaming of an Italy united under the spiritual leadership of Pius IX. The manner adopted by each prisoner was later seen by the gaolers as characteristic of two very different natures: Manin had behaved throughout with courtesy, attentiveness, even charm, while Tommaseo remained haughty, scornful and irritable.

When Giorgio Manin and his friends reached the prison they began at once to batter down the palings filling the spaces of its arcade, and started to rattle and hammer at the central gate, while Manin himself, an able gymnast, managed to clamber up to the window of his cell, appearing to 'Evviva!'s from the ecstatic onlookers. In desperation the warders now unbarred his door and urged him to leave immediately. This he refused to do – ever the lawyer – until an order of release, signed in form by Palffy, should be properly produced. As it happened, the Governor had already drawn up the document, partly at the entreaty of his wife, still shaken by yesterday's encounter with the mob. Once it was signed, he was heard to mutter, 'I do what I should not.' Was there some significance in the fact that the name he had written on the order was not 'Daniele Manin' but that of Lodovico Manin, the ill-fated last doge of 1797?

With the paper signed and delivered, the prisoners were free to leave, quitting the prison by its back entrance beside Ponte della Canonica rather than by the more public exit onto Riva degli Schiavoni. On either side of the building in any case a jubilant throng of well-wishers had now gathered. In the presence of those they first encountered, led by the Bandieras' old teacher Emilio Tipaldo, Manin and Tommaseo embraced each other. It was the only occasion on which they would ever do so. Committed to the same cause, they were soon to draw apart, the gulf between them widened by suspicion and embarrassment on the one hand and burning contempt on the other. In the same measure that their single-minded devotion to freeing Venice from Austria appears admirable, the failure of the pair to build some kind of lasting and positive working relationship – a failure for which the intransigent Tommaseo was chiefly to blame – is a matter for real regret.

For the time being this was a political marriage of convenience between the heroes of an hour which only a brief while earlier had seemed barely conceivable in Italy, let alone in Venice. The two men found themselves chaired on the shoulders of a crowd flourishing tricolour flags, sashes and cockades, which surged around the palace of the Cardinal Patriarch, along the western side of the Basilica and into the Piazza. Thence Manin was carried all the way home to his house on Campo San Paternian, where his daughter Emilia stood waving on the balcony. Yet the joy of a reunion with her and Teresa was alloyed by news the family had kept from him since his committal. Ernesta, favourite among his three sisters, the beloved 'Nello' who had been a valued confidante since his boyhood, was dead. Living at Treviso with her husband, the pianist Enrico Viezzoli, she had been shielded for several weeks from the facts of Daniele's arrest. Soon after the truth was revealed that her brother was a political prisoner with no prospect of early release, she witnessed a party of Austrian soldiers clubbing an innocent citizen to death with their rifle-butts, and the horror of the scene, together with the thought that some similar fate was reserved for Daniele, brought on a fatal heart-attack.

There was hardly any time for Manin decently to mourn Ernesta's death or worry anew over Emilia's continuing ill health. To act quickly so as to ensure the maintenance of public order was imperative, not just for him, but for those such as Venice's mayor Count Giovanni Correr, who might influence Palffy and Zichy to act in the mutual interest of the community and its occupying power. The potential for serious implosion was revealed on the very afternoon of the prisoners' release, when, to the ominous sound of cannon-fire from their barracks at San Francesco della Vigna, companies of grenadiers and Croat infantry began marching into the Piazza. Their ostensible object was to pull down the tricolour banners hoisted earlier in the day to replace the Austrian flags on the three great masts standing in front of the Basilica. Having failed to do this, they were then given the order to fix bayonets and clear the square of what was by now a considerable crowd, summoned by the enterprising patriot who had managed to get into the Campanile and toll the great bell known as 'La Marangona', whose midnight curfew, deep-toned and mournful, is still one of Venice's most evocative sounds after hundreds of years. As the knots of surly, apprehensive citizens seemed reluctant to budge, the venerable figure of Jacopo Monico, Cardinal Patriarch, was seen to emerge at the window of his palace next to St Mark's. His purpose was simply to calm the tension, but the people, knowing Monico's fervent adherence to Pope Pius IX, swarmed into that corner of the Piazza in expectation of comfortable words with some sort of a liberal spin on their spirituality. Though the soldiers drove back the throng, there were as yet no casualties. The city was growing restless and impatient nevertheless, and that evening Palffy was forced once more to confront the crowd in the square, exhorting them to stay calm and giving an assurance that he would publish details of the Emperor's newly granted constitution as soon as it arrived.

For the moment this was all the Governor could reasonably offer. Venice officially remained part of the Austrian empire and no other authority existed to challenge his own. He had reckoned without the crowd's abrupt change of mood, and may not even have been persuaded of the new realities facing him and Zichy when Cardinal Monico, 'leaving his dinner half-finished' as one observer noted in recognition of the emergency, arrived in person to ask that the troops be withdrawn from the vicinity of the Basilica. Certainly it seemed as though the administration, civil and military, was determined on a more blatant show of force when, the following morning, the crowd flocked to the Piazza in expectation of further news from Vienna. As well as details of the new constitution, they hoped for some definite assurance that Venetia would be separated from Lombardy, with the two devolved provinces then uniting to form an independent kingdom under the rule of one of the many available Habsburg archdukes. Several people present carried tricolours, and once more successful efforts were made to hoist them on the three crimson masts. The square already bristled with soldiers, and when one of the officers ordered the flags to be removed at once, the command was greeted with jeering. Two of the banners were indeed hauled down, but on a third the rope snapped and propitiously enough the flag shot back up the pole and stuck there. The onlookers hooted still louder when the Croats, always seen by Italians as congenitally stupid, gazed at the seeming miracle in dumb astonishment. Infuriated by this mockery, the officer ordered his men to open fire.

This marked the signal for action that many Venetians had been waiting for. Several, apparently anticipating trouble, had brought picks and crowbars with them and quickly prised up the paving stones, with which they ran at the soldiers who were busy reloading. As more and more people filled the square, the mood grew uglier and the embattled infantrymen lost whatever discipline might have saved the situation from degenerating into outrage. It was in vain for a young Hungarian lieutenant, Lajos

Winckler, to interpose, crying, 'If you fire, kill me first before shooting at an unarmed populace!' The troops ignored him, their second volley claiming some nine dead or wounded in the process, including a fourteen-year-old boy, Ferdinando Vianello, earliest martyr of the Venetian revolution. Even though they succeeded in clearing the Piazza, the soldiers now had to face the defiance of those clambering up to windows and roofs to rain tiles down on them as they sought to empty the thorough-fares leading from the square. Attempts at pinning down free movement across the city by marching swiftly to occupy the Rialto Bridge were rendered pointless by the gondoliers, who rallied on either bank of the Grand Canal to ferry boatloads of Venetians jeering, whistling and making ribald 'fig' signs at the apparently impotent Croats on the balustrades above.

It was exactly the kind of situation Daniele Manin most feared, a direc-tionless popular uprising which threatened attacks on life and property, and the ascendancy of demagogues bent on overturning that rule of law to which he had dedicated his professional career. On the morning of 17 March when he was carried into the Piazza by his would-be liberators, he admonished them, 'Do not forget that there can be no true liberty (and that liberty cannot last) where there is no order. You must be jealous guardians of order if you hope to preserve freedom.' The events of the next twenty-four hours must have convinced him, and others broadly sympathetic to his legal contest, that there was no further prospect of working realistically within the framework of the existing regime to achieve his aims. In this crucial moment, as the Austrian government, lacking any clear mandate from Vienna, wavered between overreaction and loss of political will, Manin identified the earliest opportunity for reviving an independent Venice, a new Republic of St Mark which should both reflect the proud spirit of its extinct forerunner and invoke democracy to help repair those manifest injustices by which the Habsburg emperors had so tormented their subjects over the past thirty years.

The idea was not universally welcomed by visitors to the house at San Paternian. Teresa later found the point worth making that her husband had not been among those instrumental in pressing Palffy for reforms during this period, and that he preferred instead to devote his time to careful consideration of ideas already formed during his imprisonment, discussing them with the friends and political associates now gathering around him. Tommaseo, for example, saw the whole issue as primarily an intellectual struggle, while Leone Pincherle, a young Jewish busi-nessman acting as agent for the great underwriting house of Assicurazioni Generali, had responded with bewilderment when Manin declared that 'in a few days we shall all be shouting for a republic'. There was besides a *bien-pensant* element to take account of, formed from the municipal congregation, the town council whose members mostly derived from the Venetian nobility, with the Mayor, Count Correr, at their head. Correr was known to have liberal sympathies – he sported the same kind of signifying chin-fringe beard as Manin – but for the time being he and the rest of the municipality preferred to wait on the news from Vienna, expecting the promised constitution to remedy earlier grievances.

The bloody encounter in the Piazza on 18 March hardened Manin's resolve to secure the city for its own people. The previous evening his friend the physician Giacinto Namias, who had loyally visited Teresa and the children each day throughout the period of his detention, had sought Palffy's consent to establish a civic guard. The proposed institution was as much symbolic as practical – armed citizens patrolling the streets suggested a reclamation of the community's right to self-government – and its presence was to mark the arrival of revolution in towns great and small across Italy in 1848. If the Governor refused Namias's request, this was doubtless because he perceived the danger in allowing the 3,500 Italians in the Austrian army stationed in the city to fraternise with professed liberals who might tempt them to join the patriot cause. To Manin the issue of the civic guard was now more urgent than ever, not simply as a means whereby the patriotic interest could gain control of the city, but as a bulwark against the kind of disorder threatened by the events of that Saturday morning.

Palffy was not in conciliatory mood when a deputation arrived at the palace in the afternoon, with young Ferdinando Vianello dead, blood on the broken pavement outside and public order in Venice hanging by a thread. The party included the notary Giuriati, Angelo Mengaldo, an elderly lawyer who had once taken part in a swimming match down the Grand Canal with Lord Byron, and liberal aristocrat Niccolò Morosini. Their request for a civic guard, at least to protect private property while the troops defended public institutions, was rejected. Palffy, on the other hand, conceded that Morosini, together with another member of the deputation, Pietro Fabris, might leave for Verona, to ask for a blessing on the scheme from Archduke Rainer, who had fled there for safety after scenting danger in Milan. This was a clear attempt by the Governor at playing for time until the political situation should clarify itself one way or the other. He must have known, or at least suspected, that Milan too was on the brink of revolution, and was presumably expecting some positive news announcing that its 10,000-strong garrison under Marshal Radetzky had quashed any likely popular upheaval with more ruthless efficiency than had met January's tobacco riots.

On hearing of Palffy's stalling, Manin now took matters into his own hands. The proper channels could still be utilised, in the spirit of the *lotta legale*, therefore he presented himself to the municipality with a request that they should use their influence on Palffy. Almost at once a formal petition was sent back to the palace. 'Excellency,' it ran, 'public safety is the supreme law. The people are agitated, seriously so. It is necessary to do what is done in all countries in similar cases, with the happiest outcome, namely to institute a civil guard. Not doing so will cause great misfortune, which the proper authorities are obliged to prevent by whatever means. The municipality begs for this needful provision: supporting it with one voice are all those citizens who cherish order.' Palffy, forced to respond to this lofty instrument of moral blackmail, offered a clever fudge. A civic guard could not be permitted save by imperial decree, but military governor Zichy (whom he had supposedly consulted) would agree, given 'hints from His Eminence the cardinal Patriarch, together with my own', to the arming of 200 of the worthiest, most honourable citizens chosen from among the various *sestieri* and responsible to the municipality, a force charged with the maintenance of public and private security. 'Such a measure, understood as *temporary* and *exceptional*, is approved on the assumption that the populace remains calm.' The town council's 'zeal' and 'patriotic ardour' would help to further this object. If it were not achieved, military force would be invoked once more.

Viewed impartially, Palffy's concession was a brilliant exercise in buck-passing. He had effectively sought to drive a wedge between the city's social echelons by engaging the upper and middle classes to police the lower. He had cynically flattered the Italian liberals by appealing to their *amor patriae*. He had been careful to duck behind the – theoretically at least – more menacing figure of Zichy, and to suggest that it was thanks to himself, aided by the peace-making Cardinal Monico, that the guard, in whatever form, was permitted at all. Yet he had taken care to warn the civic dignitaries that if anything went wrong it must be their responsibility, and that the consequence would be further cannons and bayonets in the Piazza.

Events, as before, outmanoeuvred the Hungarian. His cunning feint looked like mere weakness and he was blamed afterwards by members of his own Habsburg proconsular class, as he has since been blamed by historians, for letting the Venetian revolution happen so swiftly and easily. By early evening on that busy 18 March, the civic guard was a reality. Not 200 but 2,000 citizens had been divided into platoons, armed with every sort of weapon from a musket and a duelling pistol to an antique halberd or a sabre from some patrician armoury, and given a white sash as a distinguishing uniform. Daniele Manin himself donned the sash, took up a musket and patrolled the city with one of the companies. When Baron Call's assistant police commissioner Strobach accused him of deliberately fomenting revolt by enlisting ten times the number stipulated by Palffy, the response was thunderous. 'I am here in the name of order in the city, but if you try to prevent whatever is needed to obtain it, you yourselves will cause the revolt you so much fear.' And with these words the little man shook his musket in Strobach's face.

As the guard now enthusiastically embarked on its round of duties, a Lloyd steam packet, specially sent from Trieste, brought the news that the Emperor had agreed to constitutional government for the Italian provinces. This was a definite improvement on the promises delivered two days earlier, and apparently caused the Mayor Count Correr to weep with joy, besides giving Palffy and Zichy reason to believe they might buy a little more precious time. Palffy read the imperial concessions to the crowd and proclaimed himself delighted to be Venice's first constitutional governor. Bands played the Austrian national anthem, Haydn's 'Emperor's Hymn', in the Piazza to shouts of 'Viva l'Italia!' and 'Viva l'Imperatore!', windows up and down the town were illuminated, and the time-honoured Venetian custom was observed of festively hanging carpets from windows and balconies. Palffy and his wife had been at a hastily organised gala concert at La Fenice when the boat arrived, and as soon as the news ran round the theatre, they graciously acknowledged the audience's cheers. The next day, a Sunday, saw a general atmosphere of euphoria diffused through the city. Heavy rain meant no more flag-waving outside St Mark's and the Austrians perhaps supposed that, given a little benevolence and condescension, the patriot element would stay at home for good.

On Monday, as the rain kept up with the impacted relentlessness of a true Venetian downpour, this spurt of goodwill between governors and governed started quickly to evaporate. Rumours were circulating as to secret preparations by the Austrians to bombard Venice from the Arsenal and the barracks at San Francesco della Vigna nearby. The military presence, despite the formation of the civic guard, was undiminished, and suspicion had started to mount among the citizens once more. Hardening resolve on both sides was the amazing news now arriving from Milan where, following a hostile confrontation between government officials and a vast patriotic crowd demanding political reforms, the city had thrown up barricades and defied the troops under Radetzky's command to regain effective control. The '*Cinque Giornate*', the five days' urban resistance since famous in Risorgimento annals, had begun, and Radetzky found himself forced to pull back to positions beyond Milan's outer ramparts, where he could try to blockade and bombard the citizens into surrender. 'The character of this people,' he wrote in a letter to his daughter Friederika, 'has altered as if by magic, and fanaticism has taken hold of every age, every class and both sexes.'

Not for nothing had the Viceroy, Archduke Rainer, thought it politic to retreat to Verona, urged on by his wife. For all its residual Austrophilia, Verona, for the time being, was nearly as feverish with patriotism as Milan. Demonstrators outside the Due Torri hotel where the viceregal couple had put up insisted that Rainer should at least show himself at the window, but when at last he appeared it was to inauspicious cries of 'Down with Austria, death to the Germans!' and insults hurled at the sentries guarding the main door. The same evening at the opera house there was another flourish of defiance, with many of the female audience wearing tricolour shawls and everyone sending up 'Viva!'s for Italy and Pio Nono. 'Here,' the Archduke's son Ludwig wrote to his brother Ernst, 'everyone has completely gone off their heads. Most of them are drunk, going round the city crying "Evviva l'Italia!", embracing the soldiers like brothers and even doing the same to the officers, who are legless as well. And this is happening in an Austrian provincial town!' The next day, having blamed his own family, especially the 'idiot Emperor', the 'rapscallion Hereditary Prince' (Franz Josef, Ferdinand's nephew) and the scheming Habsburg womenfolk for the growing catastrophe, the young Archduke bitterly exclaimed, 'Goodbye, empire! We may as well join the civic guard!'

While the Austrians reeled in panic and disbelief at their overthrow throughout Lombardy-Venetia, Manin was starting to plan in earnest for a takeover of Venice. The key to any manoeuvre by either side must be the Arsenal, where the Croat garrison was belatedly receiving reinforcements, but whose Italian labour force nursed a powerful grudge against the government. The sailors and marines of the imperial fleet offered another reliable arm for any proposed revolution, and Manin had been quick to make contact, following his release from prison, with one of the naval officers, Antonio Paolucci, a friend of the Bandiera brothers and son of that same Admiral Paolucci suspected of having allowed Emilio to escape from Venice. When an unsigned letter arrived at Campo San Paternian on 21 March warning of further reinforcements being drafted to the Arsenal, Manin called an emergency meeting that night. To it came Leone Pincherle and the advocates Adolfo Benvenuti and Zilio Bragadin. Niccolò Tommaseo, soon to make a fetish of his alienation from the central revolutionary caucus, would later claim that he was absent, though

Teresa Manin noted his attendance. The scheme under discussion seems to have been the seizure of the Arsenal and the four cannon in the Piazza by trusted elements in the navy and the civic guard. Teresa recalled afterwards that the conference only broke up at half-past two in the morning, following much argument over the watchword, finally agreed upon as 'Viva San Marco!'

Pincherle had been late in arriving. His excellent excuse was that he had been making a nuisance of himself at that evening's extraordinary session of the town council, during which he had asked, as at meetings on the two previous days, whether the municipality, given the Austrian regime's likely dissolution, had the strength and courage to take over the government. As before, Count Correr and the councillors brushed this embarrassing question aside and proceeded to business. Earlier that morning three noblemen had presumed to offer the Mayor their services as additional board members in what seems to have been a fleeting attempt by Venetian patricians to reclaim the senatorial authority their ancestors had enjoyed under the extinct Republic. Correr, whatever his ancient lineage, sent them packing at once, with the announcement that he had already sought the advice of sensible people among the ordinary citizens. This was true, repeated invitations having already gone out to Daniele Manin, who had so far refused to attend the council meetings. When Pincherle presented himself at San Paternian it was with a message from a slightly miffed Correr, wanting to know why the lawyer was staying away and what his plans were. Manin's answer was simple enough. 'Indeed I have a plan, but it is inopportune for me to spread details of it around. If the Mayor wishes to know of it, he must come to my house at seven tomorrow morning.' Correr appeared at the stipulated hour and, having listened carefully to what was proposed, went on to the council session in a state of considerable alarm, refusing to disclose what was afoot except by saying that the plan was extremely serious. By this early hour Manin, managing to get very little sleep since leaving prison, had arranged with his old schoolfriend Francesco Degli Antoni to rendezvous outside the Arsenal at midday with certain civic-guard captains on whom they could rely. The guard's full support had been cautiously withheld by its commander Angelo Mengaldo, but the presence of even a few men with muskets and pistols must serve to show that Manin and Degli Antoni meant business.

Both of them were aware of the potential for violence among those who worked or were quartered behind the high walls of the Arsenal, the naval dockyard of the old Republic, its magnificent Renaissance portico guarded by ancient sculpted lions brought from Greece by the fighting seventeenth-century doge Francesco Morosini, '*il Peloponnesiaco*'. As well as Italian troops and a garrison of Croats, it contained a workforce of some 1,500 men, known as *arsenalotti*, under the overall command of Captain Giovanni Marinovich, a naval officer from the Bocche di Cattaro* on the Dalmatian coast, whose sense of duty was hardened by a family loyalty, handed down over generations, to whatever government happened to be ruling Venice. In the space of a few years as Arsenal superintendent, he had contrived to make himself spectacularly unpopular with the labourers in his charge. A martinet with little in the way of personal charm to offset his brusqueness, Marinovich was also an obsessive fault-finder, preoccupied with trying to cut costs and disagreeably alert to the prevalence of moonlighting among his workers, as well as to their old-established habit of taking perks from among the various materials and equipment used in boat-building. His clampdown on these time-honoured practices was accompanied with the threat that no *arsenalotto*, once dismissed, should ever be able to find employment within Venice. Indeed, to any favour requested of him by the workmen, his response was always a blunt 'Next week'. The Captain's reputation had suffered still further from the rumour that his strictness had helped to cause the death of the well-loved Archduke Friedrich, to whom he had been appointed watchdog when the young man was sent to cool his heels in Venice after being forced to break off a liaison with a woman judged socially unacceptable at court.

When the *arsenalotti* detected Marinovich's hand in what appeared to be a plan to bombard the city from ships in the lagoon, this suspicion – though in fact groundless – stiffened their loathing of him to a point at which his life became genuinely endangered. He was the man who had persistently refused their requests for a pay increase, the man who had forced the owners of the *squeri*, where gondolas were repaired, to deny them any odd jobs to eke out their income, and the man they held responsible for an order forbidding them to join the civic guard. On the evening of 21 March, knots of home-going workers hung about on the steps outside the Arsenal's main gate, with an obvious intention of mobbing him as he left the building, so that he was forced to await the arrival of a civic-guard platoon to escort him off the premises.

Marinovich's bravery was nurtured by his lack of imagination and his evident contempt for most of those with whom he had to deal. There

---

* Kotor, in Montenegro. Until 1797 it marked the furthest point of Venice's Dalmatian coastal territory, and its citizens were noted for their fervent devotion to the Republic.

was work to be done next morning, so it was only reasonable that he should arrive at his office at the stipulated hour. He had arranged, after all, to conduct the naval commander Admiral Martini on a tour of inspection and was punctual to his appointment. Thirty Croats now guarded the gate, but they faced an infuriated crowd. Instead of ordering them to remain at their posts, Martini dismissed the soldiers in an effort to appease the angry workers, while one of Marinovich's fellow officers, Captain Turra, had a covered gondola made ready at the side entrance. Helped by Manin's revolutionary contact Antonio Paolucci, he escorted the superintendent to the boat, and the pair were rowed to the Porta Nuova at the lagoon end of the dockyard complex. Soon enough the *arsenalotti* got wind of the escape and hastened to head off the fugitives, some in boats and a few running along the sides of the docks. Fatally for Marinovich, the gate had been locked on his orders, and a man sent to fetch the key was seized by the pursuers. It was Paolucci who urged Marinovich to hide in the nearby tower while he himself tried to turn back the enraged workmen. Marinovich climbed the wooden ladders up the inner walls to emerge on the open roof just as the crowd below battered down the doors and started clambering up after him, shouting, 'Prisoner! Prisoner!'

Looking down as the first of them reached the little room under the final ladder, the Captain called out; 'Do you want me dead or alive?' 'Alive,' came the reply. 'What will you do if I surrender?' he asked. They returned no answer, but he flung away his brace of pistols nevertheless, descended the ladder and gave up his sword. Though his courage might have impressed some of them, the rest had no mercy. A young man named Conforti, nursing a private grudge, stepped forward to lunge at Marinovich with a crowbar. Badly wounded but not yet dead, he was seized by the feet and bumped on his head down the remaining steps, 180 of them, to cries of 'Cut him in pieces! Burn him!' Thrown into one of the old Serenissima boatsheds, he remained alive for a brief space even after this barbaric ordeal, but when he managed to ask for a priest to administer the last rites, the request was met with his own catchphrase: 'Next week'. When his gondola was searched, they found, tucked under the cushion, a hastily scrawled note in his handwriting which read, 'Look after my children.'

News of the murder, carried to the town council by a workman who burst in on their meeting shouting, 'Now the bastard's dead we'll have no more Germans in the Arsenal!', convulsed Venice. Manin, horrified at its symbolism as much as by the deed itself, knew he had to act quickly to prevent further needless bloodshed. Already that morning a naval officer had arrived to warn him that plans were afoot to bomb the city into submission, though Zichy had assured the British consul that this was not true. Now Daniele donned his top-hat and white civic-guard sash, girded on his sabre and, taking Giorgio with him, kissed Emilia farewell. Teresa would not embrace them, afraid of bursting into tears at this fearful moment. All she said to her husband was, 'You may be killed.' 'Yes, maybe,' he rejoined.

Their intimate knowledge of the city made it easy for father and son to zigzag via the more remote *calli* towards the Arsenal, so as to dodge Austrian patrols, urging any of the civic guard met on the way to join them. When they reached San Giovanni in Bragora, where the Bandieras' house stood, Manin divided his followers (by now a substantial body) into two companies of fifty each, led by himself and Francesco Degli Antoni, and without undue haste they proceeded to the Arsenal's main gateway. One of the guard battalions, from San Pietro in Castello, on the city's northern edge, had already entered the yards with the object of stifling any further potential outbreaks of violence. Manin's business, meanwhile, was with Admiral Martini, who was terrified that he too might be lynched by the angry shipwrights and was correspondingly eager to offer every assurance that an Austrian plot to bombard Venice was simply a rumour. Accompanied by several naval officers, Manin, Giorgio and Degli Antoni began a careful reconnaissance of the entire installation before ordering the store of weapons to be opened and the bell to be rung which normally summoned the *arsenalotti* to work. In the presence of the assembled labour-force, Manin effectively wrested command from Martini, reassigning it among three officers, Antonio Paolucci, Leone Graziani and Giovanni Marsich – the two last being relatives of the Bandiera, a fact whose significance was probably not lost on those present.

Even at this juncture it might still have been possible for the Austrians to turn the tables. While the handover of weapons and keys was taking place within the Arsenal walls, a company of infantry from the Wimpffen regiment stationed nearby, together with a detachment of marines, had arrived in front of the gateway to find their entry blocked by the civic guard. The commanding officer, a Hungarian named Boday, ordered them to open fire, but unluckily for him the men were all Italian conscripts from villages in the Veneto, whose loyalty had been steadily chipped away over recent days by a promise that they would be allowed to go home to their families if they joined the patriot cause. As Boday gave the order to fire, one of the marine officers, Baldisserotto, flung himself in front of the troop, drawing his sabre and commanding them to lay down their arms. Boday, brandishing his own sword, rushed on him and the two began to fight. As Baldisserotto fell wounded, a sergeant, rushing to his assistance, disabled Boday with a bayonet thrust in the shoulder, while several other soldiers turned their muskets on him as he begged for mercy. Only Degli Antoni's timely arrival on the scene saved his life.

This sudden mutiny was the signal for nearly 4,000 more Italian troops in the city to lay down their arms, spelling victory for Manin as they did so. Even the Croat soldiers in the Arsenal had been talked into holding their fire, while the patriots' rallying call of 'Viva San Marco!' echoed across the broad campo outside the gate. As Teresa warned, the whole enterprise had been a gamble and there is no suggestion that Daniele foresaw the astonishingly swift process of surrender which ensued. In Piazza San Marco meanwhile, another civic-guard officer, Carlo Radaelli, leading a platoon armed with everything from pistols to halberds and two-handed medieval swords, advanced on St Mark's basilica with the intention of seizing the cannon ranged in front of it after the violence of four days earlier. Once again it was Italian soldiers who confronted the guard. Bidding them lay down their arms, Radaelli cried, 'Long live Italy! Surrender to the national guard!' and the two forces started mingling amicably as the volunteers, pulling the black-and-yellow cockades off the grenadiers' shakos, pinned tricolour favours on their uniforms instead. One of the details always remembered from that day was the sight of hundreds of these *schwarzgelber* Austrian cap-badges floating up and down the canals of Venice.

By two o'clock that afternoon the four cannon were trained, not on the square itself, but on the windows of the Governor's palace, while civic guards had replaced the soldiers on his staircase. Count Palffy was effectively a prisoner in his own palace, more isolated than ever. No fresh orders had reached him from Vienna or from Archduke Rainer, an unwelcome refugee among the Veronese. The news from the Arsenal was bad enough, and now Angelo Mengaldo, in his capacity as civic-guard commander, presented himself to issue a demand for surrender of administrative powers to the town council. True to form, Palffy refused, but invited the municipality to send its representatives to discuss the worsening situation. Shortly afterwards the commission arrived, led by *podestà* Correr, accompanied by two fellow noblemen, Francesco Michiel and Dataico Medin, together with Leone Pincherle, Paolo Fabris, another regional congregation member, and the lawyer Gian Francisco Avesani, a republican with pronounced Mazzinian views. The six men had come prepared to be firm with the Governor: time was of the essence and most of them were worried lest Manin seize more political advantages than he already had. They were taken aback therefore when Palffy, with his secretaries and advisers gathered about him, began an extended harangue on the false accusations being made against the government and the dangers of fomenting revolution.

He had miscalculated his hearers' mood and, more significantly, failed to grasp the degree to which that morning's events had already conspired to undermine his credibility. After listening with increasing impatience, Avesani, most politically *enragé* of the deputation, snapped, 'So are we here for a rebuke in your old style or have we come to negotiate?' Palffy crossly announced that he would not be speaking to Avesani, preferring to do business with Correr. He then sought to wrong-foot his visitors by declaring that earlier concessions had been made on an assurance of no further disturbance among the citizens. Correr pointed out that it was precisely in order to avoid further bloodshed that they were here now. In a gesture both threatening and truculent, he then appointed Avesani as their spokesman. Seizing his chance, the iron-willed advocate told Palffy that the moment for bluster was over, that they hadn't got time to answer his 'inconvenient preamble' or to enter into discussion as to the rights and wrongs of popular grievance or the adequacy of the government's concessions. What mattered was the simple question of whether or not the imperial authority was disposed to give up its power over Venice. 'If that is the case,' replied Palffy indignantly, 'I shall relinquish my position, and in compliance with official instructions, consign my responsibilities to His Excellency the Military Governor, so that the city will only have him to deal with.'

Avesani was not to be fooled by Palffy's implicit warning. Having already spotted Count Zichy in an adjoining room, he asked for him to be sent for in order that what had just been said could be repeated in his presence. When Zichy entered, Palffy promptly tendered his resignation, adding his hope that in carrying out official duties, the Vice-Marshal would do his outmost to spare 'this fine and monumental city, towards which I have always felt the deepest affection'. Zichy somewhat grimly protested that even though Palffy's request surprised him – he too loved Venice, his residence for many years – he had no choice but to do his duty, which might well result in him having blood on his hands. Brushing this threat aside, Avesani went on to state the municipality's demands: all non-Italian troops to be evacuated by sea to Trieste, the forts on the lagoon to be surrendered and all arms and ammunition to be left in Venice, along with the army pay-chests. To each of these terms Zichy offered some objection, but faced with Avesani's implacable firmness of purpose, gave way at last. Only on the financial issue was there some compromise, with a deal finally struck that allowed three months' pay for the departing soldiers and additional funds to cover the expenses of their transportation. Palffy and Zichy were to remain as hostages for better assurance that the terms would be properly carried out.

The newly deposed civil governor, clearly deploring his military colleague's weakness in yielding so easily, protested at Avesani's failure to trust him. 'I have always behaved like a gentleman, and don't deserve to be treated in this fashion.' 'A gentleman, yes,' came the reply, 'and admittedly well-disposed towards Venice until three months ago. Since then, however, you have committed serious errors – setting aside those which derive from the orders of the man who prides himself on being the Nestor of diplomacy, but who instead, by resisting the trend of the age, has brought the Austrian monarchy to the very brink of disaster.' The allusion here was to Metternich, no less, and though the accusation was hardly fair, Palffy and Zichy both had reason to acknowledge its kernel of truth. The latter shook Avesani's hand, offering his word of honour that the terms would be proclaimed. A document of capitulation was signed at 6.30 p.m.

To whom exactly had the Austrians surrendered Venice? Officially to delegates representing the municipality as sanctioned by the Habsburg government. For hundreds, if not thousands of Venetians the real power now lay in the hands of another lawyer altogether, one just as ruthlessly determined as Avesani, yet a focus – as he alas was not – of popular admiration for his personal courage, so lately displayed in seizing the Arsenal from under the very noses of its garrison commanders. While negotiations had been going on within the Procuratie Nuove, an extraordinary scene was taking place outside. Manin, having snatched an hour's rest at a tavern near the Arsenal, had marched triumphant, at the head of a huge crowd along the Riva degli Schiavoni towards St Mark's. On the Riva he paused to raise a tricolour banner topped by a red Phrygian bonnet, symbol of liberty and perhaps recalled by older citizens from the heady days of 'Venezia giacobina', in the wake of La Serenissima's fall, when this particular French revolutionary emblem had seemed to promise so much. To cries of 'Long live the Republic!' the throng swirled into the Piazza. It was impossible for Avesani and his fellow delegates not to have heard the jubilant voices, and this explained the eagerness with which they pressed the two governors towards a speedy surrender. The sense of the ground being cut from under them was made more obvious when Manin, clambering onto one of Florian's café tables so as to be seen above the heads of the crowd, saluted his audience with the thrilling words 'Siamo liberi!', 'We are free!' They had a double right to boast, he claimed, rather bending the truth in the process, because they had not shed a drop of blood. 'But it is not enough,' he went on, 'that we should overthrow the old government. We must put another in its place, and for us the best, I believe, is the republic, for it will remind us of our past glories, and will be all the better for our present freedoms. We do not intend to separate ourselves from our Italian brothers. On the contrary, we shall form one of those centres which will help to achieve the fusion, by degrees, of our beloved Italy into one country. Long live the republic, long live freedom, long live St Mark!'

Though Manin was then allowed to go home and snatch a brief repose, the city had not finished with him. True, Avesani was now leader of a new provisional government, hastily saluted by an official proclamation of the municipality as a miraculous achievement. The idea behind this initiative was clearly to effect a smooth handover from the Austrians to those *bien-pensant* elements which formed the city council and were generally unsettled by what had happened at the Arsenal. The simple fact was, however, that for most Venetians no government could possibly be acceptable that did not include Manin, a truth he himself fully understood. As he sardonically remarked to Degli Antoni, the only visitor allowed at San Paternian that evening, 'Well, these gentlemen will be sending for me soon enough.' The city, far from being content with the new state of affairs, seethed with anger and frustration throughout the evening, to a point at which Degli Antoni, at Manin's request, stepped out to the patriotic printworks owned by the courageous widow Teresa Gattei and asked her to run off the following notice:

VENETIANS!
I know that you love me, and in the name of such affection, I ask that in the legitimate manifestation of your joy, you conduct yourselves with that dignity appropriate to a people worthy of being free.
Your friend,
MANIN

Perhaps he honestly was worried that disorders would break out, but no gesture could have been more effective in focusing popular attention on the missing man at the centre of the regime. After midnight, with Florian's still open, a group of influential citizens gathered in the café to appoint one of their number to bring the new governing commission to their senses. A young lawyer, Antonio Bellinato, shortly afterwards entered the palace to inform Avesani that it was his duty to resign forthwith and that no government which did not include Daniele Manin could hope for popular support. At half-past three in the morning Avesani bowed to the inevitable. He had been in power a mere nine hours and the surrender of his authority must have been mortifying. Not a little of his subsequent coldness towards Manin as a political colleague was surely coloured by this experience, yet he remained deeply committed, throughout the revolution, to the liberal cause.

There was no alternative now but for Angelo Mengaldo to go in person to Manin's house and deliver him the key responsibility of President at the head of a new provisional government. Tired and ill, Manin, as so often, rallied his astonishing reserves of energy to meet the challenge of the moment. This had been an extraordinary twenty-four hours. As Teresa wrote to a friend, 'The events seemed to me like a dream, our new condition like something imaginary. My dear, can you conceive of our happiness? To get up in the morning as *slaves* and go to bed *free*? Ah, dear friend, why weren't you here? Days like this never happen more than once in the course of a single life.' She recalled the horror of waiting for news from the Arsenal, ended by the roar of the crowd distinctly audible from the Piazza, in whose cry of 'Viva la Repubblica! Viva San Marco!' she now joined. 'For the second time in five days, I saw my husband carried home in triumph. It was almost too much for me, but I suppressed my happiness just as I'd subdued my anxiety. I kissed my husband as a liberator of my country, the foremost such liberator of them all. I kissed my son, who at just sixteen had shown a courage and a calmness of bearing, and I gloried in possessing them both.'

One other detail from 22 March, that day which saw Venice improvising, from hour to hour, its nearly bloodless revolution, deserves mention. As the civic guard carried the news across the city of Manin's tabletop address to the crowd at St Mark's, they encountered, near the church of San Aponal, a venerable old man, who raised his hat when their proclamation of the republic was read out. 'All of a sudden,' noted one of the officers, 'he seized me in his arms, then drew from his bosom an ancient lion carved out of wood. "I knew that Venice would rise again one day!" he cried. "I was so certain that for fifty years I have always carried this lion with me, ready for the day when I should once more become a republican. Now I have nothing else to ask of God, and I can die in peace."' Around them the canals were bright with the discarded black-and-yellow cockades, and the streets echoed to the laughter of children pulling off the houses the Habsburg double-headed eagle signs used by the Assicurazioni Generali fire insurance company. Venice, truly – amazingly – was free.

CHAPTER 4

~

SPRINGTIME IN UTOPIA

WHILE THE VENETIANS LUXURIATED IN the novelty of political freedom after fifty years of occupation, Counts Palffy and
Zichy, now archetypal yesterday's men, prepared to leave the
city. A steamer of the Austrian Lloyd line was to carry them, with several
other civil and military officials, north along the Adriatic coast to the
port of Trieste. Both men presumably anticipated some sort of criticism
among imperial conservatives for their hasty surrender of Venice, but
neither surely guessed at the degree of scorn and execration that would
be directed at them, not just from their own Habsburg officer caste, but
from liberal foreign commentators. For Edmund Flagg, later United States
consul in Venice and author of a rambling but lively account of the revolution, *Venice, City of the Sea*, the two governors were guilty of simple
cowardice in failing to mobilise the available garrison regiments when
they had the chance to do so. They should have done their best, besides,
to prevent fraternisation between the Italian troops and the mob and
could have tried harder to block the formation of a civic guard. Flagg's
fellow American, W. H. Stiles, US attaché at the court of Vienna, claims
that Zichy, after signing the capitulation document, had declared, 'Now
I can eat my dinner in peace!', and points out how eagerly Palffy, when
summoned to an inevitable court martial later in the year, passed the
buck by saying that he was never given a chance to reject the surrender
after handing over his responsibilities to Zichy.

In the immediate aftermath of 22 March, the Austrian army's top brass
was unforgiving. Present at that afternoon's showdown between Avesani
and the two governors had been the sixty-seven-year-old Count Karl
Culoz, commanding the Kinsky regiment. Judging Zichy's action to be

illegal and unjustified by the pressure of circumstances, he had returned in a fury to his quarters in the barracks at the former hospital of the Incurabili on the Zattere, where he and his men refused to budge for four days until finally persuaded for purely practical reasons to leave while there was still time. His criticism of the military governor's pusillanimity was echoed by Baron Constant D'Aspre, commander-in-chief of the Padua garrison. Speaking of the 'shameful capitulation', D'Aspre noted the lamentable truth that 'Zichy was an upright, brave soldier, but one of those for whom everything is fine so long as they have peace'.

It was Palffy who seized on a chance, suddenly offered to both departing governors, of limiting the damage to their own reputations. On the afternoon of 23 March, he and his wife, together with Zichy and the other officers, were escorted on board the steamer *Erzherzog Friedrich*, bound ostensibly for Trieste but secretly intending to make a significant detour before it reached its official destination. To the captain, named Maffei, was consigned an important dispatch from Daniele Manin, as President of the new provisional government, containing details of the revolution which were to be passed to the Adriatic fleet based at Pola on the Istrian coast. The ships' crews, whatever security measures had been adopted since the Bandieras' martyrdom, were still mostly Italian, men who saw the two brothers and their comrades as heroic rather than treacherous. To Manin, diverting the steamer to Pola must have seemed a golden advantage to commandeer the fleet and thus see off any attempt by Austria, once its forces regrouped, to blockade the channels into the Venetian lagoon. He chose now to trust Captain Maffei, even though a trio of naval officers based in Venice advised him against passing crucial instructions directly to a mere functionary of the Austrian merchant marine, offering themselves instead as bearers of such an important commission.

Manin's act of faith was a major miscalculation. For Palffy had somehow got wind of the letter's contents, and no sooner was the *Erzherzog Friedrich* steaming out of the lagoon into the open sea than he and his fellow passengers forced Maffei to give up the document and alter course, heading immediately for Trieste. There the instructions were passed to the Governor, Count Gyulai, who immediately saw to it that loyal officers in charge of the harbour forts at Pola had their cannon at the ready to prevent the fleet from sailing. As a result, only three small pinnaces managed to slip away to Venice, captained by patriotic Italians, while measures were taken to rally Austrian vessels at Trieste from further down the coast and all suspect naval personnel were clapped in irons.

Venice was in no mood to ponder the likely consequences of her new leader's error of judgement. 'We are free,' began an exultant leader in the former *Gazzetta privilegiata*, now the *Gazzetta di Venezia*, with 'Viva San Marco!' and the holy evangelist's lion at its masthead instead of the Habsburg double-eagle. 'We belong to nobody but ourselves, we have our own motherland and can speak those sacred words "We are Italians". History in her annals has surely recorded no greater or more inspired event. Without bloodshed, amid the most rigorous constraints and the tyrannical high-handedness of military cohorts, a city, the wonder of the world, has triumphed and the oppressed citizens have shaken off their yoke. Genius has conquered and the former power lies at its feet. Courage has vanquished strength and words have blunted the bayonet's point.'

Just how much had changed, and how abruptly, was made clear to a young Austrian officer of French origin, Georges de Pimodan, who had set out from Trieste on the night of 22 March with letters from Gyulai to Zichy. As the ship headed southwards, they passed another steamer going at rather greater speed in the opposite direction. Only later did Pimodan realise it was hurrying towards Trieste with news of that day's Venetian revolution. As it was, when he stepped on deck early next morning to catch the always thrilling view of the city down the Bacino di San Marco, he was astonished, as they drew nearer, to find the Riva degli Schiavoni and the Piazzetta swarming with jubilant crowds, whose cries of 'Viva la Repubblica! Viva San Marco!' echoed unmistakably across the water.

After landing, he managed to enter the Doge's Palace, where the new provisional government was busy moving in. Here he came across an officer in Austrian naval uniform, but sporting a tricolour armband. Pimodan's immediate instinct was to address him in German, to which the man rejoined, in an accent suspiciously perfect, 'Ich spreche kein Deutsch.' The anteroom in which they both waited was a scene of absolute confusion, but finally Pimodan gained admittance to Daniele Manin himself. 'I saw a little man of about 50 [*sic*] seated at a desk. He was wearing spectacles and seemed to have spent many nights without sleep; his face was pale and worn with fatigue.' Manin's initial glance of aston-ishment on seeing a white Habsburg army tunic quickly changed to one of cynical curiosity. Opening a drawer, he drew out a bag of gold coins, began to rattle it, fixed his eye firmly on Pimodan and asked him whether he wanted to fight for Venice's freedom. Outraged, the young officer scornfully answered that he came from noble stock and was the Emperor Ferdinand's officer or nobody's. 'Very well,' said Manin in an ironic tone, 'as you wish. Meanwhile you will remain here under guard.'

Not unreasonably Pimodan demanded to be allowed to see Zichy, otherwise, given the circumstances, he might be accused of desertion. Manin agreed and had him escorted across the Piazza to the Governor's palace, where Palffy and Zichy were about to end their brief house arrest by leaving for Trieste. On the stairs Pimodan was surrounded by a group of young men who cut off the tassel of his scabbard, snatched away his cap to remove the black-and-yellow band and cockade and tried to pin a tricolour favour on his tunic. Upstairs Zichy was still in bed. The guards had failed to search Pimodan for the letters from Gyulai, providentially hidden up his broad uniform sleeves. When they brought him unceremoniously into the bedroom, he tried to signal to the old man that he had something to drop, which might be worth picking up. Poor Zichy, however, looked 'too beaten down, too overwhelmed to understand me'.

There was no point in prolonging the interview, and Pimodan realised that he had better get out of Venice while the going was good. Still carrying the letters, he was marched as far as a palace on a small campo, where the guards left him on the ground floor. At the watergate he bribed a passing gondolier to carry him to Mestre, and under cover of the gondola's black awning he got safely up the Grand Canal. Just as the boat prepared to enter the lagoon, somebody on the bank spotted Pimodan's white cloak, and a cry went up that an Austrian officer was trying to escape. A young man, 'very *comme il faut*', at the head of a civic-guard patrol, ordered the gondolier to halt. When Pimodan landed before a hostile crowd, he was asked for a permit. All he had was his official army dispatch-rider's pass. 'The young man saw it was worthless, but the danger I was in probably moved him to pity me', and Pimodan was allowed to proceed. After a hairy quarter of an hour in Mestre, where he threatened to shoot the Mayor unless he were allowed to go on, Pimodan journeyed north-west as far as Castelfranco, where he rejoined the Austrian army. The time of his life, as a young soldier hungry for action, honour and glory, was about to begin.

In Venice that same night a gala concert took place at La Fenice. There was an exuberant flourish of red, white and green in dresses, sashes, ribbons and armbands, not to speak of the decorations around the auditorium, where the gorgeously appointed box intended for the Doge in Antonio Selva's original theatre and annexed, since the Austrian occupation, by the civil and military governors, was soon to be allotted by the provisional government to ordinary citizens. 'At the centre of the stage,' reported the *Diario Veneto* (among the earliest of a crop of newspapers springing up overnight as Habsburg press censorship evaporated), 'there arose the image of Italian Unity', though sadly we are not told exactly what this looked like. The centrepiece of that evening's performance was to be the 'Ronda della Guardia Civica veneziana', a hymn with words by the Friulan patriot Federico Seismit Doda:

O fratelli! alfin si posa
La coccarda sovra il petto,
Una notte avventurosa
Lunghi affanni cancellò;
E dei popoli al banchetto
Oggi Iddio ci convitò.
  Viva la ronda della Guardia civica!
  Viva ognuno che pianse e che sperò!*

The jolly, if rather coarsely fashioned march tune to which Seismit Doda's four verses were set was the work of the veteran Sicilian composer Giovanni Pacini, who happened to be in Venice overseeing final preparations for his new opera, *Allan Cameron*. Pacini, who had enjoyed several triumphant Fenice premières over the past three decades, had staked much on the work's success, but it was destined, alas, to be upstaged by the real-life drama outside. After the first night the theatre was closed until further notice, only reopening for the occasional fund-raising concert. An accompanying ballet, whose title translated as *The Anti-Polka-ist and the Polkamaniacs*, based on the current international dance craze and starring Fanny Cerrito partnered by her husband Arthur Saint-Léon, was also cancelled. The theatre management warned the pair that they might not even be able to leave Venice for London as planned. 'Communications along the land routes are interrupted and a sea journey will expose you to grave dangers, at the hazard of your lives.' Cerrito may have reflected ruefully that it was her open demonstration of patriotism on the Fenice stage in February which had helped, after a fashion, to create what the letter clumsily called 'the present emergencies of political upheavals'.

Before the last notes of the 'Ronda della Guardia Civica' had died away, the audience burst into cheers for everyone and everything from Manin, Pio Nono and the Bandieras to France, America, 'our sister Milan', brotherhood, unity and the new republic. Yet what sort of a republic had Venice actually become? Hardly the aristocratic oligarchy of St Mark's lion with his open book, that government of procurators and

---

* 'O brothers! / At last we pin the cockade to our breast. / A momentous night / has extinguished our long sufferings / and today Almighty God invites us / to partake in the banquet of the nations. / Long live the civic guard patrol! / Long life to everyone who has wept and hoped!'

proveditors, of Othello's 'toged consuls', of the Bucintoro, the *Festa della Sensa* and solemn processions by the Doge in ermine and horn-shaped hat. Manin, like many other Venetians of his class, saw the ideal opportunity present itself for a moderate democratic constitutionalism of the sort then represented by Great Britain and the United States. There was to be a representative assembly, elected through manhood suffrage,* there were to be full civil rights for all and equality before the law; and the character of the administration was to be regulated by a utopian moral scrupulousness, which ruled out any aggressive stance towards other nations, greeted instead as brothers and friends. It was in this spirit that Manin immediately entrusted Niccolò Tommaseo to send letters to the various states, inviting them to recognise the newly independent Venetian state.

The Dalmatian did his work well, using the French acquired during his long Parisian exile. France itself was addressed easily enough with a fraternal republican handshake, but England, he had taught himself to believe, was the country of hypocrites and opportunists. British support in possible negotiations with Austria was nevertheless important, so for the high-minded one to stoop to a little flattery at this moment seemed not at all inappropriate. 'The provinces of the ancient Venetian state,' wrote Tommaseo, 'in assuming the name of Republic, have done so in obedience to the past and to present necessities. Such a nation as England, where respect for tradition is a species of social dogma, must realise how sacred is the memory, for these provinces, of former times. We do not therefore doubt of gaining the sympathy of this great nation, where the sentiment of liberty is an instinct, and which, through the grandeur of its vision and perseverance in achieving its aims, recalls better than any others the glory and success of ancient Rome.' To the United States of America the writer was probably more sincere in his appeal. 'The ocean divides us, but mutual sympathy unites us, and liberty, like an electric telegraph crossing the seas, will bring your example before us, maintaining a community of feeling more precious than that of shared interests. We have many things to learn from you, and as civilisation's eldest son, we do not blush to admit this.' To its credit, the USA granted instant recognition to the provisional government. The only other nation to do so was Switzerland, which also sent arms and troops who fought bravely throughout the subsequent war and siege.

In undertaking this diplomatic task Tommaseo had his own agenda,

---

* The possibility of extending the franchise to include women seems never to have been considered.

including the hope that Austria's Dalmatian provinces, given their large Italian-speaking populations, might be drawn into the revolution, and a firm belief in the need for a Catholic spiritual underpinning for the whole enterprise. Whatever his growing dislike of Manin, he had accepted a post in the new government as Education Minister, though without any special desire to cooperate with other members of the administration. Few of these were likely to earn his approval for their politics or their principles. Leone Pincherle, appointed Minister of Trade, he saw simply as Manin's creature, likely to adopt the other man's pragmatism. Francesco Camerata, Finance Minister, was a lightweight, appointed less for his revolutionary credentials (unimpressive, since he had been a civil servant under Austrian rule) than for his probity and professional expertise. As Secretary for the Navy, Antonio Paolucci had already proved his worth in the Arsenal episode, but he was known as an adherent of Mazzini, whose ideology earned Tommaseo's disapproval for its rejection of any role for the Church or the Pope. To his naval portfolio Paolucci soon added that of Secretary for War, when the elderly Napoleonic veteran Francesco Solera resigned after only a week in office.

Some of Tommaseo's deepest contempt was reserved for two of the newly formed Cabinet's ablest and most dedicated members. The lawyer Jacopo Castelli, Minister of Justice, was a political conservative, suspicious of the ordinary Venetians' ability to organise themselves into any convincingly workable democracy, though loyal to the government in the cause of recovering the city's ancient freedom. His spirit certainly owed something to memories of his father, a Veronese army officer who had suffered bitterly, first for opposing Venetian neutrality during Napoleon's invasion of Italy, then for trying to mount opposition to the French after the Serene Republic's dissolution. In the late summer of 1848, Castelli would find his own fate uncomfortably – and at length devastatingly – intertwined with that of Venice herself.

If Castelli possessed a true ally among other ministers, it was surely Pietro Paleocapa, to whom the rather vague portfolio of 'public construction' had been assigned. Paleocapa is a seriously undervalued figure in Venice's history. He was an engineer, hence lacking in the glamour that surrounds doges, painters and poets, yet the city owes more of its survival than is often realised to his organisation of dredging operations, flood precautions and improvements to the working of the port. From a Cretan family which moved to Venice in the eighteenth century, Paleocapa learned engineering at the Modena military academy after three years at Padua University. Immediately prior to the revolution he had completed a successful project for widening the Hungarian River Tisza and rescuing the surrounding countryside from flood damage, but though the Habsburg government was grateful, he continued to be fingered by the authorities. A police report, while noting his 'unimpeachable moral conduct' and respectable position 'owing to his knowledge of the art he professes', was suspicious of his 'affection for the past order of things' and his friendship with noted Freemasons.

Manin's appointment of Paleocapa and Castelli to ministerial office would later seem like an act of deliberate self-denial, a sacrifice of personal feelings to the greater good of the republic. For the former he had never cherished a particularly warm regard, and Paleocapa soon came to view Manin as hot-headed and dangerously impractical, but the engineer's standing with the Venetian professional class made his presence among the ministers almost a foregone conclusion. As for Castelli, he had earlier locked horns with Manin over the railway question, favouring the Bergamo against the Treviglio route. It was the kind of opposition Manin normally found difficult to forgive and impossible to forget. The two nevertheless admired each other – Castelli chose to send his son Emilio to Manin's law office for his pupillage – and only later would politics drive a more serious wedge between them.

The creation of the new government had been, of necessity, a rushed business – almost, as Manin's subsequent notes suggest, the proverbial back-of-an-envelope sketch. Tokenism in various forms played a signifi-cant part in the process, for the sake, as much as anything, of transcending the limited social qualifications imposed by the Austrians on member-ship of local authorities. Businessmen were to be included, more espe-cially those who were 'already well known and not unpopular'. For a very brief period there was a single aristocrat in the list, Count Carlo Trolli da Laveno, a former appeal-court counsellor, but his dubious political credentials soon ensured that his portfolio of Interior Minister was passed to Paleocapa. It was important, Manin believed, for there to be at least one Jew 'as a sign of emancipation'. Leone Pincherle, who became more of a pronounced republican once the revolution was an established fact, suited the position both as a dedicated patriot and as Daniele's personal friend. Later, in an unofficial capacity, another of Venice's distinguished Jewish citizens, Isacco Pesaro Maurogonato, would act as an expert adviser to the government as its financial needs became more pressing.

The administration was not, and never would be, fully representative of Venetian society at all its different levels. Manin and his friends already knew enough about the revolution currently under way in France to realise that socialism, let alone communism, in the sense in which both terms were then understood, would not fit easily into the context of the bourgeois democracy they were intent on bringing into existence. Some significant nod, however, had to be made towards the profound patriotic impulses of the Venetian working class, and with this in mind Manin nominated Angelo Toffoli to a ministry without portfolio, but bearing responsibility for labour relations. Toffoli ran a tailoring business on the Rialto and had endeared himself to the Manins during Daniele's imprisonment by offering Teresa financial assistance. He was a universally popular figure among the revolutionaries, though few of them could avoid a hint of snobbishness in the way they treated him. 'He's an amiable creature,'* declared the lawyer Giuseppe Giacomo Alvisi, 'with his small, elegant figure, pale complexion, quite lively black eyes and genteel manners without affectation; in his role as Labour Minister he brooks no arguments.' When at length he was taken to Paris by Tommaseo as assistant in what turned out to be a sadly mismanaged embassy to the French republican government, the Dalmatian simply treated Toffoli as a superior species of valet or messenger-boy, making the social distance between them abundantly clear.

To Toffoli's forethought and courage the provisional government owed the removal of a singular and quite unanticipated headache created by the departure of the Austrian military commanders and the loyal portions of the garrison. Most of the large number of Italian troops remaining in the city were not disposed to shift their allegiance automatically from the Emperor to the new republic, whatever friendly demonstrations they may have offered during the March days. The majority were not Venetian, but conscripts from the mainland villages, with an understandable wish to get back, as soon as possible, to the homes and families an accursed Austrian levy had forced them to leave behind. It was obviously not in the government's best interest either to try keeping them in Venice, where they had already begun selling off weapons and items of uniform, or to let them leave in a single body whose indiscipline might endanger civilian life and property, suggesting that the revolutionaries, with all their idealism, had failed to exert control where it was genuinely needed. For several days the troops remained without anyone assuming responsibility for their food or pay.

Angelo Toffoli now undertook the difficult task of facing down the mutinous elements in the various garrisons around the lagoon where the Italian soldiery was concentrated. At the southerly forts of Pellestrina, Chioggia and Brondolo he was joined by Manin himself, but within

---

* The word *creatura*, often used by Venetians with reference to individuals, is rather less pejorative than its English counterpart.

Venice, at the barracks of San Niccolò dei Tolentini and San Salvador, the tailor entered alone and unarmed to persuade the angry troops to wait a day or two while the government arranged for their phased withdrawal to the mainland. Though this proved easy enough at the Tolentini, the grenadiers stationed at San Salvador, near the Rialto, were less accommodating. As the 'amiable creature' entered the barrack square, several of the soldiers, engaged in plundering the stores of bedding and ammunition, took potshots at him. Toffoli, with a bravery fuelled by anger, turned to his attackers, shouting, 'So I'm still among the Austrians, am I? Last night you sold off what rightly belongs to your motherland. Now, if it's your brother's blood you're after, start with me and fire at this tricolour sash!' Abashed, the men agreed to wait three days before departing in small bands for the mainland, though the civic guard had to intervene to prevent any further looting while this dispersal was going on. A few later returned to fight for Venice, others rejoined the Austrian army or were shot for desertion according to the humour of different imperial officers, and the rest became a byword for lawlessness among the towns and villages of the Veneto.

While it may have seemed like good riddance, the soldiers' departure was regarded by many as almost a worse blunder than losing control of the fleet at Pola. Had Toffoli contrived, instead of a holding operation, some kind of deal with the malcontents which persuaded them to remain in their barracks, Venice, it was argued, would have had the nucleus of a professional defence force capable of mobilisation against an Austrian army seeking to recapture the lost provinces for the empire. Manin and Tommaseo, when challenged on this point some days later by a deputation from Treviso, offered startlingly ingenuous excuses. The former protested that the troops, by being allowed home to their villages, could better instruct their fellow countrymen in the exercise of arms. Tommaseo, appearing totally serious, declared that a single Italian tricolour planted on one of the alpine passes must be enough to prevent the Austrians crossing it.

The high-mindedness in both these assumptions seems as preposterous to us today as it did to the Trevisan delegates, yet an acceptance of the belief each implies in the better nature of ordinary human beings is essential to our grasp of what happened, not just in Venice, but all over Italy in the revolutions of 1848. Though it never found a coherent ideologue – Manin, whatever his gifts, was no Mazzini – and its only intellectual, in the shape of Niccolò Tommaseo, ultimately proved more of a hindrance than a help, the Republic of St Mark never lost sight of its purpose as a moral enterprise, an implicit riposte to the cynicism and fear of personal initiative which characterised the benign tyranny of the Habsburgs. Lasting, in its earliest form, a little more than a hundred days, it was hardly an ideal or even skilfully calculated political experiment: the speed of events would scarcely allow that. Its utopianism often looked like folly, its rhetoric could degenerate into sheer pomposity, it was guilty of fatal misjudgements, logistical blunders, panic reaction and overbearing gestures, which sinisterly reminded its critics of the very regime it was meant to have superseded. And as modern historians point out, this was an exclusively bourgeois administration – Angelo Toffoli was a shopkeeper, not an artisan – perpetually nervous of the working class as a force for disorder. Yet with all these errors and imperfections, the government was neither brutal nor tainted by corruption. The spirit of its laws and procla-mations reflected a faith in that notion of a shared public good, supported by political liberty, religious toleration and respect for the individual, which most modern citizens of evolved nation states take for granted as the enabling basis for a safe and prosperous existence.

'No communism – No social subversion – No government in the Piazza – Respect for property – Equality for all in the face of the law – Full liberty of thought and word – Free discussion without tumults – Improvement in the condition of those poor who wish to live from their work.' Thus Gustavo Modena, greatest Italian actor of his generation and fervently committed to the revolution, summed up the goals of the new republic, but not all could be met with the same success. Within a week of independence being proclaimed, there were disturbances in the tobacco factory at Santa Marta, whose workers, ready to riot for pay, were only quelled by the civic-guard commander Girolamo Gradenigo, who supplied their wages from his own pocket. The dock-workers and boatmen around the lagoon offered another potential menace, while on the lace-making island of Burano the fishermen requested the government to establish some additional industry, which should keep the community going through the winter months when the boats were unable to put out.

Many of the initial laws promulgated by the republic were therefore designed to head off more serious unrest among the working population. The hated salt duty was cut by one-third, and unredeemed pledges in pawn shops valued at under four lire could be taken back by their owners. Refuse-collectors received a pay increase, the tax on fishing was abolished and workers at the Arsenal were rewarded for rising in revolt (by the same token, presumably, for lynching poor Marinovich). In rapid succession the enormities and embarrassments of Austrian rule were corrected or effaced by the legislature. Use of the *bastinado* as an official punishment was ended, as being 'repugnant to Italian customs and to the dignity of mankind'. Stamp duty was removed from newspapers and there was guaranteed freedom of the press. Liberty of religious conscience was accompanied by entitlement to full civil rights for all. The accused in a court of law was now allowed a defending counsel, who must have free access to the relevant witnesses. Schools were recommended to teach Italian history, with special emphasis on Venice herself. Various ships commandeered in the lagoon by the government were patriotically renamed – the *Minerva* became the *Italia,* the *Ussaro* (hussar) was christened the *Crociato* (volunteer), and the *Clemenza* the *Civica* (doubtless because Clemens was Metternich's baptismal name). Domenico Moro's brothers were adopted by the state, along with the children of those killed in the Piazza on 18 March; and Baroness Bandiera, as the mother of martyrs, was granted a pension.

In this honeymoon phase of revolution there seems to have been a vaguely formed yet fervent desire on the part of almost everyone, except for a few disgruntled nobles, some (though by no means all) of the city's clergy and certain *austriacante* merchants anxious about their business prospects, to make the whole thing work. There was a widespread yearning to be part of what still seemed an astonishing sea-change in Venetian affairs. Even school pupils were made aware of their historic destiny. The headmaster of the high school at Santa Caterina was only too ready to allow those students who were old enough to enrol in the civic guard. Having enjoined them that the motherland was in need of 'an enlightened intelligence which puts disorder, ignorance, superstition and despotism to flight', he urged his 'young friends and brothers, the first to salute the dawn of so fine a day', to be equally swift in 'scattering the clouds and storms which darken our horizon'.

The upbeat atmosphere was palpable to intelligent observers such as the Modenese exile Antonio Morandi. Originally imprisoned on the lagoon island of San Severo for his part in the disastrously mismanaged revolution that had briefly unseated the Duke of Modena in 1831, he had escaped to Greece, where the government employed him to organise a gendarmerie for suppressing bandits in the Peloponnese. Given six months' leave to join the patriots in Italy, Morandi came to Venice only to pick up certain things left behind seventeen years earlier, including papers belonging to Count Pietro Gamba, brother of Byron's mistress Teresa Guiccioli. The Count had died in Morandi's arms, entrusting him with various souvenirs of the poet. Though a search for these relics drew a blank, Morandi decided to stay and help with preparing the city's defences. He admired the Venetians, the working class above all. 'There is no ordinary folk on earth,' he wrote, 'more lively, intelligent, good-natured, enterprising, steadfast, and at the same time watchful, religious without bigotry, obedient to the laws without grovelling, respectful towards authority but not basely so, and more devoted to their native soil than the Venetians.' The simplest and least educated, so he claimed, 'knew the history of Venice in detail, and the humblest gondolier could name the architects of palaces and churches'.

He rejoiced in the city's recovery of its self-respect:

> Venice arose from the waves purged of Austrian putrefaction, haughty enough never to tolerate a fresh servitude, and beautiful with that beauty the progress of civilisation brings with it. Walls and columns were covered from head to foot with patriotic hymns and odes, with government decrees inculcating order, harmony and forgiveness for particular acts of hostility, oblivion of the past and resolve for the future, with popular invocations to union, fraternity and common accord in the noble work in hand. In every street, every corner of every lane, at office doors, public buildings and churches, people were selling for a pittance, or distributing gratis, pamphlets, tracts, catechisms, handbills containing precepts for the life of every citizen under the new dispensation of freedom, equality of rights within the law, and due respect and submission to the new social compact. In the campi, on the house-fronts or along the calli were painted laurel garlands surrounding the words 'Viva Italia', 'Viva San Marco', 'Viva l'Unione', 'Equality and Fraternity the symbol of Jesus', 'Long live Manin and Tommaseo', 'Long live Pio Nono, away with the barbarians', 'Remember the Bandieras and Moro, martyrs to a love of their country'.

This euphoria was not confined to Venice. Throughout the Veneto and its neighbouring region of Friuli, town after town had made its own gesture of revolt and watched, its triumph mingled with frank astonishment, as the Austrians, with however bad a grace, packed their traps and cleared off. At Bassano del Grappa the touchpaper was lit on the morning of 19 March, when two men arrested for subversive activities in nearby Asolo were brought into the city on a cart with a police escort. News of the revolution in Vienna had arrived the previous night, and a large crowd, most of whom had been too excited to go to bed, now gathered around the gendarmes and their prisoners. To cries of 'Viva Pio Nono! Viva l'Italia!' they compelled the men's release, turning the rest of the day into a rolling demonstration. A party of working men hastily improvised a tricolour and marched to the town hall with the obvious intention of remaining there until the Mayor and councillors should offer signs of positive action. Priests gave orders for church bells to be rung, while the

police and revenue inspectors gave up their arms, put on patriotic cockades and fraternised with the citizens. Any man without a cockade simply
scribbled 'Viva Pio IX' on his hat with a piece of chalk. Amazingly, the
Austrian troops did nothing except retreat to their barracks, where they
lurked for the next three days. On the 22nd the garrison marched out,
taking with them their Italian commander Major Roccavina, whose popularity with the townsfolk had already been signalled by a serenade from
the municipal band. As the landlord of the Albergo della Luna hastily
removed from the front of his hotel the arms of Prince Metternich, who
had stayed there in 1822, Roccavina made a fulsome address to the leading
citizens before he left, praising the moderation and good conduct of the
Bassanesi.

Things were done with only a little less decorum in the city of Rovigo,
capital of the malarial Polesine district around the estuary of the River
Po. Life in this swampy delta was some of the grimmest in Italy. A change
during the eighteenth century from large-scale stock farming to cereal
production had brought increased poverty and malnutrition. Banditry
was rife, and farm labourers kept guns beside their beds to ward off
constant attempts at stealing basic commodities such as furniture, blankets, sausages and polenta. Whole villages as a result remained in an
almost perpetual state of siege throughout the period of maximum hardship during the winter months. Most of the work around Rovigo was
connected with estates belonging to the town's aristocracy, whose rack-
rent bailiffs drove many peasants to seek help from local money-lenders.
Since 1815 the Austrians had done little more than the French before them
to improve conditions in the Polesine, yet until the eve of the March
revolution there were comparatively few signs of focused discontent among
the population, more concerned with day-to-day battles for survival than
with politically reinventing itself as Italian.

Given the momentum for change set up in the wake of Pope Pius IX's
election, it was inevitable that Rovigo, a town not altogether hopelessly
off the beaten track, should be carried along by the tide of events. The
flashpoint here was the arrest and trial of Domenico Piva, a young revenue
inspector who had thrown in his lot with the Padua university students
in their battle with the Austrian soldiery on 8 February. Wounded by
bayonet thrusts, Piva managed to slip out of one of the Caffè Pedrocchi's
windows (perhaps the same one left open by poor Giovanni Anghinoni)
and was taken into hiding by a Jewish family in the nearby ghetto. With
their help he managed to get back to Rovigo, whence he was smuggled
to a supposedly safe house at a village a few miles off. Word of his where-
abouts reached the police, who took advantage of his foolhardy return to

the town on a busy market day to fling him into gaol. On 17 March, Piva was tried and sentenced to a long term of imprisonment for the double offence of subversion and abusing his trust as a public functionary (he had compounded the offence by throwing away his uniform before joining the student demonstration).

Had this happened a week or two earlier, the citizens might simply have shaken their heads and passed on. As it was, news had arrived from Venice and elsewhere which suggested the regime was beginning to lose its grip, and several of the bolder Rovigini called for Domenico Piva's release. Despite the appalling state of local roads and some recent bad weather, on 19 March the announcement got through that Emperor Ferdinand had granted a constitution, and that the newly released Manin and Tommaseo were now setting the political agenda for the established government. So when an Austrian sergeant was reported to have attacked a man wearing a tricolour cockade, a crowd positively efflorescent with red, white and green gathered to demand Piva's freedom.

Like so many others of his kind in towns across the Veneto, the Austrian Governor, Count Strassoldo, was rendered suddenly nerveless by events. Power seemed to pass more or less at once to the municipality, represented by the *podestà* Domenico Angeli (earlier described in an Austrian police report as 'generous, splendid, disinterested and dutiful, always keen to promote and put into operation every useful project on the city's behalf'), who announced the immediate formation of a civic guard. Its ranks, and those of Rovigo's revolution in general, were a good deal more widely representative than their Venetian counterparts. As well as the usual noblemen, doctors and lawyers, the patriots included a dancing master, several priests, a family of pork butchers and a market porter. The diocesan bishop, Mgr Bernardo Squarcina, sympathetic to the cause, ordered a thanksgiving mass for the new constitution and personally blessed a tricolour flag. When news of Venice's installation of a provisional government arrived on 23 March, there was a general dismantling in Rovigo of all Habsburg insignia and flags. The Austrian troops, who had been confined to barracks for several days on Strassoldo's orders, now found the civic guard and a considerable crowd of civilians under their windows, bent on persuading the Italian portion of the garrison to desert. In a short while the soldiers clambered down ropes and ladders, to muster in the Piazza Maggiore.

Their Hungarian commander Lieutenant Colonel Poschaker hurried out after them to remind his men of their oath of loyalty to the Emperor, and threatening punishment for breach of discipline. To the sound of shots the mob hustled him across the square to the town hall, where

Mayor Angeli, politely detaching the officer from his escort, led him to a room in which an act of surrender lay waiting to be signed. When Poschaker courteously but firmly refused, an ex-government official named Giuseppe Maggi rejoined curtly, 'We're not asking you, we're ordering.' That night, without bloodshed and in good order, the garrison's detachment of Hungarian hussars rode out towards Este, while a further half-battalion of chasseurs, mostly Italians, arrived from Polesella on the border with the Papal States. Their officers, promptly arrested by the civic guard, were made to don civilian clothes, while other ranks fraternised with the populace 'amid "viva!"s and glasses of wine'. Count Strassoldo, bemused by the whole business, was bundled off in a carriage the following day.

In Padua, where thousands had enlisted in the civic guard during the course of a single night, nobody was sorry to see the Austrians leave, led by their grim-visaged commander Count D'Aspre. An immediate attempt to deface their memory now began, an *épuration* sometimes carried to powerful extremes. People refused to eat potatoes, the staple food of the Croats, the Caffè Militare, where the soldiers used to drink, was closed down by order of the provisional administration, and its entrance porch was used as a public urinal. Above the doorway somebody scrawled the words: 'Whoever refuses to piss here is a spy'. To rid the town of its Habsburg taint and the breath of police and informers, altarboys went around clanking their thuribles, sending clouds of incense up and down the streets. Everyone wanted to do their bit for the cause, but though the doctors rejoiced that as a result of the stress caused by such frenetic involvement, their patient numbers were increasing, Padua's prostitutes were not so happy with the new mood of high-mindedness. If things went on like this, ran their letter of complaint to the municipality, they would die of starvation.

So often this startlingly rapid implosion of Austrian authority throughout the Veneto was helped forward by the courage, forethought and initiative of single individuals, quick to seize whatever opportunities lay to hand and armed only with the abstract weapons of dedication and single-mindedness. Manin and Tommaseo were not unique examples in this respect. Would the revolution in Vicenza, for example, have taken place so speedily without the enterprise of Valentino Pasini to empower it? Almost inevitably he was a lawyer, born in the town of Schio, where his father* had helped to establish the local textile industry. From the

* Pasini senior was christened Eleonoro – a unique instance, so far as I can gather, in the fascinating and often bizarre annals of Italian baptismal names.

outset of his legal career, Pasini had found himself either in direct conflict with the Habsburg authorities or under suspicion for being too keenly interested in the human rights of his clients. He also sought the introduction of an adequate and equitable interrogation system by police agents or judges in court, but attempts to publish his views on the matter were thwarted by the censor.

Pasini managed nevertheless to combine a distinguished career with success as a writer on jurisprudence, prison reform and political economy, a topic whose very name was generally calculated to invoke a *damnatur* from the police. He endeared himself to Daniele Manin by espousing the Treviglio route in the great railway debate, and in 1846 his standing was such that he seemed the obvious choice for President of Vicenza's Accademia Olimpica, newly revived after some 300 years. As the town's contribution to events surrounding the scientific congress in Venice (where he had helped to organise the free-trade banquet for Richard Cobden), Pasini pioneered a staging of Sophocles's *Oedipus Rex*, the drama chosen in 1585 to open the superb Teatro Olimpico, specially built for the academy by Andrea Palladio and Vincenzo Scamozzi.

It is not hard to detect a patriotic slant in this celebration of Italian Renaissance culture. When Manin, soon after taking control in Venice, sent Pasini a message saying, 'We have conquered and are free. What are you doing? What do you need to liberate yourself?', the answer was a request for 1,500 rifles. Pasini had already struck terror into the military governor, Prince Thurn und Taxis, by brazenly entering his headquarters and demanding a civic guard. When this was refused, he read the Prince the relevant concession wrung from Palffy in Venice and ordered his followers to hoist the tricolour over the palace. As armed civilians started to patrol the streets, Thurn und Taxis ordered his troops, 4,000 of them, to barracks while he meditated on some sort of counterstrike, beginning with an attempt to capture the precious rifles, promptly dispatched by rail from Venice. Pasini, getting wind of the plan just in time, coolly took a carriage two miles up the line, flagged down the train and had the arms unloaded.

When he got back to town, it was to the alarming news that General D'Aspre, commandant at Padua, had pulled out his men and was moving at some speed towards Vicenza. What most unsettled Pasini was the fact that D'Aspre, before leaving, had ordered the seizure of Padua's public funds, an act of brass-necked military insolence which the ruthless warrior would no doubt repeat elsewhere along his route. It was late at night and Vicenza's city treasurer was in bed, but Pasini had no scruples in waking him up and telling him to bring his keys to the town hall. There the pair of them found the Mayor with an Austrian official who, presumably acting on D'Aspre's orders, demanded that the coffers be handed over at once. The Italians had successfully fended this off, with the help of Pasini's legal quibbles over properly constituted authority, when the troops from Padua clattered into the city. D'Aspre, accompanied by his second-in-command Franz von Wimpffen, was in a foul temper, having just undergone an operation, apparently without mishap, on one of his testicles,* and announced his intention of going to bed immediately. At nine the next morning Pasini, with several others, called on D'Aspre, only to be told that he was prepared to use force if necessary to break open the coffers.

Knowing the General, despite his notoriously short fuse, to be a man of honour, Pasini asked him whether he really wanted to be remembered in Vicenza as a burglar and a thief. D'Aspre was duly piqued. 'Do you think me so dishonourable?' he cried. 'Yet my men – they must not die of hunger.' The soldiers, Pasini agreed, would have enough to eat, though when D'Aspre asked for 80,000 florins to cover expenses, the sum was beaten down at once to 14,000. While clerks drew up the necessary documents, the two men, having clearly developed a mutual respect during an encounter lasting a mere few minutes, discussed the political situation. D'Aspre was quite frank as to his belief, shared by the rest of the Austrian high command, that it was Metternich and nobody else who had landed them in this situation. 'Now,' he declared, 'everything is up to Radetzky. If he holds on to Milan, we'll all be back here, if not, then everything is over. The Austrian empire . . . !' Here he beat his fist on the table. 'That I should live to see it end thus!' Pasini watched as 'a great tear ran down the cheek of this haughtiest of men'. Once honourable terms had been agreed, the whole force moved on towards Verona. 'Viva l'Italia!' cried the throng of citizens watching them go, and many were moved when the soldiers gave an answering 'Viva!'

Notwithstanding a personal regard for Manin, Valentino Pasini was among many who felt that he and his associates had gone too far in proclaiming a republic once the transfer of power in Venice and other towns was secure. 'Our Manin,' he told a friend in Milan, 'wishes to recreate Italian history for the sake of a misjudged devotion to Venice.' He was reluctant for Vicenza to attach itself instantly to the kind of broad-based republican state Manin had in mind when, on 24 March, he appealed to the provincial communes, large or small, to share in

---

* Sources do not make clear whether this was for testicular cancer or for the type of scrotal enlargement known as a hydrocele.

fashioning this new political entity. Presumably aware of a possible unwillingness to sign up, or even of outright opposition based on ancient resentments and conservative disapproval of republicanism *per se*, the Venetian provisional government sugared the pill, not only by its reduction of the salt duty, but by abolishing altogether the detested poll tax whose exaction had laid such heavy burdens on peasant families throughout the province.

This concession above all influenced popular support for adherence to the new authority, though the various civic representatives flocking to Venice to find out more about what was involved seem to have hastened the process with the reassurances they were able to send back. One by one the communes, great and small, sent off their fervid declarations, liberally sprinkled with phrases such as 'patriotic love', 'banner of the motherland' and 'yoke of the detested foreigner', yet also careful to include requests for assistance in the shape of weapons or money. Some, like the village of Contarina in the Po delta, asked for advice in avoiding outright revolution among disaffected peasants. Given the large number of day-labourers cultivating the rice fields, would the Venetians kindly send 'apposite instructions to guide us securely towards the most laudable means of fulfilling our politico-economic responsibilities'? Another village, Tribano, was rather more blunt. 'Our peasants,' wrote the anonymous author, alongside an order for 200 rifles, 'are not so far educated as to have developed an unlimited and worthwhile attachment to the new order of things without needing material proof that the youthful Republic is dedicated to improving their genuinely miserable condition.' The Friulan commune of Sacile put in for a share of bullets and gunpowder, since 'we are all Italians, all brothers, and have all of us the same cause to defend and the same enemy to conquer'. Others, like the ancient ring of cheese-making villages known as the *Sette Communi*, around the Asiago plateau high up on the Dolomite spurs north of Vicenza, showed more feeling in their protestations of loyalty. Here the people were a tough breed, speaking an ancient Germanic language, which made many believe they were a remnant of the tribes who fought against the Roman general Caius Marius during the second century BC. Freedom-loving and democratic, they lived in straw-thatched mud huts, herding cattle on the alpine pastures during the summer and bringing them down onto the plain before winter snowfalls, which could last till May. To this 'very Siberia of Italy' the Serene Republic had granted special privileges and tax exemptions, creating a bond of loyalty which Austrian rule did nothing to destroy. 'How many times,' exclaimed the *Sette Communi*'s ringing declaration, 'have the hearts of our people served as a bulwark against German

invaders seeking to reach the fair land of Italy from out of the Tyrol!'
Their affection for Venice was undimmed and they rejoiced to hear 'the
roar of revolution sent forth from the Adriatic Lion'.

Contrast this with Treviso's terse little announcement that, Austrian
government being over, its own provisional administration had
commenced business. Or the extraordinary flourish, like something from
a modern tourist brochure if it weren't for the sentence structure, with
which the town of Adria, down in the Polesine, dispatched its fraternal
greetings. 'Whether for its topographical position, so favourable to
commerce, or for the fruitfulness of its surrounding territory, so very
productive now that the inhabitants have activated the necessary appa-
ratus for draining low-lying areas, or for its notable increase in population, Adria has good reason to cherish the highest expectations of a
propitious and encouraging future in the new era about to begin.'

Most of these pledges of unity arrived less than a week after Manin
had proclaimed the republic. Vicenza took longer than many towns to
determine its position. The guiding spirit was once again Valentino
Pasini, who on 29 March put the issue to a vote in the piazza, in which
those in favour kept their hats on while the opposition stood bare-
headed. Even though acknowledging the triumph of the hat-wearers, an
official letter from the city's provisional government made it clear that
this was a conditional assent, always keeping the eventual union of the
newly enlarged Venetian republic with Lombardy and other Italian states
firmly in view.

Lombardy indeed, as represented by its capital Milan, mattered more
than Manin and his colleagues had bargained for. There the revolution
had been still more dramatic than Venice's. In less than a week the entire
city, rich and poor, old and young, had risen against the imperial garrison,
throwing up barricades made of everything from café chairs, carriages,
pianos and theatrical scenery to beer casks, mirrors, flower vases and
church pulpits. Street after street was bitterly contested, the Austrians
consistently failing to make any significant gains from an infuriated
civilian guerrilla force. By 21 March the commander-in-chief, Field
Marshal Radetzky, had decided to withdraw his troops and retire eastwards, inside the circle of forts dominating the towns of Verona, Mantua,
Peschiera and Legnago and known as the 'Quadrilateral'. By this
manoeuvre, the only retreat he was ever to make, Radetzky could assemble
what remained of the Austrian army in southern Lombardy, depleted by
widespread desertion among the Italian soldiery, restore morale and begin
planning a major counterattack.

As to what kind of government should take power once the Austrians left, the Milanese were far from united. On the one hand, alongside the Mayor, Count Gabrio Casati, were ranged the city's liberal aristocracy, proud of the anti-Austrian traditions established by their caste as leaders of the Carbonarist conspiracy in 1821, yet profoundly apprehensive of the spread of republicanism in the wake of events in France. Lombard supporters of a republic, on the other side, were seriously divided. One camp, led by young radicals such as Luciano Manara and Enrico Cernuschi, had been raring for a fight, while against these stood the more moderate figure of Carlo Cattaneo, a teacher and ideologue whose rueful memoir of the Milanese revolution is one of the Risorgimento's classic texts. Though initially reluctant to join in the armed uprising, he acknowledged the astonishing success of the insurgent leaders in the street battles and threw in his lot with them. The chance soon arrived for rejecting all compromise with the nobility, who were desperate for the intervention of King Charles Albert of Piedmont at the head of his army. Now, however, Cattaneo urged the radicals to delay their proclamation of a republic in favour of a temporary council of war, to organise further fighting and deal swiftly and ruthlessly with Austrian attempts at fudging the desired surrender. From then on, Gabrio Casati and the monarchist nobles seized the advantage, declaring a provisional government on their own initiative and shuffling the political issue to one side with the realist argument that there was a victory to be won and that the Milanese had better get on with fighting for it while time was on their side. Thus Cattaneo was effectively sidelined, the victim of his own hesitation and self-restraint. The sense of bitterness all this occasioned adds unmistakable edge to his narrative of events.

To the rest of Italy the outcome of the *Cinque Giornate* gave a thrilling, if entirely inaccurate, impression of Radetzky and his staff panicking in the face of an unforeseen surge of resistless patriotic energy. What could Italians, fired by their holy cause, not now achieve? On Daniele Manin, however, it had a more sobering effect. He was faced with the possibility that in establishing the Republic of St Mark, the members of the provisional government had been too precipitate and might even look dangerously selfish in the face of a shared national emergency. Letters from Milanese friends, part of Casati's new moderate administration, warned him to wait on circumstances in the light of a growing expectation that the King of Piedmont, already mustering troops on his frontier with Lombardy, would declare war on Austria and order an invasion. How could either Venice or Milan, they argued, hope for assistance from a sovereign in whose face they flourished a republican standard? And what was Venice intending to become, some sort of Hanseatic port or else a modern avatar of its earliest incarnation in the Middle Ages? At this crucial moment Manin, for all his avowed republicanism, chose to step back in favour of a wait-and-see policy, which put any sort of drastic political reconstruction on hold until the conflict, now seemingly inevitable, should be resolved in favour of Charles Albert and his army, purporting to uphold Italy's right to self-determination.

Even those government members less than wholeheartedly republican scented possible danger in this approach. It had been important, they argued, to make the provinces feel wanted as significant elements in the new state, for which Jacopo Castelli had already drawn up plans regarding a constituent assembly. Instead the mainland towns were now to be fobbed off with a mere consultative council which, almost like the regional congregations under Habsburg rule, was to have no executive authority, a sure recipe for future discontent. Niccolò Tommaseo, forced to agree to this sudden compromise of Manin's, saw nothing but danger ahead for Venice's autonomy, achieved only a week or so earlier. Even more than Manin himself, he believed passionately in Venetian exceptionalism, cherishing the sense of Venice as somehow morally superior to the rest of Italy. For him the old republic of La Serenissima had been a state 'more ideal than England, more civilised than Rome', its laws humane and just, its people lively, intelligent, candid and emotionally secure, a community 'elegant in its gravity'. For him Charles Albert's intervention, or that of any other Italian sovereign save the Pope, could only betray this historical pride and dignity as it had been betrayed at Campoformio and the Congress of Vienna, harnessing Venice once more to the whims of a monarch. One modern historian has shrewdly discerned in this idealised vision a legacy of Tommaseo's origins on the fringe of the old Venetian empire, whose loyal Dalmatian troops had been ready to defend the Doge in 1797. Essentially he wanted to do what they had been prevented from doing and offer himself as champion of the true Venice in its hour of need. Tommaseo was like the citizens of Perasto in the Bocche di Cattaro, the old republic's southernmost territory on the Adriatic coast, who when news arrived that the state had been dissolved, took the banner of St Mark, solemnly burned it and preserved the ashes as a sacred relic.

Manin was unlikely to share in such nostalgia. His attachment to Venice was just as visceral, but it was that of a native, not an awestruck incomer, and characterised moreover by a sternly practical view of what the city needed to ensure its realistic survival. The speed with which the old Austrian hegemony over Italy was suddenly unravelling seemed to justify his caution. Pio Nono had finally granted a constitution to his subjects in the Papal States, while his ministers looked likely to conclude a defensive pact with Tuscany and Piedmont. The Duke of Modena had slipped prudently out of his capital at the first whisper of revolution, though the Modenese would eventually turn out to be less enthusiastic for the patriot cause than he feared. His cousin Duke Carlo Ludovico of Parma was more or less dragooned into playing a role as a constitutional sovereign, presiding over the formation of a civic guard and a provisional government. Only in Naples might a dispassionate observer have spotted a few unsettling portents as the various liberal elements in the government began trading accusations of bad faith, the people gradually lost confidence in the new political dispensation, and King Ferdinand, however demonised formerly, now reflected qualities of patience, moderation and good sense which made him almost admirable beside his ministers.

The signal everyone awaited was to come from King Charles Albert of Piedmont. His troops were already mobilised along the frontier with Lombardy, the Milanese nobles had begged for his help at the onset of the *Cinque Giornate* to prevent the city from falling into republican hands, and the Pope, whom he held in mystic veneration, looked likely to bless what in the eyes of many was a holy war against a foreign oppressor. That oppressor, what was more, appeared an easy enough target for the well-aimed thrusts of an invasion force vitalised by a sense of its own moral mission on Italy's behalf. The mood in Piedmont itself had swung jubilantly in favour of a swift spring campaign, before Radetzky had time to gather reinforcements. An enthralled witness to events was Massimo d'Azeglio's sister-in-law Costanza Alfieri, married to his brother Roberto. The letters she wrote to her son Emmanuele, Piedmontese minister at the court of St Petersburg, offer a shrewd and unsentimental assessment of events and personalities as the war began. All Piedmont, she told him, was poised for action:

> In those provinces cheek by jowl with Lombardy enthusiasm has been at its highest. In Novara, Mortara, Vigevano nobody sleeps, people have been out in the streets day and night waiting for news . . . Everyone wants to join up, former soldiers, teachers, husbands and fathers, even children. We are all giving money and horses, we are taking collections and making bandages. Nobody thinks of anything else but war, we just live in the streets, where little urchins selling pamphlets deafen you with crying their wares. Everyone wanders to and fro scanning newspapers and handbills, bumping into one another as they do so but not minding in the least.

On 23 March, Charles Albert issued a public declaration of intent to invade Lombardy-Venetia, describing the forthcoming Piedmontese advance across the frontier as representing 'the help which a brother receives from a brother and a friend from a friend'. In the cause of 'racial sympathy, an understanding of the spirit of the age and a dedication we all share' he ordered his troops, when entering Lombardy, to carry banners bearing the cross of Savoy on a tricolour background 'as a better outward expression of Italian unity'. Such a gesture deliberately flattered liberal opinion, as did the lofty rhetoric of the whole proclamation. How far Lombards and Venetians actually believed the King was another matter, but the war was clearly about to happen as promised. Two days later, on 25 March, Charles Albert's advance guard crossed the River Ticino into what the Austrians still regarded as the westernmost territory of their empire. The crossing of rivers has possessed symbolic significance throughout the history of warfare, and the borders of both provinces were effectively marked out by major waterways. Whether or not an army was prepared to cross the Po, the Mincio, the Piave or the Adige would become an issue of major importance in the days ahead. By directing his force of 40,000 men to enter Lombardy over the Ticino, advancing on the cities of Milan and Pavia, Charles Albert had signalled the beginning of a new and decisive phase in the struggle against Austria. For the time being most Italian liberals were prepared to trust him, linking his name with the talismanic Pio Nono as the chief paladins of Italy's deliverance.

The widely publicised slogan adopted by the King was the phrase 'L'Italia farà da se', 'Italy will go it alone'. As a watchword it carried genuine moral impact, but the mode of expression thinly concealed a warning to other European states not to meddle in the conflict. England, whose Whig government had an absorbing interest in the unfolding crisis, showed no signs as yet (beyond sending Lord Minto on his mission and an increased naval presence in Italian waters) of adopting a more openly hands-on approach, let alone of an outright break with Austria. More significant was the attitude of the new French republic and its Foreign Minister Alphonse de Lamartine. Though the poet-politician was a noted Italophile, who had served as a diplomat in Florence and Naples, his concern with the struggle was hardly altruistic. If France were to undertake any kind of intervention, or accept an expansion of Piedmont's existing borders, she must hope for some reward, possibly in the form of Savoy and the coveted port of Nice, both part of Charles Albert's kingdom. The usefulness of an enlarged buffer state between France and Austria was undeniable, but Lamartine was reluctant to countenance any growth in the power and prosperity of the existing kingdom. 'Any French government,' he told a Piedmontese Member of Parliament, 'either monarchical or republican, which would permit the House of Savoy to conquer and govern a total population of twenty-six million brave men without occupying the Alps in its own defence would be betraying France.'

The tide of French popular opinion, however, moved increasingly in favour of the Italian revolutions. Paris, even more than London, was a refuge for exiles and dissidents of all shades, and the anti-Austrian views of many of its writers and journalists had grown more marked since the return, some years previously, from St Helena to Les Invalides of the body of Napoleon Bonaparte, victor and vanquished in an earlier war against Habsburg armies. Lamartine had certainly taken note of this interventionist mood in a manifesto published in *Le moniteur universel* on 5 March. In it he announced that French assistance would be forthcoming if the Italian states were invaded by Austria, if 'limits or obstacles were imposed on their internal transformation' or if 'their right to ally themselves in order to consolidate their Italian homeland were challenged by armed might'. While he tried to dissuade Piedmont from mobilising for war with Austria, the French government proposed the formation of an invasion force, 60–80,000 strong, which might if necessary cross the alpine frontier, thereby alarming England sufficiently for her to adopt the role of mediator between the two principal combatants.

The whole issue of Franco-British mediation was to act as an irritant to Austria and a chimera to Italian patriots over the next twelve months. Where Britain was concerned, the government had no wish to be dragged into playing a central role in Italian affairs. Charles Albert, for his part, viewed France's intentions with genuine suspicion. Historically Piedmont had always mistrusted its powerful western neighbour, though making use of French aid and influence whenever advantageous. A strong conservative element among the aristocracy loathed Napoleon and execrated France as a wellspring of social upheaval, subversion and anarchy. In the spring of 1848 the French had once again overthrown a monarchy and established a republic. 'L'Italia farà da se' was thus as much a warning from Charles Albert to France as a rallying call to Italians, a keep-out notice whose spirit was shared by many others in Italy regardless of their politics.

Manin was never among them. His earnest hope, even before Austrian retreat from Venice became a likelihood, was that some sort of armed French intervention might speed the process onwards, and France was the most obvious source of weapons and *matériel* to add to whatever the provisional government might have been able to seize from the departing Habsburg regiments. What would happen in the event of these troops returning was given little thought during the first heady spring days of freedom, and almost nothing was done towards drawing up a concerted defence plan for either Venice or the cities of the *terraferma*. With the garrison regiments broken up, a large number of valuable weapons had been dispersed or purloined, while no practical attention seems to have been paid meanwhile to rearming and retraining that considerable share of the male population that had served as conscripts in the Austrian ranks. By the end of March it was widely known, in the towns and villages of the northern Veneto and Friuli, that Austria was mobilising a reserve army based on the city of Gorizia, with the presumed intention of recovering Udine, Pordenone and Belluno with their surrounding regions, yet the provisional government's answer to the loyal alacrity of these and other cities was only a strangely persistent inertia.

Ironically it had been Field Marshal Radetzky who, on the eve of rebellion, recommended the formation of a rural militia, capitalising on what he saw as an essential Italian contrast between the townsfolk, 'lazy, antipathetic, proud, arrogant and given to every kind of wickedness', and the peasantry, 'well-behaved, mild and upright, through leading a patriarchal existence in isolated dwellings'. Devised as a species of yeomanry or territorial army, led by pensioned but able-bodied Austrian officers, the new force would act as a stabilising social element, 'since these countryfolk are not infected with the poetic illusions of so-called nationalism and are more likely to trust a foreigner than a compatriot whose influence they fear'. Radetzky had no time to submit his scheme to the imperial government before the uprising in Vienna and Metternich's resignation. His assessment of peasant loyalty appears somewhat wide of the mark, based as it was on those salt-of-the-earth notions of simple but honest labouring folk that we might expect a high-ranking Austrian commander to possess. As it turned out, the response of the northern Italian rural population to the events of 1848 was decidedly ambiguous, unpredictable and influenced throughout by local factors largely unconnected with the broader political issue of 'under which king?'

A similar initiative to Radetzky's could nevertheless have been encouraged by Manin and his fellow ministers with some success, given the enthusiasm for the revolution waiting to be tapped in communities great and small throughout the Veneto. From the Brenta to the Dolomites, by the beginning of April, mobilisation in the civic guard ran to thousands, and everywhere this volunteer spirit, typifying Risorgimento Italy at its best, cried out for a coherently organised resistance to any Austrian advance, either from the north or by the troops now concentrated within the Quadrilateral fortresses. The civic battalions watched in disgust as some 6,000 ex-soldiers from imperial regiments returned home still in uniform, shouldering their muskets, but without the least intention of lending their military expertise to furtherance of the cause by even the most basic defensive measures. Appeals for rifles and ammunition to be dispatched from the still considerable stores in the Venetian Arsenal were mostly ignored, unless they came from provisional administrations in the principal cities. Anywhere smaller, and the inhabitants soon learned they must shift for themselves with the aid of blunderbusses, fowling pieces, rakes and pitchforks. Instead the provisional government preferred encouraging the recruitment of volunteers in small, lightly armed bands regulated by only the most elementary drilling and discipline, known as 'free brigades' or more colourfully, '*crociati*', 'crusaders', echoing the widely shared idea that this was a holy war under the patronage of Christendom's leader Pope Pius.

The *crociati*, as will be seen, were no paladins of medieval chivalry, and in many cases their presence turned out to be less of a help than a hindrance. By pursuing this kind of enlistment scheme rather than strengthening the hand of a civic-guard movement willing to accept orders and adequate training, Manin and his government showed a signal failure of nerve. Not only did their dilatoriness in encouraging civilian defence suggest a basic mistrust of the mainland communities, as if townsfolk and villagers, once given weapons, would turn them on the propertied classes instead of aiming them at the white tunics of Croats and Bohemians. It also implied the Venetian leaders' inability to connect adequately with the *terraferma*'s needs and aspirations, giving the fatal impression that Venice itself was all that really mattered to them. Adherence to the new republic by the city's neighbours was acknowledged as a political gesture only, not as a practical measure expecting appropriate recompense in arms, money and, not least important, morale.

The Veneto would soon make its anger or sadness audible. Even having opted to support the Piedmontese invasion, Manin still had the opportunity, during late March and early April 1848, to raise north-eastern Italy against Austrian countermarches and drive an effective wedge between Radetzky, regrouping at Verona, and the regiments now gathering under the command of Marshal Nugent in Gorizia. His reluctance to act seems wholly uncharacteristic in the light of the decisiveness he had shown on 22 March, but such inaction revealed how little he possessed, at this stage, of the war leader alongside his gifts as a politician. It reminds us too, in the element of indifference towards the rural Veneto, that here was a man who seldom left Venice unless he had to, remaining profoundly metropolitan in his thinking. At this moment Manin was not a Winston Churchill *avant la lettre*. That Churchillian quality he ultimately displayed would be drawn from him by the tyrannical imperatives of changing circumstance. For now, in the immediately unfolding drama of illusion, frustration and vain bloodshed, Venice was a mere onlooker. It was those ill-considered cities of the mainland which would count the cost, trapped as they were between two armies ginger for combat, while the rains of a northern Italian April, heavy and inexorable, began to water the troubled earth.

CHAPTER 5

～

STRIPPING THE ARTICHOKE

I N PERSONALITY, OUTLOOK AND AMBITION, no two war leaders could have been more distinct from one another than the two men whose word now governed the armies of Piedmont and Austria as they moved towards open engagement. The conduct and outcome of a war are obviously influenced by factors of greater significance than mere character traits of this or that commander, but the Italian conflict of 1848 validates Blaise Pascal's famous dictum that history would have been very different had Cleopatra's nose been a little shorter. The personal impact of King Charles Albert and Field Marshal Radetzky was crucial for the officers and men they led, and the difference in what each expected, or in what others expected of him, had a decisive effect in sealing the fate of Lombardy and Venetia in their efforts to cast off Austrian rule.

Few, during Charles Albert's early life, would have marked him out as being the stuff of which liberal standard-bearers are made. He had become King of Piedmont *faute de mieux*, since his predecessor had no legitimate heirs. His father Charles Emmanuel belonged to a cadet branch of the ruling Savoy family and had married Marie Christine Albertine, a princess of the Baltic duchy of Courland. The pair nurtured strong sympathies for the French Revolution – according to Metternich, the princess 'during the Terror danced the Carmagnole with the sansculottes of Paris and Turin' – and they were living outside Paris when Charles Emmanuel died in 1800. Their son was then aged two, and the deeply reactionary Piedmontese court at Turin grew understandably worried that he would imbibe what was loosely called 'Jacobinism' at its very source. Charles Albert nevertheless remained with his mother in France, but in 1810 the Princess married for a second time, to a French nobleman, Comte de

Montléart. The effect on the boy was traumatic and to it was later attributed much of his subsequent air of remoteness and introversion during adulthood. Circumstances were not improved when Napoleon gave the family notice that they were no longer welcome in Paris. Hastily retreating to Geneva, Marie Christine placed her son in a Protestant boarding school, under the direction of the influential pastor and educationalist Jean-Pierre Vaucher. Discipline was strict but fair, and the scholastic ethos, which encouraged an interest in science and laid heavy moral emphasis on asceticism and self-sacrifice, helped to shape Charles Albert's character and outlook.

Late in 1813 he was summoned to Turin as adopted heir to the elderly King Victor Emmanuel I. At the court, which was gloomy, stuffy and laboriously fogeyish, the boy was placed in the safe hands of Count Filippo Grimaldi del Poggetto, a loyal monarchist and a faithful Catholic, who made sure that the Prince, following his brief but significant encounter with Protestantism, was shadowed throughout his waking hours by a chaplain. These early years in Turin were bleak and directionless, made worse by the interference of Victor Emmanuel's queen Maria Teresa, who, not satisfied with Charles Albert's limited manifestations of religiosity, had sacked Grimaldi for failing to attend to this aspect of character training. His replacement, Policarpo Cacherano d'Osasco, was an aged bigot whose solicitude merely increased the young man's by now almost pathological mistrust and alienation. A single comfort was afforded by the wife chosen for him from among the available stock of Italian princesses. Maria Teresa of Tuscany was the daughter of Grand Duke Leopold II and had inherited something of her family's artistic taste and good sense. The marriage, happy and successful* produced five children, three of whom were eventually to take part in the war of 1848.

The earliest testing moment in Charles Albert's adult life arrived in 1821, when he was twenty-three. This was the age of the Carbonari, the secret societies with widespread support among aristocrats and former Napoleonic army officers in various parts of Italy, dedicated to such patriotic ideals as constitutional government and independence from foreign rule. Following Austrian suppression of what remained of an abortive Carbonarist uprising in Naples, a group of Piedmontese army officers, led by General Santorre di Santarosa, made their own demand for a constitution and a war against Austria. Charles Albert was known to have been in contact with Santarosa and his fellow dissidents, and it must have

---

* Though we cannot discount the recent suggestion that their eldest son Victor Emmanuel was the product of the princess's liaison with a Florentine butcher.

looked superficially as though he shared their liberal agenda. It was typical of him that his stance should actually have been more ambiguous, clouded by the mass of doubts, reservations and contradictions which seemed to surround everything he undertook. True, he favoured a constitution and wanted at all costs to avoid a bullying Habsburg intervention. He was no friend, on the other hand, to anything that promised the kind of drastic political solutions witnessed in the Napoleonic France of his boyhood. When the Carbonarist officers refused to moderate their demands and seemed bent on war with Austria, he retreated into his habitual gloom. King Victor Emmanuel's announcement that he was preparing to abdicate so depressed Charles Albert that he seriously considered suicide. His position as heir was now critical. Charles Felix, succeeding to his brother's crown, seemed determined to bar the Prince from succession, but was finally content with making him swear to uphold Piedmont's fundamental statutes and with sending him off to Spain to prove his political conservatism by fighting the constitutionalist rebels against King Ferdinand VII. A successful attack on the fortress of Trocadero, outside Cadiz, in 1823 won him praise from the reactionary King Charles X of France and assorted *bien-pensants* and ultras throughout Europe, and more significantly reconciled him with Charles Felix.

When at last he gained the throne in 1831, Charles Albert could scarcely have been a less appealing Italian sovereign to the liberals surrounding Mazzini. He detested the newly crowned French king Louis-Philippe, supported the claims of the conservative Don Carlos to the Spanish throne and upheld the grotesquely obscurantist Dom Miguel of Portugal, to whom he wished to send money and weapons. His desire to be seen as the new legitimist champion drew approval from Metternich, and when in 1834 the new king struck hard to prevent a wave of Mazzinian enthusiasm sweeping through the army, the Chancellor may have scented a potential 'pupil' of the sort he was wont to claim among European conservatives. He had never trusted Charles Albert, however, since their first meeting a decade earlier, in the presence of Emperor Francis I. 'He talks too glibly,' commented the Emperor. 'I don't care for phrase-makers. A man who behaves and talks as he does is either a saint or a rogue. Since there are more hypocrites than saints alive, I'll settle for the rogue.' Others would share this attitude, though, as his surrogate mother, Queen Maria Teresa of Piedmont, shrewdly perceived, his deviousness and refusal to engage directly with others owed more to a lack of necessary emotion than to calculated faithlessness. 'He is not wholly bad,' she concluded, 'but such as he is, he will remain, without enough sensibility to do anything purely for love of other people, though in himself he is upright,

proud, just and charitable.' Charles Albert nevertheless remained true to
a sincere belief in reforming Piedmontese institutions so that the Sardinian
monarchy itself should not perish. Like certain reigning sovereigns in our
own time, he was fundamentally a dedicated conservative with a fairly
limited awareness of popular feeling and aspiration, but one who also
perceived that his own advantage and that of his family must finally lie
in adapting to circumstance. It was both a crudely enduring strength and
a fatal weakness in the House of Savoy that its members should believe
so steadfastly in the significance of their dynasty and its survival.

Charm was not a noteworthy characteristic of the Savoys, any more
than a love of the arts or a concern with the life of the mind. To his
contemporaries, the King seemed a cold, almost pathologically withdrawn
figure, whose sole interest, apart from hunting, lay in cultivating a mystical
Catholic religiosity. His shift towards a more liberal outlook on the political direction of Italy was partly occasioned by an enthusiastic reading,
in 1843, of Vincenzo Gioberti's *Primato morale e civile degli italiani*, with
its theocratic federal vision of Italian states led by the Pope and the armies
of Sardinia for their shield against foreign invaders. When Pius IX was
elected in 1846, the moral impetus and seriousness of purpose the new
pontiff brought to his consecrated task offered a galvanic inspiration to
the King. Here at last was both a true spiritual father and a worthy political partner in what seemed to be turning swiftly into a God-given mission
to liberate Italy. 'If God ever vouchsafes us a war of independence, I alone
shall be in command of our army. What a magnificent day it will be
when we can raise the cry of national freedom,' he wrote in 1846 to his
aide-de-camp Count Castagnetto. It was an open letter, news of whose
contents were distributed among Piedmontese progressives at a meeting
of an agrarian association in the town of Mortara. Later in the year
Castagnetto noted that 'the King still hopes for a rupture with Austria,
an excommunication and a war of religion'.

Though personally connected to the Habsburgs through his wife and
the marriage of his sister to Archduke Rainer, the imperial Viceroy, Charles
Albert had little love for Austria. According to his cousin the Duc de
Talleyrand-Périgord, he had neither forgotten nor forgiven their treatment of him in 1821, especially that moment when the Governor of Milan,
Ferdinand Bubna von Littitz, had sneeringly paraded him before a courtyard full of soldiers, crying, 'Make way for the King of Italy!' Yet even
before the advent of Pius IX, Charles Albert had given at least one important signal that he was ready to commit himself to the Italian cause. In
1845 he was visited by Massimo d'Azeglio, who had come in search of
support for the revolutionaries in Romagna. D'Azeglio had sought to turn

aside their planned insurrection in the genuine belief that Charles Albert would strike a blow for liberty when the time was ripe. The King, an early riser according to custom, received him in audience at six o'clock in the morning, and seemed willing enough to listen to his news from Romagna. D'Azeglio was keen to emphasise the new spirit abroad among Italian patriots, disdainful of 'Mazzinian folly and wickedness' and eager for leadership from Piedmont, the only Italian power with enough military force to achieve results. He did not wholly trust Charles Albert and suspected that whatever comment he might make was likely to be 'sibylline'. To his surprise the monarch, looking him squarely in the face, said, 'Let those gentlemen [the Romagnole revolutionaries] know that they should remain quiet and take no steps now, as nothing can be done at present; but they can rest assured that when the opportunity arises, my life, my children's lives, my arms, my treasure, my army; all shall be given in the cause of Italy.'

The Romagnoles ignored the King's pledge, and the 1845 uprising was brutally suppressed. Even if a little less conservative than most of his fellow Piedmontese nobles, d'Azeglio believed that bloody revolution was not the way forward, publishing his *Degli ultimi casi di Romagna* the following year in vindication of his ideas. The *Statuto*, the constitutional charter granted by Charles Albert to his subjects in March 1848, with its pledges of bicameral government *à l'anglaise*, religious toleration and the rule of law, seemed to substantiate a growing image of the sovereign as Italy's most progressive, yet some were not so convinced. A closer scrutiny of the *Statuto*'s clauses would reveal that its distinctive focus was not on expanding popular rights and concessions, but on strengthening the royal prerogative and confirming the King's position as ultimate proposer and disposer, whether in the ratification of laws or in major political and military decision-making.

Thus when Piedmont eventually went to war against Austria, more than a few observers, Italian or foreign, were inclined to distrust Charles Albert's motives. Fear of revolution and the spread of democracy, they suspected, had driven him at last to assume the guise of Italy's deliverer. 'He did not act for love of Italy,' commented Turin's archbishop Luigi Franzoni, 'but for a wish to usurp her. He did not fight for Italy, but for the chance to become her master.' Metternich was equally unconvinced, later remarking to his friend Lord Aberdeen that Charles Albert 'lies to others as he lies to himself. He is simultaneously devout and immoral, a tyrant to his own government, yet at the beck and call of all the revolutionaries, physically brave but morally a coward.' It was widely remembered that an earlier King of Piedmont had cynically described

Italy as an artichoke from which he and his family gradually peeled off and ate the leaves. Charles Albert wanted, said Carlo Cattaneo, one of his sternest critics, 'to continue the ancient traditions of his dynasty in "following the centuries and following the Po"'. From Cattaneo's account, the King emerges as a shameless mountebank, flattering patriotic expectations by combining the white cross of Savoy with the tricolour on his regimental banners, while protesting to the European powers that the campaign was really against his better judgement and that he only undertook it to prevent the growth of anti-monarchical sentiments. Worst of all, in Cattaneo's opinion, was the fact that so many Italians should believe in him as their deliverer. 'With the promise of an avenging war on Italy's behalf, the King had effectively extinguished in their souls (either childishly credulous or else senile and worn out) the religion of liberty and memories of betrayal and persecution.'

Wreathed in the plaudits which elevated him to the level of Pio Nono himself, so that their two names were invoked like those of paired saints in the church calendar – Cosmas & Damian, Sergius & Bacchus, Hermagoras & Fortunatus, Pio Nono & Carlo Alberto – the monarch could count on the loyalty of his army and his people. Piedmont had always been a tight-knit little kingdom, depending for its survival on traditional bonds created by feudalism, a minimal level of literacy, elemental Catholic beliefs and a continuing military preparedness, which kept a wary eye on the French to the north and west and the Austrians to the east and south. The political core of the realm was formed by a numerous and deeply conservative aristocracy, French-speaking like the royal family, for whose menfolk service in the army, the Church or at court was a destined career across the generations, to the extent that a wayward scion like Massimo d'Azeglio, who announced to his family that he wished to become a painter, was considered (at least to begin with) shamefully frivolous and embarrassing. No other Italian state except Naples produced an officer and ministerial caste of such substance, and even there the sense of an absolute dedication to the Crown was not nearly as powerful or instinctive as in the northern kingdom.

A similar unquestioning loyalty to the ruler and the divinely sanctioned legitimacy that he or she embodied was to be found among the officers of the Austrian army. The principle of *Kaisertreue*, fidelity to the Emperor above everything, had to be understood – but was very often imperfectly grasped by Italian patriots – as conditioning every decision made, every order given, by the generals commanding the various Habsburg forces disposed throughout Lombardy-Venetia. Nearly all of them belonged to that nobility, German-speaking whether from Styria,

Carinthia, Hungary or Bohemia, whose names resonate through Austria's 300-year history as a European power, from the reign of Leopold I in the seventeeth century to the death of Franz Josef in 1916. Schwarzenberg, Liechtenstein, Pálffy, Zichy, Strassoldo, Spaur, Thurn und Taxis could all summon the right patrician echo, while other commanders and governors (Welden, Haynau, D'Aspre, Nugent), though boasting not quite so many quarterings in their coats of arms, came from ennobled families with sufficiently venerable records of service and an instinctive sense of duty.

Yet the army whose upper echelon this patrician officer caste provided was by no means an ideal fighting force. Training at the military academies in Vienna and Wiener Neustadt or at the various cadet schools was plodding and unimaginative, apparently designed to crush all original impulse out of the fledgling subaltern. Snobbery, string-pulling and graft were freely used, once the graduates joined their respective regiments, to secure promotion. Young officers scarcely managed to live on their exiguous pay, from which uniforms must be purchased, a batman kept, furniture hired and victuals procured. There was no compulsory retiring age since pensions, like almost everything else in the Habsburg realms before 1848, were not a guaranteed legal entitlement, and many officers chose to soldier on well beyond the point at which their counterparts in other European states were settling down comfortably to their memoirs, their smoking-room anecdotes or their treatises on gunnery and horsemanship.

In the ranks most of the men were conscripts, brutally rounded up by local commissioners and frogmarched in chains to nearby depots, whence they would be posted to some garrison often far from their home villages. Their pay was proportionally even worse than that of the officers, and the harshest penalties were meted out for everything from adverse comment on the monarch, the service or the officers to requests for hardship relief, if made by more than two men at a time. More often than not the punishments themselves were corporal, either in the form of beatings, with the culprit bowed over a drumhead, or the notorious running of the gauntlet, in which the offender, stripped to the waist, was ordered to march up and down lines of 150 men wielding birch rods. Vengeful attacks on harsh NCOs were not unknown and there was even the occasional suicide. The men could expect little sympathy from their officers, who seldom made any effort to establish contact with those under their command or to boost morale by showing proper concern for the physical and material welfare of the troops.

For most Italians, the standard image of the ordinary Austrian

infantryman was that of the 'Croat', as he was loosely called, a soldier
who might indeed hail from Croatia, but was just as likely to come from
Slovenia, Moravia, Transylvania or any region of the empire in which
Italian was not spoken and where the staple diet was potatoes rather than
polenta. Croats by long-held tradition in northern Italy were ignorant,
stupid and brutish, swilling beer, smoking foul tobacco and stinking of
the tallow with which they smeared their legs in order to pull on their
skin-tight uniform breeches and boots. In the myth-history which, as in
all great events, the Risorgimento created around it, they were to become
infamous for harshness and cruelty towards the civilian population and
for their contemptuous mockery of everything the patriotic Italians held
sacred.

In fact a sizeable proportion of the Austrian army in Italy (around
70,000 men in all) was not 'Croat', but native Italian. Marshal Radetzky,
writing on the eve of the events in Milan, had commended their morale,
while at the same time conceding that they would doubtless be unwilling
to fight against their compatriots and were likely to be 'subject to all
kinds of influences' or even to desert altogether. Indeed they did, in their
hundreds by the beginning of April, in their thousands by its end, but
it is worth pointing out that three of Radetzky's eight Italian regiments
stayed loyal throughout the campaign and that the ultimate success for
the Austrians of various battles and siege operations depended on the
steadfastness of these troops, led though they mostly were by non-Italian
officers.

What guaranteed their loyalty, or, for that matter, that of their fellow
subjects of Emperor Ferdinand, dragooned into the ranks, underfed,
underpaid and cut off from any proper contact with home and family?
The answer lay largely – though not exclusively – in the charismatic presence of the eighty-one-year-old man who had contrived their escape from
Milan and led them along muddy roads under the driving rain to Verona.
If Field Marshal Baron Johann Josef Wenzel Anton Franz Karl Radetzky
von Radetz lived for the army, it was because no other kind of life had
ever possessed any meaning for him. He had been born in the age of
powdered wigs and knee-breeches, a child of minor Bohemian aristocracy living near the town of Budweis (Cesky Budovice), which is famous
for its beer. His mother died while giving birth to him, his father followed
her when the boy was only six, and the uncle to whom he was left as a
ward soon frittered away most of young Radetzky's inheritance. With
what remained, he was packed off to the *Theresianum*, the academy for
young nobles established by Empress Maria Teresa. He was scarcely a
model scholar: his spelling remained faulty throughout his life and no

academic subject interested him except history, more especially the reigns of the Byzantine emperor Justinian and King Louis XIV of France.

Genuine distinction, once he had entered the army, did not arrive until, aged thirty, he took part in the Italian campaign of 1796–7 against the French forces led by General Bonaparte. A horse shot under him at Marengo and five bullet holes in his uniform ensured rapid promotion thereafter, and at the battle of Leipzig in 1814 he was responsible for drawing up the Austrian plan of operations. Emerging from the war as the most prudent and resourceful of Emperor Francis's younger officers (and one who was never afraid to tell his sovereign exactly what he thought), he was appointed chief-of-staff to General Frimont, whom he succeeded as commander-in-chief at Verona in 1831.

Radetzky was well aware of the Austrian army's shortcomings and cherished his own ideas for reforming it through improving the *esprit de corps*, introducing a new training programme and, most significant of all according to Emperor Francis, conducting extensive manoeuvres so that the civilian population and foreign diplomats could duly note the troops' preparedness in the face of likely rebellion or invasion. This policy had its critics. One politically dissident officer, who later joined the Viennese revolt of 1848 in its final stages, poured scorn on the wastefulness of the manoeuvres and their mismanagement by officers who saw the whole exercise as a glorified excuse for a party. The Duke of Modena's brother Archduke Maximilian censured the idleness and ignorance of the staff officers, while General D'Aspre, looking back on his campaigning experiences, wondered how Radetzky had managed to achieve anything at all, given the inefficiencies plaguing the chain of command, which resulted in a host of contradictory orders being given simultaneously.

As D'Aspre doubtless realised, a great deal – almost too much – depended on the personality of the commander-in-chief himself in his role as the grizzled old warlord whose paternal solicitude for his men earned him the admiring sobriquet of 'Vater Radetzky'. His own five sons were little better than a pack of arrogant spendthrifts living off their father's reputation. His marriage to Countess Francesca Strassoldo-Grafenberg had been a failure, based, as he admitted, on financial calculation rather than love or good sense. Outside his military circle the only two individuals whose affection and advice he valued were his beloved daughter Frederica 'Fritzi' Wenckheim, who became his chief correspondent during the war of 1848, and his mistress, a Milanese laundress named Giuditta Meregalli, on whom he fathered four children and who remained faithful to him in the teeth of opprobrium heaped on her by Italian patriots.

Otherwise Radetzky's life was centred on soldiering, and those who came across him in his professional milieu immediately grasped the secret of his impact on the troops. The French journalist Henry Blaze de Bury, meeting him after the war had ended, was instantly charmed by this 'little old man with a kind, lively face, cheerful, friendly and sociable, beaming with good nature, not just in his countenance but in his speech, characterised as it was by a native Austrian dialect'. The Field Marshal, according to the same source, had the ideal common touch, which gave him the status of 'a deus ex machina in this Homeric episode, of which anecdotes and legends made him the brave hero, humane, fatherly, and sharing in every joy and sorrow which overtook the humblest soldier in his army'. So popular was he with his officers that they purchased a goat, which they took along on campaign, to ensure that he could always have milk in his morning cup of chocolate.

What others appreciated was Radetzky's absolute lack of pretence. The diplomat Count Hübner, as the only civilian at a grand dinner in Milan just before the *Cinque Giornate*, was enchanted by the way in which the Field Marshal made sure that his guest was properly served, 'seating himself beside me and, with old-world politeness, helping me to the choicest morsels with his trembling hands'. Listening to the conversation among the officers, Hübner realised that nothing except the army could save Lombardy-Venetia for the imperial Crown and that Radetzky's inspiring presence at its head was essential not just from a military aspect, but morally and politically besides. According to another French journalist, Charles de la Varenne, it was the Field Marshal, rather than the Emperor and his ministers, who had effectively ruled the two Italian provinces since his nomination as commander-in-chief.

Some might have been forgiven for thinking that a retreat to Verona 'with bag and baggage', as Charles Albert's forces advanced towards Milan, suggested blind panic rather than inspiration. Worse still, Radetzky appeared to have no definite plan of action beyond going to earth within the relative safety of the Quadrilateral. The Marshal, however, knew exactly what he was doing. There was no realistic possibility of a counterstrike at the Piedmontese in Lombardy without adequate support from the army that General Nugent was mobilising at Gorizia, whose task, when it was ready to move, would be to mop up the rebellion in Friuli and the eastern Veneto stage by stage. For the time being Verona was as safe a place as any to hole up in. The city's little burst of Italian patriotism had not amounted to anything very impressive. A civic commission designed to exact viceregal concessions from Archduke Rainer, now ensconced in the Albergo Due Torri, had been fobbed off with a few vague promises, and the civic guard lasted only nine days before it was summarily abolished by General D'Aspre arriving with his troops from Padua. By the time they marched in, the Viceroy had slipped away, leaving his hotel by a secret staircase, then spirited out of town with a military escort. Effectively Verona was now at the army's mercy, with leading citizens, aided by the pro-Austrian archbishop Pietro Mutti, dowsing the few remaining flickers of sedition in the name of peace at any price. D'Aspre's coming, said one of Radetzky's staff officers, had instantly transformed the Veronese from ardent republicans to faithful subjects of the emperor.

Radetzky himself did not appear until three days later, on 1 April. His army, bringing with it a horde of servants, wounded soldiers from the fighting in Milan, Italian hostages and a large number of women in various capacities, took nearly a week to quarter itself in and around the city. The soldiers' morale was low, for they had left Milan without adequate provisions and there had been widespread looting in the villages en route. Their commander-in-chief offered them no illusions as to the gravity of the situation. As he told his daughter Fritzi, 'without money or provisions, without any help coming from Vienna, I cannot tell what the outcome may be. We have lost everything – only my carriage and horses have been saved. My eyes are sore, but otherwise I'm well. Trusting in God's help alone, I hope to keep the army together.' As soon as he arrived in Verona, a spate of proclamations and prohibitions began blistering the available wall space in streets and squares. Housewives were forbidden to hang out their washing in case it was being used for signalling to the enemy, inside or outside the ramparts. All doors had to be left open at night with a lamp burning above them. Gloomy and taciturn, the townsfolk went grimly about their business in a city which had become an armed camp bristling with guns, many of which pointed inside its walls.

Radetzky was taking no chances, yet he must have been well aware of the disadvantages under which the Piedmontese were labouring as they pushed further into Lombardy. Charles Albert, notorious for his indecision, had been nicknamed '*il Re tentenna*', 'the wobbly king', and the conduct of the war would fatally emphasise this tendency to haver interminably between two conflicting opinions, even if the reason for doing so was an entirely laudable one of seeking a proper perspective for a correct judgement. The army he commanded was more fervently loyal throughout its ranks than Radetzky's, its officers were professional soldiers, but in terms of military efficiency and operative infrastructure, it was no equal match against Austria. It needed, what was more, to rely on the support of other Italian forces to pin down Austrian manoeuvres in the Veneto and southern Lombardy, and its advance was based on the belief that the civilian populations of the two provinces must automatically welcome Piedmont in the person of its king as their deliverer from a hated tyranny.

Taking anything for granted as to an overall mood among the ordinary citizens of Lombardy-Venetia in 1848 was dangerously naive. In the rural areas peasants might, or more frequently might not, adopt the same standpoint as their landlords, who could be any shade from stolidly Austrophile to mildly patriotic, enthusiastic advocates of change or – and this was understandably rare – fervently anti-Habsburg and avid for war, whatever the socio-economic consequences. In the cities by no means all of the working class and lower bourgeoisie would necessarily uphold the principles set forth by the various provisional governments, whose members would scarcely claim, in any case, to speak for all local business interests or represent a common viewpoint among the town's aristocracy. What emerges from an overall perspective of northern Italy during these fretful months of marching, manoeuvres, assaults, retreats, resistance and surrender is the simple fact that the political climate varied heavily – sometimes violently – from one area to another, and that most of those who later chose to generalise on it in their memoirs of the period did so on the basis of very limited experience. The reality was that neither the Piedmontese nor the Austrians could afford to rely on the loyalty and enthusiasm of the communities whose livestock they drove off, whose wine they drank, whose crops they galloped over and whose houses they bedded down in. If the men and officers of the Habsburg army were a shade more hard-headed in coming to terms with the existence of deeply rooted resentments among the Emperor's Italian subjects, this hardly ever guaranteed that they would arrive at any grasp of a possible justification for such grievances. To the Piedmontese and other forces from beyond the Austrian provinces who later joined in the fighting, from Tuscany, Naples or the Papal States, the prevailing apathy or hostility towards 'the holy war' in many parts of Lombardy-Venetia would prove a bitter and puzzling disappointment.

While Radetzky was meditating on his next move at Verona, Charles Albert and his staff considered their options for an all-out attack and found almost none of these feasible at a moment when the fortresses of the Quadrilateral were so obviously fulfilling the defensive role originally designed for them. Verona itself, Mantua, Peschiera and Legnago were the outlying bastions of an immense citadel girdling the territory between the rivers Mincio and Adige to the north and west, the shore of Lake Garda to the north and the Po marking off the southern frontier. The only choice appeared to lie between laying siege to one of the forts after breaking through Austrian defences along the Mincio, or avoiding the Quadrilateral altogether, leading the army as far as Venice and then striking from the rear so as to drive Radetzky back into Lombardy and pin him between the Piedmontese reserves and the main force. Taking the fortresses would then be easy enough, and in the case of Verona might even rouse its fainéant citizens to give more genuine support to the cause.

The first alternative was much the easier in purely practical terms. Morale was high in the Piedmontese ranks and their seemingly unopposed thrust into Lombardy had gingered them up for a fight. Taking the advice of General Eusebio Bava, one of his abler commanders (and later one of his less charitable critics), the King decided on a swift strike across the Mincio, beginning with the capture of the three main bridges along its northern stretch, at Borghetto, Monzambano and Goito. Once these had been secured, the army could sweep the Austrians aside and advance on the forts at Mantua and Peschiera. On the morning of 8 April, Bava moved his men up the dead-straight road, the old Roman Via Postumia, towards the bridge of Goito, defended by about 1,200 Austrian infantry, a squadron of hussars and four guns, under Major-General Ludwig von Wohlgemuth, military governor of Milan until the *Cinque Giornate*.

Driving off the Jägers, Tyrolean sharpshooters, who guarded the last stretch of road, Bava began his assault on the main Austrian position in Goito village by sending in their Piedmontese equivalent, the Bersaglieri, crack light infantry whose distinctive broad-brimmed hats adorned with black cocks' feathers have since made them one of the most easily recognisable of Italian army units. It was the regiment's debut in action, but though its colonel, Alessandro La Marmora, was more than satisfied with the performance his men put up, his pleasure was marred by a bullet wound in the jaw, which knocked him out of action for several months. Once the business of flushing the Austrians out of the village was completed, it seemed easy enough to advance to the river, where the Jägers appeared to be falling back towards the right bank. This manoeuvre was no more than a hurried dash to safety, for the bridge had been mined, a fuse was touched off and a violent explosion left two of the piers in ruins.

All the Piedmontese could do was keep up a steady fire across the river, gradually wearing away Wohlgemuth's resistance and forcing him to retreat along the Via Postumia towards Verona. It was not exactly a victory for Charles Albert, since the bridge was no longer practicable for a quick crossing of the Mincio and much depended on the divisions charged with seizing the other two bridges at Monzambano and Borghetto, but it would do to be going on with. Even if, somewhat ominously in view of its later incompetence, the commissariat had failed to supply the men with any sort of breakfast before they went into action, their spirits were exalted* and a further boost was given by the news that thirty Jägers from the Italian south Tyrol had deserted on the spot to join the Piedmontese ranks.

On the very same day as the action at Goito, a far more dispiriting encounter took place some sixty miles further east, on the road from Verona to Vicenza, between the Austrians and a ragtag-and-bobtail force thrown together in the name of the Venetian defence committee and commanded by the elderly Napoleonic veteran Colonel Marcantonio Sanfermo. The Italians were almost all *crociati*, volunteers from Padua, Vicenza, Treviso and the surrounding areas, keen for a scrap but recruited in a completely haphazard fashion, untrained and hopelessly ill armed because nobody in Venice had thought it necessary to send enough muskets to the provincial committees. Mustering his 1,200 men at the neighbouring villages of Sorio and Montebello, together with 200 ex-Austrian soldiers (who had at least managed to hang on to their rifles), Sanfermo persuaded them that it would be easy enough to mop up the enemy – essentially a glorified foraging party dispatched by Radetzky to bring in more provisions – and march unopposed on Verona. Some of the volunteers may already have grasped the dangerous absurdity of this plan from a skirmish the previous evening in which the Austrians had easily beaten them off. Heavy rain during the night had soaked both the men and their powder supply. What was more, Sanfermo, unable to mount a horse, had to direct operations from a carriage, wearing an improvised uniform consisting of a black tail-coat and a top-hat adorned with an ostrich plume and tricolour cockade.

Successful at first the *crociati* proved, however, keeping the 3,000 Austrians under General Prince Liechtenstein at bay for nearly seven hours until a wave of reinforcements managed to turn the volunteers' right flank, panicking the main force on the road below the two villages. Sanfermo simply ordered a general retreat and told his coachman to head back towards Vicenza. Only a gallant university battalion from Padua and a legion from the silk-weaving town of Schio managed to retire to Montebello in good order and hold the centre of the village while the Austrians were looting and burning outlying houses before returning to Verona.

* The appropriate Italian expression, potentially confusing to English-speaking readers, is *in orgasmo*.

The action at Montebello was unimportant in the broader context of the unfolding war further west, but it revealed with an embarrassing clarity how negligent, disorganised and over-optimistic the Venetian provisional government had been in its handling of defence and mobilisation during the previous weeks. To the Piedmontese it must have looked as if the whole burden of an Italian role in the struggle now intensifying was to be laid on the shoulders of Charles Albert and his generals. The obvious irony of the situation lay in the immense reserves of goodwill, courage and determination among the people of the Veneto, simply waiting to be properly focused and guided by military leaders adequate to the situation. A volunteer spirit was alive in the most unlikely quarters, as the formation of the various civic guards had proved. In Venice, for example, a women's battalion had been set up under the auspices of the patricians Elisabetta Giustinian and Teresa Papadopoli. The main initiative here came from an aunt of the Bandiera brothers, Maria Graziani, who published a patriotic appeal to female Venetians asking whether a love of patriotism and liberty were purely masculine sentiments. 'Are we incapable of such noble affections? Let us too show a spirit of patriotic sisterhood, and dismiss the absurd prejudice which declares women to be born solely for the distaff and the needle.' Enrolment was to be made at her house in Calle del Ospedaleto, near SS Giovanni e Paolo, but for all those who signed on, there were as many who scorned the whole enterprise. One of them, Irene Ferrari, effectively stymied Graziani's efforts by distributing a sarcastic flyer pointing out that the ladies of Venice would be better off using those very same needles to sew uniforms rather than donning their own.

Some were doubtful of the whole volunteer initiative, among them the American minister to the court of Vienna, William H. Stiles. The Venetian *crociati*, so he had heard, were nothing better than a bunch of porters, gondoliers and 'all vagabonds who could find no employment in the city. The officers were composed of musicians, painters and such other artists as the times had deprived of the means of subsistence, or who, with the Moor of Venice, could exclaim "Othello's occupation's gone!"' Rumour, by the time it reached Stiles, had transformed the women's brigade into an unruly amazon band 'consisting of opera dancers and females of the most dissolute character in Venice'. Blessed by the patriot clergy, the entire outfit – male and female – had set out for Treviso and Udine, 'under no control, and indulging in every kind of license'. They might, concluded Stiles, 'more appropriately have been called Corsairs than Crusaders. So far from affording protection, they soon became a greater terror to the inhabitants than the Austrians they had enlisted to oppose.'

Stiles's informant, probably the American consul in Venice, William Sparks, had doubtless based his report on descriptions of the singular expedition which left Treviso in early April, heading towards Udine and the fortress of Palmanova. At its head marched Italy's greatest living stage actor, Gustavo Modena, and his Swiss wife Julie Calame. Born in Venice in 1803, Modena was himself the son of an actor and joined the profession after attending Padua University, where Manin was among his contemporaries. After involvement in the abortive uprising at Bologna in 1831, he went into exile in Paris, meeting Mazzini and joining his 'Giovine Italia' movement. Marrying Julie (or Giulia as she became) in 1835, he was offered an amnesty by the Austrians three years later, but could not raise sufficient money to fund a return to Italy. His theatrical forte, besides memorable interpretations of Alfieri's tragic heroes, was the recitation of cantos from Dante's *La divina commedia*, and it was this which secured him star billing at a grand concert presented for his benefit at Her Majesty's Theatre in London in 1839. Framed by extracts from Donizetti's *Roberto Devereux*, sung by a stellar line-up including Giulia Grisi, Fanny Persiani and Lugi Lablache, Modena gave 'choice specimens of Italian Declamation, among which the most beautiful passages of the "Inferno" of Dante', as the London advertisements put it.

With the money raised, the Modenas went home at last, but preferred to settle outside Venice, in a little villa near Treviso. When revolution fever swept the countryside in the spring of 1848, they were ready to take part, though neither was under any illusion as to the dubious outcome of a movement which seemed to have no proper organisation or long-term programme. When a band of local volunteers, knowing their patriotic sympathies, paraded in front of the villa, Gustavo and Giulia took this as a signal to join up at once. 'We ran to catch the *diligence*, throwing a few shirts and a pair of stockings into a bag, and reached Codroipo ahead of the marching column.' There they were formally enrolled, the actor in the ranks, his wife as a nurse, and marched into Udine under the pouring rain with Giulia carrying the flag at the head of the troop, 500-strong, including Gian Francesco Avesani's son and a group of young Venetian nobles. The city greeted them with serenades and 'Evviva!'s and Modena was invited to improvise at the theatre, where Giulia reported, 'from the boxes fell a rain of sonnets and other poems addressed to the volunteers, to Gustavo and to me'.

With this sort of enthusiasm at its disposal, the Venetian government could – and should – have concentrated on fusing the volunteers with the considerable body of Italian trained soldiers from the Austrian army to create an effective fighting force. Instead they sought the aid of the

Piedmontese general Alberto La Marmora, brother of the Bersaglieri commander at Goito, who had spent the past few years as superintendent of the naval academy in Genoa and pursuing his hobby of birdwatching. A gouty veteran of the battles of Wagram and Leipzig, he had offered his services to Charles Albert at the start of the war and was sent off to Venice on the very day of the action at Montebello. La Marmora's contempt for the *crociati* at once made itself plain. Dispatched to take stock of the situation at Vicenza, whose position gave it key strategic significance for the Austrians, he roundly told the government that he could not accept command of an army that did not exist. On 17 April he marshalled the various brigades on the city's parade ground and was horrified by the ill-armed rabble which passed in review. 'I cannot express my sorrow,' he wrote, 'in observing their condition as an armed force. Many are without rifles and barely half of those which do exist will serve for more than two hours' use in battle. What on earth am I to do with these unarmed or poorly equipped men? Where am I to place them in the event of an attack? All they can do for the present is to draw their pay and create confusion. The more I think about this the more I believe some enemy of the cause or some adverse destiny guides this business.'

Pessimism characterised La Marmora's approach from the outset, making him thoroughly unsuitable for a position which needed dash, initiative and positive thinking if the Austrian advance into Friuli was to be checked. On the very day he was wringing his hands over the condition of the Vicentine volunteers, Count Laval Nugent, Quartermaster General of the Austrian army, had begun to move his relief force of 13,000 men from their base at Romans' d'Isonzo towards Udine. This city's immediate capture was essential not just because of its command of major roads down into the Veneto, but for the likely damage to patriotic morale, in view of the apparent ease with which the Udinesi had sent the Habsburg cohorts packing only a few weeks earlier. At the age of seventy-one, Nugent had all the experience necessary to conduct the operation swiftly and decisively before engaging with an Italian army he had every right to assume was preparing to block his advance towards the equally desirable prizes of Treviso and Vicenza. Soldiering was in his blood, as a member of an Irish military family some of whom had been 'Wild Geese' Jacobites in the French and Austrian armies during the eighteenth century. He was also thoroughly familiar with Italy and the Italians, having marched almost from one end of the peninsula to the other in a successful campaign against Napoleon's brother-in-law Joachim Murat, ex-King of Naples, as well as dealing with minor rebellions in the Papal States, Parma and Modena and later overhauling the army of the restored Neapolitan Bourbons.

With Radetzky temporarily immobilised in Verona, the fate of Habsburg hegemony in Italy now lay as a heavy responsibility on the shoulders of Nugent and his men. Assembled in haste, inadequately uniformed and marching to bands gathered from among Triestine café orchestras, they were by no means an ideally constituted force, yet to preserve the two provinces of Lombardy and Venetia was a matter of honour for the entire army, from the high command down to the humblest Croat private. Despite Austria's negligent and obtuse attitude towards Venice itself since 1814, the city had its own symbolic importance to the empire. Radetzky had judged 'the disastrous and inexplicable loss of Venice' and the revolts in surrounding cities to be a far worse blow to morale than the uprising in Milan. 'Reducing Venice to submission,' he insisted, 'is of the utmost importance: all our remaining energies should be devoted to this task.' Nugent's assignment was now to restore the status quo, not just for the sake of imperial prestige but in the name of that mission, sacred as it had been to Metternich, of sustaining a conservative order in Italy against the insidious march of liberalism.

Udine, in theory at least, was not to be secured easily. On Nugent's way there lay the fortress town of Palmanova, built by the Serene Republic in 1593 on a grid plan within a carefully devised system of ramparts and bastions so as to defy possible invasion by ever-encroaching Austria or even by the Turks. Like so many other defensive schemes of its kind, the place was a white elephant. During the French invasion of Italy in the 1790s it obstructed neither Napoleon's troops nor those of Emperor Francis, but the Venetian provisional government, soon after taking office on 22 March 1848, had insisted on its seizure as vital to the military control of the region. Accordingly on the 23rd commissioners from Udine had arrived in post-chaises to demand the garrison's surrender. If they were kept waiting until six o'clock the following morning, it was because the wife of the commandant Colonel Vancha had spent most of the intervening period trying to persuade him not to hand over the fort. Her demonstration of loyalty saved him from a threatened court martial, but Palmanova was at length yielded and the Austrians marched out.

The new commandant was a man who until this moment had been languishing in the dungeons of the fortress. General Carlo Zucchi, a veteran of Napoleon's retreat from Moscow, had been serving the latest stage of a hard-labour sentence originally handed down for his part in a revolution against the Duke of Modena in 1831. Always a stickler for discipline, he had undoubtedly been made more harsh by incarceration, first in the Hungarian fortress of Munkacs, then at Josefstadt in Silesia, before being transferred to Palmanova. Those now under his command soon found themselves echoing the verdict of a contemporary, that his behaviour 'recalled the cruelty of Napoleonic militarism without reviving any of its splendours'.

Whatever these personal failings, Zucchi had done his best to prepare his forces for an Austrian assault. Besides nearly 1,000 regular soldiers formerly in the Habsburg ranks, the fort contained a small body of Piedmontese artillery, along with the local civic guard and various troops of *crociati*, including those led from Venice and Treviso by Gustavo Modena and his wife. In the village of Visco, about a mile from the walls, a brigade led by Major Giuseppe Galateo of Bologna, aided by volunteers, had driven out Nugent's pickets and occupied the houses and farmsteads. Nugent evidently saw Palmanova as a potential distraction from the main object of seizing Udine in good time, so he ordered Prince Felix zu Schwarzenberg to attack Galateo's position while at the same time dispatching two columns ahead to deal with any possible resistance from volunteer patrols. For a while Galateo's brigade held off the assault, until the arrival of two Croat battalions, followed by a few shells from Schwarzenberg's artillery, proved too much for them and they retreated to the nearby village of Jalmicco.

This was not at all what Nugent wanted. His plan was to flush out all opposition in the surrounding area and then allow Schwarzenberg to commence a siege of Palmanova while the main body of the army moved on towards Udine. Stormy weather had now set in and muddy roads would slow down the march. Having to skirmish anew with Galateo's regrouped force might allow Zucchi to launch an attack from Palmanova itself on the army's rear. Jalmicco's defenders and its inhabitants too must be summarily dealt with, in an operation that would furnish a grim warning to civilian communities elsewhere. While Visco was reduced to a smoking ruin, the Austrians, having flushed out Galateo and his men, fell savagely on Jalmicco, looting, burning and killing, and in the process offered the Italians the first propaganda victory of the war.

A horrified witness of the whole episode was the writer Caterina Percoto. The daughter of a local landowner, conventionally educated for marriage and motherhood, she had begun her literary career by translating sections of *Messias* by the German poet Friedrich Klopstock, which were accepted for publication by a Trieste magazine. Its editor, Francesco Dell'Ongaro, himself an accomplished poet, encouraged Percoto to describe her own world of rural Friuli and she soon made a name for herself as a short-story writer at a time when the form was not widely practised in Italy. She never married, owing, it was said, to the traumatic effect of a teenage relationship broken off by interfering nuns at her former convent school, who were shocked to discover that the boy in question was Jewish. Though several later lovers proposed to her, Percoto preferred her freedom, living with her widowed mother on the family estate at San Lorenzo, north of Jalmicco, wandering the farms in a battered straw hat with a pipe stuck in her mouth and collecting Friulan dialect words and traditions from the country folk, a way of life which earned her the nickname of '*La contessa contadina*', 'the peasant countess'.

From her bedroom window Percoto watched Jalmicco, its houses, barns, granaries and straw stacks going up in flames as the Austrians ran amok. 'I heard the savage cries and drunken howling of the soldiers,' she wrote. 'Under my very windows, I heard the groans of the wretched villagers, fleeing with their children in their arms to seek refuge in my house. They told me how their stock had been driven off and their cottages looted. A hundred voices told a tale of priests insulted, graves opened, holy relics profaned and altars stripped of their images. I was taken to see the house, with its roof ripped off, where lay unburied the body of Antonio Bussetto, a 70-year-old man killed because, being stone deaf, he had not been able to hear the soldiers' brutal demand for money.' The villagers later showed her a tree where another man had been stripped naked and battered to death for refusing to curse the Pope, instead crying 'Viva Pio Nono!' till he gave up the ghost. Cataloguing these and other atrocities some months later, Percoto was horrified, though probably not altogether surprised, to hear that the soldiers involved had received their share of decorations and promotions for their assiduity.

At least she herself was spared a visit from the Croats. Nugent, like his fellow generals, was a respecter of rank, and what would do to put the fear of God into the peasantry was not appropriate behaviour towards countesses, whatever their politics. Less fortunate in the aftermath of Visco and Jalmicco was the painter Ippolito Caffi. Last of the great Venetian *vedutisti* in the tradition of Canaletto, Bellotto and Guardi, he had been based in Rome when the revolutions began, and immediately joined a brigade of volunteers from the Papal States marching north to fight for the cause. His plan was to head for his home town of Belluno, where he could enlist with the *crociati*. By 16 April Caffi, going by way of Venice, had got as far as Palmanova and found himself swept up in the action around Jalmicco. Taken prisoner by the Croats, he was stripped, tied to a beam and 'beaten like Christ at the column' until timely intervention by an officer saved him from a hanging. With other prisoners he was then marched northwards to Gorizia, spending one night in a cowshed and being spat on, insulted and pelted with excrement by villagers en route, while the landowners turned out in their carriages to watch.

Barefoot and half-naked, the captives reached Gorizia only to find a ferocious mob gathered around the bridge across the Isonzo into the main portion of the town and threatening to kill them. The twenty-three men were quickly herded into a nearby barracks, where news arrived next morning that Count Hartig, Metternich's military adviser on Italian affairs, now joining Nugent's army as political administrator of the recaptured province, had decided to free them, fearing that a rebel force from Udine was intending to do the same. Caffi swooned on hearing he was at liberty, but was carried to the house of a painter friend who helped him return to Venice armed with Hartig's safe-conduct. The attitude of ordinary people towards the prisoners and the cause they represented had not exactly been encouraging – the women, noted Caffi, were the worst – and the letter he wrote, describing his experiences, to the secretary of Rome's Società Artistica seems in some sense to have been a warning against naive expectations of patriotic peasantry yearning to cast off the Austrian yoke.

Nugent meanwhile had begun his march towards Udine, leaving Schwarzenberg to embark on the siege of Palmanova, an operation less simple than either of them at present imagined. The news of the army's advance took the Udinesi completely by surprise. It was all very well plastering the city with morale-boosting proclamations announcing to the townsfolk that God was with them and that Pius IX, 'the immortal pontiff, the regenerator of humanity, the liberator, has blessed the whole of Italy'. The reality was that defences inside or outside the ramparts were painfully inadequate to the task of resisting an Austrian bombardment. In desperation the citizens stuffed the town gates with barricades made of household furniture, pillows and mattresses, and littered the surrounding roads with various sorts of farm machinery to hold up the movement of mounted troops. The defence force itself was too small, numbering only 800 regular soldiers, commanded by Major Licurgo Zannini and Colonel Giovanni Battista Cavedalis, whose brief had originally been to recruit and coordinate the activity of the various civic-guard units throughout Friuli. Udine's own guard of 1,500 men was as ready for action as it would ever be, but they were poorly armed and the government in Venice had failed, as in similar cases, to send weapons and ammunition when asked.

Neither these nor the regulars were destined to see any sort of action. Having brought his guns within reach of the city, Nugent began a steady bombardment, kept up throughout the following day. During the night panic gripped the townsfolk when a madman, managing to get hold of a pistol, rampaged through the streets killing or wounding several passers-by. The next morning, 22 April, happened to be Good Friday, and when Nugent, probably feeling he had done enough, sent an emissary to begin negotiations, the defenders professed unwillingness to enter into any arrangements on this of all days, noted for its bad luck. With a first feeler put out and rejected, an entire delegation of officers, led by a Colonel Smola, now approached the walls. Thinking that this marked the opening of a general assault, the soldiers on the ramparts opened fire. A captain was killed, Smola was hit in the foot, and a stray bullet succeeded in knocking out a lieutenant who happened to be Nugent's son. Smola picked himself up, however, and was finally allowed to hobble into the city. After an hour or so he returned, accompanied by Udine's archbishop Zaccaria Bricito, who had urged surrender to avoid unnecessary bloodshed.

Bricito, a saintly scholar and poet much loved in his diocese, was later savaged by Niccolò Tommaseo for 'betraying' the city to the Austrians, but most of those present on the occasion ruefully acknowledged the wisdom of yielding in the face of an outright attack, which could not have been adequately resisted for more than a few hours. Nugent, on the other hand, was not inclined to complacency with Udine in his grasp. He and Hartig saw their task as essentially one of conciliation once the Veneto had been recovered. At this stage the Austrian government appears to have believed that negotiation with Piedmont, leading to a forfeiture of the Lombard province, was more or less inevitable. Any damage-limitation exercise for the sake of hanging on to Venetia must therefore involve some sort of pledge to reform the political infrastructure and make liberal concessions wherever opportune. While still in Gorizia, Nugent and another government official, Count Marzani, with Hartig's later approval, had drawn up a convention document designed to coax the Italians into peaceful surrender. Its promises included a blanket amnesty, abolition of the poll tax, reduction of salt duty, more powers for provincial congregations once these were reinstated, and greater freedom in the deployment of local government finance. Hartig's role, in the wake of Nugent's reconquest, would be that of magnanimous proconsul spreading the blessings of peace.

The provisional government of Venice was in no mood to trust these Habsburg olive branches. Losing Udine so swiftly served to underline those failures of preparedness which La Marmora and the defence committees of other towns had complained of in previous weeks. To believe that Nugent would dawdle around Palmanova was a ludicrous miscalculation, while the inadequate or non-existent arrangements made for the guarding of bridges and major roads had revealed a fatal misjudgement of defence priorities. It was true that the people of Friuli were notorious for being stubborn, headstrong and unwilling to obey orders, added to which the spirit of rivalry and *campanilismo* among the various urban communities made it difficult to coordinate a proper resistance movement throughout the region. The situation was not helped, on the other hand, by the sort of gung-ho propaganda articles currently appearing in the newly liberated Venetian press, in which the *Gazzetta di Venezia* could confidently declare that the alpine passes were being energetically defended, that Nugent's forces numbered only 5,000 men 'with little stomach for a fight', that Trieste was about to fall into the hands of a regiment of Dalmatian patriots, or that General Zucchi had vowed to bury himself beneath the walls of Palmanova rather than surrender.

Zucchi had done no such thing. Admirable as his decision was to tough it out against Schwarzenberg's siege-train, he had not endeared himself either to the provisional government or to certain of his subordinate officers. Before the Austrian army arrived, he refused to acknowledge the authority and legality of the new Venetian republic and would not go to Venice to confer with Manin, pooh-poohing the idea of a serious Habsburg counterattack from Gorizia. The volunteers he judged to be pretty much useless, and he antagonised their commander Colonel Conti, whose request for reinforcements during the fine show they put up at Visco and Jalmicco he unaccountably refused. After the two villages were looted and destroyed, Zucchi had the gall to blame Conti for the disaster, sneering at 'your national guards on whom you put so much store and I none at all'.

With the forces at Palmanova now pinned down, Udine in enemy hands and Nugent preparing to march on Belluno and Feltre, it was vital for Manin and the provisional government, if they wished to maintain convincing leadership of the confederated republic, to display an adequate grasp of the situation and offer something more like a firm response. Manin was under pressure not just militarily but politically besides. Inevitable comparisons offered themselves with Milan, a city which found itself in exactly the same condition as Venice, having thrown out the Austrians and set up its own administration. With a Piedmontese army in control of Lombardy, the absorption of the province and its capital into Charles Albert's kingdom seemed to many a Milanese a desirable or otherwise unavoidable option. Sceptical voices like those of Carlo Cattaneo were overwhelmed by the predominant view, upheld among the largely aristocratic municipality led by Count Gabrio Casati, that fusion with Piedmont was altogether preferable to existence as an independent republic, with the vague threats of socialism, communism, sans-culottes and egalitarians which such a political dispensation must imply. A nobility is pointless without a sovereign, as Cattaneo doubtless realised when, on the last of the *Cinque Giornate*, he heard that a formal appeal for assistance had been sent to Charles Albert. Couldn't they bear, he angrily remonstrated with Casati and his supporters, to be their own masters for once in their lives?

Aristocrats played a fairly small part in the new Venetian government. Though many of the old *Libro d'Oro* families were deeply patriotic and their womenfolk had braved Austrian censure and arrest for taking up collections for the Milanese when news of the *Cinque Giornate* arrived, Manin's administration was largely middle-class and theoretically better equipped to cope with more democratic political structures. Added to which, Venice possessed – as Milan, with its memories of tyrannical Visconti and Sforza dukes, followed by Spanish kings and Austrian emperors, emphatically did not – a long and proud republican heritage. Certainly La Serenissima had never existed by popular suffrage, but the central principle of its ruling oligarchy was that of power conferred by election, however limited the voting rights. The Doge had been a figurehead, appointed through a complex psephological process, not a despot ruling by hereditary right.

When the Piedmontese envoy to Venice, Lazzaro Rebizzo, arrived in the city on 12 April he delivered his message in carefully chosen terms. His liberal credentials were, after all, sound enough. He was known to be on the files of the Milanese police, he was acquainted with the exiled propagandist Cristina Belgiojoso, there were political links with the reforming statesman Camillo Benso di Cavour and, most advantageous of all, he was a friend of Daniele Manin. With him he brought a letter from the Foreign Minister Lorenzo Pareto conveying the King's congratulations and holding out the offer of 'such material assistance as may be needed for the achievement of Italy's complete independence – assistance and friendship which, to use Charles Albert's sublime expression, a brother owes to a brother or a friend to a friend'. Manin was under no illusions as to what this must mean. Shadowing Rebizzo was another diplomat, Ponzio Vaglia, whose task was to sound out opinion in the Veneto as to possible fusion with Piedmont and report independently to Turin, while his fellow emissary was ingratiating himself with members of the provisional government. Charles Albert's star meanwhile appeared to be in the ascendant. Those who mistrusted his intentions, such as Manin and Tommaseo, needed to manoeuvre carefully if the republic was to maintain its autonomous identity in the face of a gathering enthusiasm for an enlarged northern Italian kingdom extending from the Adriatic to the Gulf of Genoa and from the Alps to the Po.

Rebizzo, despite his friendship with Manin, was instantly conscious of hostility in official circles to any idea of a closer link with Piedmont. When he put forward the notion of a unified state which should include Lombardy, Liguria and the Veneto, he was 'listened to as if I had been speaking in German'. He was as unimpressed as La Marmora with the state of Venetian defences and saw Manin's republic, from its very inception, simply as a device for holding on to popular allegiance at any price. 'The sole means available to the Dictator,' he noted, 'for arousing the populace, a means whose considerable success could be judged by its effect, was to cry "Viva San Marco!"' Manin was not yet a dictator, nor could he allow himself to be seen as such, but Rebizzo's terminology here shows an alertness to political straws in the wind as regarded his friend's ability to harness the loyalty of ordinary Venetians.

No sympathy whatever towards fusion was likely to come from Niccolò Tommaseo. His unshakeable confidence in Pope Pius as the destined saviour of Italy meant that he had nothing but contempt for Charles Albert, as somebody whose seemingly heroic intervention was little better than a calculated exercise in land-grabbing. When Rebizzo tried to invoke the good offices of a mutual friend, Cristina Belgiojoso, to patch up their differences, her intervention was unsuccessful against Tommaseo's intransigence. To her letter he added his own description of Rebizzo, 'a limping Genoese, an affable fellow, who came to Venice to prepare the way for Charles Albert. His gift was for poking his nose in everywhere, offering a demonstration, in all honesty not specially agreeable, of what Piedmont had to offer us.'

In this mood of reluctance and distaste, the provisional government nevertheless decided to send representatives to Charles Albert's headquarters. On 9 April, the day after the battle of Goito, Count Giovanni Cittadella of Padua and the Venetian lawyer Bartolomeo Benvenuti arrived in the Piedmontese camp. Their original brief seems to have been merely that of offering a bland acknowledgement of the King's friendly intentions, but under no circumstances to suggest that he might consider entering the Veneto at the head of his army. The news of Goito changed all this, and Cittadella was now concerned to sound out the possibility, if not of direct intervention, then of practical armed assistance against the expected movement of Nugent's forces from Gorizia. His report to the government, dispatched on 14 April, was not encouraging. Charles Albert made all the right noises about coming to aid his 'brothers' and the cause of Italian independence, but clearly disliked the very idea of a republic, a feeling shared by his ministers, generals and soldiers. The Secretary for War, Antonio Franzini, made it brutally clear that the provisional government could expect help only in return for political concessions, which must surely end in the absorption of Venice and its province into an enlarged kingdom of Piedmont with Milan as its administrative centre.

This formula, whatever acceptance it might find in Turin, was obviously not going to appeal to the Venetians. Their city's pride had been bruised enough during recent decades by its deliberate downgrading in favour of Trieste, and though there were patriotic sympathies aplenty towards the brave Milanese who had trounced Radetzky, Venice would be reluctant to oblige them by yielding precedence as a potential capital of the new state, or at least as a metropolis with equal claims to importance both commercial and historical. The council of ministers in any case decided that the whole issue must be left on hold for the time being, just as they had accepted (or been made to accept) Manin's previous decision to shelve the business of defining the republic's constitutional profile and postpone the convening of an assembly until the Austrian threat had been adequately dealt with. A new fault-line was starting to trace itself between those such as Jacopo Castelli and Pietro Paleocapa, who regarded fusion with Piedmont as inevitable, and a more intransigent republicanism espoused by Manin and Tommaseo. From the outset the fusionist camp was able to count on an increasing groundswell of support from the provincial towns, by now growing disheartened with the mixture of arrogance and disregard which had characterised the Venetian government's practical response to their initial gestures of fraternal bonding. Cities like Treviso and Padua, whose freedoms had been curtailed in the past by Venice's resistless empire-building during the late Middle Ages, scented a disagreeable whiff of La Serenissima's old domineering ways and were unimpressed by the measures – or lack of them – taken to stem the Austrian military advance. Local aristocracies and business communities became uneasy, what was more, at restlessness among the urban working class and agricultural labourers, which seemed to smack of Jacobinism and promised the sort of violent confrontations taking place contemporaneously in France and Germany.

Fears of this sort of unrest becoming universal were calculated to broaden the fusionist constituency. News of Udine's fall and Nugent's movement westwards towards the valley of the Tagliamento, with the obvious aim of seizing Pordenone, Ceneda and Belluno, only strengthened the case for intervention by Charles Albert in exchange for a surrender of autonomy. There were plenty of republicans in the Veneto, but their cause was being steadily undermined by 'Albertist' proselytes, equipped with money and the sort of social influence that counted for so much in the small-town Italy of the nineteenth century. The King, however, was not prepared to budge. Though Goito had not been followed up and Radetzky, from within Verona's walls, was still concerned to husband his resources and avoid giving battle to the Piedmontese for the time being, most of Charles Albert's army had now crossed the Mincio into eastern Lombardy. The prizes ahead of them were the big fortresses of the Quadrilateral, more especially Peschiera, on the shores of Lake Garda, and Mantua, under its pitiless and cunning commandant Karl von Gorzkowski. It was remotely possible that once these had fallen and Charles Albert had launched an all-out assault on Verona, Nugent's advance might be mopped up before he got too close to Treviso and Vicenza. A less distant and altogether more unpleasant likelihood was that the King might after all prefer, out of respect for Habsburg legitimacy, to eat merely the Lombard leaf of the Italian artichoke, leaving Venice and the Veneto as a scrap of empire to salve Austrian pride during any ensuing peace negotiations.

Somebody had to stop Nugent before he got to Radetzky, but the Field Marshal himself had not exactly been idle while awaiting his hour to strike. The day after the battle of Goito a Lombard volunteer force descended on the village of Castelnuovo, between Verona and the lake, and captured an Austrian foraging party, including many Italians who willingly joined the patriot cause. Wary of reprisals, the renegades warned their new comrades to hide in the hills, but the commander, the Genoese patriot Agostino Noaro, refused and ordered his men to commandeer carts and supplies. The atmosphere grew so tense that the village's provisional government ran off in fright, one of them contriving to send a message to headquarters at Verona. Two days later a disproportionately large force of 4,000 Austrian troops, led by Prince Thurn und Taxis, with six cannon, arrived before the village and immediately launched an attack. The volunteers put up a strong defence, but were forced to withdraw into the nearest houses and clamber onto the roofs. The infantry were ordered to fix bayonets and flush out the defenders, with additional help from grenades. Two further columns closed in on the village from either side to prevent the *crociati* from escaping. Cannon-fire meanwhile silenced the church bells.

The episode was as shameful to Austrian arms as the scenes which later horrified Caterina Percoto. After dealing with the volunteers, the troops – principally Bohemians, Tyrolese and Hungarians – became trigger-happy and shot up the village, profaning the church and massacring more than forty unarmed villagers of either sex and all ages. One married couple were shot as they lay in bed, their corpses bayoneted and the bed itself set on fire. A ten-year-old boy, Michelangelo Mischi, had his head split open with a sabre. At the house of an apothecary named Cavattoni, the inhabitants, including several friends of the family, were dragged out and all sixteen people were made to undergo a ghastly parody of running the gauntlet, walking up a hill between jeering lines of soldiery. When Cavattoni's wife fell on her knees weeping and clutching the crucifix, she was thrust roughly aside as a madwoman. The others, reaching the top of the hill, were summarily shot. Once it was noted that a woman among them named Maria Rossi had merely fainted, the firing squad dragged her to their captain Sabin Mauller, who promptly raped her. Other soldiers burst into the church, murdered those gathered there for safety and marched off with holy pictures and candelabra after desecrating the altar and flinging the consecrated host on the floor. When the villagers who had managed to flee slipped back to their homes, they found two women still alive inside a cellar, one of whom had gone mad with fright.

Thurn und Taxis later maintained that he was simply trying to dislodge the rebels as effectively as he knew how. His fellow general Karl von Schönhals blamed local priests for stirring up the villagers to rebellion. What events at Castelnuovo revealed was that Radetzky and the Austrian high command meant business and that the retreat to Verona was exactly the sort of *reculer pour mieux sauter* operation wise observers must have suspected it to be. Yet if the Venetian provisional government learned, during the next ten days, that it could not depend on Charles Albert as a disinterested saviour, then the prospect of an alternative suddenly and dramatically started to emerge. For by the middle of April a different Italian army altogether stood poised to cross the Po and present itself as the Veneto's longed-for deliverer.

CHAPTER 6

'VENGO CORRENDO!'

POPE PIUS IX HAD WATCHED with mounting concern the events unfolding in Piedmont and Lombardy-Venetia during early spring. He could scarcely be unaware of the role in which many Italians were now eager to cast him, that of numinous leader at the head of a crusade against the Habsburg cohorts. Conscious, from the very outset of his papacy, of the dignity and universal significance of his office, he was nevertheless unprepared to assume the character of a holy warrior. History indeed had its share of warlike popes. Neither Rodrigo Borgia, who became Alexander VI in 1492, nor Giuliano della Rovere, following him in 1503 as Julius II, was the type of man likely to appeal to their fastidious nineteenth-century successor, yet the importance to Pius of his temporal sovereignty made his possession of an independent army into a major political issue. He would not emulate the two Renaissance pontiffs by donning a breastplate, mounting a charger or directing a siege, he had not yet openly echoed Julius's famous cry of 'Away with the barbarians!', but his command of a fighting force now took on more than nominal significance.

The papal army before 1846 had been little better than a small, badly organised internal defence corps. Apart from the Swiss Guard, whose officers knew a thing or two about discipline and efficiency, the 7,000-strong force could not have entered the field with any credibility against an invader. It was barely fifty years, after all, since it had been a pushover for battalions of the French Directoire during Napoleon's successful campaign against the Austrians. When Pius IX became Pope, reform of the army was not among his priorities, but the Consulta, the assembly he set up to offer advice to his ministers, made this its main concern in

the light of a developing emergency, especially following Austria's reinforcement of its garrisons during the winter of 1847-8. Officers were
therefore summoned from Piedmont to take the various regiments in
hand, with the object, at least as far as Pius understood it, of presenting
an effective resistance to any imperial show of force which should violate
the sacred independence of the Papal States. Whatever liberals may have
hoped or believed, he had no intention of declaring war on his fellow
sovereigns. His broader sympathies lay at this stage with the patriots –
he had, after all, openly invoked God's blessing on Italy and was known
to favour the idea of an Italian federation – but whatever nation emerged
from the conflict would have to face the truth, that its political destiny
was less important to Pius than the sanctity of that God-given trust
committed to him as a ruler both spiritual and temporal.

The new commander of the papal forces was not inclined, however,
to see himself as merely the overseer of some glorified territorial army or
home guard. Though Giovanni Durando came, like his friend Massimo
d'Azeglio, from one of those Piedmontese clans whose children were
brought up in an unbending tradition of service to Church and king, his
family was distinctly liberal in its politics. One of his brothers had been
imprisoned for belonging to a secret society; another, while living abroad,
had written a controversial book on Italian nationality, which a third
sibling, who happened to be a royal chaplain, had given to Charles Albert
to read at proof stage. The monarch, just then rather nervous of Austrian
opinion, warned the author not to return home for a while, but hinted
at his own approval of the work, as did Giuseppe Mazzini, who sent a
detailed critique.

When Durando took up his Roman command in 1848, he was forty-
four, a seasoned campaigner who had served in the civil war in Portugal
between the reactionary Dom Miguel and his cousin Dom Pedro, had
then joined the army of Queen Cristina of Spain to fight against the legitimist claimant Don Carlos, before returning to the Piedmontese service.
The political climate in which he found himself when summoned to
Rome was increasingly influenced by the presence of other officers from
Charles Albert's army, including Massimo d'Azeglio. Their fighting talk
encouraged an idea that the new papal army would eventually be given
its proper role in the patriotic struggle. By the end of March its ranks
had been swelled by *crociati* brigades from all over the Papal States, especially Romagna, that nursery of rebels, which had not forgotten the brutal
reprisals against the failed revolt in Rimini three years previously. In addition came four civic-guard brigades from Rome and Bologna, a substantial corps of student volunteers and two further units of around 600 men

each, the whole division under the command of Andrea Ferrari, an elderly Napoleonic veteran who had seen service in the French Foreign Legion and against the Carlists in Spain.

The mood of the entire force, its two divisions amounting in all to 18,000, was fervently enthusiastic, but by the end of March Pius's orders were only that they should march to the frontier along the River Po and prepare to defend themselves if attacked. Such instructions put the senior officers in an impossible position, since it was almost inevitable that the men under their command would wish to cross the river and enter the theatre of war as fully involved combatants. On the 24th Durando's division set out on its northward march, followed the next day by Ferrari and his brigades. There was no love lost between the two generals. Durando had given Ferrari the volunteer battalions in an implicit attempt to downgrade him, and Ferrari, a Neapolitan, despised Durando as an ingratiating Piedmontese whose leadership lacked any practical merit when it came to managing a serious military campaign. This mutual mistrust was not a good omen, any more than the disunity which developed almost at once between the army's professional sector, stiffened by its Piedmontese officers, and the *crociati*, badly equipped and insufficiently trained to withstand attack from a disciplined enemy. During the march there was every opportunity for Durando's officers to school their opposite numbers in Ferrari's division, but such vital consolidation of the army into a credible fighting force was simply neglected.

By the time the papal troops – *i papalini* – reached Bologna, Durando evidently felt that he was far enough from Pius and his ministers to adopt an altogether less cautious line on the issue of direct participation. On 5 April an extraordinary harangue was issued, in the guise of an order of the day, signed by Durando but actually written by Massimo d'Azeglio, attributing to the Pope 'the supreme argument of kings', namely armed force, as 'the only one that is righteous and possible'. Pius was threatening, claimed d'Azeglio without a shred of authority, to excommunicate the Austrians, who were 'enemies of God and of Italy', while Radetzky was 'waging war on the Cross of Christ', and any attack on them would be not merely patriotic but Christian. For that reason the soldiers were to wear crosses on their uniforms and their war cry was to be that of the Lombards who had joined the First Crusade in 1095: 'Dio lo vuole', 'God wills it'.

Pius was naturally outraged at this open usurpation of his authority. The customs union concluded with Tuscany and Piedmont in 1847 had been the first step in his project for a league of Italian states, an idea presented to Charles Albert by Giovanni Corboli Bussi, the clerical patriot dispatched on 10 April as Rome's special envoy to Piedmontese head-quarters. Neither the King nor his ministers particularly favoured the idea, feeling that it looked too much like a get-out device to free other Italian states from the responsibility of providing troops for the armed struggle, while leaving Piedmont to shoulder the burden of the actual fighting. At the same time Charles Albert himself was wary of any poten-tial challenge to his central role as champion of the patriot cause. The whole principle of 'l'Italia farà da sè' seemed to have been vindicated by Radetzky's withdrawal to Verona and the Piedmontese victory claimed at Goito. Durando's intemperate proclamation, appearing in all the news-papers at Bologna, where it was issued, made the proposed league even less likely, but its more serious effect was to frighten the Pope into believing that a veritable Pandora's box had been opened with the army's north-ward march. D'Azeglio, as author of the offending document, thought it a huge joke. 'Now, my noble priests, go and say that we are not to cross the Po!' The supreme pontiff, as far as he was concerned, had been a mere lever to manipulate the devout Charles Albert, and d'Azeglio's principal aim during his stay in Rome throughout the previous year was to promote Piedmont as an obvious leader of the national crusade appar-ently blessed by the Church. 'If Pius IX wishes it, if he consents to what public opinion is making of him, the Papacy will become the century's guiding force. Should he refuse, I cannot tell what may happen. Providence never offers such an opportunity more than once.' He could not, or would not, see how the gesture must prejudice Pius's position as Holy Father to several million Catholic Austrians as well as to their Italian co-religion-ists. In addition it had destroyed the trust which ought to have been taken for granted by the pontiff in his army's commander-in-chief. Henceforth the issue was not whether Durando, high-handed and disobedient as he now appeared, would cross the Po, but when.

The approach of a potential deliverer offered consolation to the Venetian provisional government kept waiting by Charles Albert and disappointed in its efforts to secure foreign aid. As soon as the regime was established, it had sent representatives to France and England to sound out the likelihood of practical support. Tommaseo's letters to these supposedly friendly powers, artfully phrased as they might be, were not calculated to do the business on their own. Going first to Paris, the envoys – Giacomo Nani and Angelo Zanardini – got little joy from the French Foreign Minister Alphonse de Lamartine when they visited him on 9 April. In the manner of politicians, he was glib and reassuring, but when, two days later, an order was issued permitting the Venetians to purchase a thousand rifles from the arsenals of Toulon, Montpellier and

Grenoble, the weapons were limited to rifles of a model rendered obsolete in 1840, and payment for them was allowed only in a currency acceptable to the French national bank. Thus baffled – as Lamartine perhaps intended they should be – Nani and Zanardini crossed over to London, where the British foreign secretary Viscount Palmerston received them at eleven o'clock in the evening and stated the government's position candidly enough as being that of an interested spectator. There was no likelihood of an armed intervention against the Italians, given the strength of British public opinion, at this stage, in favour of the rebel governments in the various states. Venice must remember, nevertheless, that Great Britain was officially Austria's ally, according to compacts made at the Congress of Vienna, and Palmerston, his low opinion of the Metternich system notwithstanding, was keen to preserve the alliance as a counterpoise against the French. In the light of this neutrality, the envoys were wryly amused by his hint that though the British government could not officially supply them with arms, they might apply to a private contractor. 'He suggested Birmingham; see how the mercantile spirit reveals itself; in England, what a statesman cannot openly do for political reasons he allows himself to do in the interests of commerce.'

If European powers beyond the Alps would not ride to Venice's rescue, the papal army advancing so purposefully towards the Po looked as if it might do the business. At the provisional government's request, Durando agreed to cross the river as long as Venice was prepared to defray the expenses of the campaign. It was a reasonable enough condition, if not on the surface distinguished by a spirit of patriotic self-sacrifice, since the General must have realised that Rome itself, in the wake of his proclamation, would hardly be willing to fund any unauthorised expedition. Together with the necessary money, Manin sent him a letter pointing out the implied insult to the brave Friulans if the defensive line along the River Isonzo were to be abandoned. By doing so, 'we should cause Europe to say, or to suppose, that in the midst of this memorable Italian movement there is something lacking, namely the correspondence of wishes with intentions, and that where promised aid is most needed, it is precisely this spot at which it is most lacking'. Durando would have good reason to remember this final admonition in the weeks to come. The letter was dated 11 April, and it took him another ten days before he got his divisions across the river. Even then they were directed immediately to the Piedmontese camp at Ostiglia, at the junction of the main roads to Mantua and Verona, rather than moving on into the Veneto to block General Nugent's advance.

This had been the idea of La Marmora, still charged with organising

the Venetian republic's land defences, his pessimism at Vicenza notwithstanding. Charles Albert, to whom, as Piedmontese subjects, both he and
Durando owed allegiance, had different notions, and was determined that
for the time being the papal brigades should support his projected march
on Verona, whenever this might take place. The Austrians had meanwhile
reinforced the garrison of the fortress at Legnago, commanding the road
south along the Adige towards Rovigo, so that Durando had felt it necessary to station at least part of his force between these two places at Badia
Polesine, to head off foraging raids of the kind Radetzky's men had been
making further north. General Ferrari was still at Bologna, waiting with
his volunteers for instructions that Durando was mystifyingly reluctant
to transmit. There had been no reply to Ferrari's suggestion that the two
divisions should be reorganised, allowing the inexperienced volunteers to
be mixed in with the professional element so as to give each regiment an
adequate framework as a practical combat unit. In a second letter, Ferrari
repeated this request, adding a baleful warning that if such a measure
were not adopted, the pair of them, as officers commanding, must bear
the blame for whatever went wrong.

In this unpromising atmosphere the news arrived of Udine's surrender
to Nugent. There could surely be no suggestion of Charles Albert tempor-
ising any further on the issue of sending troops into Friuli. Manin now
addressed a genuine cry for help to Piedmont's Minister for War, Baron
Antonio Franzini. 'In the name of Italy, of humanity, of justice, we demand
immediate assistance.' The letter was fraught with warning as to the likely
effect on public confidence of any further delay, especially in the battle
zones, and the writer took pains to allay Charles Albert's suspicion of
Venetian republicanism. This would not be the last time that the provisional government came face to face with the reality of the King, its
supposed ally, as a chronic ditherer, endlessly mulling over the various
aspects of a political or military problem rather than dealing with it in
the nick of time. The fact was that nobody at Piedmontese headquarters
had honestly believed that Austria could possibly scramble together such
a vast reserve force as Nugent's, let alone in little more than a fortnight.
To make matters worse, La Marmora, supposed to be preparing a suitable resistance to any Austrian advance on Pordenone, had made no movement of any kind and was roundly rebuked by Manin for his lack of
confidence in the volunteers. 'Fill them with the courage which inspires
you yourself, and lead them into battle. Whatever the outcome, your
honour is not likely to suffer, but that of Friuli and many other places
will be tainted by this present inactivity. You are aware of what is currently
being said on the subject. It is important to avoid providing a pretext for

Emperor Ferdinand I of Austria, Venice's sovereign ruler from 1835 to 1848. A shy, sensitive man unsuited to his role, but not the complete imbecile his critics liked to claim.

(*Above left*) Baroness Anna Marsich Bandiera, from a contemporary photograph.
(*Above right*) Emilio Bandiera (*Below left*) Attilio Bandiera.
(*Below right*) Domenico Moro. The engraved portrait, like those of the Bandiera brothers, was
made from a sketch by their companion Giuseppe Pacchione.

Leaders of the Venetian revolt
(*Right*) Daniele Manin
(*Below*) Niccolò Tommaseo

Manin's triumphal entry into Piazza San Marco, from a painting by the Venetian artist Alvise Nani, 1876.

Manin and his son Giorgio saying farewell to Teresa and Emilia before leaving for the Arsenal. Giorgio is wearing the 'Ernaini'-style hat favoured by the revolutionaries.

The Wounded Volunteer, drawing by Giulia Targione Tozzetti for a special album presented by patriotic Florentine women to the Piedmontese politician Vincenzo Gioberti, 1848.

Alessandro Gavazzi

Ugo Bassi,
from a drawing by Angelo Lamma.

Bassi and Gavazzi preaching in Piazza San Marco.

Austrian Generals
(*Above left*) Laval Nugent (*Above right*) Karl Culoz
(*Below left*) Constant D'Aspre (*Below right*) Ludwig von Welden

The War-Leaders
(*Above*) King Charles Albert of Piedmont
(*Right*) Fieldmarshal Radetzky

such opinions.' Even when La Marmora managed to destroy the bridge over the flooded River Tagliamento, which Nugent's troops were bound to cross, the General had a new one hastily thrown together from scaffolding being used to repair a nearby church, and the army got over in three days. With horrifying ease and rapidity, Friuli, on whose grit and resolve in withholding any Austrian invasion the patriots had hoped to rely, seemed to be falling before the conquerors without the least show of any fight.

Finally, on 24 April, Charles Albert agreed to release the necessary troops – not Piedmontese, it was noted, but Durando's papal brigades – and the General now busied himself with trying to move his men as quickly as possible down the Po by boat to Polesella, and thence to Rovigo, marching them north via Treviso and directly into the Friulan war zone. Treviso was now a key rallying point for the various volunteer forces. Ferrari's division based itself there, alongside several hundred Venetians, a battalion from Belluno, 150 Sicilians led by Colonel Giuseppe La Masa, civic-guard units from as far away as Ascoli Piceno in the Marche region of the Papal States, and an international brigade composed of French, Polish and Italian *crociati* which had found its way from Marseilles. In this last respect the liberation struggle of 1848 was both the Spanish Civil War *avant la lettre* and a vigorous echo of the Greek independence movement in the 1820s. Idealism drew foreign volunteers from every conceivable background. Some were professional soldiers like the widely respected Colonel Forbes,* a Briton who later served under Garibaldi. Many were bruised and hardened by their own nationalist uprising, such as the Pole Onufry Korzeniowski, whose legion of exiles, having tried and failed to return to Poland earlier in the year, now offered to fight for the Italian cause. When Durando's regiments arrived, the combined number was almost more than a town like Treviso could sensibly cope with – 8,000 regular troops, a further 3,000 volunteers commanded by Duke Lante di Montefeltro, and a brigade of university students from Bologna led by one of their professors.

Theoretically, given that the size of these combined forces more or less equalled his own, Nugent should have faced a difficult task in his planned move westward to the River Piave, and thence down into the Veneto plain. He had been assisted, however, from the very start of his advance

---

* Angelo Giacomelli, serving alongside '*il prode colonello Forbes*' in the defence of Treviso, describes him as 'devoted to the Italian cause like the best of us, a courageous and most honest soldier'. He apparently wore a white top-hat and had a notoriously short temper.

from Gorizia by the hopeless state of his enemy's military intelligence. La Marmora was already being criticised for his failure to establish proper liaison with local communities, and Durando was to suffer similar accusations. It would not have been difficult to organise information as to troop movements in the area or rough estimates of numbers being mobilised for a given operation. In fact nothing more was undertaken than the simplest *ad hoc* reconnaissance, thus allowing the Austrians to take full advantage of the element of surprise in their day-to-day marches. Not even the volunteers' destruction of a wooden bridge across the Piave north of Belluno was able to deter Nugent's resolve. Belluno itself was not as well garrisoned as Udine had been, and when the local defence committee realised that the Austrians merely planned to move down the east bank of the river and attack the city head-on from across its own bridge, made of stone, they yielded after the briefest of bombardments. On 7 May a brigade led by General Culoz (earlier so critical of Zichy's surrender of Venice) hurried south to seize Feltre, whose defenders had foolishly assured Durando and Ferrari that they would hold it till their last drop of blood. Choosing to believe this, the two generals concentrated their troops along the valley below, making it easy enough for Culoz to pounce from the heights behind the town, which gave in without even a first drop of blood being shed for the holy cause.

Had he chosen, Nugent could now have outflanked the *papalini* altogether by moving still further westwards and dropping down into the Veneto along the road that followed the River Brenta to Bassano. Instead he preferred to advance due south towards Treviso, a far more important strategic prize than any of the towns reoccupied so far, a place whose capture would secure control of the northern Veneto, threatening Vicenza and Padua and cutting off a major supply line to Venice itself. The old Irishman had a personal reason for choosing this route. News had reached him that his daughter, Countess Dorsee, happening to be in the city with her husband at the time of the March revolutions, had been captured while trying to escape and was likely to be used as a prime hostage in any possible negotiation. It might be feasible therefore to thrust aside the papal army and fall on Treviso with his large force relatively intact, once again making use of the swiftness and surprise that had served him so well in Friuli.

He was helped furthermore by Durando's mistaken idea that Bassano, rather than Treviso, would be the object of the main Austrian attack, and by the confusion which appeared to govern the movements of the two papal divisions. Ferrari, having arrived with his volunteers, had initially been requested by Treviso's provisional government to march up to

Primolano on the road from Feltre, to block Nugent's likely advance and move northwards in order to link up with Durando. The two commanders met at Pederobba, on the east bank of the Piave. Here Ferrari renewed his demand for professional battalions to stiffen his volunteers' resolve, and on this occasion Durando grudgingly conceded him a small squadron of dragoons and five cannon, before setting off towards Bassano to meet what he presumed would be the principal Austrian thrust into the Veneto plain. A successful attack by Bassanesi volunteers on a party of reconnoitring Croats had further convinced him that Nugent's main force could surely not be far behind. The townsfolk meanwhile looked forward excitedly to a major engagement in which, if all went well, the Habsburg reserves would be seen off for good and all, with Radetzky left unsupported down in Verona.

A battle there certainly was, and decisive it turned out to be, but the time and place were emphatically not of Durando's choosing. It was Ferrari's brigades, unschooled and inexperienced as they mostly were, who now had to face the full impact of the Austrian advance guard. Late in the afternoon of 8 May some 300 papal volunteers encountered more than 1,000 enemy troops at Onigo, just south of the commanders' meeting point on the Piave the previous morning. Though the Austrians retired under the Italian fusillade, Ferrari at once thought to inform Durando, while not at this point summoning reinforcements. The volunteers had done well to hold back such a substantial force, supported as it was by rockets and a platoon of mounted lancers, but an Austrian night raid flushed them out of strong positions on the hillside above the Treviso road, and by ten o'clock that evening they were concentrated further down the valley, around the village of Cornuda. Ferrari brought up further battalions from Montebelluna, where his division was based, telling Durando that he meant to hold out, on the assumption that his commander-in-chief would move instantly to support him. The whole force at Cornuda was not much larger than 2,300 men, with infantry positioned along the slopes and two squadrons of cavalry in the fields below.

Because the messenger had at all costs to avoid Austrian pickets by taking a long way round, Durando did not receive Ferrari's first message until six o'clock the following morning. Still believing the main attack was coming down the Brenta valley, rather than from further east along the Piave, he answered that he was moving to Crespano, more or less halfway between the two rivers, to mount an assault on the enemy's left flank. Though the news would hearten Ferrari's men, it was to be followed by a second note indicating that Durando meant to return to Bassano that evening. By the time it arrived at Cornuda, the battle had well and truly begun.

Around dawn on the morning of 9 May, an Austrian force of some 2,700, with six guns and four rockets, under the command of General Culoz, had advanced on Ferrari's positions around the village. The Italians met the attack with spirit, and for almost six hours the enemy failed to make any headway against their steady fire. By midday however, it was imperative that some sort of back-up should arrive with Durando's presumed eastward march along the road from Bassano. Ferrari had hurriedly scribbled a second message to Durando, urging him to move as quickly as possible. The Austrians meanwhile had called up a fresh battalion, and though the *papalini* had confounded all expectations by their courage under fire, everything now depended on the arrival of re-inforcements. So as to play for time and bring up his artillery, Ferrari tried the diversionary tactic of sending in the cavalry to clear the main road along the valley. What ensued was a sort of 'Charge of the Light Brigade' in miniature. Fifty papal dragoons now fell on the Austrian line, easily scattering it and riding in pursuit of the lancers, but just when Culoz's force seemed to be feeling the full impact of this manoeuvre, a well-placed Austrian grenade was lobbed into the midst of the charging cavalry. Domenico Barnaba, a volunteer from Udine, describes the resulting chaos. 'The terrified horses all bolted, and disorder made its sinister influence felt. Running off in every direction, they knocked down those who failed to get out of the way in time. Many of them, having thrown their riders, crashed into one another, trampling on the men who lay beneath. The artillery, amid such confusion, could not advance to take up its positions. So much noise was there that orders could not be heard, discipline was thrown to the winds and it became every man for himself.' Of the original squadron, just ten got out alive.

By now, as if to mock Ferrari's expectations still further, another message had arrived from Durando. It consisted of precisely two words – 'Vengo correndo!' meaning 'Coming at the double!' – yet throughout the after-noon there was no sign of a relief force on its way. Marshal Nugent himself had appeared among the Austrian lines to encourage his men, while two battalions from Prince Schwarzenberg's regiment moved up to bolster their advance and harass Ferrari's right flank. Around five in the afternoon the General realised that nobody was riding to his rescue, at the double or otherwise, his men were worn out and demoralised, ammu-nition was running low, and in a matter of hours the Habsburg force they continued to hold back so tenaciously had more than doubled its numbers. In good order, the papal brigade retreated to Montebelluna, with 140 men wounded and thirty dead. Mercifully the Austrians, though with a much smaller casualty list, did not choose, for the time being, to follow up the victory.

The battle of Cornuda gained a notoriety which made it one of the most hotly discussed actions of the entire war. Durando's failure to arrive as promised was to dog him for the rest of his career, even if his subsequent conduct meant that he was able to avoid any kind of official disgrace. In the inevitable apologia issued soon after the event, he spoke of 'my honour, too dishonestly torn to shreds' and protested that he could never have held on to what remained of Friuli with a mere 8,000 men. His deliberate strategy had been to capitalise on the local revolutionary spirit by marches and countermarches, thereby trying to convince the Austrians that a much larger division was in the field. He blamed everybody – the Piedmontese high command, Charles Albert, the War Minister Franzini, the Venetian provisional government for not supplying enough munitions, Nugent and Culoz for having too many soldiers – everybody, in short, except himself. His claim was that a patrol sent on from Crespano had arrived at Cornuda during a brief lull in the firing, from which its commander concluded that the battle was over. Almost as soon as the officer came back to report, a message from Bassano announced that 3,000 Austrians were moving down the Brenta from the direction of Feltre. This may have seemed an adequate pretext for leaving Ferrari in the lurch, yet why did Durando not inform him of the change of plan?

Durando had his defenders, among them loyal members of the Piedmontese military establishment writing the campaign history over succeeding decades. Massimo d'Azeglio, the faithful friend who declared that 'a braver man or one more active and steadfast never existed', willingly took up his fluent pen on the General's behalf, portraying him as the victim of intrigue, indiscipline and ignorance of the facts. For those who bore the brunt of the fighting at Cornuda, however, Durando was simply the leader who had abandoned and betrayed them at a moment when their hitherto untested mettle seemed about to furnish inspiration for patriots throughout Italy. Who could blame Ferrari for his aggrieved recriminations? 'I expected you to support me, since your note gave me to understand that you would arrive by midday at the latest. Whatever your motives, in the eyes of my men your conduct has been inexcusable, especially as you only had fourteen miles to cover in order to get there.'

Shattered and angry, the volunteers lost all semblance of discipline as they entered Montebelluna. Many chose not to halt there, moving on instead to the relative security of Treviso, where Ferrari led the rest of his division the day after the battle. The town was still thronged with Italian troops of all kinds, professional and irregular, and its government, led by the enterprising mayor Dr Giuseppe Olivi, was in close touch with Venice. In many respects this was a more 'democratic' administration than its Venetian counterpart, Olivi himself being already noted, as one member put it, 'for his more or less openly acknowledged Italian sentiments, enjoying public respect for his intellectual capacity, rectitude and integrity of character'. Sensibly the government had kept the Austrian garrison commander General Ludolf as a hostage and was indeed, just as Nugent feared, hanging onto the Marshal's daughter Countess Dorsee and her husband. They had been spotted trying to escape, using forged passports, by the patriot poet Giovanni Prati, who recalled having met them both in Padua, and were now under house arrest in Treviso's Palazzo Pola.

Even before Cornuda, the Trevisans had looked askance at the papal army passing through the city on its way north. 'We realised,' commented one witness, 'that the presiding spirit in the organisation of these troops, as well as their general bearing, was not that of a corps adapted to warfare. It could scarcely have been asked of men brought up to say mass and sing vespers that they should appreciate the needs of soldiers and the finer points of military art.' The volunteers had made an especially bad impression, 'composed as they largely were of dubious individuals with sinister faces, dressed in odd-looking uniforms, some of which were nothing of the sort, given their variety of colours and fashions. Many of these people, who seemed to have broken out of gaol, lacking honour or discipline and disposed to every kind of excess, were a real rabble, simply hoping to reap personal advantage from the unsettled situation and going into battle to loot rather than rescue the motherland.' Small wonder that people were now quoting the distich 'Cinque soldati del Papa/Non valgono una rapa' – 'Five soldiers of the Pope/Aren't worth a radish'. Some of those Ferrari had left behind in Treviso had further disgraced themselves by a murderous assault on three of the Duke of Modena's agents, discovered hiding in a cellar, 'livid with terror'. The Duke owned property in the Veneto, but he was no more popular than his recently dead father, who had succeeded in making Modena a byword for repression, and since the family was Habsburg, its servants were bound to fall under suspicion. Olivi and his fellow government members decided that they should be taken to Venice for questioning. As they were about to leave, a mob of *crociati*, crying 'Death to the traitors, death to the spies!', unhitched the horses, hauled the carriage into the nearby corn market, dragged the three men out and stabbed them to death, after which the corpses were hacked into pieces and the bleeding fragments paraded through the town.

Perhaps to vindicate the honour of his battalions, Ferrari ordered one more attack on the Austrians before they got too close to Treviso. On the morning of 11 May, Nugent had sent a proclamation to the citizens, counselling surrender rather than the horrors of a siege. In tones which echoed the Trevisans' shared spirit of patriotic defiance and optimism, the government answered, 'Whoever you may be, we must inform you that having secured our liberty, we are resolved to defend it with that courage and national sentiment which should inspire every citizen.' In the same mood, Ferrari led out four infantry battalions, a party of chasseurs and half a gun battery to confront Major-General Schulzig's brigade as it moved down the dead-straight road from the little *borgo* of Spresiano. The Italians marched 'to the sound of the mournful "Hymn of Pius IX"', and it must have been obvious to many of them that the expedition was a gamble with very long odds. Though they drove back the Austrian advance guard easily enough, they were unprepared for the murderous fire with which the roadsides suddenly blazed, from the rifles of the Croats closing in around them. The ditches at either edge were too deep for the papal troops to escape and, as at Cornuda, panicking cavalry set off a disorderly general scramble towards the gates of Treviso, a rout on which Schulzig did not deign to capitalise.

Disgusted by his men's cowardice, Ferrari handed over his command to General Alessandro Guidotti, leaving 3,600 men in his charge and retiring to Mestre with the rabble of broken volunteers he somehow still hoped to knock into sufficient shape to produce an adequate fighting force. Guidotti was a Bolognese aristocrat who had won battle honours in Napoleon's Spanish and Russian campaigns and had allied himself, after 1815, with every Italian patriot venture going, spending several years in exile as a result. Cornuda and the abortive campaign surrounding it, together with the collapse of morale among the *papalini*, had plunged him into a deep depression – exacerbated, it was later maintained, by an unhappy love affair with a female cousin. He was also said to be smarting from a reprimand received from Ferrari for not having properly defended one of the Piave bridges four days earlier. Whatever the truth, no sooner had Ferrari left Treviso than Guidotti in his turn passed on the command to a fellow officer, the Duke of Lante di Montefeltro. Lante was eager enough to exploit such fighting spirit as remained among the various brigades, and set about planning a series of sorties against the Austrians. On 13 May, Guidotti made one on his own account. Snatching a carbine from one of the defenders of the city's north gate, he walked out alone onto the road, ignoring the pleas and remonstrations of astonished onlookers. Some of them followed him a little way, until Austrian bullets drove them back. Angelo Giacomelli, a young member of the provisional government, describes what happened next. 'The general went on, unafraid, down the middle of the road. Scarcely had he advanced a short distance than a musket ball brought him to the ground. Apart from a slight trembling at the lips, he offered no further sign of life. The shot had caught him in the chest, at the very centre of the tricolour cross adorning his uniform. This worthy citizen and valiant soldier had for some time been sad and disheartened, and with good reason. He wished to die and had seized the first opportunity to do so.'

There was another possible cause for Guidotti's depression: the arrival of news which must certainly have increased his sense of isolation and was undoubtedly responsible for further undermining the papal soldiers' confidence in the validity of their current mission. For in Rome on 29 April Pope Pius IX had issued an extraordinary public statement, known according to the unique taxonomy of Vatican official pronouncements as an 'Allocution', setting out his principles in relation to the struggle against Austria and his anticipated role in this. The Allocution firmly repudiated not merely the suggestion that Pius should act as political leader of a federated Italy (as many devout patriots sincerely wished), but the expectation that he would declare war on Austria and such allies as she still possessed. His role, he declared, was to be that of a peacemaker and conciliator, and it was his hope that Italians would shun the cunning blandishments of journalists and republican agitators by remaining loyal to their various sovereigns.

The pressures on Pius to issue a statement of this kind had been increasing ever since Durando and d'Azeglio had produced their hot-headed order of the day on 5 April. He had never been convinced that Italians were ready to embrace free representative government along the British and French models for which revolutionaries throughout Europe were now in arms, yet as Lord Minto, still in Rome on his extended mission, observed, 'he seemed to accept his share of it very frankly, and with the desire to contribute as far as it is in his power to its success'. Pius was personally disappointed by the failure of his scheme for a league of Italian states, which the customs union with Piedmont and Tuscany had been intended to foreshadow, but which neither Charles Albert nor Grand Duke Leopold now seemed disposed to accept. The Grand Duke, what was more – full of excellent intentions for his subjects, but increasingly unnerved by the current crisis – had started pressing the Pope for moral support through a firmer line in the face of liberal demands. Pius was further concerned by the intolerable stresses placed on the Church through the reaction in various quarters to its traditional alignment with political conservatism and the old legitimist status quo. The Jesuit order, for example, had always been viewed by liberals as the shock troops of obscurantism, and the pontiff was much hurt by outrages against them in Genoa and Sardinia, as also by their recent expulsion from Naples. Still worse were the attacks aimed at him, from a different direction, by ordinary Austrians in Vienna, accusing him of being their enemy and having started the war, charges he was bent on refuting in the Allocution's opening paragraphs.

Pius had prepared his text at least a fortnight before it was officially issued. In the original version he had shown himself to be much more pro-Italian and less favourable to Austria, but his Secretary of State, Cardinal Giacomo Antonelli, whom many later saw as less of an ordinary eminence than an *éminence grise*, made sure that the wording of the Allocution was suitably toughened by the time of publication (though evidently with Pius's approval). The truth seems to be that the Pope, however much he genuinely desired an Italy for Italians, never meant to go as far as he was thought to have gone along the liberal path. His reforms, he claimed, were simply those his predecessor Gregory XVI should have carried out in response to hints from Metternich and Palmerston in their 1832 memorandum. What patriots failed to understand until too late was that for Pius the rights and interests of Holy Church must always take precedence over every other consideration. Constancy to this principle was, for many Catholics, the secret of Pius's greatness as a pontiff, yet it was this same exalted concept of his role as God's Vicar, nurtured by what appears to have been a strong personal vanity, which would ultimately destroy the papacy as an independent sovereign power.

The Allocution, as Pius might have predicted, went a considerable way towards doing exactly this. By salvaging the dignity and validity of his office as Holy Father of the worldwide Catholic ecclesia, Pius had sacrificed his role as spiritual leader of a national Italian Church. His agony after issuing the statement was, if anything, worse than it had been during the previous weeks. Rome erupted into ugly demonstrations while the pontiff sought vainly to clarify his position, the civic guard was on the verge of mutiny and several cardinals were threatened or insulted by the mob. What frightened many Romans, just as it later unmanned the *papalini* in the Veneto when tidings of the Allocution reached them, was the immediate political impact on the army of Pius's refusal to declare war. By thus disowning his soldiers, he had effectively denied them their status as belligerents, hence allowing them to be shot like common brigands if they were taken prisoner. Only by requesting Charles Albert, two days after the Allocution was issued, to take the brigades into his service was the Pope able to reverse this situation, but the damage was done and the shockwave of disillusion throughout Italy was profound. Pius's name continued in many places to be sounded with the accompanying 'Viva!', but this was now more of a reflex than an indication of any enduring hope that he might yet preside over a nation united under God.

Disheartened though the *papalini* were by the Allocution, they and everyone else in Treviso could take comfort from the news of Piedmontese victories over the Austrians, which had filtered in from the main theatre of war south and east of Lake Garda. On 28 April at Pastrengo, Charles Albert's army of 13,000 men overwhelmed a much smaller force under General Wocher, driving it back behind Radetzky's curtain of defences around Verona. Meanwhile the King had decided to blockade the great brick fortress of Peschiera, at the edge of the lake, one of the Quadrilateral's key strongholds. If captured, it would represent a prime trophy in military terms, and its fall must isolate Radetzky still further, making Nugent's decision to halt before Treviso that much more frustrating, given the possibility of a Piedmontese breakthrough into the very heart of that small square of Italian territory still controlled by Austrian arms.

There was more good news for the patriots when a fresh addition to their fighting force in the Veneto seemed about to arrive in the shape of a Neapolitan army, led by the elderly but indefatigable Guglielmo Pepe, a general with impeccable revolutionary credentials. Even before King Ferdinand was compelled, as the constitutional monarch he had now become, to declare war on Austria in early April, volunteer contingents had set off from Naples to join the Piedmontese invasion. Further parties of officers and men had already reached Venice and Treviso. Pepe's brief was to march the main body of the army, about 40,000 men, through the Papal States and up to the Po. Among them was the poet Alessandro Poerio, from a Calabrian family of fervently revolutionary aristocrats. For several years he had suffered from chronic hiccups, brought on, according to his doctor, by 'perverted functioning of the pneumogastric nerves'. The same physician saw this complaint as inherently psychosomatic, related to Poerio's naturally depressive temperament, and felt that the distractions offered by travel would probably clear it up. The poet saw his northern expedition as an ideal chance to combine patriotism with therapy. Writing to his friend Niccolò Tommaseo in Venice, he announced that 'I want to pay my debt to the motherland, hoping to heal or at least lessen my nervous illness, long declared incurable at Naples, and reaching a point at which I have become no good for anything.' Poerio was one of the comparatively small number who actually crossed the Po under

Pepe's command. Of the notional 'tens of thousands' expected to march, only about a quarter of the proposed Neapolitan force actually reached the frontiers of Lombardy-Venetia, and an even lower proportion followed Pepe to the defence of Venice. The importance of the news from Naples at this stage lay in its effect on the morale of both sides in the conflict. For the patriot brigades, it was heartening to feel that fresh legions of their Italian brothers were on the move in the name of the holy cause. Equally, it threatened to undermine any more complacent assumptions the Austrian high command might have made as to the smooth running of its current pincer operation by Nugent and Radetzky.

It was a Neapolitan officer already at Treviso whose exhortation had stiffened the resolve of both the citizens and the wavering *papalini*, who were contemplating a wholesale southward dash across the frontier. On the steps of the cathedral, he had harangued his fellow volunteers, proclaiming, 'The Neapolitans will never forsake an Italian city thus. Men, swear after me that you will die defending it!' The papal contingents shamefacedly moved to show their solidarity with the gallant southerners, and Lante di Montefeltro was thus able to lead an efficient sortie against the Austrians, well supported by artillery. Treviso was proving more of a stone in Nugent's shoe than he had foreseen. In addition, the reserve battalions he was expecting had not yet arrived. Durando and his reserve force were still at large in the countryside between Asolo and Castelfranco; several officers were urging the Marshal to ignore Treviso as a necessary evil and move on at once to relieve the pressure on Radetzky at Verona; while he himself was feeling the combined effects of age, exhaustion, an ongoing worry over the fate of Countess Dorsee, and the recurrence of an old head wound sustained during the Napoleonic Wars. By 18 May, when another letter arrived from Radetzky telling him to hurry up, Nugent had turned over his command to General Count Thun, who promptly moved off with the greater part of the army westwards along the old Roman road towards the crossing of the Brenta at Fontaniva, with the object of capturing the apparently ill-defended city of Vicenza.

In Venice meanwhile the prevailing mood was more upbeat than expected. The defeat at Cornuda had genuinely shocked many who believed, like the Modenese exile Antonio Morandi, that Nugent's army was simply a ragtag-and-bobtail force inadequately uniformed or provisioned. Yet the news from Treviso was encouraging; peevish old General Zucchi, still holding out in the fortress of Palmanova, had lured the Austrian besiegers close to the walls before battering them to pieces, killing or wounding some 800; and on 18 May the Neapolitan fleet, consisting of seven frigates and a brig under the command of Admiral Cosa, hove into view down the Canale di San Marco. Watching them was Alessandro Poerio, who had first received Venice's request for naval assistance in the shape of a letter from Niccolò Tommaseo, which he passed on to the new liberal government in Naples. Now he wrote excitedly to his mother: 'I cannot describe to you the spectacle of that magnificent Piazza San Marco. The square was packed with civic guards, young men dressed in Italian uniforms made of velvet and wearing plumed hats, as well as a joyful crowd sporting tricolour ribbons, cockades and crosses. Huge tricolour standards flew from the top of the three masts, while on the balconies of the Procuratie stood ladies dressed in the height of fashion. There was loud clapping of hands, a fluttering of handkerchiefs, and above all else, a genuine pleasure lighting up every face.'

This was the kind of festive occasion the Venetians adored, and the provisional government wisely encouraged any excuse for a celebration, so as to keep up the townsfolk's spirits. Patriotic victories were acclaimed, national holidays associated with the various foreign consulates (such as Queen Victoria's birthday and 4 July) were marked with parades, and even funerals offered a chance for uplifting addresses, with suitable emphasis on sacrifice for the motherland, and much flourishing of red, white and green. Most popular of all were the flag-blessing ceremonies of the various volunteer brigades. The banners themselves were sewn with much love and devotion by the womenfolk of Venice's patrician families. Such an activity had of course been proscribed under the Austrians, and several of the needlewomen may have remembered the case, surely not a solitary one, of Rosa Testi Rangoni, who in 1831 had been sentenced by the ducal government of Modena to perpetual confinement in a nunnery for having embroidered a patriotic flag. The public benediction of such standards was attended with the usual crowds and bands, and the priests who gave the blessings used every opportunity to harangue the crowd on behalf of the Italian cause, punctuated with answering 'Viva!'s for Pio Nono, 'the magnanimous Charles Albert', the civic guard, the motherland and the Virgin Mary. Even on seemingly routine religious festivals, the parochial clergy were unfailingly patriotic. At the exposition of a reliquary in the Frari containing Christ's blood, the preacher Don Giovanni Turotti told the congregation that just as Our Lord had shed his blood for mankind, so the martyrs of the revolution had given their lives 'to free you from your oppressors and restore the Motherland to your keeping'.

In spite of the Pope's Allocution, the Church, both inside Venice and beyond, numbered dozens of priests and not a few bishops whose ardent Italian sentiments were unlikely to be crushed by Pius's candle-snuffing attempt at salvaging his authority. The Patriarch, Cardinal Monico, it is true, was mistrusted by Manin and Tommaseo for his links with the political status quo ante. Manin used to refer to him as 'old friar-face', and Tommaseo, in a memoir of the revolution, sneeringly describes him as 'not lacking in alms but without the bowels of charity, a seminarist with a taste for theology and fine wine, fond of his evening card parties with Governor Palffy'. The Cardinal had nevertheless done his best to help engineer a peaceful transference of power during the March days, thereafter urging the Venetian clergy to back the revolution with spiritual comforts, parish collections or in certain cases even with the loan and purchase of weapons, though he drew the line at priests taking an active part in the fighting. In May, Tommaseo had received an anonymous plea from certain seminarists to be allowed to serve with the volunteers. It was impossible, so they claimed, to suppress their patriotic fervour, given the noble examples of it which surrounded them. 'We must all conquer or die for our country. To love, protect and rescue it from the enemy is the duty of every citizen. Great is our desire to fight in this most just of wars.' Tactfully Tommaseo passed the petition on to Monico, who assured him that it had certainly not originated in Venice and that in any case he could not possibly agree to priests engaging in military service.

Holy Church, for the Patriarch, represented not just an institution, but an immutable set of values, transcending all worldly political fluctuations and responding solely to the ordinances of its shepherd, the Pope. Monico's thoroughgoing conservatism in ecclesiastical affairs was rooted in a genuine horror of a world without religion, something that the pace of change in the nineteenth century looked like making a genuine possibility. While Pius IX was prepared to endorse the Italian revolutions in their opening phases, his faithful cardinal would broadly support the provisional government, though recoiling from certain of its more liberal measures. He locked horns with Tommaseo, for example, over the appointment of the Bandieras' former teacher Emilio Tipaldo, a figure of real distinction and unimpeachable character, as official inspector of schools, simply because he was not Catholic, but Greek Orthodox by religion. Tommaseo administered a magisterial dressing-down to the Cardinal, adding, 'I beg you, in God's name, not to give credence to troublemakers, but to hear my voice, a severe one maybe, yet that of a true son of the Church. Pray for us all!'

Far from being surrounded by *austriacante* 'troublemakers', Monico found himself in the midst of a markedly patriotic set of clergy at St Mark's. The basilica's archpriest, Monsignor Balbi, was described as 'a doughty republican, enemy of the former government'; the patriarchal

Chancellor, Giovanni Battista Ghega, was 'a red-hot Italian'; the Cardinal's secretary, Don Pietro Dolfin, was reluctant to put on the black chasuble fringed with yellow customarily worn at funerals, because these were the Austrian colours; and the diocesan lawyer, Ignazio Zorzetto, always sported a tricolour cockade, a lion of St Mark and an image of Pio Nono. As for Don Vincenzo Marinelli, an ex-Dominican from Dalmatia whom Tommaseo, probably not without regard for their shared background, had nominated as chaplain to the civic guard, he had already gained a reputation as a Mazzinian and believed his duty, together with that of other clergy, was to unite 'the sword and the cross under the flags of Italy and Pope Pius'. The fervent Catholic faith of most fighters for the revolution was never in doubt, despite growing disillusion with the Pope's political stance, and Marinelli was correct in maintaining that the presence of chaplains in the ranks was essential for raising morale.

The two most memorable churchmen among the revolutionaries were not native Venetians. Father Ugo Bassi had already enjoyed a nationwide reputation for saintliness and eloquence, enhanced by the official censure he received for his wholehearted espousal of the Italian cause. Born to a poor family in the town of Cento* near Ferrara, he had fallen in love, while a student at Bologna, with a young noblewoman whose premature death had caused him to turn for comfort to the Church. He joined the Barnabite preaching order, but his sermons in the great church of San Petronio proved too radical for the local church hierarchy, and in 1840 he was inhibited and sent by Pope Gregory to a small town in Calabria, where he could do less harm. His patriot sympathies were strengthened during a stay in Milan two years previously, and when Gregory was succeeded by Pius IX, he was able to return to Bologna and channel his activities as a priest working for political reform. Bassi's charisma was enhanced both by his striking good looks and by a personal courage which never failed him even when, during the last months of the revolution, he was condemned to face an Austrian firing squad. His sincere spirituality sat easily, if incongruously, alongside an extraordinary foppishness and theatricality. His cassocks were flawlessly ironed, he used cosmetics, spent money on hairdressers for his blond curls, and when on the mainland cut a dashingly unclerical figure on his white horse. While in Venice, he lodged with the Manins and forged a friendship with Daniele as deep as, to all appearances, it was unlikely. Manin, the cool pragmatist not given to Catholic fervours, admired Bassi's integrity and was grateful for

* From the ghetto of this same town came the family of Isaac D'Israeli, father of the British statesman Benjamin Disraeli.

his counsel and support. For his part, Bassi believed that in Manin he had met a genuinely heroic personality.

A fellow member of the Barnabite order, Alessandro Gavazzi encouraged him to join Durando's march into the Veneto as a regimental chaplain. From a solidly revolutionary Bolognese family, Gavazzi had been inhibited from preaching in Venice by the Austrians as long ago as 1836, when the police were made nervous by an inflammatory series of Lenten sermons he gave at the Frari. After publishing some suspect observations on steam navigation in the proceedings of the scientific congress meeting at Turin, he was banished from Piedmont, while a further preaching veto was administered by the Cardinal Legate of Bologna, and Gavazzi was made to take up a prison chaplaincy. His experiences as a political suspect, constantly under surveillance, rebuked and harangued by his superiors for liberal opinions, made him sympathetic to the convicts' plight, so that he set up a rehabilitation service for prisoners and their families, which was quite possibly unique in the Italy of his epoch.

Gavazzi was certainly not frightened of making enemies. Becoming a kind of wandering evangelist for the revolution among the towns of the Papal States, he continued to raise official hackles with his inflammatory sermons, and after one notably outrageous piece of rabble-rousing in Ancona he was confined to a local monastery. As soon as Pius IX's 1846 amnesty set him free, he hastened to resume his former role as patriot orator. At Recanati, the family gathered at the funeral of the impeccably reactionary Count Monaldo Leopardi, father of Italy's greatest romantic poet, was scandalised by the friar's funeral address. 'Instead of listening to a eulogy on our poor papa,' wrote the Count's son Pierfrancesco, 'we were treated to a bitter criticism of his opinions, contrary as these were to modern progress and Pius IX, with remarks on the inadequate education of the nobility of his period etc., with a great many exhortations to the people of Recanati not to do less than those of other cities [i.e. in the way of patriotism].' It was Pius's brother Giuseppe Mastai Ferretti indeed, a friend of the errant Barnabite, who arranged for a papal audience, but the pontiff was less than encouraging, ordering Gavazzi to give up preaching politics on pain of interdiction.

The opportunity for which he had been waiting arrived with the departure from Rome of Durando and Ferrari at the head of their papal brigades in April 1848. Alerted to his presence as chaplain with the force, Niccolò Tommaseo invited Gavazzi to Venice to boost morale and rattle the collecting tin, not just in the city itself, but through the Veneto as a whole. The friar arrived with a troop of volunteers, including the Pope's nephew Ercole, on 5 May, and the next evening preached his first sermon to a large crowd in the Piazza. Among those present was the Bolognese *crociato* Augusto Aglebert, impressed enough by Gavazzi's fund-raising rhetoric to describe its effect on ordinary Venetians in a letter to his sister-in-law: 'Wretched sailors pulled from their ears the rings worn as sacred objects since childhood. Weapons of all kinds were offered, rifles, sabres, pistols. One young man, in giving his rifle for the cause, was so carried away that he fell into convulsions. The fervour and exaltation exceeded anything in nature. When Manin's wife came to present the few modest ornaments which adorned her, there was an astonishing commotion, more especially since her family, though it is that of the republic's president, lives in very straitened circumstances.' According to Edmund Flagg, American consul in Venice immediately after the revolution, Manin himself gave a silver snuffbox, 'ladies resigned their jewels, and even the lower classes tore off their bracelets and those fine Venetian chains called *jasseron*, manufactured and sold by the yard by the goldsmiths of the Rialto Bridge, and gave up even the large silver pins which the poorest possess and which serve to confine and ornament their masses of night-black hair'.

Gavazzi's fervour, according to Manin's friend Carlo Leoni, was enough to frighten the more timid members of the Venetian clergy into imitating his example. It was amusing to watch them trying desperately to quieten the loud 'Evviva!'s from the congregation which greeted his more resounding harangues. 'So magical an effect must have wrung tears from the coldest of mortals.' The next day Gavazzi moved on to Treviso, where he was joined by Ugo Bassi, who had contributed his share of fervid harangues in Venice and now prepared to take the field alongside the volunteers. It was he who had the sad task of bringing the last rites to General Guidotti as he lay dying from his longed-for bullet wounds.

The zeal of the Venetians, more especially among the working classes, in giving so freely to the patriot cause was an encouraging augury both for the provisional government and for Manin personally. During his imprisonment, the little man in spectacles had become, and would remain, the people's hero, and it was this unwavering loyalty to the demagogue that provided Venice with a moral resource beyond value at a time, not long distant, when the city was to find itself standing alone against the Austrians. So far, under his leadership, the government had done its best to rule justly, with a strong sense of its more progressive measures carrying with them an implicit rebuke to Habsburg obscurantism. It was not universally beloved, however, and continuing discontent among poorer sectors of the working population, such as boatmen, porters and street vendors, ruffled the apparent consensus in the administration's favour, hinting at likely exploitation by radical agitators and a lurch towards socialism or even outright anarchy.

Manin was worried enough by this, as by the increasingly critical position of the republic's finances, whatever the generosity of individual Venetians. On 14 May a forced loan was announced, to be raised among the cities of the Veneto, 'in consideration that the war now being waged for Italian independence requires an immense expenditure'. A more insidious menace to the very survival of an autonomous Venetian state was the pressure starting to grow, as a result of Nugent's advance and the Cornuda disaster, for some sort of fusion, initially with the neighbouring province of Lombardy and ultimately with the kingdom of Piedmont itself. As several of the republic's leading ministers, such as Jacopo Castelli, Pietro Paleocapa and Leone Pincherle, began to favour the idea of a united Lombardo-Venetian assembly, the progressive democratic state which Manin and Tommaseo had brought into being suddenly began to seem a utopian construct, notwithstanding its espousal of individual liberty, equality before the law and the reduction or abolition of unjust taxes.

The provincial towns, what was more, following their initial revolution-springtime declarations of brotherhood and amity with Venice, had not unreasonably relapsed into a traditional wariness of what looked like being a revival of that domineering arrogance they had known all too well as subjects of the old Serenissima. Leading citizens of these mainland communes, many of them old nobility, disliked the bourgeois character of the new Venetian government and felt that the landowning interest was inadequately represented in the consultative assembly through which Venice had sought, though with little success, to conciliate them. Swiftly the various cities started making their own decisions on the fusion issue. By the second week of May several, including Padua, Vicenza and Treviso, had addressed letters to the Lombard assembly in Milan, urging its leaders to press the Venetians into acceptance of a full union between the two provinces. On the 12th, despite Manin's serious reluctance (almost leading to his resignation) and Tommaseo's outright refusal to sign the document, Venice officially agreed to fusion with Lombardy.

As it turned out, there was no need for such a gesture. For some time the Milanese government had been largely in the hands of a group of conservative nobles favourable to a union with Piedmont, which should save vested interests in Lombardy from the egalitarian menaces of republicanism. They were savagely criticised by opposition leaders such as Carlo Cattaneo, who later subjected them to scarifying appraisal in his incisive analysis of Lombardy's 1848 *L'insurrezione di Milano*, and whose view of the government as essentially a stalking-horse for Charles Albert's ministers and agents was by no means exaggerated. Both sides had signally failed to rouse the province for the revolution, the pro-fusion camp (known as *albertisti*) because they needed to tread carefully so as not to frighten off the King, and the opposition through reluctance to attach Lombard freedom-fighters to a royal army. Besides which, as the Neapolitan socialist commentator Carlo Pisacane sardonically observed, neither Charles Albert nor the aristocratic caucus in Milan had really offered the working classes an adequate motive for revolution. Unlike its Venetian counterpart, this provisional government only overhauled the Austrian tax system under pressure, moved less by genuine goodwill than by a fear of popular uprising. 'A hatred of the present state of affairs and a need for improve-ment are both of them deep, universal and apparent,' wrote Pisacane, 'yet though this feeling is enough to produce an insurrection, it is incapable of lasting.' Since March, the peasantry composing the bulk of Lombardy's population had gained no adequate representation in government, and discontent at the sluggishness or absence of reforms had erupted into sporadic violence throughout the province. Cries of 'Viva Radetzky!' expressed anger with the landlords rather than indulgence towards the Austrians, an anger more likely to be felt by those owners of large estates, who actively sought to prevent their labourers joining the national guard and prayed, not altogether secretly, for the Field Marshal's ultimate victory.

Though the Milanese government was in no sense bound to keep faith with the Venetians, the latter were entitled to assume that their sister province under former Austrian rule would march roughly in step with them, and the fusion vote on 12 May was made in good faith. That very day, however, Milan jumped the gun. Silver-tongued pledges of the Piedmontese monarch's liberal benevolence had been sent from Turin to appease the doubters and the more hesitant *albertisti*, and now the govern-ment announced a general plebiscite to determine whether Lombardy would indeed become part of Charles Albert's kingdom or continue to go it alone. In the manner of many such votes before or since, the real issues soon got lost under a fog of propaganda and distortion. The Albertist lobby throughout the province did its job thoroughly, persuading the peasant majority that the simple choice lay between the King and Emperor Ferdinand. Out of 60,000 adult males, more than 50,000 declared in favour of fusion with Piedmont.

Once news broke that Lombardy was preparing to stage the plebiscite – implicitly rejecting the original policy adopted, for their part, by Manin and the Venetian provisional government of deferring any sort of polit-ical integration until the war was over – the Veneto communes, large and small, hastened to mount their own referendums, with only a small handful staying loyal to Venice for the time being. The general impulse seems to have been that of a rush for cover under the sheltering Piedmontese wing, a keeping-hold-of-nurse entirely understandable at a time when Austria's reserve army was putting out dangerous tentacles towards the cities of the central Veneto, and when those it had somehow bypassed in its southward push had little but prayers left to save them. What was the point of waiting any longer on events, when a political destiny appeared to be deciding itself with such ruthless speed and simplicity? By 20 May the Habsburg vanguard, under General Prince Thurn und Taxis, had arrived under the walls of Vicenza. Four days previously the townsfolk had voted for fusion with Piedmont, but Charles Albert's army, in whom they now trusted for deliverance, was nowhere to be seen.

CHAPTER 7

∾

THE CAT-EATERS' LAST STAND

'I NACTION, THAT IS WHAT DOES real harm to our army at present,'
wrote Costanza d'Azeglio to her son Emmanuele at the end of May.
'When it is a question of fighting, everybody takes part willingly,
afraid of nothing, but when they have little to do, this evil makes itself
felt, especially among the married men, of whom there is a great number.'

Emmanuele had recently been expelled from his post as a diplomat in
St Petersburg by Tsar Nicholas I in protest at Charles Albert's invasion
of Lombardy. After a nightmare voyage to Copenhagen, in which his
luggage had been washed overboard in a storm, he was unlikely to be
much heartened by the increasingly disillusioned tone of his mother's
letters as she continued to report on the progress of the war. The real
problem, Costanza rightly perceived, for the Piedmontese forces spread
so thinly across the plains between the Rivers Mincio and Adige was the
men's lack of suitable provisions, shelter and clothing. 'Officers and
soldiers are living off polenta and sleeping on the bare ground, though
they are not very demanding and they fight like lions.' On this score the
Milanese provisional government had seriously let them down, having
failed to deliver promised supplies to the army. 'After the victory at Goito,
the troops were given nothing to eat, the officers were as badly treated
as the men, there was no straw to sleep on after their forced marches,
and the horses got no oats. This was not done deliberately, but simply
as a result of inexperience in military matters.'

All war involves a heuristic acquisition of wisdom among the combatants from their immediate involvement in the unfolding campaign. A
military academy, however meticulous its training methods, cannot hope
to prepare its cadets completely for the experience either of battle itself

or of the complex developing relationship between armies and the civilian context of settled populations, built environment and local agriculture within which their movements against one another almost always take place. Doubtless the Piedmontese high command ought to have foreseen the difficulties ahead during the frantic weeks of mobilisation leading up to the advance into Lombardy, a period when, as Costanza d'Azeglio's Italianate French expressed it, 'l'orgasme était au comble', 'excitement was at its height'. The naive assumption by the generals had been that the troops could easily manage to live off the country once the invasion had been properly launched and that, given the speed with which Austria's resistance in both its Italian provinces had seemed to collapse in the wake of the Milanese *Cinque Giornate*, the campaign would be an affair of weeks rather than months. If it was not quite a case of 'lions led by donkeys', the Piedmontese rank-and-file, tough, courageous and loyal, deserved better leadership than many of their senior officers, overconfident and inexperienced, were willing to give them.

The decision made by Charles Albert at the end of April to besiege the fortress of Peschiera on Lake Garda would prove a serious mistake. While Radetzky busied himself, behind his defensive curtain around Verona, with strengthening fortifications and stockpiling weaponry and provisions, there was time for the Piedmontese to launch a head-on attack, as well as cutting off the main Austrian supply lines. Instead the King preferred to concentrate a major initiative on seizing the fort, significant both as a symbol of the Habsburg grip on Lombardy-Venetia and as a crucial component of the defensive system between Garda and the Po. Radetzky for his part, aware of Charles Albert's intentions, was prepared for the time being to let Peschiera go, so long as the major route out of the Alps and down the Adige valley to Verona could be kept open by Austrian forces.

The Piedmontese victory at Pastrengo on 28 April had no lasting impact. Charles Albert showed his usual courage under fire, volunteer units fought bravely throughout, yet the Italians failed to block an Austrian retreat towards Verona. Soon enough the King realised that something more was needed to spoil Radetzky's waiting game. A direct assault on Verona was now an imperative, not merely in terms of drawing the old fox out of his earth or of consolidating Piedmontese positions around Peschiera, but of bolstering the Italian reputation in the eyes of England and France as each began to consider brokering a peace between the combatants. Charles Albert had been assured, by revolutionary cells still hanging on within the city itself, despite a saturation presence there of Habsburg military, that he needed only to appear before its walls for the citizens to rise up and cast out the Austrians for good and all, as the Venetians had done. In addition, the garrison contained large bodies of Italian and Hungarian troops who, it was believed, would mutiny at the slightest provocation.

Charles Albert's plan was to attack the ring of villages along the heights around Verona's western side, which Radetzky had been occupied in fortifying during the past three weeks. Once these had been taken and proper reconnaissance made, it should have been easy enough to fall upon the city, whose patriots would ensure that the gates were flung open. Unfortunately the details – especially the essential fact that this was an initial move on Verona's outlying defences, rather than a full-scale storming of the town – were badly understood by the Piedmontese generals, whose transmission of orders to their staff muddled matters yet further. At a meeting on 5 May, General Bava prudently suggested that the advance be delayed for twenty-four hours until the officers had properly considered all the implications and an order of the day had been clearly set out, but he was overruled by the arrogant and domineering War Minister, Count Franzini. On the following morning, when the attack was due to start, nobody seemed any the wiser as to a precise operational schedule, and regiments started moving off haphazardly, their officers vaguely aware that they were to march on the three villages of Santa Lucia, San Massimo and Croce Bianca. For whatever reason, Franzini had chosen to ignore the outlying positions at Chievo and Tombetta, held by nearly 4,000 Austrian troops.

Predictably therefore the ensuing battle became a shambles. Not only was the absence of even the most basic synchronisation of movement among the various divisions fatal to the success of the King's plan, but astonishingly there had been no attempt to reconnoitre the intervening terrain. If Pastrengo was a picnic, this had been partly due to the physical nature of the battleground, composed of open fields and vineyards on fairly gentle hillsides. At Santa Lucia the vines alternated with large, sight-obstructing mulberry trees (feeding silkworms for the local textile industry), much of the steeply sloping ground was broken by coppicing, clumps of bushes and dry-stone walls, and the Piedmontese had reckoned without the efficiency of Austrian communication lines along the road running from end to end of the defensive semicircle. Even though a breakthrough was successfully effected at Santa Lucia itself, the Austrians proved ferocious defenders of their other positions, while admiring the heroism of their attackers in the heat of battle. Young Georges de Pimodan, now one of Radetzky's aides-de-camp, was among those who marvelled at the sheer tenacity of the Piedmontese. 'At every point in the fighting we saw their officers rush forward, urging on the men to attack. "Allons! En avant! En avant! Courage! La victoire est à nous!" we heard them shouting in French. These fearless men were Savoyards from the Aosta brigade, as I could tell later from letters we found on their dead bodies.'

When Charles Albert himself arrived on the heights at Santa Lucia, he had the chance to rally his centre and turn both Austrian flanks at San Massimo and Croce Bianca, forcing them to retreat towards the safety of Verona. If he failed to seize this opportunity, it was because he was still clinging to the idea of the whole costly operation as essentially one of reconnaissance and was awaiting a clear signal from within the city that the promised revolution had begun. An uncanny silence brooded over its roofs and towers as the King scanned them through his field-glasses in the May afternoon. Evidently there was to be no uprising, among either the populace or the garrison. Radetzky, detecting a mood of unease in the streets, had ordered all civilians indoors and dispatched patrols throughout the town to enforce discipline. A proclamation, in the tradition of those about which the local satirist Cesare Betteloni had been so scathing, soon followed, declaring that any show of rebellion would be a signal for the artillery surrounding the city to launch a bombardment, wholesale and without mercy. The Field Marshal meant what he said. The Roman amphitheatre, the Arks of the Scaligers, 'Juliet's Tomb' and the great churches of San Zeno and Sant'Anastasia would all have been reduced to rubble. Hence the Veronese made no move and Charles Albert headed back towards Peschiera, his men hungry, puzzled and demoralised, with 500 of their comrades dead or wounded to no obvious advantage.

The pointlessness of the Santa Lucia action must have confirmed what the Austrians suspected, that Charles Albert's strategy was to show fight for its own sake rather than contrive a properly mounted thrust across the Adige to join up with Durando's papal brigades and keep General Nugent busy in the northern Veneto. For Radetzky and his generals, however, the outcome of the war was far from settled or even predictable. Just as so many Piedmontese had followed their king into battle for honour's sake rather than in the cause of freeing Italy from foreign thraldom, so too for most Austrian officers the issue was one of morality, of devotion to the empire, of keeping faith with the sovereign they had sworn to serve (regardless of poor Ferdinand's physical handicaps and lack of charisma) and of restoring the lost provinces to what most of those dwelling in the imperial heartlands believed was their proper place under the Habsburg crown. Radetzky knew perfectly well the depth of hatred for Austria throughout Lombardy-Venetia, whatever the pockets of resentment among the peasantry against their patriot landlords. 'Italy has never loved us and will never do so,' he was heard to say. His simple duty, and that of his generals, was to rescue the empire. 'God bless us and preserve us, that is my motto!' he declared, in an unshakeable assumption that the Deity must always be on the side of whatever in Austria was *kaisertreu*, *schwarzgelber* and unimpeachably conservative.

By the end of May it was starting to look as if Radetzky might have to do God's work for him. With Metternich in exile (currently living in London's Eaton Square, he was preparing to move to a seaside villa in Hove), the imperial family seeking refuge at Innsbruck, and the government in Vienna effectively in the hands of radical university students, the burden of restoring the status quo lay firmly on the octogenarian warrior's shoulders. Clouding the political horizon still further was the possibility of a negotiated peace between Piedmont and Austria, with Britain or France as the go-between. The Austrian government now seriously considered the likelihood of having to surrender at least part of its Italian territory, even if there were those among its members who shared Metternich's belief that Britain was 'the most active instrument of the ruin of our affairs in Italy'.

The villain of the piece, according to him, was the British foreign secretary Viscount Palmerston. 'Since the creation of the world there has never been a situation like that which now exists. To see a great power like Britain putting itself at the forefront of a radical revolution and following the inspirations of a madman is indeed a novel circumstance. Lord Palmerston has placed himself at the head of every upheaval in continental Europe. It is he who, with the help of revolutionary sects, lights the blaze which calls out the fire brigade and then presents himself as the moderator needed to damp down the flames.' For Metternich this outburst was unusually exaggerated.* Though Palmerston was unquestionably eager for change in Italy, it was because of his realistic grasp of the unpopularity of Austrian rule among Italians, rather than through any radical sympathy with the revolutionaries. At sixty-four, he was at the height of his powers, the most colourful, enterprising and shameless British politician of the mid-nineteenth century, convinced of his country's greatness and of her right to safeguard and pursue her own interests abroad without interference, a man whose relaxed morality in private life was counterbalanced by the dedication with which he threw

---

* In the same letter to the Austrian ambassador in London Metternich names Sir Robert Peel, Lord Minto and the British envoys to Turin and Naples as revolutionary agitators.

himself into ministerial office as Home Secretary, Foreign Secretary and ultimately as Prime Minister.

Palmerston was currently apprehensive of the role the new French republican government might be preparing to play in the affairs of a new Italy that was likely to emerge from the current wave of revolutions. Fear of France as the ultimate loose cannon of European politics would always dominate his outlook on the international situation, making him favour an enlarged kingdom of Piedmont as a desirable buffer state, to block French influence in northern Italy. Its recent aspiration to at least some of the aspects of a constitutional monarchy, with parliamentary government and Charles Albert's *Statuto* document setting out the basis of his rule, offered an effective counterweight to the more negative effects of Austrian hegemony among the other Italian sovereign states. What was more, if diplomatic negotiations were now afoot, Palmerston was anxious that France should be prevented from snatching all the major initiatives from under Britain's nose and emerging as the international peacemaker.

He had no wish to see Austria collapse altogether, whatever Metternich's demonisation of him, but her desperate attempts at holding on to the Italian provinces seemed a recipe for disaster. The Alps, Palmerston believed, were the Habsburg empire's natural frontier, and it was pointless to cling, even for the sake of national honour and treaty obligations, to territory whose inhabitants would never learn to love the Emperor and his proconsuls. As he told the Ambassador to London, Karl von Dietrichstein, 'I doubt you will ever manage to pacify or quietly govern provinces in which so implacable a hatred has been expressed against you. By continuing the war, you risk bringing an auxiliary army from France onto your soil.' The French general Charles Oudinot indeed, having taken command of the Armée des Alpes stationed on the Piedmontese border, had alarmed Austria still further by his sabre-rattling proclamation expressing 'profound sympathy for the Italian populations', referring to Italian soldiers having shared in Napoleonic *gloire* on 'immortal battle-fields' and to a possible renewal of such martial comradeship.

In the wake of Charles Albert's victory at Pastrengo, the Austrians decided to send the diplomat Karl von Hummelauer on a peace mission to London. The solution he had to offer was a species of home rule not unlike that promulgated forty years later for Ireland by William Ewart Gladstone. Lombardy-Venetia was to be governed by an Italian administration from top to bottom; there was to be a special ministry for Italian affairs; the provinces would be given their own army, not to be used against other Italian states; and advantageous adjustments would be made to tariffs, customs and commercial legislation. It all sounded politically feasible and was in essence an attractive package, designed to save Austria's face and acknowledge concerns of the type voiced by Manin and Tommaseo in their fateful 'instances'. It failed nevertheless to confront the very same reality which had brought Hummelauer to London in the first place, namely the ongoing war and the groundswell of popular support among the aristocracy and bourgeoisie of Lombardy-Venetia for a complete separation from the empire. Most bizarre of all, in Palmerston's view, appeared the proposal that Prince Ferdinand of Modena, in his role as an Austrian archduke, should be appointed Viceroy of the newly consti-tuted domain. As the Foreign Secretary reasonably pointed out, the Prince was a brother of Modena's Duke Francis V, no better loved among Italians than his recently dead and unlamented father had been. Why not instead cede Lombardy to Piedmont, send Archduke Rainer (the present Viceroy) into honourable retirement, and put Venetia under a new governor charged with applying the home-rule programme?

Hummelauer at first refused to accept this amendment, but then agreed that Lombardy should be let go, as long as Venetia remained Austrian. By now – it was the last week of May – the proposals had been run past the Piedmontese government, whose Foreign Minister Lodovico Pareto immediately rejected them. His hand had been strengthened by the fusion vote in Lombardy and by assurances wrung from Charles Albert by the Milanese provisional government that he would never make peace as long as an Austrian remained on Italian soil. The British vice-consul in Milan, Charles Campbell (pro-Italian, unlike his chief, Clinton Dawkins, in Venice), told Palmerston that 'His Majesty declared the war at the head of which he had put himself to be Italian, and one which he could not call finished until every part of the Italian territory was evacuated by the enemy; he confirmed his former pledge not to lay down his arms until the Austrians were driven beyond the Alps . . . and expressed his convic-tion that when Verona was conquered, Venice would be free.'

This same belief, despite the failure of Piedmontese arms at Santa Lucia, was what encouraged the 'Albertists' in Venice itself. Daniele Manin was not nearly so convinced, and on 29 May he sent another of his subtly probing letters to the King, seeming to praise his achievements in the war so far, while implicitly urging him to hurry up and finish the busi-ness that Durando, Ferrari and their *papalini*, not to speak of La Marmora, had so far bungled in attempting to liberate the Veneto. As he told Massimo d'Azeglio, he was suspicious of the way in which Durando seemed to imply that Charles Albert's intervention was by no means disin-terested, and of the fact that 'a cloud of Piedmontese agents' was now travelling across the country, spreading proclamations of a very different character from those of Charles Albert and essentially giving the lie to the royal word of honour. If these were not true, then surely it was up to d'Azeglio and others to discredit them. Perhaps d'Azeglio really did believe, as he claimed, that the King had no intention of insisting on fusion as the price of intervening, and maybe he was right to blame the high-handed Franzini for such ruthless political horse-trading, but Manin was unlikely to accept these reassurances.

For either side the whole situation in northern Italy was now so volatile, such a matter of living from day to day, that any long-term strategy for preserving the integrity of the Venetian republic was impossible. Even if the Austrians had managed to wrest back most of Friuli, the castle of Osoppo and its fortified village, north-west of Udine, continued to defy attack from a Habsburg force mostly consisting of loyal Italians. To mounting astonishment, it would hold firm for at least another five months under its dashing and resourceful Bolognese commander Licurgo Zannini, with a garrison of 400 men. At Palmanova Carlo Zucchi was in no mood for the time being to yield the fortress to the brigade that Nugent had left behind weeks earlier on the assumption that a successful siege operation would be a matter of a few days. Bassano, Rovigo and Padua were still in the hands of their provisional governments, but yet more galling to Radetzky was the freedom enjoyed by Vicenza and Treviso, both of which controlled the supply lines from the north upon which the Quadrilateral forts depended.

In surrendering his command, Nugent had split the reserve army into two divisions, one of them intended to deal with the problem of Treviso, and the other, led by Prince Thurn und Taxis, supposed to set off immediately towards Verona. Thurn, to his credit, made a determined effort to seize Vicenza on his way south, but was beaten back by furious resistance from a combined defence force of Durando's *papalini* (including a redoubtable Swiss brigade), a battalion of Roman volunteers and the citizens themselves, who had thrown up a line of highly effective barricades across the town's main thoroughfares. Keen to clear the stain of defeat at Cornuda, Durando made a further attack on Thurn's column as it moved onwards, but was driven off after two days' skirmishing along the road. The undoubted hero of this follow-up action was General Giacomo Antonini, commanding a legion of exiles he had personally recruited in France. Described as 'a true republican, honest and loyal as any old soldier of Napoleon's empire', he had a respectable patriotic record, having at one stage been arrested as a supposed accomplice of the Bandieras. While riding after the fleeing Austrians, he was hit by a cannon ball, which smashed his right arm and knocked him from the saddle. 'Let it go,' he said of the damaged limb as he contrived to remount, 'so long as Italy triumphs.' Amputation was inevitable, but remarkably, given the medical standards of the time, Antonini survived the primitive surgery, involving not much more than a brandy bottle and a surgeon's saw. The arm itself, brought to Venice by an intrepid housemaid named Beatrice, who acted as a messenger between Venetian families and their menfolk at the front, was placed in the church of San Biagio as a sacred relic – surely a unique example of such a blasphemous blurring of the divide between religion and revolution. Following Austria's repossession of Venice in 1849, it was removed from the church, inside its specially designed metal container, by the patriot Maddalena Montalban Comello, who then had to surrender it to the police. Later it found its way into the Risorgimento collection of the Museo Correr, where it presumably still rests.*

When at length this division reached Verona, Radetzky's welcome was less heartfelt than expected. The arrival of the belated reinforcements meant 18,000 extra mouths to feed in a Verona whose hungry citizens were growing restive, despite the threat of bombardment made before Santa Lucia. Thurn and his whole force, decided the Field Marshal, must go back and take Vicenza, clearing out Durando and his brigades in the process and mopping up any volunteer resistance in the surrounding countryside, so that the whole north-western Veneto should now come under Austrian military control. Thurn's task was to seize the key vantage point above the city formed by the range of hills known as Monte Berico, on whose northern spur stand Andrea Palladio's famous Villa Rotonda, the Villa Valmarana 'ai Nani', containing a magnificent Tiepolo fresco cycle, and the baroque basilica of the Madonna del Monte commemorating a miraculous apparition of the Blessed Virgin. Amid these buildings Thurn could place his howitzers, rockets and cannon and batter Vicenza into submission. On the night of 23 May his main column would mount an attack on the town gates, with the full bombardment scheduled to start at dawn the next day.

Already emboldened by their earlier success in driving his men off, the Vicentines were not to be caught napping on this occasion. Further barricades had been erected, and on the south side the waters of the River Retrone, already high from an uncommonly rainy spring, had been allowed to flood the open plain beneath the Monte, on whose heights patriot troops were stationed in anticipation of the Austrian pincer attack.

---

* As is often the way with Italian museums dedicated to the Risorgimento, this one has been 'in course of rearrangement' (i.e. closed indefinitely) for many years.

The inundation did its work, forcing Thurn's infantry to make such an elaborate detour that they failed to capture the crucial hill. Now the General ordered heavy shelling from his artillery outside the main gates, but the three-hour pounding, which lobbed nearly 3,000 projectiles into the town, made no real impact and the citizens seemed more excited than alarmed. During the night assault, Giuseppe Fogazzaro, a priest who formed part of Vicenza's provisional government, noted 'lights at all the windows, shops with their shutters wide open as if it were day, the church bells, those trumpets of the people, ringing frantically from every tower, and the populace, men, women and children, scattered through the streets, applauding in a dignified fashion those who left their offices, their workshops, their gilded halls, their humble hovels, with rifle in hand to rush to the barricades and face death'. Massimo d'Azeglio, among those directing defence operations, remarked on the way everyone sat about in the cafés chatting and laughing as the shells whistled into the town, and praised the courage of a group of women who helped in shifting 250 barrels of gunpowder from a dangerously exposed magazine near one of the main gates. By nine o'clock in the morning Thurn und Taxis was compelled once again to acknowledge defeat at Vicenza and gave the order to retire.

Radetzky, true to form, would bide his time before planning another attempt on the Palladian city. Something needed to be done meanwhile to break up Piedmontese defences along the Mincio, thereby relieving pressure on Peschiera. His scheme, prepared with the help of Heinrich von Hess, his Quartermaster General* and most astute officer on his staff, was to move no fewer than 40,000 troops from Verona to Mantua, under Charles Albert's very nose, and then start a systematic sweep up enemy positions from the south, taking advantage of the concentration of royal forces around Garda lakeside. The King, obsessed with capturing Peschiera as a trophy, had withdrawn brigades from stations west of Mantua and replaced them with a battalion of Neapolitan troops and 7,000 Tuscans, partly regulars of Grand Duke Leopold's army, but many of them young volunteers from Pisa University.

Keen as mustard, the students had enlisted, alongside several of their professors, in the teeth of disapproval from the Tuscan government, liberal though its inclinations officially were. When the professors, including the respected geologist Leopoldo Pilla, were told they must give up soldiering

---

* The rank was largely honorific. Hess's main roles, where Radetzky was concerned, lay in planning strategy and drafting public proclamations, orders of the day and morale-boosting messages to the troops.

and return to the lecture halls, as the annual season of final exams was at hand, one of them answered, 'Decorum and the sense of duty, which has sent us over the Apennines, demands that we follow our pupils and stay with them. Many are the parents who, solicitous of their children's welfare, are happy enough for their teachers to accompany them.' In fact, like so many of the *crociati*, they were better equipped from a moral and ideological point of view than in purely practical terms, some indeed marching without proper boots and most of them sporting hastily improvised patriotic badges and sashes rather than a proper uniform. For these lads, however, it was a revolutionary springtime, and they were happy enough to be fighting for a new Italy, whatever that might turn out to be. Their teachers felt similarly elated. Giuseppe Montanelli, soon to become a leading figure on the Tuscan political scene, acknowledged some years afterwards that it was 'still a pleasure, like that of a first love, for an exile's thoughts to return to memories of campaigning: of nights spent on watch by the poetic banks of the Mincio, where Virgil and Sordello* sang, of those impetuous dawn raids, often as far as Mantua itself, of mass celebrated to the sound of a military band, with all ranks present and armed, those Mantuan towers standing dark before us upon which we hoped to be the first to raise the tricolour flag – and in the silent night the far-off call of the enemy sentinel mixed with the sweet warbling of the nightingale'.

The Tuscan force was commanded by General Cesare De Laugier, a Belgian with a Florentine mother; resourceful and courageous, he was determined to knock his men into shape as quickly as possible. Their youth and ardour, he realised, could be put to good practical use with a little basic drilling, and by the time Radetzky began his southward manoeuvre, the brigade had received its genuine baptism of fire while repelling a fierce Austrian attack launched on 13 May. The positions to which the Tuscans had been assigned, defending the Mincio crossing at the villages of Curtatone and Montanara, were vulnerable to shelling from artillery south of Mantua, and in the event of any major action would always have to depend on support from Piedmontese troops remaining in the area, led by General Eusebio Bava. There was no love lost between the two officers. Bava had the usual suspicion of volunteer interlopers in the war, whatever their fighting potential, and adopted the condescending

---

* The troubadour Sordello (1209–1270), Provencal by family origin, was born at Goito (where the two 1848 battles took place). Dante hailed him as a patriotic reformer, and the Italophile Robert Browning, in 1844, made him the subject of a long and notoriously incomprehensible poem.

attitude customary among Charles Albert's officers towards their opposite numbers from other Italian armies. De Laugier, whose supreme command was only confirmed by the Tuscan government on 26 May, already felt overburdened by tasks he was unable to delegate without properly trained subordinates. There were uniforms to be ordered, local mayors and farmers to be kept sweet, lists of dead and wounded to be filled up and letters to be written to the men's families, as well as the day-to-day business of sustaining discipline and morale. The Piedmontese reluctance to cooperate struck him therefore as positively damaging in the climate of what purported to be a nationwide struggle to liberate Italy.

Such unhelpfulness was the last thing De Laugier needed as the Tuscans prepared, on 29 May, to meet the first of Radetzky's two columns advancing from Verona. Bava had passed him the news of the Austrian troop movements as he received it, promising the necessary back-up as long as the troops at Curtatone were ready to stand firm. As a last resort, the Tuscans were to fall back on Goito, scene of the first important battle two months previously, where Bava once more guaranteed support. By the small hours of the following morning he seems to have panicked, as the size of Radetzky's army – forty-three infantry battalions, fifty-four cavalry squadrons and 150 pieces of artillery, marching along two parallel roads about twenty miles apart – became clear. Seeking advice at headquarters from Charles Albert and Franzini, the General was directed to concentrate his force at Goito in the expectation that the new enemy brigades, once arrived in Mantua, would hastily turn themselves round and push on to attack Piedmontese positions along the southern reaches of the Mincio.

The idea that a small semi-professional force could keep the Austrian cohorts at bay while Bava frantically massed troops further north to hold the line against the threatened roll-up was not altogether preposterous, given the ardour and pluck already shown by the Tuscans during raids and skirmishes. Or were they, as many of them later supposed, simply being thrown to the wolves through a callous delaying tactic, which saw them as expendable casualties in the more important business of saving Piedmontese forces to meet the big attack? Whatever the truth, De Laugier, as Bava's subordinate, had his orders, and on the morning of the 29th stood ready with his 5,400 men, now including two Neapolitan infantry battalions and another of volunteers, to meet an enemy at least four times superior in numbers. The main Italian concentration was at Curtatone and Montanara, with reserves of cavalry and grenadiers, together with the Pisa University volunteers, at the nearby hamlet of

Grazie and a Florentine civic-guard battalion holding the road along the left bank of the Mincio. It must have been immediately obvious to the advancing Austrian infantry brigade, led by Prince Felix zu Schwarzenberg, that the Tuscan line between the two villages was far too weak to sustain a frontal assault, and that its four field pieces were no match for the twenty-four cannon and howitzers brought up by the imperial artillery. The logical tactic would have been a two-pronged attack on the Tuscan positions. Instead Schwarzenberg chose first of all to engage at Curtatone, the better-defended of the two and surrounded by deep ditches across which it was impossible to drag the guns.

De Laugier's imperative was now to delay the Austrian right wing with a series of feints and sudden forward dashes, while the brigade over at Montanara coped as best it could with the pincer movement formed by an advancing wave of 4,000 infantry and a rearguard action led by Schwarzenberg's second-in-command Prince Liechtenstein, who had deliberately swept his cavalry squadrons a mile or so southwards before veering round to pounce on the Tuscans. In one sense the battle, as it unfolded, was a grim re-enactment of Cornuda three weeks earlier. Just as Ferrari's men had fought doggedly on, in the belief that Durando would turn up in the nick of time, so De Laugier hoped against hope for reinforcement from Bava. When at last a message arrived from Piedmontese headquarters ordering a northerly retreat, the fight had already started and it was too late for the Italians to pull back without falling into Liechtenstein's trap.

Astonishing to both Habsburg commanders was the heroic intrepidity of the two little forces opposing them. Tuscans and Neapolitans, regular or volunteer, remained staunch against continued pounding from Austrian infantry, guns and cavalry, and the Pisa University brigade even burst into song when advancing from Curtatone. Georges de Pimodan was among the officers who paid tribute to the 'courage héroïque des braves Toscans', admiring, in addition, De Laugier's resourcefulness in digging in so strongly around the villages, crenellating the perimeter walls of outlying houses and piling farmyard manure and rubbish sacks in front of doors and gates. Even the hard-bitten and cynical General Schönhals, reviewing the battle in his account of the campaign, was moved to praise 'the stubbornness and valour, against every expectation, of the Tuscan defenders'.

The ultimate gesture of Italian bravado came during the second Austrian attack on Curtatone, in the afternoon. De Laugier, riding up to the single remaining gun battery, discovered a scene of devastation. 'Twice the gunpowder had been set on fire by Austrian rockets and made tragic havoc of all who stood near it. Various gunners and soldiers, burned,

blackened and scorched, were rushing away, screaming and tearing their
clothes off as though they were mad. A good many men and horses lay
dead and wounded around the shattered gun carriages and broken wheels.
The guns themselves, overturned on the ground, could no longer be used.'
At least one artilleryman thought otherwise. A Pisan student, whose name
is variously given as De Gasperi, Cipriani or Elbano, he had had his
uniform blown off by a congreve rocket hitting a powder keg. Naked as
he was born, he managed to right one of the guns and carried on loading
and firing single-handed until the order for retreat was given.

By early evening it became clear that while Bava, at the head of a
Piedmontese cavalry regiment, was only nine miles away, no back-up
from him would be forthcoming, even though De Laugier had sent a
rider to ask for it and heartened his men with the prospect. Bava's subsequent excuse was that the messenger had announced an imminent pull-
back rather than requesting support. Of the two generals' accounts, De
Laugier's is always the more credible. His bitter riposte to Bava's published
memoir invokes the battle of Curtatone e Montanara* as a symbol, both
of what might have been achieved by Italian arms against Austria in 1848
and of why the war in Lombardy ultimately failed, its initiatives crippled
by wrangling, time-wasting, name-calling, snobbery and the conflicting
ambitions of those who should have pooled their resources of manpower,
energy and talent in the concerted repulse of a common enemy.

As Liechtenstein's cavalry closed in on Montanara, De Laugier's second-
in-command, Colonel Giovanetti, began a hazardous withdrawal, his men,
even in retreat, impressing the Austrians with their bravery as they turned
and fought along the roads northwards. At Curtatone, De Laugier himself
rallied his dragoons in a last desperate charge, but was denied the glory
of leading it when an Austrian bullet toppled his horse and he narrowly
avoided death as his cavalrymen galloped over him. Only when he gave
the order to retire did the Tuscans' nerve crack, as they jostled one another
to escape across the single bridge over the canal flowing into the Mincio.
Otherwise Curtatone and Montanara represented the Thermopylae of
1848, an archetypal glorious defeat. Tuscan and Neapolitan, volunteer and
professional, had fought side by side as Italians, led by a capable general
and inspired by their officers' example, holding positions against impossible odds throughout an entire day and earning unstinted praise from
adversaries normally so grudging and contemptuous in their attitude
towards Italian rebels in arms.

Bava refused to grasp any of this, let alone acknowledge that De Laugier

---

* The battle is always referred to by the names of both villages.

and his men, by making their stand instead of falling back as originally directed, had bought him precious time in which to mass a Piedmontese force of sufficient size to meet the expected Austrian push up the west bank of the Mincio. In fact Radetzky failed to move as anticipated. The victorious troops at Curtatone and Montanara spent the remaining daylight hours rounding up fugitives and counting prisoners, and when the main body of the army, under the Field Marshal's personal command, began to advance the following morning, it was in an encircling sweep too ambitious to allow proper liaison between the various columns and misjudging both the location and the strength of the Piedmontese. Bava's disposition of his forces was adequate rather than ideal, but when Goito once more witnessed an encounter between the two armies, he was able to take advantage of Austrian overconfidence, and Radetzky, after fierce fighting and the loss of 600 men, was compelled to retire. While Charles Albert was acknowledging the cheers of his men, news arrived from Peschiera that the fortress had at last been taken and the soldiers cried out, 'Long live the King of Italy!'

Bava's failure to follow up the victory at Goito by pressing Radetzky back against Verona was widely criticised, but both sides pleaded the impossibility of making any significant movement along roads reduced to quagmires by the torrential rain which fell during the next three days. Radetzky was now on the ropes. In London, Hummelauer was still discussing peace terms with Palmerston; the fusion between Lombardy and Venetia would seem to have clinched both provinces' resolve to quit the empire, whatever the swelling pockets of pro-Austrian feeling in rural areas; and, to make matters worse, news arriving from Vienna suggested that students and radical democrats had now seized firm control of such government as purported to exist there. The Field Marshal's duty, as he clearly perceived it, was to rescue and preserve whatever he could of the battered empire and seek to hold it together. Understood as a conservative political abstract, Austria at present existed only in so far as Radetzky and his generals were able to keep the army in being and scotch for good and all Charles Albert's roll across the Adige to Verona and ultimately to Venice.

What could no longer be neglected were those stones in the Austrian shoe Vicenza and Treviso. Each was still obstructing the supply lines, and Radetzky wanted to avoid any repeat of the privations that had forced Peschiera to surrender, supposing other Quadrilateral garrisons were forced to endure a prolonged siege during midsummer. Vicenza above all required taking out, not just for its nuisance value, but because its most recent resistance had been accomplished with such insolent success on the part of a substantially civilian defence force. The honour of Habsburg arms was at stake, and Radetzky now prepared to authenticate this in a massive swoop on the city, which should cut it off altogether from the rest of the Veneto and reduce it to rubble if the citizens once again showed fight.

Almost a week after their repulse at Goito, the Austrians began moving northwards with the same swiftness and secrecy as had characterised the march to Mantua, so that by 9 June more than 40,000 troops and 124 guns formed a tight semicircle around Vicenza. They faced defiance from a considerably larger force than had seen off Thurn und Taxis at the end of May. Giovanni Durando, as garrison commander, had martialled 6,000 regular soldiers, 4,000 of the civic guard and several volunteer brigades. Alongside him stood his fellow Piedmontese, Colonel Alessandro Avogadro di Casanova, together with Massimo d'Azeglio, who repeated here the glamorous impression he had made on the women and girls of Treviso. One of those, Luigia Codemo, recalled him 'seated on a beautiful sorrel horse, upright in the saddle, in his polished boots and cocked hat, its plumes nodding in the breeze. Haughty yet full of animation, he glanced at the cohorts passing before him, reining in his prancing steed but more obviously controlling himself, for his artist's enthusiasm must not be allowed to overpower his soldierly bearing.'

D'Azeglio's apparently inexhaustible reserves of dash and energy matched the prevailing mood in Vicenza, which was surprisingly buoyant given the realisation that the city was now effectively under siege from a large and well-equipped army, determined, on this occasion, to stay and finish the job. Some of this cheerful defiance was due to the skill with which Durando and his officers had managed to sustain morale during the period immediately following the 25 May bombardment. Diverted by patriotic illuminations and rousing band concerts, the Vicentines joked that the Austrian shells, far from ruining their town, had improved its appearance. Pietro Soga, faithful major-domo to a local marquis, sent occasional bulletins to his master, who had retreated to his country villa for fear of a second attack. On 6 June he reported ecstatically, 'I can assure you that Vicenza, since ever it was Vicenza, has never witnessed so many different spectacles! Every night two bands now play in the square, with shouts of "Long live Italy, long live Pio Nono, long live unity and liberty!"' And Domenico Barnaba, who had fought under Ferrari at Cornuda and afterwards quitted Venice in disgust at what he considered the citizens' heartless attitude to the papal volunteers, found an altogether nobler spirit prevailing here, in a city whose inhabitants the Venetians scornfully derided – and continue to mock – as 'magnagatti', 'cat-eaters'. The women were cheerful and courageous and the children playing in the streets sang patriotic songs.

The ultimate test of this collective nerve was now at hand. In the earliest glimmer of dawn on 10 June 1848, General Karl Culoz, who had marched his 5,000 men up from Verona three days earlier, began advancing along the spine of Monte Berico to attack Durando's outlying positions, carefully watched by Radetzky. The Field Marshal was keen to husband his resources until all his units along the roads leading east and south, to Treviso, Padua and the Euganean hills, were ready to swing into action. Swiftly flushing out Durando's men, Culoz set fire to the wooden fort, known as the Bella Vista, at the end of the hill closest to the town, but below this he encountered stiff resistance from Italian troops inside the villas adorning its wooded slopes. Palladio's magnificent Rotonda, defended by Paduan university students, had to be bombarded and stormed; the Villa Valmarana was the scene of a struggle between Austrian infantry and a civic-guard battalion from the Romagnole town of Faenza; and the neo-classical Villa Guiccioli, in its *parco inglese*, was staunchly held for several hours by a combined force of Italians and the Pope's Swiss Guards.

By early afternoon all Radetzky's troops had come into play, and the sheer strength of Austrian fire-power was making itself felt along the entire stretch of the Monte. Domenico Barnaba recalled the whole operation as a simple matter of pounding the Italian positions with successive shellings and wave upon wave of infantry. The Austrians, he says, 'were falling in their hundreds, making the ground so slippery with blood that it was all their comrades could do to follow them up the hill'. Slowly but inevitably the Italians began falling back towards the basilica of Madonna del Monte, the domed baroque sanctuary with its tall *campanile* over-looking Vicenza's southern gate. Durando was now frantically directing the defence, assisted by Massimo d'Azeglio, who ordered what turned out to be a disastrous counterattack by the Swiss, aimed at recovering what remained of the burned-out Bella Vista fort. Austrian artillery mowed down the advance guard, d'Azeglio himself was too badly wounded to stay in the field and a bayonet charge finally drove the Swiss back towards the church.

A fight to the death ensued in the sanctuary itself, as men from either side stabbed and shot one another amid the aisles and altars. The very monks from the attached Servite monastery had taken up weapons along-side the patriots, and several died or were taken prisoner in the battle. As the fighting slackened, General Prince Liechtenstein, whose manoeuvre at Curtatone e Montanara had settled the gallant Tuscans' fate, rode his horse through the great main doorway of the church to survey the scene. At that moment a wounded Italian chanced to raise himself sufficiently to level a shot at the Prince, killing him instantly before himself falling back dead on the marble pavement. It was this juxtaposition of insensate carnage with one of the most beautiful manmade prospects in the world that rendered the battle of Vicenza ('le Waterloo de la Vénetie' as a French friend of Manin's later called it) unforgettable for many of those taking part. Georges de Pimodan, Radetzky's aide-de-camp, would always recall that bizarre amalgam of horror and loveliness under the failing light of an Italian summer afternoon, writing:

> Never have I seen, or shall I see, a spectacle finer or more terrible as the Austrians made ready to batter the city into surrender. The town lay at our feet, drowned under a blue vapour of cannon smoke pierced by the flames of burning houses. The sun, with its last rays, gilded the mountains of the Tyrol. The waters of the Brenta reflected sunset's vivid colours, while beside me a regimental band played the Emperor's Hymn, and hundreds of candles taken from the sanctuary of the Madonna lit up the rose-gardens and jasmine of the terrace. The soldiers, drunk with the heat of battle and the scent of gunpowder, were dancing among the corpses of their dead comrades. Sixty-two pieces of artillery swept the city, filling the air with thunder, smoke and flame, while the fearful screams of the citizens and the call of bugles mingled with our shouts of triumph. The town was ours and it lay within our power to reduce it to ashes.

Inside the church, 'tides of blood' stained the white marble of steps and pavements. The next day a band of vengeful Croats, angry at Liechtenstein's death and the presence of the fighting monks, would burst into the refectory of the monastery and with their bayonets slash the splendid painting of 'The Banquet of St Gregory' by Paolo Veronese into thirty-two pieces.*

There was no need for the Austrians, however, to wreak destruction on Vicenza itself. A little more pounding, Radetzky realised, and Durando and Casanova must see sense. Just before seven that evening the white flag of surrender was hoisted, to the fury of the citizens. Most of those carrying rifles took potshots at it, and the 'fearful screams' Pimodan had heard earlier changed into a chorus of booing and whistling. Durando had not been inclined to take further risks. Military intuition perhaps enabled him to grasp that Radetzky's object, having fallen upon Vicenza

---

* In Vienna Austrian public opinion was sufficiently shocked by this attack on the picture for the government to agree to paying for its repair. 'In those days there were still limits to the vandalism of war.' (Trevelyan: *Manin* p.193)

with such drastic speed and thoroughness, was to be able to hurry back as quickly as possible to Verona. Thus the terms of a capitulation were unlikely to be as harsh as the defenders might have feared, though once again Durando's good name was in danger of being compromised among the more fervid patriots.

The problem, once the white flag was up, became that of getting through to the Austrian generals. It was eleven at night before Eugenio Alberi, Durando's chosen negotiator, managed to arrive safely at Villa Balbi, three miles beyond the city, where General D'Aspre was enjoying a late dinner with some of his officers. The old man greeted him warmly, saying, 'Between brave soldiers, a strong handshake first of all!' Alberi refused to dine, but accepted a glass of claret while they hammered out the details, assisted by Prince Bartolomeo Ruspoli, whom Durando had shrewdly ordered to accompany Alberi, both because his mother Leopoldina Khevenhuller-Mersch was Austrian and because his rank as a member of one of Rome's grandest families was calculated to tickle the snobbery of the Habsburg officers. There was a glitch in the proceedings when the details had to be referred to Radetzky, who failed to reply, setting off D'Aspre's famously short fuse. Another occurred when General Hess, after much *Almanach de Gotha*-seasoned genealogical chitchat with Ruspoli, told both the Italians that as officers in the Pope's army, officially not at war with Austria since Pius's April allocution, neither they nor their men were protected belligerents and so ran the risk of being shot. Both problems were ironed out (it was neither the first nor last time D'Aspre had openly censured Radetzky), as was the issue of whether this surrender arrangement constituted a capitulation or a convention. The latter was agreed upon, its essence being that Durando and the papal brigades must leave forthwith, returning across the Po and agreeing not to fight against Austria or its allies for three months. They were allowed to march out with military honours, taking weapons and baggage – the Austrians feeling well able to indulge the luxury of magnanimity and relieved to get rid of what, despite its unspectacular performance as a fighting force, had proved a serious military obstacle in recovering the Veneto for the empire.

Pimodan watched the *papalini* leave the next day, with a large number of civilians following in their wake. 'The soldiers were almost splendid-looking, with dark eyes, aquiline noses, jet-black hair and moustaches. Handsome though they were, when they passed before our Croats, tall and upright with their hard, wild countenances, all these Romans seemed soft and effeminate beside them.' A great many of the accompanying carriages contained well-dressed ladies, some of whom angrily brandished their fans at the Austrians, though most of them seemed suitably down-cast. General Karl van Schönhals, also present at the scene, caught sight of the firebrand preacher Alessandro Gavazzi, who had come to Vicenza, welcomed at the railway station with flags and the civic guard, to hearten the rebels by his missionary zeal. Now he marched out in step with a regimental band, 'majestic as Moses'. Rather more meanly, Schönhals, in noting the ladies' presence, described 'numerous Amazons in medieval costume, among whom our hussars recognised more than one former acquaintance whom they jocularly taxed with her infidelity'.

The civilian exodus from Vicenza was a gesture that would cost some families dear. D'Aspre, assuming command as military governor, was determined to bring the citizens politically into line and would tolerate nothing which bore the stamp of disaffection towards restored Habsburg rule. After a week during which it was expected that the erring patriots would have second thoughts and start drifting homewards, he found it necessary to issue an order, via the Mayor and town council, that unless those concerned came back at once, their property would be forfeited to the government. Eight days' grace was given to those who had fled else-where within the province of Venetia, fifteen to fugitives into neigh-bouring provinces, and a month for those wandering further afield. 'The Municipality, confiding in H. E. Lieutenant-Marshal Baron D'Aspre, can confidently reassure absent citizens that they will be treated, on their return, according to the benevolent principles guaranteed by the Government in Article III of the capitulation.' Yet many courageously chose to stay put in their self-imposed exile.

Schönhals can be forgiven, in his summing-up on the battle of Vicenza, for calling it 'one of the finest and most skilful operations in military history'. Allowing for such exaggeration, Radetzky had managed the whole affair with lethal efficiency, achieving his main strategic object within the space of twenty-four hours. Verona, during his absence, had been left with what seemed like a skeleton force to protect it, but the Field Marshal had deliberately bamboozled the Piedmontese by simulta-neous troop movements in and out of the city, designed to lure Charles Albert into the long-meditated all-out attack for which Santa Lucia had been such a costly rehearsal. On 11 June, the royal army prepared to advance, with the aim of cutting off any attempt by Radetzky at getting back inside Verona as swiftly as he had left it two days previously. The troops begged, however, for the opportunity to pass in review before their sovereign as a prelude to what promised to be the campaign's decisive moment. Against his general's advice, Charles Albert agreed; the parade commenced at 9 a.m. and it was not until mid-afternoon that regiments began marching in earnest. By this time sheets of rain were making the roads almost impassable, and news had arrived of Radetzky's precipitate return to Verona at the head of 8,000 men. The chance had come and gone, but though this sense of lost opportunity left the Piedmontese embittered and demoralised, it is doubtful whether the operation could have succeeded without improved levels of reconnaissance and liaison throughout the army.

War in the Veneto was not quite over. Despite Nugent's mopping-up initiative in May, several towns, large and small, were still in Italian hands, if only for a little while longer. Rovigo, for instance, which had undertaken a go-it-alone poll for fusion with Piedmont on 1 June, had sent a mixed Lombard and Neapolitan force on its way to Vicenza a week later. Three days after the flag-blessings and opera tunes had seen these heroes off, a hangdog column of refugees and *papalini*, the remains of Durando's brigades, began drifting through the town in the direction of the frontier along the Po. Many of them rested for the night in the main square, hitching their mounts to the pillars of its arcade and stretching out beside them on the pavement, while such of the wounded as had managed to survive the march were carried to the local hospital. 'It was a sight to make stones weep!' commented one of the doctors. A few days more and the town had fallen, without serious resistance, to the Austrians.

Further north, Bassano, Asolo and Conegliano had already surrendered. In Padua, where the Venetian provisional government had posted 5,000 troops, principally Neapolitans under the command of General Guglielmo Pepe, the citizens naturally assumed that after Vicenza their turn would come next, and seem to have been ready enough to put up a fight. To their fury, Venice announced its decision to pull out Pepe's brigades and abandon Padua to its fate, a measure prompted by purely practical considerations, but inevitably smacking of that immemorial high-handedness which the Veneto towns had so resented under the Most Serene Republic. Panic spread through the city, and when, on 13 June, even the fire brigade slipped away, taking all its equipment, an enraged mob broke into the offices of the local defence committee to seize any available weapons. Only quick thinking by the civic-guard commander Andrea Cittadella prevented total anarchy. Thus it was easy enough for a few hundred Austrians to regain control on 14 June, but the Paduans would always resent Venice for denying them an opportunity to demonstrate their true patriotism, of which the old university city had proved, during last February's events, that it had plenty in reserve.

During recent weeks Radetzky and his generals had chosen to ignore the ongoing problem of Treviso, heavily garrisoned and an obvious rallying point for the various Italian fighting forces still at large in the Veneto. The city, on 30 May, had voted overwhelmingly for fusion with Piedmont, and it was presumably in the hope that Charles Albert would advance triumphantly across the Adige, sweeping all before him, that its defence committee had rejected an offer of peace and amnesty made the next day by General Ludwig von Welden, moving south at the head of a fresh reserve army from the Tyrol. Welden did not attack forthwith, preferring to concentrate on wiping out pockets of resistance in the towns and villages of the Dolomite foothills first of all. In overcrowded Treviso the atmosphere grew decidedly edgy as the realisation dawned that no assistance would be forthcoming from the Piedmontese and that the city was effectively pinned down between encroaching Habsburg armies. General Nugent's daughter, Countess Dorsee, was still a prisoner, the object of adoring poems from the guard of handsome young Sicilians with whom she flirted under her husband's nose, but her value as a hostage had markedly decreased. The fall of Vicenza became Welden's cue to pounce, and at dawn on 13 June, with another pacific overture rejected, he ordered the bombardment to commence.

As that morning was hot and muggy, the cellars and church crypts in which the Trevigiani took cover were a doubly welcome refuge from the 500-odd projectiles which battered their town for the next eleven hours. Disdaining any such shelter was the Mayor, Giuseppe Olivi, who stayed at his desk issuing orders, sustained by coffee, bread and soup sent in from nearby *trattorie*, while the civic-guard band occasionally played rousing marches in his honour. The prayers of those women and children gathered in the cathedral to beg intercession from Treviso's patron saint, the fifth-century hermit Liberale, fell on deaf ears, however, and at six that evening Olivi sent two representatives in a carriage with a white flag to offer surrender to Welden. On entering the city, the General was astonished to find it garrisoned chiefly by well-disciplined volunteers rather than the regulars whose presence had always been assumed by Austrian intelligence. He was a more humane character than several of his fellow generals and could see no reason not to be magnanimous, allowing the patriots to leave with full military honours, accompanied, as at Vicenza, by civilians in carriages. For some of those who stayed behind, the contrast between the shabby, makeshift appearance of the valiant *crociati* and the smart Habsburg soldiers at the victory parade was altogether too painful. 'This was a strong, compact army,' wrote one observer, 'properly uniformed and provisioned, which marched to the sound of fanfares and the roll of drums, their hated banners floating in the wind and their caps adorned with the conquerors' laurel sprigs.'

Nothing now remained to stall the Austrians' wholesale recovery of Venetia for the empire, save Venice itself and the two forts of Palmanova and Osoppo. The former, under its martinet commandant Carlo Zucchi, had successfully held off the siege force left there by Nugent six weeks earlier, and there were many within the fortress town who believed it strong enough in supplies and munitions to carry on a convincing resistance. Giulia Modena, who had stayed to nurse the wounded while her husband Gustavo was in Venice, calculated that enough food remained for a least two more months. Yet after the fall of Vicenza, Zucchi could no longer rely on external support; the discipline among his volunteer brigades was showing serious cracks; and his ex-Austrian troops were troubled by rumours of punishment and execution meted out to recaptured deserters on Radetzky's orders. On 24 June he managed to arrange favourable surrender terms, though at a considerable cost to the defenders' sense of honour. The article which rankled most was that acknowledging the error of Palmanova and its inhabitants in rebelling and their readiness humbly to submit to the Emperor's sovereign clemency. With a bad grace the defence committee at length agreed to this, so as to avoid having to shoulder the cost of the substantial repairs needed to fortifications and civic buildings. Giulia, calling Zucchi 'that imbecile', believed he had simply caved in to 'the prayers of a few rich families and those of various officers who, it seemed, had already arranged to rejoin the Austrian service'. A month previously she claimed to have caught him discussing terms with an Austrian agent who promised a safe-conduct and a Habsburg barony if he consented to flee. On Guilia's tip-off, the *crociati* made sure Zucchi stayed at his post, but she became convinced that he was deliberately encouraging wastage of ammunition stocks.* When the final handover took place, General Welden was delighted with the fortress's 'very considerable arsenal, with over 120 cannon and a large stock of gunpowder'. The 1,500-strong garrison marched out, with Giulia Modena riding after them in a carriage, dressed in black but defiantly sporting the volunteers' scarlet cross.

At Osoppo, high up the Tagliamento valley north of Udine, the commanding officers were better able than Zucchi to capitalise on the determination of their men to die in the last ditch. The fort, a sixteenth-century castle originally built by the Savorgnan family, occupied an impressive position on top of a crag above a village which could, if necessary, be defended. During the last week of April its commandant, Giovanni

---

* Similar accusations were made against Zucchi in December 1848 by volunteers who had served at Palmanova.

Battista Cavedalis, had left to join General La Marmora in organising the Veneto's anti-invasion forces. His deputy, the altogether admirable Bolognese colonel Licurgo Zannini, seized his chance, managing to mobilise some 400 men and instilling them from the outset with patriotic values. 'Osoppo,' he told them, 'now relies upon our love of Italy and our loyalty to the finest of causes, blessed by God and his Vicar on earth, the venerable Pius IX. Think of the glory of being able one day to boast to our brothers "I was at Osoppo, among the defenders of the fortress"!' All around the village the Austrians, mostly Italian troops loyal to the empire, adopted a scorched-earth policy, burning crops and pulling down houses and farm buildings to open up their field of fire. But Zannini, assisted by his lieutenant Leonardo Andervolti, a native Friulan, held firm, keeping his men busy with lessons in tactics and gunnery, cultivating a meticulous discipline throughout the ranks and constantly heartening them with a sense of their own bravery in what he must have known was an increasingly impossible situation.

The sense of standing heroically alone when defeat all around seemed imminent was not confined to the Italians. Radetzky and his staff were well aware that even as they successfully completed their task, face-saving diplomatic manoeuvres which might undermine it were being energetically conducted in Vienna, Turin, London and Paris. The generals' isolation was heightened by a lack of genuine support from central government. Johann von Wessenberg, Austria's newly appointed Foreign Minister, believed, as did Baron Hummelauer, returning on 12 June from his London mission, that Lombardy would have to be surrendered to Piedmont. Italian sympathisers in Lord John Russell's Cabinet, including the Prime Minister himself, had forced Palmerston to harden his original stance on the whole question, demanding the cession of both Austrian provinces. In France, Alphonse de Lamartine, still seeking to influence policy though no longer holding ministerial office, implied that his country's government would be willing to accept a compromise, with Lombardy offered to Charles Albert in return for the frontier territory of Savoy, which the French saw as a legitimate reward for the military intervention that was still hoped for by Italian patriots.

The day after Hummelauer's return, Wessenberg sent a dispatch to Austrian headquarters in Vienna ordering Radetzky to prepare for an armistice. It was forty-eight hours before the letter reached the Field Marshal. According to one of his officers, its effect on him was devastating. 'A 36-pound cannon ball falling at his feet would have seemed like the dove from Noah's Ark compared to this unfortunate communication.' In that two-day period the final stages of Vicenza's reoccupation were completed, Treviso had fallen to Welden's army, and the Austrian general staff felt, like their chief, understandably less disposed to conclude a truce with their work more than half done and the scent of victory in the air. They might have been encouraged, what was more, by the news that the Lombard provisional government had rejected peace feelers tendered on Austria's behalf by Karl von Schnitzer, a diplomat with some experience of Italian affairs. He had guessed correctly that France was using Savoy as its bargaining counter, but was surprised by the high-mindedness of the Lombards in insisting that since they had voted over-whelmingly in favour of fusion with Piedmont, there was no question of making a separate agreement without Charles Albert's assent. They were also unwilling to abandon Venice, following its earlier gesture of solidarity in voting to amalgamate with Lombardy, even if they them-selves had rendered this pointless in their haste to place themselves under the King's protection.

Belief in Charles Albert's altruism remained touchingly constant. The Lombards would have been outraged by the contents of a letter he had sent to one of his ministers only a week or so earlier. 'I seriously believe,' he wrote, 'that if we can obtain the surrender of Lombardy as far as the Adige, together with the two duchies of Parma and Modena, we shall have conducted a glorious campaign, and that a state as small as ours, challenging the might of the colossal Austrian empire, will have achieved superb conquests, almost unheard-of in history.' The leaves of the Italian artichoke, in his ancestor's phrase, were to be enjoyed one at a time, and neither Venice nor the Veneto had ever formed a serious part of the King's territorial calculations.

Perhaps Radetzky guessed at these limited intentions more exactly than the noblemen in Milan who had sent Schnitzer about his business.* He was determined, at any rate, that there was to be no compounding with Piedmont while the Austrian army was so effectively engaged in demonstrating the weakness of Charles Albert's grip on eastern Lombardy, notwithstanding the much-trumpeted capture of Peschiera. The crucial error of the King and his generals had been to treat the Veneto campaign as a mere sideshow, allowing Radetzky to consolidate his strength in Verona and obliterate any further rearguard action by Italian forces. Now the Field Marshal prepared to make a stand against the show of weak-ness by ministers and diplomats in Vienna. On 18 June one of his most

---

* Radetzky told the French journalist Blaze de Bury that Charles Albert had never enjoyed popular support in Lombardy, having been 'duped by revolu-tionary intrigue and at the same time blinded by his own ambition'.

intransigently conservative officers, Prince Felix zu Schwarzenberg, was sent to the imperial court in refuge at Innsbruck to announce that there would be no armistice, whether according to the terms proposed by Wessenberg or on any conditions whatsoever. Schwarzenberg, dashing and unscrupulous had both the necessary *physique du rôle* (somewhat enhanced, in the circumstances, by a wound sustained at Goito) and considerable diplomatic experience. His brief was to explain the realities of the current military situation, demand 25,000 extra troops and secure a free hand for the Austrian high command to pursue the campaign to its promised outcome.

Steamrolling Wessenberg's objections that there was no money left to manage the war and that the troops which would almost certainly need to be raised among the German-speaking provinces must prove less reliable than the loyal Croats and Bohemians, Schwarzenberg persuaded him at least to defer the armistice, taking time, while at Innsbruck, to draw up a detailed memorandum supporting the army hard-liners. A peace based on the cession of Lombardy to Piedmont would not last, he argued, because the Italians would want the Veneto as well. Security for Italy and Europe lay in cutting Charles Albert down to size. As for finances, would it not be cheaper in the long run to maintain hostilities on their present basis, rather than have to start a fresh war against an augmented Piedmont? Wessenberg, accepting these cogent points, finally agreed to send further reinforcements from the empire's Slavic provinces and bowed to Radetzky's demands.

Ironically, the ultimate reward for the Field Marshal's determination would come, not from Vienna, but from Paris. There the economy had collapsed in the wake of February's revolution; a massive local unemployment crisis had been staved off, but not solved, by the dissident journalist Louis Blanc, acting as unofficial Labour Minister; and to make matters worse, hordes of the jobless had descended on the capital, lured by government assurances of the right to work. Elections for a new constitutional assembly resulted in a representative body top-heavy with aristocrats, rentiers and political moderates, which was bound from its inception to see the so-called 'national workshops' set up for the unemployed as dangerous nests of socialism. Early in June the assembly closed them down, with draconian penalties threatened against any equivalent organisation. The workers took to the streets, throwing up barricades while the government rallied support from among the provincial bourgeoisie and made haste to call up 60,000 troops commanded by the War Minister, General Eugène Cavaignac. In four days of fighting, 1,460 lives were lost, mostly among the insurgents. Cavaignac declared himself powerless to restrain his men from brutal reprisals, as Paris became an armed camp, its streets, open spaces and public buildings policed and inhabited by the soldiery. Proclamation of martial law marked the start of a violent political lurch to the right, enforced by the assembly's offer of dictatorial powers to the general whose prompt action had foiled the threatened triumph of socialism.

These Parisian June days created a major turning point in the course of the 1848 revolutions across Europe. A menacing image of the French capital plunging headlong into anarchy overrode for many those unimpeachable aspirations towards political reform and improved civil rights which, five months earlier, had prompted uprisings everywhere from Palermo to Berlin. A sense of better-the-devil-you-know now encouraged a more benign view of the forces of conservatism that were formerly challenged or despised, whether in the shape of ruling dynasties, aristocrats as hereditary guarantors of social stability or the armed forces as ultimate preservers of that civic order which shielded property and allowed commerce to flourish. In this new climate Radetzky and his staff seemed not just heroic in their refusal to accept the defeatist solutions proffered by the diplomats, but essential to the recovery of Austria's national prestige, let alone its survival as an empire. 'The revolutionists of Paris had in fact come to the rescue of the Austrian imperial forces in Italy,' as a modern American historian succinctly puts it. The army would fight on, there was everything to play for, and Venice – trophy city of the Habsburg Crown – still maddeningly revelled in her liberty.

CHAPTER 8

❧

'AND WHAT ABOUT US?'

FROM ITS VERY FOUNDATION VENICE has been as much an ideal city, imagined or conceptualised, as a physical entity created from brick and stone. To the Middle Ages and the Renaissance it represented power and autonomy based on immeasurable wealth, while for the eighteenth century there was an obvious moralising connection to be made between its loss of empire and international influence on the one hand and its role, on the other, as a pleasure-drome, vibrant with the annual rhythm of masquerades, operas, puppet-shows, gambling and gossip. Brought low after the Treaty of Campoformio extinguished the Serene Republic, the city became the dream-world of Romantic travellers, a place without present or future, its past darkened by *la leggenda nera*, an inhabited ruin magnificently symbolising the pointlessness of human endeavour, '*la Bella Dominante*' reduced to a forlorn old pensioner living off her memories.

This emblematic potential was seldom more in evidence than during the revolution of 1848–9. Venice's destiny, during these two years, was guided to a significant degree by her role as an abstract embodiment – the focus, for some, of hopes, ideals and long-forestalled ambitions; the object elsewhere of resentment, suspicion and anger. While the Austrians came to view the city's recapture as their ultimate goal, 'the turning point in the drama' as Felix zu Schwarzenberg later declared, it was Venice's iconic status as a beacon of liberty in a world of confusion and compromise that inspired her republican citizens, with Manin and Tommaseo at their head. For the latter, bitterly intolerant of the way in which others tended to let practical considerations corrupt ideological purity, it was easy to revere Venice as a utopian historical construct. By the time he was born in 1802, Sebenico (Sibenik), his native city, belonged to Austria, but all around the growing boy in the Dalmatian port lay images of Venetian imperial power, such as the superb Renaissance cathedral of San Giacomo, the colonnaded town hall, the triangular fortress of San Nicola and the seven-gated girdle of ramparts. Spiritually, Tommaseo belonged to the metropolis of this lost empire, as to nowhere else in his long and almost entirely peripatetic existence. A modern Italian cultural historian has called him 'the last citizen, or one of the last, of the old Venetian Republic'. For the Dalmatian in 1848, 'the moment had arrived when he could turn towards St Mark and offer the Republic that defence which the Slavic regiments, notwithstanding their wish to do so, had been prevented from offering in 1797'. That he shared the devotion of those Croat troops who had panicked the senators with their loyal salvo during the Grand Council's final session is shown in a touchingly sentimental poem in which the city appears variously as the bride, mother, sister, father and brother to whom the writer dedicates life and love: 'Just as your gospel, O Mark, has brought virtue down the ages, so may health and strength be given to my Venice by heaven's angels.'

For Daniele Manin, the idea of what Venice was or ought to be lay grounded more strongly in immediate realities. Writing to the Piedmontese Foreign Minister Lorenzo Pareto on 21 June, he proudly pointed out that while the *terraferma* towns had fallen one by one to Austrian arms, 'Venice alone retains its independence, regained on 22 March. Protected by its natural ramparts, the patriotism of its citizens and the bravery of the volunteers, this city can stand firm against enemy attack.' What mattered now was that the 'ancient bulwark of liberty' should be preserved from danger in the name of a shared Italian cause, and that all those involved in the ongoing struggle should be able to depend on its abiding freedom. To ensure this, reasoned Manin, two things were necessary: reinforcements and money. The swift dispatch of some of those 'valorous, battle-hardened Piedmontese troops' would be in everybody's interest (these last two words were underlined) and their military attributes would be an inspiration to younger, less experienced soldiers. The letter ended with a candid acknowledgement that the government's finances, already substantially drained by having to maintain the existing force of 18,000 men, were likely to be exhausted altogether by the end of the first week of July, even with the help of two forced loans raised from among Venetian citizens and the proceeds of the May fund-raising drive so successfully carried out by Ugo Bassi and Alessandro Gavazzi.

A further strain was placed on these dwindling resources by the presence of the two fleets, Piedmontese and Neapolitan, which had been cruising the lagoon for the past two months in support of the Venetian navy. The cost of that fatal error made when Governor Palffy was shipped out of Venice on 23 March, which had resulted in the loss of the ships at Pola, was now being counted by the provisional government, as the Austrians started blockading ports large and small, forcing merchant vessels to sail to Trieste. Such naval resources as the Venetians could muster – a brace of corvettes, two brigantines, a schooner and a flotilla of smaller craft – were expanded with the help of Arsenal shipwrights, who built a third brig and ran up a forty-gun frigate, besides fitting up several other boats as vessels of war. For all the festive enthusiasm that had greeted the Neapolitan squadron of five frigates and a twenty-gun brig, a cloud of rumour and suspicion hung over its elderly admiral Raffaele De Cosa. Though King Ferdinand of Naples, running with the political tide, had officially given his blessing to the expedition's departure for Venice on 27 April, he was said to have whispered in De Cosa's ear, 'Remember you are old and have a family to take care of.' This sinister warning was meant to reinforce the monarch's secret order that the fleet must on no account attack Austrian shipping. From the Neapolitan War Minister, Francesco Del Giudice, came a slightly more flexible set of instructions, allowing De Cosa to fire on enemy vessels in the open sea, but not attempt any action against ports or along shore-lines.

De Cosa has been routinely traduced by Risorgimento historians as a mere creature of the detested 'King Bomba'. In fact he had never enthusiastically supported the Bourbon regime and was unwilling to accept his present command, precisely because he mistrusted Ferdinand's intentions. His sincere patriotism, had Venetian detractors realised it, contrasted notably with the ambivalent attitude to the enterprise adopted at this stage by his Piedmontese counterpart, Admiral Giovanni Battista Albini. The brief given to the combined fleets was to sail to Trieste and commence a blockade, but it was easy enough for foreign consuls in the port, led by those of Britain, France, the United States and Greece, to persuade Albini that by seeking to harm Austria he was effectively damaging their subjects' commercial interests. Added to these voices was that of Lieutenant Ippolito Spinola, Piedmont's naval attaché to Venice, fearful of the fire-power from the Austrian shore-batteries and damning the blockade as imprudent.

Only when news came that General Nugent had been busy mustering a fresh reserve force to bombard contumacious Palmanova into submission did Spinola change his mind, imagining this would leave Trieste undefended from the land. By now, however, coal supplies for steam-powered

vessels were running short, and the whole idea of combined naval operations had been thrown into confusion by the dramatic counter-revolution
that took place in Naples on 15 May, later called 'one of the most causeless instances of slaughter and bloodshed ever recorded in history'. King
Ferdinand, having sworn to uphold a constitution, now found himself
and his new government faced with a radical opposition determined at
any cost to undermine what it saw as maintenance of the status quo with
modish political frills attached. On the night of 14 May rioting broke
out in the streets of Naples, which Ferdinand did his best to halt by
agreeing to concessions in exchange for all barricades being removed in
the space of three days. Just before midnight, when neither side showed
any signs of yielding to the other's demands, a single shot accidentally
fired by a civic-guardsman triggered off six hours of fierce fighting between
the *barricadisti* and such army units as were not yet posted north to take
part in the war, while the *lazzaroni*, the Neapolitan mob from the warren
of slums around the port, went on the rampage and many unarmed citizens were killed in the crossfire.

Ferdinand, whatever his shortcomings, scarcely deserved the blame
heaped on him by his contemporaries. He continued to act with moderation, going ahead with the project of constitutional government, treating
the most *enragé* of the street fighters with greater leniency than he had
shown towards the Bandieras and their accomplices, and visiting and
comforting the wounded of both sides. What Italian patriots never forgave
him was the order issued on 18 May to all Neapolitan forces in the
northern theatre of war that they should return home at once. The blunt
truth was that events had played into the King's hands. He was running
out of funds to sustain his army's contribution to the war, he was reluctant to antagonise Austria any further, and the way lay open, in the
context of an abruptly changed political order in Naples, for recovering
Sicily, most of which had been lost to his rule since the Palermo uprising
in February.

The response from his troops, mainly concentrated at Ferrara, was
mixed. Several regiments turned tail almost at once, but a significant body
of committed patriots, some 1,400 in all, remained dedicated to the cause
and followed their elderly commander Guglielmo Pepe across the Po to
aid the Venetians. As one of them put it in a letter to Manin, the issue
lay between disobedience to their sovereign and an infamous betrayal of
the trust reposed in them by other Italians. In the case of one officer,
anguish over the choice brought on a stroke, while two others were driven
to suicide. Alessandro Poerio, having committed himself to the revolution, wrote home in disgust, 'I assure you, dearest mother, that as a

Neapolitan it is most bitter for me to see our soldiers' reputation thus sullied. Such deliberate infamy is enough to make one die of shame.'

For Admiral De Cosa it ought to have been a simple matter of obeying the order dispatched by King Ferdinand's new War Minister Francesco Ischitella, and turning his navy's head towards Naples forthwith. To his credit he temporised, claiming that to leave now would shame both officers and men. A second assault on Trieste was being planned, Ippolito Spinola having told his superiors in Turin that inaction by the combined fleets, at anchor outside the port, was damaging naval morale and making a very bad impression in Venice. The Austrians had utilised the delay to build up Trieste's defences, and the commercial objection put forward by the consuls was surely invalid, given the attacks on various cities currently being carried out by land forces. Three days later, while the blockade continued, fresh orders from Ferdinand arrived, expressly commanding his ships to return home. Since the officer who brought the letter immediately published its contents throughout the fleet, De Cosa had no choice but to obey. Humiliated, he asked to resign, but was met with an official silence. By the time his ships rounded the Calabrian coast, his tone had changed its professional moderation for a greater asperity. It is not difficult to read, between the lines of his second offer of resignation, a deep sense of alienation and betrayal. He could not go on to Sicily (as presumably he would be required to do), bomb his fellow Italians and carry out what he saw as a deliberate suppression of long-postponed freedom. 'I prefer rather to retreat into private life than compromise the reputation which my efforts and well-attested record of service have procured for me.' Once returned to Naples, De Cosa was as good as his word, rejecting invitations to court, snubbing overtures from the King and government, and cursing the Bourbon dynasty from his deathbed.

Left without the Neapolitans, Piedmont's Admiral Albini, urged on by Spinola, grew somewhat more enthusiastic about bombarding Trieste. Unprovoked firing from the shore-batteries gave him an adequate pretext, and on 15 June he and the Venetian fleet stepped up the blockade. The Austrians, instead of trying to batter their way out, artfully turned to international law for help by appealing to the Frankfurt Diet, the democratically elected parliament assembled from the representatives of the various German states, which had opened on 18 May to journalistic fanfares and high European expectations. Trieste's special status was invoked, and the Diet was happy enough to claim the prosperous Mediterranean entrepôt as part of the German confederation, thus retaining neutral status. For the Piedmontese government this absurd technicality, by which Albini was forced to reduce the blockade, offered a handy get-out. Charles Albert had already been embarrassed by pressures from Palmerston to give up the idea altogether, since Trieste, according to the Foreign Secretary, contained 'a great quantity of British property, which would of course be destroyed by such an attack, and thus British interests would suffer severely. Feelings hostile to the Italians and especially to the Sardinian [i.e. Piedmontese] government would be excited in the public in this country, not to mention claims to which losses so occasioned might give rise.' Thus, it might be said, the slender majority on which Lord John Russell's Whig administration survived in Parliament and the continuing crisis on the London money market were to play their parts in thwarting the best-laid schemes of the Italian patriots.

There was no question of Albini leaving the Adriatic while Venice seemed increasingly poised to surrender its boasted autonomy to Piedmontese control. As for Spinola, he saw it as his job to square the crews of the various Venetian vessels in favour of immediate fusion, following the example of the Lombards and the mainland cities before their recapture. In the light of events during early June and the news from Paris, which seemed to rule out any possibility of French intervention, becoming a part of Charles Albert's swiftly expanding realm looked, to many Venetians, not so much an attractive option among several, as the only recourse left. Fusion now became the word on everyone's lips, whether invoked as the ultimate safeguard of liberty or blasted as the latest device for enabling the Piedmontese sovereign to nibble at yet another leaf of the Italian artichoke. The issue was in any case far from simple. As one dialect rhymster put it:

Non intendo ben sto termine
    Che sento dir: *Fusion*;
Me par che i se desmentega
    De metter prima un *con*.

'I don't fully understand this word "fusion" I'm hearing: it seems as if people are forgetting to put a "con" before it.'

Confusion of one kind or another as to Venice's relationship with Piedmont had set in almost from the new republic's inception. From Milan the aristocrats forming the government warned Manin concerning the unacceptable nature of a republican administration to the Piedmontese, yet initially they seemed to support his wait-and-see policy of leaving the fusion issue in abeyance until the war reached a successful outcome. Within Venice itself, the fault-line among his Cabinet swiftly revealed itself, with the Justice Minister Jacopo Castelli lining up beside

Pietro Paleocapa, the illustrious engineer-turned-politician, to back an immediate union once news began arriving of Charles Albert's advance into Lombardy and Radetzky's withdrawal towards the safety of the Quadrilateral. They were supported by the conservative Gian Francesco Avesani, who – whatever his intransigence in spelling out surrender terms to Palffy on 22 March – was suspected of pro-Austrian sympathies for having earlier retracted an instance to the central congregation under police pressure, thus refusing to go the way of Manin and Tommaseo towards honourable imprisonment.

Against them stood Daniele Manin himself, opposed to fusion not just because he clung to the notion of Venice's independence as something infinitely valuable in itself, but challenging it also on the typically legalistic basis that so serious a step needed a proper consultation process and suitable reference to the views of ordinary citizens. Niccolò Tommaseo, for his part, was still backing Pope Pius IX as 'the single counterweight to Charles Albert', whom he thoroughly despised, holding him personally responsible for having, 'with his usual generosity', left the Tuscans fully exposed to the Austrian onslaught at Curtatone e Montanara. Tommaseo's profound aversion to any closer links with Piedmont than circumstances warranted was shared by more openly republican Venetians, including Carlo Radaelli, who was later to write his own history of the revolution; the lawyers Giandomenico Giuriati and Antonio Bellinato; and the soldier priest Antonio Torniello, a doughty fighter at the head of his own legion at Treviso. In April they had started meeting as a club, dedicated to defending 'the principle of democratic republicanism', and their fears regarding Charles Albert's darker purpose found an echo among several thoughtful voices outside Venice itself.

Chief among these was Giovanni Battista Castellani, the provisional government's envoy to Pope Pius. Essentially a federalist, he had been strongly in favour of the idea of a constituent assembly, to be held in Rome by representatives from various Italian states – a revival, as it were, of the medieval league of communes that had defied Emperor Frederick Barbarossa in Lombardy during the twelfth century.* In a letter to the government on 23 June, Castellani articulated the anti-fusion case:

> Before Charles Albert began to stir himself, our people had driven the last foreigner beyond their frontiers. It was faith in him which dampened

---

* This same episode provides the theme for 'La battaglia di Legnano', Giuseppe Verdi's only opera directly linked to the events of the Risorgimento, first performed in Rome in 1849.

enthusiasm and rendered our armed struggle useless; it was his supporters who destroyed our union; it was he who, introducing a political question from the outset, replaced with mistrust the generous confidence of citizens in their governments, and substituted for the broad initiative of so many the narrow vision of a mere few. It would have been infinitely preferable had Venice acted of its own accord, Lombardy also, and every other Italian state, since the mistake was made of failing to acknowledge provisional governments from the start and concluding agreements with them. Now instead we resort to fusion, the origin of weakness since, by opposing union, it crushes and destroys that individuality which is the true basis of strength. To free Italy they wish to change its very nature. Italy thus betrayed will be unworthy of history, ambition or hope.

Such arguments cut little ice with the fusionists, the *albertisti*, represented mostly by the patricians and the bourgeoisie, increasingly frightened by the rough-and-ready republicanism of the Venetian working class – fishermen, gondoliers, shipwrights at the Arsenal – who passionately revered Manin as a kind of Roman tribune and 'father of his country'. Their opportunity to put a fusionist case more forcibly arrived in June, when Venice witnessed its first ever democratic election,* for membership of an assembly that should give greater legality to the provisional government. Representatives were invited from mainland towns and villages, and votes were cast according to parishes, with much nudging given in one direction or another by local priests. It was not strictly a partisan election, but the preponderance of bourgeois members (including many Jews, whose full civil rights were guaranteed by the revolution) meant that Albertist views would be strongly canvassed when the assembly was scheduled to open its first session on 3 July.

Manin had postponed the opening from its original scheduled date, 18 June, because one more chance had seemed to present itself, after the loss of Padua and Treviso, to seek military intervention, either by France or other Italian states, so as to head off the inevitability of fusion. It was this two-week put-off which ironically gave the Piedmontese time to stir up the Venetians in favour of surrendering their independence to whatever administration Charles Albert might impose. While Ippolito Spinola propagandised energetically among the crews of the fleet, a more insidious agent of the monarchy arrived in the city with a clear

---

* Under the Serene Republic the Doge was elected by the complicated system whose use of small ivory or wooden balls, *balote*, gives us our English word 'ballot'. The franchise was limited to members of the Golden Book nobility.

agenda for slipping Venice into the King's pocket as easily and quickly as possible.

Count Enrico Martini presented himself to the provisional government offering promises of money and military aid in return for immediate fusion. Arrogant and snobbish, he appears to have been completely taken aback, to begin with at least, by the lack of what he deemed an appropriate submissiveness on the part of Manin and his ministers, in view of Venice's current disadvantages. He despised the individual members of the administration as mere bourgeois pen-pushers, refused to deal with them personally, and was not above distributing bribes or invoking the bugbear of a recent Austrian assault on Marghera (strongest of all the lagoon forts) to blackmail the government into surrendering its authority to royal commissioners.

Martini's hand was visible to many in a major demonstration by the civic guard in favour of fusion, which took place in the Piazza on 29 June. Their commanders, especially Angelo Mengaldo, could be easily manipulated, and it was obvious that *albertisti* such as Jacopo Castelli and Pietro Paleocapa had engaged to do their share in encouraging the guardsmen, during a review by General Pepe (whom Martini wrote off as a nincompoop), to raise a cry of 'Viva la fusione, abbasso la repubblica!' Manin, on hearing the tumult, was incensed, telling Mengaldo that 'while the lowest classes of the people have restrained themselves and are calmly awaiting the imminent vote of the assembly', the guard had disgraced itself in trying to influence the outcome, 'thus endangering the very public order they are meant to be preserving'. Time was now against the republicans, as news of the Paris riots and the Austrian troop movements made union with Piedmont not so much an option as an absolute necessity for the Venetian bourgeoisie, if their city were to survive. The fall of Palmanova added further urgency to calls for fusion by the demonstrators in the Piazza. Pietro Contarini, who later published a diary of events in Venice during 1848–9, noted that for the first time the cry, unimaginable two months earlier, of 'Death to Manin and Tommaseo!' was heard among the civic guard.

It was not in Manin's nature to accuse his fellow citizens of ingratitude. Nobody could claim that the provisional government's record was perfect. The collapse of its goodwill among the mainland towns, the disbanding of the Italian regiments and the lack of military coordination in confronting Nugent's advance marked serious political failures of judgement from whose effects it had no chance of recovering. Worse still, there was no coherent programme with which to follow up the expulsion of the Habsburg governors and the proclamation of liberty on 22 March. The crisis-management nature of the new regime revealed itself, what was more, in its continuously nervous attitude towards demonstrations by the Venetian working class in search of improved pay and conditions. Though Manin needed – and was given – enthusiastic support from artisans and labourers, he remained fearful, from the very day of his release from prison, as to the possible spread of communism and anarchy within any kind of social vacuum left by the departing Austrians. Splendid in conception, daring in execution, the republic had been hustled into existence without an adequate constitutional basis or any clear sense of its intentions being effectively realised via the operations of the various armed forces at Venice's disposal. Once the central machinery of Austrian government in the Veneto was dismantled, no proper bureaucratic framework materialised to take its place. The immemorial rivalry and mistrust dividing Italian cities began showing themselves almost as soon as the earliest fraternal 'Evviva!'s had died away. Feltre and Belluno, Vicenza and Treviso, Padua and Venice, all were reluctant to bury historical differences. There could be no common cause, in any case, throughout a province in which the political ratio of patriotism to Austrophilia varied so markedly between regions, communities and social echelons.

Yet from that purely moral aspect nowadays so often ignored by the executive of a liberal democracy, the government had been exemplary in promoting a culture of openness and accountability lacking under the Habsburgs. Liberty of expression and opinion was symbolised by the mushroom crop of newspapers sporting every shade of politics: some of them, like the *Speranze del Popolo*, the *Martiri Italiani*, the *Utile e Dilettevole* and the *Ficcanaso*, surviving for only a few issues; others, like the witty, iconoclastic *Sior Antonio Rioba*, its woodcut cartoons alive with a devilish knowingness, hanging on to push the new press freedom to its very limits. The sessions of the council of ministers were open to observers and were more than once inopportunely broken off by over-zealous patriots such as the young Veronese, representing a volunteer brigade, who begged to be allowed to march against Radetzky and free his native city; he was politely recommended by Jacopo Castelli to head north for Bassano, where he and his fellow *crociati* would be rather more useful.

This incident was one of several representing the kind of dialogue between the executive and the people which had not taken place in Venice since the days when the Jacobins had hoisted a liberty tree in the Piazza, and probably not even then. The ultimate luxury which the provisional government, whatever its mistakes, guaranteed to everyone was that 'eternal spirit of the chainless mind'* whose existence Austrian rule, by

* This lapidary phrase is Byron's, from his poem 'The Prisoner of Chillon'.

its very essence, was bent on crushing. When news of the Viennese revolution in March had reached Trieste, the civil governor Prince Salm had announced that 'His Majesty has graciously conceded freedom of thought', to which the journalist Pacifico Valussi retorted, 'Thank you, but we had that already.' In Venice there were those who believed, not without reason, that to give away to another monarchical regime the basic freedoms assured by 22 March was to forfeit anything of value achieved in the course of the revolution so far.

On 3 July the inaugural session of the newly elected assembly was due to take place after morning mass at St Mark's. Manin, aware of his vulnerability as leader of the anti-fusionists, sent a note, as soon as he arrived at the Doge's Palace, to his wife Teresa and their children Emilia and Giorgio regarding their presence at the forthcoming debate. 'I take it as understood that no member of my family is to show any sign of approval, disapproval or impatience. If you think that you will be unable to restrain yourself, you should remain absent. I am confident that in this solemn moment you will not add to my sorrows that of being disobeyed by my wife and children.' As far as we know, the order was obeyed, though the fact that Teresa kept the document among her papers suggests that the family was fully conscious of the occasion's momentousness and of its likely outcome.

It was Gian Francesco Avesani, impatient as ever, who hustled the fusion debate into being, after Manin had insisted on the importance of a cast-iron legality as the foundation of all the assembly's proceedings and a proper verification of the electoral process. 'Let us hurry and get this over with,' snapped Avesani. 'The city is in torment.' When he started his next sentence with the words 'We wish', their implication proved too much for Niccolò Tommaseo, who sarcastically observed that the honourable deputy doubtless really meant 'I wish', but that in any case he could scarcely wish to force a precipitate decision which would dishonour them in the eyes of both Italy and Europe. What besides, asked another republican, Giovanni Ferrari Bravo, were the anxieties and perils to which Avesani seemed so anxious to draw everyone's attention? The assembly needed to remember that barely half a century ago, in this very same Sala del Maggior Consiglio, timidity on the part of the Venetian Senate had brought about the Serene Republic's fall and precipitated fifty years of civil and military despotism. 'A Venice revived and regenerated must be dignified and not pusillanimous when it comes to pronouncing on her destiny.'

When Manin rose to speak again, it was to deliver, in his concise fashion, a résumé of the tumultuous events of the past three months, emphasising the propriety and altruism of the provisional government in determining Venice's course across an increasingly complex political terrain, reminding his audience of the resolution (made on 22 April) not to engage with the fusion issue until the war was successfully concluded, and pointing out that Lombardy and the Veneto towns had jumped the gun with their various referendums on the question, effectively detaching themselves from Venice even as the Austrians began the recapture of the surrounding province. 'Ponder your deliberations carefully,' he warned them, 'so that they may increase Venice's strength and safety, while assigning her the honourable rank which is her due in an Italy unified and independent. The motherland demands from you, citizen represen-tatives, an act of civic wisdom. May inspiration descend upon you within these sacred walls!'

The following morning the deputies gathered an hour earlier, at 9 a.m., in the clear consciousness that a decisive moment in the history of reborn Venetian liberty was upon them. When the republican Samuel Olper sought to reinforce Ferrari Bravo's words as to the importance of standing firm and showing courage in adversity, Manin – prophetically as it turned out – claimed that if Austria were to attack the city, all political divisions would disappear amid the unity of its defenders and that 'if there were anybody who dared to speak of surrender, the whole populace, myself foremost among them, would crush such infamy and treason!' Olper's speech was an effort at making some sort of running against the fusion-ists by appealing to patriotic sentiment. Manin now switched to a subtler tactic, that of outlining the various prevarications and failures to respond positively with which other Italian governments had answered Venetian requests for financial assistance and advice as to possible French inter-vention. That cash reserves had started running perilously short was borne out by reports on the army and navy budgets now produced by Jacopo Castelli and Antonio Paolucci.

At this moment Niccolò Tommaseo chose to weigh in, with a speech whose elaborate disingenuousness would have been judged a masterstroke by any other audience than this one. Had not Charles Albert, he argued, promised them his protection? Had he not come to their aid without demanding any pledges in return, making a solemn engagement not to sheathe his sword 'while a single Austrian bayonet should reflect the light of the Italian sun'? Could the assembled deputies honestly believe that His Majesty would behave any worse than King Ferdinand of Naples, traitor to his word and murderer of his subjects? Surely, by refusing to accept union with Piedmont, Venice offered Charles Albert a chance to fulfil his promise by performing the noblest and most generous of acts.

The monarch himself knew that if the struggle were not detached from all vulgar dynastic considerations, he would never triumph. They must grant him, therefore, the opportunity to silence his detractors by showing himself ready to fight without setting a price on the spilling of blood. 'May God,' ended Tommaseo, 'fulfil my wishes for this beloved land and give the lie to my gloomiest forebodings.'

Everybody present must have known what the Dalmatian honestly thought of Charles Albert. It was the engineer Pietro Paleocapa who, getting to his feet immediately, sealed the republicans' doom through an obvious contempt for Tommaseo's brilliant forensic flourishes. 'Accustomed as I have been, over forty years, to the fatigues of battle and public affairs,' he began, 'I can only offer you the words of a man of action, a man without the gift of being able to raise his imagination to lofty heights, a man who values not only his country's independence, but its prosperity as well.' Internationally successful within his profession (though 'the fatigues of battle' played very little part in the bridge-building and river-widening projects with which he had been chiefly involved), Paleocapa could command respect among Venetians in general as someone who had dedicated much energy and ingenuity to improving the infrastructure of the port and helping to revive the city's commercial life. He believed sincerely in the acceptance of fusion as the key to Charles Albert's seemingly mysterious inaction over providing immediate military and material assistance. Now he dismissed Tommaseo's arguments, barely taking the trouble to examine them in detail, and brushed aside Manin's original recommendation that the issue be deferred until the end of the war. If they were to emulate their valiant forefathers during fourteen centuries of Venetian independence, they must remember 'these men's practical knowledge, their willingness to ponder their actions in conformity with the true needs of the nation, setting aside abstract ideas and all this political vapouring, which easily gets lost in the clouds and, like the clouds themselves, can turn into a storm'.

Paleocapa's speech, artfully punctuated with further references to his plain-man's practicality in comparison with the visionary rhetoric of earlier speakers, was greeted with such fervent applause that Avesani, who had planned to support him with a blistering exposé of the government's incompetence and mistakes, simply urged the deputies to accept union with Piedmont and sat down. Tommaseo, having originally prepared a second address, warning that the Piedmontese would simply treat Venice like a conquered territory and advocating an Italian federation of self-governing provinces, realised that Paleocapa had knocked the wind out of his sails and ostentatiously took up a set of galley proofs to correct during Avesani's brief address. He would never forgive either of them for the success with which they had steamrollered the republican case. Equally unpardonable, in his eyes, was the attitude of Daniele Manin, whose extraordinary altruism at this moment was not of a kind to flatter Tommaseo's intransigence. Instead of making a further bid to retain the political status quo, the lawyer surprised everybody by urging them, whatever their politics, to accept the reality of the situation. There was now, he argued, a serious threat of civil war within the city over the fusion issue, strife that could only be avoided by a major sacrifice of long-held principles.

'Let us give the lie to the enemy at our gates, counting on our disagreements. Let us forget party divisions. Let us show him that today we forget whether we are monarchists or republicans, that today we are all of us citizens.' It was scant comfort to the anti-fusionists for Manin to add that the real future of a united Italy would be decided by a constituent assembly in Rome. When he had concluded this noble yet fateful gesture of reconciliation in the name of civic order, a storm of cheering shook the hall, deputies rushed to embrace him, and Jacopo Castelli, leader of the *albertisti*, cried, 'The motherland is saved! Long live Manin!' Tommaseo, grinding his teeth, prepared to damn Castelli to perdition in a vitriolic sketch included in his memoir of 1848, summing him up as 'a fine orator and not altogether uneducated, a good father, a good man indeed, but exquisitely contemptible'.

Just then, according to the Friulan poet Francesco Dall'Ongaro (a political weathercock currently in republican mode), something sinister happened. It was 4 July, and since the United States of America were always friendly to the provisional government, a festive salute had been ordered from the cannon ranged along the mole of the Piazzetta. As the deputies inside the palace proceeded to a vote, they can scarcely have failed to recall that other salvo, fired in loyal sadness rather than joy by Dalmatian troops, which so shook the senators of the Serene Republic on 12 May 1797 and panicked them into voting for their own dissolution. The result of the present poll was an overwhelming triumph for the fusion lobby, 127 votes in favour with only six against and no abstentions. Venice was now declared part of the mushrooming kingdom of Piedmont, which, in a few weeks, had grown to more than twice its original size. Remembering that July morning, Dall'Ongaro noted one other significant detail. Among those watching and listening intently to the proceedings was Maddalena Montalban Comello, devotedly patriotic wife of a leading Venetian merchant. When the vote was declared, she covered her face and wept. 'This woman,' observed the poet, 'was a better representative of Venice than all the elected deputies of its assembly.'

The provisional government was now officially at an end, its powers transferred to a caretaker administration, which would preside until the Piedmontese had formally accepted control of Venice and its territory in the lagoon. Manin's name headed a list of possible ministers within this temporary political framework, but he could not conscientiously accept any kind of role in a monarchical government. 'I beg my fellow citizens,' he told the assembly, 'not to force me to do something so foreign to my beliefs. I have made a sacrifice, but I have not given up my principles.' Besides, he was so worn out by the stress of the last few months that physically he scarcely felt equal to the task. Cries of 'No, no! Viva Manin!' filled the hall, but he stood firm, and Jacopo Castelli, rather more appropriately given his fusionist enthusiasm, became head of the new government, to be joined by Paleocapa, Paolucci and Giovanni Battista Cavedalis, former commander of rebel forces at Udine and now settled in Venice, a thoroughgoing conservative among patriot leaders.

Cavedalis appears to have accepted his portfolio as War Minister with some misgivings, sharing Manin's original opinion that now was not the time for make-or-break decisions and that in any case Venice's role as a last bastion of liberty might become genuinely significant if Piedmont lost the war and patriots needed a rallying point. His doubts were shared by the Venetian public, whose response to the assembly's decision was not as ecstatic as some of the more convinced Albertist deputies might have wished. There was a gala concert, hastily thrown together at the Teatro Gallo di San Benedetto, with hymns praising the King, for the umpteenth time, as Italy's deliverer, and the officers of the combined fleets threw a party on board a Piedmontese warship with appropriate speeches and toasts, but the atmosphere in the city remained curiously tepid. Perhaps it was true, as the *austriacante* Count Cicogna confided to his diary, that the whole process had been urged forward for the sake of practical advantage and of hanging on to independence, rather than through any real desire for the Veneto to become a province of greater Piedmont.

News of the vote was carried to Turin by Pietro Paleocapa, while three ambassadors whose patrician names – Grimani, Donà dale Rose, Boldù-Dolfin – were calculated to charm the ears of the snobbish Piedmontese set off for Charles Albert's camp at Marmirolo, north of Mantua. The King had his own reasons for receiving them with indifference, announcing that he would delegate to his government the responsibility of making a suitable reply. He had no interest in Venice save for its undeniable value as a bargaining counter in any peace negotiations with Austria, and would have been happy to settle for Lombardy and the two duchies of Parma and Modena rather than pushing his conquests beyond the natural frontiers of the River Adige. The fortunes of war were beginning to run against him. Radetzky's success at Vicenza, the strategic uselessness of Peschiera on whose capture he himself had staked so much, the failure of his generals to break or even seriously dent the Austrian line along the Mincio, were each of them galling enough to make him eager for peace. The offer of Venice at this moment was thus little better than an embarrassment, but, given the importance of Charles Albert's current incarnation as Italy's deliverer, he could not very well refuse it, and the matter was duly was referred to his government in Turin.

The absence of any real Italian patriotism in the King was obvious to the republicans in the former Habsburg provinces, even if they knew nothing, at this point, of his desire to bring the war to a speedy close by cutting a deal with Austria. According to the Milanese writer and politician Carlo Cattaneo, who referred to his 'jesuitical' deviousness, Charles Albert had gone to battle solely for the sake of enlarging his family domains and to stave off the rise of a republicanism which reflected Italy's historical traditions. He had entered Milan, claimed Cattaneo, ostensibly as the people's champion, but in reality as a conqueror. In taking control of Lombardy he had treated it like a subject province rather than seeking to conciliate public opinion, even if titles and honours of various kinds had been distributed with the aim of keeping useful citizens onside.

In Venice the republicans, having lost the contest over fusion, were certainly not going to keep quiet, whatever the efforts of Castelli and the caretaker administration at maintaining order and calm throughout the city until the Piedmontese parliament and Charles Albert should graciously assent to its incorporation within the kingdom. A few days after taking office the new regime ordered the suppression of several of the more hard-line anti-monarchist newspapers. As Justice Minister, Castelli had already banned the virulently republican *La Staffetta del Popolo*, defended in vain by Tommaseo. Now, as premier, he added to the list *Sior Antonio Rioba* (later permitted to resume publication) and *Fatti e parole*, whose distinguished editorial board included the Friulan journalist Pacifico Valussi, his brother-in-law Francesco Dall'Ongaro, the actor Gustavo Modena and that most fervent of republicans Samuel Olper. The excuse given for such a deliberate violation of the freedoms guaranteed by Manin's government at the outset of the revolution was that such papers 'tended to destroy whatever was achieved through general goodwill, contributed towards subverting order within the state and undermined public tranquillity'. Valussi promptly resigned his editorship of the official *Gazzetta*, but a protest from his fellow journalists to the relevant ministry fell on deaf ears.

Unmistakably audible by now from across the lagoon was the sporadic rumble of Austrian gunfire. Venice was not yet fully under siege, but her position was more obviously imperilled than at any time since 22 March. Ludwig von Welden's 20,000-strong reserve army, once its business around Treviso was finished, had moved swiftly to occupy the towns and villages along the coast. One of Radetzky's most efficient generals, Welden was not wholly uncritical of his chief, having censured his failure to ensure an adequate level of military preparedness in the Tyrol, an area many perceived as crucial to Austria's success in keeping a tight rein on its Italian provinces. Now, without further ado, he began stretching a line, offensive and defensive, as far south as the river estuaries below Chioggia, seizing the fort at Cavanella, on the mouth of the Adige, which overlooked a fertile zone of orchards and market gardens. The Croats had no sooner marched in than foraging parties began commandeering the fruit and vegetables normally sent to the markets of Venice. To recapture the fort was the aim of General Pepe's Neapolitan force encamped nearby, urged on by Chioggia's mayor and the town's military commander, that same General Andrea Ferrari whom Durando had so wretchedly left in the lurch at the battle of Cornuda.

Pepe's plan was for a pincer attack on the fort, to take place early in the morning of 7 July. The weather had turned from the heavy rains of previous weeks to a fierce heat, heralded in the dawning hours by a blanket of thick mist across the plain. Ferrari, commanding a mixture of volunteers, the remnants of his papal army and a brigade of Sicilians, was to move in support of the Neapolitans, supported by 500 Lombard volunteers, spearheading the main assault. Unfortunately the mist cleared too quickly and Ferrari's men found themselves disagreeably close to the walls, where they were sitting targets for the Croat artillery. Pepe's force meanwhile lacked enough boats to get from their base at Brondolo to the mouth of the river and failed to arrive in time. As at Cornuda, Ferrari was compelled to retreat after putting up a gallant show, and the usual round of name-calling, so frequent in the Italy of 1848, began. Some blamed ancient mutual suspicion between Neapolitans and Sicilians, others maintained that an 'Austro-Jesuitical' faction in Chioggia had tipped off the defenders, and several believed that Pepe had only devised the expedition in order to show the government in Venice that he was a man of action rather than words, thereby increasing his standing with both soldiers and civilians.

Guglielmo Pepe had been appointed commander-in-chief on 18 June, as part of a government reshuffle by Manin while still premier. Physically a giant of a man, he had the expansive personality and public profile to complement his stature. He was the last of twenty-four children born to a Calabrian noble family,* and several of his older brothers had preceded him into the Neapolitan army. As a boy of sixteen he fought against the reactionary horde led by Cardinal Ruffo, which overturned Naples's Parthenopean Republic in 1799. Later he supported Joachim Murat, brother-in-law of Napoleon, in trying to regain the kingdom wrested from him by the restored Bourbons, and in 1821 he had played a major role as divisional army commander in ensuring the success of a revolt in favour of turning the Two Sicilies into a constitutional monarchy. Austrian troops led by General Nugent had crushed the rebellion, driving Pepe into exile in London. Thomas Adolphus Trollope, brother of the more famous Anthony, meeting him during the 1830s, described Pepe as 'a remarkably handsome man, but not a brilliant or amusing companion. He had a kind of simple, dignified, placid manner of enunciating the most astounding platitudes, and replying to the laughter they sometimes produced by a calm, gentle smile, which showed how impossible it was for his gentle soul to imagine that his hearers were otherwise than delighted with his wit and wisdom.' Women adored him, but though he enjoyed the flirtation and lionising of London salon hostesses, he remained devoted to the Scottish heiress Anna Gilchrist Coventry whom he married in 1822. Back in Naples in 1848 following King Ferdinand's amnesty, Pepe was flattered to be given command of the expeditionary force dispatched to the war in Lombardy. According to the writer and political activist Luigi Settembrini, whose polemic played a key role in the revolution, the King, in yielding to his officers' request to be led by so intransigent a liberal, consoled himself with the reflection 'Well, he'll probably make the same kind of mess he contrived in 1821.' When Ferdinand ordered the army's return following the royalist counter-revolution in Naples on 15 May, Pepe's refusal to budge was supported by more than 1,000 of his men. 'You could not see and obey without loving him,' said a senior officer, and the General's experience and charisma were undeniably useful to Venice's new government, as they had been to Manin.

Though the ravages of malaria in the army prevented Pepe from organising further raids for the time being, he was determined to knock the large body of volunteers now at his disposal into a creditable fighting force. In Venice itself, meanwhile, the civic guard continued its valuable

* Apparently Pepe was born in a bivouac where his mother was sheltering after an earthquake destroyed the family palace in the town of Squillace.

task of policing the city, its commanders careful to keep their brigades in the best possible trim. On 22 July they issued a lengthy catalogue of the physical handicaps and ailments disqualifying potential recruits from enlistment. Scurvy, hernia, piles, faecal incontinence, herpes and rectal prolapse were all noted as disadvantages, and so too were syphilitic ulcers, fistulas, varicose veins, inoperable tumours, dropsy and epilepsy, though it may have seemed a little hard to some that stammering and chronic foot odour were added to this bizarre assemblage. Daniele Manin's serious short-sightedness does not seem to have counted against him, however, and he was seen performing sentry duty like a sincere patriot. On the same day that the guard issued its warning to would-be members, the Modenese exile Antonio Morandi watched Pepe's volunteers parading in the Piazza. 'Wearing clean uniforms, their weapons glistening as if fresh from the makers', cheerful in countenance, proud and carefree in their bearing, healthy, robust and bearded, they looked like brothers from a single family – as indeed they were, united by common sentiments, as one in their hearts and wishes, so that every city in Italy might have counted them among her champions. Therefore, with one accord, this legion chose as its name 'Italia Libera', 'Free Italy'.

A week earlier these home-defence forces had been joined, according to an agreement made as part of the fusion package, by 2,000 Piedmontese troops. Their presence, together with that of Admiral Albini's fleet, would seem to have guaranteed a greater safety for Venice, though Welden's threatened squeeze on the *terraferma* was stymied for the time being by the same marsh fevers plaguing the volunteers. It looked at least as if the trust reposed by the Albertists in their newly acquired sovereign was properly justified, and that Venice was now receiving the attention denied her by the King during the rule of the provisional government. All that remained was for Charles Albert to make a final thrust into the heart of the Quadrilateral and chase Radetzky over the mountains into the Tyrol.

Yet only a day after the Piedmontese disembarked from their transports on 19 July, Alessandro Poerio, who had refused to go home with the Neapolitan troops, preferring to stay by Pepe's side, was shaking his head dubiously over a letter received from his uncle Raffaele, commanding a Lombard brigade in the royal army. The rank and file among the King's troops, he allowed, were fine, spirited fellows, 'but with few exceptions their generals are wet blankets,* with no practical sense of their profession,

---

* The word he uses – *caccadubbi*, literally 'doubt-shitters' – has no comparably powerful equivalent in English.

lacking energy and hazarding nothing. There is not a single commander among them capable even of devising a plan of campaign.' Alberto La Marmora, still in Venice but nobly refusing to take sides in the fusion issue, believing that soldiers had no right 'to add the weight of their rifles to either pan of the scales in political questions', sardonically noted that 'the theatrical intrigues of prima donnas and ballerinas are as nothing to those I witnessed among generals wearing the same uniform'. Several Italian officers serving with the Piedmontese forces criticised the rank snobbery governing military appointments, which seemed to depend more on royal favour and titled connections than on tactical and strategic know-how. 'The army,' commented Francesco Anfossi, a Mazzinian from Lombardy, 'embarked on its campaign purely in order to fight for the King, wearing the leaden mantle of aristocracy which for so many years had weighed upon its shoulders.'

Others perceived the real weakness to lie in the lack of ambulances and medical supplies, a wretchedly inadequate commissariat and not enough uniforms. General Eusebio Bava, whose account of the war industriously heaps blame on everybody but himself, describes basic provisions as 'always the principal stumbling block in our enterprise. Often they did not arrive in time or simply did not appear at all. It was not that the stores were empty, but that the transport wagons, drawn by oxen, moved with infinite slowness.' Around Mantua, according to one officer, the troops were practically in rags. Civilians, as much as soldiers, were conscious of these shortcomings. Writing to her son in Copenhagen, Costanza d'Azeglio told him that 'our troops suffer more from privation than from gunfire. The soldiers rarely get anything in the way of hot soup, and more often than not they have to bed down in the mud.' According to Alberto La Marmora's brother Carlo, the ultimate blame rested with Charles Albert's War Minister Franzini, whose combination of arrogance, stubbornness and stupidity rendered him 'positively worse than mediocre'.

Doubtless this was true, but throughout the war the King retained an unshakeable confidence in this figure, who was otherwise incapable of arousing much enthusiasm in those who worked alongside him. Whoever might be responsible, the progress of the campaign was scarcely encouraging, whether to Charles Albert's own subjects or to the millions in Lombardy-Venetia who had opted to join them under the white cross of Savoy. A kind of stalemate had settled on the armies of Piedmont and Austria during early July, and there had been little in the way of encouraging news from the battle-front. Peschiera remained in Piedmontese hands, for what such a trophy was worth in practical terms, but Radetzky was not going to waste his resources on trying to get it back, preferring instead to coax Charles Albert into advancing under pressure from Italian expectations of an easy victory. To the Field Marshal, conscious of the inadequacies of both the Piedmontese high command and the army's operational infrastructure, it was a matter of maintaining low-level attrition while seeking to lure the enemy deeper into the country around Verona and Mantua, from which effective Austrian counterstrikes could be launched.

Radetzky's forces, moreover, were stronger than Charles Albert's, numbering some 83,000 men divided among front-line units, support troops stationed in the Tyrol, the garrisons of the three Quadrilateral forts remaining in Austrian hands, and two reserve brigades from Vienna. Military intelligence, as we have seen, was a low priority among the Piedmontese commanders, unaware until too late of how far Austrian resources extended. Honour required some sort of headline-grabbing forward thrust if the King's reputation with his new subjects was to be sustained. Fatally Charles Albert decided to focus his attentions on Mantua, well defended as it was, leaving a relatively small force of 28,000 around Verona. This kind of concentration effectively split the army in two, with nothing save a few cavalry divisions to hold the line beyond the east bank of the Mincio between Villafranca, to the south of Verona, and Mantua itself, where the King had sent nine crack brigades to blockade the city. For Radetzky this represented an open invitation. The little army outside Verona could be pushed back easily enough, with Peschiera recaptured in the process and the Piedmontese driven towards the Po, the frontier of the Papal States, whose territory beyond the river was currently being policed by Austrian troops.

On 22 July Radetzky set his plan in motion by attacking enemy positions along the hills between the Adige and Lage Garda. Though the Piedmontese were initially forced to retreat, fresh brigades arrived to dislodge the Austrians. The following morning the Field Marshal had to judge his tactics more carefully when turning his attention to the rolling country west of Verona, held by a small force of 8,000 men and twenty guns. In a sequence of flanking manoeuvres on the three main positions, the Austrians shattered the centre of the Piedmontese line, effectively separating the northern command from the main body of the army gathered outside Mantua. Charles Albert's best hope, with Radetzky's battalions hurrying on towards the Mincio, was to abandon his siege operations and seek to halt the Austrian advance by hitting his left flank. By the afternoon of 24 July he had brought his finest brigades, two of them led by the Crown Prince Victor Emmanuel, onto the plain between Villafranca and the vineyard-covered hills topped by the village of Custoza* which

* Unique among Italian place names in not duplicating its letter 'z'. The 'o' is lengthened as a result.

gives its name to the dry white wine of the region. The Piedmontese confidently scattered the Austrian defenders along the slopes, pushing up onto the plateau, where they prepared to face Radetzky's main army the next morning. It was scarcely an equal contest. Though Charles Albert's men displayed exemplary courage, and the King himself was, as always, disdainful of his own danger, sheer grit was useless against the Habsburg force's numerical strength and its officers' disciplined cooperation, initiative and élan. Among the Piedmontese generals there was the usual lack of communication, the men were exhausted by rapid marching and countermarching the previous day, provisions were in short supply and many had no water to slake their thirst in the stewing heat of a Lombard summer afternoon. By 5 p.m., when yet another Austrian reserve brigade slammed into the royal ranks already decimated by heatstroke, the final retreat was sounded.

Custoza was now the name of a battle as well as a wine. News of the Austrian victory reached General Welden at Mestre the following day, and he lost no time in sending the Venetian government a smug notification of the event. 'After fierce fighting over a period of three days,' it ran, 'the army of Charles Albert has been completely destroyed. Our forces have reached the River Oglio. I am a man of honour. Lying would be unworthy, and indeed useless, since little time must be necessary for you to verify the news. This might therefore be the moment – another is unlikely to present itself – for you to debate your cause before it is wholly lost.' As President, Jacopo Castelli returned a courageous answer. 'We beg your Excellency to reflect that we are not at all competent to be the judges of a cause we hold in common with the rest of Italy. Now, however, that this appears confined to the city of Venice alone, we must hope to furnish you with proof that it is far from being lost.'

Custoza was a blow from which Charles Albert would never adequately recover. Any realisation of this, however, made almost no impact on Venice for at least a week after the Piedmontese army started its general retreat across the Mincio. Opponents of fusion were much more concerned, during the last days of July, by the government's assault on dissident opinion in shutting down the contumacious newspapers and acting against public meetings by republicans critical of the new administration. Soon the nucleus of a republican club had begun to form, its members including leading anti-fusionists such as Samuel Olper, Giuseppe Giuriati and the volunteer leader Antonio Mordini, as well as the Neapolitan general Girolamo Ulloa and Giuseppe Sirtori, one of the most striking and well-regarded figures of the Italian Risorgimento. A devout Christian who had trained for the priesthood, Sirtori renounced his vows following a crisis of faith and left his native Lombardy to study at the Sorbonne. When the 1848 revolution broke out in Paris, he had his first taste of battle while manning a street barricade, but hastened home once news of the Milanese *Cinque Giornate* arrived. The Lombard fusion vote made it impossible for such an ardent republican to remain in Milan, so he joined a volunteer battalion leaving for Venice and quickly gained respect among the defenders of the fort at Marghera for his coolness under fire – 'loved by all,' according to Francesco Dall'Ongaro, 'as the personification of valour, modesty and common sense'.

Meeting in the Casinò dei Cento in Campo Santa Margherita, the new club called itself the 'Circolo Italiano'. The government tried to discredit it at once by spreading a rumour that its sessions were a front for pro-Austrian activity. An ugly incident, fomented by Castelli, involving a threatened attack on the secretary and members by a huge mob of drunken workmen armed with clubs, was defused in the nick of time by Samuel Olper, who spotted an acquaintance in the crowd, embraced him and encouraged others to enter the building and listen to the debate. The Circolo survived in the teeth of continued suspicion from monarchists and, more significantly, from the moderate type of republican represented by Daniele Manin, for whom the Mazzinian ideas espoused by Sirtori and Mordini enshrined the sort of political extremism he most dreaded.

The ex-premier was not exactly awaiting his hour, for there was no likelihood just at present that he would be called upon to make a triumphal return to government. His popularity with ordinary Venetians, however, was of a kind that anybody more vain or unscrupulous would instantly have tried to exploit in the increasingly fragmented political climate of the city during the late summer of 1848. Neither Castelli and his ministers nor – surprisingly – the Circolo Italiano members went out of their way to court the favour of the humblest and poorest of their fellow townsfolk, who continued to believe in Manin as, in some sense, one of their own because he spoke to them, whether literally or figuratively, in terms they understood. So was his appearance on 30 July in the uniform of the civic guard as a sentry in the Piazzetta a calculated I'm-still-here publicity manoeuvre, as one of his bitterest critics suggested? His notes on this, made a year after the siege, furiously rejected the accusation. 'Lies and calumny. I never chose the day, the time or the place. No sooner out of government, I joined the guard unit of my *sestiere* so as to carry out my civic duty and set an example to others who were failing to do so. I performed this assiduously and exactly, obeying my commanding officer. When they detailed me to serve in the Piazzetta, I obeyed as usual.' His presence certainly created an impression, and the comments of several hundred passers-by that day made it clear that they shared the opinion of the Paduan patriot Carlo Leoni, who noted in his diary, 'This man is destined for great things.'

While Castelli and his colleagues were perturbed by the role that Venice seemed rapidly to be assuming as a haven for patriots in arms, especially those from regions of Italy whose revolutions were either stalling or had totally failed, the arrival on 5 August of the Piedmontese royal commissioners ought, in theory at least, to have strengthened their Albertist resolve. The two functionaries, the distinguished jurist and historian Count Luigi Cibrario and the one-legged Vittorio Amedeo Colli da Felizzano, an army officer and civil servant, were entirely sincere in their intention to proceed with the formal annexation of Venice to the kingdom of Piedmont, as if the battle of Custoza had never happened or at any rate on the basis that their royal master was not yet completely vanquished. On 7 August the handover ceremony took place in the upper hall of the Biblioteca Marciana, with its luminous ceiling panels by Titian, Veronese and Tintoretto. Present were Cardinal Monico, General Pepe, Admiral Graziani (uncle of the Bandiera brothers) and the Mayor, Giovanni Correr. The commissioners' acceptance document stated that a free press, liberty of association and a civic guard would continue to be guaranteed, existing laws were to be upheld and the Castelli government was to remain in a consultative capacity for the purpose of ratifying new laws and treaties. Outside, the tricolour flags were hauled down from the masts in the Piazza where they had flown so proudly since 22 March, and replaced by new ones bearing the arms of Savoy superimposed on the Italian colours. Bells rang, bands played, but the popular mood was decidedly grim. By degrees the reality of Charles Albert's critical position had started to kick in, subduing any potential excitement at the idea of forming part of a new Italian kingdom.

Three days previously, the King's tattered and exhausted army had reached the gates of Milan, with Radetzky hard at its heels. Retreating into the city following a desperate rearguard action in which Charles Albert had once again demonstrated a dogged bravery, they found its defenders in a state of hopeless muddle and unreadiness. There was no point, reasoned the Piedmontese generals, in a fight to the death when their own ammunition wagons had gone missing and, almost inevitably, the commissariat had barely enough food to go round. A surrender was the only option, but once Radetzky had dictated his terms there was the problem of breaking the news to the Milanese. When, on the morning of 5 August, General Bava spelt out the situation to the defence committee, the whole town erupted into panic and rage. A heaving mob, crying

'Betrayal!', surged around Palazzo Greppi, where Charles Albert had passed a sleepless night. Numbers of them took care to smash up his carriages to prevent him leaving, and eventually they burst into the building to find the monarch sitting 'impassive as a statue, without moving or showing so much as a twitch of his face. In his soft, slow voice, supported by gestures from his long, fleshless hands, he bade them be calm and leave, undertaking to answer them in a few minutes.'

Playing for still more time, he drafted a proclamation announcing his desire to stay where he was and fight alongside the citizens. He knew, as did everyone else with any common sense (Piedmontese or Lombard) that Radetzky's forces could easily overwhelm any further show of resistance. Worn out by fatigue, privation and the sheer enormity of his failure, he agreed at length to face the crowd and tottered onto the balcony. When his voice gave out as he started to address them, the response was anger rather than pity, and somebody even took a potshot at the fatally tall and distinctive figure of the monarch, who accepted this as a signal to withdraw. Further bullets began peppering the palace, its gates were set alight and only the timely arrival of an infantry battalion with two heavy guns saved his life.

The armistice concluded with the Austrians is always known by the name of the officer who signed it on Charles Albert's behalf, General Carlo Canera di Salasco. Its terms were basically those of a suspension of hostilities lasting for six weeks at least, with a complete Piedmontese evacuation of Lombardy, Venice, the duchies of Parma and Modena and the fortress of Peschiera. The army was to withdraw across the River Ticino, while Radetzky guaranteed mildness in the reimposition of Habsburg authority over Milan. For Italian patriots the document was a veritable catalogue of national humiliation. Even the fusionist champion Pietro Paleocapa, now permanently based in Turin as the King's Minister of Public Works, was moved to condemn his new masters for the grovelling fashion in which they had accepted the Field Marshal's demands. What angered him most was Salasco's readiness to disregard the political aspects of such a negotiated peace. Why had he ignored the whole issue of fusion and the presence of the royal commissioners in Venice, leaving it to the enemy's mercy like a rebel city? This would simply encourage the triumph of the Venetian republicans, the outcome that Paleocapa, by now a convinced monarchist, dreaded above all.

'Salasco,' wrote a friend of the engineer's from Paris, 'has assured himself of a unique place in modern history, and his name will now stand as a synonym for imbecility. His stupidity is such that I cannot even view him as a traitor.' Most galling of all to Venetian patriots, in or out of

Italy, was the Piedmontese negotiators' treatment of their city as if it had been an Austrian possession throughout the war, its independence and subsequent voluntary submission to Charles Albert having counted for nothing. General Welden cannot be blamed for sending another of his smirking little notes, this time to the royal commissioners, dated 11 August and accompanying a copy of the armistice. 'I have the honour to enclose an official document just received. Persuaded that the officers charged with carrying out its articles will arrive shortly, I leave you the choice, sirs, of ceasing or continuing hostilities.'

Welden's missive, with its ominous attachment, arrived in Venice from his Paduan headquarters that same morning. The day before, republican newspapers had launched scathing no-confidence assaults on the government: now it looked as if Piedmont and Austria between them were about to fulfil the hopes of Tommaseo, Olper and Giuriati by causing the new administration, officially only four days old, to melt away entirely. To the credit of commissioners Cibrario and Colli, supported by Jacopo Castelli, they made no attempt to prevent news of the Salasco armistice spreading through the city. Cibrario had earlier assured Manin that if Piedmont surrendered, Venice would not be handed over, adding, 'I had rather be torn in pieces first.' The question was how any of them would face what threatened to be an indignant and terrified crowd now gathering in the Piazza outside. Castelli rose to the occasion by pointing out that Venice's adherence to Charles Albert had always been conditional, and that since the conditions themselves had never taken effect, the city would resume its former independence and not submit to unjustly applied force. Cibrario and Colli agreed to resign once Welden's news was confirmed (he could, after all, have been pulling an elaborate bluff) and a defence committee was to be formed as soon as possible.

As the August afternoon wore on, the crowds gathered in the Piazza waited anxiously for some sort of dispatch from Lombardy. A Genoese newspaper brought by a passenger on a steamer from Ravenna contained an article on the capture of Milan, and when Colli read this out, a voice from the throng in the square cried, 'So it is true that Milan has surrendered? On what conditions? What about the fleet? What about us?' Colli frankly admitted that he could no longer guarantee the continuing presence of the Piedmontese warships. 'His words,' wrote one of those present 'were like oil thrown on a fire.' The crowd started shouting, 'Down with the traitors! Death to the commissioners!', and several of the younger republicans, led by Giuseppe Sirtori and Antonio Mordini, began making towards the doorway into the apartments in the Procuratie Nuove, where Cibrario and Colli now lodged. As they did so, the civic-guard commander

Angelo Mengaldo gave the order to sound an alarm, but bugles and drums were drowned out by the whistling, hooting and howls of execration which filled the Piazza.

Hurrying up the staircase, the young men burst into the room in which the two commissioners sat together with Jacopo Castelli. Colli and Cibrario found themselves seized and dragged towards the window, where Sirtori intended to force them onto the balcony to announce their resignation from office. Colli, however, refused to budge. 'What sort of violence is this?' he cried. 'Do you think I'm afraid? I left one of my legs on the battlefield, I have offered four sons to the motherland as soldiers, and I intend to die at my post. I shall not resign until I receive official notice of the armistice.' To which Cibrario merely added. 'And neither shall I.' At this critical moment the one person capable of saving the situation entered the room. Earlier that day Castelli had called on Daniele Manin, bearing details of the armistice as given by Welden and asking him to come to the Procuratie Nuove at eight-thirty that evening to advise the commissioners on the most effective measures for Venice's safety. Manin, evidently still wedded to the idea of some sort of intervention by France, whether military or diplomatic, proposed a rendezvous with the French consul under the Campanile at six to discuss this. About half an hour previously he had stepped into a bookshop in the Merceria to rest for a while when his friend Giorgio Casarini, horrified at the chaos in the Piazza, came swiftly to find him. The pair rushed towards St Mark's, entering the Procuratie in the nick of time to rescue the two Piedmontese from their captors and, if possible, defuse a menacing situation. Colli, who had never before met Manin, introduced himself, asking. 'What do you want from me?' Before Manin could answer, one of the republicans broke in, 'It's we who want you to resign your power, it's we who don't want to serve anyone any longer, especially this king who has betrayed us.'

Whereupon they seized the commissioner once again and pushed him towards the window. Casarini sought to tug him back, and Manin himself, whom regular exercise made well able to hold his own, squared up to Colli's captors. Jacopo Castelli, coming hastily into the room, now took Manin by the hand and led him, rather than poor Colli, onto the balcony. The mere sight of their champion, barely tall enough to be visible over the balustrade, was sufficient to pacify the crowd. A dramatic stillness fell upon the square as he started to speak. His words were simply a request for a few moments' calm while he deliberated with the commissioners, but a rousing cheer suggested to those inside the window that valuable time had thus been bought. Meanwhile Colonel Cavedalis, commander of military forces within the city, had arrived and took the opportunity to see off the surly republicans, angrier still at losing their unique opportunity to establish some sort of Mazzinian government within the city. When he pointed out that the people had a right to know precisely who was taking control at this crucial instant, Sirtori angrily rejoined that the issue would be decided soon enough. 'Remember,' said Cavedalis grimly, 'that I am determined and ready to prevent anarchy.' Sirtori took the hint and backed off.

A hurried discussion saw Manin trying without success to persuade Castelli to remain alongside him in any administration he might be called upon to lead. The French consul was shown into the room, and appears to have made the right kind of noises concerning support from Paris for the new government, whenever it should materialise. After barely more than quarter of an hour, Manin stepped once more onto the balcony to address the throng. 'I have come to assure you,' he told them, 'that France will listen more willingly to the appeal of a people than to that of a king. From this moment onwards the royal commissioners have declared themselves ready to resign. The day after tomorrow, the assembly will convene to appoint a new government. For the next forty-eight hours I alone am in command.' Thunderous applause greeted this announcement. 'Viva Manin! To the forts, to the forts!' rose the cry. On his pledge that civic-guard units would be sent immediately to defend Marghera, the crowd declared that if only he would give them arms, they would all rush to its defence. 'You have arms already,' he answered. 'For a people wishing to defend itself, everything serves as a weapon. Remember those with which you drove out the Austrians on 22 March. Now clear the square and go home. You need silence and calm to provide for the needs of the motherland.'

This last response of Manin's provides a telling illustration of his ability to manipulate the Venetian populace through a well-judged mixture of lawyerly sophistry and patriotic uplift. His skilful implication was that they were all in this together, with a shared responsibility for maintaining order. In a single brief moment he had assured the survival of democratic government in Venice and the continuance of an armed struggle against the Austrians. He had thwarted, for the time being, any attempt by the Mazzinians to make capital out of the Salasco armistice, and had succeeded in channelling the anger of his fellow citizens into the practical business of shoring up defences around the lagoon against a possible assault by Welden's troops, keen to exploit the atmosphere of confusion and weakness occasioned by Charles Albert's defeat. What was more, he had saved the lives of Colli, Cibrario and Castelli, all of whom had behaved honourably in a critical hour. That very evening, according to Giuseppe Giuriati's son Domenico, a changed atmosphere of hope, energy and resolve was palpable throughout the city. 'Oh shining night of August 11,' he recalled, 'how you are etched upon my memory in characters of fire! With what fervour we hastened to inscribe our youthful names in the lists of volunteers! With what confidence in saving the motherland we stayed up to watch the dawn breaking over the railway bridge and the battered vessels of our fleet!' With Manin restored as her leader, Venice made ready to fight on.

CHAPTER 9

~

WAITING FOR THE FRENCH

O N 4 AUGUST IN THE city of Udine, now under Austrian military government, the proprietress of a toyshop chose to exhibit a new array of dolls in her window. One feature of their costume was unusual, possibly unique, in the annals of doll-dressing. Instead of the customary miniature adult clothes, such as ballgowns or frock-coats, they were clad in the uniforms of Piedmontese soldiers and loaded with fetters. The most handsomely attired of all bore the label 'Charles Albert, a prisoner and in chains'. This openly mocking display was not destined to last for long. An angry crowd collected outside the shop, smashed the window and its offending figures, seized the wretched owner and dragged her to the nearest city gate, whence she was thrown out onto the road. Cries of 'Viva Carlo Alberto! Viva l'Italia!' had an unexpectedly alarming effect on the Austrian troops, who withdrew to the citadel, where their commanding officer issued a proclamation threatening to bombard the town if such disorders continued.

The warning made its desired impact, but the episode was eloquent of the confused emotions created by the news of Piedmont's defeat at Custoza. For all those who mistrusted the King and his generals, there were as many who needed to believe that some kind of integrity could be salvaged from the debacle. In Piedmont itself, Costanza d'Azeglio was still hopeful. 'This is the end of our forlorn Iliad,' she told her son. 'Without seeing clearly what kind of fate is reserved for our generous and excellent nation, we can at least say that honour is safe. Here is our consolation, and we must hope that justice will be done to us in this respect.' Horrified by the condition of the soldiers returning from the war – 'veritable mummies, their skins dry and blackened, their eyes fixed, the tortures they have endured plainly visible' – she blamed over-ambitious politicians at home for pushing the army beyond its practical limits. The Prime Minister Vincenzo Gioberti, Costanza believed, was a visionary living in an imagined world, while the Foreign Secretary Lorenzo Pareto and his satellites 'dreamed only of Italian unity, without taking account of the time needed to achieve this, supposing it were possible'.

Few outside Piedmont's borders were prepared to shed tears either for the kingdom's famished, misdirected troops or for their battered self-respect, once the terms of the Salasco armistice were published. Charles Albert's rallying call at the beginning of the conflict, 'l'Italia farà da se', was now fraught with tragic irony, yet the fact of his fighting force laying down its arms, giving up all its conquests and retreating within Piedmont's historical borders by no means spelled the end of the patriotic struggle. Others had made still less of an effort to keep faith with the patriots. With his counter-coup in May, Ferdinand of Naples had seemed to betray the liberals' trust, and Pope Pius had begun losing credit fast in the wake of his notorious April Allocution. Now, during the early autumn of 1848, a fresh phase of the revolution saw so-called democrats, left-wing lawyers and journalists, supported by workers' cadres, seizing control from the moderates who had believed so earnestly in an Italy united under a single monarchy or a benign Catholic theocracy. Far from the *crociati*, the amateur soldiers, falling away, a new breed of volunteer arose, no less fuelled with idealism, yet believing now in a radical alternative to rule by kings and popes – that of a constituent national assembly embodying general assent to the creation of an Italian republic. Ironically those young hard-liners, Sirtori and Mordini at their head, who broke in so peremptorily on the Piedmontese commissioners in the Procuratie Nuove would have fared much better in Florence, Leghorn or Rome than in a Venice prepared to entrust itself to the unfashionably moderate, even timid republicanism professed by Daniele Manin.

The flaw in so many calculations by Italian patriots in 1848 was a belief that somehow the sheer strength and certainty underpinning revolutionary ideals must be enough to ensure their triumph in practical terms. If Manin, and whoever he might now choose to stand alongside him in the re-established autonomous government, were to save Venice, much would henceforth depend on an awareness of immediate needs, hard choices and the imperatives created by circumstances which all the flag-blessings, death-or-glory declarations, odes to Italy and patriotic anthems could hardly magic away. The Austrians had won the war with the help of discipline, professionalism, grit and patience, unassisted by anything more romantic than a dogged loyalty to the Habsburg throne, regardless of whether or not its occupant – in the shape of the brachycephalous semi-invalid Emperor Ferdinand – was an especially plausible object of devotion. Radetzky was not a Napoleon or a Wellington. Much of his success had been achieved by a clever concentration and deployment of his forces, well-judged periods of inactivity and a continued strategy of attrition, rather than brilliant manoeuvres, costly set-piece battles and high-profile offensive operations of the sort that had undoubtedly been expected of Charles Albert and his army. Though his staff were by no means uncritical of their chief, there was a general feeling that the old Field Marshal had well deserved the Grand Cross of the Order of Maria Theresa, brought to him on the Emperor's orders during the days following Custoza, as he pursued the Piedmontese towards Milan. Ferdinand himself, says Schönhals, took the medal from his own coat to sent to Radetzky. 'We shall always remember seeing the tears of joy streaming down the old man's cheeks. We had long foretold this honour for him, and it was a day of rejoicing for us, feeling as we did that we ourselves had been decorated in the person of our general.'

In Vienna even the more enthusiastic liberals were ready to worship Radetzky as the saviour of the empire. The dramatist Franz Grillparzer, a protégé of Metternich who had nevertheless dabbled in revolution, addressed a hymn of praise to the Field Marshal, in which the line 'In deinem Lager ist Österreich', 'Within your camp lies Austria', seemed to sum up the essential conservatism of the nation. Johann Strauss,* Vienna's leading composer of dance music, cobbled together a march, using popular songs of the day, for a grand victory celebration. At its first performance the 'Radetzky March' was not much liked, but after Strauss altered the key and tinkered with the ending, the piece became the unofficial anthem of imperial Austria and as such is still cherished by the Viennese.

Radetzky was now at leisure to concentrate on restoring an Austrian presence not merely in Milan, where the palaces of rebel nobility were looted and turned into barracks and stables, but in the two duchies of Parma and Modena. To the latter he returned its Duke Francesco, not greatly loved but preferable, apparently, to the Piedmontese forces which had occupied it for the past three months. In the former, while Duke Carlo Ludovico still stayed away, he installed a military governor. The little matter of retaking the fortress of Peschiera, meanwhile, was resolved with characteristically ruthless thoroughness by General Julius von

---

* Known as Johann Strauss Vater, to distinguish him from his more famous son, 'the Waltz King', of the same name.

Haynau, shortly to become notorious as the most inhuman of all the Austrian generals in the Italian campaign. A brief siege laid to the fort, with its 3,000-strong Piedmontese garrison, was concluded by blowing up the magazine and training fifty-two cannon on what remained of its defences. On 10 August, as Haynau was handed his copy of the armistice text, a white flag was hoisted on the ramparts and Peschiera soon resumed its role as a key defensive element in the Quadrilateral.

Some time after this surrender, the English poet Arthur Hugh Clough was among those who passed close to its great brick bastions, originally raised by the Venetian republic in 1553. The fortress became an image for him of heroic failure, of the victory in defeat characterising so many episodes in Italy's 1848 revolutions:

> The tricolour – a trampled rag –
>   Lies, dirt and dust; the lines I track
> By sentry boxes yellow-black
>   Lead up to no Italian flag.
>
> I see the Croat soldier stand
>   Upon the grass of your redoubts;
> The eagle with his black wing flouts
>   The breadth and beauty of your land.

Out of these verses, with their familiar refrain, ''Tis better to have fought and lost/Than never to have fought at all', evolved the yet more famous companion poem, which begins:

> Say not, the struggle naught availeth,
>   The labour and the wounds are vain,
> The enemy faints not, nor faileth,
>   And as things have been, things remain.

The Austrians may be forgiven for having anticipated an easy victory over Venice, now almost alone in its resistance and, as it appeared, easy prey across a mere quarter-mile of railway bridge. Events after all seemed to be developing in their favour throughout Italy, 'with the swiftness,' as Schönhals exultantly observed, 'of a set of magic lantern slides'. The reality was in fact not nearly so propitious to the Habsburg forces as he imagined. Piedmontese vessels still patrolled the lagoon, despite their officers' clear awareness of the armistice terms. Whatever Admiral Albini's vacillation over the business of blockading Trieste, he was sufficiently honourable and patriotic to refuse to budge until orders arrived from Genoa on 21 August. Even then he was able to use the excuse – not especially convincing, as it happened – of bad weather in order to stay put for at least another three weeks, until expressly commanded to hoist sail for Ancona. On the shores of the lagoon itself, Welden's troops were laid low by malaria and dysentery, and affairs were little better among the patriot defenders of Marghera and the smaller forts and batteries dotted around the city. Austria's hand, in any case, was stayed from any decisive action against Venice while the possibility of an international peace conference, to resolve the issues of the Salasco armistice, delayed any threat of more aggressive Franco-British intervention in Italian affairs. For the rest of August a kind of 'phoney war' atmosphere took the place of that full-scale siege operation Venetians had dreaded in the wake of the Custoza debacle.

Manin's first action on assuming control of the government was to make a direct appeal to France for military aid. What Charles Albert could not achieve with his Italian army must surely be attainable with help from a friendly republic, so far broadly sympathetic, but unforthcoming with any serious contribution to the patriotic war. There was a decided feeling among certain Venetians that by formally recognising the existence of their new state (as the United States and Switzerland had done), a nation which had inflicted on the Serene Republic the shame of Campoformio would redeem itself handsomely enough. To this end, Manin dispatched a heartfelt plea to General Cavaignac and his ministers in Paris. Addressed to Foreign Secretary Jules Bastide, this ended with the ringing words, 'The existence of a people which has contributed so much to European civilisation depends henceforth on the prompt assistance granted to it by the heroic French nation.' The envoy Manin selected to take the letter to Paris was Niccolò Tommaseo. A fluent French speaker, with useful Parisian contacts established during his years in exile, he seemed an ideal choice, but was initially unwilling to accept when Giorgio Casarini brought him the proposal on the tumultuous evening of 11 August. Tommaseo had never forgiven Manin for what he saw as an ignoble compromise in the fusion debate, choosing thereafter to retire from public life to concentrate on his translation of the four gospels into Italian. This looked like the sulk it indeed was. If Tommaseo was to accompany Casarini to the Procuratie Nuove that night, it would simply be to refuse the offer of the embassy. Manin's warm embrace of him on arrival was not reciprocated. Tommaseo must by now have heard of the new President's announcement that 'For the next forty-eight hours I alone am in command', and he chose this as a further basis on which to found a grudge, unaltered for the rest of his life, against his former colleague. No doubt Tommaseo resented the dictatorial implication of Manin's words, but it looks unavoidably as if other, less noble feelings were at work here, among them a deep-rooted envy of the other man's standing with ordinary Venetians and of his talent, which the Dalmatian scorned to cultivate, for reacting pragmatically to the turn of events.

Tommaseo, going home, may have been satisfied with the snub thus delivered. Manin, however, was not, and again sent to him with the offer of a Paris mission. On this occasion the influential figure of Emilio Tipaldo, inspector of schools for the provisional government, happened to be present, and his persuasion eventually brought Tommaseo round. By three o'clock the following morning he was on his way to France, by a somewhat zigzag route taking him via Ravenna and Forlì to Florence and thence to Leghorn, where he boarded a ship to Marseilles. Had Manin made the proposal as a means of getting a tiresome curmudgeon out of the way? Tommaseo always chose to believe this, and it is likely that any notion of him as the best man for the job was balanced by some awareness that at a time when republican extremism seemed to threaten stability within Venice, his continuing presence as a focus of opposition was potentially dangerous.

His appointment, together with the contents of the letter to Bastide, was ratified by the Venetian assembly, gathered in force on 13 August for its first session under the new administration. Aware that *albertista* sentiment was still strong in the city, Manin must have been heartened by the deputies' refusal to listen to a proposal from one of their number, Carlo Trolli, that the royal commissioners be called upon to resume their duties. His own appeal for unity at a critical moment – 'We must recognise only two sides in the struggle, Italian and Austrian' – was acclaimed with prolonged 'Viva!'s. Further approval came when he magnanimously lauded the conduct of Colli and Cibrario during the handover of power, indicating that a message of affection and esteem from the deputies was the very least the two men deserved.

It was on the ensuing tide of applause that his friend Bartolomeo Malfatti first used the words '*il nostro Manin*', 'our Manin', soon universally applied to a man the Venetians increasingly saw as their only convincing champion. The republican Antonio Bellinato, as if to confirm the worst fears of the absent Tommaseo, now proposed that the premier should assume dictatorship of the city. It was an offer Manin was sensible enough to reject, ostensibly on grounds of military ignorance. Instead, leadership of the government was to be divided between himself as Prime Minister, Giovanni Battista Cavedalis as commander of the army and

Attilio Bandiera's father-in-law, Admiral Leone Graziani, at the head of the navy. According to Manin's view of the political situation, Venice, having seized the initiative opened to her by the Salasco armistice and the resignation of the Piedmontese commissioners, could hold her head high among nations. 'We must tell France,' he said, 'that since all peoples have a right to regain their independence from usurpers, then we too possess such a right.' Tommaseo's task, by implication, would be to assert this claim. The Venetians would discover soon enough whether he possessed the necessary diplomatic skills.

Among the republicans, sidelining the Dalmatian (if such had really been Manin's intention) had no appreciably dampening effect on the growth of Mazzinian enthusiasms. Though Sirtori and Mordini had lost their initiative on 11 August, neither they nor their friends were prepared to glad-hand Manin into the sort of Cromwellian role others seemed eager to confer upon him. When he informed the assembly that the March republic was not to be restored and that the new government was provisional to the extent of being wholly apolitical, he meant to emphasise the current situation's urgency as something transcending party divisions and demanding unity of purpose. For some republicans this declaration carried an ominous ring, while others, including Pacifico Valussi, Samuel Olper and Francesco Dall'Ongaro, editors of the newspaper *Fatti e parole* (*Deeds and Words*) were ready to give him some measure of support. Mazzini himself meanwhile, from his refuge in the Swiss town of Lugano, where he had fled after Austria's reconquest of Lombardy, sought to stir up radicalism in Venice by sending his associate Pietro Maestri to make contact with Manin and by urging all true-hearted republicans throughout Italy to 'destroy the monarchs who up to now have been the vermin which have sapped our strength' and dispatch arms and assistance to Venice.

This was not at all what Manin wanted. As long ago as 28 May he had sought politely to deflect Mazzini's efforts to involve himself more directly in Venetian affairs by refusing his offer of a Franco-Italian legion to defend the city. With elaborate disingenuousness he had flattered the other man concerning his powers as a polemicist. Words rather than bayonets were needed, 'the moral assistance of the free, authoritative discourse of eminent and famous men such as yourself'. Let Mazzini lift up his voice to mark the cowardly machinations of Charles Albert and show how the great cause was endangered when national issues became merely dynastic. 'Defending us you defend the cause of Italian liberty, which until now has had no shelter beyond the Venetian lagoon. This same cause, which throughout your glorious life you have always sustained, summons you yet again as its champion.' If this was buttering-up, then Manin was laying on the butter by the trowelful, but Mazzini failed to take the hint. Under his auspices a Polish legion, led by the great national poet Adam Mickiewicz, soon arrived in Venice. Tommaseo welcomed them with a resounding image of Italy and Poland as 'two sisters in the same prison', and they were sent off to join Durando's brigades in the final struggle for Vicenza. Later the provisional government decided it could not afford to employ the Poles, so they quitted Venice for Rome, to play a distinguished role under Garibaldi in the defence of that city against the French the following year.

Manin's distaste for a thoroughgoing popular revolution, led by tribunes of the sort Mazzini himself would later become in Rome, had increased during the six weeks he had spent out of office in July and August. He had friends among the more dedicated republicans, but the existence of their club, the Circolo Italiano, with *Fatti e parole* as its newssheet and with regular meetings, first at Santa Margherita and then in the Sala Camploy at San Luca, began to alarm him considerably. His own hold over the Venetian working class was an important political asset, even if he was heard to refer to them as '*un popolaccio*', 'a rabble', and was thought by various observers to be afraid of them en masse. The idea that they might be effectively mobilised by activists independent of his influence – in the name, what was more, of a socialist reaction to the failures of Charles Albert as a national leader – jarred with his increasingly narrow vision of a bourgeois consensus as the sole guarantee against a breakdown of civic order.

The whole republican issue, where Manin was concerned, represented a perilous distraction from his principal goal, that of securing the support which Charles Albert's ministers had discouraged the French from offering while Piedmont was still at war with Austria. Now nothing existed to prevent the Venetians from seeking to draw France more closely into the struggle. Letters went to the French ambassador in Rome, asking for warships to be sent to the lagoon, and the distinguished figure of Angelo Mengaldo, ex-commander of the civic guard, was dispatched to Paris in Tommaseo's wake, bearing a letter to Jules Bastide pointing out that Venice was once again a free agent, Piedmont's commissioners having renounced their task. In Turin meanwhile, Pietro Paleocapa, who had remained there after bringing news of the fusion vote in July, made sincere attempts to engage the sympathies of French diplomats by outlining Venice's parlous situation following the armistice. His faith in Piedmont had been badly shaken by the cavalier fashion in which Salasco and the other generals seemed ready to dispose of Venice via the terms of the agreement, as if fusion had never taken place and she had not in fact been accepted as an addition to the realm. The apparent legality of the transfer of power in July was thus a sham, with Charles Albert seeming quite prepared to bundle Venice back into Austria's pocket without any idea of having betrayed its citizens' trust by doing so.

'The energy of despair will sustain her,' Paleocapa foretold of the city he loved, but would never set eyes on again. It was genuine expectation rather than despair which fuelled the vigorous diplomatic initiative Manin focused on Paris during the early autumn of 1848. He too was determined that Venice must always remain a separate issue in any negotiations between Austria and the ministers of France and Great Britain acting as mediators. 'The independence of Venice,' he instructed Tommaseo on 20 August, 'cannot be a matter for discussion. It must be established as a preliminary condition. Besides the fact that Venice possesses historical, legal and moral rights, she alone, among all the rebel cities, remains free.' Manin clearly hoped to exploit a build-up of liberal sympathies in France following Piedmont's defeat. During an audience given by General Cavaignac to the British ambassador Lord Normanby in the first week of August, armed intervention in the Venetian cause was indicated as a distinct possibility. In London *The Times*, whose attitude to the revolution was generally unfavourable, published a witheringly scornful first leader calling its readers' attention to 'a floating idea that France is sooner or later to be absorbed in the Italian gangrene' and to the notion that 'sixty thousand Gauls are to purge a classic soil from the barbaric invasion'. There was revolution, declared the anonymous scaremonger, 'in every step of that army, from its inaugural review in the Champ de Mars to the Te Deum of victory in the cathedral of the Doges'.

Unfortunately for the Venetians, by the time Tommaseo left for Paris the French position had shifted from an initial enthusiasm for mobilising in the cause of liberty to an altogether more oblique and cautious approach. In part this was due to the pressure placed on Cavaignac and Bastide in those same crucial August days by the Piedmontese envoys Alberto Ricci and Antonio Brignole Sale, determined as their government was to prevent a French republican army from succeeding where Charles Albert's troops had failed. Italy, if it could not make itself, was not to be brought into being by an alien power that had sent its lawful monarch into exile disguised in a wig and green spectacles under the alias of 'Mr Smith', and whose fiat was the will of the people. Licking his wounds after Custoza, Charles Albert detested republicans as much or even more than before, and the French were Piedmont's historical enemies. He was still looking, however unrealistically, for some sort of territorial concession from Austria – a reward, as it were, for having invaded its provinces and sustained a four-month campaign against its armies. Unwelcome as a belligerent against the Austrians, France would prove useful as a mediator with them, and it was on this basis that the Piedmontese diplomats now approached Bastide.

Characteristically, '*il re tentenna*' changed his mind once Ricci and Brignole got to work. Influenced by the former leader of Milan's provisional government, Gabrio Casati, he agreed to a letter being dispatched to Paris soliciting what was euphemistically termed 'cooperation' from the French. Cavaignac meanwhile was all too conscious of the pressure of public opinion in favour of some positive move towards blocking Austria's drive towards recovering her Italian hegemony complete. Paradoxically, according to the British ambassador, 'the friends of peace and order' in the French national assembly were now the most eager interventionists, 'saying that if something was not done within the next few days, a further reverse on the part of the Italians would create such an indignation throughout France as would for the time overbear all prudent considerations'.

Normanby knew that his chief at the London Foreign Office, Lord Palmerston, wanted at all costs to prevent the outbreak of a major European war in northern Italy. British commercial interests had inevitably been damaged by the volatile Italian situation, with the home markets already suffering what the Prime Minister Lord John Russell vaguely defined as 'a money crisis'. Yet both Russell and Palmerston remained committed to seeking some kind of diplomatic solution that should benefit the Italians. They were aware that Austria, flushed with victory, had stiffened its resolve since Baron Hummelauer had arrived from Vienna in May with his devolution proposals. Palmerston, anxious at the prospect of a completely reimposed status quo ante in Lombardy-Venetia, now sought a more sidelong and conciliatory approach to obtaining Austrian concessions. France was to be persuaded that mediation in Piedmont's favour was preferable to outright aggression. Normanby, on his own initiative, had already run the idea past Cavaignac of an enlarged Piedmontese kingdom incorporating Lombardy, and Palmerston gave his approval to this on 8 August. News of the fall of Milan arrived in Paris the next day, but by that time the French government, on Britain's advice, had accepted the path of peaceful negotiation.

In Normanby's proposals to Cavaignac, the fate of Venice was to be settled through the simple expedient of returning it to Austria. The French premier had given the go-ahead to the joint initiative, and it was now up to the Austrians to consider the terms. Official wheels in Vienna always ground slowly, but doubtless the imperial ministers, with everything to play for in Italy, were further heartened by the British parliamentary debate taking place on 17 August, when the Tories, led on this occasion by their rising star Benjamin Disraeli, pressed Austria's case hard with the government. As soon as the exiled Metternich had arrived in London several months earlier, Disraeli had called at his hotel to imbibe conservative wisdom, in its purest essence, from the elder statesman and delight in his reminiscences. Metternich in his turn was seriously impressed when this latest in a long series of political pupils savaged Palmerston during the debate for his preoccupation with 'modern and new-fangled' nationalism, so alien to everything the brilliant young Tory held dear.

By now Tommaseo had embarked on the mission for which not a few Venetians considered him wholly unsuited. Paleocapa, for instance, referring to him as 'that boaster', exclaimed, 'Poor Venice, if her fate were to depend on the political fantasies of an oaf like him! The wretched man thought that the negotiations undertaken in order to induce Austria to accept mediation were all designed to fulfil his influential instructions. What fools our men of letters are!' Elsewhere he was described as impatient, hopelessly unworldly, insufficiently in command of the facts and too inclined to let personal considerations influence his judgement. Others criticised his patronising treatment of Angelo Toffoli, the tailor who had been Employment Minister in the provisional government and who now accompanied the Dalmatian to Paris. 'Poor Toffoli leads a pitiable existence here,' a friend wrote to Manin, 'he isn't a secretary but a servant. I don't know how he has had the patience to remain with Tommaseo all this while.'

The pair of them, though staying at the Hotel Bristol, had to resort to the classic expedient of smuggling food into their rooms rather than spending money in restaurants. Tommaseo lunched off bread and apples, whose cores he managed to hide from the staff. The city was swarming with Italian patriots of every political colour. There were Piedmontese diplomats, various Lombard envoys, official and unofficial, and four additional Venetian representatives. Besides these, and Carlo Cattaneo representing Mazzini, there was the ever-arresting presence of Cristina Belgiojoso, re-established in the Paris where, during the 1830s, she had presided over a brilliant salon and befriended everyone from Balzac and George Sand to Liszt, Heine and Musset.

This Lombard princess was also an ardent patriot, and her 1848 so far had been notably eventful. In Naples she hired a steamer and took on board more than a hundred volunteers, while King Ferdinand watched from his palace window, glad that this 'boring eccentric', as he called her, was leaving so soon. A triumphal arrival at Genoa was followed by a no less festive progress to Milan, with Belgiojoso sporting a Calabrese bonnet and tricolour cockade and riding in a carriage at the head of her *crociati*. On behalf of the city's government, Gabrio Casati went through the motions of welcoming her, while confessing in a letter to Charles Albert that his heart sank at the prospect. Dashing and romantic as she appeared, the Princess had a common-sense grasp of the military situation's more unpleasant realities, a practical awareness transcending that of most other Lombard leaders at the outbreak of war. Via her own twice-weekly newspaper *Il Crociato* she was freely critical of the prevailing incompetence in the organisation of local volunteer forces, advocating a people's war of guerrillas and partisan bands aimed at lightning swoops on Austrian positions, at sabotage and swift manoeuvres – the very opposite, in fact, of the kind of campaign undertaken by Charles Albert and his generals, which explicitly belittled or cut out altogether the role of the enthusiastic and committed amateur.

To begin with, Belgiojoso was a defender both of the King and of Pius IX, yet always as a means towards achieving Italian unity rather than as enemies of republicanism. Her pragmatic approach was simultaneously respectful towards Mazzini and unsparing of his less practical expectations as to what patriotic Italy, with all its deeply incised fault-lines, could currently accomplish. It was she who attempted, via leading government figures in Turin, to forge an effective liaison between him and Charles Albert. Historic compromise of this kind was doomed to fail, but to Belgiojoso's credit she was able to keep some sort of dialogue going among them for several weeks. What finally shook her faith in the King was his refusal to make a final stand against the Austrians at Milan itself, where she had been tireless in mobilising a defence force among the citizens. When Charles Albert ignominiously took flight after the near-anarchy of 5 August, Belgiojoso left the city, alongside two-thirds of its inhabitants and accompanied by her friend Giacomo Antonini, hero of Vicenza and Treviso, whose left arm now lay in its reliquary on a Venetian altar at San Biagio. She had the grace to apologise to her republican acquaintance for having upheld the King's cause among the Milanese. 'Now we belong to the same party,' she told Carlo Cattaneo, 'and I repent, I repent for leading my fellow citizens astray. I beg forgiveness from my country and I shall do anything in my power to expiate my mistake.'

Among those ready to forgive Belgiojoso was her old friend Niccolò Tommaseo. The pair of them went back a long way, to the days when, as a fellow exile in Paris, she had told him not to worry about his shabby boots when visiting her salon. During his period as a provisional government minister in Venice he had invoked her aid in trying to procure arms and ships for the republic. She complained of his impracticality – exactly what munitions were needed and how many? – warning that Venice was wasting precious time by sending ten men on missions for which one was sufficient. She would have done well to repeat such advice, for by the beginning of September the number of Venetian envoys in France had risen from two to six, all apparently with conflicting ideas as to their instructions and status.

For his part, Tommaseo lost no time in putting the republic's case roundly to the French. Foreign Secretary Bastide was emphatic in declaring that France wanted Austria out of Italy bag and baggage, but insisted that mediation rather than intervention must be the answer. The truth was that the unfolding diplomatic situation now threatened to embarrass his government, especially since Austria, having considered the terms offered by France and Britain, was starting to blow hot and cold on the mediation idea. Convinced that popular opinion among the French remained strongly in favour of a positive move on Italy's behalf, Tommaseo now went into print with an open letter to the government entitled 'An Appeal to France'. His fluency as a writer was never in doubt, and it required very little to set him going, but on this occasion such facility appeared decidedly hazardous. The tone of the 'Appeal' was hectoring and reproachful. Tommaseo reminded France that she not only had a right, but a duty, to intervene. Radetzky's victories had been achieved less by his own skill than by his enemies' incompetence and treachery (an obvious dig here at the Piedmontese generals). It was the people, rather than their leaders, who had made the revolution work, and it was this same people who demanded some gesture of solidarity from the French. By the end of the letter Tommaseo's manner had grown decidedly bullying. 'I say to France and I say to England that it would be a disgrace for humanity to let the sword of a decrepit Brennus* decide a nation's fate. Our cause is yours. Help us in our hour of danger, otherwise you too will perish.' Such words were calculated to put Cavaignac on the spot, since Austria now chose to reject a peace conference, on the reasonable pretext that its reconquest of Lombardy made any further discussion of its future pointless. France must therefore honour its promises to Italy by sending troops and warships, or else back down altogether from its stance as self-appointed champion of republican liberties.

The announcement of Vienna's new hard line by the imperial

---

* The reference is to a Germanic chieftain who attempted an invasion of Italy in 102 BC and was defeated by the Roman general Gaius Marius.

Chancellor Baron von Wessenberg was accompanied by the disingenuous assertion that Austria 'aspires only to confer on its Italian provinces the benefits of peace, together with political institutions which have liberty and nationality as their foundation'. Words like 'liberty' and 'nationality' sound odd coming from the mouth of a Habsburg minister. Surveying the changed situation, Palmerston was reluctant to believe any such pledge, convinced as he had already become that the Austrian empire must eventually give up its Italian domains under pressure from the sheer loathing of the regime felt by Lombards and Venetians. When Queen Victoria, influenced by Prince Albert's abhorrence of the Foreign Secretary he nicknamed 'Pilgerstein',* spoke of Austria's 'right' to Lombardy-Venetia, Palmerston was quick to point out that the only right in question had been established at the Congress of Vienna, in which the Italians had had no say, and that such a claim was now re-established solely by force of arms.

Given Britain's constant fear of a northern Italy transformed into a French client state, it was imperative for Lord Normanby as Ambassador in Paris to do what he could to restrain Cavaignac from sending an expeditionary force once Austria had dug in her heels over mediation. At Marseilles 3,000 troops were being mustered in readiness as the Mediterranean fleet began preparing for a voyage to Venice. Manin and his fellow ministers in Venice meanwhile, though deeply embarrassed by Tommaseo's 'Appeal to France', were certainly not going to fall over themselves in trying to persuade their allies to move more slowly in the direction of renewing a patriotic war with Austria. Cavaignac had assured Angelo Mengaldo that he had Venice's interests very much at heart and wished to know everything of the current situation in the city, the mood of its defenders and the length of time they could hold out before a relief force arrived. No wonder the *Times* leader writer on 5 September saw the French essentially as cat's-paws in the hands of Manin's envoys.

The unnamed British journalist need not have worried. Normanby's attempts at playing for time had paid off the previous day, when the French council of ministers, meeting in camera, split evenly on the issue of armed intervention and Cavaignac gave his casting vote against. He was surely influenced by British reluctance to sanction the initiative, even as a means of forcing the Austrians to resume the mediation process. Palmerston, it was true, favoured a joint expedition, advising Queen Victoria that it was better for France to act under Britain's moderating

* 'Palmer' is an old English word meaning 'pilgrim' – German 'pilger' – and 'stein' is the German for 'stone' – thus Pilgerstein = Palmer-stone.

hand than to be allowed a free rein in Italy. The Queen and Prince Albert in fact believed that he was simply using France as a stalking-horse to wrest the reconquered provinces from Habsburg hands. He was over-ruled, however, by both the Cabinet and the Prime Minister. Lord John Russell's Italophilia was stronger than Palmerston's, but on this occasion he chose restraint, perhaps fearing a clash with the Queen over royal assent to any military venture, and possibly suspecting that the mere rattling of French sabres might be enough to bring the government in Vienna as far as the negotiating table at which it had not yet conde-scended to sit down.

To some extent this idea was correct. Anticipating a major interna-tional crisis, Wessenberg signified a willingness to return to mediation, and it was with some relief that the French hailed this change of heart. The Austrians were in no real mood for compromise, however, their resolve stiffened by the arch-autocrat Tsar Nicholas I of Russia, who insisted on their right to teach Italy a lesson and threatened a serious cooling of relations with France if she were to go to war on behalf of his ally's rebel subjects. It became obvious to Palmerston that Wessenberg was simply stringing the mediators along, in the hope of favourable results from military operations in Italy and Hungary, where Habsburg forces were now heavily committed. Cavaignac and Bastide, having fluffed their opportunity to put fine words into positive action, were ready to accept Austria's reversal at face value for the sake of salvaging the French govern-ment's damaged international credit.

The hope against hope that France might suddenly emerge as the saviour of patriot Italy never wholly died in the hearts of the Venetian rebels. Far from feeling inclined to recall Tommaseo, Toffoli and Mengaldo, Manin permitted or encouraged them to stay in Paris, and on 8 September sent Valentino Pasini, former leader of Vicenza's provi-sional government, to join them. It was assumed that he would take part in any forthcoming peace negotiations and he was briefed accord-ingly, with instructions as to the future democratic character of a free Venetian state and the possibility of establishing an Italian federation, which should constitute 'a single moral entity, taking its political place among other nations'. Pasini's responsibility, by no means an easy one, was to act in concert with Tommaseo to achieve the best available outcome not just for Venice but for Italy. The envoys remained en poste throughout the winter, but the sole practical good which emerged from the long diplomatic waiting game between Venice and the Cavaignac government was the continuing presence in the lagoon of two French warships, whose role was to act as suitably menacing symbols of what might happen, were the Austrians to attempt a full-scale naval assault on the rebel city.

There was no likelihood, for the time being, of anything in the way of a serious siege being mounted while General Welden's army, in its encampment around Mestre, was so ravaged with malaria, that inevitable scourge of nineteenth-century Italy's marshlands and river deltas. Austria was reluctant, in any case, to commit further troops to the enterprise of subduing Venice while warfare threatened in another part of the empire altogether. Hungary, having embarked on its March revolution a week earlier than the Venetians, had already pushed ahead with a radical reform programme, spearheaded by the lawyer and journalist Lajos Kossuth, designed to modernise not only the administration of the kingdom,* but also its ancient taxation system, rooted in the medieval feudalism of vast landed estates. The ministers of the new parliament in Pest were not loved by the more reactionary members of the Habsburg imperial family, and any opportunity to undermine their achievements was eagerly exploited by Emperor Ferdinand's ambitious and manipulative sister-in-law Archduchess Sophie, mother to the heir-apparent Franz Josef. Her way grew clearer once it became obvious that the Hungarian magnates, for all their liberal zeal, had no intention of papering over the historical racial and nationalist divisions between the Magyars and the various Slavic peoples they dominated. Among these, it was the Croats above all whom they despised, as stupid semi-savages whose only practical use lay in their historical role as dogged defenders of the south-western frontier with the Ottoman empire, an extended military zone bordering the northern edges of present-day Serbia and Bosnia.

The Habsburgs had no qualms at this stage in using one imperial subject race to subdue another. This set-a-sprat-to-catch-a-mackerel principle was as self-evidently useful in Hungary as it had proved in Italy, where the Croats had no real grudge against the revolutionaries in terms of racial or cultural oppression, and simply acted as the loyal cohorts of empire they had always been. With the Hungarians, however, the quarrel was genuine, based on a long history of slights and grievances. When, during the revolutionary spring, the Croats found their leader in Josip Jellačič, colonel of a frontier regiment and fervently loyal to the Habsburg throne, Hungary, to whose Crown lands most of Croatia belonged, hastily sought some kind of workable arrangement with him. Jellačič stalled long enough over compromise with the government in Pest to reassure Archduchess Sophie

* Hungary was a separate kingdom under Austrian rule, and remained so until the collapse of the Habsburg empire in 1918.

and her conservative faction, winning her praise with his personal declaration of fealty and a manifesto enjoining all Croat soldiers in Italy to
serve the flag faithfully. Appointed supreme commander of all troops within
Hungary's borders, he marched into the heartland of the kingdom with
the idea of reclaiming it, but his bungling generalship merely encouraged
Kossuth's newly reorganised army to stiffen its resistance, and by the last
week of September Jellačič turned tail and fled back to the borders.

A few days later the imperial court, in its refuge at Innsbruck, was
convulsed by news of a revolution closer to home. In Vienna a grenadier
regiment ordered to join Jellačič's army had mutinied, while a mob
composed largely of workers and students broke into the Ministry of War,
dragged out and lynched the aged minister Count Baillet de Latour and
strung his body from a lamp-post. Once more Emperor Ferdinand and
his family retreated, this time to the Moravian town of Olmutz
(Olomouc), where they were followed by most of the moderate government ministers and many of their sternest critics among the camarilla
surrounding Archduchess Sophie. A punitive expedition, mounted by
Prince Windischgrätz with Jellačič's help, set out meanwhile to take the
capital by storm. Windischgrätz, himself an intransigent loyalist, had no
hesitation in bombarding the city, burning its suburbs and allowing the
Croats free rein in looting and summary executions. The recovery of
Vienna spelt the end of any significant opposition within German-
speaking Austria to restoring the imperial regime, though a form of democratic government was suffered to continue for the time being.

With the Hungarian revolt seriously stretching Habsburg resources, it
was all Welden could do as regional commander in the Veneto to maintain any sort of meaningful encirclement around Venice's principal points
of communication with the mainland. Radetzky, busy restoring imperial
authority in Lombardy and the duchies, was short-handed enough and
the returning Austrian garrisons were being kept busy by the contumacy
and surliness of a civilian population which had resigned its freedom with
a very bad grace in many cases. As at Verona in April, curfews were
imposed and streets patrolled at night, often so rigorously that even
doctors and midwives were forbidden to go out on call, and priests were
prevented from administering the last rights to the dying. In the province
of Rovigo additional taxes were levied for the billeting and victualling of
soldiers, and a rumour ran around Padua that Welden was charging to
the municipality not only his barber's bill, but his wife's account at the
smart dress shop of Zatta. Things were not improved as autumn drew
on by the military government's resort to using volunteer corps from
Austria's German-speaking heartland. An anonymous Paduan commentator

sarcastically described a newly arrived battalion of dirty, ill-clad Styrians as 'the flower of courtesy, educated in the philanthropic establishments of prison and the galleys'. Their behaviour was predictably thuggish. One man was beaten up for singing in the street, another for talking to his yoke of oxen as he led them. Learning the names of 'patriotic' shops and cafés, the Styrians smashed their windows and furniture. Welden was at length forced to intervene when they murdered one of the former defenders of Palmanova, hacked another civilian to death with their sabres and gang-raped a woman, before stabbing her in the eye and cutting her ring-fingers off.

Even those inclined to welcome the reinstatement of Austrian rule were shocked by the military's callous triumphalism. Don Giovanni Renier, parish priest of Mestre, noted sorrowfully that the local garrison had summoned from Padua and Treviso 'a veritable herd of prostitutes', organising dances which soon became 'orgies so disgraceful that the pen shrinks from recording them'. This was hardly unexpected among soldiers eager for a little relaxation after a summer of war, but as the cold weather set in, their contempt for their humbled foes took on a more serious aspect. A house-to-house requisition of blankets and bedcovers was instituted, and the answer to any kind of protest was to ransack the premises from attic to cellar. The order had come not from Welden, but from General D'Aspre, still very much in command at Treviso. When Renier went in person to beseech compassion for his parishioners, the old soldier's reply, a chilling amalgam of brutality and preposterousness, said everything needful as to the prevailing attitude among the officers towards the Emperor's rebel subjects. 'I did not order winter to arrive,' D'Aspre told the priest, 'it was you Italians who started this war.'

Emphatic as their presence on the mainland was, the Austrians were reluctant to take action against Venice while talks about talks were still in progress. As far as they were concerned, the city was rightfully theirs and it was merely a matter of waiting until the terms of the armistice were properly fulfilled. The issue of whom the city belonged to, raised by Manin in a spirit of what Schönhals calls 'Machiavellian hair-splitting', came to the fore once again when General Alberto La Marmora, bowing to political pressure, consented at last to evacuate his three Piedmontese battalions by sea to Ancona and thence to Genoa. La Marmora's was not an especially distinguished war – having conspicuously failed to halt Nugent's march into Friuli, he made little significant contribution to the armed struggle in the Veneto thereafter – but his heart was in the right place, and it was with real reluctance that he issued an order to pull out. As if determined to do right by the Venetians, he sent a letter to Welden informing him that the regiments were about to leave, adding at its close a lengthy paragraph objecting to Austria's evident preparations for an attack and declaring that a Piedmontese withdrawal did not guarantee surrender of the city to Austria, still less justify an assault on it.

An ostensible pretext for delay had been given to La Marmora by his naval opposite number Admiral Albini, pleading bad weather as an excuse for remaining anchored in the lagoon for at least a fortnight after the relevant orders arrived on 21 August. He too had been slated for inaction, denounced as philo-Habsburg or merely written off as a poodle of Charles Albert and the Turin government. Sympathy and admiration for Venice in its present plight encouraged him to advise the triumvirs, before he was due to leave, that their city was not invulnerable from the sea, that the Austrians were preparing to step up their somewhat desultory blockade of the lagoon entrance channels, and that they should take advantage of a lull in the fighting to lay in necessary provisions for what might prove to be a lengthy siege.

It was well-meant advice, none of which, as so often happens in situations of this kind, was taken seriously. The Venetian Naval Minister, Leone Graziani, let slip the opportunity to build up a defensive presence around the channels at either end of the Lido by fitting out more vessels, while his vice-admiral Giorgio Bua maintained that supplies could easily be brought in from the river estuaries of the Brenta and Piave. It was well known, after all, that the imperial navy at Pola and Trieste had few seaworthy ships, that its officers were lazy and its sailors, mostly Italian in any case, unenthusiastic about the blockade. Manin, while freely acknowledging his ignorance of military matters and wary of warlike preparation while the French seemed poised to move, disregarded the whole naval issue in favour of allowing the War Minister Cavedalis a free hand in pulling the land forces into adequate fighting shape.

The incompetence of military and naval commanders and the Venetians' general unpreparedness for confronting a full-scale siege were just the sort of sticks for beating the government for which the Circolo Italiano had been looking. On 1 October the republican newspaper *Fatti e parole* stepped up its criticism with an acerbic article by Francesco Dall'Ongaro accusing the generals and admirals of squandering the fruits of victory and warning them that 'the People, undisciplined, imprudent and fearless' could quite easily stage another, more violent revolution than the almost bloodless coup of 22 March. An ever-growing number of non-Venetian army officers now belonged to the Circolo, which had elected Tommaseo, *in absentia*, as its President. The club, as a Mazzinian power-base, seemed calculated to challenge the authority of Manin and his fellow triumvirs, so the sooner it was dealt with, the better. The day after Dall'Ongaro published his attack, several prominent Circolo members were arrested and expelled from Venice, and the poet's own turn came a few days later. As a sop to liberal opinion, outraged by what seemed like a return to the worst days of a Habsburg police state, Manin announced that the assembly would be convened on 11 October to elect a committee 'which should deal with the current political situation and nominate a new government, whenever the emergency should cease which had brought about the present dictatorship'. An overwhelming confidence vote among the members consolidated Manin's position, and though a move towards free elections was agreed, it was to be another two months before the appropriate legislation enabled them to go ahead. 'And thus,' noted Cavedalis gleefully, in his current capacity as the President's strong right arm, 'were the malcontents and ill-intentioned persons defeated.'

Astute and hard-working, Cavedalis cooperated effectively with General Pepe to develop that infrastructure of coordination and discipline on which any army needs to depend. What bedevilled them, as it tested the patience of everyone labouring to sustain the reality of Venetian freedom, was an increasing lack of funds. The various forced loans and jewellery collections made during the summer by the provisional government had yielded temporary relief, but more substantial sums were now needed for everything from the purchase of arms and the payment of workers in the Arsenal to the salaries of envoys abroad and dole for the rising number of unemployed. The national savings bank established in July issued its own 'patriotic currency' and shares in the Venice–Milan railway were put up for sale. Having presided over an administration that initially set out to reduce or abolish taxes established by the Austrians, Manin found himself in the unenviable position of having to sanction fresh duties, imposed on tobacco and the brewing of beer.

On 31 August, as an ultimate demonstration of the seriousness of its current fiscal position, the new government decreed that a national loan of ten million lire be guaranteed by the mortgaging of buildings and treasures considered to be the most precious exemplars of Venice's artistic patrimony. A special commission of art experts was set up to consider the feasibility of so unprecedented a measure, and at the end of October its report was submitted. Not surprisingly, the committee had serious doubts as to the likely advantages to Venice of the proposed scheme. If the works to be mortgaged were not finally redeemed, tourism would drop off, art students would be seriously inconvenienced by a lack of classic reference points, and one of Venice's principal claims to international importance would be removed at a stroke.

Practical considerations weighed even more powerfully. How were ceiling panels, for example, such as those by Titian in the sacristy of Santa Maria della Salute, to be removed, and where could they be re-installed to the correct measurements? What would be the fate of such enormous works as the same artist's 'Assumption of the Blessed Virgin' or Veronese's 'Feast in the House of Levi', whose sheer size made transportation almost impossible? What allowances were to be made for the effect, over several centuries, of the Venetian climate, with its humidity and saline deposits, on a whole range of canvases and panels currently displayed inside damp churches? The list of these artistic hostages to fortune included, as well as the Doge's Palace and its contents, many of Venice's most treasured paintings. Bellini's 'Virgin Enthroned with Four Saints' at San Zaccaria, Tintoretto's 'Miracle of St Mark', Veronese's three canvases from the presbytery of San Sebastiano, Carpaccio's St George cycle from the Scuola Dalmata and Bartolomeo Vivarini's St Mark triptych in the Frari would all have gone under the hammer. No wonder the committee, despite internal disagreements, concluded unanimously, 'we pray the government to consider carefully the dangers involved, the time, the expense and probable lack of a successful outcome, before making any firm decision as to this important issue'. Later generations may be thankful that several of the richest Venetian merchants came forward immediately to redeem the debt.

Among the most effective agents in raising popular awareness of the economic crisis were Venice's parish priests. The impact made by the Barnabite preachers Ugo Bassi and Alexandro Gavazzi during their fund-raising drive in May had been considerable, and the clergy responded eagerly to Cardinal Monico's latest pastoral letter, circulated on 14 September, underlining the moral duty of all parishioners to support their community at such a critical moment by giving freely to the cause. The Patriarch instituted a new service, to take place an hour before sunset every day for a month, when the litany according to the rubric 'In quacum tribulatione' ('In whatsoever tribulation') was to be sung. There were to be no candles or instrumental music, but a collection could be taken at the close. Even Monico's sternest critics among the patriots could hardly have quarrelled with his closing words. 'What sort of a nation is ours, my beloved children? A city which is the very cradle and fortress of liberty, the mother of heroes and saints, nurse of immortal genius, preceptress of every worthy discipline, former mistress of the seas, triumphant over barbarous peoples, jealous protectress of the one true Faith, now giving shelter to Italian hopes, with every eye in Europe fixed upon her.'

This was a pardonable exaggeration on Monico's part, one that might have given some comfort to those who felt that the principle of charity beginning at home was not being taken seriously enough by the rest of Italy. It was true that the Roman government had failed to honour its earlier promise to pay compensation for the maintenance of Durando's *papalini* during the Veneto campaign, but a more encouraging response was expected from Genoa, forever fretful under the Piedmontese rule imposed on it in 1815 and currently angry at Charles Albert's failure to achieve results. In September, the poet Arnaldo Fusinato arrived in the city. As commander of a volunteer force raised in his home town of Schio, he had led his men in a desperate attempt, reinforced by the civic guard from the nearby spa of Recoaro, to stop the Austrians crossing the mountain pass of Pian delle Fugazze. His assistant as fund-raiser was another poet, the youthful Genoese prodigy Goffredo Mameli, writer of the hymn 'Fratelli d'Italia', which is now Italy's national anthem. The gala benefit evening in which both took part at the city's Teatro Carlo Felice, organised by a committee of noblewomen, featured the talents of two prima donnas who later created roles in operas by Verdi.* Such a stellar occasion was given its ultimate significance by Mameli's declamation of a poem including the words: 'Spare a coin for Venice: the noble beggar has nothing but water, courage and seaweed, since she is the friend of the sea. Alone amid so many infamies, she remains our glory. The listening world would hear yet another ignoble story if our Illustrious Pauper were to die of hardship – 'Venice asked for bread, but nobody gave her any'. Though kings may choose to sell her, may God and the People be her defenders!'

The programme was a great success, attracting pledges totalling more than one million lire, but the Piedmontese government effectively vetoed Genoa's initiative before any practical help could reach the Venetians. Much more promising was the reaction of individual givers and small communities to Venice's current plight, highlighted as this had been in an article published in October by the novelist Alexandre Dumas in the French journal *Le Mois*. A fervent supporter of the Italian patriotic cause (he was to join Garibaldi's expedition to Sicily in 1860), Dumas was only too happy to speak up for the rebel Venetians. 'The beggar queen', as he called Venice, had stretched forth her hand to the nations and withdrawn it empty. France herself had done nothing for 'this heroic city', which was 'living off its own entrails'. The defence of

---

* Teresa De Giuli Borsi and Marietta Gazzaniga, creators of Lida in *La Battaglia di Legnano* and Luisa in *Luisa Miller*.

Venice was now, he maintained, a question of money as much as feats of arms.

Others throughout Italy had similarly noble impulses. In a poor village near Ravenna the inhabitants had devoted the funds set aside for their church feast day to 'the immortal lagoons', praying that 'on the towers of St Mark the banner of Italian independence may flutter uncontaminated'. Four ladies at Civitavecchia clubbed together to make bandages for the wounded and take up a collection in the town. The civic guard at Cesena, the citizens of Bagnacavallo and Aosta, a Lombard priest, a Milanese duke and the wife of a Jewish merchant from Leghorn all contributed to the cause. Charity concerts were organised in the Emilian town of Fiorenzuola and at Sassari in Sardinia, and donations came in from as far afield as Istria and Egypt. In Paris, meanwhile, the era's leading baritone Giorgio Ronconi presented an operatic gala at the Théâtre des Italiens.

Yet to many in Italy, such bursts of generosity were not enough. It took Giuseppe Mazzini, as moral conscience of the resurgent nation, to step forward, reminding patriots of their duty to assist. 'Venice,' he declared, 'needs three million a month to survive, and three million Italians can provide this. She is today the heart of Italy, by virtue of her unyielding will, of the holiness of her intentions, of her glories, her hopes and her misfortunes . . . Whoever refuses to pay this national levy in Venice's favour will pronounce her doom and will shamefully have deserted the cause of freedom and the motherland.' Not the least among the Venetians' bitter experiences as autumn drew on would be to realise how little their fortitude mattered to those whose help – whether with guns, money, diplomacy or moral support – might have counted for most.

~

CHAPTER 10

THE MAKING OF HEROES

AT LEAST UNTIL THE MIDDLE of October, the Venetians were not quite alone. High up the Tagliamento valley, north of Udine, the fortress at Osoppo, perched on a hill overlooking the village, had continued miraculously to hold out against its Austrian besiegers. Back in March, Colonel Cavedalis, then commanding patriot forces in Friuli, had ordered the stronghold to be made ready for a possible attack from whatever detachments Nugent might care to throw at it. Summoned to join La Marmora in his inspection tours of the volunteer forces, he handed over command of the fort to the Bolognese officer Licurgo Zannini, who gathered together a 400-strong garrison, consisting mostly of fugitives from Udine. He and his second-in-command Leonardo Andervolti proved inspiring leaders, though their task was made no easier by the constant intrigues of a fellow officer, Captain Enrico Francia, who sought to discredit their achievements in the eyes of the other defenders, subsequently presenting a serious threat to both men's professional reputations. Odious as he proved, Francia was no coward, contributing, like the rest, to a heroic resistance lasting almost six months.

At first, not merely the fort, but the village as well withstood the Austrian assault. The Habsburg troops, themselves mostly Italian, had carried out a scorched-earth strategy in the neighbourhood, driving off cattle, burning crops and pulling down houses to facilitate their artillery's field of fire. By June, the daily rations for Zannini and his men had been reduced to three ounces of pasta or five of rice to make broth, five ounces of meat, four of bread, three-tenths of an ounce of lard and a glass of wine. When Major Tommaselli, directing the siege, called upon Zannini to surrender, he was given a firm refusal, on the grounds that 'all these valorous defenders have declared their wish to preserve this rock uncontaminated, to the greater glory of Italy'. Exasperated, Tommaselli threatened to burn the village, and several of its inhabitants hurriedly retreated to the safety of the fortress. One who did not was Giovanna Savio del Cet, the indigent mother of six children, all by now in serious need of food. Driven by despair, she took it into her head to approach one of the Austrian outposts and beg the soldiers directly for bread. A Croat sentry, encouraging her to come nearer, held out a piece of pumper-nickel on the point of his bayonet. The wretched woman trustingly grabbed hold of it and called two of her little girls to join her. The Croat's response was to pull the embroidered scarves off their heads and shoot all three dead.

Happier by far was the experience of Domenico Barnaba, who, after taking part in the battles of Cornuda and Vicenza, had been forced to give his parole not to take up arms against the Austrians. Returning to his family's house at Buia, south of Osoppo, he found his mother Francesca at the centre of a bizarre situation. During May she had been visited by an Austrian officer anxious to use her carriage in order to reach the nearby town of San Daniele. He had none of the brusqueness and arrogance usually displayed by the Habsburg military in its dealings with Italians, and offered to pay for hire and feeding of the horses. Francesca Barnaba declined the money, but though her daughters afterwards reproached her for not refusing the request altogether, she let him borrow the vehicle.

Her trust was rewarded. Not only did the officer, a Bohemian named Prohaska, send back the carriage, but a few days later he gave her an anonymous tip-off that the house was due to be searched. She and the two girls hurriedly hid or destroyed a multitude of compromising objects, such as tricolour cockades, suspect books and pictures of Garibaldi, Mazzini and Lajos Kossuth. Just before dusk came the expected knock at the door. An officer and a dozen men began a thorough turn-over of the villa and its farm buildings, examining the kitchen, lavatory, stables, harness room, granary and servants' quarters over the barn. While the soldiers rummaged outside, one of the Barnaba daughters had the pres-ence of mind to tear a picture of Radetzky out of an almanac and stick it in a frame, prominently displayed in the *salotto* where the women nerv-ously awaited the officer's findings. In halting Italian, he delightedly recog-nised 'nostro brafo marescial' and was pleased to accept a glass of wine and an exchange of pleasantries before giving the signal to depart. As Francesca stood at the door to see him off, he whispered, 'Captain Prohaska sends his kind regards.'

Next morning the Captain himself arrived. 'What was I to do? Shut the door in his face?' Francesca later told her son. 'He had treated me kindly. Was I to show him ingratitude? In the end, while respecting his sentiments, I remained true to my own, those of a good Italian.' Prohaska then confessed to a personal motive for his visit. Signora Barnaba's goodness was well known in the neighbourhood, and she reminded him of his own dear mother, whom he had not seen for four years. Might he then pay them an occasional call? 'You will think me weak and unworthy of being a soldier,' said he. 'Ah, signora, I cannot and must not forget that before I became a soldier, I was a son.' Moved by this, and recalling her own boys absent fighting for the cause, Francesca agreed. Every Sunday for the next few weeks, Prohaska came to eat a plate of risotto with the family and talk about gardening, on which he had some useful tips.

When Domenico Barnaba got home after the Vicenza debacle, he was naturally appalled to find an enemy officer at his ease in the villa. Francesca nevertheless managed at length to introduce the two men, and Captain Prohaska, true to form, commended Domenico for putting filial loyalty before politics. 'Serving your country is a sacred duty.' He concluded, 'but a mother has her rights as well. Depriving her of the help of both her sons was too much.' Touched by this, Domenico shook his hand, noting afterwards how greatly Prohaska was now respected by the family's servants and farm workers. This little truce did nothing, however, to lessen Domenico's contribution to Osoppo's resistance. He managed to smuggle food into the fort and at one stage to acquire a hundred pairs of boots for its defenders. Suspecting the Barnabas' involvement, but never quite managing to prove it, Major Tommaselli imposed a levy on the family of 1,000 lire. After Domenico paid up, Prohaska sardonically let slip that the money would certainly go into the Major's pocket, but that without its prompt payment the villa would probably have been ransacked and set on fire.

Tommaselli was not moving quickly enough for the Austrian high command, to whom Osoppo's doughty stand seemed an irritating stone in the shoe. In September he was replaced by Lieutenant-Colonel Friedrich Van der Null, who came determined to finish matters for good and all within the next month. On 8 October his troops burst into the village, sacking and burning the houses, making a bonfire of the historic archives of the Savorgnan family, the castle's former owners, and turning out all inhabitants. Those too old or infirm to move were simply bayoneted where they lay. In the fort, Zannini and Andervolti realised surrender was near, but refused at first to agree to Van der Null's terms. Their fellow defenders supported them, declaring to Zannini that having come thus far, they would blow up the magazine and bury themselves under the ruins. 'This response,' wrote one of them, 'accompanied by the firm and resolute demeanour of everybody concerned, had something fierce and terrible within it. A tear, as of wonder and shame, was quickly dried from the bronzed cheek of the brave soldier.'

Wisely deciding that his men were more useful alive than dead, Zannini dragged out the negotiations, a process which had the unforeseen result of persuading them that their officers were making a secret deal with Van der Null while preparing to let the rank and file shift for itself. After a riot broke out in the garrison and a private shot his corporal dead, Zannini was left with little choice but to speed up the surrender. On 14 October the heroes of Osoppo, ragged and half-starved, were allowed to leave, taking their tattered colours with them. Once outside the fort, the officers decided to pay a courtesy call on the Barnaba family to thank them for their assistance during the siege. While taking some much-needed refreshment, they were startled by a roll of drums. It was Captain Prohaska and his platoon of Croats who had come to salute them, presenting arms to honour the brave Italians. Drawing his sabre, the Captain said, 'I greet you today, you and your valorous men, as an admirer of your heroism. Tomorrow, as your adversary on the battlefield, I shall show you my sword-point, ready to wound.'

The courage of Osoppo's defenders was upheld as an example to the patriots manning the fifty-four forts which encircled Venice and commanded its approaches from the mainland. Most of these had been built by the Austrians and were either simple brick octagons enclosing gun batteries, a line of which extended from north to south along the westward side of the lagoon, or larger fortifications like those guarding the entrance to the Lido. Most imposing of all was Marghera (often written as Malghera), a typical Vaubanesque construction dating from the early eighteenth century and rebuilt under Napoleon, its angled outer bastions containing gun emplacements and forming a star shape, which enclosed an inner moat surrounding a central stronghold built to the same pattern. Commanding the nearby Ferdinandea railway line running across its marble viaduct were two smaller forts: Rizzardi, with the adjacent 'Speranza' battery, and the defended position formerly known as Fort O or Eau, now christened 'Manin'. An additional reinforcement which became particularly valuable during the next few months was the fortified islet of San Giuliano, at the entrance to the so-called military canal parallel with the Ferdinandea. A further canal, leading north-west to Mestre, allowed boats to bring supplies directly into Marghera's moat.

To get at Venice itself, General Welden, commanding the currently depleted Austrian army stationed on the mainland, realised that he would have to deal with this entire defensive system first of all, sustained as it now was by the energy and fervour of what soon turned out to be the most resoundingly effective of all Italian forces mobilised in the patriot cause during the 1848–9 revolution. Its personnel was by no means exclusively Venetian. Many officers were Neapolitans who had stayed on with General Pepe rather than obeying King Ferdinand's summons to return home following his 15 May counter-coup, and it was these men who supervised engineering operations, gave lessons in gunnery and knocked the volunteer corps into fighting shape. In addition there were Roman and Bolognese professionals from the papal army units formerly led by Durando and now commanded by Livio Zambeccari, a handful of Piedmontese disdaining the order to leave with La Marmora, and a Hungarian brigade led by Lajos Winkler, formerly of the Austrian Kinsky regiment, who had bravely defied the order to fire on the crowd during the confrontation in the Piazza on 21 March.

La Marmora's view of the volunteers during the early weeks of independence had been dim enough, and by the beginning of September, despite their baptism of fire in the various phases of the Veneto campaign, the condition of certain legions looked far from encouraging. The 3,000 Paduans who had enrolled by torchlight at a café table on Piazza delle Erbe in the space of a single night now appeared little better than beggars. 'I noted with real sadness the state of squalor and misery which prevailed among these young soldiers,' wrote one of Pepe's officers at Brondolo. 'Their uniforms in rags, their health poor, one could no longer perceive in them those bold, robust youths who had marched into the estuary region. Barely 35 were now in a condition to move.'

The lull in hostilities during the period of Anglo-French mediation had nevertheless enabled many commanders to bring their battalions up to strength, give them fresh uniforms and prepare them for the new kind of defensive warfare in which they were likely henceforth to be engaged. The mixed origins of these corps enhanced a genuine feeling among the men of being involved in a national enterprise transcending old rivalries and suspicions among cities, regions and states. Ex-defenders of Osoppo and Palmanova, for instance, formed a Friulan legion with no obvious tensions of the kind existing between neighbouring towns in the area at the start of the war. Another regiment was made up of Tommaseo's compatriots from the Italian-speaking ports along the Dalmatian coast. The Capuchin friar Antonio Torniello had founded his own brigade of sharpshooters, leading off with a grand flag-blessing ceremony at SS Giovanni e Paolo led by the charismatic Father Gavazzi. After being forced to lay down their arms at the recapture of Treviso, they had retreated disgruntled across the papal frontier to Ferrara, until they successfully badgered Cavedalis into allowing them back to Venice to form a new unit, known as 'Italia Libera'. Many ex-members of Italian regiments in the imperial army, what was more, joined the patriot forces in the lagoon. The former Venetian garrison battalion, made up of old or wounded soldiers, became the National Veterans' Corps, doing sanitary chores, guarding prisons and manning the more remote forts. Others provided the city with its gendarmerie (most of the Austrian police having resigned or made themselves scarce), but were ready to take part, when needed, in mainland sorties or foraging expeditions. The Venetian defence force could even boast a cavalry regiment, 200 lancers led by the patrician Jacopo Zorzi. Dressed in dark-green tunics, red-striped trousers and gilt-trimmed shakos sporting white plumes and tricolour cockades, they were a dashing but ill-assorted bunch of Venetian and Neapolitan sprigs of nobility, and it was not long before a new officer, Guglielmo Diaz, was ordered to take Zorzi's place and turn them into something a little less like an opera chorus.

Everyone who could handle a weapon was welcome to join the defence force. Besides Winkler's Hungarians, non-Italians fighting for Venice included the eighty-strong Swiss brigade led by Major Johann Debrunner and all hailing from the canton of Torgau. Debrunner was strongly committed to the cause, and the Swiss in any case had a bone to pick with Austria, which had sought a year or two earlier to interfere drastically in their country's politics. When they first arrived in Venice the citizens gave them a frosty welcome, supposing, because they spoke German, that they must be Austrian prisoners. To begin with, they were lodged in barracks at San Salvador, where their Swiss cleanliness was outraged by the large population of fleas in the blankets and palliasses. Debrunner took a dim view of the Italian volunteers, especially the university students. Once they received new uniforms, 'their magnificent attire and general turn-out proclaimed a brilliant intellectual culture', he remarked witheringly, but they were wretchedly undisciplined, always complaining and disobedient towards their officers. Having no mess of their own, they ate in *trattorie*, where they got drunk and swarmed through the streets picking fights and behaving like hooligans.

Other foreign nationals in the Venetian ranks hailed from Germany, France and Spain, and we know of at least four Britons who enlisted: one of them the much-admired Colonel Forbes, who was later to fight for Garibaldi; another named John Oates from Sheffield, who had joined Pepe's expeditionary force in Naples back in April; a certain 'Odoardo Davis' mentioned as part of the Italia Libera outfit; and a lieutenant in the Treviso 'Cacciatori del Sile' brigade called James Campbell. Was he a relative, perhaps a son, of the pro-Italian consul in Milan, Robert Campbell? It would be nice to think so, in view of the intractably pro-Austrian stance of the latter's consular superior in Venice, Clinton Dawkins.

Of all the various corps, the Bandiera e Moro artillery regiment became the crack unit among the volunteers. Its very title, taken in memory of the martyrs of 1844, would seem to guarantee a certain glamour, and both officers and men distinguished themselves throughout the siege by their mixture of conspicuous gallantry and practical resourcefulness. The regiment was especially favoured by young members of the 5,000-strong Venetian Jewish community, which had already contributed so much in moral and material terms to the revolution's success. Looking down the muster roll, we find names such as Emanuele Levi, Leone Tedesco, Gabriele Finzi, Gismondo Jakia Ferrara, Arnoldo Pavia and Michele Treves, men whose grandparents only fifty years earlier had been compelled by the Serene Republic to dwell in the ghetto and whose parents had been denied full citizenship of the Habsburg empire by Francis I.

Life in the forts, more particularly at Marghera, was by no means disagreeable, to begin with at least. Boats were constantly plying to and fro with provisions, and one of Venice's leading restaurateurs was engaged to provide a *trattoria* whose meals supplemented the soldiers' basic rations. 'With a dish of rice or a good soup,' recalled the Modenese officer Antonio Morandi, 'a piece of boiled meat with or without vegetables, a roll or two and a drop of light wine, the whole costing 50 or 60 *centesimi*, a man could leave with a full belly.' Other traditional consolations of the soldier were not forgotten. After the siege was over, an American consular official censoriously noted the very high incidence of venereal disease among the volunteers, and a contingent of whores (probably larger than the 'herd' servicing the Austrians, which so scandalised Mestre's parish priest) appears to have been an established feature of life in Marghera and doubtless in some of the other forts besides. Their presence depressed Don Vincenzo Marinelli, whom Cardinal Monico had asked Pope Pius's permission to make principal chaplain to the army. He had not been happy with the readiness of itinerant clergy like Bassi and Gavazzi to converse directly with the prostitutes, and felt that the two priests' odd attire, let alone their beards and moustaches, was in some way linked to this unorthodox conduct. What alarmed Marinelli most of all was '*il vizio sodomitico*', seemingly brought into the barracks by 'those idle young boys who pass to and fro selling strong drink', and who were all too easily seduced by 'the beastliness of depraved sinners'. Having become soldiers themselves, 'they contaminated others with the detestable practice'. According to Don Vincenzo, such homosexuality was merely part of a conspiracy by the Austrian police 'to introduce Asiatic softness into Italy, so as to render Italians unwarlike and thus susceptible to tyranny by a foreign power'. Now, he declared, Italy must do everything possible to recall her sons to their ancient dignity, rendering them worthy of the freedom conferred by God.

The chance for the soldiers to prove that, whatever their private vices, public virtue was still in generous supply came at the end of October 1848. Though Osoppo had surrendered, the position of the Austrians on the mainland was not necessarily encouraging. General Welden, recently retired through illness and soon to be made military governor of Dalmatia, had left his troops seriously ravaged by malarial fevers, which continued to take their toll throughout the winter. The imperial navy, awaiting an adequate commander, had failed to make the anticipated breakthrough into the waters of the lagoon, where French warships in any case rode at anchor as a pledge of their country's good intentions on Venice's behalf, even if a landward intervention was not guaranteed. There was talk of a peace conference to decide affairs in northern Italy for good and all, and Britain had warned Austria not to embark, supposing resources allowed, on any major offensive for the time being. The weather, besides, was scarcely ideal for campaigning: heavy rains had turned the eastern Veneto plain into a quagmire and flooded the streets and *campi* of Venice itself.

Inside Fort Marghera, however, spirits were undampened. Its defenders, itching to take a crack at the Austrians in the form of a properly organised sortie, were receiving gunnery lessons from Major Musto, a Neapolitan veteran of the Greek independence struggle during the 1820s, much respected by his men. Clinton Dawkins and his French opposite number as consul, anxious to preserve a stand-off between Austrians and Italians while the mediation process was at a delicate stage, complained to Manin, although he seems to have done nothing to halt Musto's preparations and those of his fellow officers Morandi and Zambeccari. Whatever the chief triumvir's Micawberish hope that something would at length turn up in the way of material assistance from Paris, beyond two or three ambiguously minatory battleships, he was shrewd enough to appreciate the value of a successful operation against the imperial army, in terms both of its effect on morale and of its potential for increasing Venice's international prestige at a time when the revolutionary impetus throughout Italy seemed in danger of stalling.

The earlier stirrings to action came on 22 October, when an expedition was launched, not from Marghera itself but from Treporti, on the south-western end of the long spit of land jutting out from Jesolo as far as the northern entrance to the Venetian lagoon. Nowadays a seaside resort, it was then largely occupied by market gardens and fishermen's huts. Austrian troops had recently moved as far as the little village of Cavallino, where 400 of them dug in with the evident design of establishing a bridge-head on the peninsula from which to menace shipping, besiege the fort at Treporti and maybe even launch an assault on Venice. The object of the patriots' expedition was to flush them out, driving them back towards Jesolo and the canal by which the River Piave enters the sea.

The operation was three-pronged, involving the use of cannon mounted on boats rowed along a channel on the north side of the narrow penin-sula, a detachment of troops sent to attack Cavallino from the north, and the advance of an armed column, 500 strong, drawn from the Cacciatori del Sile brigade, mostly men from Treviso, led by Major Daniele Francesconi. Under heavy rain, the march down the single muddy road to Cavallino was made even slower by a need to keep level with the gunboats, and by the thick blanket of fog covering the surrounding fields. Initially the Italians were taken by surprise when a rattle of fire told them they had reached the outlying houses, but the cannon on their little oared vessels were put swiftly to work, and it was easy enough for the *caccia-tori* to charge the barricades, chase the enemy from their trenches and seize the two pieces of artillery with which the village was defended. Though the pursuit was halted by the onset of night and further bad weather, this Cavallino action was a good excuse for a parade in the Piazza the following day, with the customary review of troops by General Pepe, the captured Austrian munitions on prominent display, and a general feeling among Venetians that the army was achieving concrete results.

This was not a major feat of arms, but as Major Carlo Radaelli, respon-sible for planning the assault, observed, 'the simultaneous attack by land and sea and the valour demonstrated by the troops were happy auguries of greater exploits'. Earliest among these was one of the most successful actions of the entire patriotic campaign, the sortie launched against Austrian positions at Mestre on 27 October. A dramatic example of how well the mixed professional and volunteer force could fight, if given adequate drilling, sound leadership and proper coordination, it achieved epic dimensions in the annals of the Venetian revolution, being remem-bered as one of those unsurpassable I-was-there moments.

Radaelli himself was mainly responsible for the operation's initial outline, aided, in the council of war, by Pepe, Cavedalis and the Neapolitan colonel Girolamo Ulloa. None of them anticipated an easy victory. Only one road led to Mestre from Marghera, and this was dotted with Austrian gun emplacements, while snipers were placed in the windows and on the roofs of neighbouring houses. On the south side of the canal ran the railway track to Padua, joining the Treviso branch line at the station, which Welden, in establishing his military base, had taken care to fortify. Between this and Fusina, the old landing stage for the ferry to Venice at the mouth of the River Brenta, lay an entrenched camp containing some 2,800 Habsburg troops.

Radaelli's original plan was to land the Cacciatori del Sile, blooded as they now were from Cavallino, at Fusina, accompanied by a light artillery division, with the object of capturing the enemy's cannon and keeping the defenders busy while the main attack from Marghera and neighbouring Fort Rizzardi was thrown against the town of Mestre itself. Zambeccari, with his gallant Bolognese and Romans of the Italia Libera brigade, was to lead the thrust at Mestre; Antonio Morandi, heading a force mostly made up of Lombards and Romagnoles, was ordered to capture the station; and the naval division charged with landing the men at Fusina was under the direction of Captain Antonio Basilisco. Much depended, as in the raid from Treporti, on the vagaries of the weather, more especially the lifting of autumnal fog blanketing the lagoon, and at its thickest where the Cacciatori del Sile were due to disembark.

In the dawn hours of 27 October, this damp grey curtain seemed more impenetrable than ever, and it was some time before the *cacciatori* could begin their silent advance on the trenches at Fusina. A single cannon shot from the shore had been plainly audible as a pre-arranged signal to Pepe at Marghera, who now gave the order for the main attack to commence. The Austrians appear to have had some intelligence of the operation, but Zambeccari's men found it easy to storm the defences, bayoneting the gunners, seizing their cannon and driving the enemy back onto the town. At the railway station Morandi faced a tougher fight, and it was only through sheer weight of numbers flung against the palisades surrounding the building that the Austrians retreated, with some ferocious hand-to-hand combat in the process. Even when Morandi's force broke through and managed to join up with Zambeccari's brigade, a disagreeable surprise awaited them all as they entered Mestre's main square, divided by the little River Oselino. On the opposite bank more than 1,000 infantry and four cannon were drawn up, with extra artillery placed on the single bridge, the earliest rays of morning sunlight glinting on bayonets, cap badges and epaulettes. It was now that Major Musto's rifle drill came in handy, as the best marksmen were detailed to pick off the Austrian gunners while their comrades poured onto the bridge. Once more the Austrians gave fight for a while before they broke and fled into the neighbouring streets, eventually forsaking the town altogether in a headlong rush to the greater safety of Treviso, some twelve miles distant.

This left the troops formerly defending the station to shift for themselves, as a sequence of skirmishes began within Mestre itself. General Pepe rode to and fro among the Italian ranks, a distinctive figure in his cocked hat and gorgeous Bourbon uniform patriotically adapted. The combat was bloody and intense, the Austrians' desperation tempered by awareness that their attackers from the north and east were inadequately supported by those on the town's southern fringes. Though the *cacciatori* eventually managed to flush the enemy out of the trenches and push the retreating infantry as far as the outskirts of Padua, their triumph was less conclusive in terms of its timing, upset by the fog. Holding on to Mestre was less important, in any case, than bringing back to Marghera a considerable quantity of captured weaponry, ammunition, wagons and supplies, as well as some 600 Austrian prisoners. Pepe ordered an honourable withdrawal, and the success of the whole operation, considered purely as a sortie with the aim of ruffling Austrian complacency and showing what stuff Italian patriots were made of, resounded throughout Venice.

Stiff resistance by the imperial force only enhanced their enemy's valour, given that at least half of those involved on the Venetian side were volunteers. Plaudits and honours were liberally bestowed; Pepe's customary Neapolitan exuberance, in this context, now seemed more appropriate than the hard-boiled northern reserve displayed by Cavedalis who, as War Minister, had not taken a direct role in the raid. Praise went to everyone: Zambeccari, Morandi and Ulloa, the Lombards under their Mazzinian commander Agostino Noaro, the lads of the Bandiera e Moro brigade, the 300-strong Venetian civic-guard detachment, and above all to the Bolognese battalion led by Captain Carlo Bignami. 'Thanks to sound discipline,' wrote one of its officers, 'there were only three or four wounded in the regiment. Ah, these men are astonishing! Bologna is the greatest city on earth and its people are the finest. What use are words when facts speak so plainly?' The action at Mestre was, he added, 'one of the best days of my life. There is poetry even in war, and the heady delight of victory is yet sweeter for this.'

His fellow citizen, Friar Ugo Bassi, after bravely risking his life at Treviso during the summer, was equally fearless now in bringing help and consolation to wounded or dying men. Mestre's parish priest Don Giovanni Renier had taken a dim view of the patriot preacher, censuring him as an '*oratore di modà*', all too popular with 'light women', an arch-poseur with his moustachioes and long, curly hair oiled and perfumed with much effort each day, sporting a pair of pistols on the saddlebow of his 'fiery steed'. Can it really be true, as Renier declares, that 'among his superabundant portmanteaus and trunks', Bassi included a dressing case 'full enough with unguents and scent bottles to put the most elegant lady to shame'? Something of a dandy this peripatetic Barnabite may have been, but he remained unflinchingly dedicated to the Italian cause, for which he was soon to suffer a martyr's death.

The troops and sailors bringing the captured Austrian guns entered Venice as heroes on the morning after the raid. Under bright sunlight a jubilant crowd filled the Piazzetta on either side of a processional route towards St Mark's, outside which Manin, Cavedalis and Pepe stood ready to greet them. Heading the parade was a singular figure, that of a child carrying a tricolour standard under whose folds he almost disappeared. His name was Pietro Antonio Zorzi, a cabin boy on one of the armed pinnaces guarding the transports that had carried the Cacciatori del Sile to Fusina. The flag had originally flown from his vessel, until a cannon-ball sent it flying into the sea. Antonio at once plunged in, seized the precious banner and scrambled up the mast to tie it firmly back on, crying 'Viva l'Italia!' With him marched the fourteen-year-old drummer of the civic-guard's 3rd Brigade, Giovanni Battista Speciali. During the fighting, when a boy beside him was wounded in the hip, he took the lad on his back and continued rattling the tattoo, before carrying his comrade back to Fort Marghera. The young heroes embodied a spirit of resilience that would remain undimmed throughout the Venetian revolution, and many other children in the city were ready to follow their example.*

For some there was no festive homecoming. Estimates of killed and wounded on either side vary wildly in Italian and Austrian sources. Manin himself mentions thirty-five dead and seventy-two wounded, with 200 casualties among the imperial troops. Radaelli puts the Italian casualty list at sixty, with the Austrians at 350. One early twentieth-century historian, Vincenzo Marchesi, places the former as high as 244 and the latter at 200. As regards medical resources, Venice was no better equipped than any other nineteenth-century European city, but a general desire among its citizens to help the cause in whatever way they could meant that at least there was sufficient space in convents and palaces for hospital treatment, even if hygiene and nursing standards were far from ideal and many an amputation resulted in the patient's death. There were plenty of good

---

* Pietro Zorzi was subsequently rewarded by the government with a free place at the Venetian naval academy.

doctors in the city, led by the much-respected Giacinto Namias, friend of both the Manin and Bandiera families, and the hard-working hospital superintendent Paolo Callegari. Teresa Manin herself had joined together with a group of patriot noblewomen to set up a serious nursing scheme for the soldiers, which should involve not merely palliative and post-operative care, but the provision of adequate food, bedding and bandages, regular ward visits and a supply of books for those who wanted them. This 'Pious Ladies' Society for Military Assistance', as it was called, strikingly anticipated many of the professional reforms carried out by Florence Nightingale some six years later during the Crimean War. The ladies established a scale of performance-related pay for the nurses, but had no scruples about rolling up their own lace sleeves as volunteer cooks, cleaners and wound-dressers. To the dying they brought comfort and ensured that men about to leave hospital were given material relief and clean uniforms and had their weapons restored to them. Patricians such as Teresa Papadopoli and Elisabetta Giustinian, whose family palaces were sufficiently large, converted them into temporary convalescent homes for the recovering wounded.

Those who did not survive either the Austrian bullet or the surgeon's knife were commemorated in a special service taking place with great pomp in the basilica of SS Giovanni e Paolo on 31 October. Over the Gothic portal at the western end of the church hung a memorial banner bearing an inscription whose political tendentiousness could scarcely fail to strike any worshipper who paused to read it. 'Brothers! Brothers!' it ran, 'Let us pray for repose and perpetual light for the souls of those heroes who with their blood splashed upon the barricades of Mestre contrived in some measure to purge the stain – not theirs indeed! – of the Italian army, proving to an Italy now moribund through diplomatic manoeuvres that through blood alone she may return to a life of true and lasting freedom.'

This implied criticism was taken by some to refer specifically to Charles Albert and the Salasco armistice. Among many who had damned the agreement was the Neapolitan poet Alessandro Poerio. Having chosen to remain with General Pepe in Venice rather than return to Naples, he had found his loyalty to the cause strengthened by the tide of anger sweeping the city at the King's unworthy compromise. When his mother wrote to ask whether the Venetians had accepted the terms, he answered, 'Venice obedient to the shameful and treacherous convention? What! Would a city which is a natural fortress reinforced by art, a city restored to Italy by Providence through the miraculous expulsion of the Austrians, readmit its fiercest enemies at a mere nod from Charles Albert? Was fusion, which it so longed for, merely a prelude to a return to Austrian rule? No, Venice will stand firm, a steadfast and glorious champion of Italian independence.'

To this conviction, the forty-six-year-old poet had remained constant, frankly acknowledging, in one of his finest lyrics, that he adored Venice more than his native Naples. 'O Venice, never has passion drawn a more heartfelt song from me! I never felt the luxury of tears so deeply as when I looked upon your sweet face! . . . Chosen by nature for art, glory and misfortune, you were my supreme desire, and nowhere else could I find shelter or refuge.' Poerio's love affair with his adopted city was tragically ended by his death following the attack on Mestre. At Pepe's side in the thick of the fighting, he was struck on the right leg by a musket ball. Determined to soldier on, he plunged further into the struggle, but his short-sightedness fatally caused him to mistake a party of Austrians for his own men. A further shot hit him in the knee, and some Croat soldiers, after hacking him about the head with their bayonets, left him for dead.

After lying for nearly an hour in a pool of his own blood, Poerio was found and carried back to Venice. There, at Pepe's own quarters in Palazzo Soranzo, he submitted to an amputation, writing to his mother afterwards that he would gladly have offered his life for his country, 'so it does not grieve me to remain with one leg the less'. Popular as he was with the Venetians, more especially the patrician families, for whom he had become emblematic of noble selflessness in a caste until lately associated with indolence and time-wasting, his recovery was a matter of general concern throughout the city. The operation, alas, was botched, gangrene set in and the poet made ready for death, telling the priest who brought him the last rites, 'Yes, I am at peace with all men, I love all, I love Italy – I only hate her enemies.' The funeral cortege, attended by those Neapolitan fellow officers who themselves would reaffirm Poerio's dedication to Venice through their own heroism, took the body to the island cemetery of San Michele. His tombstone was paid for by the noble-women who had harmlessly worshipped him: the inscription calls them 'sisters to the deceased in their love of the motherland'.

High-minded and courageous, Alessandro Poerio was the ideal Risorgimento martyr. Plenty of those present at Mestre were prepared to follow his example, but for the time being the government was unwilling to commit its military resources to further raids on the mainland. Magnificent as the achievements of 27 October were in the short term, they had gained nothing substantial. The Austrians had almost at once returned to Mestre, behaving with their customary harshness towards the reconquered population. Shops such as tobacconists and confectioners were looted and their owners bastinadoed for daring to protest. Private houses were entered and turned over for anything valuable before being commandeered as barracks, in which the soldiers made good use of the barrels in the wine cellars.

It must have been obvious by now, to even the most naively optimistic of patriots, that the imperial forces, however overstretched and underpaid, would remain on the edges of the lagoon for as long as it might take to bring Venice to her knees. In the rest of Italy the political situation offered no likelihood of a patriot army marching to the rescue. Radetzky, in regaining control of Lombardy, had wrung a crippling indemnity from the moneyed noble families he held principally responsible for having fomented the revolution. Martial law was imposed; a whole series of emergency penalties, large and small, was introduced by local garrison commanders; and the province was reminded, in no uncertain terms, of its undutiful conduct displayed towards a benign and fatherly emperor. Austrian forces, meanwhile, having restored the Dukes of Parma and Modena to their thrones, remained to guarantee the status quo. As for Tuscany, whatever unity of purpose might have inspired the heroes of Curtatone e Montanara had long ago collapsed under the weight of ideological conflict and political in-fighting between so-called democrats of various shades from Catholic to communist. Watching developments with anger and dismay, Grand Duke Leopold looked enviously in the direction of Naples, where King Ferdinand was busy reasserting monarchical authority, and began to consider his options.

For Pope Pius IX, the course of revolution merely simplified the issues before him. Having distanced himself from the Roman liberals in the wake of his Allocution against the war with Austria, he dismissed their leader Terenzio Mamiani, and in September appointed a new chief minister, Count Pellegrino Rossi. Impatient and high-handed, archetypally a man who never suffered fools gladly or bothered to make himself agreeable, Rossi was a reforming conservative, dedicated to upholding the papacy's temporal authority while purging the government of abuses, sorting out the tax system and dealing sternly with offences against public order. Though one of his sons was serving with the Roman volunteers in Venice, he was generally unsympathetic to the cause of Italian unity, and when no less a figure than Giuseppe Garibaldi, fresh from skirmishing with Radetzky's troops in the alpine foothills, advanced towards Bologna with his brigade, Rossi determined to isolate him as a dangerous troublemaker. The chosen agent of coercion was General Zucchi, martinet defender of Palmanova, who had returned to Rome after the siege ended with his much-criticised surrender of the fortress. His present mission was to block Garibaldi's progress across the Tuscan frontier into the Papal States, thereby preventing him from recruiting in Romagna, that nursery of Italian revolutionaries over the past thirty years.

When Zucchi was called away to deal with trouble in Ferrara, Garibaldi was allowed to enter Bologna, on condition that his men remained at the border. Popular outrage at Zucchi's conduct forced his hand, and he eventually agreed to a compromise arrangement whereby the *garibaldini* should be allowed to march as far as Ravenna, where they would then travel by ship to Venice. Tempting as it is to wonder what might have happened had Garibaldi accepted, his refusal was equally momentous in its consequences. The prospect of an unworthy and pointless civil war in the Pope's eastern provinces now loomed as the revolutionary commander began his recruiting drive, Swiss Guard regiments marched on Ravenna to reinforce Zucchi's orders, and instructions were given to the officer commanding in Bologna to arrest the always controversial figure of Father Alexandro Gavazzi, who was initially responsible for raising the city in Garibaldi's favour.

Such tension only heightened the already perilous position of the Pope's chief minister. Pellegrino Rossi had now shown his hand as a determined opponent of liberal initiatives and earned no favours in Rome by his draconian enforcement of law and order. On 15 November a hostile crowd gathered outside the Palazzo della Cancelleria, where the Council of Deputies was scheduled to begin its latest session. Contemptuous of danger, Rossi stepped from his carriage and crossed the piazza towards the palace steps. Among the waiting throng were several ex-volunteers from the Lombard campaign, who started jeering as he came forward. When one of them moved to hit him, Rossi turned his head slightly and in that moment was struck down by a dagger-thrust in the neck.

The assassin appears to have been Luigi Brunetti, son of the bizarrely nicknamed demagogue Ciceruacchio, a man of immense influence in Rome, and his attack was hailed by many as a genuine blow for liberty. Nothing was done at this stage to bring him to justice, since Rossi, in his short spell as minister, had made himself widely loathed even among the clergy, whose privileges he had sought to curtail in attempting to modernise the state. It was Pope Pius who interpreted the murder as a final outrage against his own divinely appointed sovereign authority. The event provided, in some sense, the pretext he sought for effectively disowning the burdensome status of patriotic icon. In the days following the assassination, Pius and his closest advisers, led by Cardinal Giacomo Antonelli, devised an escape plan, in consultation with the French ambassador, by which the pontiff could slip out of Rome disguised as an ordinary priest,* taking the road to Civitavecchia, where he would board a ship to Marseilles.

The truth was that Pius had no intention of putting himself into the hands of the republican French. The Ambassador was merely a convenient accessory before the fact, and doubtless the circumstances sufficed to absolve the Holy Father from the sin of lying to him. As it was, the waiting carriage sped, not west towards the sea coast, but south across the Neapolitan frontier to the ancient fortress town of Gaeta, on its promontory overlooking the gulf of the same name. In making this choice, the Pope had declared his hand once and for all. His protector now was the Bourbon King Ferdinand, seen by the liberals, ever since his counterstrike in May, as the champion of everything reactionary. Pius would remain at Gaeta for almost a year, playing with great spirit and dignity the role of the wronged exile in which he was content to be cast, while hardening his conservative stance both on the issue of his temporal rights and privileges and on matters of Church doctrine.

News of the Pope's flight convulsed his subjects and was received by many Italians elsewhere with emotions ranging from astonishment and sadness to anger and outright contempt. For Mazzini and Garibaldi it was a heaven-sent opportunity to create a republican citadel from the place which history seemed to indicate as the obvious capital of a united Italy. For Tommaseo, disapproving of Mazzini's secularism, Pius would continue, for the time being, to remain the ideal leader of a free Italy. He chose to take a long historical view of this new polarisation between a defiantly reactionary Vicar of God and the forces now gathering around the two leaders into whose hands papal intransigence seemed to be delivering Rome. It was a return to the old division between Guelphs (supporters of the papacy) and Ghibellines (upholding a secular sovereign in the shape of the Holy Roman Emperor), which had rent Italy asunder during the Middle Ages. Believing Pio Nono to be too plainly the victim of external influence – whether that of King Ferdinand or of Austrian agents – Tommaseo tried, without success, to urge the French to offer the Pope a refuge in their own country.

Daniele Manin, for his part, had never been sympathetic to Tommaseo's neo-Guelph idealisation of Pius as Italy's redeemer, thaumaturge and priest-king, and the flight to Gaeta merely confirmed his scepticism. Among those severely shaken by the news was his house guest at San Paternian, Ugo Bassi, now preparing to leave Venice and join Garibaldi's

---

* Some sources maintain that Pius escaped in female disguise, as a children's nurse.

forces as they in their turn set off for Rome. Coming across him in the Piazza, Manin was shocked by his sorrowful appearance and gave the priest a warm hug to cheer him up. Bassi was so moved that later that day he sent a short note of homage. 'My thanks, beyond all expressing, for the precious testimony of affection you gave me this morning. Ah, if you knew how much that meant and how I felt my whole being filled with enthusiasm! I, who never chose to abase myself before monarchs, adore Manin. *After* God and Italy, *before* Pius IX, Manin! Ugo Bassi, humble servant of the greatest of Italians.' On the morning of his friend's departure, Manin had said a hurried farewell before leaving for his office. When Bassi left the house, he was observed to kiss the brass nameplate on the door. The two men never saw one another again.

Perhaps the most dramatic impact made in Venice by the tidings from Rome was on the city's aged Cardinal Patriarch, Jacopo Monico. His attitude towards the revolution had always been conditioned by unswerving fidelity to the Holy Father, and the surge of patriotism among certain of his Venetian clergy had often discomfited him. Pio Nono's rush into the Bourbon embrace left Monico in something of a quandary. He could either follow the pontiff's example by retreating into total reactionary intransigence, or work out some kind of compromise position whereby his integrity as a churchman remained undamaged, without forfeiting his position as spiritual leader of Catholic Venice. The issue became no easier when the radical newspaper *Sior Antonio Rioba* issued a damning leader on the papal tergiversation. Monico had already expressed his unease as to the 'immorality, irreligion and scorn for the most venerable and sacred persons and things' and the prevailing anti-clericalism of many of the public prints. Now, having failed to move the government to take action against *Sior Antonio Rioba*'s editors, he issued a decree effectively excommunicating all those who bought or read the paper.

Instead of bringing pious Venetians to heel as he intended, the Cardinal succeeded in stirring up a hornets' nest. On 3 December, the day after his warning appeared, a crowd gathered in the Piazza to listen to one of the last sermons preached in Venice by Ugo Bassi, in which he roundly berated Monico and those closest to him as 'Jesuits and Austrophiles'. The friar seems genuinely not to have foreseen the effect of his harangue, which was to send an infuriated mob in the direction of Palazzo Querini Stampalia at Santa Maria Formosa, where the Cardinal now lodged,* with the intention of burning it to the ground. Only prompt action by the

---

* His official residence, on the north side of St Mark's basilica, had been given to the civic guard as a barracks.

civic guard and Bassi himself prevented the outrage, but, as we shall see, neither Monico nor his borrowed palace was safe from further attack.

Since Monico detested Bassi as a contumacious agitator, the implicit irony must have been hard to swallow. The next day another paper, *San Marco*, roundly condemned the Cardinal for his obscurantism, describing him as 'dragging forth from some antique, worm-eaten volume the kind of excommunication our present century no longer sanctions, in a city moreover which never feared such a proceeding even during the ages of ignorance'. The reference here was to the Republic of Venice's sturdy defiance, in 1606, of Pope Clement VIII over the issue of ecclesiastical privilege, which had resulted in a year-long interdict. As it now happened, the government was in no mood to knuckle under to Monico either, and its Committee of Public Vigilance invited him to reconsider his action in the light of the threatened disturbance. Meanwhile the various newspaper editors, in an effort to calm ruffled feelings, composed a joint letter, beginning with the words 'We Catholics', saying how sorry they were that *Sior Antonio Rioba* should be seen as in any way lacking in respect for religion, and promising to be more circumspect in future. Monico's response was merely to redraft their address in an altogether more abject vein and return it to them for a signature he could not realistically have expected. In a letter to his own parish clergy he declared that press freedom was no guarantee of liberty of conscience, and reminded the priests where their real duty lay. Here, for the time being, the matter rested. If the Patriarch was able to reconcile himself to a nominal endorsement of the political status quo in Venice, it was only because he believed in the Church's capacity to transcend secular government through its own unshakeable authority, based on doctrine and scripture. His angry and ill-considered attempt to counter free expression with spiritual blackmail had done permanent damage, however, to his moral standing within the Venetian civic community.

As the year drew to its close in one of the coldest and stormiest winters Venice had ever known, Manin had more to worry about than this latest instance of the eternal collision between liberal humanism and the Catholic Church. In November the Habsburg Emperor Ferdinand I had been prevailed upon to abdicate in favour of his nephew, the eighteen-year-old Archduke Franz Josef. The new emperor was conscientious and hard-working, imbued with an unshakeable conviction in the significance of his imperial role and of the deference due to him and his family. He was also obstinate, unimaginative and profoundly suspicious of anyone whose initiative and intelligence threatened in any way to upstage him, as various of his relatives and ministers would learn to their cost during his sixty-eight-year reign. Having seen action during Radetzky's Italian campaign and admired the Field Marshal's strength of purpose, he was not prepared to make more than a handful of initial, largely cosmetic concessions to rebel elements within the empire, until the time (not far distant) should arrive when he could deal in suitably ruthless fashion with them all.

Ferdinand's abdication ceremony took place on 2 December. 'Be good, and God will protect you!' said the Emperor to his nephew, before retiring to Prague to enjoy the rest of his long life in the indulgence of his twin passions of gardening and book-collecting. On acceding, Franz Josef was initially cautious in his dealings with the Reichstag, the parliament which, after Windischgrätz's suppression of the October revolution in Vienna, had removed itself to the Bohemian town of Kremsier (modern Kromerice). A manifesto issued at the start of his reign and circulated throughout the empire (the Italian version found its way to Venice) featured such weasel-worded assertions as 'On the bases of true liberty, of equal rights for all subjects of the empire and equality of all citizens under the law, not to mention the involvement of popular representatives in the legislative process, the fatherland will rise once more.' The new emperor declared himself 'firmly resolved to maintain the splendour of the crown unsullied and the whole monarchy intact, but ready to divide our rights with the representatives of our people', while praising the loyalty of faithful subjects and 'the valour, fidelity and perseverance of our glorious army'.

The manifesto's author was the forty-eight-year-old Prince Felix zu Schwarzenberg, a veteran of the war in Italy, newly appointed as the Emperor's chief minister. Schwarzenberg had already achieved notable success as a diplomat in St Petersburg and Naples, where he was Ambassador at the outbreak of the revolution before heading north to join General Nugent's reserve army in its invasion of the Veneto. His various attempts to stiffen the resolve of the Austrian government during the uncertain period following Custoza and the armistice were as much the fruit of impatience as of loyalty to the Crown. Never a diehard reactionary, he had no special reverence for his own caste, and was prepared, on becoming Prime Minister, to ride roughshod over time-honoured privileges wherever these impeded his designs for strengthening the Emperor's position as sovereign ruler, as opposed to the constitutional monarch his subjects currently seemed to want. There was an element of cynical calculation in him that others found decidedly chilling, and he was not one to suffer fools gladly.

The whole atmosphere of international diplomatic manoeuvres

surrounding the Italian question, and more particularly those of sovereignty over Venice, was to change dramatically once Schwarzenberg took the ministerial bit between his teeth. At least one of his guiding principles was a visceral detestation of Lord Palmerston, who had vetoed his proposed appointment as Austrian ambassador to London in 1833. The Foreign Secretary considered Schwarzenberg 'a silly & conceited fellow', who had in any case blotted his diplomatic copybook in England some years earlier by conducting a notorious love affair with the wife of a Cabinet minister.* Schwarzenberg, for his part, despised Palmerston's continuing dalliance with liberalism, contesting his right to meddle in Italian affairs and embarking on a strategy of trying to win over the French, cutting out Great Britain altogether, which events in Paris during the late autumn of 1848 made considerably easier.

Throughout the early phases of the revolution in France, a figure of real consequence, if not necessarily of great personal glamour, had been lurking in the wings, awaiting his hour. Prince Louis Napoleon Bonaparte, nephew of the great Emperor, had originally proposed himself as a candidate in the June elections which preceded the rioting crushed with such chilling efficiency by General Cavaignac. It was not until September that he took his seat, but when the new assembly voted for a revised constitution introducing a four-year presidency, Louis Napoleon saw a perfect opportunity to present himself as the ultimate champion of order, in the context, what was more, of an overt appeal to Bonapartist nostalgia. However shabbily dressed and insignificant he may have looked, the man's personal magnetism was undeniable. His nonchalant ease of manner hid a steely determination which, on 20 December 1848, won him a stunning four-million-plus presidential majority over Cavaignac, leaving the republicans Ledru-Rollin and Lamartine trailing far behind.

Eventually the Prince-President, as he was styled, would stage a dramatic *coup d'état* and proclaim himself Emperor as Napoleon III. He had always been absorbed with the political future of Italy, a place where he had spent several years and maintained significant connections with patriots of various political shades. At the apogee of his empire (1852–70) he would become crucially involved in shaping Italian destinies, including

---

* This was the celebrated Jane Digby, married to Lord Ellenborough, the Lord Privy Seal. Another of her lovers was Colonel George Anson. Since a horse called 'The Colonel' was beaten into second place at that year's Derby by the favourite 'Cadland', Schwarzenberg became known as 'Cad' for short. His callous treatment of Jane and their two children gave 'cad' and 'caddish' the meanings they have since retained.

that of Venice herself, but for the time being he was concerned solely with establishing a power-base amid the powerful constituency of devout French Catholics by seeking a role for France as potential saviour of the currently beleaguered papacy. Hence, for Manin and the Venetians, there was even less to be hoped for than during the Cavaignac government. Austrian forces in the lagoon now numbered 24,000 men, and their new commandant, General Karl von Sturmer, had ordered the raising of fresh defences around Mestre following the debacle of 27 October. Within Venice itself the government's financial position was, as ever, serious; that it was not entirely hopeless owed much, if not everything, to the generosity of individual citizens, rich or poor, which manifested itself again and again during the cruel months about to follow. The forced loans, the two kinds of paper currency issued by the government and the municipality, and the contributions made by individual donors to the exchequer were supplemented by yet more personal donations and initiatives. Mortgaging Venetian Renaissance artworks was no longer an option, but General Pepe offered a painting from his own collection (a portrait of Cesare Borgia attributed to Leonardo da Vinci) and Marchesa Carolina Bevilacqua, on behalf of her son who had died in battle, presented the family castle as 'a sacrifice on the altar of the motherland' (it was later burned down by the Austrians). Teresa Manin agreed to part with her silver dishes, coffee pots and spoons, gondoliers' wives offered their brooches and pins, and the poorest old women gave their earings and wedding bands. To cele-brate the attack on Mestre, La Fenice was reopened, after staying dark ever since the cancelled première of Pacini's *Allan Cameron* in March, for a 'Grand vocal and instrumental academy', which included choruses from Verdi's *Macbeth* and Bellini's *I puritani*, the prayer from Rossini's *Mosè in Egitto* and the great 'Gathering of the Cantons' scene from the same composer's *Guillaume Tell*, with its stirring evocation of an oppressed people united against Habsburg tyranny of an earlier era. The performers were mostly amateur, including a number of patricians, and though the house was not altogether full, a goodly sum was collected from the evening to purchase winter greatcoats for the troops at Marghera.

If Austria was still not ready to make seriously threatening gestures towards Venice and begin a siege in earnest, the citizens, in making these practical gestures of solidarity, were more than ever conscious of their isolation from other Italians sympathetic to the cause. Giovanni Battista Cavedalis, as Minister of Defence, began making calculations as to the food and other supplies that would be needed when the serious business of fighting for Venetian life and liberty should begin. Flour, sugar, coffee, rice, lard, fresh vegetables, beef, salt cod, cheese, sardines, wine, brandy, grappa and vinegar were all still being brought in under the noses of the Austrian fleet, but this run of luck could not last for ever, given the increased vigilance of patrols among the coastal villages from which boats set out to run the blockade. Cavedalis was a practical man with no illusions, but on the evening after the Mestre raid, when Venice still rang with 'Evviva!'s and patriotic songs, he had been struck by a chilling omen. Lying awake, unable to sleep, he had caught the sound of singing from a gondola on a canal some way off. It was no ordinary song, he realised, but one scarcely heard in the city for more than fifty years, the famous chanting by the gondoliers of stanzas from Torquato Tasso's epic poem *Gerusalemme liberata*, which had so enthralled Goethe on his visit to Venice in 1787. 'The faint, far-off voice which touched my ear,' says Cavedalis, 'seemed to be addressing me personally.' Distant though it was, he shuddered as he caught the words:

Misero, e di che godi! o quanto mesti
Fieno I trionfi ed infelice il vanto!

'Wretched man, what do you celebrate? How miserable your triumphs will make you and how unhappy your boasting!'

~

CHAPTER 11

ONLY A MAN

S TILL ANXIOUS TO CONCLUDE SOME kind of agreement with Austria that should go at least part of the way towards conciliating liberal Italy, Lord Palmerston had not looked kindly on the Mestre adventure. Consul Dawkins had outlined the events of 27 October in a letter whose studied detachment failed to mask his lack of sympathy towards both the initiative itself and the revolution as a whole. For rather different reasons, the British Foreign Secretary was equally doubtful. The Venetian government, he wrote back, must be warned at once that any attack on Austrian forces was in flagrant breach of the Salasco armistice terms, on which the whole surviving impetus for mediation seemed to depend. How was it possible, he reasonably objected, for Austria to refrain from staging a full-scale assault on Venice in the face of such unprovoked hostility? And why add insult to injury by mustering a Hungarian legion in the city, given the current insurrection in Hungary itself?

Italians both during and after 1848 tended to blame Palmerston for dragging his feet and aiming, none too covertly, at a sell-out to Austria, now that General Windischgrätz, that snarling mastiff of restored Habsburg absolutism, had seized control of Vienna and Radetzky was busy avenging the dishonour of the *Cinque Giornate* by humiliating the vanquished rebels of Lombardy. This view of the British minister as a closet legitimist, determined on nothing more than upholding the European peace treaties of 1815, takes no account of the pro-Italian stance expressed in his correspondence with British diplomats and personal friends, let alone of his subsequent enthusiasm for Garibaldi. Though Palmerston saw the Habsburg empire's survival as essential to the balance of power in Europe, and remained deeply suspicious of French interference in Italian affairs, he continued to question the practical purpose (not to speak of the moral and political justifications) behind a continuing Austrian hegemony over Lombardy-Venetia. 'The real fact,' he told a senior British diplomat, 'is that the Austrians have no business in Italy at all, and have no real right to be there. The right they claim is founded upon force of arms and the Treaty of Vienna.' Austria had always regarded Italy as a conquered territory, the ruling imperial echelons disdaining to mix with those they dominated. 'She has governed it as you govern a garrison town, and her rule has always been hateful.' Yet neither, after Charles Albert's defeat, did he place much reliance on the principle of 'l'Italia farà da se'. To Ralph Abercromby, British minister at Turin, he confided sadly, 'As to the warlike announcements of the Italians, they must, I fear, end in smoke or defeat. I heartily wish that Italy was *piu forte*; but weak as she is, a contest singlehanded with Austria would only lead her to more complete prostration.'

British political attitudes to the revolution had always been seen by Manin and other leading Venetians as crucial to its success, even if cultural affinities and geographical closeness, as well as republicanism, made France a more natural focus of expectation regarding practical support. The issue was complicated by the presence as Consul – and sole official source of communication with London – of the pro-Austrian Clinton Dawkins, whom the government in Venice instinctively mistrusted. Where negotiations with Vienna were concerned, Venice's independence might not have seemed so troublesome for Palmerston had Dawkins not viewed the revolutionaries, their aims and achievements with such enduring distaste. What strikes us in reading his consular dispatches is just how little, in their bald matter-of-factness, they convey of the volatile atmosphere accessible to us through other contemporary sources. It was not a case of the writer, as a British diplomatic official, merely doing his job as a detached witness, but that he loathed having to do it at all in a place where his own political alienation, as one of a disapproving minority praying for the reinstatement of Habsburg rule, made him so vulnerable. If London failed to respond as positively as Manin hoped, this was due in some measure to Dawkins's inability or outright reluctance to communicate anything of the revolution's wider basis in long-standing grievances against the imperial government or in the aspirations of Italian nationalism.

At home the Consul could have found powerful support for his negative position from the Tories, heartened as they were by the continuing presence in England of Prince Metternich, and just as significantly from Queen Victoria and Prince Albert. The latter detested Palmerston, referring to him as 'the Immoral One', and the Queen readily echoed this antipathy. Their blessing on Lord Minto's 1847 mission to promote liberal government among Italian sovereigns was long submerged beneath a deepening alarm at the sheer speed of revolutionary meltdown during the year that followed. With her lifelong envy of any sovereign who threatened to upstage her, Victoria resented Charles Albert's presence in the limelight during the war in Lombardy and criticised Palmerston's pursuit of a liberal foreign policy to secure greater influence for Britain in Italian affairs. Misunderstanding his attempt at drawing France into the mediation process as an attempt to threaten Austria, when in fact it was designed to halt possible French plans for armed intervention, she defined his guiding principle as 'Italian Nationality and Independence from a foreign Yoke and Tyranny' and complained to her uncle, King Leopold of the Belgians, that the Foreign Secretary's partiality was seriously compromising Britain's position in Europe. '*What* a very bad figure we cut in this mediation!' she exclaimed. 'Really it is quite immoral, with Ireland quivering in our grasp, and ready to throw off her allegiance at any moment, for us to force Austria to give up her lawful possessions! What shall we say if Canada, Malta etc. begin to trouble us? It hurts me terribly.'

The Irish card, as the Queen realised, was an embarrassingly easy one for foreign politicians to play against England. It had already been dealt by Metternich and other Austrian ministers, and would prove useful to Pius IX and Ferdinand of Naples when British diplomats threatened to become too sanctimonious on the subject of Italian politics* Schwarzenberg had no hesitation in using it when Palmerston complained of Austria's harsh treatment of reoccupied Milan, though the Foreign Secretary gave as good as he got by comparing the Prince's remonstrance with 'the outpourings of an enraged woman of the town when arrested by a policeman in the act of picking a pocket'. What offended Victoria's conservative interpretation of international justice most of all was the way in which Palmerston and his satellites, led by Britain's minister to Paris, Lord Normanby, were using Venice as a bargaining counter with Austria. The city, she correctly claimed, 'was to have been made over to the Austrians by the Armistice, and now that this has not been done, Austria is not even to retake it, in order (as Lord Normanby says) to keep something in hand by which Austria is to make further concessions. Is all this fair?'

---

* After 150 years, Ireland remains an internationally useful stick with which to belabour British governments disposed to criticise the harshness of other regimes. During the period of writing this book it has proved opportune to figures such as Saddam Hussein, Robert Mugabe, Slobodan Milosevic and Ariel Sharon.

Quite possibly it wasn't, but the value of Venice as a final concession to the imperial government, if the long-delayed peace conference were actually to take place, explained Palmerston's unwillingness to encourage Manin in seeking to deter an Austrian military build-up on the main-land. The defence force at Marghera was certainly equal to a repeat performance of the attack on Mestre, though the fierce winter weather made its members grateful for the military greatcoats purchased with the proceeds of the Fenice charity gala. Among the volunteers was Manin's son Giorgio, whose mother, whatever her patriotic self-denial in other respects, yielded to every normal solicitude for the boy's welfare. He was her favourite, just as his sister Emilia was Daniele's. When he wrote asking for extra clothes, Teresa answered. 'Darling, if only you know how I adore you! You are everything, or only a little bit less than everything to me, and I am sending you a shirt, two pairs of socks, your good thick shoes, your vest and four handkerchiefs. Write if you need money. A big hug and a thousand kisses from your mamma.' On New Year's Day 1849, when the thermometer on household barometer at San Paternian had dropped to five degrees below zero, she knew it must be worse for the men out at Marghera, but urged Giorgio to be staunch for the glory of their 'holiest cause'.

In fact the defenders of Marghera were probably better off in their cosy barrack-rooms than many ordinary citizens toughing out the bitter weather at the other end of the railway viaduct. The journalist Pacifico Valussi, for example, filed copy from his bedroom, where he remained tucked up until lunchtime, whereas Jean Debrunner's Swiss legionaries kept out the cold by tucking bags of roast chestnuts into the gussets of their trousers. Everywhere food prices were rising steeply, money was running short and unemployment had reached dangerous levels. Tourism, that mainstay of Venice's economy in the decades after 1815, had come to a halt with the outbreak of the revolution, and the canals were notice-ably less lively with the traffic of passing gondolas. Though the cafés in the Piazza – Florian, Suttil, Quadri and others – kept busy, their clien-tele now consisted of soldiers from the volunteer brigades, the occasional party of naval officers from French and British warships on observation duty in the lagoon, and Venetians keen to read the newspapers and pick up what scraps of information managed to get through the Austrian lines. During the autumn, however, the marble-topped café tables and folding chairs, on which tourists had formerly lounged with a cup of coffee, an ice cream and a copy of Murray's *Guide to Northern Italy* or Lecomte's more comprehensive French handbook, became dosses for groups of young people, some of them mere children, who had spent the day begging in the zone around St Mark's. At the Arsenal boat-building work was only sporadic, and elsewhere in Venice and among the islands the lighter industries, such as lace-making and the weaving of luxury fabrics, were near to collapse altogether. During the January of 1849 glass-blowers on Murano went on strike for a minimum wage and sickness benefits, obtained after prolonged negotiation, and a month later bakery workers in Venice itself secured a similar victory over their employers.

What frightened Manin and other assembly members was the intensifying of those nightmares of socialism and communism that had worried them at the revolution's outset. To foil the onset of such movements was the task of the Committee of Public Vigilance, whose six members had been kept busy in recent months by mounting discontent among various sectors of the city's working community, with jobs or without. Carpenters, builders and stonemasons had all been noted as ready to mount demonstrations in the Piazza if their demands for more work were not soon met, and further warnings came of trouble brewing among the casual labour force employed on strengthening the lagoon forts in readiness for possible siege operations. 'We note a growing resentment among the not inconsiderable number of working people in the city who, being without jobs and lacking money, have begun to make threatening complaints. They associate, what is more, with ill-disposed persons likely to spread among them the fatal principles of communism.' Similar apprehensions seem to have prompted the committee to issue an appeal to those more affluent Venetians maintaining large households of servants to carry on employing them if they could. A palace on the Grand Canal full of footmen, maids and gondoliers might formerly have been seen as merely a sybaritic status indicator; in the present crisis, such an establishment became a valued source of private charity, rescuing the municipality from an obligation it could no longer decently fulfil.

Venice, it had become obvious, was wholly unprepared for coping with the situation brought about by the realities, political and military, of Piedmont's defeat and the collapse of the fusionist settlement. Holding the community together was now a task of paramount importance for the triumvirs and those working alongside them in the Doge's Palace. The flag-blessings, parades, band concerts and celebrations of church festivals continued, as did the occasional patriotic gala evenings at the theatre. La Fenice was reopened for a benefit evening on 1 December, and on 13 February 1849 at Teatro Apollo an actress named Rosalinda Caruso declaimed a poem 'To our Italian brothers' by an anonymous soldier, and singers performed arias from Mercadante's *Il bravo*, Verdi's *I due Foscari* and Rossini's *L'italiana in Algieri*, as well as selections from

Donizetti's *Anna Bolena*. The poet Arnaldo Fusinato recited his topical lyric 'The Exile's Lament', and the whole performance kicked off with 'a grand overture played by the National Band', presumably the civic-guard's musical outfit. Yet the morale-boosting buzz created by news from the battle-fronts or the arrival of the latest volunteer battalion had vanished. The heroics of Mestre could not last for ever in popular memory with nothing to follow them up, and the Venetians were forced by swift degrees to fall back on their native reserves of character, grit and resourcefulness in order to sustain the integrity of their newly won freedom.

What seems extraordinary to us, as it did to so many at the time, was the city's collective willingness to endure, and the dedication shown by almost everybody to the increasingly grim imperative of resistance to the Austrians, triumphant now in the mainland towns and determined to humiliate those who had caught them unawares in the revolutions of March and April. There were those in Venice who prayed for a Habsburg restoration, but until the last days of the close siege soon to begin they were largely a silent minority. The truth was that 'the eldest child of Liberty' was still a young enough slave of empire to cherish the sweetness of autonomy, even in the half-remembered form of a republic of brocade-togaed oligarchs. For fifty years this race-memory had lasted, unquenched either by Napoleon's burning of the Golden Book patrician register and stripping-down of the Bucentaur, the Doge's ceremonial galley, into saleable fragments, or by '*la leggenda nera*', so eagerly propagated by supporters of the Habsburg government after 1815. Money the 1848 republic might never have enough of, stocks of weapons and ammunition would dwindle inevitably, but Venice's pride in her own inheritance never ran short.

If Daniele Manin stood at the apex of this Venetian patriotism, his position was never unchallenged. The whole issue of the Circolo Italiano and the arrest and expulsion of its leading members had underlined his determination to root out anything that threatened to split too plainly the public consensus on which his governance of the city needed always to depend. He was not yet a dictator, and showed no signs of wishing to assume the airs and persona so dubiously appropriate to the role. There were those in Venice, however, who resented what they saw as his high-handedness and authoritarianism, and who viewed the current triumvirate administration as a missed opportunity to embrace a more full-blooded republicanism in the wake of the Piedmontese commissioners' departure on 4 August.

Among these was the young lawyer Marco Antonio Canini. Before the revolution he had enrolled as a trainee with the Austrian police, but soon fell out with his superiors and went instead, as a mature student, to read law at Padua University. Here too he offended the authorities, by suggesting that Niccolò Tommaseo, in the city at the time, should be invited to pronounce the funeral oration of the recently deceased university rector. Fleeing to the more liberal atmosphere of Lucca (which had recently changed sovereigns), he wrote a tract praising Pio Nono and urging the creation of two new north Italian mega-states, a Lombardo-Piedmontese amalgam under Charles Albert and an enlarged Tuscan grand duchy, which should include the Veneto (a sort of East and West Pakistan arrangement *avant la lettre*). Quickly disenchanted with the Pope, the King and Grand Duke Leopold, Canini was imbued with socialist idealism inherited from his Jacobin father and influenced by the French theorists Fourier and Saint-Simon. Returning to Venice in 1848, he took a clerical job in the offices of the provisional government, but gave notice when the fusionists triumphed, enrolling instead in the artillery section of the Marghera garrison.

Here his political activity, as the founder of a republican club for his fellow soldiers, was immediately seen as suspect by his commanding officer, who drew attention to a law forbidding such associations within the armed forces. Undaunted, Canini proceeded to criticise not only the restriction itself, but the system appointing those who enforced it. Officers of all ranks, he maintained, should be elected by their troops on the basis of personal esteem, professional ability and the nature of their political opinions. There should be no differentiations in the pay scale, with the same salary awarded to the humblest soldier as to the commander-in-chief. Such ideas were unlikely to commend themselves to anybody managing an efficient defence force, let alone one with its back so obviously to the wall. Manin, backed by his fellow triumvirs Cavedalis and Graziani, dismissed the proposals as dangerous moonshine, and Canini prudently left Marghera to take up a secretarial post with the army procurement minister Count Alessandro Marcello, himself a noted republican sympathiser.

During the December of 1848, Canini found a more fruitful outlet for activism in the predominantly working-class area of Cannaregio on Venice's north-western edge. Here he was joined by the Neapolitan officer Cesare Rosaroll and the irrepressible Father Gavazzi in founding a political club, the 'Circolo Popolare'. It was not, he later claimed, a subversive organisation, though its meetings undoubtedly played on the mounting impatience among Venetian liberals with a government so apparently unwilling to shift towards the democrats and republicans now managing the revolutions in Tuscany and Rome, with their project for

Princess Cristina Belgiojoso, keen participant in the 1848 revolution and one of its shrewdest critics. From a painting by Henri Lehmann.

Daniele Manin in the uniform of Venice's Civic Guard.

Tuscan gallantry: the naked gunner at the battle of Curtatone.

Austrian troops storm Palladio's La Rotonda during the battle of Vicenza.

Prodi Volontarj!

Dai campi della Spagna, dalle montagne della Grecia vengo a Voi, primizie dell'Italia libera, pieno di fiducia nel vostro valore, certo del trionfo della sacra causa che difendiamo.

Avvezzo ai prodigi dei Palikari e dei Guerriglieri, mi riprometto altrettanto e più da chi prese la croce e impugnò l'armi per l'indipendenza e la libertà della patria.

Attendo da Voi non la disciplina meccanica del soldato: ma la docilità del milite che sa necessario l'accordo ad evitare il pericolo, ad ottenere la vittoria.

Mi avrete fra voi, vostro capo prima del conflitto, vostro compagno nell'ora del cimento.

Militi volontarj, giuriamo dinanzi a Dio ed all'Italia l'esterminio dell'oppressore. Vile chi depone le armi prima di aver raggiunta la meta, e ricacciato lo straniero fuori della cinghia dell'Alpi.

Noi combatteremo, noi vinceremo!

Viva l'Italia libera!

Treviso, 27 Maggio 1848.

IL COLONNELLO COMANDANTE

A. MORANDI

Treviso, dalla Tipografia dipartimentale di G. Longo.

An order of the day, couched in typically florid patriotic style, issued to the defenders of Treviso by the Modenese patriot Antonio Morandi.

The attack on Mestre, 27 October 1848. General Pepe, leading the Venetian forces is the mounted figure on the right.

Commanders at Marghera
(*Left*) Giuseppe Sirtori, diehard
republican and political opponent
of Manin.
(*Bottom*) Girolamo Ulloa,
the Neapolitan general who later
accompanied Manin into exile.

Julius von Haynau, commanding Austrian forces during the first phase of the close siege of Venice in the spring of 1849.

PROCLAMA

Conforme al Proclama, pubblicato dal sig. Tenente maresciallo Conte Eltz in data 5 Aprile a. c., deve esser noto a tutti gli abitanti, che la città di Verona è dichiarata in istato d'assedio, e devono anche esser note tutte le conseguenze che ne risultano.

Pertanto, a fine d'impedire qualunque equivoco, viene ordinato quanto segue:

1. Tutte le case particolari, locande, osterie, alberghi e caffè in generale dovranno senza eccezione essere chiusi alle ore dieci di sera, e tutti gli abitanti della città essere a quest'ora ritirati nelle loro abitazioni;

2. In caso d'allarme, che sarà annunciato con tre colpi di cannone dal forte S. Felice, nessuno potrà più fermarsi per le contrade, ma dovrà celeramente recarsi al suo domicilio. Chiunque si fermerà ad onta di questo ordine in istrada o si aggrupperà con altri individui, sarà trattato con tutto il rigore delle leggi militari;

3. Succedendo l'allarme di notte tempo, dovranno essere illuminate tutte le finestre, al qual uopo dovrà ognuno provedersi anticipatamente dell'occorrevole. Le case non illuminate saranno sforzate, arrestato il contravventore e sottoposto al giudizio militare. I contravventori restano responsabili per tutti i disordini, che potessero da ciò derivare.

Veronesi! vi dò l'amichevole consiglio di tenervi, come fino ad ora, tranquilli; chiunque mancherà agli ordini su espressi dovrà ascrivere a se medesimo la colpa delle conseguenze, poiché sono fermo nell'intenzione di mantenere con tutti i mezzi possibili la quiete e l'ordine in questa città.

Verona il 25 Luglio 1848

I. R. COMANDANTE MILITARE E CIVILE

HAYNAU

TENENTE MARESCIALLO

Dalla Tipografia Provinciale di Paolo Libanti

A typical menacing proclamation issued by Haynau. This one warns citizens of Verona to stay indoors after curfew and keep their houses illuminated.

Prince Felix Schwarzenberg, ruthless architect of Austria's political victory in 1849.

The Austrian high command and its foreign guests on the tower at Mestre, from a painting by the specially commissioned war artist Franz Adam.

Rocket attacks on the partially-ruined railway viaduct during the siege.

Austrian bomb balloon. Satirical in intent, the picture is still precise in its details.

Venetians fleeing from their city's heavily-bombarded Cannaregio district.

The exiled Manin and his family boarding the French warship *Solon*.
Emilia, on the right, takes a last look at Venice.

Emilia Manin, her father's 'beloved angel'.

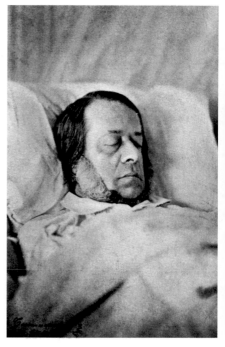

Daniele Manin on his deathbed.

an Italian national constituent assembly. It was not, however, as if others outside the Circolo Popolare, in the newspaper columns and the cafés or up and down the *calli*, did not freely air similar discontents, questioning the value of any further dependence on the mediation process and possible help from France for which Manin still hoped.

The Committee of Public Vigilance was nevertheless unhappy. Not just extremist politics but education was being dispensed to the workers gathered at the Circolo, and within a matter of weeks it had become a flourishing institution in the Cannaregio quarter. On 11 January, Canini issued the first number of a newspaper whose very title, *Il Tribuno del Popolo*, carried challenging echoes of the Jacobinism of his father's era. It was produced by a people's co-operative, based on equal payments by the journalists and printshop workers into a central fund, and carried, under the masthead slogan 'Religion, Motherland, Family', the epigraphs: 'In church and state let those worthiest govern, elected by the people', 'Every man must work: the fruits of labour should be shared in proportion to the capital and the work of mind and body which have contributed to them', and 'Long live Italy free and united! Long live the Italian Constituent Assembly, elected by all Italians!' The paper's content was not exceptionally subversive and it was clearly sensitive to the deep-rooted Catholic religiosity of the average Venetian, but its proposal to circulate a mini-edition, by whatever means, through the towns and villages of the Austrian-controlled mainland may have been the eventual spur to action by the Committee. The last thing Manin wanted, after all, was for the enemy to seize on such material as proof that Venice was a hotbed of socialist agitation. On the day following publication therefore, Canini and Gavazzi were both arrested.

With no reason given for his detention, Canini was imprisoned in the former House of Correction on the Giudecca. Gavazzi meanwhile was dispatched under police escort to the edge of the lagoon and told to board the next boat, never to return. It was the most churlish of dismissals for this unimpeachably courageous and sincere man, who, eccentric as he was in dress and manner, had dedicated himself unstintingly to the Italian cause and to Venice in particular. The rebuff thus administered could not exactly have been sweetened by the letter Manin sent after him. Assuring Gavazzi of the writer's personal regrets, it emphasised 'the sacred task of defending Venice *at any cost*' – this last phrase was to reverberate more significantly on a later occasion – and the consequent danger to public tranquillity of associations like the Circolo Popolare, with their 'seductive theories' calculated to mislead the city's 'excitable and ignorant artisans'. Witness what had happened in France, added Manin. How much more fatal must such ideas be to Venice, with the enemy at its very gates. Austrian agents could easily use such divisive elements to foment serious discord among the population. 'It pains me, I repeat, that such measures should have offended you, but every consideration and affection must yield to the duty of rescuing the motherland.' If only Gavazzi had discussed all this with him earlier! 'I could have shown you how your name, your popularity and your great talent might have been useful in achieving an outcome far removed from your subsequent intentions.' Though Manin was content, from a safe distance, to praise Gavazzi as 'one of the most fervent apostles of Italian freedom and independence', it is hard not to wonder whether the earlier – and voluntary – departure of Ugo Bassi might not have made it easier for him to get rid of this more embarrassing of the two patriot friars. Bassi had worked willingly alongside Gavazzi and would almost certainly have used his friendship with Manin to protect his younger colleague.

The disingenuousness of the letter suggests that once Bassi had left, Manin was grateful for any opportunity to rid Venice of someone he considered a mere political embarrassment. We might ask why, even though Gavazzi had not long returned to Venice before the Circolo Popolare started its activities, Manin refrained from inviting him to take part in the kind of discussion mentioned. The friar, a better Christian than many of his fellow clergy, was likely, in due season, to have forgiven the Venetian President. Marco Antonio Canini, on the other hand, was a professed atheist and was not disposed to pardon the draconian strictness with which he was henceforth treated. Three days after his imprisonment on the Giudecca, he was transferred to the island prison of San Severo. Six weeks went by without any official notification of a tribunal pending. His friends were discouraged from intervening on his behalf and a petition from his family was ignored. Canini's own surviving messages make pathetic reading. A letter written to Manin on the day after his arrest demands respect for his civil rights and a fair hearing in front of the Committee of Public Vigilance. Somewhat more bluntly, a message to his family deploring his imprisonment among 'robbers, murderers and traitors' proclaims that 'the infamy committed against me will go down in history'.

After removal to San Severo, Canini dispatched a longer address to Manin, claiming that Venice was in the hands of three dictatorships, one of which was formed by the existing government, another by the vigilance committee and the third by 'a clique of informers and rumourmongers, cowardly and base'. Was it credible that Manin should trust such people? 'I am a Venetian citizen,' Canini protested, 'I too have suffered hunger, danger and disease along with the other defenders of the forts, and I am ready to give my blood for the motherland.' His pleas were supported (vainly as it turned out) by his former ministerial chief Alessandro Marcello and by Jacopo Zennari, the trusted principal secretary to the government. After nearly two months on San Severo, Canini found himself accused of high treason against the state. The case was never brought to trial. Released and immediately rearrested, he was given the choice between perpetual imprisonment or exile. Choosing the latter, he set off for Rome, where he made himself useful to the republican administration under Mazzini. Ironically, the Circolo Popolare was allowed, for the time being, to continue its activities, though under close supervision by the authorities.

This whole episode was the single genuinely discreditable moment in Manin's career, and not one that patriot historians of a later generation chose to dwell upon. In the light of his own experience of imprisonment under Austrian rule, without reasons given for his arrest, why was Manin prepared to sanction an even harsher proceeding against somebody guilty of no worse a crime than his had been? Admittedly he was terrified lest the moderate revolutionary consensus within Venice should fall apart. Civil strife would destroy the framework of public order, opening the way for an easy reconquest by the Austrian cohorts massing on the edge of the lagoon. Yet his treatment of Canini as a common criminal, without fundamental rights to justice or humane consideration, suggests the presence of certain more personal agenda. Others had noted Manin's hard edge of vindictiveness and that, once crossed, he never forgot an injury. Did he perhaps see in Canini a challenge to his own command of popular support among the Venetian working class? Was *el nostro Manin*, the people's friend who spoke their dialect, to be faced down by a socialist demagogue? There was room for only one champion in Venice, so Canini had to go, punished the more severely for his audacity in setting up as a potential rival. It was the nearest Manin ever came to the authentic vulgarity of a tyrant

Canini never forgave him. In a memoir published in Paris in 1869, more than a decade after Manin's death, he set about rubbishing his reputation. The lawyer, so far from being a hero, was 'an eleventh-hour opportunist'. While other Italian patriots had suffered in prison, in exile or on the battlefield, Manin had remained cosily ensconced in the bosom of his family at San Paternian. Even allowing for his moments of glory, he was essentially a mediocre individual, claimed Canini, lacking in greatness as an orator or the talent to transcend the limits of his ambition. 'He appropriated other people's ideas and succeeded in believing they were his own. He thirsted for absolute power without having what was needed to exercise it properly, save for a tenacious determination and an imperious manner.' From this supremely jaundiced viewpoint, Manin emerges as that all too familiar figure of twenty-first-century politics, the control freak, obsessed with command and unaccustomed to any sort of dissent.

Setting aside our impression of Canini gleefully kicking the corpse of the man responsible for his needless suffering and indignity, there is a significant truth in this accusation. He was not the sole victim of Manin's resolve to suppress any sort of political initiative that menaced the status quo. The Committee of Public Vigilance continued to monitor and swoop on anything which smacked too dangerously of radical activism or an attempt to undermine the loyalty of the Venetian working class, most crucial of all constituencies in the fight to maintain the city's independence. In a conscious gesture towards reinforcing this bond with the populace, Manin paid a visit to the Arsenal. It was 18 January, ten months to the day since the murder of the wretched Colonel Marinovich had almost tipped the city into bloody anarchy, a situation redeemed by the President's own fearlessness. 'The great citizen,' wrote an anonymous reporter, 'toured our vast boatsheds and workshops, humming with activity. He enquired into our needs and, substituting his animated manner and lively discourse for the cold and detestable Austrian bureaucratic pedantry, he exchanged ideas, proposals and sentiments with those he governs.' The *arsenalotti*, according to the same gushing journalist, flocked around the great man, 'hanging upon his lips like sons heedful of a tender father's voice' and eager for his notice, so that his eyes were seen to brim with tears at such proofs of affection. An honour guard was formed to see Manin out at the great gateway, with the workmen waving their red scarves, and later in the day a naval band serenaded him under the windows of the Procuratie Nuove. From the balcony he addressed the crowd, congratulating them on becoming 'a strong, free and sovereign people', whose spirit of sacrifice made it a model not just for Italy, but for all Europe.

Such elaborate gestures of mutual admiration between the people and their dear leader were not calculated to please Niccolò Tommaseo, whose deliverance from Austrian bondage was also being commemorated. He returned from Paris at the end of January thoroughly disgruntled both at the French government's eternal vacillations and at what he saw as the uncooperative attitude of those very Venetians who should have supported him. Once back home (for, of all the various cities in which the Dalmatian ever lived, Venice was dearest to his heart) he published an accusatory pamphlet listing in nit-picking detail his expenditure of the funds committed by the republic to him and his hapless deputy Angelo Toffoli during their Parisian stay. They had received 10,321 lire, he stated, of which 3,450 had been paid to persons on official business. Expenses were noted for travel, postage, lodgings and clothing, which Tommaseo insisted on itemising down to the very last pairs of socks, drawers and gloves, a top hat and an umbrella. The object of this bizarre publication, typically, was to make the government and the wider public aware of his scrupulousness and self-denial in the cause of diplomacy. Having issued his statement of account, he then returned all the purchased items to the relevant department, adding the coffee percolator without which no good Italian could possibly have survived a prolonged sojourn abroad.

It was not Tommaseo's fault that the French had so consistently failed to come through on Venice's behalf. True, he had behaved insensitively towards those he ought to have flattered and cajoled. General Cavaignac, for example, was unlikely to look with favour on a letter which more or less dictated what he ought to say in his forthcoming address to the national assembly. An unwavering belief in Pio Nono must have seemed merely eccentric after the pontiff's flight to Gaeta, and another article contributed to *L'Ère Nouvelle* urging support for the Holy Father as an apostle of change consolidated Tommaseo's by now distinctly minority position. Yet nobody could accuse him of insincerity or lack of effort. With help from others, most notably Cristina Belgiojoso, he had sought to stir the conscience of liberal France by appealing to the Catholicism which the nation purported so ardently to cherish. Ironically it was this very same French Catholic constituency whose supposed scruples would shortly be invoked as an excuse for dealing a major hammer-blow to the survival of Italian independence.

Daniele Manin had never been more than a nominal Catholic, and it was a matter of some distaste therefore when he learned that the editor of *L'Ère Nouvelle*, Frédéric Ozanam, had invoked blessings on the traditional piety of the Venetians and suggested that they would be only too happy to welcome Pope Pius as a refugee, 'thereby protesting against the conduct of Italy towards the sovereign fugitive from Rome'. Pius would surely rather have perished than seek safety in a city at the forefront of opposition to restoring his temporal rule. This was beside the point. What irked Manin was Ozanam's implicit attempt to contrast Venice's devout religiosity with the ingratitude shown towards the Holy Father by other Italians. To this Venetian at least, it looked as if a conscious wedge was being driven between his people and those elsewhere, in Rome, Tuscany or Sicily, still fighting to retain their freedom.

In a rousing article published in the *Gazzetta Veneta*, Manin scouted the notion of Venice as being in any sense separated in her Catholicism from the wider national struggle. Yes, the Venetians were truly devout and their devotions were wonderful to observe. 'No movement towards freedom, no celebration of any kind takes place unrelated to religion: people move constantly between the church and the front line and vice-versa. The patriotic sacrifices made for Venice by all classes of society are literally placed upon the altar of the Lord.' The city would never stoop to welcome the horde of reactionary diplomats, Austria's allies, whom Pius had dragged along with him to Gaeta. 'Venice never desires to separate her cause from that of Italy at large. Grateful as she was towards Pius IX when he bade the Germans return to their natural boundaries, Venice protests against the miserable councillors who have now driven the pontiff formally to repudiate this earlier declaration.' A rhetorical schedule of similar protests followed, against the King of Naples, against Charles Albert for abandoning Venice to the Austrians, against the lies and prevarications of foreign journalists and politicians, and against the sacrifice gradually being made of the Venetians by those who promised much, but achieved little. 'The true friends of Italy, the religious men, the *Christians*, are those, and only those, who hurry to set their brothers free and cause those tortures to cease under which they languish.'

The *Gazzetta* article, published on 22 January, appeared unsigned, but Manin's authorship was instantly attributed. For all his noble scorn towards a new strain of Catholic conservatism forming among the faithful in the wake of Pius's tergiversation, there is an audible note of panic, even a hint of despair, resounding within the text. He had surely scented the danger of a rising tide of political reaction, natural enough among those disillusioned by the ill-kept promises or outright failure of the revolutions across Europe and anxious to re-establish a framework of public order in which the economy could safely recover. Was Venice at risk of being abandoned altogether to its fate, while those who might have helped to keep its freedom intact piously wrung their hands? Manin's emphasis on the importance of keeping faith with Italy underlined his own awareness of how much Venetians needed to feel cherished and remembered by their fellow Italians. More than simply a rejection of the unwelcome new scenario proposed for it by Ozanam, the article was a cry for help from the beleaguered city.

By later generations Manin was accused of too obviously putting Venice first, ignoring the broader picture of Italian independence. Doubtless this was true, though we need to understand just how visceral a devotion to their city burned in most of those standing beside him. If Niccolò

Tommaseo (born on the other side of the Adriatic), the Education Minister Emilio Tipaldo (a Corfiote Greek) and even the recently dead Alessandro Poerio (raised in Naples among a family of Calabrian origin) could salute Venice as their city of the heart, then how much easier it was for Manin to love the place he had hardly ever left and whose pride in its ancient political integrity he had so successfully reawakened.

Yet if Italy was expected to unsheathe a sword or at least dig deep in its pockets on Venice's behalf, then the Venetian government must make its own adherence to the Italian cause more wholehearted. Ever since the revolutions began there had been talk of a constituent assembly, 'la Costituente', whose members should represent the interests of a freely voting electorate based on adult male suffrage (Italian women did not gain the vote until 1946). At first the idea for such a body was confined to local revolutionary initiatives in Lombardy and Tuscany, but with the triumph of democrats and republicans after Charles Albert's defeat, it provided a rallying call for radical politicians throughout Italy as the long-desired blueprint for federalism. After Pope Pius's retreat to Gaeta and the leftward shift of political power in Tuscany and Rome, the dream looked like turning into reality, with the papal capital city itself providing the appropriate setting for the assembly's sessions. Therefore Giuseppe Garibaldi, instead of marching his legions to defend Venice as originally planned, moved south towards Rome, picking up an enthusiastic following in the towns of the Romagna, where the government, during Rossi's ill-fated premiership, had originally intended to pin him down. Other radical exiles and fugitives hurried to the city, and on 9 February 1849 Rome was proclaimed a republic, with a pledge that the first hundred deputies elected to its new administration should also serve as representatives in the projected national constituent assembly.

The Costituente was now on everybody's lips, though a significant minority viewed it as a forum for dangerous radicalism or, like Tommaseo, disapproved of any kind of government in Rome that should exclude Pius IX. Venice's envoy to what had been the Papal States was the politically sagacious Giovanni Battista Castellani, who saw his role as that of maintaining a carefully calibrated neutrality that was conciliatory to moderates and conservatives while personally favourable towards the republicans. Putting such sympathies aside, his advice to Manin, in a letter of 29 January, was to hang fire before committing Venice to any closer links with the assembly, whenever it should eventually be convened. 'The Costituente, you should be aware,' he wrote, 'does not compel us to any course of action. Before Venice sends any deputies to it, we should see how matters turn out.' If the revolutions in Rome and Tuscany were suppressed, Castellani pointed out, the Venetians would hardly gain credit internationally for having supported something so obviously associated with republican extremism.

It was a ticklish issue, made more difficult for Manin by the need to retain foreign governments' respect while some faint hope remained that Austria might be brought to the negotiating table. Venice, what was more, continued to depend on the presence in the Adriatic of Piedmontese warships and on the monthly subsidy of 600,000 lire recently voted to her by the parliament in Turin. Even though Piedmont's new Prime Minister, Vincenzo Gioberti, was busy pushing forward a democratic agenda that included adherence to the Costituente, Manin was unwilling to commit Venice to the assembly without proper acknowledgement of her independent status by other Italian governments. If she were to be represented, it should be by a number of deputies proportionate to the significance of her present position as the only city currently offering armed resistance to the Austrians.

He was uncomfortable too with the growing political instability in Tuscany, a state which, apart from its brief moment of glory at Curtatone e Montanara, had contributed almost nothing of any value, in terms of military resources, money or ideas, to the broader movement towards an independent Italy. Order in the region seemed to be breaking down under pressure from the democrats for closer links with the new Roman republic. Rioting broke out in Leghorn and Lucca, there was a run on the banks by frightened investors, and the government, headed by Giuseppe Montanelli, found itself strapped for cash to pay the army and navy. At the centre of events stood the always well meaning but now decidedly muddled figure of Grand Duke Leopold II, a wholly Italianised member of the Habsburg family who had done his best to conciliate liberal opinion, but shrank at this moment from endorsing the Costituente and the politics of a Rome without Pope Pius. On 26 January, as news arrived that no less a representative than Giuseppe Mazzini had been chosen by the republicans of Leghorn to speak for them in the national assembly, the grand Duke wrote in despair to the archbishops of Florence, Pisa and Siena, begging for spiritual advice. Their reply came in the form of a protest to the Tuscan chamber of deputies against the insults offered to religion in the wake of Pope Pius's flight. The next day Leopold left Florence for Siena, where he had sent his family for safety. Even here there were ugly scenes as crowds gathered on the Campo to await news of the government's fall. Leopold stoutly refused to accept either Montanelli's dismissal or adherence to the Costituente. On 5 February a letter arrived from the Pope at Gaeta, absolving him of any moral responsibility for the current political crisis. Montanelli meanwhile had followed Leopold to Siena with the text of the proposed assent to the Costituente, which merely awaited his signature. Two days after receiving Pius's letter, the Grand Duke, preparing to go for a drive in the country, told Montanelli that he would sign on his return. He had no intention, as it happened, of signing, still less of returning, and set off with his entire family into the Maremma towards the port of Santo Stefano. There, after a further fortnight of proclamations, letters of solidarity to Pius and Ferdinand of Naples and a warning to his son-in-law Charles Albert (timely as it turned out) not to meddle again in Italian affairs, Leopold, his wife and children boarded the British steam frigate *Bulldog*, which took them – inevitably – to join His Holiness at Gaeta. 'Here,' wrote the Grand Duke, 'lay order, strength and faith.'

Leopold's flight, only two months after Pius had left Rome, was naturally seen as an act of panic and treachery, essentially playing into the hands of those who saw the Italian sovereigns as irredeemable in their conservatism and subservience to the Austrian-dominated old order. With hard-line republicans now making the political running in Tuscany, Manin felt less at ease with the whole notion of the Costituente. He was surely not unaware of the conservative counter-currents building throughout Europe and the boost to Schwarzenberg's diplomatic push which the bunching together of three major Italian rulers must provide. The idea of a national assembly had by no means lost its allure for many in Venice, however, and there must have been considerable disappointment when on 5 February the Costituente held its opening session without a significant Venetian presence on its benches. While an amateur performance of Verdi's opera *I Lombardi alla Prima Crociata* was being staged at the Teatro Gallo by the gallant 'faithful remnant' of the Neapolitans in Venice, one of the most prominently displayed banners of the medieval crusaders was seen to bear the anachronistic legend 'Viva la Costituente italiana'. Loud cheers filled the auditorium, 'as if in this inscription all our future destinies were summed up'. Whether Manin was present is not recorded.

Venice's own democratic assembly was of far more importance to him, both for what it symbolised in terms of the city's ability to manage her own affairs and for its role in facilitating the decisions taken by himself and other key figures, political, financial and military. Its usefulness to Manin was highlighted in a cynical letter written on 10 January by the actor Gustavo Modena to a member of the Committee of Public Vigilance who had asked him to return from Tuscany, where he currently lived, and stand for election. Modena first of all poured scorn on the Costituente as a mere time-waster and talking-shop, predicting that Venice's home-grown version would be 'the usual collection of lawyers, journalists and *poetical* gentlemen', no better than these 'educated fleas in old wigs at the last session of the Serene Republic's Grand Council'. It would exist, he claimed, simply to rubber-stamp Manin's decisions. As for the leader himself, what was he? Certainly not an Italian in the Mazzinian mould, but more like a decent local mayor, 'a loyal and watchful commandant, incapable of betrayal or dishonourable capitulation'. Modena wanted something greater for Venice, a more positively asserted role as bulwark of Italian freedom, before he would condescend to join an assembly in which his outspokenness must almost certainly earn him a similar fate to those of Mordini, Dall'Ongaro and other members of the Circoli. An earlier remark by Manin to Modena, that 'whenever he met me, I always looked as if I were playing the comedian', had not helped. 'Believe me, this ignoble farce acted out by our professional gentlemen [i.e. the Venetian assembly] will end in renewing the power of despotism.'

Others were not so disparaging. Elections took place on 20 January, using a list system of the kind that became familiar throughout Italy in the decades after unification and remained in force there until the electoral reforms of our own day. Several non-Venetians gained seats, such as Girolamo Ulloa, representing the Arsenal district, Pacifico Valussi for Santa Maria Formosa, and the Triestine lawyer and poet Antonio Somma for the Frari.* Manin, representing the soldiers serving in the forts, did as well as might have been expected; Tommaseo, standing alongside Ulloa at the Arsenal, picked up votes which owed much to his hallowed status as a former political prisoner; but military supreme Giovanni Battista Cavedalis managed considerably better than his naval opposite number Leone Graziani, whom everyone was currently disposed to blame, as Admiral, for the timorous conduct and ill preparedness of the Venetian fleet.

Modena, in the letter quoted earlier, had spoken of the need for proper representation of the working class. 'Give me an assembly of market stall-holders, sailors and ferrymen, ready to cut out all manoeuvres, dodges and Jesuitical hypocrisy, acting instead like those brave *arsenalotti* who cut through uncertainties with their axes and drills.' If the new representative body was not quite so democratic, then many members were satisfied with its overall make-up. Even Pacifico Valussi, hardly one of

---

* A respected lawyer, Somma was also a successful playwright, later responsible for adapting Eugene Scribe's French libretto *Gustave III ou le Bal Masque* for Verdi as *Un Ballo in Maschera*.

Manin's warmest supporters, was pleased. 'Our assembly was truly representative of every social class. There were many of the old nobility, several from more newly ennobled families, property owners, merchants, lawyers, engineers, scientists, journalists, soldiers and sailors, teachers, priests, friars, Jews and some from beyond the city representing Venice's links with the mainland.' Overall, the moderate republican interest achieved greater successes than the radicals from the Circolo Italiano and the Circolo Popolare, though such a triumph did nothing to prevent a demonstration in favour of the Costituente taking place in the Piazza on 13 February, two days before the new assembly was due to open at the Doge's Palace. This was yet another chance for Manin to do what he did better than anyone, to address the crowd in simple terms, warn them of the dangers of factionalism at a time when a need for unity was paramount, and send them home with their tails between their legs. Nevertheless, the issue of Venice's closer affiliation with the new governments in Florence and Rome would remain a bone of contention between conservatives and democrats over the following months.

It was the ostensible purpose for which the assembly had been summoned in the first place. At its opening session on 15 February, the earliest business of the day was that of appointing a Speaker, his deputies and four secretaries. For the first of these posts Niccolò Tommaseo was initially nominated, but declined at once on grounds of failing eyesight and general poor health. Whether anyone believed this was another matter. Had he accepted, his integrity would at once have been compromised, and the whole experience of diplomacy in Paris must have convinced him that he was not cut out for the role of a government functionary. As a backbencher, on the other hand, he could freely indulge his opposition to Manin (whom he now believed was engaged in secret dealings with the Austrians), while never descending to any sort of vulgar *ad hominem* attack. Though he had assured his former fellow prisoner that 'because Venice is better governed than any other part of Italy' he would do nothing to upset 'the concord necessary for the well being of the state', he continued to assail and harass the administration, for motives which had more of selfishness in them than of patriotism.

Once again the difference between the two men was marked by their approach to the crisis in hand. Manin, ever the realist, urged the assembly at once to accept the proposal made by the new Deputy Speaker, Giovanni Minotto, that the existing triumvirate should continue to exercise the special powers conferred on it after the crisis of last August. Having assured the members that international relations were going according to plan and that a mediation conference was due to take place in Brussels under Franco-British auspices, he moved swiftly to the issue of the city's finances, always scrupulously administered whatever their parlous situation. Even if others disagreed with his politics or his methods, nobody could doubt Manin's firmness of purpose or his genuine faith in the viability of a free Venice as an example to the rest of Italy.

Yet he by no means managed to win over all his hearers with this inaugural address. A surly Tommaseo, snarling from the columns of the free newspaper *Fratellanza dei Popoli (Brotherhood of the Peoples)* that he distributed to everyone from soldiers and priests to fishermen and gondoliers, could easily be contained, but the republican left had produced a more effective opposition champion in the shape of Giuseppe Sirtori. At the head of his fellow Mazzinians, he had challenged Manin for control of the government on 4 August. In the new assembly his aim was that the radical left should set the agenda, despite forming a parliamentary minority. He began by spearheading a motion that each act, once passed, should open with the words 'In the name of God and the People'. Though this was voted through, it suggested to moderates such as General Cavedalis that the assembly 'had plainly declared in favour of donning a Mazzinian garb'.

Sirtori now had the bit between his teeth. With the backing of a petition from the two political clubs, Italiano and Popolare, he pushed his advantage by demanding that a special military and naval commission be set up 'to study the swiftest and most effective means of harassing the enemy with frequent sorties'. The radicals wanted action rather than containment, a rerun of the glamorous Mestre affair perhaps, but certainly some kind of initiative which would make the Austrians bedded down on the mainland a little less comfortable, and see off for good the admittedly not very efficacious enemy naval presence being maintained along the Lido and the outer lagoon islands. When Manin sought to brush the petition aside, Sirtori implicitly accused him of overriding the sovereignty of a democratically elected parliament. The tide of support for this new radical activism at length forced the triumvirs, so recently reinstated, to offer their resignation. Giovanni Ferrari Bravo, a member of the Circolo Italiano, proposed that their place be taken by a nine-man junta, which should 'ensure the enjoyment of all those liberties and fundamental guarantees which, according to democratic principles, must determine the form, organisation and mode of internal government in the exercise of legislative and executive powers, as well as the duties and rights of citizens in conformity with the present needs and conditions of the state'.

It was not merely the breathless circumlocution of Ferrari Bravo's proposal which prompted the assembly to defer a vote for two days. Quite possibly several of the more moderate members had begun to suspect Sirtori and his associates of trying to take over the government, capitalising on a popular desire for military action rather than a supine policy of containment. The mood on which such a gamble depended was much more ambivalent than the radicals realised. Even if the talk was of the need for further strikes at the Austrians from Marghera, or of an attack on the imperial ships of war forming the blockade line, nothing could shake the confidence of the average Venetian in Daniele Manin as leader in a time of crisis. As the assembly dithered, rumours spread that the members were actually considering his outright dismissal from a role in the government. It now looked as though two distinct political parties had begun to form at a time when Venice, for all the openness of its democratic procedures, needed a fundamental unity of purpose. As so often in previous months, Piazza San Marco became the echo-chamber of popular feeling, while the war of words conducted via a rash of angry posters, so typical of Risorgimento Italy, broke out yet again across the walls, doors, house fronts and column-drums of the city.

On the morning of 5 March, as the deputies inside the Doge's Palace gathered to debate Ferrari Bravo's motion, a hostile crowd started to fill the Piazzetta, the open space outside the palace, dominated by the two tall pillars between which the Serene Republic had strung up the bodies of traitors. The civic guard, drawn up as usual to protect the entrance to the building through the Gothic Porta della Carta, and evidently receiving orders not to offer serious resistance, had removed the bayonets from their rifles. Soon those nearest to the gateway began surging past them into the great courtyard, crying, 'Death to Sirtori!', driven by a genuine but bizarre belief that the rebel deputy intended to betray the city to the Austrians. At this moment Manin himself appeared at the top of the Scala dei Giganti, the marble steps leading up to the loggia on the first floor. One hand clasped that of his son Giorgio, the other brandished a sword. Behind him stood a civic-guard platoon in a more obviously businesslike mood than its fellow outside. The apparition served to calm the mob, but only for an instant. 'Citizens, my honour is in your hands!' cried Manin. 'It will look as though I deliberately caused you to rise in revolt. If you love me, go home!'

When they refused to listen, he tried once more to speak, but only after a third attempt did he manage to persuade them, and both palace and Piazzetta were eventually cleared. The unnerved assembly swiftly voted down Ferrari Bravo's proposal. Now it was time for Gian Francesco Avesani, who nearly a year earlier had been forced aside by popular support for Manin as leader of the new revolutionary government, to present a counter-measure. A moderate and a supporter of fusion with Piedmont, he sought to head off further radical intervention by proposing unlimited powers for the triumvirs. Though the motion was eventually rejected, Avesani had managed to deflect any meaningful challenge to the political status quo, leaving Manin as President of a new administration whose members predictably included Cavedalis, Graziani and the indefatigable Isacco Pesaro Maurogonato as Finance Minister. 'We are forced to admit,' remarked the baffled Sirtori through gritted teeth, 'that here in Venice there is no such thing as the people, but only a man.'

Had Manin's confrontation with the mob been anything more than a carefully staged piece of political theatre? Several historians and memorialists of the revolution suspected that government agents had deliberately spread a rumour of a betrayal of Venice to the Austrians being supposedly planned by Sirtori, plastering the city with posters calling for his death and Manin's instant appointment as dictator. Others believed that the President had been personally responsible for rousing the rabble, so as to frighten the more conservative deputies into backing him as representative of law and order. No definite evidence exists for his direct involvement, but the fact that he should have sought to adjourn the assembly for a month almost as soon as he took office suggests his fear of the power wielded by the radicals, whatever their minority role. Dissuaded from such a step by his friend Bartolomeo Malfatti, who urged him instead to concentrate on gaining the support of potential waverers, Manin obtained a week's suspension as a necessary cooling-down period for all concerned.

His address to the assembly after taking office was brief and very much to the point. He was conscious, he acknowledged, of his own daring in accepting the presidency, and appealed (however disingenuously) to their united confidence and affection. 'We have been strong, respected and praised until now because we have been entirely in accord with one another. I appeal to those virtues in you which are scarcely poetic in character, but are of immense practical usefulness. I appeal to your prudence, your patience and your perseverance. By these virtues, together with concord, love and faith, we shall triumph!' The assembly's new secretary Antonio Somma noted 'ardent applause' at this point, and even the Mazzinians could scarcely have dissented from either the spirit or the wording of the speech.

They would be heartened during the next few days by news that Mazzini himself had reached Rome, to assume the role of President, alongside Garibaldi, in the government which ruled the city after Pius IX had left for Gaeta. Meeting him soon after his arrival, the American writer Margaret Fuller Ossoli noted admiringly that 'he looks more divine than ever, after all his new, strange sufferings', and this air of deep spiritual purpose would cling to him throughout the brief but unforgettably dramatic period (scarcely longer than four months) of the Roman republic's existence. Mazzini had a mission and was determined to fulfil it as completely and as exemplarily as possible. He wrote of 'the sense of awe, almost of worship' with which he entered a place that 'in spite of her present degradation was to me the temple of humanity'. From Rome, he believed, would spring 'the religious transformation destined to bestow moral unity upon Europe'. As he passed through Porta del Popolo, he felt 'an electric thrill run through me, a spring of new life'. His government in Rome, in terms of its basis in an idealistic appeal to the better nature of human beings when trusted to exercise their democratic freedom, would offer sharp contrasts with that of the hard-headed Manin in Venice. Mazzini's programme was succinctly set out as 'No war on classes, no hostility to existing wealth, no wanton or unjust violation of the rights of property; but a constant disposition to ameliorate the material condition of those least favoured by fortune'. Though the latter part of this manifesto was hardly supported by the dire state of Roman finances, the government was able to vote a subsidy of 600,000 lire to the Venetians, in return for the gift of four cannon to be dispatched at once to Ravenna. This town, together with the port of Ancona, was an important point of supply for provisions to be shipped northwards to Chioggia and Venice, so for Manin and his fellow ministers guns were an obviously practical quid pro quo.

When the Venetian assembly reconvened on 14 March, Sirtori and his supporters sensed the political tide of revolutionary Italy running strongly in their favour. There was a real chance, with Piedmont neutralised and still licking its wounds after last year's war, that republican democrats in Rome, Tuscany and Venice could act together to thwart any return to the idea of an Italian monarchy under the house of Savoy. Sirtori took the earliest opportunity to propose a solidarity pact with the two other states. 'To undertake such an agreement,' he declared to the assembly, 'will not compromise Venice's political destiny. We shall obtain a great advantage by it, and by the same token express our willingness for national unity, so dear to all our hearts.' Scenting danger, Manin instantly protested that an issue like this one, obviously a matter of party politics, must be set aside in the interests of national defence. Somewhat unexpectedly, it was Niccolò Tommaseo who sought to lower the temperature of the debate by proposing that an official letter be sent to the governments in Rome and Florence, thanking them for the efforts they had so far made on

Italy's behalf and giving them every good wish for the future, while simultaneously calming Manin's fears of creeping extremism and taking a discreet step towards the greater solidarity that Sirtori and his friends now looked for. Doubtless Tommaseo had in mind the sort of letters he had composed with such well-weighed eloquence when the newly born republic of 22 March had sought to establish ties with other European states.

The next day parliament was due to vote on his proposal. When the deputies gathered in the Sala del Maggior Consiglio, however, they were informed by their Deputy Speaker Giovanni Minotto that the assembly would be adjourned for a fortnight. The reasons for this decision, he announced, must be understood by everybody and would in any case be fully explained at the next meeting, if events had not already made such an explanation unnecessary. The great ceiling of the chamber, with its painted panels by Tintoretto, Veronese and Palma Giovane, representing the victories of Renaissance Venice over its enemies eastern or western, echoed to thunderous applause. For everybody present had heard the news, arriving in the city the previous night, that King Charles Albert and his ministers in Turin had officially denounced the Salasco armistice. Piedmont was once again at war with Austria.

~

CHAPTER 12

WHATEVER THE COST

CHARLES ALBERT HAD NEVER BEEN happy, either with the terms of the Salasco armistice or with having to remain idle while the democrats took control across Italy and the Pope and Grand Duke Leopold fled from their respective capitals. Lord Aberdeen, writing to Metternich in February 1849, thought it quite likely, indeed, that the King would soon be off to join them in the reactionary paradise of Gaeta. Those six months and more during which the international talks about talks had dragged on, with France and Britain blowing hot and cold while Austria grew more peremptory and intransigent, had merely served to exacerbate a sense of impotent humiliation among the Piedmontese. By the beginning of December 1848, when Vincenzo Gioberti's government took office in Turin, feelings were running high enough for the British ambassador Ralph Abercromby to tell Palmerston that 'the real policy of the Sardinian Government is to avail themselves of the first opportunity to withdraw from the Mediation and eventually to resume the War'.

By the end of January it had become clear that the peace conference scheduled to take place in Brussels to iron out the differences between Piedmont and Austria would simply be a face-saving operation. Even if the British prime minister Lord John Russell maintained that 'the mere fact of the Brussels Conference having met would have a most beneficial effect upon Public opinion in Europe, and would greatly tend to the maintenance of the general Peace', neither side seemed ready to make even the most cosmetic of conciliatory gestures. Radetzky and his no-nonsense approach to reoccupying Lombardy were realities as unpleasant as the growing concentration of troops along the mainland shores of the Venetian lagoon or the stiffening of resolve among the imperial blockade fleet by its newly appointed supreme, the Danish admiral Hans Birch Dahlerup. Piedmontese sword-arms began twitching dangerously at each more bellicose pronouncement from Charles Albert.

When war was finally declared on 17 March, the King's motives were as pointedly ambiguous as they had been the previous year, when at more or less the same time he had ordered mobilisation along the Lombard frontier. It was not simply a matter of avenging the honour lost in what Costanza d'Azeglio had memorably termed 'our sorry Iliad'. Charles Albert was determined once again to wrong-foot radical opposition to Austria in whatever form it might exist and to head off any fresh attempt by republicans to seize the revolutionary initiative in the name of Italian unity. The royal denunciation of the armistice was made in the secure knowledge that, assuming everything went according to plan, there would be no need to deal with troublesome volunteers, uncooperative Milanese, rogue Mazzinians or any of those other inconvenient outgrowths of patriotism that had pestered and obstructed the Piedmontese army on the previous expedition. Among the King's more publicly professed reasons for rejecting the Salasco terms, the chief was that Austria had failed to honour her various pledges, including the removal of troops from the duchies of Parma and Modena, returning the siege guns captured at Peschiera and lifting the blockade of the Venetian lagoon.

'Whatever happens,' remarked Metternich to Aberdeen a few weeks before the denunciation, 'Charles Albert is lost. He belongs to those sad encumbrances of our age whose number is completed by Palmerston.' According to the ex-Chancellor, who had moved from Hove to Richmond and was finding his English exile not unenjoyable, the new war was really Palmerston's fault for making no effort to restrain the King. Was the royal manifesto, he wondered, legitimate in any case, proceeding as it did from the government rather than directly from the sovereign? Certainly the reopening of hostilities, if not overtly welcomed by Austria, played conveniently into her hands. Ever since Franz Josef's accession as Emperor, Felix zu Schwarzenberg, his chief minister, had been determined on taking a far tougher line with the various surviving revolutionary governments, whether in Italy or in Hungary. The new emperor proved exactly the kind of ruler conservative Austria felt it needed in order to counterbalance the effects of its brief fling with liberalism and revolution under Ferdinand. Though Schwarzenberg initially supported the Kremsier Reichstag, he soon came to reject its more sweeping constitutional proposals and, with the help of the Interior Minister Franz Stadion, drafted an alternative constitution aimed at buttressing the monarchy while guaranteeing the survival of parliament and the accountability of individual ministers. At the same time his aim was to re-establish imperial authority, repairing Austria's damaged prestige as a European power. A firm line was therefore to be taken at once against nationalism, constitutionalism and liberal reform, with help from the soundly reactionary Cabinet gathered around the Prime Minister, buttressed by the unwaveringly loyal upper echelons of the Habsburg army.

Schwarzenberg had little interest in pursing the issue of mediation in Italian affairs, save in so far as it allowed him to drive a diplomatic wedge between France and England. The former, under its new president Louis Napoleon Bonaparte, now looked more determined than Cavaignac's government to wring concessions from Austria, and the whole issue of Venice's status under the Salasco armistice terms appeared to weigh heavier with French public opinion in early 1849 than it had done for many months. To separate the two mediating powers by alarming France with the possibility of a northern Italian kingdom under British influence on its very doorstep was not merely in Austria's national interest, but also satisfied the profound loathing (on the part of both Schwarzenberg and Franz Josef) for Palmerston and everything he stood for. By digging in their heels on the binding nature of the treaties made at the Congress of Vienna in 1815, guaranteeing Habsburg possession of Lombardy and Venetia, they could put to the test his faith in the validity of such agreements, unshaken despite his genuine sympathy with the Italians and his belief that Austria had largely mishandled its responsibility to its subjects as an imperial power.

The Foreign Secretary's position on Italian affairs had become increasingly delicate since the beginning of the year. With Tory critics of government policy towards Austria growing more outspoken, and the anger of Queen Victoria and Prince Albert swelling at what they considered Palmerston's meddlesome arrogance, Lord John Russell, as Prime Minister, was driven to contemplate some sort of damage limitation, such as sending him to Ireland as Viceroy, to rescue the Whigs from political embarrassment. He was not helped by the deliberate snub administered by Franz Josef to the Queen on his accession to the throne, in failing to observe the accepted custom among sovereigns of sending a family representative to announce the fact. Worse still, it emerged that the incorrigible 'Pilgerstein' had authorised the transfer of weapons controlled by the Ordnance Office to Sicilian agents for use against the Bourbon government, so that Russell, harassed by a salvo of furious letters from Windsor, had to compel him to apologise personally to King Ferdinand. By the end of February, when the peace conference in Brussels was scheduled to open, Schwarzenberg could be satisfied that Palmerston had painted himself into a corner. Austrian intransigence and his own rashness made any settlement impossible, except one which confirmed repossession of the disputed provinces, keeping Piedmont firmly within its own borders and guaranteeing Habsburg claims to Venice and whatever pockets of surrounding territory in the lagoon were still managing to hold out.

Piedmont in any case looked likely to render the Brussels conference pointless. A kind of desperation appeared to have seized Charles Albert, according to foreign observers, and both Palmerston and France's Foreign Minister Edouard Drouyn de Lhuys warned him to back off from any attempt at renewing the war. The French, however, ultimately refused to support the suggestion made by Ralph Abercromby that a direct threat of armed intervention might be issued by both the mediating powers if Turin pushed plans for aggression against Austria any further. When the King finally issued his declaration of war, the catastrophe Palmerston most feared – a major European conflict involving Habsburg forces actually invading Piedmont, and France riding to her defence – seemed about to develop. Yet ironically it was Schwarzenberg who defused it by forbidding Radetzky to cross the border from Lombardy as he had originally intended, and by sending that most practised of Viennese diplomats Count Josef von Hübner to Paris on a mission designed to restrain Louis Napoleon from precipitate action in Charles Albert's favour. The French were to be assured that Austria required nothing beyond the acknowledgement of a right to reclaim its Italian provinces, and despite a little sabre-rattling in the national assembly and an impatient anti-Austrian outburst to Hübner by the Prince-President, their neutrality was preserved for the short duration of the war.

For the Austrians victory was a foregone conclusion. The defects of the Piedmontese army had made themselves obvious during the previous campaign, and support for the war among Charles Albert's subjects was by no means universal. In the eyes of Radetzky's aide, Quartermaster General Karl von Schönhals, the *casus belli* was too dubious in itself to offer a clear divide between right and wrong as far as many Italians, let alone the Piedmontese, were concerned. For the King, 'the memory of his defeats was insupportable to so proud a prince. It gave him sleepless nights and pursued him like a ghost.' What finally drove Charles Albert to make war, according to Schönhals's reading of the situation, was the influence of that host of political exiles (including, among the Venetians, Jacopo Castelli and Pietro Paleocapa) that had gathered in Turin since the summer of 1848. The wiser counsels of his generals as to the impossibility of resuming the fight with an army only partially reorganised after its last battering at Custoza were ignored, in favour of those engaged in salving his bruised ego with the prospect of military honour finally avenged via a swift campaign, which should end with the decisive trouncing of Radetzky and the Habsburg forces.

The mistrust with which Charles Albert now viewed his staff was openly expressed by his appointment of a foreign officer, the Polish general Wojciech Chrzanowski, as commander-in-chief. A substantial number of exiled Poles had found shelter in Piedmont and in January 1849, with royal approval, they formed their own legion. By February Chrzanowski, a veteran of Borodino and the revolution of 1831, was given charge of the entire royal army. He was not a fluent speaker of either French or Italian, and relations with the Piedmontese generals were made more problematic by the fact that Charles Albert had designated him 'general major' rather than 'general commanding', denoting a status effectively subordinate to several senior officers, Alberto La Marmora and Giovanni Durando among them, whose chief he supposedly was. Within a relatively short period, nevertheless, Chrzanowski raised morale, improved discipline and overhauled the logistical infrastructure of the whole fighting force; but a plea to the King for more time fell on deaf ears, and the army that set off to war was hardly the unified, dedicated and cheerfully optimistic host which had swept into Lombardy the previous March. The ranks held plenty of doubters, the Italian cause was no longer so sacred to men who saw their former efforts derided or belittled by civilian critics in Turin and Genoa, let alone in the rest of Italy, and the onus on Chrzanowski to deliver an easy victory was made the greater by a widespread contempt for those who had overseen the botched opportunities and outright failures of the previous campaign.

As Austria's generalissimo in Italy, Field Marshal Radetzky had no such problems. His available force, given the need to maintain large garrisons in the Quadrilateral fortresses and to keep up pressure on Venice from the mainland, was considerably smaller than Charles Albert's, at around 90,000 to the latter's 130,000, but as Schönhals points out, discipline and experience were both on the old man's side, exactly as they had been the previous year. His staff were mostly veterans of the earlier war, including, besides Schönhals himself, Generals Hess, Thurn und Taxis, D'Aspre and Wohlgemuth, all of whom had proved their worth during the fighting in the Veneto and eastern Lombardy. When news of the King's denunciation of the armistice was brought to Radetzky at his headquarters in Milan's Villa Reale,* it was greeted by everyone with shouts of joy. A proclamation was immediately drafted by Hess, under the Field Marshal's

---

* Now the city's gallery of nineteenth- and twentieth-century art.

signature, accusing Charles Albert of hypocrisy and ingratitude towards Austria, which had rescued the royal House of Savoy on several occasions in the past. The King, it declared, 'is working to destroy his throne and his dynasty, as though he were Mazzini's principal agent'. On the parade ground soldiers excitedly renewed the Austrian military tradition of the *feldzweig*, the green twigs stuck into capbands to symbolise hope of victory at the start of a campaign. Their chief was serenaded by regimental bands outside the villa while 'the air resounded with cries of "Long live the Emperor! Long live Radetzky!" Tears in his eyes, the old warrior stepped into the midst of his men, who gathered round him as their father, forcing him to don the *feldzweig* too', and parading through the streets of Milan chanting the Emperor's hymn, Haydn's tune that became the national anthem of Austria and later of Germany.

Nobody had ever thought of Charles Albert as a father, especially not his eldest son, the fat, pug-faced Victor Emmanuel, Duke of Savoy, who now accompanied him to war. The Duke's division had been ordered to take up positions to the south west of the town of Novara, only thirty miles from Milan and viewed by Chrzanowski as the perfect launch-pad for a strike against the Lombard capital. Ignoring the advice of his other generals, who suspected the Austrians were planning a direct advance into Piedmont across the Po and saw wisdom in stretching a defensive cordon along the right bank of the river where it joined the Ticino south of Pavia, Charles Albert supported his new commander-in-chief's strategy of concentrating the main army at Novara. To pin down any Austrian troops advancing northwards from the newly recovered duchies of Parma and Modena, La Marmora was sent to police their northern borders with a force of 7,000 men.

The King's crucial mistake was to believe that Radetzky would adopt the same delaying tactics he had exercised so successfully in the war of 1848. Even in defeat, the Piedmontese had derided the Field Marshal for avoiding battle wherever he could, though his attitude was simply one of common sense in view of the need to husband his resources, especially during the earliest phase of the campaign when Nugent's reserve force was just beginning its march into Friuli. On this occasion his plan, prepared with help from Hess and Schönhals, was for a speedy offensive, cutting off the small enemy force left to defend the sensitive area around the junction of the Po and Ticino, blocking any attempted advance on Milan and carrying war, if necessary, to the gates of Turin itself. Details were kept secret until the last moment from all but the most senior officers, and on 18 March regiments started moving out of Milan towards Pavia, where the Piedmontese would doubtless assume that Radetzky intended to go to ground, much as he had done at Verona almost a year ago to the day. The old Lombard university city, however, was no more than a staging post, whence Austrian units poured across the two rivers, brushing aside General Ramorino's 6,000 infantry and sixteen guns during the next two days, to advance north to the little town of Mortara. For the Piedmontese the manoeuvre's surprise was total. Only a swift push south from Charles Albert's main army could stop Radetzky marching on Turin.

Whatever exultation the rest of Italy may have felt at the prospect of a decisive drubbing for Austria was swiftly subdued as the Habsburg war machine hurtled into Piedmontese territory. Should Rome and Tuscany send troops? While their governments dithered over the issue, Venice had no doubts as to where her duty lay. Despite the misgivings of the War Minister Cavedalis, General Pepe succeeded in gathering together a 4,000-strong force at Chioggia with the idea of flushing out the Austrians from the Polesine delta country to the south. The assumption was that La Marmora's little army, having completed its work in Modenese territory, would soon be marching to join them, and news was current of 9,000 papal troops ready to advance from Bologna under the command of General Luigi Mezzacapo, the Neapolitan who had been mainly responsible for turning the Bandiera e Moro brigade into such dedicated and disciplined fighters at Mestre.

As so often in the campaigns of 1848, report and reality failed to match. By 20 March, when Pepe was ready to give his men their marching orders, the Roman government had not made any final decision as to whether Mezzacapo was to leave Bologna for Ferrara, where he hoped to overwhelm its relatively small Austrian garrison. With what seemed to Pepe's officers an unwarranted optimism, their irrepressible general issued instructions for his entire corps to begin its advance from Chioggia across the various rivers, Brenta, Adige and Po, towards Ferrara, with the aim of joining Mezzacapo's force whenever it should arrive. The scheme was typical of Pepe in its mixture of bravado and impracticality, and the officers, led by Major Carlo Radaelli, sought to talk him out of it as energetically as they could. The rivers, Radaelli pointed out, especially the Adige and the Po, would be difficult to cross without danger, and the delta terrain, with its network of deep channels and tall embankments, was not made for fighting. A more prudent expedition would move north into the Veneto, stirring up the province to rebellion and driving the enemy back across the Piave. Pepe, as they might have guessed, pooh-poohed these objections. Before the troops could set out, however, a message arrived from the tiny village of Conche, west of Chioggia, warning that Austrian troops were attacking the mixed force of Lombards and Romans which occupied the entrenched camp guarding the approach to the crucial ferry across the Brenta at Brondolo. After heavy losses, the Italians, considerably outnumbered, began to withdraw, but two of Pepe's best officers, Giorgio Rizzardi and Agostino Noaro, hurrying to the scene, managed to turn them round and renew the fight. The struggle for the trenches grew desperate, and the Austrians paid a considerable price for their ultimate victory. Two days later, those of the patriot defenders who had survived the dangers of drowning in ditches, as well as a further peppering of rifle fire when they retreated, gathered under the command of Giuseppe Sirtori, returned to Conche, launched a lightning assault on the Austrians and successfully pushed them back across the Brenta canal.

Their courage turned out, alas, to be pointless in the wider context of the new war. The Austrian advance on the town of Mortara on 21 March, directed by General D'Aspre at the head of 15,000 men, was bitterly contested by 25,000 Piedmontese, but the imperial troops stood their ground as failing light confused the enemy gunners. The following day the resourceful General Ludwig von Benedek, who had helped to save Mantua from attack the previous year, forced a passage into the town, pinning six Piedmontese battalions into the central nexus of streets and squares with hastily erected barricades made of broken carriages and dead horses. All main roads to Turin were now in Austrian hands, and Chrzanowski was forced to make a hurried revision of his original plan to fall headlong on Milan with the entire centre of Charles Albert's army. Novara, designed simply as a springboard for the grand offensive, suddenly became a wall against which the ill-fated Polish veteran now turned to face his increasingly confident foe. As one Austrian officer pointed out with gleeful prolixity:

the stout-hearted resolve to unite all our resources unencumbered by any sort of frivolous fanatical amateur element [i.e. unlike the Italians], the positively comical surprise of our sham manoeuvres, the audacity by which Radetzky brought his columns across the Ticino, with the precision of threads through the eye of a single needle, notwithstanding the dangers of such an operation (a union of forces imperceptible until the very last moment, when their respective powers could make themselves felt as effectively as possible), the exemplary use of the time at his disposal, the lightning speed and unpredictability of our attack, in short, the very decision to move the whole army towards Novara in full consciousness of the risks involved, all these things point to the Fieldmarshal's sovereign mastery of warfare, regardless of the ravages which age had made upon him.

Quite possibly, on 23 March 1849, as dawn broke over what remained of Novara's medieval fortifications (it was, to all intents and purposes, an open city), Charles Albert realised the truth that Radetzky, in little more than three days, had out-generalled him. Those three huge columns marching north in perfect order from Mortara wrote the death-warrant, not only of Piedmontese pride and the revived expectations of thousands of Lombards and Venetians, but of the King's own credibility as a military leader. By midday battle had been joined between the Austrian advance guard and the *bersaglieri*, the Piedmontese sharpshooters whose skill had made such an impact in the two actions at Goito in 1848. Now they proved far easier to scatter, though the Savoyard regiment which hurriedly took their place mounted a strong counterattack, reinforced by a division under the command of the King's second and favourite son, Ferdinand, Duke of Genoa. D'Aspre, directing operations at this early stage, realised too late that he had miscalculated the sheer size of the Piedmontese force gathered around Novara itself, yet there was no option but to fight on, relying on transfusions of support from the various units in the marching columns whenever these managed to arrive.

By mid-afternoon such sorely needed reinforcements were being sent into the front line amid a prevailing atmosphere of disbelief among their officers as to the nature of the combat in which they found themselves engaged. Far from being the kind of textbook pitched battle the Austrians anticipated, the whole engagement, developing from D'Aspre's headlong rush on what he had imagined to be merely the rearguard of an army spread out westwards along the road to Vercelli, had become a murderous free-for-all in which the continuing forward surge of one Piedmontese regiment after another could be checked only by frantic tactical extemporising on the part of the imperial commanders.

Everything now depended on Radetzky's own arrival in the field, at the head of the artillery and six battalions of grenadiers. At around five o'clock, just as Chrzanowski prepared to launch a crucial flanking attack by his under-used left wing, the Field Marshal had come up, ready with the order to move on the Piedmontese centre, keeping a promise he had given the grenadiers the previous day that they should have their fair share of the action. The gunners meanwhile pinned down the enemy's right flank, while Archduke Albert's infantry, which had seen hot work at the start of the battle, gathered to check any attempt by Chrzanowski to put his long-awaited *coup de main* into execution. None other than General Durando, still looking to redeem his reputation after his failure to support Ferrari at Cornuda, directed the Piedmontese advance, but this quickly turned into a rout as the Archduke forced him swiftly back into the suburbs of Novara. Radetzky's presence seemed to clinch the outcome of the battle, and as dusk started to fall over the plain he ordered a general advance of the whole Austrian line. Some of the Piedmontese battalions, those of the royal guard and the *bersaglieri*, showed fight to the last, but the rest fled towards the notional safety of the town itself, where Charles Albert, heedless of falling shells, had watched from the walls as his ruin unfolded. When Durando begged him to withdraw to a safer vantage point, the King rejoined gloomily: 'Let me die! This is my last day, let me die!'

The end he craved – and, as it seemed to some, had always looked for – was denied him. At around nine o'clock that evening he summoned his two sons and his principal officers to receive his decision, clearly premeditated and irrevocable in the event of a defeat, to abdicate the throne in favour of his heir, Victor Emmanuel, Duke of Savoy. While several of those present burst into tears, he said calmly, 'Gentlemen, I am no longer your king. As you have been faithful to me, give your loyalty and devotion to my son.' Two hours later he set out in a travelling carriage for the headquarters of Count Thurn-Valle Sassina, who had led the left column in Radetzky's three-pronged northern march. The Austrian officers were gathered in the kitchen over coffee when Charles Albert, announcing himself as the Comte de Barge, a Piedmontese cavalry officer, stepped into their midst. Nobody, it seems, recognised the King, though his distinctive image can scarcely have been unfamiliar to them from a whole variety of printed likenesses of various sorts. He asked for a safe-conduct to visit his estates near Nice, and Thurn, interested by his account of the battle, was ready to oblige. After further discussion of the day's events, the visitor pocketed his pass and his carriage set off at a gallop.

Nice was to be only a brief halt on the journey through France and Spain which took Charles Albert, accompanied by a single attendant, to the Portuguese city of Oporto. In a gesture of austere fatalism whose inhumanity only someone so bizarrely removed from everyday considerations could possibly justify, he had forbidden his wife Maria Teresa to join him in this self-imposed exile. She appears to have borne the injunction stoically, and proved her devotion after his death, which took place some months later, by acquiring all the furniture of the room in which he died and having it re-upholstered for reverent display in the royal palace at Turin.

A peace treaty between Piedmont and Austria would not be signed until 7 August, after lengthy negotiations over payment of an initially crippling demand by the victors for indemnity. Writing to her son Emilio,

Costanza d'Azeglio expressed what must have been a fairly general feeling among the Piedmontese. 'Imagine, my dear boy, what a misery we now feel! We have fallen from so lofty a height! Only a few days ago our army was so splendid, so well prepared. Now the country is laid waste, the state humiliated and every family desolate. If we were wrong, then God has punished us for it.' With her customary candour and perceptiveness, she acknowledged the enemy's courage and once again berated those responsible for the physical condition of the fighting troops. 'They say the Austrians never struggled so fiercely, whole lines being immediately replaced where they fell. They were superior in numbers [sic] properly rested, well-nourished, some even drunk. Ours were worn out by marching and lack of victuals. Always the same incompetence and neglect! Now, having been disbanded, they [the Piedmontese] are pillaging the countryside.'

The day after the battle of Novara, while General Thurn ruthlessly continued to bombard the town, refusing the citizens' request for a truce because, as he claimed, the commander-in-chief had not yet ordered him to desist, Radetzky took stock of the victory. If the whole engagement, considered in purely military terms, ought never to have happened, with D'Aspre's unquenchable – often insufferable – pride forcing the issue before the main army prepared to launch into action, it was the old Field Marshal's own appearance on the scene which gave the various units already in the fray their ultimate boost against what in any case was a hopeless last gamble by the outmanoeuvred Chrzanowski. Radetzky could afford to be magnanimous, and apart from the indemnity issue, his armistice terms offered to the new king, Victor Emmanuel II, were surprisingly mild. There was to be a withdrawal of Piedmontese troops from Lombardy; the strip of territory from Novara to the Po would be occupied by 20,000 Austrians; and all foreign combatants (Hungarian, Polish or Italian) were to be sent packing with a guaranteed amnesty. Following Prince Schwarzenberg's instructions, no attempt was made at pushing on to Turin, though many in Vienna would have rejoiced at any such symbolic grinding into the dust of the already humbled foe.

'God,' Radetzky told his son-in-law Karl von Wenckheim, 'has guided me, bringing victory upon victory.' News of Novara heartened political reactionaries throughout Europe. In London it was first heard at a court drawing room at Buckingham Palace, where a delighted Queen Victoria and Prince Albert hastened to congratulate the Austrian ambassador Count Colloredo. Everyone present followed suit except for Lord Palmerston, whose pointed silence was seen as a diplomatic gaffe worthy of yet another dressing-down from his party chief, Lord John Russell.

The Tories, led by Aberdeen and Disraeli, were cock-a-hoop. 'The justice of the Austrian cause must indeed be manifest,' wrote the former to an exultant Metternich, 'when all our natural impulses are reversed, and we sympathise with the strong instead of with the weak.' Disraeli, for his part, had always believed that revolutionary Italy was in thrall to secret societies 'which now cover Europe like net-work', engaged in 'war against property and hatred of the Semitic revelation'. He might have been a shade more sympathetic towards Venice in this respect had he known what profound personal sacrifices were being freely offered to the patriot cause by its Jewish population. His friends the Metternichs meanwhile, now ensconced comfortably in the old palace at Richmond, saw an end to their exile in sight. Some months earlier the ex-Chancellor had written Disraeli a long diatribe against the forces of nationalism, fraternity and progress. It was the Austrian army alone, he claimed, which had stood firm against everything the pair of them so hated and despised in the new Europe. 'Austrian soldiers swear an oath, excluding all the rest, to the *flag*, and any other kind of devotion, *even to the Emperor*, is forbidden them while under arms. A cry of 'Hurrah!' is a crime severely punished. The previous generation – to whom organising the Austrian army is due – were great psychologists, without needing to consult a professor on the subject.' What Disraeli called 'the serene intelligence of the profound Metternich' never believed itself to be mistaken, and in this case Radetzky's triumph seemed to offer yet another proof of his statesman-like sagacity.

English reactions mattered less to Italians, especially Daniele Manin, than those of the French. Austria was keeping a weather-eye on the government of Prince-President Louis Napoleon, and Schwarzenberg was keener than ever, in the wake of Novara, to sound out France's position. As so often in the past, the sabre-rattling on Italy's behalf was a great deal louder before the battle than after it. For a brief instant, when the news reached Paris, it had seemed as if mobilisation were imminent, but Radetzky's moderate armistice terms quickly subdued the fighting talk. The three-hour harangue to which the French foreign minister Drouyn de Lhuys had earlier subjected Austria's ambassador Baron Hübner was forgotten in mutually conciliatory noises between both governments. A subsequent attempt by Drouyn to browbeat Schwarzenberg into reducing the Piedmontese indemnity by threatening an occupation of Genoa was not what Piedmont itself wanted, but at least it persuaded the Austrians that having their former enemy onside by lowering the demand must be better than a French army elbowing its way into Lombardy. The Prince-President meanwhile was starting to ponder intervention of a very different kind in Italian affairs, but it would be several weeks before the devastating reality of this new project made itself plain.

In Venice, on the day before the battle of Novara, an exuberant commemoration took place to mark the anniversary of the republic's proclamation and the expulsion of the Austrians. The streets were festooned with tricolour flags; Cardinal Monico presided as patriarch at a solemn mass in St Mark's at which the Te Deum was sung; Manin reviewed companies of troops and the civic guard in the Piazza and afterwards addressed the crowd, exhorting them to preserve their courage and dignity, to prepare for further sacrifices and to support the war effort in whatever ways they could. It was another four days before a message arrived which indicated, in as chilling a fashion as possible, that such an effort, where Piedmont was concerned, had ceased to exist.

The author of the note delivered to Manin on 26 March was the sixty-three-year-old Austrian general Julius von Haynau. Following Welden's transfer to Dalmatia during the autumn, he had taken over from the temporary commander in the Veneto, Karl von Stürmer, and immediately imposed his iron will on the exercise of authority by the restored Austrian regime in the province. Like most of his fellow generals he was well born – the son, in fact, of a morganatic union between Duke William IX of Hesse Cassel and the daughter of an apothecary. Perhaps the fact that his father was a nephew of Britain's King George III served to heighten the bullying arrogance in his dealings with everybody, soldier or civilian. Schönhals, his admiring biographer, observed that Haynau was born for opposition. 'It was noteworthy,' he writes, 'that a man who made such rigorous demands on his subordinates' obedience should be so ready to resist the orders of his own superiors.' Acting on an unshakeable conviction of perfect judgement, the General led his life in an almost perpetual state of antagonism and contention, making permanent enemies in the army, the court and the government. Only two men, says Schönhals, honestly saw enough in him to merit their undying respect. One was the late Emperor Francis and the other was Radetzky. 'Without these, Haynau would have been lost to the service of his sovereign.'

Probably not a sadist in the accepted sense of the term, Haynau nevertheless carried his casual brutality well beyond the standards acceptable in the Austrian army. While commanding in Verona he had visited a civic hospital where military patients had been taken for treatment. Irritated by one of the doctors who had tipped his hat rather than doffing it fully, the General struck him across the face with his cane, barking, 'Learn to salute me better in future!' The whole town soon trembled under his rigorous curfew, like that imposed by Radetzky in Verona, which forbade even midwives attending women in labour or priests bringing the last rites to venture forth after 10 p.m. Without any of the Field Marshal's avuncular charm and courtesy, Haynau established himself at once, on taking over from Stürmer, as somebody whose impatience to get on with the task in hand – that of bringing the Italians firmly to heel – would brook no kind of restraint. The whole lingering issue of mediation, which had forced him during the winter to pursue a strategy of mere containment where the rebels were concerned, was a tiresome obstacle to his plan for an outright assault on Venice and its forts. If there was any practical usefulness in this period of enforced passivity, it lay in the opportunities offered to call up reinforcements, consolidate positions around the lagoon and make improvements to victualling and medical services for the troops.

Haynau had distinguished himself in the war of 1848, winning the coveted Order of Maria Theresa for his generalship at the battle of Custoza. His estimate of the Italians in arms was surely no less cynical than those of his fellow officers, though Austrian tributes to the courage of the Piedmontese were mostly designed to heighten awareness of the Habsburg army's indomitable hardihood in seeing off a tough adversary. He had no reason to believe that the Venetians, alarmed by the news of Novara, would not lay down their arms, and like any prudent commander, he was unwilling to waste ammunition by forcing the issue with an immediate bombardment of the forts. Accordingly the note he sent to Manin from headquarters at Padua was in the nature of a practical formula for submission without fuss, invoking the inevitable consequences if such an obvious hint were not immediately taken by the Venetian government. Enclosing Radetzky's official bulletin announcing victory at Novara, Haynau warned of its likely impact on Venice. 'The provisional government must now understand that it cannot long survive, and that a maintenance of the existing state of affairs, burdensome as this is to Venetian citizens of all classes, must be attended by the irredeemable ruin of what was formerly such a flourishing community.' Inviting the government to restore the city to its legitimate sovereign, 'the august Emperor of Austria', the General underlined the advantage of doing so as early as possible. 'Otherwise, if the town persists in revolution, I shall be forced to adopt extreme measures whose regrettable outcome I would rather avoid for Venice's sake.'

Not only in its tone, threatening Armageddon with such icy politeness, but in the simple fact it imparted of Piedmont having been brought to her knees with no obvious prospect of rising once more, this letter was the most ominous Manin had yet opened in a year as leader of the new Venetian republic. Even if Radetzky was known to exaggerate the magnitude of Austrian triumphs for propaganda purposes, the implication of both his official communiqué and Haynau's accompanying menaces could scarcely be doubted. The latter had been backed up, what was more, by a savage proclamation threatening death to anyone found collecting for the Venetians or sending food and money into the city. At once Manin sent orders to General Pepe to pull back from any further military initiatives around Chioggia and concentrate on securing Marghera and its satellite forts. Yet another message was dispatched to the government's envoy in Paris, Valentino Pasini, frantically seeking clarification of France's possible role as guarantor of Venetian independence. 'It is now time for France either to fulfil our hopes by coming to our aid or else to declare openly that she is ready to abandon us to our fate.' As wild rumours began flying around Venice declaring that Charles Albert had not really abdicated, but was simply dodging Austrian patrols to recover his scattered forces, that Radetzky's army was cut to pieces or that the rebel Hungarians had come riding to Italy's rescue, the citizens grew desperate for news, but Manin could do little enough to allay their mounting anxiety over the next few days.

Only on 1 April did he receive any confirmation from the Italian side. A letter from a friend, Sebastiano Tecchio, who had formed part of Vicenza's defence committee and then sought refuge in Turin, detailed the woeful reality of defeat, the King's abdication and the apparent triumph of a peace-at-any-price faction within the Piedmontese government. If further evidence were needed, it came in the form of a dispatch from Admiral Giovanni Battista Albini, commander of the Piedmontese naval squadron at Ancona, whose presence along the Adriatic coast had reduced the impact of an Austrian blockade. His formal announcement of King Victor Emmanuel's succession to the throne was followed by the words: 'I am at this moment prey to sorrow of a kind I never felt before; this is shared, to the most intense degree, by the entire squadron.' Despite his failure to act decisively against the fleets at Pola and Trieste the previous year, Albini had always sought to keep faith with Venice, and his grief was surely as much for the likely fate of the city – now that the armistice dictated recall of Piedmontese ships from the Adriatic – as for his sovereign's humiliation.

Patiently, under the drizzling sky, the crowd in the Piazza listened as Manin gave them such details as he could from these letters. A new mood of resilience and determination gradually replaced the desperate credulity, panic and anger which had threatened to overwhelm Venice as the first ominous messages from the mainland began to arrive. The Venetians had never forgotten who they were or abandoned their robust singularity, even if the glories of the Most Serene Republic were extinguished everywhere but in the memory and the imagination. It was at this moment that all the grit, resolution and courage which, a thousand years earlier, had secured their freedom and laid the basis of their empire on sea and land, stood ready to combat the greatest challenge to Venice's survival – if Haynau's note meant anything – that the city had ever confronted. The howitzers, cannon and mortars of the Austrians threatened more than the Frankish host of King Pepin, the galleys of Genoa or Bonaparte's all-conquering army. In token of their willingness to endure and of their perfect grasp of the moment's tremendous implications, the Venetians presented their government with a single request, whose symbolic significance demonstrated better than anything else the city's readiness to confound what seemed to be an inevitable fate.

It was a demand, to which the Patriarch Cardinal Monico acceded, that the most holy icon in the Basilica of St Mark, the wonder-working image of the Blessed Virgin known as the 'Nicopeia', supposedly painted by St Luke, should be exposed to view upon the high altar. *Nicopeia* is Greek for 'Bringer of Victory', and the picture's role as a kind of banner carried at the head of an army was validated by its other Greek name, *Odegetria*, meaning 'Guide' or 'Instructor'. Like so many sacred objects in medieval Venice, it had been looted from Constantinople, probably on the orders of the blind warrior-doge Enrico Dandolo, who led the notorious pillage of the Byzantine capital by the crusaders in 1204. Once borne before emperors marching to battle, the painting is covered in jewels and set in an ornate frame featuring images of the saints. From the moment of its installation in St Mark's, it was accorded the utmost reverence, being shown to the people only on certain feast days and at moments of national emergency. Venice worshipped the Virgin in many capacities – as '*Mater Domini*', as Our Lady of the Miracles, the Presentation, the Visitation, of Health, Pity and Weeping, of the Lily and the Bean – but it was in her role as champion of embattled Venetian warriors facing a barbarian horde that the patroness of this devoutly Catholic city was now summoned to its aid.

The renewed spirit of resistance among Venetians made itself felt in Manin's reply to Admiral Albini's dispatch. Curtly he acknowledged receipt and noted the contents. The disaster at Novara had been immense, but Providence, he believed, would not abandon 'so great a people in quest of its independence'. It was not altogether clear whether this reference applied to Italians in general or to the Venetians alone. The next paragraph seemed to indicate that he meant the latter. 'Venice,' it ran, 'will persist in her glorious resistance, continuing to count on the aid of its Italian brothers, on your personal sympathies and on the brave men of the squadron under your command.' On that rainy morning of Sunday 1 April yet another bulletin was added to the collage of posters, manifestos and government notices adorning the city. An official proclamation of Charles Albert's defeat, it put paid to any hope that the news from Piedmont might have been false or in some way distorted, undermining for good the desperate illusion that Italian patriotism must somehow triumph simply by virtue of its moral integrity. At a brief meeting of the assembly in the Doge's Palace that afternoon, held in camera, Manin seemed rather less confident of the political outcome, reading a printed copy he had received of the armistice terms, but preferring to hold a new session the following day with the idea that the members should spend the next twenty-four hours carefully considering Venice's options in the light of the current situation.

The assembly which gathered that fateful Monday afternoon was prepared for a long debate. Several of its representatives, for various reasons, found themselves wishing that a response to Haynau's note could be framed which would enable the city to return itself to Austrian rule via some sort of honourable compromise. Others still hoped against hope that Piedmont's fortunes would revive and that Victor Emmanuel would ride to the rescue, or that the newly formed republics in Rome and Tuscany might rally to help their beleaguered sister. A few supported some more sweeping military enterprise than the raid on Conche which had taken place the previous week. However, apart from a suggestion by the republican Samuel Olper that the government should encourage the Romans and Florentines by its own aggressive example to adopt a more energetic approach to resisting foreign invaders, none of these private wishes declared itself, and the whole parliament seemed grimly united. In just a few minutes Manin had asked the crucial question. 'Does the assembly wish to resist the enemy?'

'Yes!' came the answering cry.

'Does it wish to resist whatever the cost?'

'Yes, whatever the cost.'

'Bear in mind that I shall demand enormous sacrifices from you.'

'We shall make them!'

Even at such a stirring moment, Manin's iron practicality did not desert him. Resistance at any price, he warned them, required a strong government, one which could only work effectively with unlimited powers. The emergency could become so serious as to demand an iron hand, and it might even be necessary to repress those elements opposed to the struggle. Giovanni Minotto, the assembly's President, therefore proposed giving

Manin unlimited powers, and after some discussion members voted unanimously in favour of both this motion and the formula 'Venice will resist Austria whatever the cost'.

Thus the momentous session ended 'in a state', noted one witness, 'of calm and reasoned enthusiasm, altogether impossible to describe'. Outside the palace the crowd gave rousing cheers as the members stepped into the Piazzetta, welcoming Manin's reassuring presence among them to proclaim the two resolutions, urge a spirit of perseverance and prepare them for the inevitable sacrifice. Not everyone would approve of his eleva-tion to what was, in effect, the status of a dictator. Niccolò Tommaseo, for example, was perpetually resentful of the new arrangement. The Tuscan envoy Carlo Fenzi had cynically noted that in meetings of the assembly, Manin 'can scarcely open his mouth without a storm of applause' and believed that some kind of gerrymandering must lie behind the dema-gogue's hold over the populace. Nevertheless he trusted 'the talent, the integrity and pure patriotism of Manin', and it was these qualities which were to stiffen Venetian resistance during the coming months. Where the city and its people were concerned, Manin would never betray their trust, and the bond thus created would remain unbroken till the end.

As to when that should be, the Austrians had less reason to be sanguine than they imagined. True, the arrival from Copenhagen of Admiral Dahlerup, commissioned to overhaul the inefficient and demoralised Habsburg fleet, threatened a more extensive blockade of the lagoon, while on land Haynau was busy placing his gun batteries and readying his troops for an all-out assault across the railway bridge, that former symbol of peaceful progress uniting Venice to Italy, which now looked like being the instrument of her destruction. Yet, as Carlo Fenzi noted, the city, ostensibly so impoverished and without friends, faced its attackers confi-dently: its forts well manned, its substantial navy aided by a flotilla of smuggling vessels, and with an army of 20,000 men at its disposal. Gunpowder mills had been set up on the island of Le Grazie, on the edge of the city, and the Neapolitan artillery officers made careful inspec-tion of the ordnance, even as further supplies of rifles were brought in. Stores of basic foodstuffs like salt fish, maize flour and rice had been laid up the previous year in anticipation of a siege, but wine and oil were still available and bread, eggs and vegetables were brought in from Chioggia or further afield.

The only commodity which took time to reach Venice during these first days of her armed struggle was news from elsewhere in Italy. Thus it was at least two weeks before Venetians learned that the threats implied by Haynau's letter of 26 March were grounded in a chilling reality. Soon after he dispatched it, the General had been sent a desperate message from the garrison commander in the town of Brescia, on the hills west of Lake Garda, announcing that the citizens had risen in revolt and calling for reinforcements. While the Austrians retreated to the citadel, troops were hastily sent up from Mantua, led by one of Count Nugent's sons, while Haynau himself left Padua at the head of three infantry battalions, a squadron of cavalry and a mortar battery. Any new uprising in Lombardy must jeopardise a major siege operation against Venice, and this prompt reaction aimed at nipping any such patriot resurgence in the bud. What the Brescians, startled in any case by the speed with which these reinforcements arrived, could hardly foresee was the insensate ferocity with which Haynau had determined to carry out his task.

Issued on 31 March, his ultimatum to the townsfolk was more peremptory than his earlier message to the Venetians. Unless Brescia were handed over by noon that day, the city would be sacked and 'left a prey to all the horrors attending such devastation'. A deputation from the rebels had failed to move him. 'Brescians, you know me, I shall keep my word!' ended Haynau's proclamation. On reading it, the citizens became angry rather than fearful, and began final preparations for a street battle, the women taking an active part by ripping tiles off the roofs to hurl at the soldiers and keeping cauldrons of boiling water in readiness. At three o'clock the Austrian bombardment began, but even when a cannonade successfully smashed through one of the city gates, imperial troops were unable to force an entry into the well-defended streets beyond it. The following morning, which was Palm Sunday, they managed to burst in and the serious street fighting commenced. The soldiers knew their general was as good as his word, and no sort of restraining order had been issued. As the army gradually gained control, a massacre began on a scale not witnessed in Italy since the warfare of the early sixteenth century. Every civilian, regardless of age or sex, was fair game for the Austrian bayonets. Children were thrown in the air and hacked to death; an entire class of primary-school pupils watched in horror as their teacher was shot, after which they themselves were butchered; women were raped and mutilated, and jewellery was ripped from them; any house discovered to be containing weapons was immediately set on fire.

Still the Brescians refused to yield. Five times the white flag hoisted on the town hall was torn down to be replaced by a red one, and it was several days before the city was completely subdued. The slaughter and looting, in the meantime, had continued unabated, with more than a thousand citizens either killed or wounded and the corpses, on Haynau's orders, left in the streets unburied until the rebellion was crushed. As a final punishment, an immense fine was imposed on the municipality, which was expected, in addition, to foot the bill for the ammunition used in bringing Brescia to heel. Would such horrors, for which Haynau was to become notorious throughout Europe, repeat themselves in Venice? Had the assembly's resolution to hold out whatever the cost been a gesture of quixotic bravado, a mere operatic fanfaronade of which Italy's 1848 revolutions had already thrown up too many? As old Count Cicogna, longing for the Austrians' return, sardonically noted in his diary, 'Should we understand by the words "at any price" even the destruction of the city? The truth is that we shall resist as long as there is money and food.'

His doubts were not shared by the majority of Venetians. One of the more extraordinary aspects of this unique moment in their history is that the consensus among those without power or influence in the community should so unwaveringly have supported resistance, even as the odds piled higher against anything like victory. Toughing it out in the spirit with which their ancestors had stood firm against the might of the Ottomans, the presumptions of the papacy, the envy of Spain or the machinations of other Italian states became, for the people of Venice, a cause within a cause, their own affair of honour, setting at naught the Black Legend and its attendant notion of them as idle slaves in a disinherited realm of ghosts and memories. In the days immediately following the fateful assembly of 2 April, a fly-poster appeared in the streets which read, 'Venice must resist, making up for lack of money with silver and bells from the churches, precious jewellery from the ladies and brass utensils from the kitchens.' This was no vain demand. A readiness to give everything or anything to the new war effort – from family plate and scrap metal to tresses of hair for use in stuffing hospital pillows – was even more pronounced now than it had been when the earliest appeals were made by the provisional government in 1848. Such offerings were also pledges of faith. Venice, buckling herself against an imminent siege, began as she meant to go on.

To mark this shared sense of momentousness, of a turning point after months of waiting on events, the government ordered that a commemorative medal be struck. Nobody was inclined to criticise the gesture or object that the bronze used could surely serve a more practical purpose. Its obverse showed the figure of Venice herself, defending the Italian tricolour, with a quotation from Dante's *Inferno*: 'Ogni viltà convien che qui sia morta', 'It is fitting that all cowardice should perish here' – while on the reverse were the words of the 2 April resolution and the names of Manin and other leading members of the assembly. Outside St Mark's, meanwhile, there appeared the ultimate emblem of heroic defiance. A red flag, symbolising war to the death, was hung from the top of the Campanile, whence it would be clearly visible to the Austrians across the lagoon. Taking this as their cue, Venetians everywhere began to sport scarlet ribbons, men pinning them to their lapels or shirt fronts, women to the edging of their bodices. Hearts were high, convictions were staunch, and every day during its month-long exposition in the Basilica processions of the faithful from various parishes came to pray before the wonder-working icon of the Nicopeia. So immense a quantity of candles had never been seen before, and on 22 April the procession of naval personnel from the church of San Biagio numbered almost 1,000 people. The following Sunday, Manin himself, with the rest of the government and the town council, came to mass, and two days later the entire assembly went in solemn concourse to the Basilica from the Doge's Palace. The city's fighting spirit was summed up by a poor old woman who, during these late spring days, used to visit Manin, saying that the Madonna herself had given her personal assurances that all would be well. Fear of the Austrians was at this stage neither palpable nor even remotely serious. For everyone knew that before Haynau and his cohorts could begin trying to fight their way across the railway viaduct, they would have to deal first of all with Fort Marghera.

CHAPTER 13

∿

THESE DEAR ITALIAN YOUTHS

'I N THE ITALIAN DRAMA,' OBSERVED Austria's new prime minister Felix zu Schwarzenberg, 'Venice serves as a theatre to the play's misadventures. The Venetian insurrection is in truth the sheet anchor to which are linked the hopes of that party busy fomenting anarchy in Italy.' While the government of Venice and the 'so-called Republic of St Mark' continued to exist, offering asylum to revolutionaries who had failed elsewhere, 'ideas of order will not take hold in the rest of the peninsula'. Austria's duty to its reconquered Italian provinces was both moral and economic, but she could achieve nothing 'while the fires of resentment and resistance are being fed by the example and, what is more, the incessant activity of the City of the Lagoons'.

Schwarzenberg had reckoned without the inspiration offered by the new government set up in Rome, led by Giuseppe Mazzini, but in other respects he was not far wrong. His comment on the significant presence of an alien revolutionary element in Venice identified one of the key nerve-centres of the city's resistance. For little could have been achieved in practical terms without the presence of that loyal and dedicated band of Neapolitans who, eleven months earlier, had disobeyed King Ferdinand's order to abandon the patriotic war effort and head for home. Guglielmo Pepe was still their leader, as commander-in-chief of the entire Venetian army, charismatic and swashbuckling as ever, totally committed to the Venetian cause and well respected by his troops, whatever the misgivings of certain officers as to his professional competence. Others trained like him at Naples's military academy of La Nunziatella, a veritable nursery of revolution where 1848 was concerned, had harnessed their talents to improving the efficiency of the defence force and sharpening the accuracy of the gunners who would now bear the brunt of Haynau's planned assault.

At Marghera the Neapolitans fighting for Venice made their truest mark. The fort's garrison now numbered 2,744 men, including 300 artillery, the 127 members of the elite and largely self-regulating Bandiera e Moro brigade, 200 marines, fifty members of the civic guard and a complement of engineers. Joining these were two Venetian infantry battalions and the Cacciatori del Sile regiment, recruited from volunteers who had managed to slip into Venice, under Austrian noses, from the mainland area around the town of Treviso. Its citizens' heroism in keeping the Habsburg forces at bay for so long the previous year was now a bitter memory, soured in many cases by a wave of denunciations to the police from those currying favour with the restored regime; by the departure of a host of voluntary exiles, which had undermined the local economy; and by violent resentments between families who had suffered for their patriotism and others poised to profit from their downfall. Years afterwards Luigia Codemo, who as a young woman had experienced this atmosphere at first hand, could write, 'Among all the tears shed in the revolution, I still keep a few lodged like drops of lead within my heart.' At least some of the fierce bravery among the Cacciatori del Sile was due to a wish to keep faith with Venice, as their Neapolitan comrades were doing, whatever the grudges and bitterness stirred up after Treviso's surrender.

Against Marghera, its bastions and ramparts bristling with 137 guns, General Haynau had mustered a formidable army: 30,000 troops now staked out a fifty-mile blockade line stretching from the River Adige in the south to the banks of the Piave north of Treviso. From his new headquarters in a villa at Marocco, outside Mestre, belonging to the Papadopoli family (whose principal representative, Spiridione, was currently an assembly member and a guarantor, from vast personal funds, of the republic's paper currency), the General called up additional artillery from regiments recently serving in Piedmont and from the arsenals at Verona, Mantua and Palmanova. While the cities and farms of the Veneto were being ransacked for supplies, engineers were busy organising trenches and ringing the fortress with gun batteries, howitzers and mortars. Nothing was to be left to chance, though even Haynau could scarcely dictate the vagaries of the weather. True to form in an Italian April, the rain fell relentlessly for the first three weeks, filling ditches and canals, flooding entrenchments and hampering the movement of cavalry and gun teams across the already spongy terrain. Radetzky, obsessed by now with the recapture of Venice for the sake of imperial honour, had already given orders for siege operations to begin, but it was not until 4 May that

Haynau could be satisfied that his disposition of forces was sufficiently advanced to carry out a serious attack. The Field Marshal himself, accompanied by three Habsburg archdukes, had come up from Verona to observe events from the top of the campanile of Mestre's principal church. With them were two of Radetzky's foreign enthusiasts, the Russian Prince Aleksandr Troubetzkoi and the Prussian General Willisen. So convinced of a speedy victory were they all that a painter was commissioned to travel with them to make preparatory sketches for a grand canvas showing their anticipated triumphal entry into Venice. Radetzky was confident enough that Marghera must fall by 7 May to order bottles to be thrown into the lagoon containing a report announcing this as a *fait accompli*.

The resourcefulness of the Italian staff officers inside the fort had already given the lie to any such expectations. As soon as the Austrians started digging in, a series of night raids on their trenches was begun by the Cacciatori del Sile, and orders were given to destroy some of the 222 arches of the great railway viaduct to prevent any sort of surprise thrust by Haynau's troops against the city itself by making a dash across the railway bridge. Admiral Graziani, Manin's naval triumvir, had wanted to demolish the whole structure, but neither the time nor the amount of explosives necessary was available. On Cavedalis's orders, however, several of the arches were mined, and it was up to Marghera's commander to decide when to detonate the charges.

The whole issue of the command was a tricky one, if only because of the variety of political tendencies favoured by the defenders. There were radical and not-so-radical Mazzinians, some moderate republicans, a few ex-Albertists and at least some whose devout Catholic religiosity kept them loyal to the old concept of an Italian federation headed by that ultimate broken reed of the revolution Pio Nono, whenever he should decide to return from Gaeta. For some time the majority formed by Mazzinian officers had been running a smear campaign against the current commander Captain Antonio Paolucci, whose father had been involved in the Venetian phase of the Bandiera affair and who himself had been instrumental in helping Manin seize control of the Arsenal on 22 March. His critics were growing impatient with his unwillingness to commit troops to the kind of heroic sortie which had caught the Austrians napping at Mestre in October. The last straw came when, during the earliest phase of the struggle for Marghera, Paolucci gave orders not to waste ammunition by firing when the enemy was still at too great a distance to offer a vulnerable target. This was sufficient ground for charges of treachery and of willingness to open the fort gates, especially since it was already known that the Captain's brother-in-law was a general in the Habsburg army. Pressure was stepped up by journalists and members of the republican clubs, and posters appeared all over Venice warning: 'Dear Manin, watch out for Paolucci!' The prime suspect, who, far from betraying his trust, had been instrumental in strengthening Marghera's defences, quietly stood down, yielding his place to one of General Pepe's staff officers, Girolamo Ulloa, and spent the remainder of the siege in hiding on the French warship *Pluton*.

In the late morning of 4 May 1849, the Austrian artillery launched its first bombardment. The plan at this stage, according to Karl von Schönhals, was to aim at the fort's interior rather than directly at the walls, so as to panic the garrison into speedy submission. Almost at once the realisation started to dawn on the distinguished company of brass hats, assorted archdukes and 'embedded' journalists and military historians gathered on the tower at Mestre, as it had dawned on those manning the batteries a mile or so off, that for accuracy and effectiveness the Venetian gunners could give as good as they got. After a few hours, during which the Italians were able to pinpoint the weaknesses in the current disposition of Austrian gun emplacements, knocking out at least one of the batteries, Haynau gave the order to halt the cannonade, while Radetzky began pondering the likelihood that if Marghera would not yield so quickly, the government within Venice itself might be persuaded to capitulate behind the defenders' backs. That evening he and his staff at Villa Papadopoli began preparing a singular document offering grace and clemency to the people of Venice (if not to their leaders), but reminding them that he was 'ready to let fall upon you the scourge of war *to the point of extermination* if you persist in following the path of rebellion, thus forfeiting any right to mercy from your lawful sovereign'. Total surrender of forts, ships and all materials of war was demanded, with a pardon to be given to non-commissioned officers and the rank and file. Twenty-four hours only were allowed for consideration of the various articles.

As a calculated insult to the Venetian government and to Colonel Ulloa as Marghera's commandant, Radetzky and Haynau had the document run off as a proclamation and sent, under flag of truce, as an open letter. Their idea was that those receiving it in the first instance would be bound to pass on the news and thus create a willing constituency for surrender. Once again the Austrians in their arrogance had misjudged the situation. Manin's response was a magnificent combination of politeness with implicit scorn for mere army officers as valid negotiators in a complex diplomatic process. As far as he was concerned, the international mediation involving Britain and France was by no means over, but he was willing to deal directly with a minister of the imperial government, 'should Your Excellency judge it opportune to reach a quicker and easier solution'. It was up to Radetzky, under the circumstances, to end hostilities so as to avoid useless bloodshed while the necessary talks were under way. Ulloa, on the other hand, was bluntly uncompromising in his answer to the copy of the proclamation he had received from Haynau. 'Without orders from the Venetian government I do not consider myself authorised to suspend hostilities; I shall therefore sustain my fire with renewed vigour, since you have plainly abused the proposed truce by continuing your engineering operations. Equally contrary to the rules of war is a dispatch of open letters to the commander of a besieged fortress. I am honoured to advise you that our sentries have formal consent to treat the bearer of any such letter as a spy and to deal with him accordingly.'

If Haynau was furious at Ulloa's defiance, Manin's letter to Radetzky, ending with a derisive flourish of civility – 'I beg Your Excellency to accept the expression of my highest esteem and perfect consideration' – sent the old Marshal, for his part, into such a paroxysm of rage that it was all the attendant archdukes could do to calm him down. His earlier mixture of blandishments and menaces having failed, he dashed off a few curt lines to the Venetian president, which should leave no doubt of his intentions. 'His Majesty our sovereign' – the 'our', as far as Radetzky was concerned, included the rebel Manin – 'having decided on no account to allow the intervention of foreign powers between him and his rebellious subjects, any such hope on the part of the revolutionary government in Venice is vain, illusory and calculated merely to deceive the unfortunate citizens. I shall therefore refrain from any further correspondence, deploring the fact that Venice should be fated to undergo a war.' In one respect at least Radetzky, by taking him at his word and refusing to treat with him directly, had outmanoeuvred Manin. An outright war footing meant that any government envoy hoping to negotiate directly with the imperial ministers would be denied a safe-conduct through Austrian territory. Since Manin was now planning to send the indefatigable Valentino Pasini, Venice's leading diplomatic representative in Paris, to Vienna, the only solution was to arrange diplomatic immunity via the French ambassador to the Habsburg court, a process which might take several weeks.

The mediation issue currently meant a good deal more to Manin than to most of his fellow Venetians. What mattered to them above all was that Marghera – its walls so ostentatiously bedecked with red-white-and-green Italian flags, the scarlet trousers of its officers so irritatingly visible to the archdukes on their tower – should be allowed to prove its worth as the citadel of Venice's freedom. When Radetzky's proclamation was being pondered by the triumvirs, Cavedalis seriously considered the idea of withdrawing the garrison from the fort to the railway bridge. The plan was quickly dropped when Ulloa, past whom he had run it, warned that such a decision must have a disastrous impact on morale, and that were it to be adopted, he would resign his command. Cavedalis needed to understand, he added, that the defenders were currently relishing their technical superiority over the enemy, hence it was not likely that any order at this stage to abandon everything and head for the viaduct would be obeyed. Cautious proposals from Cavedalis such as this one only served to contribute, in the minds of many patriots, to a growing idea of him as a pro-Austrian fifth-columnist, busy laying the ground for future surrender.

Ulloa had judged the mood correctly. When the enemy opened a fresh assault the next morning, the Italian gunners put up a still tougher fight than they had shown two days before. The Tuscan envoy Carlo Fenzi, who had resumed the post among the volunteers that he had occupied in 1848, praised the garrison's discipline and good order. 'In a few moments everyone had mustered and gone to their various bastions to man the guns. A formidable enemy bombardment was kept up until four o'clock. Cannon balls, bombs, grenades and musket shot came flying from all directions, as well as an immense quantity of congreve rockets, of which the Austrians make such wasteful use.' This time, with a few brief intervals, the pounding kept up for three days. At night, under torrential rain, Haynau's engineers dug out his next intended line of trenches, but volunteers on an Italian raid to spike the batteries opened the sluices of the nearby canal and flooded the new parallel before the attackers could make good use of it.

> Son passato per piazza Malghera,
>   tuto 'l sangue scoreva per tera;
> i tedeschi à perso la guera,
>   i 'taliani i è sta' i vincitor.

'I passed by the stronghold of Marghera, where the earth was covered in blood; the Germans [*sic*] have lost the war, the Italians are the victors,' wrote an anonymous Venetian dialect poet. It wasn't yet quite the truth, but the overall feeling among those inside the city was that stranger things had come to pass. Radetzky and his entourage were not the only ones watching the struggle for control of the fort. The bombardment and its answering salvoes had become a spectator sport for the people of Venice,

thronging the *fondamenta*,* clambering up to their roof terraces or
huddling in the bell towers of churches to view the ongoing drama from
what at this stage was a safe distance. In their midst was the gifted young
painter Luigi Querena, son of a teacher at the Accademia delle Belle Arti,
who had joined the volunteers defending the Lido and seems to have
served, for a time at least, in the Bandiera e Moro brigade.** His speciality
was tempera sketches of Venetian scenes, and since, at a period when
photography had barely come into its own, not a single camera appears
to have been available to record aspects of the siege, Querena's meticulous paintings, some of them on tiny pieces of paper three inches by five,
are among the most precious visual impressions of the entire episode we
possess. In them we can distinguish, like the anxious watchers from
Cannaregio, those plump little smoke clouds made by exploding shells;
fragments of shattered masonry hurtling into the air as an Austrian gunner
scores a direct hit on the ramparts; the zigzag trail of rocket fire; white-
tunicked imperial soldiers scrambling to rescue a gun battery; horse-drawn
supply trains clattering along the viaduct; the Italian flag fluttering from
rooftops and the masts of shipping; and – since Querena also took his
views from the landward side – the city of Venice, towered and domed,
for which the battle was now so fiercely on.

Anyone observing the Venetians going about their ordinary lives during
this phase of the siege must have realised how vain Radetzky's hopes had
been of reducing the town to a speedy surrender, by whatever principles
of carrot-and-stick. Carlo Fenzi wrote to his father, 'You cannot imagine
the tranquillity which reigns in Venice amid all this commotion. If it
were not for the continued rumble of gunfire brought to us when the
wind is in the appropriate quarter, it would be impossible to conceive
that we were living in a city under siege, cut off on every side. Piazza
San Marco remains the resort of an elegant crowd, strolling and taking
the air, happy in the assurance of better days to come.' Among the strollers
in the Piazza there was of course a perpetual hunger for news, and cafés
like Florian, Suttil and Quadri (where patriots now sat on the chairs once
exclusively occupied by Habsburg officers) were always busy with people
scanning the papers, poring over maps or simply studying the expressions
on others' faces for indication of some fresh triumph or catastrophe.

---

* A Venetian word without a plural, meaning a street running alongside a canal
or else, in the case of the long Fondamenta Nuove, beside the waters of the
lagoon.
** Details of Querena's military service during the revolution remain obscure,
and he himself may slightly have embroidered them in later years.

Outside in the colonnades of the Procuratie, the pillars were plastered with notices, manifestos, government bulletins and decrees, poetic tributes or snatches of important news from elsewhere in Italy. The sense of living from day to day had never been greater, but it was to increase as Venice became ever more aware that she was being abandoned by other Italian cities and states formerly in revolt, to carry the torch of liberty alone. Piedmont was still reeling from the humiliation of Charles Albert's last campaign, the duchies of Parma and Modena had been regained for their sovereigns with the help of Austrian troops blooded from Novara, and now another Habsburg army, under General Wimpffen, was marching into the northern area of the Papal States, known as the Legations, to seize Bologna, that nursery of patriot insurrection.

All this was ominous enough, but worse news was arriving from Sicily, Tuscany and Rome. The island realm of the Bourbons, cradle of the 1848 revolutions, had finally been recovered for King Ferdinand, and its liberal leaders dispatched to the various prison islands. In Tuscany meanwhile, the radical government had quickly exhausted its credit with the electorate through failure to achieve any sort of practical unity in the face of Austrian menaces to independence. Contemptuously Italy's greatest satirical poet, Giuseppe Giusti, dismissed his fellow Tuscans as 'slaves under the cloak of liberty'. The panic induced by Novara saw the onset of a counter-revolution, and on 24 April General D'Aspre, having proclaimed martial law in Parma, began advancing towards the Apennine frontier dividing the two states. Negotiations were now opened between the new moderate administration in Florence and Grand Duke Leopold, who had beguiled his self-imposed exile at Gaeta by engaging his daughter Isabella to a younger son of his host the King of Naples, in an attempt to tighten the already powerful family bonds between Italy's sovereigns. Though the radical stronghold of Leghorn would hold out for a few days against the invading Austrians, the rest of Leopold's domains prepared to welcome him as a lost father. When he eventually re-entered his dukedom, it was with Habsburg troops at his heels and a pledge to himself that he would govern as an absolute ruler, 'awaiting illumination and guidance from the spirit of the time and the example of other sovereigns'. Watching the Grand Duke's return to Florence from her house near Palazzo Pitti, the English poet Elizabeth Barrett Browning gloomily pondered the collapse of revolution under:

> Austria's thousands. Sword and bayonet,
> Horse, foot, artillery – cannons rolling on,
> Like blind slow storm-clouds gestant with the heat

Of undeveloped lightnings, each bestrode
By a single man, dust-white from head to heel,
Indifferent as the dreadful thing he rode.

At Gaeta, Leopold had left Pope Pius waiting on events. Ironically it was not Austrian guns but those of France that were now preparing to batter Mazzini's Roman republic into submission. The Prince-President Louis Napoleon had been anxious both to safeguard French influence in Italy against a revived Habsburg ascendancy and to secure support from Catholics eager for the sovereign pontiff's full restoration. In an unctuous official statement, the Foreign Secretary Drouyn de Lhuys announced that the dispatch of a 10,000-strong expeditionary force to Civitavecchia under General Oudinot would enable His Holiness 'to be placed in a situation which must guarantee both Europe and Italy against fresh perturbation, without harm to either the balance of power or the independence of Italian states'. On 25 April Oudinot's force disembarked with orders to march on Rome, where they would be welcomed as liberators, reconciling the Pope to his erring subjects. Force must only be used if the revolutionary government offered armed opposition. The barely credible prospect now unfolded of republican France, guardian of revolutionary values, becoming the champion of legitimist reaction. What Oudinot and his government had not bargained for was the potency of feeling within Rome itself against any restoration of the papal regime on its former footing. Added to which, two days after the French landed, no less a figure than Giuseppe Garibaldi marched his legion into the city, raising its armed strength to 17,000 men. As Mazzini saw it, a crucial battle was about to commence for Italy's soul, with Rome forming the symbolic centre of the struggle.

Where Daniele Manin was concerned, the fact that France's military intervention, so long delayed, had finally taken place in favour of restoring a despotic government ought to have dealt a death-blow to one of his most cherished expectations. As it was, he persisted in hoping against hope that somehow the French must at length weigh in on Venice's side. The old obsession with legality conditioned his view of the current situation. If France – and possibly Britain – could offer some sort of diplomatic counterpoise to Habsburg strong-arm tactics, the Venetian government might gain considerably from the recognition of its legitimate status that would surely follow. Manin seems to have had no adequate briefing on the changed nature of the Austrian administration now that Emperor Franz Josef had assumed the crown. Though the French chargé d'affaires replied sooner than expected to his request for Pasini's safe-conduct, it was to announce, with what seemed like genuine regret, that the government in Vienna remained inflexible in its determination not to deal directly with what it considered a rebel regime. If Manin and his fellow ministers wished to open negotiations, Schwarzenberg had curtly answered, these had better be with Radetzky, who had been given the appropriate powers.

The sole response Venice was likely to give the Field Marshal lay in the mouths of Marghera's guns, but after a dawn reconnaissance raid by the Italians into the Austrian lines on 9 May, both sides confined themselves, for the next two weeks, to a campaign of attrition. Haynau's strategy took the form of offensive parallels, a sequence of gradually advancing lines of attack. When the second of these was opened up only 500 yards from the outer ditches of the fort, he took care to replace the soldiers who had dug out the earlier line of trenches with more easily expendable forced-labour gangs of local peasants. Meanwhile the battery at Campalto, an Achilles heel in his first attempts at reducing Marghera, was reinforced with thirty-two heavy cannon of the type known as 'Paixhans',* and Ulloa's raiders could do little to hinder the ongoing siegeworks.

Behind the ramparts the mood of defiance hardened as the Austrians consolidated their next major onslaught. Though everyone praised the bravery of the Neapolitans, they received more than adequate support from the various Venetian corps they had helped to knock into shape. A positively cavalier attitude to the shell-bursts and explosions around them endured even among those gravely wounded, as they were rushed to hospital in the horse-drawn ambulances plying to and fro across the viaduct. One man having his arm amputated sang Mercadante's 'Chi per la patria muor', the very same operatic anthem to which the Cosenza martyrs had walked to face the firing squad; another, whose leg was being sawn off, heard a friend cry out 'Courage!' and called back at once, 'You are the one who needs courage, I have done my part!' before slumping back dead. When Giuseppe Finzi of the Bandiera e Moro brigade caught a heavy fragment of shell in his thigh, he asked for his father to be present during the inevitable amputation at the Santa Chiara hospital, so that he could be comforted by the recitation of Hebrew psalms. Finzi endured the surgeon's saw with exemplary courage, but died from loss of blood, to the sound of his weeping parents pronouncing verses from the Book

* From their inventor, the French general Louis Paixhans. First used in 1822, they had a maximum 28 cm calibre and were a cross between a cannon and a mortar.

of Job. His comrade Domenico Baroni of Rovigo was no luckier. His knee smashed by a cannon ball, he too was rushed to theatre, only to die 'with the word "Italy" on his lips'. A happier fate, for the time being, attended Pietro Salgaro, a young miller from the village of Arzignano near Vicenza. After joining one of the volunteer corps fighting alongside General Durando's army, he served under Garibaldi in the alpine foothills around Lake Como before becoming a gunner at Marghera. Wounded in both legs, he was brought to Santa Chiara for amputation, and the right limb was successfully removed. This operation was conducted without anaesthetic, and Salgaro was understandably doubtful as to having to undergo the whole ghastly process once again. From somewhere in the hospital, however, a supply of ether was produced, and with the help of mustard plasters to revive him, Salgaro came through for the second time.

Among other Jewish boys serving with Giuseppe Finzi in the Bandiera e Moro artillery was Alessandro Levi, who had devised a novel means of communicating with the family he was unlikely to see while the assault on Marghera was reaching its critical phase. His pet dog, managing somehow to evade Austrian bullets and grenades, was sent home each day with messages tied to its collar, and would return to the fort with little cakes, batches of biscuits and other goodies prepared by his mother. One afternoon the animal failed to appear outside the door, and Signora Levi, realising at once what had happened, began frantically searching the wards for her son. Bed after bed revealed unfamiliar faces, and she had almost given up hope when she noticed a telltale sign peeping between the bandages swathing an otherwise indistinguishable figure. It was the *tsitsith*, the girdle of fringes worn by orthodox Jews, and underneath was Alessandro, barely conscious but at least alive. What had become of the dog is, alas, not recorded.

Conditions at Venice's six hospitals had notably improved since the Ladies' Committee began its work the previous autumn. Until then the wards had been overcrowded, the beds were flea-ridden straw mattresses, doctors cultivated indifference in order to deal adequately with the maximum number of emergency cases as opposed to minor injuries, and the nurses were so badly paid that they tried to make extra money by selling food and drink to the patients. A dead soldier's property was seen as a perk of the job. 'No sooner has he breathed his last,' wrote the Swiss colonel Jean Debrunner, 'than the nurses rush upon him like hungry wolves, bundling his effects together and seizing the little money he has been able to hide under his pillow.' The body was often flung naked into the grave because there was nobody to see to the making of a coffin, but Debrunner's largely Protestant contingent was less worried by this prospect than by the ministrations of the Capuchin friars, who prowled the wards seeking to redeem heretics from the damnation that Catholic teaching viewed as otherwise inevitable. 'So as to flatter themselves on having snatched a soul from the devil, these propagandists tormented the wounded man on his bed of pain. Even in his final moments they did not cease from pestering him.' At length Debrunner managed to gather his Swiss into a single ward, which became known to the nurses as 'the heretics' room'.

Some consolation for the heroes of Marghera was afforded on 16 May, when General Haynau was transferred from directing the siege to leading the army Austria had prepared to send into Hungary against the spectacularly successful operations of rebel forces under Artur Görgey. A chemistry student from Prague University, Görgey had no military experience beyond a brief spell as a subaltern in a Bohemian regiment. Though he antagonised most members of the Hungarian revolutionary government now based in Debreczen, including its leader Lajos Kossuth, he showed an improvisatory brilliance against the Habsburg troops which unsettled Franz Josef and Prince Schwarzenberg, who were congratulating themselves on having almost completed the task of pacifying Italy. They were forced at length to call for help, both financial and military, from Tsar Nicholas I of Russia to recover the breakaway Hungarian realm, while Haynau was brought forward as an ideally uncompromising carrier of fire and sword among Görgey's rebel hosts and the peasantry that supported them.

Kossuth, effectively Hungary's dictator, acted swiftly to forge links with other governments either hostile to Austria or likely to favour his people's bid for freedom. Venice was an obviously promising contact, and Manin had already given some assistance by issuing a proclamation urging Italian soldiers in imperial regiments serving in Hungary to lay down their arms. In addition, an entire Italian patriot legion had set off to join Görgey's insurgent army, beside whom it would fight bravely until the rebellion was crushed by combined Austrian and Russian forces. Meanwhile Kossuth sent General Jan Bratich as chargé d'affaires to meet Venetian representatives at Ancona, with instructions to 'do whatever may be opportune to harm the Austrian army, whether by making use of Hungarian soldiers fighting in the imperial ranks in Italy or else by concluding military alliances with Italian states currently at war with Austria'. Kossuth's broader plan, set out in the agreement eventually reached at Ancona, was for an offensive-defensive alliance which should involve Hungarian seizure of Austrian warships at Fiume, an invasion of Friuli through Slovenia and northern Croatia, and a corresponding attack on Austrian mainland positions by the armed forces concentrated within Venice.

The whole wildly ambitious scheme depended on Görgey and the other Hungarian generals, Klapka, Bem and Sandor, being able to sustain the splendid impetus that had driven the Austrians back almost to the gates of Vienna. For the Venetians it was more than a crumb of comfort during the summer of 1849. The government's paper currency – *la moneta patriotica* – picked up in value in expectation of Hungarian subsidies, and rumours of the arrival of Görgey's army outside Trieste or even in Vienna itself continued to hearten the beleaguered city. The truth, alas, was that once Schwarzenberg and Tsar Nicholas had concluded their pact, the Ancona articles were worth no more than the paper on which they had been written. The only Hungarians Venice would ever see were the members of Lajos Winkler's little legion of renegades. By professional soldiers Winkler himself, far from being hailed as a hero for his noble forbearance on 22 March, was despised for disloyalty to his sovereign as a serving officer (a case, among the Neapolitans, of the pot calling the kettle black, given their own refusal to obey King Ferdinand's orders). As for his fifty-six followers, according to Debrunner they were a wretched crew, ill disciplined, slovenly and generally unreliable, fit only for service in 'soft' positions around the lagoon, such as the islands of Murano and Burano.

Haynau's successor as Austrian commander in Mestre was Lieutenant-Field Marshal Count Georg Thurn von Valle Sassina, who had already distinguished himself by his dogged insistence on obeying Radetzky's orders to the letter at Novara. The weather during mid-May did not help the Austrian siege effort, with heavy rain flooding the trenches and turning roads into quagmires, but Thurn was determined to carry on as Haynau had begun. By 23 May nineteen batteries of eighty-eight guns in all were ready for action, while inside the fort the Italians made final preparations for the bombardment they realised must decide Marghera's fate as the front-line redoubt of Venetian defences. Spirits had been lifted by the news, received a day or so earlier, of two dramatically successful foraging raids from the forts at Treporti and Brondolo, at either end of the lagoon. The former's commander, Francesco Baldisserotto, was able to round up several hundred cattle, pigs and chickens from under the noses of the Austrians, and at Brondolo a 1,200-strong force under Antonio Morandi secured barrels of wine and baskets of eggs in addition to livestock, managing to take eight prisoners. All of them, it was noted, were suffering from scurvy.

At daybreak on 24 May the ninety-six cannon, twenty-four howitzers and five mortars of the Austrian artillery opened fire on Marghera, answered by an equally ferocious cannonade from the fort guns. The thunder of the batteries shook the earth, the houses of Mestre and that very tower on which the archdukes and historians had once again gathered to observe the siege. At one time eighteen to twenty projectiles per minute were counted whizzing to and fro under the drizzling sky. In less than two hours, seventeen of the patriot guns were knocked out, three powder magazines were blown up and 130 of the defenders killed or wounded. Against this ominous background the citizens of Venice continued their devotions on behalf of the garrison. 'It was a moving spectacle,' remembered General Cavedalis. 'As an answer to the rumbling of the guns echoed by the four winds from land and sea, and to the sacrifice and misery inflicted on the whole community, came the daily ringing of the bells, the chanting of the priests and the prayers of the faithful to the God of battles.'

When not praying, as many as possible crowded to the rooftops and bell towers to watch the bombardment, taking their telescopes and opera glasses with them. Under the cloudy sky, or as night fell, the Austrian flares offered a bizarre enchantment. At a given altitude a little cotton parachute would open, revealing a brilliant yellow flame. For a moment the flare remained suspended in the air before slowly descending and illuminating a surface area 'as if with the most beautiful moonlight'. Among those captivated, while simultaneously chilled by the whole spectacle, was the German businessman Friedrich Bertuch, watching from the *altana* of an apartment belonging to a painter friend in the enormous Palazzo Pisani on Campo San Stefano. 'What a scene we beheld through all the dust and cannon smoke! The impact and explosion of the shells in the courtyards of the fortress were easily visible, as were the people standing nearby who threw themselves to the ground. Seldom did all of them then get up again. When the wind dropped, however, there was little to be seen beyond the thick masses of gunsmoke and the whirling clouds of dust raised by the bombs striking walls and towers.'

At dusk the cannon ceased firing, but howitzers, mortars and shrapnel grenades kept up their pounding throughout the night. By the evening of 25 May, another 150 men were *hors de combat* in the fort, and the spectacle presented to Luigi Girardi of the Bandiera e Moro legion was one of barely imaginable horror. 'Cracked heads, shattered breastbones, broken arms, splintered legs, blood and brains squirting, spraying and bouncing up into your face, induced a sensation of searing pity mixed with rage, a desire to weep like a baby mixed with the bloodlust of a lion.' In the red dawn of the following day, with continued flashes of fire from the bombardment, the lagoon, through the stifling blanket of smoke, 'looked like the mirror of hell'. The great bastions of the fort lay all in ruins, the central barrack square was pitted with huge craters and the barracks themselves totally destroyed. Girardi's disgust was heightened by the reflection that defending Marghera had been pointless from the start, an act of folly on the part of the government, solely in aid of sustaining Venetian popular morale. Manin, he believed, was entirely unsuited to the post of dictator to which the assembly had summoned him in April.

Clearly he knew nothing of the original disagreement between Cavedalis and Ulloa, in which the former's recommendation to quit the fortress and concentrate on defending Venice from the railway bridge had been brushed aside by the latter as wholly unacceptable to those under his command. After another day's relentless battering from the Austrian guns, with the patriot artillerymen exhausted, provisions running low and the drinking water contaminated by shell fragments and falling masonry, even the most fervent of the defenders were beginning to grasp the hopelessness of their position. It became obvious, what was more, that the navy could no longer provide adequate support, as there were not enough sailors to man the *trabaccoli* used to carry provisions and ammunition. On the afternoon of 26 May therefore, after spies had reported further troop movements and reinforcement of the batteries, Manin, Cavedalis and Pepe, with Ulloa's reluctant consent, took the decision to evacuate Marghera. The process was to start that very evening, as soon as darkness fell, and in order to distract the enemy, the batteries of the smaller fort to the south-west (formerly known as 'Eau' or 'O', but now rebaptised 'Manin') were to keep up a desultory fire.

In danger from continued shelling by Austrian howitzers and mortars, the 800 surviving members of the defence force carried out their retreat under Ulloa's direction with that mixture of fearlessness and iron discipline which had characterised them throughout previous weeks. First the gunners of the southern bastions slipped away into boats moored in the nearby canal; an hour later the Cacciatori del Sile, Colonel Galateo's brigade and the naval volunteers left via the railway bridge; and finally the remaining artillerymen, Johann Debrunner's Swiss and the civic-guard battalion followed them. Ulloa, Sirtori and a few others stayed to organise transferring the wounded to boats and ambulances. The very last person to leave was Cesare Morosini, a member of the Bandiera e Moro brigade – appropriately, given its special association with Marghera. Waiting to set off across the viaduct, he had been standing beside his pal, Jacopo Da Lio, a young law student who had come through all the major action in the Veneto last summer, only to die now when an Austrian shell blew off his head. Morosini dragged the body to a waiting gondola, but finding the boatman drunk, he seized the oar like a good Venetian and steered through the rain of shellfire and the gleam of parachute flares to the mortuary at Santa Clara.

In the darkness outside the shattered walls Girolamo Ulloa had an important task to perform. When at the beginning of May Cavedalis had originally suggested abandoning the fort, he had also given orders for the landward arches of the viaduct to be mined and told Ulloa that he could detonate the charges at his own discretion. If the bridge was now to become Venice's front line against the Austrians, its basic function – the very same that John Ruskin had so deplored on its opening three years previously – as a communication link with the mainland must be rendered useless forthwith. Along the whole structure the architects, Giovanni Battista Meduna and Giovanni Duodo, had constructed a sequence of open spaces with larger *piazzali* at either end. Gun batteries had been set up in several of these, and it was from the landward *piazzale* that Ulloa now lit the fuses for the mines, destroying the whole western section of the bridge. Militarily this was by no means an ideal solution, since the Austrians could easily scramble together a defensive position out of the heap of ruined masonry, but at least it ruled out any further possibility of an attempt to rush the viaduct and force an entry into the city.

Not only Marghera itself, but Forts Manin and San Giuliano were both to be evacuated. At the latter, most of the garrison had panicked and fled, leaving just twelve men to maintain a token defence until Sirtori arrived to supervise their departure. Once they were ready to leave, he spiked the guns and booby-trapped the little fort's powder magazine as a savage act of revenge for the dishonour forced upon his companions by the superiority of Austrian fire-power. The bombardment kept up through the night, until a party of Styrian chasseurs, assuming the Italian guns had fallen silent as a prelude to surrender, edged towards Marghera's ramparts in the earliest light of dawn and realised its defenders had melted away. Those arriving at San Giuliano soon afterwards were less fortunate. Sirtori's trap worked with lethal precision, killing the first four of a sixty-eight-man detachment together with their commander Captain Kopecky. Despite this, the Austrian officers were generous in their praise of the Marghera garrison. Schönhals, despite rubbishing the evacuation procedure as thoroughly chaotic, states that 'our enemies fought with an admirable heroism and our soldiers, surveying the desolation within the ruins, gave unanimous homage to adversaries so well worthy of them'. A Viennese newspaper correspondent spoke admiringly of 'the brave garrison', praising 'the men who could maintain a fire so well directed'. One of the Austrian officers entering the fort on the morning of 27 May read into the devastated condition of walls and bastions sufficient evidence of courage under fire without needing to invoke it as proof that Italians could fight if they wished, or to mark Marghera's fall as a feather in Radetzky's cap. 'As I advanced further amid the ruins, the scene appeared ever more dismal,' he wrote. 'It is impossible to give any idea of the state to which this place has been reduced. Every two paces one comes across a shell hole. The ground is littered with shit and all the heavy guns have been rendered unserviceable. We must give honour where it is due: the Marghera garrison behaved valorously and everyone here acknowledges this. No other force could have sustained the defence for as long as they did.' Even Clinton Dawkins, not exactly noted for his generosity to the patriots, felt able to tell Palmerston, 'I must take this opportunity of acknowledging that during this siege, the garrison of Marghera displayed a courage and firmness which I did not anticipate and which the opinions I have frequently expressed may not have led Your Lordship to expect.'

In Venice itself, though commendation of the defenders' heroism was universal, and suitable plaudits were given to Debrunner's Swiss, to the doctors and medical orderlies and the various priests who braved flying shells to minister to the wounded and dying, serious doubts were raised as to the usefulness of holding Marghera in the first place. Cavedalis, for instance, maintained that the evacuation had only just been managed in the nick of time. 'One day more and Venice would have been lost.' Debrunner, never easily impressed by the military professionalism of the Italians for whose cause he and his Swiss from the Protestant cantons had chosen to fight, noted sardonically that the Austrians immediately made use of the ruined bridge arches as the foundation for a new gun battery.

Had the month-long struggle for Marghera been after all so pointless? Not if we consider both the damage to Austrian complacency and the drain on the besiegers' resources, whether of ammunition or of manpower. Haynau, Thurn and Radetzky had been unprepared for such a determined and lethal resistance, whose day-by-day effect was that of emphasising the more unimaginative aspects of their strategy for the benefit of the Italians. Much could be learned as to Austrian defects in the deployment of artillery, the use of trenches and attempts at cutting off the defenders' links with the city or the wider lagoon. Surely the most significant aspect of the whole affair lay in the simple fact that the forts had never actually been surrendered in any formal sense. The patriots had contrived merely to slip away under cover of night, mocking their attackers in the process, with Sirtori's death-dealing practical joke at San Giuliano providing a ghastly coda to what had been a most accomplished performance. Thus, without dishonour, the surviving defenders could fight on, in the batteries along the railway bridge, the smaller forts on the Lido or on the edges of the city itself. General Pepe could freely praise the bravery of what he called 'these dear Italian youths' and urge them to take as their motto Milton's maxim in *Paradise Lost*: 'Better to reign in hell than serve in heaven'.* Jubilantly Niccolò Tommaseo hailed a psychological victory for the patriot actors in Felix Schwarzenberg's 'theatre of the play's misadventures'. Had they not, after all, avenged the shame brought on Venice fifty years earlier by the Treaty of Campoformio? 'You young men who fought at Marghera, you have salvaged our honour in the name of this ancient city. From the not inactive silence of my study, where love of my country keeps me prisoner so as to remove all excuse for trivial discords, I bless you on behalf of every generous soul. Even when abandoned, Marghera is more than ever ours by right, since it was won through the shedding of our brothers' blood. That blood shall not have been spent in vain. Such losses are more honourable than victories.'

Tommaseo's point was not lost on the Venetians. Far from unnerving them with the capture of their guardian stronghold, the Austrians had engendered a new spirit of stubborn defiance within the very populace which they and their supporters among European legitimists and conservatives had believed it easiest to subdue, the supposedly exhausted, nerveless inhabitants of a city controlled by a caucus of demagogues misguidedly seeking to revive its political autonomy. With Marghera's fall, the siege – from being a spectator event in which soldiers, professional and amateur, performed daily in front of a civilian audience – now became everyone's affair, from the oldest to the youngest, from the patrician in his palace on the Grand Canal to the beggarwoman crouched at the nearby bridge-foot, from the lawyer and the priest to the fishwife, the market girl and the gondolier. Admittedly the resulting burdens of hunger, homelessness, disease and death would not be gladly endured by everyone in the name of a sacred cause, and the image of universal fortitude purveyed by Risorgimento chroniclers and artists following Italy's unification is to some degree misleading. What remains impressive, nevertheless, is the continued readiness of most ordinary Venetians to believe in the essential value of the struggle, even as the odds became more heavily stacked against them. The oldest lesson of siege warfare, invariably ignored by those massed

---

* Pepe had conveniently forgotten – or perhaps not – that the original speaker of these words is Satan.

outside the walls ready for the final assault, is that even if history records a city's successful capture, far less kudos accrues from this than from the moral victory earned by the courage of its vanquished defenders.

'Radetzky's sabre-rattling,' observed the French consul Vasseur, 'has produced exactly the opposite effect to what he anticipated. Dread of being subjected to the mercies of the Croats has inspired the more timid members of the populace to take their places alongside the most determined partisans of resistance.' Three days after the evacuation of Marghera, Daniele Manin sat down to compile a list of personal bequests to his family and friends, a species of codicil to his will clearly inspired by a sense of the challenge now confronting him as dictator of beleaguered Venice. At its close he wrote the words, 'La vita sta in man di Dio, l'onore in man nostra', 'Life is in God's hands, honour in our own'. For better or worse, this principle would guide him through one of the most glorious, terrible and astounding moments his city had known in the thousand years of her existence.

CHAPTER 14

∾

AUSTRIA PLAYS FOR TIME

FOR MOST VENETIANS WITH ANY feeling for history – and these, according to foreign visitors, included even the poorest and least educated – the relationship between their city and the sea whence it arose was an eternal symbiosis, a bond whose emblematic significance could never fade even when Venice as a trading emporium declined, its maritime empire became a dead letter and the island fishing communities sank into poverty. It was the sea that had brought wealth and power to the medieval republic long before its grip extended across the north Italian mainland; it was on the sea that Vettor Pisani and Carlo Zen, in 1380, had led the Venetian fleet to a decisive victory at Chioggia against their commercial rivals, the Genoese; and it was the oared galleys of Venice which, in 1571, had borne the brunt of the great battle of Lepanto, in a combined operation by the navies of the Catholic powers of Europe against that of the Turkish sultan Murad.

Lepanto in fact did no lasting damage to the Ottomans in their successful bid to seize what was left of La Serenissima's Mediterranean empire, but for the Venetians the fight became symbolic of that mastery of the waves which their doges already enacted in the magnificent Festa della Sensa, the republic's marriage to the Adriatic, staged with the utmost pomp each year on Ascension Day. The waters had saved Venice from the Turks, just as they had protected it from the Frankish host of King Pepin or from the marauding Magyars, and rescued its earliest inhabitants from Attila the Hun. Thus it was not unreasonable for the Venetians of 1849 to hope that the maritime connection might once again baffle the city's enemies. Something of the old naval spirit, remembered from the Serenissima's last years, might perhaps revive. The disastrous mishandling, after 22 March 1848, of the process whereby the Austrian fleet at Pola could easily have been induced to declare for the provisional government had led easily enough to a naval blockade of the lagoon by imperial ships. Venice, however, had its own fleet in being, and there was no reason why it should not be put to good use, now that the grip of a major siege operation began tightening around the city.

The truth was that during the previous autumn and winter Venice had learned to live with the blockade. The Austrian naval arm, stretching along the narrow spit of island and shoreline running with brief inter-ruptions from Treporti to Chioggia, consisted of two frigates, a corvette and a pair of brigs, watching from a safe distance on the open Adriatic as six steamers, requisitioned from the Triestine Lloyd line and converted to gunboats, plied up and down on continuous patrol. With an obvious finger-snap in the face of the Italian revolutionaries, the imperial govern-ment had carefully renamed several of the ships after land battles won by Radetzky and his generals: *Curtatone*, *Custoza*, and so on. Throughout 1848 their function, nevertheless, seems to have been confined to the purely representative. Fishing vessels came and went through the chan-nels into the lagoon at Chioggia, Alberoni and Punta Sabbioni, and though foreign merchant ships were prevented from entering the port, a surprising amount of supplies continued to reach Venice by the agency of intrepid smugglers, with whom the provisional government soon reached a mutually satisfactory accord.

Once the new regime of Franz Josef and Schwarzenberg had taken over in Vienna, Radetzky had consolidated his recapture of Lombardy, and Haynau had taken control of operations in the Veneto, imperial desperation to recover Venice meant that the blockade must both do and be seen to do its intended work. The trouble was that Austria, with Admiral Bandiera retired in chagrin at his sons' dishonour and his fellow commander Paolucci disgraced for allowing Emilio Bandiera to escape to Corfu, had nobody to replace them. Marinovich from the Arsenal might have stepped efficiently into the breach, had he not so inconveniently been murdered on the eve of the revolution. The sole remedy, humili-ating though it appeared on the surface, was to commission a competent foreigner, preferably from a power not tainted (as Britain and France undoubtedly were) by suspect political sympathies – a power that had not experienced such serious internal disorder during the past year that its armed forces could no longer be relied upon to carry out their tasks without question or prevarication.

Denmark, with an old-established naval tradition, was the obvious choice. Austro-Danish relations had always been cordial, and in sending to Copenhagen for a spare admiral, Schwarzenberg, with his keen sense of irony, must have been tickled by the reflection that it was the Danes to whom Emperor Francis I had originally sold off the battleships of the Serene Republic when he assumed control of Venice and her territories. Vienna's special envoy, Count Karolyi, set out for the northern capital during February 1849, and by the end of the month the rank of rear-admiral, commanding the imperial navy on its Italian stations, had been offered to Hans Birch Dahlerup, an experienced officer who used his southward journey to identify the precise difficulties facing him in his new post. In Hamburg he met Marshal Marmont and his wife, frightened out of Venice the previous March after threats were made against them following Manin's release from prison, who gave him some idea of the background to the current situation. At Vienna he listened attentively to General Welden's warning that discipline and morale in the fleet had totally collapsed, its officers now spending their time hanging around the cafés and theatres of the various ports they visited. In Trieste, Dahlerup (who spoke very good English and had produced an Anglo-Danish seaman's manual) was told by the captain of HM frigate *Ardent* that he would have his work cut out among the various crews. 'A greater set of rascals I never saw in my life! If you can make anything of them, you will certainly deserve the greatest honour!'

Dahlerup turned out to be an excellent choice. His lively memoir of five months spent directing the blockade reveals a man of integrity and good sense, loyal to his new masters yet well aware that the enemy on the other side of the lagoon was not simply a crew of posturing fanatics, but a people prepared to show fight in the name of their dedication to a common cause. He had no illusions as to how much work needed to be done before the fleet was ready to tackle those jobs of interception and patrolling in which it had so far failed to make a serious impact. A more sophisticated navigational system was introduced, discipline was shaken up and the crews were issued with boat cloaks, pea jackets and uniform caps, where many of them before had gone almost naked. Something needed to be done, as well, about their slackness on watch. At sunset they were in the habit of settling down to sleep on deck, but Dahlerup soon introduced a system of night patrols to create an unslackened cordon along the lagoon's eastern littoral. Sailors were rewarded with improved pay, and the new admiral prided himself on instituting regular meals, with better food. 'For breakfast,' he notes with pride, 'instead of stinking sardines and cheese, I ordered hot coffee, sugar and bread.'

The army officers in Mestre were delighted with these improvements. Visiting headquarters, Dahlerup was surprised and not a little amused at having to receive enthusiastic kisses from both Haynau and Radętzky, the latter exclaiming, when the Dane offered a diffident cheek, 'No, on the mouth, on the mouth! This is a comrade's kiss, a brother's kiss!' He was taken up the tower to meet the archdukes and historians, and admired the splendid view across the Austrian entrenchments, with Marghera and the railway bridge in the middle distance and the prospect of the city beyond, as unforgettable as it was unget-at-able.

Nevertheless, for all Dahlerup's skill in making the blockade a working reality by the end of April 1849, it ought to have been possible for the rebel fleet to sustain some kind of low-level attrition against Austrian vessels so as to break the stranglehold at various points, if not actually do serious damage to any of the larger craft involved. In spite of the blockade's increased effectiveness, a breakthrough from the open sea to attack Venice was impossible without proper command of the channels through the lagoon. The Venetian navy, besides policing these, might easily have ventured out beyond the Lido to offer a serious menace to the new system of coastal patrols. Nearly ninety ships of various kinds stood ready, from the corvettes and brigs seized on 22 March to the gunboats which had managed to cut loose from Pola and a whole flotilla of armoured fishing smacks and sailing barges. These could have ensured the free passage of arms and food supplies, spirited in by venturesome captains from ports in the Papal States and even from the smaller coastal towns in the Kingdom of Naples. As it was, the entire contingent was destined, for the time being, to lie idle, mocking the expectations of those who saw it as the ultimate agent of Venice's deliverance. To make matters worse, the patriotism of the crews themselves was in many cases suspect, composed as these often were of Istrian and Dalmatian sailors. During the early months of 1849 as many as seventy men were committed for trial on disciplinary grounds and at least one was shot as a traitor.

By the time the Austrians regained Marghera, accusations of treachery against members of the assembly, against priests, merchants and even several of the fort's most gallant defenders, let alone against the foreign consuls (more especially the unsympathetic Clinton Dawkins), were two a penny among the Venetians. A week after the army had retreated to the batteries on or around the railway bridge there occurred one of the most unfortunate examples of such hysterical finger-pointing. A building labourer named Agostino Stefani, moved by no more ignoble impulse than simple patriotism, came to see General Ulloa asking to be allowed to touch off the remaining mines at the western end of the bridge. Failing at his first attempt, Stefani courageously determined to try again, but this time his boat capsized and he was forced to swim towards the Piazzale battery as Austrian bullets peppered the water around him. Instead of being hailed as a hero by the Italian officers who happened to be supervising fortification work on the battery, he found himself placed under arrest and carried once more into Ulloa's presence. When they accused him of trying to swim towards rather than away from the enemy, the poor man, by now traumatised both mentally and physically, was unable to speak and could display his outraged denial solely through gestures. As Ulloa had only given permission for the first of Stefani's bids to touch off the fuses, he thought it best to clear up the matter with the government's Committee of Public Vigilance, and arrangements were made to take the prisoner to the relevant office within the city.

A boat set off towards the entrance to the Grand Canal, but as it crossed the lagoon, Stefani recovered his powers of speech sufficiently to protest to his guards that the second attempt had indeed been officially authorised, this time by a senior officer whom he could only identify by the fact that he wore spectacles. This was none other than Ulloa's fellow Neapolitan Colonel Enrico Cosenz, who, having learned of the arrest, now jumped into another gondola in the hope of catching up and verifying the prisoner's good character. Too late, alas, for the rumour of treachery had swept with horrifying swiftness across the bridge into Cannaregio, and as the boat carrying Stefani came to land, a waiting mob dragged him onto the quay and hacked him to death as a spy. To Niccolò Tommaseo, who demanded that the state take charge of the victim's family and composed his memorial inscription, to Ulloa, who doubtless regretted his haste in ordering the committal, and to Manin, for whom popular sentiment was an important barometer, the whole episode served to warn of a new and menacing volatility in the civic mood, as Venice braced herself against what seemed likely to be the first all-out Austrian attack on the city itself, fuelled by a surge in confidence following the triumphant repossession of the forts.

The assumption that Thurn, encouraged by Radetzky, would lay on a major offensive was legitimate enough, but in reality the Habsburg army, far from preparing to capitalise on its new advantage, was counting the cost of nearly a year spent as a largely inactive force engaged in an attenuated holding operation against a surprisingly resilient enemy. The imperial government had always lived well beyond its means, and the maintenance of 20,000 troops during Welden's spell as area commander had been expensive enough. Under Haynau's vigorous reorganisation, an extra 10,000 men had been brought up from Milan, Mantua and the garrisons charged with ensuring restoration of the old order in the duchies of Modena, Parma and Tuscany. Their material well being could not easily be guaranteed. The commissariat, while scarcely as chaotic as it had been among Charles Albert's regiments, remained a problem for the quarter-masters in traditionally impoverished regions such as the eastern Veneto or the always benighted Polesine to the south. Sedentary concentrations of troops brought additional hazards created by inadequate sanitation and personal hygiene. Epidemic diseases like typhus, cholera and dysentery, having undermined the effectiveness of Welden's force, continued to ravage the augmented siege army. Add to these anxieties the current success of Hungary's rebel generals against the army that Haynau had recently been summoned to command, and it was no wonder the government in Vienna should have begun to ponder negotiation with Venice as a reasonable alternative to bombardment.

A skilful plenipotentiary stood ready in the person of fifty-year-old Karl von Bruck,* Finance Minister in Schwarzenberg's administration and one of the most able and imaginative figures on the Austrian political scene after Metternich's fall. Well acquainted with Italian affairs as a busi-nessman in Trieste (where he had founded the Lloyd steamship line), Bruck was centrally involved in the affairs of the Venice–Milan 'Ferdinandea' railway and became a trusted friend of Radetzky. The Field Marshal had put forward Bruck's name as a possible negotiator, but if Schwarzenberg concurred, it was perhaps owing to the reflection that little had so far been achieved by the high command's brusqueness in its dealings with the rebels. A polite and conciliatory civilian representative, apparently ready to work out an acceptable agreement (which could always be torn up once the city was in imperial hands), might yet engineer the submission which Marghera's fall and Thurn's renewed strategy of pounding the viaduct batteries had failed to achieve.

On 31 May Bruck had sent a brief but courteous note to Manin as follows: 'In your response, dated 5 May, to the proclamation made by H. E. Marshal Radetzky, you alluded to the possibility of direct negotia-tions with the imperial government so as to reach the most prompt and easy settlement available. Though ignorant as to the desirable character of such dealings, I am authorised to inform you that I shall be at headquar-ters [Villa Papadopoli] near Mestre until eight o'clock tomorrow morning.' The minister had originally addressed this to 'Signor Manin, Lawyer, Venice', but the Italian officer into whose hands it was delivered refused to accept the message, saying he knew nobody of that name save the

---

* In contemporary Italian sources his name is always Gallicised as 'De Bruck', and is given as such by both Trevelyan and Ginsborg.

President of the Venetian government. Bruck, at this stage, was prepared to sacrifice a formality or two, and the document, suitably redirected, found its way to Manin just before a meeting of the assembly in the Doge's Palace.

It was a tense moment for the President as he began outlining the current state of affairs, after reading Bruck's note to the members. Mediation by France and England was now dead in the water: Valentino Pasini had so far been denied all possibility of journeying to Vienna in person to put the government's case, and his interviews in London with both Palmerston and the Austrian ambassador Count Colloredo had produced no positive result. The Foreign Secretary was clearly hampered by the slenderness of his party's majority, with a Tory opposition scenting blood in the wake of Charles Albert's defeat, while Colloredo had politely but firmly made clear his government's intention of crushing all rebellion in Italy and Hungary before any idea was raised of consulting the subject populations on their future within the Habsburg empire. Piedmont, meanwhile, edging closer to a full peace settlement with Austria, was in no position to threaten interference. Any hopes of aid arriving from Hungary were clouding fast with the intervention of Tsar Nicholas's Russian army in support of Franz Josef.

Writing to Schwarzenberg soon after meeting Pasini, Colloredo was at pains to underline his belief that the Venetians, as much as the Austrians, now sought a convenient diplomatic escape from the current military impasse. 'My impression is that they feel their position to be no longer tenable, that they wish to free themselves from it as swiftly as may be, assured, in the process, of the merit in so doing.' In Venice itself a similar interpretation of the government's attitude had been made by Clinton Dawkins. Together with the French consul, Vasseur (whom he mistrusted as a meddlesome liberal), Dawkins had gone at the beginning of May to see Manin with the intention of urging him to give up the struggle. His arguments in favour of surrender were reasonable enough: without foreign assistance, and confronted by Austria's ruthless determination to bring them to their knees, the rebels had no chance of victory in any form. 'To all my representations, though received in a friendly and grateful manner,' he told Palmerston, 'Signor Manin's constant reply was "It is impossible – I cannot surrender – I cannot surrender – I cannot trust the Austrians – I am here to resist."' Two weeks later a further meeting suggested that the President had at last started to consider the available options, but he now maintained that by surrendering on Radetzky's terms, he would forfeit his influence over the Venetian populace. 'Though such a loss was personally indifferent to him, it would lead to consequences he shuddered to think of.'

It was Manin's old fear of a breakdown in public order as the ultimate menace, against which his singularly effective relationship with the
crowd in the Piazza formed the final rampart. Dawkins's belief that 'the
great majority of the peaceable inhabitants are but too ready to yield',
echoed on several other occasions in his consular reports, was now being
tested, not least by the assembly's reponse to Karl von Bruck's note of
31 May. This and other relevant documents – including an outline of
possible terms for negotiation, which Pasini had submitted to the French
government – would, at Manin's suggestion, be considered in camera
that same afternoon by a commission consisting of Tommaseo, Avesani,
Ulloa, Sirtori and five other members. It would then refer its judgement
to the full parliament, reconvened for 6.15 p.m. What emerged, in the
careful phrasing devised by Giovanni Battista Varè, was a statement
affirming the constancy of purpose among Venice's defenders and lauding
their courage, while at the same time freeing Manin to open talks with
Bruck. As a correspondent for the *Gazzetta di Venezia* pointed out, the
assembly was not being harassed in its deliberations by the presence of
a crowd in the Piazza – the daily stroll along the colonnades had scarcely
begun – and the civic guard, which might otherwise have imposed an
unwelcome constraint, maintained a low profile at its stations around
the palace. 'Our representatives, so as to remain faithful to their mandate,
had no other encouragement than the voice of their conscience, and no
other inspiration than patriotism.' Out of 109 members, ninety-seven
gave their approval to the statement, with eight votes against and four
abstentions.

Varè, like Tommaseo, had seen the need to put a patriotic spin on
the announcment, 'in order not to alarm the troops'. Some bad feeling
there undoubtedly was when the Venetian representatives, Giuseppe
Caluci and Giorgio Foscolo, made their way, under a flag of truce, to
Mestre, and a few stray bullets were fired at them from riflemen on the
viaduct. Neither man was likely to be deterred by such a gesture. Foscolo
was devoted to Manin, whose children he had tutored, and Caluci had
already done good service to the republic by organising the transfer of
vital funds from Piedmont during the summer of 1848. With them they
carried the President's letter to Bruck, a simple indication that he was
ready to talk. As far as a swift outcome was involved, nobody in Venice
held their breath. The white-coated imperial infantry and artillery
continued their attempts to force a passage onto the railway bridge, while
Pepe and his staff organised a recruiting drive to fill the gaps left among
Marghera's former garrison, now holding three main defensive positions:
at the Piazzale on the bridge itself, at the islet of San Secondo to the

north, and at the Carlo Alberto and San Marco batteries, closest of all to the city.

Abandoning Marghera, San Giuliano and Fort Manin had merely hardened the resolve of the patriot forces. Expert training from the Neapolitans, and all the good use to which it had lately been applied, now gave the gunners of the Piazzale a lethal effectiveness. On 5 June they targeted an Austrian powder magazine, and two days later the munitions store only just re-established at San Giuliano was easily disposed of. On this occasion at least one detachment of an otherwise inactive fleet was able to offer more than adequate support to the artillery on the bridge. A small gunboat, the *Euridice*, commanded by a young lieutenant named Pozzati, kept up a steady fire on the fort throughout the night, while a squadron of armed *trabaccoli*, the small sailing vessels of the Adriatic coast, harassed the Austrian batteries on the ruined bridge piers.

Watching these and other actions from various vantage points along the viaduct was the painter Ippolito Caffi. After his hair-raising experience of captivity during Nugent's march into Friuli the previous April, he had returned to his home town of Belluno before setting off for Venice to enrol in the civic guard. The city which, before the revolution, had seen him splendidly renewing the tradition of urban view-painting created in the eighteenth century by Canaletto now inspired him to adopt the role of war artist, the earliest important example of a figure more familiar to us from the global conflicts of the twentieth century – the painter whose task is to observe and record military life in the front line without seeking in any way to glamorise it. Gaining the necessary permits and safe-conducts from the Committee of Public Vigilance and the various battery commanders, Caffi moved freely among the defence posts, making a series of quick, vivid pencil and ink sketches, later touched up in watercolour, capturing every aspect of the operations: gunners loading and firing the cannons, soldiers piling sandbags, going through rifle drill or shouldering arms to go on sentry duty, officers haranguing their men, smoke clouds drifting across the lagoon and the shattered viaduct stretching towards Mestre. Inside the city, his eye caught the shapes and colours among the crowd thronging the Piazza, a pair of women in bonnets and bright shawls, the jaunty tasselled caps of sailors in their boat cloaks, blue-uniformed Neapolitans among a group of men in top hats and frockcoats. These '*memorie*', as Caffi called them, as well as being the most intimate visual record of the siege in its closing phases, are an example, more fascinating for being until recently completely unknown, of the nineteenth century's marriage between art and journalistic reportage that is familiar from magazines such as the *Illustrated London News*.

While the struggle for control of the viaduct continued, Caluci and Foscolo had their first conference with Bruck. The minister was notably courteous, even welcoming, assuring them that Austria now was a different kind of state from the one with which Venice had parted company last March, and inviting them to explain in detail the reference in Manin's letter to 'a convenient political condition' for the city. The envoys made it clear that the government's demand was for complete independence for Venice and 'a strip of territory which should render its existence economically viable'. It was not Mazzinian fanatics alone, they insisted, who were aiming at such a political outcome, but all those who feared the prospect of losing their new-found freedom. Such a sacrifice, Bruck begged them to understand, was essential before any concessions could be offered. Only after Austria had completed her task of recovering Venice for the empire would a new Lombardo-Venetian monarchy (for drafting whose constitution he was personally responsible) be created, and on this basis alone a suitable measure of liberty was to be granted. The scheme proposed was not exactly flattering to Venetian ideas of primacy among the cities of north-eastern Italy, since the capital of the new joint province was to be Verona. The Emperor was to be sole sovereign as before, dashing the hopes sustained by some assembly members for a state ruled by a branch of the imperial family, a prince of Piedmont or even a brother of the new Duke of Modena. Equally unchanged was the office of Viceroy, supported by a council of state. There would, however, be the novelty of a bicameral legislature, composed of a senate and an elected chamber of deputies, from whom nothing more than an age qualification would be demanded. Its powers would embrace every area of law-making save those relating to war and foreign affairs. Devolution, in short, was now on offer, and if Venice (let alone Milan) were to feel genuinely insulted by Verona's exaltation to metropolitan status, then, according to Bruck, the Emperor was prepared to create two separate devolved administrations for Venetia and Lombardy, with their capitals as before.

Manin was not inclined to dismiss this package out of hand, but directed the envoys to seek greater clarification of the accompanying details. Meanwhile Bruck left for Milan, whence he answered Caluci and Foscolo in a letter mixing official prevarication with several shrewdly placed hints as to what Venice might yet achieve for itself by a quick surrender. While he was at present unable to do more than outline the new project, they were asked to believe that it included a broader autonomy for the municipal governments large and small, greater emphasis on freedom under the constitution, and a concession of certain unspecified 'fundamental rights' with 'such modifications as might be better adapted to the national genius, principally as regards the independence and supremacy of the Catholic church' (a reference to the privileges conceded some seventy years earlier by the reforming Emperor Joseph II). To make the proposals more attractive, Bruck warned the Venetians not to push so hard for liberty that Venice itself ended up in the same position as Trieste, whose peculiar status as a free city of the empire was unenviable in view of its geographical position among 'bare mountains and barren plateaux'.

The two plenipotentiaries were not convinced, and made their scepticism plain enough, reminding Bruck of the broken promises disfiguring Austria's relationship with her Italian subjects since 1815. Still, they had clearly been struck by the minister's patience and civility in his dealings with them so far, and complimented him on his overall approach. 'If Your Excellency continues as you have begun, then you will reap the blessings of the Italian people and earn an honoured name in the history of our epoch.' Time, however, was starting to run short for both the parties involved. Bruck, with all his appearance of urbane flexibility, was immovable on the issue of Venice's ultimate reincorporation into the Habsburg domains. Caluci and Foscolo were equally adamant that a simple capitulation was impossible, given those 'sacrifices of blood' that had been made so as to preserve Venice's new-found liberty over the course of some fifteen months. The assembly, what was more, had grown preoccupied with the question of whether, in the light of the recently concluded pact with the Hungarian revolutionaries, any sort of unilateral surrender agreement could be honourably concluded without ratification from Kossuth's government first of all.

This assumed, of course, that Hungary remained independent and in arms against the imperial troops, something Manin and his ministers no longer had any means of ascertaining. Almost nothing in the way of news, from Europe let alone from Italy itself, now penetrated the siege cordon surrounding Venice. Most citizens would have been unaware that King Charles Albert of Piedmont had recently died in his self-imposed Portuguese exile. Few would have heard of the earliest attack on Rome by General Oudinot's French army on 30 April, which had been repulsed with such dedicated courage by brigades under the command of Giuseppe Garibaldi, or of the latter's subsequent victories during May over King Ferdinand's Neapolitan troops at Palestrina and Velletri* It was a long time too before tidings arrived of Oudinot's contemptible violation of

---

* Trevelyan (*Garibaldi's Defence* p.156) delightfully remarks of the Bourbon forces that Garibaldi was 'deeply impressed by their incapacity'.

the peace agreement arranged between Mazzini with his fellow Roman triumvirs and the official French representative, Ferdinand de Lesseps (better known for pioneering the Suez Canal project). The siege of Rome, beginning in the small hours of 3 June 1849 and continuing for four weeks, was to become part of Italy's Risorgimento hero-mythology. That of Venice, which had already lasted far longer, would make no impact whatsoever on Italian popular consciousness.

Though little detailed information was currently getting through, Manin and his ministers were at any rate aware that no material support was likely to come from those areas in which, only a few months earlier, patriotic voices had been loud with fraternal greetings and promises of money. Even Piedmont, whose capital Turin sheltered a significant number of exiles – among them Venetians such as Pietro Paleocapa and Jacopo Castelli who were unable to return to their city – was unwilling to pass even the slightest backhand contribution for fear of upsetting the Austrians, with whom it was anxious to conclude a suitably honourable peace in the wake of Novara. All Venice could now rely on, therefore, was the iron determination of its defenders to sustain the kind of resilience which had so impressed the imperial troops outside Marghera. On 16 June, to harden this still further, a new military commission was appointed, composed of Girolamo Ulloa, the naval lieutenant Francesco Baldisserotto and Giuseppe Sirtori, whose cool-headed management of the evacuation of the forts had made him indispensable, whatever his opposition to Manin and the bourgeois moderates within the government. The initiative was partly designed to combat growing criticism of the armed forces among members of the republican clubs and the Mazzinians, for whom Sirtori was a political as well as a military hero. To begin with, General Pepe was not included among the commissioners and, feeling decidedly piqued, made preparations to resign. Ulloa, tactful as always and realising that Pepe, whatever his failings, deserved respect for his wholehearted attachment to the Venetian cause, managed to get him appointed the commission's president. Honour was thus satisfied, and the other members could embark meanwhile on the important tasks involved in streamlining defensive operations.

Their combined energy and efficiency had an obvious impact. Negligent and incompetent officers were forced to make sideways moves or dismissed, demands for extended leave were rejected as unpatriotic, and the process of court martial for disciplinary offences or suspected collaboration with the enemy was speeded up. Valour, on the other hand, was properly recognised. The Bandiera e Moro volunteers, for example, found themselves dignified with official regimental status under Colonel

Carlo Mezzacapo, an Amalfitan nobleman who had served as liaison officer with Charles Albert during the 1848 campaign before taking over as artillery commander at Marghera. Although there seems to have been no talk of introducing conscription, a serious recruiting drive was pursued among the still considerable number of young Venetian males who had not taken up arms on their city's behalf. Even as a simple exercise in consciousness-raising, this had a beneficial effect on civic morale. That apathy of which Dawkins and other foreign observers had accused Venice in the past seemed to have vanished altogether, supposing it had existed as anything more, in the first place, than an excuse evolved among pro-Austrian opinion-formers to justify the continuance of Habsburg hegemony.

One or two dissentient voices among the patriots were heard to criticise the commission's new-broom zeal. War Minister Giovanni Battista Cavedalis plainly resented the sidelining of his authority by officers (Ulloa among them) who judged him too cautious and suspected his political leanings. 'I opposed some of these arrangements but the commissioners did exactly as they pleased, without seeking my assent,' he notes crossly in his *Commentaries*, blaming 'the exaggerated notions of incompetent demagogues'. He has the grace, on the other hand, to praise the women of Venice, whose contribution to the war effort had by now become symbolic of the way in which an entire populace was shouldering the burdens of resistance. Pepe and his Neapolitans had already been captivated by the mixture of charm and no-nonsense efficiency with which the Ladies' Committee went about its self-appointed tasks. To his wife Anna the old general had written jocularly of the distractions they offered. 'They are better at this sort of thing than the French women. I am made to feel like a Nestor who has somehow fetched up on Calypso's island.' Women of ancient lineage, beautiful and young, added Pepe, went fearlessly into the hospitals to visit the sick and wounded. On the wards their work had gathered strength, as teams of amateur nurses learned to dress wounds, administer medicine and food and bring comfort to the dying. In houses up and down the city sewing-bees gathered together to run up sheets and pillowcases and make bandages. Many women offered their fashionable ringlets of hair as stuffing for the pillows themselves. There was hardly a family in Venice, however impoverished, that could not offer something to the cause – a bed, a mattress, pans, dishes or objects of scrap metal – and even without these, says the veteran soldier Carlo Radaelli, the women could make the ultimate self-denial by persuading their husbands and sons to enlist. 'So many virtues and so many sacrifices!' he exclaims in his memoir of the siege, 'yet how wretchedly they were to be rewarded!'

It is to Radaelli that we owe the story of one of the more bizarre episodes in the Austrians' increasingly frantic efforts to wrest Venice from its citizen defenders. They had tried menaces, they had offered bribes, they had held out attractive pledges of increased civil liberties and flexible political solutions, they had scattered leaflets and launched proclamations in bottles on the waters of the lagoon – all to no avail. Somebody among General Thurn's staff in Mestre now had the inspired idea of using the charms of a handsome woman to snare the susceptible Italians. A certain Signorina Puttimato, 'dissolute in her habits but most alluring in her person' as Radaelli expresses it, had suggested herself as the ideal siren, and the scheme was quickly taken up by the Austrian officers. 'La Puttimato was very beautiful,' adds Radaelli, 'blonde-haired, an expert flatterer practised in feminine guile, perfectly fashioned to seduce those whose hearts were too softly-tempered.' Promising her honour and privileges should she succeed, the officers gave her a false passport under the name 'Teresa Manini', presumably chosen as a deliberately vulgar insult to the pre-eminently virtuous Teresa Perissinotti Manin, Daniele's wife.

Spies somehow secured details of the plan to launch Puttimato on Venice as a Mata Hari. Her assignment, after all, was to fascinate not mere soldiers, but the highest-ranking members of the government. For some time the Committee of Public Vigilance had been stepping up its watch over suspected pro-Austrian elements within the city (Consul Dawkins among them) and one of those fingered was an officer in the civic guard, Count Giulio Pullè. Identified as the blonde temptress's contact some days before she slipped into Venice, he was arrested and flung in gaol, while an army lieutenant named De Capitani took his place, an easy enough task since neither the Count nor the good-time girl was known to one another personally. A suitably dashing young military article, De Capitani proved a fatal distraction for Puttimato. Precious time which could have been spent on gaining access to various ministers, or perhaps even seeking, as 'Teresa Manini', to replace Teresa Manin in the dictator's affections, was wasted in a whirlwind romance with the all-too obliging officer, who had no difficulty in coaxing out of her the essential details of her mission and her real name. Radaelli discreetly hints that the bogus 'Count Pullè' was eminently satisfying to his mistress from a sexual aspect, while abstracting from her luggage the necessary letters and documents. After several weeks, when the committee had gathered enough evidence, the siren, along with certain others of her *austriacante* contacts, was arrested and taken to prison on the island of San Severo. What happened to her thereafter is unknown.

Whores of a more patriotic tendency continued to solace the troops on furlough from the batteries. The immorality that had so distressed the forces chaplain Vincenzo Marinelli in 1848 had predictably increased under the stresses of war, but several of the earlier writers on the siege were rather too readily shocked by what, for a number of Venetian women, must have been an easy means of acquiring payment in kind with precious army rations to eke out dwindling household supplies. Such commentators were appalled besides by the frankness with which the soldiers were prepared to admit to using the prostitutes' services, or by the sheer blatancy with which the sex workers (some of them male) drummed up custom. Edmund Flagg, United States consul in the years immediately following the siege, noted the serious increase in venereal disease during early 1849, while the anonymous author of a blistering attack on the revolution in the English conservative *Quarterly Review* ascribed to the volunteers 'an atmosphere of licentiousness not to be described. Vices practised at first with some attempt at concealment arrived at length at such a pitch of barefaced extravagance that observation was rather courted than shunned.' Much of the subsequent mortality attributed to cholera, he claimed, was 'the natural effect of intemperance and debauchery'. The American chargé d'affaires at Vienna, W. H. Stiles, was only too happy to flatter the puritanism of his readers in the United States by plagiarising the entire relevant paragraph from the *Quarterly* article.

Prostitutes, like everyone else in beleaguered Venice, had their crust to earn. The whole issue of food shortages had now become serious enough for the government to extend the activities of the committee established the previous year under Gian Francesco Avesani to regulate prices in the various flour mills and bakeries of the city. On 29 May controls were officially applied to all kinds of sausages and preserved meats, cheese, oil and rice. A week later a more detailed series of tariffs was issued, adding *baccalà* (salt cod), herrings, beans, peas, pasta and lard to the prosciutto, salami and mortadella and the pecorino, lodigiano, Emmenthal and Dutch cheeses already listed. Where bread was concerned, Venice's mayor Giovanni Correr had issued health and safety instructions concerning the dangers of adulteration, but by the middle of June the bakers were finding compliance with these impossible. When the Provisioning Committee managed to get hold of a large stock of rye flour, plentiful and cheaper loaves were soon on offer, but the new bread was decidedly not to Venetian taste. 'It looked like mud, tasted disgusting and was seriously indigestible,' declared one dissatisfied customer. Shown a sample after the siege was over, Admiral Dahlerup noted that it 'had the appearance and consistency of builders' rubble'. Though fish were always available, even if boats could not venture beyond the Lido's blockaded channels, and fruit and vegetables could be brought in from the orchards and market gardens of the lagoon islands, most citizens preferred trying to continue with their traditional meat-and-cereal diet. The brave posse of smugglers slipping up and down the coast, having managed to avoid Dahlerup's cordon, occasionally brought supplies of beef and pork, and hence it was possible for the Tuscan envoy Carlo Fenzi, even as late as mid-July, to write to his father that he had just eaten a good if expensive restaurant dinner of soup, fish, boiled meat, a pudding, fruit and coffee, accompanied by bread and a bottle of wine.

More serious for the defenders at this stage was the maintenance of ammunition supplies, especially the gunpowder store. Projectiles of various types lobbed into the city could be recycled, and Edmund Flagg records the courage of the Venetian boys who chased the cannon balls as they fell and carried them back to the batteries to be reused.* The stocks of powder could be kept up only with an available supply of nitre, but as this ran low, the Military Commission began to investigate the possibility of using nitrous material from the lavatories of private houses. A gunpowder mill had been set up on the small island of Santa Maria delle Grazie (known as 'La Grazia'), south of San Giorgio Maggiore, whose convent and neighbouring Gothic church had been suppressed by the French in 1810. On 19 June a massive explosion shook the city and echoed across the lagoon as 1,400 bags of powder exploded, though the mill itself appears to have remained intact. Rumours of sabotage started at once, and the next evening a large crowd gathered in the Piazza, threatening death to the traitors, whoever they might be, and demanding immediate dismissal of the Provisioning Committee over the black bread fiasco.

Crowd control was becoming an ever more significant feature in Daniele Manin's public life as the siege continued and the potential increased for adverse propaganda and sheer panic to work on the popular imagination. Now, from his window in the Procuratie Nuove, he spoke to the frightened citizens in his usual tone of fatherly reproof mixed with rhetorical appeals to their better nature. 'Venetians, do you really believe that this conduct is worthy of you? You cannot be the people of Venice I know, not even the smallest part among them. I shall never stoop to obey the caprices of a rebellious mob, but submit instead to the vote of our legally appointed representatives. You will always hear the truth from

* See Flagg p.136 'It is idle, as it is unjust, to denounce "Italian cowardice" with hundreds of examples of intrepidity and hardihood like these, even in the children, with which the bloody chronicles of 1848–49 abound.'

me, even when your guns are aimed at my breast and your daggers lifted to strike. Now leave at once, all of you!' Mingled shame and admiration drew loyal cheers from the throng below and the Piazza emptied immediately. Nobody else in Venice could have faced down an enraged mob with so much coolness and command, but the raw volatility underlying the situation showed Manin how much Venice had to fear from within its own confines, let alone from the pounding of Austrian guns.

The turmoil in the square had been underscored by the ongoing thunder of falling shells as the summer night darkened across the city. For several days now the enemy batteries at San Giuliano and the western end of the viaduct had stepped up their fire, and on 13 June the buildings of Venice itself were hit for the first time. As so often in wartime, it was several of the town's poorer quarters which bore the brunt of the attack. The Cannaregio district north of the railway station took a heavy battering from grenades, many of them falling as far eastwards as the church of the Madonna dell'Orto, while cannon fire tore into that part of the San Polo *sestiere* closest to the Grand Canal, around San Giacomo dell'Orio on its broad rectangular campo. Even the black flag flying outside the Santa Chiara hospital did not command the respect traditionally accorded by combatants to signals of this kind. General Ulloa believed, indeed, that it was deliberately targeted by the Austrian gunners.

Their work, however, was hardly noted for its accuracy, and the seasoned Venetian artillerymen took a generally scornful attitude towards General Thurn's strategy and the clumsy nature of its implementation. The sheer force and volume of the increased barrage, and the fact that the town itself was now in the firing line, made new demands on the resilience of the defenders along the railway bridge. On that morning of 13 June civilian Venice learned that the war was no longer a spectator sport, to be quizzed from *altane*, belfries and high windows with the aid of telescopes and field-glasses. Yet an undoubted boost to the patriot morale was given by the Austrians' failure to seize any sort of naval initiative within the stretch of the lagoon between the mainland and the viaduct's outermost redoubt.

Why, Ulloa wondered, were they doing nothing to clear this crucial channel of the flotilla of small vessels with which the Venetians continued to harass the imperial artillery and carry ammunition to the Italian gunners on what remained of the bridge? Why had Radetzky not ordered floating batteries to be constructed at Verona and brought up by train, to be assembled and launched at Mestre? Where were the boats which could have been pressed into service from Lake Garda or the various larger rivers? For rather different reasons, Consul Dawkins was surely asking himself the same questions. He had been heard to remark that as soon as the first bombs fell on Venice itself, the government would hoist the white flag, and he made no secret of his anger when no move towards surrender was made, the red banner continued to wave defiantly from the top of the Campanile and, in celebration of enduring resistance, the principal battery at the Piazzale was named in honour of St Anthony, whose feast day is 13 June. 'The persons in power,' he spluttered in a dispatch to Palmerston, 'appear determined to hold out to the last moment, trusting to the Chapter of accidents, and utterly regardless of the misery they are entailing on the inhabitants.'

Manin may have been having a few second thoughts, but the defence force was in no mood to give up when faced with the challenge of a tougher Austrian assault. Death from a sniper's bullet, a shell fragment or a cannon ball was instantly glamorised by the rhetoric of martyrdom and sacrifice; and few officers manning the makeshift ramparts were more honoured through such a process than forty-year-old Cesare Rosaroll, who was hit while rallying his men after a series of explosions, on 27 June, threatened to shatter the Sant'Antonio battery beyond repair. The son of a Neapolitan baron, he had fought in the Greek independence struggle and alongside the Spanish constitutionalists before returning to Naples in 1833 to join a conspiracy against King Ferdinand. With a fellow officer named Lancillotti, Rosaroll was arrested and committed for trial. The pair made a suicide pact in prison, but while Rosaroll's pistol bullet killed Lancillotti, he himself was only wounded. On his hospital bed he received news of his death sentence, and as soon as he could walk, he was marched to the scaffold. A last-minute commutation doomed him to gaol with forced labour, and it was another fifteen years before Ferdinand's 1848 amnesty set him free.

Rosaroll flung himself with predictable enthusiasm into the Neapolitan revolution. After fighting bravely alongside the Tuscans at Curtatone, he led his band of volunteers to Venice, where Ulloa praised his 'soul of iron' and his insatiable thirst for action and danger. His gallantry had been conspicuous in the attack on Mestre and throughout the defence of Marghera. As the Sant'Antonio battery's new commander, it was only to be expected that after a shower of grenades blew up the powder magazine, disabling four Italian guns in the process, he should rally his men and personally seek to hoist the tricolour flag over what remained of the ramparts. As the three cannon still in action began answering the Austrians' fire with what, under the circumstances, seemed a surprising effectiveness, Rosaroll, in the act of planting the sacred banner, was caught by a stray bullet, but managed to order his gunners to stand firm before he was carried across the bridge to Santa Chiara. The wound was mortal and a priest arrived to administer the last rites.

'Do you die at peace with everyone?' asked the confessor. 'I have no enemy in the world,' answered Rosaroll, 'save the Austrians and the King of Naples.' To General Pepe, who stood nearby, he murmured, 'Give your thoughts not to me who am dying, but to our Italy.' Pepe, devoted to his officers, ordered a splendid funeral for the hero at St Mark's, where the Venetians, with their instinctive sense of occasion, crowded to watch. Soon afterwards the battery at San Secondo, north of the viaduct, was solemnly baptised '*La batteria Rosaroll*'.

By the end of June, when Rosaroll was killed, the food situation had grown noticeably worse. The cows kept in various parts of Venice to supply fresh milk were slaughtered for their meat, there was almost no butter available and the rye bread which had given such offence earlier was being adulterated still further by the use of oats and barley. Long queues outside the bakers were now a familiar sight, which, as Niccolò Tommaseo remarked, 'mixed wonder, terror and pity in the spectacle of wretched folk crowded outside a shop, with pregnant women and those carrying babies in arms waiting patiently for their rations, in an orderly and uncomplaining manner'. Tommaseo became obsessed with the idea that hoarding was going on among the *austriacanti* and those whose patriotism was on the wane, and in his recently adopted role as a sort of revolutionary loose cannon, trying to embarrass the government from the vantage point of a seat in the national assembly, he may well have been responsible for stirring up a more widespread suspicion among his fellow citizens as to the squirrelling away of precious comestibles. Soon enough the dignified behaviour of the bakery queues relapsed into quarrels and fighting; several sausage shops believed to contain more than they were prepared to sell got looted; and particular anger was reserved for those who sought to mark up their prices despite the Provisioning Committee's new regulations. One woman on the Rialto who asked a massive twenty-five lire for a pair of guinea fowl was chased from her stall, never to be seen again. She was luckier than a fellow market-wife lamenting the disappearance of the eggs she customarily sold. Heard to wish that the government would give up the fight, she found herself set upon by the other stallholders, who beat her and pulled out handfuls of her hair.

The besiegers, in truth, were faring scarcely better than the besieged. In the official Austrian report on the Italian campaigns, published in 1854, we can read what Schönhals and the anonymous *Allgemeine Zeitung* correspondent airbrushed from their too fervently upbeat accounts: that malaria was cutting a broad swath through the Habsburg ranks, that the local hospitals were so overcrowded that 1,200 men had to be sent on to Verona for treatment, and that many of those untouched by disease had succumbed to heatstroke as the scorching summer of the Veneto plains gathered intensity. In Verona itself cholera, scourge of nineteeth-century Italian cities with their heavy-density populations and inadequate sanitary infrastructure, had begun its first onslaught, killing 493 people in a single week. Worst placed of all were the troops forming the southern extremity of the siege cordon, on the Brenta estuary below Chioggia. There was hardly any drinkable water and almost all the men had been fever-stricken at one stage or another. The heat made sleep impossible, flies and mosquitoes swarmed over every area of exposed skin, and only in the brief period when the dawn light drove the insects off could the harassed soldiers snatch some rest.

Doubtless Karl von Bruck bore these factors in mind even while choosing Verona for his next meeting with the Venetian envoys on 21 June. Giorgio Foscolo had now been replaced by Vincenzo Pasini's brother Lodovico, who had negotiated the friendship treaty with the Hungarians. Yet whatever ideas he and Giuseppe Caluci might have entertained, as to Bruck's gradual softening on the matter of special treatment for the Italian provinces, were doomed to disappointment. There were, after all, to be no extraordinary provisions made for either Lombardy or Venetia. Whatever was offered would simply be a corollary of the constitution granted by Franz Josef on 4 March (for what such a document was now worth, given the intransigence of both the Emperor and Felix zu Schwarzenberg). The concessions of human rights and press freedom, of which Bruck had spoken earlier, turned out to be conditional on the outbreak of war or internal 'disturbances', when they might easily be revoked. In short, the entire notion of home rule, which the minister had appeared so eager to dangle in front of them, was nothing but a mirage. As if echoing Metternich's repeated enunciations of his 'Italy-is-only-a-geographical-expression' mantra, Bruck made it clear that the sole nationality tolerated within the realm was Austrian, and that by the same token, subjects from anywhere else within the empire might reasonably expect to occupy major administrative positions in Venetia-Lombardy. Adding insult to injury, he pointed out that taxes and customs dues raised within the two provinces would not be earmarked for strictly local expenditure.

By the time Bruck informed the envoys that the terms of the constitution would only come into force when Venice had submitted to an interim Austrian military government and after 'the complete re-establishment of tranquillity in Italy and Europe', they had heard enough. All that remained was to make clear, supposing he had not grasped the true significance of the issues at stake, that without proper regard for what they termed the Italians' 'national dignity', this diplomatic game of promises made only to be modified or withdrawn was pointless, since it was 'so little adapted to the moral needs of the epoch and the nation'. Manin, on learning from Caluci and Pasini of the Austrian conditions, had barely enough time to express his disgust before a fresh communication arrived from Bruck. This took the form of an ultimatum setting out what were in effect surrender terms, though guaranteeing all civil rights established by the provisional government and not demanding any indemnity from Venice's inhabitants. The government was given eight days to consider the offer, and Bruck, with a characteristic final flourish of amiability, added, 'It will be infinitely agreeable to me to have contributed towards saving Venice from the disasters to which she has been most unhappily compelled to succumb through the present war.'

Supposing, of course, that Venice wished for such a salvation. An in-camera session of the assembly on 30 June listened in silence as Lodovico Pasini gave his account of the negotiations and the reasons for their breakdown. Manin declared the whole Austrian initiative towards seeking an honourable peace nothing but a sham; another member, Giovanni Ruffini, demanded that the report and Bruck's letter should be made public; and Giovanni Battista Varè proposed that on this basis they should move towards a vote. He offered no definite wording for the motion, but some kind of formal rejection of Austria's proposals was taken for granted.

At this point the first serious voices of dissent were raised against the policy of resistance at all costs that had been so ardently espoused on 2 April. They were those of two patricians, the eminent philologist Pietro Canal and Niccolò Priuli, an equally distinguished figure who had acted as Vice-President during the 1847 scientific congress and edited the three magnificent presentation volumes of *Venezia e le sue lagune*. His reasonable suggestion was that instead of rushing headlong to a vote, the assembly should appoint a commission to examine the available resources for continuing the struggle and report as soon as possible. Canal, while supporting Varè's line in principle, backed Priuli's proposal and felt it should receive priority. Varè saw the amendment as being essentially a threat to Venice's honour, of which this parliament was guardian. Canal then widened the moral dimension by accusing the rejectionists of sacrificing the good of the community to their own interests. Debate grew so heated that the assembly's speaker, Giovanni Minotto, suspended the session for a quarter of an hour. When it reconvened, the meeting was open, and it was via a challenge from Manin's friend Leone Pincherle to

Canal to name names that the rest of Venice learned of the two deputies' courageous objections. Later that evening Priuli and Canal had their windows smashed by a mob hurling stones and accusations of treachery.* The assembly meanwhile had proceeded to a vote, once more in secret, on the motion 'That between Austria and Venice, Europe should be the judge'; 105 members voted in favour to thirteen against.

Europe was no longer especially interested. England could only recommend to Manin that he submit to Austria's demands, and his letter to the French foreign minister Alexis de Tocqueville, begging for 'a generous demonstration in favour of liberty' and flattering the celebrated political commentator by saying that his ministerial tenure at one of history's most important moments could scarcely be accidental, met with nothing useful by way of an answer. In Vienna, Schwarzenberg, having at last graciously allowed Valentino Pasini the necessary passport to travel as the Venetian government's spokesman, roundly informed him that only after the rebels had offered total submission would Austria consider honouring its various promises. 'In the end he has no other object,' wrote Pasini, 'than to edge us little by little towards unconditional surrender.'

The one ally who might genuinely have come to Venice's aid, insurgent Hungary under Lajos Kossuth, was being hard-pressed between General Haynau's reinvigorated imperial army and Tsar Nicholas's Russian expeditionary force. In Italy itself the port of Ancona surrendered on 19 June, after a two-week siege, to General Wimpffen's Austrian troops. Barely a week later Giuseppe Garibaldi, 'his red shirt covered with dust and blood, his face still moist with the sweat of battle, his sword so bent that it stuck halfway out of the scabbard', entered the Roman republican assembly to inform Giuseppe Mazzini and the other triumvirs that the heroic defence of Rome he had led for the past month against Oudinot's French cohorts could no longer continue. On 2 July Garibaldi, accompanied by his Brazilian wife Anita, left the city in the first phase of an escape whose combination of hair's-breadth good luck, fortitude and pure tragedy added a new dimension to the epic aspect of the Risorgimento. A few days later Mazzini himself fled into exile. The great ideologue's work was by no means over, but his moral integrity would never again be given the chance to show itself to such inspiring effect.

Venice was thus completely alone, the final bastion of all those hopes in whose promise of speedy fulfilment Italy had roused itself to revolt against the Habsburg superpower a year and a half ago. There were to

* Cicogna, in his diary, witheringly refers to the window-breakers as 'some 40 or so of the very cleanest persons'.

be no more fraternal greetings, no more festive arrivals of volunteer regiments, no more patriotic collections in the fashionable salons of Paris or the theatres of Genoa, no more poems about driving barbarians over the Alps and no further subventions from the treasuries of neighbouring governments. Nothing now stood between the city and her former imperial masters save the courage of her defenders, the steadfastness of her people and the resolution of a little man in spectacles, who, whatever Consul Dawkins might believe, was not ready to give up just yet.

CHAPTER 15

~

'ALL'ULTIMA POLENTA'

T HE CRUCIAL MOMENT IN DANIELE Manin's leadership of Venice
had now arrived. Whether he was ready to confront its challenges,
or whether he believed any longer in the validity of accepting
them, was doubted by several of those who had dealings with him during
these summer months of 1849. Clinton Dawkins, for example, persuaded
that 'the great majority of the peaceable inhabitants are but too ready to
yield', thought the President, 'having unquestionably deceived the people',
was experiencing his own form of disillusion with the process of revolt
and the false expectations which sustained it. 'The veil,' wrote the Consul,
'is now torn from his eyes, but he can scarcely yet believe the truth, and
still less can he undertake the task of making it known to those to whom
he has always held a different language.' Emerging from Dawkins's version
of events – the only one then available to the British government – is
the sense of Manin as a sort of baffled impresario, determined that the
show must go on, whatever the dwindling resources of his cast and production team, for fear of the audience's hostility if the curtain is brought
down.

His abiding horror of anarchy was certainly one of the forces inspiring
him to carry on the struggle, yet the success of the military commission,
led by the radical Sirtori, seemed calculated to encourage precisely those
hard-line attitudes which could detonate the worst sort of urban disorder.
Judging from the popular reaction to the request made by Priuli and
Canal for careful consideration of Austria's proposals, the feeling for resistance was still strong among the defenders, and in the vote on Varè's
motion of 30 June, the number of dissentient voices had been notably
small. Manin, however, was no Mazzini. Throughout the existence of the

Roman republic, following Pius IX's retreat to Gaeta, Venice had notably failed to establish close links with the Pope's former capital and its new rulers, warned off by the government's envoy Giovanni Battista Castellani, whose reports took a sceptical view of the Roman triumvirate's ability to manage the emergency created by France's armed intervention. Manin's own shade of republicanism was emphatically not Mazzinian, and the exalted spirituality of the older revolutionary appeared completely alien to him. His outlook was rational and pragmatic, based not on visions of the brotherhood of mankind, but on what it had seemed possible to obtain in the way of legally guaranteed civil rights and improved economic conditions from the Austrian government at a moment when its guard was down and its power weakened. He would not send men to battle in the name of an ideal without practical support and some possibility that they might be able to defend themselves and outmanoeuvre the enemy. Just as Mazzini's Christlike charisma was lacking in Manin, so were the good looks which, in the case of the former, proved so fascinating to women. Manin – essentially unromantic as a happily married bourgeois paterfamilias, with his small stature, his myopia and his pointedly un-Mazzinian growth of beard – was hardly an attractive or convincing incarnation of the rebel demagogue. Yet the astonishing episode in the life of Venice now about to unfold, touched as it was with glory and suffering, was defined by his presence both physical and moral. Towards its close he was no longer a completely committed participant, but its peculiar character, as the very last act in that Italian drama of which Schwarzenberg had spoken, is unimaginable without him as its hero.

Comedy rather than tragedy was in the air – literally, as it turned out – when on 7 July the Austrians resorted to their latest device for bringing the city to its knees. Anyone at the northern end of Riva degli Schiavoni that day and glancing in the direction of the Lido might have noticed the sky suddenly being covered with scores of small balloons. Constructed at Treviso, these had been launched from Admiral Dahlerup's blockade vessels and contained explosives operated by timed fuses. As far as can be ascertained, this was history's earliest recorded attempt at aerial bombardment, but it was destined to inglorious failure. Some of the balloons burst and fell into the lagoon, while the rest were carried away on a south-easterly wind to Mestre, where they discharged their bombs on the Austrians. The Venetians found the whole enterprise funny rather than frightening, and sent up loud cheers as echoes of the various explosions reached them from the *terraferma*. Further attempts at balloon-bombing took place a fortnight later, with similarly unpromising results. On this occasion the whole city turned out to watch in silence as the death-dealing aerial squadron drew closer to the city. When once again the wind proved favourable to Venice and a further series of friendly-fire disasters took place over the Austrian lines, there were jubilant cries of 'Evviva!', 'Bravo!' and 'Buon appetito!' from the crowds.*

Many were heartened by the imperial forces' continuing inability to dent the resistance of the gunners on the railway bridge. By now several more of its arches had been blown up, and the Austrians were growing desperate in their efforts to force a passage onto the remaining stretch so as to rush the city's inner defences from the head of the Grand Canal. A few minutes after midnight on 7 July a tremendous explosion was heard from the direction of the canal linking Mestre to the lagoon. As the artillerymen at the Sant'Antonio battery crowded onto the parapet to peer into the dark, a swarm of Austrian infantry surged out of the shadows, pushing them back towards their redoubt. An alarm was sounded, and Enrico Cosenz, rallying whatever men he could find from the various units, drove the whitecoats off with a bayonet charge. A combined naval assault was met with gunfire from the other Italian batteries, whose commanders had somehow received notice of the operation from the spy network which continued to pass on information throughout the siege concerning many, if not all, of Thurn's intended moves.

Sinister and mystifying to the patriot defenders, however, was the gradual diminution of the Austrian bombardment following the failure of this night attack. Over the next few days the guns fell almost completely silent, apart from an occasional burst of firing designed to warn the Venetians that the imperial army was still occupying its positions as before. Only at Brondolo were troops withdrawn for the purpose of reinforcing the fever-ravaged regiments further north along the line of attack. During the retreat, farms and crops were destroyed and whatever livestock remained was driven off, but the patriot garrison of Brondolo's fort made various successful sorties in order to prevent the Austrians opening the sluice-gates of irrigation canals to flood the whole area. By 16 July all enemy artillery in the batteries closest to Venice itself had suspended its fire, prompting Ulloa, Cosenz and Sirtori to suspect that some fresh initiative more deadly in its effectiveness than proclamations in bottles, the luscious Signora Puttimato or bombs dropped from balloons, was now being got ready.

They were not wrong. The newest Austrian plan was for an adjust-

---

* There is some confusion as to the dates of these balloon attacks. Contarini places the first of them on 7 July. Marchesi, quoting Cavedalis as his authority, pushes this forward to the 25th.

ment in the angle of fire to forty-five degrees so that heavy guns could target central areas of the city, causing maximum damage not merely to the houses and property of ordinary Venetians, but to the surrounding churches, *scuole* and public buildings. There was to be no further respect accorded to the ancient fabric of Venice's historic core, to the myriad art treasures it sheltered, or to the lives of innocent men, women and children in its narrow streets. Implied by this outright devastation were the fury of Radetzky, Thurn and Bruck at the failure of earlier strategies, their irritation at the revolutionary government's intransigence, and a deliberate attempt to alienate the civilian community by realising that scenario of misery and chaos which their successive communiqués had foretold as an inevitable consequence of rebellion. Memorialists of the siege, such as Ulloa and Radaelli, describe this new phase of total war in terms that suggest something positively unsporting and dishonourable in Austria's hardening of heart. Radetzky and his generals can scarcely be blamed, however, for seeking to complete, as expeditiously as possible, the task they were summoned to perform. Venice had now assumed the position – glorious or unenviable, depending on political alignment – of the stone in the imperial shoe, where resumption of Habsburg control over Italian affairs was concerned. Piedmont was not yet the challenger to this hegemony it would shortly become under the guidance of its ministerial rising star Camillo Cavour, and France's intervention on behalf of Pope Pius was hardly seen, at this stage, as an augury of a greater international menace. Schwarzenberg's government, having given Radetzky a free hand in the management of the Italian campaign, had every right to expect him to use any means in his power to return the rebel city to what most Austrian opinion, however liberal, considered her rightful allegiance.

While Thurn and the battery commanders made their final preparations for the new offensive, the Venetian assembly continued its deliberations, firmly believing in the need to sustain a framework of democratic government whatever the mounting emergency. The deputies' collective nerve had undoubtedly been shaken by a second explosion in the powder mill at La Grazia. Eleven workers were taken, badly burned, to the hospital in the monastery of San Giorgio Maggiore, and suspicions of arson seemed rather better justified than previously, though nobody was actually charged with the crime. Business, whether in the Doge's Palace or in the town as a whole, must be seen to continue as usual, hence the announcement of a fresh round of elections for a new parliament, to take place on 4 August. The sense, nevertheless, of an administration with its back to the wall dominated the secret session of the assembly which opened on 28 July. Sirtori, for example, may have been moderately optimistic as to the improvements wrought by the military commission, but he was in agreement with Manin concerning a need to suppress, for the time being, any exact statistics relating to available food and ammunition resources. The fear in this case was not so much of panicking the citizenry as of handing a propaganda advantage to the enemy. The Capuchin friar Antonio Torniello, who had taken a major role in fund-raising for the cause and led his own volunteer brigade into battle, asked anxiously for news from Venice's allies among the Hungarian rebels. To this Manin returned the mournful answer that the blockade was so effective, where news was concerned, that no communications of any kind were getting through, let alone the food, money and arms promised by the Ancona agreement. Gian Francesco Avesani was more upbeat, reminding the assembly that the Hungarians were still holding out against both Austrian and Russian armies. He added that the presence of a French army in Italy, despite its avowed intention of restoring the Pope, was a positive advantage and that Piedmont had still not concluded the peace negotiations with Austria begun in the wake of Novara.

It was Niccolò Tommaseo who cut short an exchange between Ulloa, speaking on behalf of the army, and the lawyer Bartolomeo Benvenuti, pressing for more drastic offensives in the vulnerable Brondolo sector, by reminding his colleagues that 'what matters above all today is that we should know what to say to the people'. They owed a degree of honesty to 'this population which suffers and waits, yet hears not a single consoling word from either the assembly or the government'. What must emerge from this meeting, he declared, was a proclamation which should rouse the energies of both the city and the army. Once again the fundamental difference in outlook between him and Manin came to the fore when the latter brusquely rejoined that no such public statement could be made until the assembly itself had resolved on a course of action.

Though nobody among those present in the Sala del Maggior Consiglio that day cared to say it in so many words, an obvious split was starting to develop between the idealists and optimists on the one hand (figures such as Sirtori, Avesani and Baldisserotto, keen to sustain the struggle to the last ounce of powder in the barrel) and those more practical or simply sceptical members (such as Finance Minister Isacco Pesaro Maurogonato) who warned that without another forced loan, money supplies must run out by 20 August, or those (such as Cavedalis) concerned that their deliberations should address the realistic issue of whether or not the fighting was to be carried into the streets of Venice itself. By the end of the afternoon the first faction had triumphed, in a resolution ratifying the announcement, originally made on 2 April, that the city would resist at any cost, though the division on the vote (sixty-five in favour, thirty-eight against) was significantly narrower than any of its predecessors.

Neither the assembly members nor the citizens they represented had long to wait before this motion was put to the test. Austrian preparations were now complete, the guns had been tilted to their maximum elevation, and on the night of 29 July the first heavy bombardment of Venice began. We should not imagine the kind of saturation fire-storm assault familiar from twentieth-century warfare. The projectiles launched were shells and cannon balls of various sizes, inflicting damage only in the precise spots where they fell, as opposed to heavy explosives designed to spread destruction over a wide area, causing extensive casualties in the process. Comparatively few Venetians actually died as a consequence, nor was the entire city under threat. Cannaregio continued to bear the brunt of the attack, but elsewhere the balls fell thickest on two broadly identifiable sectors. One was the region to the south-west of the Grand Canal, stretching from San Polo and the Frari to San Barnaba and its adjacent parishes as far as the Zattere. The other was a semicircle on the north side of the Canal, enclosed by the parishes of Sant'Angelo, San Samuel, San Luca and San Salvador, whose outer edge at San Gallo lay cheek-by-jowl with the Piazza itself.

Wherever the bombs fell, fires were inevitable, more especially since many of the projectiles launched were deliberately heated for incendiary impact. There were some distinguished architectural casualties as a result. Various of them, including Palazzo Labia and the neighbouring church of San Geremia, lay outside the main danger zones, but San Moisèe, SS Giovanni e Paolo, the church and *scuola* of San Rocco, the Frari and the Madonna dell'Orto all suffered damage, as well as Teatro Malibran and many of the palaces on the Grand Canal. In the Doge's Palace such paintings as could be taken down were made safe, rather more so than at the Accademia, where, though Titian's great 'Assumption of the Virgin' was packed in wadding, falling bombs destroyed several other pictures, including Bonifazio de'Pitati's 'Adoration of the Magi'.

The effect on Venice as a whole was hardly the intended Armageddon. Though, according to some accounts, panic broke out immediately as a mass evacuation began from the stricken areas to safer districts around St Mark's and in the north-eastern *sestiere* of Castello, others describe a more sober and resigned mood, as 'the people, surprised by this visitation while they lay sleeping, left quietly for the open spaces of Castello and other less vulnerable spots. Apart from one or two women very occasionally making complaints and desiring a speedy surrender, everyone was calm and good-humoured, only now and then cursing the Austrians' cruelty. With their children on their backs, and with many singing as they went, the citizens headed towards safety. It was an indescribable spectacle. Even those opposed or different to the Italian cause must have been moved by it.'

Many of the poorer refugees sought shelter under the arcades of the Doge's Palace and in the narthex of St Mark's, where the journalist Pacifico Valussi, entering the Piazza in the early glimmer of dawn after being kept awake by the rumble of cannon, found a crowd of mothers suckling not merely their own babies, but those of other women unable to lactate owing to shock. Elsewhere people moved in with friends across the city, several settled down on the decks of boats moored out of range of the bombing, and those who could afford to took whatever rooms were available at the hotels. Countess Memmo Martinengo, for example, wife of a major in the civic guard, fled her family's palace for a berth on a *trabaccolo*, while another patrician, Marina Albrizzi Persico, removed her three children, a nurse and two maids to the comfort of the Albergo Danieli. Certain inhabitants, on the other hand, deliberately chose to stay put. At the smartly appointed headquarters of the Bandiera e Moro brigade in Palazzo Mocenigo on the Grand Canal, a group of legionaries lay asleep on their pallet beds that first night of the bombing, a fine, warm summer evening. Just after 11 p.m. a massive crash shook the building* and the soldiers awakened to find the room filled with black smoke, through which a hole in the ceiling and an enormous cannon ball on the floor were faintly visible. They saw no reason for shifting quarters, and the palace received little serious damage thereafter.

Carlotta Cattonari, who lived not far off in Campo San Stefano, had more reason to be afraid. Twelve people were dwelling in the house at the time, several of them old and infirm and one a five-year-old girl. Herself still young, Carlotta first grew uneasy on realising how much closer the cannon shots sounded than those she had been used to hearing while the attack was still concentrated on Marghera and the Piazzale. The flashes of fire too seemed unnervingly bright, and the fearful whistling of the shells seemed to herald 'ruin, destruction, desolation and death'. Hurrying downstairs, she found her uncle and two aunts cowering close to the dining table, which stood under a lighted glass chandelier. While they sat there, 'an indescribable crash was heard as the ceiling suddenly burst open and the lamp shattered into tiny fragments, which, mixed with pieces of plaster, shot into every corner of the room'. Hearing screams from upstairs, they found another of her aunts prostrate on the floor,

* The palace, on the San Marco side of the Canal, is actually several structures knocked into one. It was the lodging, in 1818–19, of Lord Byron and his entourage.

bruised and shocked from the explosion. Even the family dog was so traumatised that it was unable to bark. This was the signal for them all to quit the house and join the crowd fleeing towards St Mark's, from where they moved on to find shelter among friends at San Giovanni in Bragora.

In the great square itself, a Piedmontese reporter for a Turin newspaper, observing the huddled throngs of women and children under the brilliant moonlight, wrote, 'Whoever, walking here on this evening, beautiful and calm, might witness this sad and silent multitude must have thought himself transported to the fall of Missolonghi.' An allusion here to the Greek independence struggle some twenty years earlier was gloomy enough, but the stubborn courage of the Venetians was to impress many witnesses during the days to come. The Florentine Carlo Fenzi praised them for 'showing the world what a people is truly capable of when it has the will, and what it can bear in the cause of proving itself worthy to obtain independence'. Like the Londoners during the Blitz of the Second World War, they not only learned to live with the daily barrage, but made a continual sport of it, laughingly referring to the incendiary bombs as 'Viennese oranges' and hurling insults at the '*Fioi di cani!*' – 'Sons of dogs!' – who dared to harm their beloved city. Children ran to and fro chasing the smaller shot as it fell, waiting for it to cool and carrying it to government agents, who paid one lira apiece for every recyclable projectile. At Ponte dei Fuseri, near Campo San Luca, an aged beggarwoman who, just like those in modern Venice, kept her station at the bridge-foot, cackled with delight as she picked up a cannon ball. 'Look, look!' she cried, 'Radetzky's giving me charity!'

'*Resisteremo fino all'ultima polenta!*' was the general cry – 'We'll hold out till the last slice of polenta!' It had not quite come to that, but the situation, as Fenzi perceived, was growing critical. Remaining stocks of maize flour were being mixed with crushed beans to make 'patriotic bread', and the troops were being issued with horse meat. The restaurant at which he had eaten so agreeably ten days earlier was closed, along with most of the others, and Florian's café, that bastion of patriotism, was sedulously following the government's bakery regulations. Water was laced with whatever brandy was available in an attempt to purify it, and supplies of wine had run out altogether. The Provisioning Committee reckoned that while oil and cheese might be stretched out for as long as two months, the stocks of rice and vegetables could only last a few weeks more. Hunger, as much as any nobler impulse, may have moved Clinton Dawkins on 2 August, three days into the bombardment, to write Daniele Manin a letter (its principal sentence is 115 words long) calling on the government to open its eyes 'to the far greater evils that must ensue from a perseverance in the course in which they are now engaged'. He appealed 'in the sacred name of humanity' for an end to resistance and warned its members to 'weigh well the responsibility of involving in destruction the lives and fortunes of their fellow citizens'.

Dawkins appears to have hoped, like the Austrians with whom he was suspected by some of plotting as well as sympathising, that the sheer horrors of siege warfare now being visited on the Venetians would induce them to agitate for surrender. For the time being he had misjudged the situation. As so often in beleaguered towns, the greater the duress, the more buoyant grew an impulse to outwit the enemy and defy him to do his worst. Just as at Lucknow in 1857, Mafeking in 1900 and the legation quarter at Peking during the Boxer Rising, a heightened sense of honour and shared resolve bound the defenders together, regardless of hierarchical and socio-economic differences. Venice was determined to maintain, at however rudimentary a level, some semblance of her ordinary life and of the rhythms of civil society. Thus on 1 August, notwithstanding the bombs, Teatro La Fenice was reopened for a scratch performance of Rossini's *Guillaume Tell*, an opera that ends with the defeat of Austrian tyranny and an ecstatic hymn to the radiant dawn of liberty. The occasion was in honour of a raid carried out that same day from the fort at Brondolo on the Austrian positions. Masterminded with his usual intrepidity by Giuseppe Sirtori, it had aimed at seizing as much as possible in the way of provisions from what was always the weakest sector of the enemy's front line. Surprised by the swiftness of the Italian assault, the imperial troops simply melted away, scattering their knapsacks and even their weapons as they ran. One battalion, not content with abandoning all its baggage, left the regimental flag behind, a morale-boosting trophy to be added to the 200 cows, fifty boats full of provisions and several prisoners borne back in triumph to Venice.

Perhaps Sirtori had recalled the letter he received some weeks earlier as a member of the Defence Committee, from an anonymous correspondent exclaiming, 'There's no bread, for God's sake!' and reporting scenes of panic in Campo SS Giovanni e Paolo, where women were being robbed in broad daylight of whatever jewellery they had not already given to the patriotic collections. 'Give us food as quickly as may be. As a result of the new provisioning regulations, we're passing from the frying pan into the fire.* It is up to you, who hold the city in your hands and

---

* Italians say 'Dalla graticola alla pentola' – 'from the griddle to the saucepan'.

who are responsible for it before God, the Motherland, Italy and Europe, to provide for us. The people are growing restless and demand a sortie.' Certainly, according to the Swiss officer Jean Debrunner, the apparent success of the Brondolo raid (though the captured victuals were only enough for three days when distributed among the citizens) encouraged talk of further expeditions, and a growing anti-surrender faction began to gather. Debrunner, with grisly humour, refers to it as 'the cannibal party', since, if starvation hit the city as seemed likely, human flesh would be all there was left to eat.

As if famine and the bombardment were not miseries enough, a fresh horror now threatened the Venetians in the shape of Asiatic cholera, the killer epidemic disease of close-packed urban communities throughout the nineteenth century. Italy's port cities had always been particularly vulnerable to its onslaughts since its arrival in Europe during the 1830s. In 1849, just as before, the eruption of cholera in the city was part of a wider pandemic spreading westwards from Afghanistan across the Middle East. The causes of *cholera morbus* were at this stage attributed to a poisonous miasma given off by bad drains, cesspits and overcrowded dwellings: it would be another ten years before the London doctor John Snow identified its real source, during a virulent epidemic in one of the poorest areas of Soho, as drinking water contaminated by human excreta. Given the fact that the Austrian siege force was already being ravaged by the disease, it was not difficult for either side to ascribe its appearance to noxious vapours from a mainland heavily occupied by large concentrations of troops. Veneto towns such as Rovigo and Bassano, what was more, already lay in the grip of extensive cholera outbreaks.

Considering the thinness of the average Venetian diet during July and August of 1849, it might have been possible to believe, with the correspondent of the Paris *Journal des débats*, that some of the earliest so-called cholera cases in the city were more likely to be owing to a lack of meat and proper bread or to overmuch consumption of vegetables. Whatever the truth, the thirty-six cases recorded on 1 August had risen to 140 the following week, with fifty-six dead. These statistics are sinisterly noted in a little green notebook preserved among Manin's papers in the Biblioteca Correr. By 6 August so many corpses were waiting to be ferried to the Christian cemetery at San Michele or the Jewish graveyard on the Lido that it had become necessary to double the number of boatmen and increase the sextons' salaries. Hospital mortuaries were full to overflowing and bodies had to be dumped unceremoniously in surrounding *calli* and *campi*. Once again San Pietro di Castello bore the brunt of the epidemic.

By 15 August the anonymous compiler of the green notebook noted 402 fresh cases, with 247 dying in a single day on the 17th. The Public Health Commission calculated the total number of deaths at this stage as 1,249 and it was to be another month before the epidemic ceased to offer a serious threat (though as readers of Thomas Mann's *Death in Venice*, published some sixty years later, will recall, outbreaks would continue in the city – the most recent, at the time of writing, recorded in 1994). Set up expressly to deal with the new emergency, the commission painted a bleak enough picture of the situation. Doctors and pharmacists were worked to exhaustion and many cholera victims were at risk for lack of basic medical attention. 'Certain individuals,' ran the report, 'are lying huddled together in damp ground-floor rooms without light or ventilation, among those dying or dead, the latter unburied for want of gravediggers or because such people refuse to enter areas in which they become exposed to falling shells.' Implied by such words was an obvious plea for surrender negotiations to begin.

That the end was near in any case, and that further suffering might be avoided by prudent negotiation with the Austrians, had occurred to others besides Niccolò Priuli and Pietro Canal, in their bold attempt at an amendment during the debate of 30 June. On 2 August, Count Girolamo Dandolo, described by a contemporary as 'an odd fish, testy and restless, one of the few patricians with a drop of the old heroic blood in his veins', presented a petition – an 'instance', indeed, such as Manin's had been in the December of 1847 – to the municipality of Venice, urging its members, led by Mayor Giovanni Correr, to persuade the government to surrender. The impetus behind this, as much as destruction, hunger and disease, had been a realisation that Schwarzenberg actually meant what he said in announcing to Valentino Pasini that there could be no deal made with Venetian representatives until the city itself had yielded unconditionally. Correr, however, would not accept a request with only a single signature attached, and Dandolo promptly went in search of others. Sources do not agree on exactly how many names he managed to gather, but it was probably around eighty.

They included that of the Cardinal Patriarch, Jacopo Monico. His loyalty to the cause had been suspect long before his condemnation of *Sior Antonio Rioba* in December, yet he had never openly declared support for the Austrians and continued to encourage the clergy's cooperation as regarded special prayers and parish collections linked to the activities of the army or the government. Monico's refusal, on the other hand, to confront political issues from any but a strictly orthodox ecclesiastical standpoint, determined by his unbending devotion to Pope Pius, made him a generally unsympathetic figure to the revolutionaries. Thus when news of the petition was leaked by members of the assembly to whom it had been presented, the Patriarch's temporary residence at Palazzo Querini Stampalia offered an obvious focal point for popular discontent, and on the morning of 3 August a crowd of several hundred people gathered in the little campo outside the palace, on the south side of the church of Santa Maria Formosa.

The building housed a superb library and picture collection gathered together by Count Giovanni Querini Stampalia (later bequeathed, together with the palace, to the municipality of Venice as a cultural foundation, still flourishing today). Querini and his family were living in the palace at the time, but could have had no inkling of the grotesque episode that was about to involve them. Led by the lawyer Giuseppe Giuriati, by Michele Caffi, ringleader in the window-smashing dealt out to Priuli and Canal, and by an engineer named Manzini, the mob surged onto the bridge over the canal dividing the palace from its campo, and broke open the doors. An orgy of looting and vandalism began, its damage estimated at 100,000 lire. Books and objets d'art were hurled out of the windows, and among the pictures ending up in the canal was Giovanni Bellini's beautiful 'Presentation in the Temple'. A portrait of Pius IX was hacked to ribbons, funds of which Monico acted as custodian were stolen, and mirrors, lamps, chandeliers, Japanese vases, clocks and the Count's important collection of coins and medals were all carried off, as well as a set of furnishings formerly adorning the boudoir of the French queen Marie Antoinette. Only the arrival of forty police, led by Niccolò Tommaseo and his fellow deputy Jacopo Bernardi, rescued Monico from the lynch-mob martyrdom he was preparing himself, on his knees at prayer, to face with suitable courage. Setting aside his enduring contempt for the Cardinal, Tommaseo faced down the rioters, assuring them that the government was not contemplating a cowardly surrender and warning that episodes like this merely played into Austrian hands.

Suitably terrified, Monico shifted his quarters once again, this time to the Armenian monastery on the island of San Lazzaro, refusing Clinton Dawkins's offer of shelter aboard a British ship. The Consul had almost certainly lent his support to Dandolo's petition, and it was presumably more than coincidental that his letter to Manin should have been sent on the same day. Amid profound misgivings and sharply conflicting priorities, the assembly gathered in secret session on 5 August. Officially this was to be its final meeting before a new parliament assumed office following an election even then supposed to be taking place. In fact that familiar modern democratic ailment known as 'voter apathy' had seized hold of the citizens, though for different reasons from those complained of nowadays. Evidently far fewer potential electors thought the process was worth taking seriously, and some observers believed this was a message to the government to consider surrender before Venice sank absolutely to her knees in terms of human and material resources.

If Manin had imagined that the force of circumstance would make it easier for him at least to recommend an honorable submission, he was mistaken. Though Ulloa, dignified and realistic as ever, appeared decisive on the point that the city could no longer be supplied with food from the mainland, and Cavedalis wearily emphasised the absurdity of Venice and Chioggia tottering to their ruin without managing to rescue Italy in the process, their warning voices were overwhelmed by those of diehards like Varè and Tommaseo, urging a more proactive form of armed resistance. Varè seized eagerly on Cavedalis's suggestion that a dictator be appointed, but Manin, seeing which way the wind blew, was quick to point out that if such a man were to lead the people, he must be someone who wholeheartedly believed in fighting to the end. Without such a conviction, he must be no better than a liar. When Varè demanded to know why he had not so far consulted these very same ordinary citizens as to their wishes on the matter, Manin answered with chilling bluntness, 'Because I desire that on my wretched tombstone be inscribed the words "Here lies an honest man."'

His position was now as clear as he could possibly make it. After Tommaseo's demand for a more rigorous analysis of the naval and military resources still available, the session was suspended for an hour. When it reconvened, another deputy, Giovanni Minotto, reminded his fellow members that they were gathered there to deal with the prevailing emergency, not to discuss surrender. They needed therefore to elect a leader 'incapable of a cowardly act or of condemning the city to a pointless destruction'. His motion was 'that plenary powers should be conferred upon Daniele Manin, to provide, as he thinks best, for the safety and honour of Venice'. It was Giuseppe Sirtori, predictably, who at once objected, claiming that 'neither the people nor the army have complete confidence in him'. Once more Manin gained advantage from his own candour, acknowledging that his popular support was not what it had been, but blaming this implicitly on the assembly's own failure to back him in recent weeks.

Sirtori now took a step too far, and in doing so produced the very situation he had striven to avoid. 'In my opinion Manin cannot be given sole charge of the government,' he declared scornfully, 'because his very name will signify immediate capitulation.' Far from stopping the

President in his tracks, as Sirtori had intended, this insult was the cue for him to accept Minotto's proposal. Yes, he would assume the proffered dictatorship, but only with the assembly's moral backing and the grant of unconditional authority. His recent presidential role had meant little more than 'serving as a passport for ideas which were not my own'. Now Manin wanted complete and undivided power. Further objections from Sirtori and Tommaseo were in vain, and the parliament adopted Minotto's motion by fifty-six votes to thirty-seven, with the proviso that any decision concerning surrender must be ratified by the full assembly. Given the number of 'no' voters, Manin naturally felt constrained to ask for a guarantee of cooperation from this significant minority. After a prolonged silence, Sirtori declared the request needless. Manin paid tribute to this honourable reply, and all those present, whatever their political tendencies, agreed to unite in the common cause.

The outcome of this dramatic session of 6 August had both seen off the challenge to Manin's authority from the radicals and left him in a more exposed position. An obvious indication of the change occurs in an episode outlined in letters written from Venice at this time by Paul-Henry de Belvèze, commander of the French naval squadron in the Adriatic. His flagship, the *Panama*, was now moored in the lagoon, and he was a natural channel of communication with Admiral Dahlerup and the Austrian fleet. It helped that, like France's consul Vasseur, Belvèze should at least have begun by admiring Manin. 'What characterises him and does him honour is his sense of order and discipline, as well as that benevolent spirit which fourteen months of siege have done nothing to undermine.' Belvèze was broadly sympathetic, what was more, to Venice's desire for independence, but saw surrender as inevitable. The Venetians themselves he considered 'passionate and versatile', yet 'their political education has still to be achieved, and they will succumb, in the end, to the combined action of material forces'.

On the basis of this judgement, Belvèze had begun discussions with Dahlerup as to the likely fate of the government leaders once the siege was over. After agreeing that refuge on French warships might be offered to the revolutionaries, were they to be exiled, Dahlerup found himself pressured by Radetzky and Thurn to keep a greater distance from the supposedly neutral Belvèze, whom they suspected of allowing provisions into the beleaguered city. Consul Vasseur, after all, had courageously smuggled supplies of quinine to Venetian hospitals. There was no evidence of French vessels directly trying to break the blockade, however. Belvèze contented himself with marvelling at the toughness and courage of ordinary Venetians as cholera, hunger and Austrian bombs hit ever harder.

'The calm, the patience, the strange determination to resist among most of the population subject to such grim ordeals is, in my opinion, one of the most incredible and extraordinary things it is possible to witness.'

On 4 August the commander had a meeting with Manin, who told him quite frankly that surrender must come very soon and invited him to act as intermediary in what he referred to somewhat mysteriously as 'the counter-project', details of which would soon be forthcoming. It is not clear from Belvèze's correspondence what the outline of this scheme was, but he seems to have known enough of it to discuss the matter with Dahlerup, who was eager to help by carrying the proposals to Radetzky whenever they should arrive. Feeling understandably heartened at the prospect of a diplomatic breakthrough, succeeding where so many others had failed, Belvèze returned to Manin to finalise arrangements. It was 7 August, the fateful assembly had come and gone, and Manin was a dictator with unlimited powers. His reaction now, far from being encouraging, was one of positive annoyance. If an Austrian spokesman were to arrive, he declared, there would be nothing to offer him. Equally angry at what he considered an extraordinary volte-face, Belvèze withdrew, and the next day penned a curt note 'putting an end to this whole intrigue'.

Following this, his view of Manin was a little less charitable. He came to believe, as Clinton Dawkins already believed, that the President had become a mere tool of the radical *enragés*. 'M. Manin has lacked the necessary courage to withstand the discontent of anarchists and ambitious persons who pushed for resistance to the uttermost, and he has thus allowed one of the most useless acts of devastation to be carried out.' Was this altogether just? Had Manin, by standing up to Sirtori and accepting, in the process, his position as dictator, simply painted himself into a corner from which there was no escape, condemning Venice, meanwhile, to further ruin and suffering? A more likely interpretation is that having assumed his new authority, he resolved to act honourably by the assembly members who had placed such a symbolic trust in him, as well as by the Venetian working class with whom his role as unchallenged leader would greatly enhance his standing.

What they had always admired in '*nostro Manin*' was his refusal to put on airs and his readiness to take part alongside them in facing the hardships of the siege. A memorable instance of this unselfconscious fellowship with the citizens whose destiny lay in his hands was offered on 14 August. The bombardment was now in its third week and fire-watches were being kept over the city from the highest *campanili* of its various churches, especially that of St Mark's. Joining a civic-guard patrol near the Frari, Manin helped to put out a blaze started by falling shells, following which the men celebrated with a few loaves of bread, 'two white and three black as night', and a bottle of Valpolicella somebody had managed to find. The parish priest of the Frari, an intrepid patriot, showed them his collection of bombs and cannon balls and invited Manin to join the celebrations to be held the next day at the nearby church of San Rocco for the saint's feast day. Manin could hardly refuse – had he not been born, after all, in the adjacent parish of Sant'Agostino? – so the following morning, under the whistle of grenades and 'Viennese oranges', his gondoliers set out. When they reached the canal leading towards San Pantalon, the church directly to the south of San Rocco, the bombing grew so heavy that the boatmen were reluctant to continue. 'Go on!' ordered Manin. 'We're not cowards! The priest is waiting to add our prayers to his, that God may favour this oppressed city.'

As stocks of ammunition began running low, and as food supplies dwindled and deaths from cholera mounted, divine dispensation was about all the Venetians had left to trust in. Writing to Manin on behalf of an overburdened fire brigade, who in a single night on 12 August had managed to extinguish sixty conflagrations, their chief Giovanni Sanfermo, praising their courage under the bombing, compared the abandoned and devastated areas of Venice to 'Pompeii, a city of the dead', almost as if the Black Legend were reaching its ultimate ghastly fulfilment in a total nemesis of the 'sea Sodom'. Everywhere houses and shops were boarded up, with notices such as 'Closed owing to owner's joining the defence force' or simply 'Closed owing to the death of the proprietor'. The Austrians having now contrived to block the supply of fresh water to various parts of the city, attempts were made at digging artesian wells, but the water they produced was so rank-tasting that it needed to be mixed with a drop or two of whatever brandy or grappa might still be available. The crash of shells was unceasing, and on 14 August one of them found no less prestigious a billet than the bed of Her Britannic Majesty's consul Clinton Dawkins, falling neatly between his legs as he lay asleep. Save for a minor burn, he was unharmed, but news of the accident sped through the city in a flash and patriots were gleeful at his expense.*

Cheerfulness in the face of disaster somehow managed to persist. A gondolier working the *traghetto* (ferry) across the Grand Canal at San Beneto thanked God for dropping a cannon ball close by so that he could take it to the Arsenal for money to buy bread. By the same token, the owner of one of Venice's many small gardens, flattened by a hailstorm of

---

* The offending ball is still in the possession of the Dawkins family.

bombs, could philosophically conclude, 'Well, the Croats may destroy my flowers, but at least they've made me rich.' Watching a shell burst, a little girl was heard to say to her friend, 'I'll be able to tell people about this when I'm grown up.' And there is no reason to doubt the story, retailed by Francesco Carrano in his account of the siege, of the young mother whose arm was blown off as she snatched up her baby to flee. 'I've got one left for you, my darling,' she cried through her pain, 'and that's enough as long as I don't have to see those ugly mugs of the Croats any more.'

Rumour and panic presented a more insidious danger than Austrian guns to Venetians in this defiant mood. Advocates of a direct military offensive, to be launched from the city across the railway bridge, had gathered support during the earliest phase of the bombardment, and on 7 August a large crowd gathered in the Piazza demanding that 'the people of St Mark should be allowed to advance in a body against the enemy'. Quite what this meant in practical terms was unclear, and Manin, appearing at his customary window in the Procuratie, was quick to exploit such ambiguity so as to wrong-foot the agitators. 'You wish to fight?' he asked them. 'But how often have I urged you to join the volunteers? Alas, to our common shame, I must say that I have come to expect words rather than deeds from you all, and now you make this useless uproar, like effeminate weaklings. I repeat, action is needed. If you want to fight, you can. Go and find a leader.' In a few minutes he had entered the square and called for a table and a register. Knowing exactly what he was doing, he announced, 'Let all who wish to fight inscribe their names.' Only eight men came forward. As they did so, the Austrian cannonade rumbled even louder and the crowd started to melt away.

The peril of such mass hysteria remained. The following day, a certain Tondelli fly-posted the city with the announcement of a proposed attack on the Austrian positions to be carried out by every able-bodied male not currently engaged in holding the forts and batteries. At midnight that evening there was to be a grand patriotic victory-or-death oath-swearing ceremony in the Piazza. Tondelli was said to be mad, but the mob collected as before. This time they were greeted by a handsome youth dressed in peasant clothes, who claimed to be an adjutant of Giuseppe Garibaldi, known to be somewhere on the Adriatic coast following his dramatic escape from Rome. In a rousing speech, full of 'Viva!'s, 'Death to Austrian sympathisers!' and 'Away with foreign oppressors!', he announced the imminent arrival of the patriot hero. This was enough for the crowd, which dispersed in happy anticipation. Quite possibly Manin himself believed this, though Cavedalis thought it was a ruse cooked up by the

Committee of Public Vigilance to fox the agitators. Certainly the *garibaldini* had intended to reach Venice on fishing boats from Cesenatico, but Austrian patrols had intercepted them and, as they retreated into the marshes and pine forests of the Po delta, Garibaldi's wife Anita, already frail and exhausted, fell mortally ill and died in his arms. Some contact with the fugitives was nevertheless maintained by Sirtori, though after Anita's death Garibaldi decided to head south towards Ravenna rather than trying to reach Chioggia as originally planned.

Among the defence force itself, Tondelli's proclamation and rumours of Garibaldi's coming threatened to erode both discipline and morale, the latter already affected by the destruction of two raft-mounted gun batteries at San Secondo and the bursting of a cannon at the Piazzale, killing eight artillerymen. On 10 August Girolamo Ulloa, as commander of the forts, used his authority to disperse an ugly gathering in the Piazza of men from the Bandiera e Moro brigade, but they planned to meet again at the Hotel Gran Bretagna to prepare a massed sortie. General Pepe now intervened, first of all ordering senior officers to handle the situation, and then, when it became obvious they had lost control, agreeing to receive delegates from among the mutinous regiment. The old man's charm and friendliness persuaded the hotheads to face the practical impossibilities and intrinsic wastefulness of the proposed operation, but he had no compunction in adding that quite enough loyal soldiers remained in the ranks for him to have his visitors shot, if he chose.

Between them, Ulloa and Pepe now sought to head off any further breakdown in disciplne by instituting an emergency procedure. Officers were to meet Pepe for orders each evening until further notice; the civic guard was to maintain an emergency detachment in the Doge's Palace, alongside 150 police and four cannon; and all Neapolitan troops were confined to barracks. A plea was sent to Ulloa to permit the meeting at the Gran Bretagna to go ahead as planned, with assurances of good conduct throughout, but he begged the leaders not to plunge Venice into a fratricidal struggle. Once they had backed down, fifteen officers were arrested and dispersed to imprisonment in various forts around the lagoon.

Manin read the situation as yet another threatened collapse of public order. On 13 August, standing on his usual balcony reviewing four battalions of the civic guard in the Piazza, he harangued them on their loyalty to Venice, demanding an affirmation of their continuing confidence in him. Loud cheers broke from both the guard and the watching crowd. 'Your steadfastness fills me with sorrow,' he told them. 'It makes me feel your sufferings the more strongly. You must not rely on my moral or physical strength, but on my devotion to you. This alone abides, deep, infinite, immense, and ending only with my life. Whatever happens, supposing I must live and die far from you, say "This man lied to himself" but never "This man lied to us". Never have I deceived anybody, never did I try to foster illusions which I did not share, or cry "Hope!" when I myself could hope no further.' At this point, overcome with sheer emotional exhaustion, Manin collapsed and was helped from the balcony into the room behind. The entire crowd was now in tears and he himself was weeping. Beating the table with his fists, he exclaimed, 'To be forced to yield, with such a people!' Whatever his critics – the Caninis, Sirtoris and Tommaseos – might lay to his charge, Manin's visceral attachment to Venice could never be in doubt, and this affirming moment between the populace and the man who had suffered most on their behalf held a pathos the greater because so many of those present must have known how soon the end would be at hand.

One resource, however, had so far remained untested. Threats of mutiny notwithstanding, the army had performed prodigies of valour, but nothing so far had been seriously asked of the navy, or indeed offered on its behalf. Soon after the abandonment of Marghera, supreme naval command had passed from Leone Graziani (Emilio Bandiera's father-in-law and an experienced officer who had done his best to enlarge capacity by converting fishing smacks and sailing barges to gunboats) to Achille Bucchia, a corvette captain much respected by Admiral Albini during the Piedmontese fleet's long stay in the Adriatic. Bucchia, almost as soon as he took over, cast doubt both on the seaworthiness of available ships and on the discipline among their crews. On the cruiser *Pio IX* the men had grown surly and insubordinate enough to alarm the council of war, which ordered three arrests and had one of the prisoners shot. Most of the best officers elsewhere had forsaken the service to join the gunners at the batteries and forts, and few of those left behind honestly believed that the Venetian fleet, for all the number of its boats and the sailors' keenness to take a crack at Dahlerup's blockade, could match the Austrian vessels for either speed or effectiveness of armaments. A handful of minor actions had taken place during recent months, but nothing genuinely calculated to dent the Danish admiral's confidence.

Ironically, this was no longer what it had been when his reforms were carried out during early spring. Cholera and malaria had taken their toll on the various Austrian crews – the brig *Oreste* was so short-handed, indeed, that she could only execute the simplest of manoeuvres – and one frigate, the *Vulcan*, was currently at Trieste being refitted after a storm during which several of her cannon had to be thrown overboard to prevent capsize. Bucchia nevertheless mistrusted reports of such losses brought to him by a government envoy returning from Ravenna, and was reluctant to allow even a dash through the southernmost Lido outlets at Alberoni and Chioggia to gather in sorely needed provisions from down the coast. It was all he could do to dissuade even the most navally expert members of the government from urging a token expedition so as to silence critics in the army, led by Ulloa and Sirtori, who believed the fleet could do its bit if it chose. After all, they reasoned, it was not as if a warship could easily pursue the lighter Venetian craft through the channels of the lagoon – a fact which, as much as the demoralised incompetence of Austrian sailors in pre-Dahlerup days, explained why the city had never been seriously menaced from the water during the whole revolution.

While Dahlerup was writing anxiously to Schwarzenberg's Minister for War, Count Gyulai, to say that if Venice managed to hold out a month longer he could no longer guarantee an adequate blockade or resist a naval assault, Bucchia was busy warning Manin and his colleagues not to risk any kind of maritime adventure. 'I dissociate myself entirely,' he told them, 'from the opinion of those who believe in the usefulness of a desperate attempt made against the enemy by sea, expecting some sort of national advantage thereby. I do so the more strongly in the knowledge that such an action, far from promoting our glory or that of Italy, would be merely a pointless shedding of blood. I have no desire that my memory should be blackened by the curses of mothers, sisters, wives and entire families, simply through the sacrifice of those under my command.' His plea fell on deaf ears. What Jean Debrunner called 'the cannibal faction' was in the ascendant, carrying Manin along with them, and though sailors and officers throughout the fleet proclaimed their unshaken confidence in Bucchia, the majority were determined on immediate action. Urged on by one of Niccolò Tommaseo's fly-posted effusions, headed 'Address to the Venetian Navy' and declaring that the inhabitants of Istrian and Dalmatian ports would welcome them with open arms (some obvious wishful thinking here), they prepared to set sail, despite inadequate provisioning, insufficient water and very little money with which to pay the crews, should they indeed break through into the open Adriatic.

One officer, Luigi Fincati, who, like Bucchia, had been fingered by the Austrian police at the time of Emilio Bandiera's escape, was prepared to stick his neck out against Tommaseo and those in favour of immediate action. His defence of the navy's refusal to budge was also an arraignment of the government's failure, over many months, to arm the fleet adequately and overhaul its command structure. He accused those in charge of the Arsenal of wasting valuable wood supplies, which could

have been used for ship-building, for the construction of beds and barricades, and he was keen to remind the Venetians (in danger, as it seemed,
of forgetting) that numerous vessels of different kinds had played an indispensable role in supporting the land actions at Treporti and Conche, not
to speak of their part in the defence of Marghera and the other forts.

Bucchia was forced to bow to the popular mood, and on 8 August
crowds gathered to wish the fleet God-speed. For the next two days the
larger ships kept up a desultory cannonade, returned by Dahlerup's
gunboats, but neither navy made any sort of move towards a close engagement. The Danish admiral later acknowledged that if, instead of finally
retreating behind the sea-wall at Malamocco, the Venetians had ventured
out into open water, they could easily have cut through the already
maimed blockade cordon and sailed on towards the Istrian coast, where
provisions were freely available. Instead, Bucchia appears to have stuck
to the instructions issued by Francesco Baldisserotto, on behalf of the
Military Commission, ordering him to stay within sight of land, since
the army might suspect, once the ships were over the horizon, that a
mutiny had broken out. According to Emanuele Cicogna, still indefati-
gably keeping notes for his diary, a rumour was afoot in the city that the
Austrians were offering an amnesty to officers as long as they refrained
from direct attack. Bucchia's subsequent claim that the force of the sirocco,
getting up as dawn broke, made fighting impossible was suspected by
several as being merely a convenient pretext to mask an already determined course of action.

Whatever the truth, the force on which Venice had staked her final
throw turned tail and headed back to port. Bucchia had been all too
accurate in stating that the crews, in several cases, were unfit for combat.
On the corvette *Lombardia*, for instance, her 110 men already on the verge
of mutiny, fifty-three went down with cholera during the three days spent
out in the lagoon. 'In truth,' remarks Carlo Radaelli, recalling the miserable news of the ships' return, 'it seemed as if the God who rules the
destiny of nations had turned away his face. The hapless Queen of the
Adriatic was now undergoing the most hideous torment recorded in
history. The martyrdom of Venice served to show what extremes of super-
human virtue might be reached through the patriotism of a people confident of its rights, proud of its honour and powerful in its unity.'

None of these splendid abstractions availed against the practical necessities of a battered and semi-deserted city, whose inhabitants now faced
further ravages of starvation and disease in the furnace blast of a full-on
Italian summer. Help from anywhere outside the siege lines was unimaginable. On 11 August Field Marshal Radetzky issued a proclamation to

the Venetians from his Milan headquarters, announcing that a full peace agreement had officially been concluded between Emperor Franz Josef and King Victor Emmanuel of Piedmont. 'By degrees tranquillity and order will provide happiness for the rest of Italy, whose population, so recently a prey to anarchy, will turn its gaze towards a new era. The faction now oppressing you Venetians has arranged matters so that you alone among all the rest are continuing in your unjustifiable resistance to a Government offering every guarantee of order and rational progress, of a kind you have expected in vain from the rebel administration.' Exhorting them to surrender, he repeated the terms presented three months earlier, before the attack on Marghera began.

Radetzky must have been heartened by the news arriving from Hungary. Under General Haynau, the Austrian army – its nerve stiffened by support from Tsar Nicholas's Russian expeditionary force – had swept across the rebel kingdom in a spirit of righteous vengeance, looting, burning and hanging, while General Görgey sought to make terms with the Russians rather than surrender to Habsburg justice. On 11 August Lajos Kossuth resigned as leader of the civil government, and two days later the 160,000 soldiers under Görgey's command laid down their arms at Vilagos. Though he himself was spared, the Russians promptly rounded up the Hungarian officers to hand over to the Austrians. Nearly 400 were sent to prison, several others were stripped of their rank and made to serve as privates, thirteen were hanged and a hundred more were shot. Haynau in Hungary was as barbarous as he had shown himself at Brescia, ordering women to be stripped and flogged, and pursuing a policy of wholesale conscription checked only when it was pointed out to him that the fields would soon have nobody left to work them.

The news from Hungary took five days to reach Venice. Meanwhile, together with Radetzky's proclamation, there arrived another letter from Milan, written by Karl von Bruck but couched in terms far chillier than those in which he had sought to engage Caluci and Pasini during July's abortive peace negotiations. Manin was addressed as 'Signor Avvocato', the customary form when writing to Italian lawyers (*avvocato* is the English 'advocate') without any reference to his position as head of state. Bruck's object was merely to introduce the proclamation, warning that a failure to make it public would constitute a betrayal of Venice and its honour. Assuming the conditions listed were acceptable, he would journey to Mestre in person, 'most happy to see the intentions of the worthiest of monarchs carried out, and the city of Venice participating in the general pacification of Italy'.

On the evening of 16 August, the day after Manin had attended mass at San Rocco, where the liturgy was drowned by the thunders of the bombardment, a secret meeting took place in the Doge's Palace between government ministers and the Military Commission, to choose possible envoys for deliberation with the Austrians. Further discussions next morning with Vasseur, Belvèze and Clinton Dawkins led to them agreeing to accompany three representatives, Dataico Medin, Niccolò Priuli and Giovanni Battista Cavedalis, to the mainland under a white flag. Rumours of the proposed truce got out at once, and the crowd in the Piazza demanded Manin's presence on the balcony. Prepared to admit that some sort of peace process was under way, he nonetheless assured them that any negotiations would be conducted with honour. 'The mere suggestion that I should act basely on Venice's behalf is itself unworthy. I could not make such a sacrifice.' Yet even as he spoke these words, a voice cried, 'We're hungry!' Furious, Manin shouted back, 'Let the hungry man come forward.' There was no answer. Shame rather than anger ran through the throng below. 'We are Italians! Long live Manin!' exclaimed several of them. 'Hunger does not yet exist in Venice,' he declared, once more challenging the doubter to come forward. After a few more 'Viva!'s, the crowd dispersed.

Manin was lying, and his hearers knew that. It was essential, if anything like acceptable terms were to be secured for Venice's submission, that as few details as possible should be allowed to get out regarding the actual state of her resources, or more properly the lack of them. By publicly rebutting rumours of impending starvation, Manin hoped to prevent the enemy from exploiting any obvious sense of despair among the citizens, so as to exact the most humiliating penalties. As negotiator for the imperial army, after all, Schwarzenberg had chosen General Karl von Gorzkowski, as robustly efficient an officer as Haynau, but without his readiness to indulge a wanton brutality in suppressing revolt. Gorzkowski had earned praise during the 1848 campaign for keeping Mantua safe from Piedmontese attack, and his swift response to such emergencies made him the ideal replacement for Thurn von Valle Sassina, whom Radetzky had transferred to a fresh command. The new supremo, as anxious as anyone to bring the whole siege operation – costly in men and money alike – to an end, frankly despised the Italians and would offer exactly the kind of tough conditions that Manin sought to avoid by making him believe that Venice still had the wherewithal to resist a while longer.

Gorzkowski presented his first obstacle on 18 August by refusing to meet Vasseur, Dawkins, Belvèze or any other representatives of foreign powers intending to act as mediators. The last illusion was thus destroyed of a free Venice as an international issue. By implication the matter was one merely for the victorious Austrians and the rebel subjects they were now about to bring to heel. That morning therefore, three men alone, Medin, Priuli and Cavedalis, stepped into the gondolas moored at the mole of the Giardinetti Reali, behind the Procuratie Nuove. The guns on the batteries had fallen silent and the boats carried white flags, but the crowds thickly clustered along the Canale della Giudecca, watching the gondoliers heading out into the lagoon towards Fusina, still cried, 'Viva Venezia!' On landing the trio were ushered into carriages and taken to Mestre, where Gorzkowski appears to have assumed that the surrender could be wrapped up in a matter of minutes. Angry at the negotiators' perfectly reasonable request for clarification of certain points in Radetzky's schedule, including the fate of the defence force and the number of those to be sent into exile, he abruptly broke off discussion and gave orders for the bombardment to resume within three hours. Cavedalis's request to be allowed to visit Radetzky in person at Verona was impatiently rejected. As the baffled envoys returned to their gondolas, a regimental band contemptuously struck up the Habsburg anthem 'Gott erhaltet unser Kaiser', and amid the opening peals of a dramatic thunderstorm, they returned to Venice as the rumble of cannon started again.

To add to their frustration, there was every sign that mounting uncertainty concerning the city's fate threatened a breakdown in public order. True, the red flag still fluttered on the Campanile at St Mark's:

> Sora la tore di Samarco al vento,
>> Scarlata come 'l sangue una bandiera
>>> Subito à sventolà!*

and officially resistance continued, but the soldiers were growing concerned over their pay in a Venice whose paper currency now had no financial back-up, save private guarantees from the more generously patriotic among richer citizens. Desertions were now becoming frequent among all ranks, and Manin, having visited the batteries in person to hearten those who remained, frantically consulted with Cavedalis as to what money might yet be available, not just to settle army accounts, but to offer a bonus to each man still in uniform. Meanwhile cholera continued to scourge the population: on 20 August Carlo Fenzi told his father that in the past twenty-four hours 136 people had died of the disease. A riotous

---

* 'Above the tower of St Mark / a blood-red flag flutters'. The Venetian dialect lines are by Luigi Vianello.

crowd on the Giudecca had broken into a warehouse where rice was stored for feeding patients in the now hopelessly overburdened hospitals, and carried off every sack and every other foodstuff they could find. The simple matter of holding Venice together until its fate should be settled now became Manin's most urgent concern.

The Austrians were quite as anxious to reach a settlement. Evidently feeling that Gorzkowski had been needlessly brusque with the three Venetian plenipotentiaries, the government in Milan dispatched more practised diplomats in the shape of Karl von Bruck and Heinrich von Hess, Radetzky's quartermaster general and military *éminence grise*, to help hammer out surrender terms. The crucial meeting on 22 August took place, as before, in Villa Papadopoli at the village of Marocco outside Mestre on the Treviso road, the same imperial army headquarters where Dahlerup had admired Haynau's nine-inch whiskers and received the 'brother's kiss' from Radetzky. Here Priuli, Medin and Cavedalis were joined by Giorgio Caluci and a merchant named Antonini to represent Venetian business interests, and by early afternoon conditions had been agreed for handing over the city. Radetzky's revised proclamation, issued the previous week, with its general pardon for all non-commissioned officers and private soldiers and its blanket permission for those who wished to leave Venice, was to be adhered to; however, exile was decreed for officers formerly in the Emperor's service, foreign military and naval personnel of whatever rank, and those civilians named in a list handed to the envoys. The Lombard battalions would leave on 24 August, forts and batteries were scheduled for handover the next day, the city itself would be reoccupied on the 27th, but the Neapolitan troops had to wait until the 30th to make their departure.

In the Emperor's name, Gorzkowski and Hess put their signatures to the document, followed by the five Venetian commissioners. Such an act by no means guaranteed an end to the bombing, since the government in Venice had not yet ratified the terms and the Austrian high command was nothing if not pedantic in seeking to ensure total compliance from the rebels. From the Venetian artillery, what was more, a desperate cannonade was returned – a final flourish, as it were, to show the enemy how much the essence of the struggle would endure even after freedom had vanished. Under the dawn light of 23 August, the defenders on the railway bridge watched a single gondola approach from Fusina. In it sat General Cavedalis, bearing the instrument of surrender. He called up to them to cease fire and hoist a white flag. At six o'clock that morning the guns at last fell silent.

There was another reason for the anger of those final Italian salvoes. On the 22nd, as news of a likely capitulation agreement had spread across the city, certain of the soldiers began to panic at the prospect of Austrian reprisals and the possibility that the government, on the verge of dissolution, would duck any obligation to pay them whatever money might be owing. Later that morning in the Piazza a group of malcontents, their ranks soon swelled by sailors from Bucchia's fleet, summoned Manin to the balcony with demands for three months' wages, some of them even proposing a final crazy sortie against the Austrians. To the deputation they sent up, he explained that any such expedition was impossible, and that despite his efforts, together with those of Cavedalis, to gather enough for a fair settlement, the money available was still insufficient. Out of a fighting force which, at the end of March 1849, had been numbered at 25,000, there were still 11,000 men on active service, let alone the civic-guard battalions, some of whose members were entitled to expenses.

Disgruntled, the ringleaders returned to their comrades in the square. For several hours Manin and the Military Commission officers waited nervously for the soldiers' next move, and at around five o'clock that afternoon news arrived that several hundred men had seized control of the Roma battery at the landward end of the viaduct (or what remained of it) and were threatening to mount their own bombardment of the city unless their demands were met. For the very last time Manin resumed his customary blocking position in the gap between order and anarchy. Leaders of the mutiny called on him to publish the outcome of the negotiations at Mestre. Calmly he told them to wait until an official publication of the surrender terms next morning. Then, roused to anger by the surliness of the crowd, he demanded, 'Are you Italians? Do you wish to deserve freedom, perhaps soon within your grasp?' 'Yes, yes!' came the answer. 'Well then, drive out from among you the infamous agents of these disorders. I have told you already that our situation is serious, even terrible. I had the courage – and God knows I needed it – to declare this to the Assembly. Yes, our situation is difficult, but not so desperate that we must yield unconditionally. I would rather die than sign a dishonourable agreement. If the enemy's superiority in numbers, our hunger or the fact that Europe has abandoned Venice should force us to yield, we know how to submit while preserving the Venetian banner without a stain!'

With a final burst of his old fervour, he had successfully turned the crowd. Cries of 'Manin! Manin!' echoed across the Piazza as he appeared under the colonnade, a drawn sword in his hand. The sheer implausibility of this figure, the little lawyer in his frock-coat and spectacles wielding the brand of the warrior, must have frozen some of the mob with astonishment. 'Let all true Italians,' he announced, 'follow me and help to maintain order!' The emergency was indeed as serious as he had feared. As well as seizing the battery, the mutineers had placed a guard on the main thoroughfares across the western side of the city, and Manin, having gathered enough men together, found his path blocked by sentries on the bridge over the main arterial canal through Cannaregio, linking the Grand Canal with the lagoon. Ulloa now issued a general order for all men to return to quarters, while he and Jean Debrunner detailed their officers to man the bridges closest to the railway station. This hastily devised holding operation, isolating the rebel troops in the batteries until they had time to ponder the realities of the situation, mercifully succeeded, but it was perhaps a wonder that the angry gunners thus pinned down did not take a potshot at Cavedalis as the fateful gondola carried him past the viaduct and on towards the Grand Canal, with the surrender articles and Venice's doom in his hands.

At two o'clock that same afternoon of 24 August Daniele Manin put his signature as President to the last official decree issued by the government of an independent Venice. The document ran as follows:

> Considering that an imperative necessity has brought about a state of affairs in which neither the representative Assembly nor the powers emanating from it can be expected to take any part, the Provisional Government of Venice declares:
> 1. That the Provisional Government itself shall cease to function.
> 2. That the powers of the Government of all the territory administered by it shall pass to the Municipality of Venice.
> 3. That public order, tranquillity and the safety of individuals and their property shall be entrusted to the protection of all citizens, to the patriotism of the Civic Guard and the honour of the armed forces.

In some lines he later added to a copy of this document, Manin, with obvious pride, noted that by 24 August 1849 Rome had already been occupied for six weeks; Grand Duke Leopold of Tuscany had regained his throne two months earlier; Piedmont had signed her peace treaty with Austria on 6 August; and Görgey's Hungarian army had surrendered to the Russians on the 13th. Those last ten days of the siege ought therefore to have earned Venice the admiration, not just of Italy, but of all liberal Europe. As it turned out, her sacrifice – whether in blood, money, mortality from hunger and disease or the unquantifiable yearning for freedom – would all too soon be reduced to a footnote in the history of the Risorgimento or, among Italians, be remembered only by the words of a single poignant poem.

Commemorating the end of the siege, 'A Venezia', or 'Addio a Venezia' as it is sometimes called, was written by the poet Arnaldo Fusinato, born in the Veneto textile town of Schio, who had so tirelessly drummed up charitable donations for the provisional government while in Piedmont after the 1848 armistice. Later he had joined the defence force in Venice itself as a member of the small garrison on the island of San Lazzaro degli Armeni, and it was here that he steeled himself to face the likely collapse of armed resistance. A few days before the siege ended, he wrote his best-known poem, mingling profound wretchedness and anguish with an ardent dedication to Venice all the deeper for being an outsider's. Sitting disconsolately on a balcony at San Lazzaro as dusk falls, Fusinato seems to hear 'a last sigh from the lagoon'. A gondola passes and he asks for news:

> Il morbo infuria,
>   Il pan ci manca,
> Sul ponte sventola
>   Bandiera bianca!

'Disease rages, we have no bread, and on the bridge flutters the white flag.' The final hour has arrived for Venice, but the poet knows that hunger and not cannon shot has brought this about. 'While freedom still exists, I give you my last song, my last kiss, my last tear.' Italian sunlight must not shine on such misery, now the city, 'that illustrious martyr', is lost for ever. He will carry Venice with him in the temple of his heart, like the image of his first love. The same passion felt by Poerio and Tommaseo, by Ulloa and Cavedalis, by Sirtori, Bassi and Gavazzi under-scored the melancholy beauty of Fusinato's verses. He had guessed all too shrewdly at the ways in which, for many a native Venetian, it must soon sharpen the bitterness of exile.

~

'ONLY A TEAR FOR VENICE?'

O N 25 AUGUST 1849 GENERAL Gorzkowski, accompanied by the
Habsburg Archduke Sigismund, was escorted by Cavedalis to
San Secondo, first of the forts in the lagoon to be reoccupied
by Austrian troops, a process that continued throughout the day. Next
morning they entered the Arsenal and assumed full control of Venice
itself. Henry de Belvèze noted the atmosphere throughout the city that
day, encapsulating it in a sentence more memorable in the original French
than in translation: 'La ville est calme et morne, les magasins sont fermés,
on attend.'* It was he who had arranged with Gorzkowski and Dahlerup
to carry those listed in the surrender articles towards the first stage of
their exile, on the British-administered island of Corfu. There were forty
names in all – the imperial government was bent on seeming magnanimous towards its erring subjects – including, besides Manin and
Tommaseo, those of Giuseppe Sirtori, the civic-guard commander
Mengaldo, the lawyers Giuriati and Avesani, the fighting priest Antonio
Torniello, Leone Pincherle, who had played so important a part in
managing the regime's finances, and the patriot politicians Benvenuti,
Varè and Comello. At first Belvèze had been reluctant to accept
Tommaseo, Sirtori and Giuriati on board, since they were 'noted for their
exaggerated opinions, the violence of their acts and the constant expres-
sion of their hatred towards France'. In the end Giuriati would go his
own way, leaving Tommaseo and Sirtori to join the rest on the warship
Solon, scheduled to leave the lagoon on the afternoon of the 28th.

Accompanied by Teresa, Emilia and Giorgio, Manin had boarded the

---

* 'The town is calm and sombre, the shops are shut, people are waiting.'

Solon the previous evening. While they prepared to leave the house at San Paternian, which only one of them would ever see again, a throng of ordinary Venetians, the kind of crowd he had so often harangued in Piazza San Marco, gathered on the campo to watch their departure. The family at length appeared at the door, and as they moved towards the gondola, Manin distinctly heard a voice say, in Venetian dialect, 'Here's our dear master, poor fellow, who has suffered so much for us. God bless him!'* Soon such tributes were to be stifled with the threat of fines, the *bastinado* or imprisonment, but when Gorzkowski later ordered the stone name-plate on the house to be smashed in pieces, its fragments were quickly gathered up as souvenirs. The Manins, though unable to take much in the way of luggage and personal belongings, were not, for the present at any rate, wholly without money. On their behalf the Mayor, Count Giovanni Correr, who had resumed control of the city at the head of the municipal council, scraped together 24,000 lire from his fellow citizens, most of whom had very little left to contribute after the privations of the siege. 'When, to soothe the pangs of exile,' he wrote, 'you recall to mind those days in which your intrepidity and courage preserved Venice from the greatest disasters and maintained order under the most difficult circumstances, you may remember at the same time that Venice herself will always retain the deepest affection and gratitude towards you.'

The exiles were not allowed to leave before the humiliating reappearance of white-coated Austrians in the Piazza on 28 August had sealed the empire's repossession of Venice as an ineluctable fact. Again it fell to Cavedalis to accompany Gorzkowski and Archduke Sigismund with their flotilla of gondolas from Marghera, but once across the open lagoon he ordered his own boatmen to row him into a side canal, where he could avoid the distasteful sense of triumph inevitably surrounding such a procession into the conquered city. He need not have worried unduly. The progress of the cortège down the Grand Canal was marked by a silence among those who witnessed it as glacial as it was dignified. There were no unseemly demonstrations, there was no booing or whistling, but even the most sanguine or determinedly insensitive among the victors must have perceived the absence of enthusiasm for a reinstatement of that status quo ante they represented. What had already astonished the Austrians, and would continue for some while to amaze them, was the way in which most Venetians had clearly been able to live with bombardment, cholera and semi-starvation over a long period without more than

* 'Qua ghe xe el nostro bon pare, poareto, el ga tanto patio per nu. Che Dio la benedissa!'

sporadic outbreaks of popular discontent. Nothing had prepared Gorzkowski and his men for the devastation their own artillery had wrought within the city, but they were correspondingly impressed by the evident efficiency with which the Italians had maintained the forts and batteries until the very last. Still more surprising to them was the scrupulousness with which the public accounts had been managed, both by the provisional government and by the municipality, from the very first days of independence. Though the bureaucratic machinery had worked with difficulty because of the number of clerks enlisting as army volunteers, the bookkeeping remained sedulously exact throughout. As if in disgust at not having been able to find fault, Gorzskowski was heard to remark, 'I didn't think such republican trash could be so honourable.'

This did not stop him from imposing massive financial penalties on Venice. If, as a matter of imperial policy, the rebel city could not be punished with the same harshness Radetzky had meted out to the Milanese, it would be made to pay the price in a more literal sense for seeking to break free. Thus the government's paper currency, the *moneta patriotica*, was gathered in and publicly burned, in the presence of a specially convened group of Austrian and civic authorities, under Sansovino's Loggia, while the money issued by the municipality in November 1848 was reduced to half its value before being gradually phased out.* The burden of reconstruction throughout Venice was laid upon its already exhausted, impoverished and depleted population, and a final humiliating twist of the knife was supplied by a demand that 100,000 Austrian lire were to be paid, in compensation for hardships experienced, to the family of the detested Colonel Marinovich, whose murder at the Arsenal had accelerated the transfer of power on 22 March. Gorzkowski arrested and hanged those involved in the killing, and others far less deeply involved incurred his summary justice. For example, having been told of some rusty rifles found in a cupboard at the hospital of SS Giovanni e Paolo, he rounded up the director, almoner and head porter and had them all imprisoned.

The final confirmation of Venice's restored status as a fiefdom of the Habsburgs was given on 30 August, when Field Marshal Radetzky entered the city in triumph. He had already taken care to praise the besieging army for its steadfastness in sustaining a campaign that had lasted more

---

* See Effie Ruskin, in a letter of 15 November 1849: 'The other day an immense Fire and a large cauldron was put in the Square where they burned all the paper money issued by the Provisional Government here while it lasted. I saw the ashes of above 2,000,000 of notes.'

than 500 days. Promising 'peace under Austria's stainless flag', he saluted his men as 'leaders on the path of honour and duty'. One of his many virtues as a commander was a notable lack of professional vanity, and he was well aware that, however much success had depended on his immovable resolve to keep the Italian provinces within the empire come what might, it was the courage and loyalty of his generals and their regiments that had ensured this final victory. To the strains of Haydn's 'Emperor's Hymn', Radetzky crossed the Piazza hand in hand with Admiral Dahlerup – 'The pair of us must walk together,' he insisted – to be formally greeted by Mayor Correr and Cardinal Monico, the latter unashamedly delighted by the regime change. In St Mark's itself, a solemn Te Deum celebrated the restoration of Venice to 'its legitimate sovereign'. According to an anonymous writer in the London *Quarterly Review*, whose contempt for the revolutionaries suited the magazine's uncompromising Toryism, 'the entrance of Marshal Radetzky was performed amid the silence of a bewildered population, who felt at their deliverance a joy their fear compelled them to conceal'. This is wishful thinking on the part of the conservative reviewer. That evening's festive illuminations in the Piazza, outside the palace where an Austrian governor, in the shape of Gorzkowski, had once more taken up residence, were ordered, and not spontaneous, and there is no evidence of widespread exitement or relief occasioned by the restoration of imperial power, save among a handful of unreconstructed *austriacanti*. Among them was the elderly chronicler Count Emanuele Cicogna, who, while acknowledging that he was happy to serve his native city whatever its rulers, and to respect whoever might be in command, confessed, 'I must always, for the sake of gratitude, prefer the Austrian government, under whom I have been favoured with office and honours.'

Three days before Radetzky's arrival, the exiles had left Venice, most of them for Corfu, others on a roundabout journey to Piedmont via the Papal States, since a progress across Lombardy-Venetia was judged too potentially contaminating by the nervous imperial police. Among this latter group was Giuseppe Giuriati, accompanied by his son Domenico. The pair set off up the Grand Canal in a gondola bound for Marghera, together with Giovanni Battista Varè, Francesco Degli Antoni and Bartolomeo Benvenuti, all of whom had played prominent roles at various stages of the revolution. As they emerged from beyond Cannaregio into the lagoon, they could see the waters around them crowded with vessels moving landward like theirs, while in the opposite direction came the large oared transports carrying imperial troops. At Marghera they were duly informed of the ban on the movement of exiles through Lombardy.

When Varè suggested that they might be allowed to return to Venice and board a ship to Greece, they were told that their passports were valid only for land travel. The documents seem to have been inadequately detailed, since one of the officers had to ask Benvenuti whether his name featured in the list of forty exiles stipulated by the surrender agreement. When he answered yes, the official gave him two heavy blows across the face.

For Manin, Tommaseo and the others bound for Corfu, the leave-taking, if not so rough, was just as bitter. Eight vessels had been chartered by Consul Vasseur to carry away more than 600 voluntary exiles, but it was an especially distinguished group that boarded the French warship *Solon* on 27 August. Girolamo Ulloa and Enrico Cosenz were there, alongside General Pepe, the Army Minister Alessandro Marcello, Leone Graziani, Antonio Paolucci and Leone Pincherle. When eventually Tommaseo joined them, the Dalmatian was decidedly unhappy about the company he was expected to keep. 'Not only were there members of the most recent provisional government and certain representatives of the first one, who had been colleagues of mine, but also police officers, minor officials and even certain Jews.' That Tommaseo makes this last distinction begs the question of whether his earlier plea for improvements in Jewish civil rights had been altogether sincere.

Once the *Solon* had sailed out of the lagoon into the open Adriatic, the exiles were transferred to a second French ship, the *Pluton*. Its captain was only too anxious to offload his passengers, mindful of the cholera still present in Venice, and after a two-day voyage they were landed at Corfu's *lazaretto*, the quarantine station maintained in all Mediterranean ports. The Ionian Islands were a British colony, and its High Commissioner Lord Seaton was as suspicious of Italian exiles as his predecessor had been five years earlier during the Bandieras' brief sojourn. Seaton had grown more nervous since the autumn of 1848, when his attempt to conciliate the islands' native population, eager for union with the newly formed kingdom of Greece, by granting a constitution and a free press had got disastrously out of control. A revolt on Cephalonia had ended with the imposition of martial law and the execution of twenty-one ringleaders. Thus there was no question, even after cholera clearance, of most of *Pluton*'s party being allowed to remain. 'You will have the goodness to understand,' warned Seaton:

> that this concession must not serve as a precedent for any future case of a similar nature; that the government cannot consider itself justified in admitting, within a small and impoverished community, a swarm of

refugees without means of existence; that it cannot allow the peace of these islands to be troubled by foreigners newly emerged from nurseries of revolution on the Continent, and that in offering a temporary hospitality, it is with the requirement that such persons should abstain from any involvement in the external affairs of these islands, and that they should prove, by their tranquil and judicious conduct, that they merit the exception the government has agreed to make in their favour.

Gratitude for such condescension, with all its officious verbosity, can hardly have been uppermost in the exiles' minds as they faced the prospect of a dismal semi-imprisonment on a small islet off the northern coast of the little peninsula occupied by Corfu's capital, Kerkira. For the Manin family, the wretchedness of saying farewell to Italy from the deck of the *Pluton* had been made worse by the open hostility of Niccolò Tommaseo, who pointedly refused to take his meals with them, and by the continuing recurrences of Emilia's epilepsy. At the *lazaretto* they were afforded some relief by a Catholic priest, Don Spiridione Campi, who gave Manin two mattresses with some sheets and pillows. The others had to stretch out on the floor. Once the three-week quarantine period was up, they were allowed to land and wander about Kerkira, seeking relief among the Italian community. It was barely fifty years since Corfu had been part of the Venetian empire under the Serene Republic, and the sound of street vendors crying their wares in the accents of the Merceria and the Rialto made Tommaseo very wretched. He had determined all the same not to return to Venice, 'whatever the outcome of human events', a vow he kept sternly for the rest of his life.

During early September boats appeared with more exiles, including Manin's Anglo-Italian nephew George Merryweather, but on the 14th, when the last shipment arrived on the *Icarus*, Seaton forbade them to land, ordering the captain to sail for the Greek port of Patras in the northern Peloponnese. A few hardy spirits on board nevertheless took one of the launches and rowed to the *lazaretto*. On the way they spotted another boat, approaching from the harbour, and on seeing their former leader among its passengers, they sent up a cry of 'Viva Manin!', which was echoed to the skies by those on board the *Icarus*. Teresa's brother Antonio Perissinotti commented afterwards, 'That cry, in those waters and under those circumstances, was both the epilogue of the revolution and its crowning moment.'

Even had the British not been so anxious for them to move on, the exiles could have lingered only a short while among an already over-large refugee population, with no proper financial assistance for its poorest

members. The luckier ones might have followed the example of the
Anconetan poet Luigi Mercantini, who published and sold copies of his
patriotic verse while on Corfu. Some, like the Capuchin 'sharpshooting
friar' Antonio Torniello, who became Catholic chaplain on the island of
Lefkas and was able to purchase his own parsonage house, were sustained
by their private fortunes. The Manins, on the other hand, quickly ran
through the donation raised by the Venetian municipality and, as the end
of September drew on, prepared to leave. Noting the sorrowful farewells
on the quayside, the republic's former Education Minister Giuseppe Da
Camin remarked that 'everyone clung to each other so fervently that they
had to be torn apart by force'. The single and predictable absentee was
Niccolò Tommaseo. Curmudgeonly to the last, he had shunned all contact
with Manin and would not let bygones be bygones even at an instant
like this. It was Antonio Perissinotti, in remembering the occasion, who
pronounced a judgement on the Dalmatian's moral weakness that many
were likely to have shared. 'The man who, at such a moment, allows
himself to be dominated by a mean-spirited amour-propre, and will not
acknowledge as his brothers those unhappy creatures who are compelled
to part from him en route to exile, forgetting every former rancour – oh,
he is indeed unworthy and must be punished with much sorrow!' On
hearing the news that Tommaseo was to remain in Corfu for an indefi-
nite period, Perissinotti crushingly remarked, 'Let him stay. Everywhere
on earth he wanders, he will carry the scourge of his vanity and envy
with him.'

Where could the Manins find refuge? All the Italian peninsula except
Piedmont was barred to them now that the sovereign rulers had resumed
their thrones. Daniele, still a republican at heart, would not have fitted
easily into the new monarchist Italy that was now beginning to evolve
within the limited pseudo-democracy of King Victor Emmanuel's realm,
managed by Massimo d'Azeglio and the increasingly dominant figure of
Camillo Cavour. All three of them were determined to avoid a repetition
of what one modern historian has aptly termed 'Charles Albert's preten-
tious failures'. Later ages would imbue the negotiations between the new
king and Radetzky, following the battle of Novara, with the myth of the
young sovereign's dedication to preserving the spirit of the constitution
set out by his father's Statute of 1848. In fact he had been eager to assure
the Field Marshal of his readiness to crush the remaining democrats and
revolutionaries once he had secured the respective loyalties of his subjects,
of the army and of a parliament whose members he had no scruples in
coercing. In a Turin where the patriot émigrés formed a nation within a
nation, mostly detested by the conservative Piedmontese, a political figure

as clear-sighted and articulate as Manin must always have been unwelcome, even supposing the government, nervously mending fences with Austria, were prepared to tolerate his presence.

London, that haven for many an Italian exile, he seems never to have considered, perhaps because of the dominant presence there of Giuseppe Mazzini, to whose political stance Manin was basically unsympathetic, even if at one stage during the summer of 1848 he had contemplated inviting Mazzini to Venice to bolster the anti-fusion case. The experience of dealing with Clinton Dawkins and Palmerston's consistent failure to encourage the Venetian revolution were not calculated to foster much warmth towards England, and the deliberately unwelcoming, move-along-please attitude of the administration in Corfu did not help matters. The final straw was probably contributed by the government of Malta, another British crown dependency, where Henry Lushington, a highly influential secretary to the Governor and apparently so liberal in his views on Italian politics, was yet reluctant to countenance any further settlement of patriot exiles on the island.

Thus the Manins headed for France, the nation which more than any other had disappointed or actively betrayed the hopes of the Italian revolutionaries in 1848, but in whose potential as a bringer of liberty Daniele held a faith the more touching for being so untypical of his otherwise sceptical outlook. The Italian exile community in Paris, sheltering several of their friends, including the tailor Angelo Toffoli, token artisan and Labour Minister in the first provisional government, would make them welcome. Yet, as if it had not suffered enough, tragedy awaited the family on landing at Marseilles. The French port, with its links to Egypt and the Levant, was a danger zone for cholera epidemics, and the disease was currently rife in the city. By the cruellest of ironies, Teresa Manin, having survived its visitation of Venice during the siege's final months, fell a victim soon after her arrival and died on 11 October 1849. Manin was shattered by the loss of a partner who had been far more to him than a loyal and dutiful wife. She had shared his strength of purpose, his practicality, his courage and a certain inability to suffer fools gladly, which had inspired her attempt, during his imprisonment, to take on the Austrian authorities at their own legal game and combat their obstructiveness and pomposity.

On the eve of their departure from Venice, Teresa had written to a friend in Padua. 'It is all finished, everything save honour is lost. I leave now for a foreign land, for the sight of unknown faces and the sound of an alien tongue. My own most beautiful language I shall never, never hear again.' It was indeed as a teacher of Italian that Daniele Manin now settled in Paris with his son Giorgio and his daughter Emilia. Their lodging was on a gloomy *entresol* of a house in rue des Petites-Écuries, where they lived, if not quite in abject poverty, then certainly in modest circumstances. As far as he was able, Manin refused to accept charity from his fellow exiles and earned his living from daily lessons and occasional journalism. Among his pupils were the novelist Charles Dickens,* a frequent visitor to Paris during the 1850s, and the three children of Countess Marie d'Agoult, a writer who several years earlier had become the mistress of the composer and piano virtuoso Franz Liszt. Their second daughter Cosima is better known to us as the woman who left her husband Hans von Bülow for the more glamorous embraces of Richard Wagner. Part of the latter's *Tristan und Isolde* would later be composed in Venice, where he was a firm supporter of the Austrian regime.

Dickens had been introduced to Manin by a mutual friend, the painter Ary Scheffer, who, like several others, had fallen deeply under the spell cast by poor, stricken Emilia. 'She seemed to flourish even amid grief and misery,' he wrote, 'spreading happiness, gaiety and hope around her. There was no subject, however abstract or profound, which she could not discuss with a wondrous acuteness and sagacity. Those big, fantastic eyes of hers assumed an incomparable fervour, and she could speak of Italy's misfortunes with such stirring accents that we were moved to tears.' Her health inevitably suffered from the privations of their life in rue des Petites-Écuries, and in 1854 she sensed the approach of death. 'Can you picture to yourself this wretched girl,' wrote the aged poet Jean-Pierre de Béranger during her last days, 'thinking of the pain her disorder gave her worthy father, clasping him with her withered hands and asking his forgiveness for the martyrdom she caused him?' Scheffer, who had sketched Emilia on her deathbed, arranged for her to be buried in his family tomb in the cemetery of Père Lachaise. Among those at the funeral were Marie d'Agoult, the Tuscan politician Giuseppe Montanelli and two veterans of the siege, Girolamo Ulloa and Giuseppe Sirtori. For Manin himself the parting with his daughter proved even more agonising than Teresa's death. 'From the time she was five years old,' he once said, 'I perceived that we understood each other.' And in some sense his continued involvement with the cause of Italian freedom became a homage

---

* Dickens left no record of his meetings with Manin, though a possible avatar in his fiction is the Italian refugee John-Baptist Cavalletto in *Little Dorrit*. Wilkie Collins, who accompanied his friend and fellow novelist to Paris on several occasions, almost certainly used Manin as a model for the diminutively athletic Professor Pesca in *The Woman In White*.

to that patriotic intensity which Scheffer had so admired in Emilia while she lived.

For three more years the bereft father endured, living now in an apartment in rue Blanche (near the modern Gare St Lazare), a focus of admiration among the exiles and their Parisian friends. A visit to London in the summer following Emilia's death brought him invitations from the growing pro-Italian caucus among liberal British politicians. Staying at Schill's Hotel in Albemarle Street, he was invited to meet Lord Palmerston, currently out of office after a general election had returned the Tories to power, led by that arch-Austrophile the Earl of Aberdeen. Manin had conversations with the Whig leader John Russell, with a future foreign secretary Lord Clarendon and with William Ewart Gladstone, whose recent pamphlet blasting the treatment of political prisoners by the Bourbon government in Naples had not altogether justly turned King Ferdinand II into a tyrannical ogre. Alas, no record of any of these meetings survives, but the mere fact that such highly placed figures were willing to see Manin suggests that a distinct shift was taking place in British attitudes towards the Italian question.

In Paris once more, Manin, despite his essentially republican outlook, allowed his pragmatism to persuade him that the only solution to the problem of displacing Austrian hegemony in Italy was to try and persuade King Victor Emmanuel, if necessary by dragging Piedmont into another war, that a move towards unification would ultimately benefit the royal House of Savoy. A close association with the Lombard exile Giorgio Pallavicino saw the two of them working towards the formation of what became known as the National Society, based in Turin under the leadership of the Sicilian journalist Giuseppe La Farina, with later support being offered by Garibaldi. Neither Manin nor Pallavicino was under any illusions as to the possibility that the King – no more sympathetic than his father had been towards constitutional government, unless forced upon him by circumstance – would miraculously emerge as a democrat, but his figurehead status was invaluable. Worth everything else was the favourable attitude of his ambitious and resourceful chief minister Camillo Benso di Cavour, who saw the National Society, with its newspaper, its funds and its energetic networking among patriots in other Italian states, as a useful propaganda tool, not least in the way its members chose to distance themselves from Mazzini and his followers.

When Manin first accepted the need to place Piedmont at the centre of the struggle for Italy, Pallavicino declared that his name alone was worth legions. Dedication to the cause needed a physical stamina to match it, and Manin's health, never strong at the best of times, began to ebb.

The death of Emilia, while not breaking him wholly, had left a permanent wound. 'Nobody loved me or will ever love me like that blessed angel,' he wrote on the anniversary of her funeral. 'I accompanied her to the cemetery, saw her laid in the grave and cast a handful of earth upon her. And whenever it rained, I used to think of the water drenching the wood of her coffin . . . My sweet soul, my good girl, my darling, my saint, my angel!'

On 22 September 1857, Daniele Manin died at the age of fifty-three, having signed, on his deathbed, the articles of the Italian National Society. It was an ultimate act of political abnegation in the name of what he and many others at the time believed to be Italy's greater good, but dying came in the end as a simple release from physical exhaustion and personal sorrow. As the British historian G. M. Trevelyan says in his study of the Venetian revolution, 'he had lost and suffered too much to regard death as anything but a friend'. Giorgio, the son who had been Teresa's favourite, led the funeral cortège to the church of La Trinité, having given assurances to an alarmed Parisian prefect of police that there would be no political demonstrations at the ceremony. 'Invitations have not been issued solely to the Italian émigré community,' reported an official of the Ministry of Justice. 'Most of them are addressed to the numerous friends M. Manin had acquired by virtue of his honourable character.' Once again it fell to Ary Scheffer to organise the burial, and Daniele was laid to rest beside his beloved Emilia.

In Venice itself the official *Gazzetta* curtly noted that 'the exile Manin died of heart disease today', but another paper, *La Sferza*, somehow managed to evade censorship with an obituary praising him for his integrity and 'uncommon talents'. No memorial service was permitted, but on 30 September a huge crowd, mostly dressed in black, assembled in his parish church of San Luca. The police had forbidden midday mass to be celebrated, but as the clock struck twelve the whole congregation fell to its knees in prayer. Similar incidents took place at other churches across the city, and on the island of San Michele there was even a sort of mock-funeral, with a gondola procession and prayers in the church, which the authorities were unable to prevent.

By now others were gone who had stood at Manin's side. Ugo Bassi, the priest who venerated him as a hero, had died at Bologna before an Austrian firing squad. In 1855 General Guglielmo Pepe, seeking well-earned repose through studying Plutarch in a Piedmontese country villa, had fallen mortally ill. 'I believe the greatest sacrifice I ever made to Italy,' he once wrote, 'was that of remaining in Venice.' His faults, such as they were, had long been forgiven by the many who served under him, and he was a man whom both Manin and Tommaseo were equally able to admire. The latter spoke at his funeral in Turin's neo-classical church of Gran Madre di Dio, to which the tricolour-draped coffin had been escorted by massed bands, a guard of honour and a huge international crowd. Praising Pepe's great-heartedness and generosity, Tommaseo shrewdly added, 'Yours was the talent for a spiritual, almost invisible unity of leadership. You allowed all to enjoy their moments of glory freely. You prevented petty jealousies, you encouraged positive ambition, and being confident of your own established reputation, without insisting on the importance of rank, you made sure there was room for everyone to flourish.' Two weeks later Tommaseo gave a similar discourse to a group of Venetian women exiles who had come to lay a metal wreath on Pepe's grave. The old general had always basked in attentions from the ladies, especially the members of the nursing committee during the siege, but his love for Anna Gilchrist Coventry, the Scottish wife he had married in 1822, the year after his banishment from Naples, remained steadfast till the end. His last words, when she asked him on his deathbed if there was anything else he wanted, were 'Your company.'

His loyal Neapolitan officers Girolamo Ulloa and Enrico Cosenz would eventually pass into the Piedmontese service. During the campaigns of 1859–60 against Austria and Naples that effectively created the new Italian kingdom, Ulloa (made governor of the port of Leghorn following the precipitate flight of Grand Duke Leopold from Tuscany) was accused of favouring a French candidate for the ducal throne rather than immediate unification with Piedmont. Disgruntled, he returned to Naples to join the army of King Francis II, eventually following him to exile in Rome. In 1866, when Italy went to war with Austria, he sought a fresh commission, but was not unreasonably turned down and spent his old age in Florence writing military history. Cosenz, on the other hand, after getting his fingers burned by throwing in his lot with the socialist Carlo Pisacane in a disastrous Bandiera-style attempt at starting a revolt in Calabria, followed the orthodox career path of an officer in the new Italian army and was soon loaded with honours. Though his heroism in the defence of Marghera was not forgotten, a political move to the right was inevitable, but his posthumous reputation was scarcely enhanced by the last act of his life, the dispatch of a congratulatory letter to General Fiorenzo Bava Beccaris for his notorious massacre, in 1898, of a group of unarmed demonstrators on the streets of Milan.

On others the Venetian revolution made an altogether more lasting personal impact. Felice Orsini, for example, who had served with Zambeccari's Bolognese brigade at Treviso and Vicenza and taken part in the 27 October action at Mestre, lost nothing of his belief in the moral victory won by Italian patriots even after the overthrow of Mazzini's Roman republic. He would prove his commitment in the most drastic way imaginable when, a few years later in Paris, he prepared an 'infernal machine' to kill Emperor Napoleon III and Empress Eugénie en route to the opera. The imperial couple were unhurt in the blast, but the bomb killed eight bystanders and wounded 142 others. It was the first major use of high explosive in an assassination attempt, and would prove deeply inspiring to a rising generation of political murderers throughout the world. Though Orsini was executed, his gesture, made in the name of an enslaved Italy, undoubtedly influenced the Emperor in forging closer links with Piedmont as the only respectable alternative to Mazzinianism in championing the aspirations of Italian patriots.

For Alessandro Gavazzi, the Barnabite friar whose preaching had roused the Venetians to volunteer and the citizens of Treviso to stand firm, the experience of revolution was, in however different a sense, equally traumatic. Having been forced out of Venice by Manin, he had gone almost at once to Rome, where he worked tirelessly during the siege as superintendent of an ambulance unit. Escaping after the French arrived, he went to London, where he began to evolve a dissident theology in reaction to what he viewed as the treachery and weakness of Pope Pius IX in rejecting the ideals of a national movement towards a united Italy. Gavazzi never actually embraced any of the various Protestant communions, Baptist, Methodist or Free Church of Scotland, which reached out eagerly to welcome the renegade so liberally critical of the pontiff and his authority. In joining the movement against a Catholic revival in Britain, the United States and Canada (the last two of which he toured as preacher and lecturer), the ex-friar, a Savonarola reborn amid gaslit lecture-halls and earnest mid-Victorian pamphleteering, sought a church that might rediscover its roots in the teachings of the early fathers, renouncing its obsession with absolute control over the lives of its adherents. Controversial to the end, he returned to Italy in 1860 as a fighter with Garibaldi's invasion force in Sicily and infuriated the Roman hierarchy still further by publicly denying the historical accuracy of St Peter's journey to Rome and the Apostle's status as guarantor of papal authority over the Church.

Like Manin, many Venetian exiles determined to make the best of their surroundings and resources, whatever their experience of economic hardship, personal sorrow or living on the margins of an alien society. Most of them would have remembered the lines written by that earlier Italian outcast Dante Alighieri in his *La divina commedia*:

Tu proverai si come sa di sale
Lo pane altrui, e com'è duro calle
Lo scendere e'l salir per l'altrui scale.

'You will discover how bitter the bread of others tastes and what a hard road it is up and down others' staircases.' The same melancholy determination to endure that had sharpened the medieval poet's inspiration gave courage and hope to Angelo Toffoli, the tailor on the Rialto whom Manin had made Labour Minister in the first provisional government. In Paris he not only founded a relief fund for the exiles, enlisting the help of his friend the composer Gioacchino Rossini, but used his experience of Venice under threat of Austrian attack to encourage the Parisians during their own siege in the Franco-Prussian war of 1870. Another refugee, the painter Ippolito Caffi, settling in Rome, had to deal *in absentia* with the false accusation laid against him of having taken part in the looting of Palazzo Querini Stampalia on 9 August 1849, a charge which had led to his inclusion in the list of forty exiles. The real culprit, Michele Caffi (no relation), had wriggled out of court by offering his services as an informer to the police, and it was only after the artist's mother Teresa had petitioned the Emperor that an unconditional pardon was granted. Caffi solaced eight years' absence from his beloved city with a series of spirited impressionist oil sketches of Roman prospects, but soon after he returned to Venice his career was tragically cut short. A patriot to the last, he enlisted in the Italian navy in 1866, during another war with Austria, and was drowned during a battle off the Dalmatian coast.

One distinguished figure among those chased from Venice by Austria would never go back. To a friend Niccolò Tommaseo wrote, 'Since 1849, having left Venice, I made a vow not to set foot there again, whatever the outcome of earthly affairs.' The reasons for this decision have never been made clear, but it seems likely that they were connected with the shock to his profoundly emotional relationship with the city brought about by the experience of revolution. To exorcise this, once Manin and the others had left Corfu – sent on their way, as it were, by the negative energy of his churlish no-show on the quayside – Tommaseo sat down to write his memoir of the whole affair. Cast in a strangely clotted, pedantic Italian, which makes it anything but a pleasure to read, this ugly, angry book, unpublished during his lifetime, is less a record of experience than a sustained cry of frustration at the failure of reality to live up to the author's ideals. Through it all runs Tommaseo's inarticulate and deep-rooted envy of the man with whom he was briefly compelled to share the limelight, Daniele Manin, variously represented as calculating, insincere, ruthless, cowardly, vain and ungodly.

Tommaseo revised nothing of his judgement as the years passed. Devout as his Catholic faith was, he could evidently never accept the ultimate Christian challenge of forgiveness, whatever obscure hurt he might suppose himself to have suffered through the ascendancy and popular glorification of Manin. He stayed on in Corfu until 1854, having married his landlady Diamante Pavullo in order to legitimate their bastard daughter. Gradually blindness, symptomatic of the syphilis contracted during his exile in Paris during the 1830s, overtook him, but in Turin and later in Florence he continued to write or dictate poems, reviews, philological studies and works on education and politics, as well as producing one of the finest nineteenth-century Italian dictionaries. Respected but always remote within his carapace of uncompromising single-mindedness, Tommaseo died in 1874, following a seizure while out walking on the Lungarno. Where Venice was concerned, he had kept his word and stayed away.

In the attitude of the Venetians themselves, whom he had once angrily dismissed as 'a race of slaves', he would have found something to admire as they prepared once again to knuckle under to their Habsburg masters. That supposed 'joy their fear compelled them to conceal', attributed by the British Tory journalist to the crowd in the Piazza on the Austrians' return, manifested itself among no more than a handful of the population. Failure on so public a scale as that of revolutionary Venice is not heroic for Italians. By the same token, the heroism of a whole people in giving all they possessed in order to defend their city created a bracing folk-memory which filed the edges of resentment. Conciliating gestures made during the 1850s, such as a visit from Emperor Franz Josef and his young bride Elizabeth of Bavaria, or the arrival of his brother Maximilian as Viceroy, armed with even more good intentions than those of the ineffectual Archduke Rainer, were forgotten in the climate of despair that followed the war of 1859–60. While Napoleon III's French army helped Piedmont to realise Cavour's project of an Italian kingdom under Victor Emmanuel, a hastily concluded peace treaty at Villafranca between France and Austria allowed the latter, while handing over Lombardy, to retain control of Venetia. This was both a face-saving gesture and respectful of an idea, fostered by Prussia, which had threatened to enter the war on Austria's side, that the province, rather than being Italian, somehow represented part of a greater Germany.

The English poet Elizabeth Barrett Browning, who had watched with a sinking heart the entry of Habsburg legions into Florence in 1849 to restore the Grand Duke, had passionately espoused the Italian cause, and now published a sheaf of indignant poems pouring scorn on the French emperor's sordid compromise. One of these, 'A Court Lady', was based on a true anecdote of a noblewoman in Turin who, as a hospital visitor, had dressed herself in her finest clothes to honour the wounded soldiers. In Barrett's poem, she enters the wards resplendent in satin and diamonds, to offer a consoling or encouraging word to each of the men – Lombard, Romagnole or Tuscan. It is when she comes to 'one with a face from Venetia, white with a hope out of mind' that the lady is momentarily unable to speak:

> Long she stood and gazed, and twice she tried at the name,
>   But two great crystal tears were all that faltered and came.
> Only a tear for Venice? – she turned as in passion and loss,
>   And stooped to his forehead and kissed it, as if she were kissing the
>   cross.

Such mute compassion was not exaggerated, and Mrs Browning's empathy with the Italian cause had accurately divined the feeling among most Venetians as the new kingdom of Italy, setting up its capital in Florence, began the unification honeymoon party without them. The Austrians, however, were all too well aware of the failures of military leadership that had left them with only half an Italian empire and four of their sovereign allies or clients in exile. There was no Radetzky left to save the Habsburg lands. The old field marshal had died in Milan, the city to whose nobles he had proved such a merciless Attila, on 5 January 1858. His last request, made two days before his death, was for a special payment to be given to the soldiers in his memory. After a funeral service in the Duomo, his body was taken to Venice, carried by battleship to Trieste, and received further honours at a magnificent funeral in Vienna, with massed bands, artillery salutes and the tolling of the city's church bells. Emperor Franz Josef had wanted the saviour of his empire buried in the Kapuziner-Gruft, the vault in which members of the Habsburg imperial family were traditionally laid to rest. Radetzky himself had asked for interment in the military mausoleum at Klein-Wetzdorf, where two of his generals, Wimpffen and D'Aspre, already lay. The monuments raised here and in Vienna (a lively equestrian statue by Kaspar von Zumbusch on the Stubenring) bear witness to the kind of numinous status accorded him by Austrians then and since as the ultimate *schwarzgelber und kaisertreu*, commemorated likewise by Grillparzer's poem and Strauss's march.

Radetzky's comrade-in-arms Julius Haynau made a less serene descent to the grave. In 1850, while staying in London, he took it into his head to visit one of the capital's largest breweries, the Southwark firm of Barclay & Perkins. Popular sympathy for the Italian patriot cause had grown appreciably during the past two years, and Haynau's role as 'the beast of Brescia' was not forgotten. Somebody in the brewery recognised him by the exaggerated length of his white whiskers (a feature that amused Admiral Dahlerup on the two men's first meeting in Mestre) and he was immediately set upon by a mob of angry coopers and draymen shouting, 'General Hyena!' Bruised and terrified, he managed to escape into the street and hid in a nearby shop until the police arrived. Even the Tories seem to have felt the drubbing was deserved, and though Queen Victoria spoke of 'lynch law' and complained that Palmerston's apology to the Austrian government was insolent rather than fulsome, she conceded that Haynau had only himself to blame. He died the following year, apparently unrepentant, though the publicity resulting from the whole episode had damaged Austria's prestige internationally.

When Venice, which Haynau had helped to regain, was at length united with Italy, it was via a sidelong diplomatic manoeuvre rather than as the result of conquest or of a renewal among the citizens of the spirit of 22 March. In 1866 Prussia, with Italy at her side, went to war against Austria. The Italian contribution, by both land and sea, revealed an embarrassing level of incompetence, and the conflict need never have happened at all, since the Austrians, before hostilities began, had offered to hand over Venice in return for a guarantee of neutrality. After Franz Josef's army was decisively annihilated by the Prussians at Sadowa, the ensuing peace settlement arranged that the city and its surrounding territory should be handed over to France, which would then transfer it to Italy. Having won all their battles against Italian forces, including a second victory at Custoza and a naval action in which an admiral's flagship was sunk, the Austrians could not honourably yield to a loser. Thus Venice joined the new nation in the guise of a present bestowed upon King Victor Emmanuel by Emperor Napoleon III.

The King arrived by rail on 7 November 1866, to be greeted at the station by an assembly of international dignitaries, among them Lord John Russell, the British prime minister whose government had proved so notably unenthusiastic in its response to overtures from Manin in 1848. He now sported an immense tricolour cockade. Other survivors of the revolution present in the city on this occasion included Valentino Pasini, a tireless diplomatist for the republic; Gian Francesco Avesani, key negotiator in the surrender of 22 March; Isacco Pesaro Maurogonato, the former Finance Minister; and the apparently ageless Count Emanuele Cicogna, still keeping up the diary précis of notable events within the city which he had begun fifty years previously. In the procession down the Grand Canal to St Mark's, Victor Emmanuel was accompanied by Giorgio Manin, the sole survivor of his family, who had slipped into Venice unannounced several weeks earlier. He was not exactly comfortable at the monarch's side. A naturally modest man, who had spent his early years in Paris working as a railway engine-driver before leaving to join Garibaldi's dashing 'Thousand' in their 1860 invasion of Sicily, he was apparently much concerned lest anybody should suppose him guilty of exploiting his father's status as an iconic figure of the revolution.

Giorgio was present, however, when, precisely twenty years to the day after the proclamation of independence on 22 March 1848, Daniele Manin's mortal remains were brought home to Venice. En route from the French frontier, the honours paid to the dead patriot may have been perfunctory, as Marco Antonio Canini, whom he had exiled for subversion, was happy to point out – 'the indifference of the majority of the Italian people towards him is his punishment' – but the Venetians themselves were ready to do him proud. An immense crowd thronged the landing stages, wharves and *fondamenta* along the Grand Canal, watching in respectful silence as a cortège of boats, accompanied by bands playing solemn music, escorted the coffin to St Mark's. 'It was beautiful,' noted the correspondent of the *Gazzetta privilegiata*, 'to observe how, when dusk began to fall, a mass of fire created by the torchlight seemed to advance slowly down the Canal amid a quiet interrupted only by the plash of oars and the band's funeral melodies, with over a hundred gondolas following, decked in mourning and lit with candles and lanterns.' There was a lying-in-state on a dais erected before the Campanile, a guard of honour surrounded the Piazza, and the catafalque absorbed the impacted reverence of civic functionaries and Manin's admirers and friends.

Only the Church failed to set aside past differences and resentments in its attitude towards the dead man. Though Cardinal Monico, sworn enemy of liberalism by the revolution's close, had long gone, his patriarchal successors were no less intransigent, and when the Kingdom of Italy confiscated Church property and dispersed religious communities, an impulse to seize any opportunity for petty revenge against the secular arm was understandable, if in this case not especially Christian. The clergy of St Mark's basilica simply refused to allow the body of Daniele Manin to be buried inside the church. Whether this was also due to Manin's Jewish origins on his father's side, to his fairly nominal status as a Christian or to the riot at Palazzo Querini Stampalia (which Monico, its principal target, neither forgot nor forgave), it meant that a man whose constancy to his principles and whose pattern of life had excelled those of many a *soi-disant* believer, was denied the final honour Venice owed him. A marble sarcophagus containing his remains, to a design by Luigi Borro, was placed in the apse at the end of the north portico, where it still stands.

On 18 June 1867, a year before Manin's body was brought home at last, the monks and priests of SS Giovanni e Paolo behaved rather more generously towards three other Venetians whose names had been talismanic throughout the revolt of 1848–9. Whatever remained (and, after the Bourbon authorities' treatment of the bodies, this was probably not much) of Attilio and Emilio Bandiera and their companion Domenico Moro was given a solemn funeral in the great Dominican church, pantheon of the Serene Republic's doges, generals and admirals and a suitable resting place even for paladins as hopelessly rash and incompetent as these had been. To the astonishment of many, their mother, the same Baroness Anna who had sought in vain to dissuade them from their enterprise, was still living, now aged eighty-one, in the little villa at Carpenedo near Mestre to which she and her husband the Admiral had retired in sorrow and shame after their sons' deaths. Now she was determined, whatever the personal cost, to look at the bones before the coffin lids were shut and sealed for ever.

Not long before Victor Emmanuel's triumphal entry into Venice the previous year, the old woman had been a guest of honour at the ceremony of renaming Campo della Bragora as Campo Bandiera e Moro. A plaque on the grey-shuttered house where the family had lived commemorates the martyrs, but in the early years of the twenty-first century what does its presence mean to those who cross the square? 'I thirst for immortality,' Manin, as a young man, once wrote. 'I desire to help my fellow men. Lazy as I am, I love my neighbour and long to do something on his behalf as long as it can be done without tiring me.' His fame had been purchased at a price unimaginable when he recorded these thoughts, and whatever faults contemporaries might lay to his charge, idleness in Venice's hour of greatest need was not among them. Yet though united Italy named streets and squares after him in cities such as Rome and Milan, the stand he and his fellow citizens made in the name of liberty was quickly forgotten.

Historians of 1848–9 preferred to remember the heroic resistance put up by Mazzini and Garibaldi in defending the Roman republic. Thus the siege of Venice quickly became a kind of 'also-ran' postscript to their achievement, the vignette or colophon (if mentioned at all) in any summary of the revolution's final moments. Many of Manin's contemporaries chose, in any case, to belittle his role or to question its moral basis. Lazzaro Rebizzo, Piedmont's envoy to Venice in April 1848, saw his proclamation of the new Venetian republic as simply a demagogic ruse for securing power over the mob. The Neapolitan critic and novelist Vittorio Imbriani was still more devastating. Manin, as dictator of 'a microscopic and ephemeral mini-republic', would have been forgotten had it not been for his support of the Italian National Society. 'This was what helped to unify and liberate Italy, revealing a greater strength of will than any displayed in the seizure of the Arsenal or the defence of Venice. Without this, his life would simply have been that of a revolutionary activist, one among many.' Imbriani, good Neapolitan that he was, attributed the patriotic triumphs of the siege exclusively to Pepe and his officers. Manin, allowing for his personal integrity and good intentions, was just a lawyer 'who imposed himself on the people and the various revolutionary assemblies, without the least touch of seriousness or practical ability, let alone administrative skill, a credulous and naive figure'.

Some of us might beg to differ. Yet perhaps Marco Antonio Canini, sniping at Manin from the safe distance of twelve years after the latter's death, was correct in saying that Italian unity mattered less to him than securing a unilateral independence for Venice analogous to that of German Hanseatic ports like Hamburg and Bremen. Or maybe it was simply that the myopic attorney, small of stature and short of breath, possessed none of that *bella figura* abundantly displayed by such charismatic Risorgimento icons as Mazzini and Garibaldi. Even the cut of his beard was not quite what a dashing rebel leader, whether ideologue or paladin, required. Hence the elaborate myth-history of the struggle for Italian unification could find no room for a man who, whatever his occasional mistakes and pardonable failings, showed a courage, integrity and dedication which deserve, in the context of Italy's subsequent historical experience, to be cherished and celebrated.

It has been the partial object of this book to counter the widely accepted view of the Venetian revolution, together with the subsequent siege, as a side-show, not just in the drama of the Risorgimento, but in the wider theatre of Europe's 1848 experience. It mattered to the patriots of the age, thousands of whom from all over Italy (and several who were not Italian) came prepared to offer their energy, their money and their lives in the cause of keeping Venice free, and it was of vital significance to the Austrians, who themselves were ready to devote all they possessed in terms of men, time and resources towards recovering a city whose subjection symbolised the ultimate triumph of Habsburg imperial power. For us also the whole episode, considered as something more than a highly coloured narrative ending in tears, has a continuing resonance, in an age when democracy and its kindred liberties are abused by opportunists and the forces of extremism, when cynicism and apathy combine to devalue political commitment, and when media censorship, imprisonment without trial, a minister's lies or a public servant's obfuscations can all be invoked as benign instruments by a government claiming to act in the name of national security.

Is Venice herself prepared to remember? In a city on which the burden of a triumphal and glittering past lies so heavily, the tragedy of 1848 is easily ignored. Roaming the *calli* and *campi*, we shall find comparatively few reminders of the siege or its dramatis personae. Manin's statue on Campo San Paternian, the work of that same Luigi Borro who designed his sarcophagus in the basilica, is by all accounts a good likeness, but unsatisfying in the context of the shabby-looking space that surrounds it. Five minutes' walk away in Campo San Stefano, a less successful monument commemorates Niccolò Tommaseo. The craggy-featured sage is curiously posed with the hinder-skirts of his frock-coat resting on a pile of books, representing part of his voluminous oeuvre. Venetians, with their age-old irreverence, refer to the figure as '*el cacalibri*', 'the book-shitter'. In Campo Sant'Angelo, the enormous open space dividing these two, there used to stand a statue of the patriotic engineer Pietro Paleocapa, Manin's Minister of Public Works who spiked his guns in the fusion debate, but during the 1930s it was transferred to the public gardens opposite the railway station.

On the great viaduct itself, where Rosaroll died, where Caffi did his quick-fire sketches of the gunners at their work, and where the brave fisherman Stefani blew up the arches, a modest memorial cenotaph stands, not easily visible am ong the dusty plantations of oleanders between the railway line and the parallel roadway. A scattering of other plaques across the city itself – to Enrico Cosenz at San Provolo, for example, and to Carlo Mezzacapo and his volunteer legion on the façade of Palazzo Mocenigo overlooking the Grand Canal – honours the rebel heroes; and behind the Piazza, next to the central post office, a sequence of bronze reliefs commemorates everybody from Gian Francesco Avesani, the man who gave Zichy his marching orders, to the Hungarian renegade Lajos Winkler. In the lagoon itself stand the crumbling remains of the various gun batteries, Campalto, San Secondo and the rest, haunting in their forlorn solitariness amid the waves. Here and there an Austrian cannon ball still lies embedded in a wall, as at the church of San Salvador near the Rialto, and a pile of them is artistically arranged as a memorial to the siege close to Teatro La Fenice. Still more projectiles are stacked up on a landing of the Museo Correr, whose Risorgimento display, including a preserved sample of the terrible 'patriotic bread' eaten during the siege, has been closed to visitors for more than a decade. A reopening is not imminent, probably no longer economically viable, and would hardly draw the throngs of visitors who swarm into St Mark's or the Doge's Palace, but Manin and his companions deserve at least this act of piety from the city they adored.

Perhaps their truest memorial lies in the essence of a Venice still managing to endure the impossible exigencies of mass tourism, the corruption and intrigue without which Italian public life cannot function, and the ravages of nature in an era of global warming. The Piazza upon which Manin looked from his balcony in the Procuratie Nuove, the Sala del Maggior Consiglio which echoed to his voice, and the view across the lagoon towards the Lido which Dahlerup's ships blockaded are still basically, give or take a few modern installations, much as they were in 1848. The stones abide, so too do the handsome, confident faces of native Venetians – a far smaller number now, since so many who work in the city live outside it – and their raucous singsong accent, which Manin loved to hear. Walk back from the grey-shuttered house of the Bandieras, back into the crowds along the Riva and try to remember that this is still a city worth dying for. Should you happen to be wearing a hat, follow the example of those who strolled these pavements in the January and February of 1848 and doff it as you pass the prison next to Ponte della Paglia. The bridge once crossed, try not to walk between the two columns in the Piazzetta – Venetians say it brings bad luck. But thread your way between the tables of the café at the end of the colonnade closest to the water and take a careful look at the pillar just to the left in front of the ice-cream stall looking out towards the Giudecca. On the marble drum's brown surface you can still see, very, very faintly, the most poignant of all memorials of the siege. It is a simple inscription, stencilled in red letters, which reads: 'Viva San Marco, viva la Repubblica!'

ACKNOWLEDGMENTS

Writing this book has fulfilled a long-cherished ambition. The siege of Venice in 1848–9 is one of the less familiar episodes of Italian history, even to Italians themselves. Only two studies have ever been written in English on the subject. My aim was to produce a straightforward account of the events, personalities and issues involved, in an attempt at doing justice to the pluck and determination of both sides in the struggle. I have tried to be fair to the Austrians, but essentially this narrative is a tribute to the gallant citizens of Venice and those from different regions of Italy and other countries who joined them in defending their newly-won freedom and their aspiration to become Italians rather than subjects of the Habsburg empire. The unified Italy emerging from the Risorgimento was probably not the kind of nation state many of them would have wanted, but in the light of subsequent historical experience their courage and idealism surely deserve to be remembered.

Doubtless this would have been a better book had I been furnished with the necessary grants and sabbaticals to extend my research. Possibly I should have finished writing it much earlier had these been available. As it is, the work was undertaken as an adjunct to a day job. My hours spent blowing the dust (literally) off manuscripts in Venetian libraries were limited by school holidays and a teacher's salary. Given these restrictions – and also because of them – I have hugely enjoyed writing the book. It is by no means a complete picture: I have not found room for the guerrilla war in Cadore, for example, I have dealt far too summarily with the whole issue of the Venetian provincial government's finances, and regrettably I was forced to dispense with a section on Browning's 'Pippa Passes' and what it can teach us as to the atmosphere of a Veneto provincial community during the 1830s. I came across David Laven's study of Venice under Austrian rule too late to adjust the balance of my early chapters under the influence of his groundbreaking revisionism. Nevertheless, since this era of Italian history remains intensely vivid for me, I hope that some of my passion for the world of the Risorgimento, not to speak of my love for Venice itself, will rub off on the reader.

I have been fortunate in the help and good wishes received from a great many people. My first thanks must go to Mary Sandys, in whose house at Harbord Street I first conceived the project over twenty years ago. Since then it has been warmly encouraged by various friends, especially Robin Lane Fox (who kindly read the first complete version of the text), Nick Byrne, Rupert Christiansen, Mark Elder, Tim and Danuta Garton Ash, Alan Hollinghurst, James Loader, Gerard McBurney, Sandra Raphael and Jon Rayman.

I am grateful for specialist assistance and advice from John Clark on nineteenth-century Italian phraseology, to Jamie Bulloch for a balanced view of Emperor Ferdinand, Adam Zamoyski for details of the Polish contribution to the Risorgimento, Michael Rose for a stirring rendition of Pacini's 'Ronda della Guardia Civica', the late Patrick Whitmore for help with military matters, Emma Tristram for locating Dantean allusions, Paolo Ferrante for an uncompromisingly legitimist perspective on revolutionary Italy, Tim and Lizzieboo Llewellyn for the gift of a valuable catalogue, Claire Tomalin for a tantalizing clue as to the existence of a novel about the Venetian revolution and Adrian Lyttelton for wisdom as to everything from Massimo D'Azeglio's personality to the correct pronunciation of Carlo Cattaneo's surname.

In Italy my brother Timothy Keates provided illuminating insights, useful books, excellent food and patient companionship. My special thanks to Thekla Clark, under whose roof at Terzano part of this book was written, to Hugh Honour and the late John Fleming, to Rosanna Montorsi, Piero Crida, Dr Piero Pasini and the late Gianni Guidetti.

My thanks to the staff of the following institutions: in Venice, the Archivio di Stato, the Biblioteca Correr and the Biblioteca Marciana: in Florence, the Biblioteca Nazionale and the Gabinetto Vieusseux: in Modena, the Biblioteca Estense: in London, the London Library, the British Library, the City of London School Library. I am particularly grateful to the Taylor Institute and the Bodleian Library at Oxford. My special thanks to Vera Ryhajlo for her inexhaustible patience and consideration over several years in dealing with my frequently tiresome requests and enquiries.

Elsewhere, my thanks to Joseph and Anne Rykwert, John Julius

Norwich, Sheila Hale, Paul Holberton, Tom Henry, Angela Bohrer, Giles McDonogh, Christopher Ryan, Claudiu Ramba, James Fenton and Darryl Pinckney, Angelo and Laura Hornak, Patrick O'Connor, James Boyes, Marina Warner and my fellow members of Kindlings, and Mrs G. Fallows. The History department at the City of London School has been invaluable in providing books and information of various kinds: my thanks to Lionel Knight, Gary Griffin, Noeleen Murphy, Andrew McBroom, and Helen Pike. I could not have written this book without the goodwill and long suffering of my colleagues in the English department, George Phillipson, Richard Blanch, David Dyke, Stephen McConnell, Tom Wingate, Josh Norman and Tony O'Sullivan.

Finally I must thank Jonathan Burnham for commissioning this book, Jenny Uglow, most sensitive of editors, Poppy Hampson and my agent Felicity Bryan.

BIBLIOGRAPHY

DOCUMENTS

Venice, Archivio di Stato: Governo provvisorio
Venice, Museo Correr: Documenti Manin, Cicogna diary.
London, British Library: Stanmore Papers, Aberdeen Papers
London, National Archive: Consular despatches of Clinton Dawkins, F.O.
   7. 356

PRINTED SOURCES

Adesioni delle provincie, dei distretti, communi, uffici, corpi ed individual al governo provvisorio della repubblica veneta. Venice 1848

Agrati, Carlo: *Giuseppe Sirtori, il 'Primo dei Mille'.* Bari 1940

Anfossi, Francesco: *Memorie sulla campagna di Lombardia del 1848.* Turin 1850

Anon: *Ministero della Guerra, Comando del Corpo di Stato Maggiore, Ufficio Storico: La Campagna del 1849 nell'Alta Italia.* Rome 1928

Archivio triennale delle cose d'Italia dall'avvenimento di Pio IX all' abbandono di Venezia. 2 vols. Milan 1974

Aricò, *Angela Caracciolo: Censura ed editoria (1800–1866).* Storia della Cultura Veneta 6, ed. G. Arnaldi & M. Pastore Stocchi. Vicenza 1986

Ashley, Evelyn: *The Life of Henry John Temple, Viscount Palmerston 1846 - 1865.* 2 vols. London 1876

Aspesi, Alessandro: *Ombre e luci del nostro Risorgimento. Carteggio del Generale Giacomo Durando (1847 – 1867.)* Turin 1952

Assedio di Venezia. Venice 1849

Baillie Cochrane, Alexander: *Young Italy*. London 1850

Baldini, Alberto: *La Guerra del 1848–49 per l'indipendenza d'Italia*. Rome 1930

Barbarich, Eugenio: *Cesare De Laugier e le armi toscane alla prima Guerra d'indipendenza italiana*. Rome 1896

Barbarich, Eugenio: *Memorie storiche sull'assedio di Osoppo*. Udine 1902

Barbaro, Giuseppe: *Niccolò Tommaseo, ministro per la istruzione pubblica*. Venice 1882

Barbiera, Raffaello: *Voci e volti del passato (1800–1900)* Milan 1920

Barbiera, Raffaello: *I fratelli Bandiera*. Rome 1923

Barbieri, Vittorio: *I tentative di mediazione anglo-francesi durante la Guerra del '48*. Rassegna storica del Risorgimento XXVI 1939

Barié, Ottavio: *L'Inghilterra e il problema italiano nel 1848–9*. Milan 1965

Barizza, Sergio: *Il Comune di Venezia 1806 - 1946*. Venice 1982

Barizza, Sergio: *Storia di Mestre*. Padua 1994

Barnaba, Domenico: *Da 17 marzo a 14 ottobre 1848, ricordi*. San Vito al Tagliamento 1891

Battaglini, Tito: *Il traditore dei fratelli Bandiera secondo I documento ufficiali borbonici*. Rassegna storica del Risorgimento *XXVII* 1940

Bava, Eusebio: *Relazione delle operazioni militari dirette dal Generale Eusebio Bava, comandante il primo corpo d'armata in Lombardia nel 1848*. Turin 1848

Belgiojoso, Cristina di: *Il 1848 a Milano e a Venezia*. Milan 1977

Bell, Herbert C.F.: *Lord Palmerston* . 2 vols. London 1936

Beller, Steven: *Francis Joseph*. London 1996

Belvèze, Henry de: *Lettres choisies dans sa correspondance 1824–1875*. Bourges 1882

Benko von Boinik, J.: *Geschichte der K.-K. Kriegs-Marine während der Jahre 1848 und 1849*. Vienna 1984

Benzoni, Gino & Cozzi, Gaetano ed.: *Venezia e l'Austria*. Venice 1999

Berengo, M.: *L'agricoltura veneta dalla caduta della Repubblica all'Unita*. Milan 1963

Berkeley, G.W.: *Italy in the Making*. 2 vols., Cambridge 1940

Bernardello, Adolfo: *La prima ferrovia fra Venezia e Milano*. Venice 1996

Bernardello, Adolfo: *Veneti sotto l'Austria. Ceti popolari e tensioni sociali (1840–1866)* Venice 1997

Bertoli, Bruno: *Le origini del movimento cattolico a Venezia*. Brescia 1965

Bertolini, Francesco: *L'Italia nella tempesta del 1848–49 (Venezia e Daniele*

Manin) in *Pensiero ed azione nel Risorgimento italiano*, Citta di Castello 1898

Bertolini, Francesco: *Storia del Risorgimento italiano*. Milan 1899

Bertuch, Friedrich: *Beitrage zur Vorgeschichte der Einheit Italiens*. Halle 1909

Bezzola, Guido: *Niccolò Tommaseo e la cultura veneta*. Storia della Cultura Veneta 6 Vicenza 1986

Bianchi, Celestino: *Venezia e i suoi difensori*. Milan 1863

Bianchi Giovini, A: *L'Autriche en Italie*. 2 vols. Paris 1844

Biscaccia, Nicolo: *Cronache di Rovigo dal 1844 a tutto 1864*. Padua 1865

Blaze de Bury, Henri:'Verone et le marechal Radetzky.' *Revue des Deux Mondes* 1850

Bonafede, Antonio: *Sugli avvenimenti de'Fratelli Bandiera e di Michele Bello in Calabria negli anni 1844 e 1847*. Gerace Marina 1894

Bonghi, Ruggiero: *La vita e i tempi di Valentino Pasini*. Florence 1867

Bourgin, Georges: *La mort de Manin*. Rassegna storica del Risorgimento IV-V 1915

Bourne, Kenneth: Palmerston, *The Early Years 1784 - 1841*. London 1982

Bowring, Sir John: *Report on the Statistics of Tuscany, Lucca, the Pontifical and the Lombardo-Venetian States etc*. London 1837 (Parliamentary Papers 1839)

Boyer, Ferdinand: *Le problème de l'Italie du Nord dans les relations entre la France et l'Autriche. Rassegna storica del Risorgimento XLII* 1955

Boyer, Ferdinand: *Les derniers jours de la République de Venise (Aout 1849) d'apres un officier de la Marine Française. Rassegna storica del Risorgimento LVI* 1969

Brentari, Ottone: *Storia di Bassano e del suo territorio*. Bassano 1884

Broglio Solari, Catherine, Countess: *Venice under the Yoke of France and of Austria &c. by a Lady of Rank*. London 1824

Brunello, Piero: *I mercanti di grano nella carestia di 1846–47 a Venezia. Studi Storici* 20 1979

Brunetti, Mario,Pietro Orso, *Francesco Salata eds.: Daniele Manin intimo, lettere, diari e altri documenti inedite*. Rome 1936

Brunetti, Mario: *L'Opera del Comune di Venezia nel 1848–49*. Archivio Veneto 78 1949

Caffi, Ippolito: *La mia prigionia. Lettera di Ippolito Caffi*. Venice 1848

Calimani, Riccardo: *Gli ebrei a Venezia dopo l'apertura del Ghetto*. Storia della Cultura Veneta 6. Vicenza 1986

Caluci, Giuseppe: *Documenti inediti relativi al primo periodo della rivoluzione italiana nel 1848*. Atti del R. Istituto Veneto 29 1870–1

Canini, Marco Antonio: *Vingt Ans d'Exil*. Paris 1869

Cappello, Girolamo: *Alcune pagine di patriottismo della famiglia Cappello di Venezia.* Rassegna storica del Risorgimento *VI* 1915

Cappello, Girolamo: *Le famiglie Bandiera e Graziani nel Risorgimento d'Italia.* Rocca S. Casciano 1911

Caputi, Mauro: *Esposizione dei fatti relativi alla partenza dei fratelli Bandiera da Corfu per la Calabria nel 1844.* Bari 1883

Carci, Luigi: *La spedizione e il processo dei Fratelli Bandiera.* Modena 1939

Carrano, Francesco: *Della Difesa di Venezia negli anni 1848–49.* Genoa 1850

Carte Segrete della Polizia Austriaca in Italia, estratte dall'Archivio di Venezia e pubblicate per commissione di D.Manin. 3 vols. Capolago 1851

Carteggio diplomatico del Governo Provvisorio di Venezia etc. Venice 1849

Casarini, Luigi: *Sulla origine, ingrandimento e decadenza del commercio di Venezia.* Venice 1823

Castelli, Emilio: *Jacopo Castelli ovvero una pagina della storia di Venezia nel 1848.* Venice 1890

Cattaneo, Carlo: *L'insurrezione di Milano.* Milan 1986

Cattonari, Carlotta: *Storia di Carlotta Cattonari e sua famiglia al tempo di bombardamento di Venezia, scritta da lei medesima.* Venice 1850

Causa, Cesare: *Vita dei Fratelli Bandiera fucilati a Cosenza il 25 Luglio 1844.* Florence 1888

Cavedalis, Giovanni Battista: *I commentari* ed. Vincenzo Marchesi 2 vols. Udine 1929

Cervellini, G.B. ed.: *Cornuda, 9 maggio 1848. Relazione inedita del volontario pontificio avv. Nicola Pavolinelli.* Archivio Veneto 79 Venice 1950

Cessi, Roberto: Carlo Alberto, *Venezia e il problema della fusione.* Archivio Veneto 53 1953

Cessi, Roberto: *Come nacque la Repubblica di Venezia nel 1848* (frammenti e polemiche) Archivio Veneto 62–63 1948

Cessi, Roberto: *Il mito di Pio IX* (dal carteggio di G.B. Castellani) Udine 1953

Cessi, Roberto: *La capitolazione di Venezia del 22 Marzo 1848.* Atti dell' Istituto Veneto di Scienze, Lettere ed Arti 106 Venice 1948

Cessi, Roberto: *La missione Martini a Venezia nel giugno 1848.* Archivio Veneto 51 1952

Cessi, Roberto ed.: *La Repubblica Veneta nel 1848–49.* 2 vols. Padua 1949

Cessi, Roberto: *Studi sul Risorgimento nel Veneto.* Padua, 1965

Cessi Drudi, Maria: *Pietro Paleocapa nel 1848–49 . Archivio Veneto* 81–82 1951

Charles Albert, King of Piedmont: *Scritti e lettere di Carlo Alberto.* Ed. Nicomede Bianchi Turin 1879

Chiappini, Luciano: *La Guerra del 1848 nel Veneto in un carteggio del Marchese Giovanni Costabili.* Scritti sul Risorgimento a Ferrara. Rovigo 1953

Ciampini, Raffaele: *Vita di Niccolò Tommaseo.* Florence 1945

Codemo Gerstenbrand, Luigia: *Fronde e fiori del Veneto letterario in questo secolo.* Venice 1872

Codemo Gerstenbrand, Luigia: *Pagine famigliari artistiche cittadine(1750–1850)* Venice 1875

Codice Penale Unihversale Austriaco. 2 vols. 2nd edn. Milan 1815

Communications from the Austrian Government as to the Territorial Arrangements and Political Conditions of Italy etc. Accounts & Papers vol LXV, London 1848

Contarini, Pietro: *Memoriale Veneto storico-politico, dal 18 Marzo 1848 al 26 Agosto 1849.* Documenti della Guerra Santa d'Italia 9 Capolago 1850

Cosenz, Enrico: *Custoza e altri scritti inediti* ed. Francesco Guardione Palermo 1913

Costello, Louisa Stuart: *A Tour to and from Venice by the Vaudois and Tyrol.* London 1846

Curato, Federico ed.: *Gran Bretagna e Italia nei documenti della missione Minto.* 2 vols. Fonti per la Storia d'Italia. Rome 1970

Curato, Federico ed.: *Le relazioni diplomatiche fra la Gran Bretagna e il Regno di Sardegna* 3rd series: 1848–60. Vol.1 *Fonti per la Storia d'Italia.* Rome 1961

Cusani, Francesco: *Venezia e le citta venete nella primavera del 1848.* Milan 1848

D'Agostini, Ernesto: *Ricordi militari del Friuli* . 2 vols. Udine 1881

Dahlerup, Hans Birch: *Mit Livs Begivenheder: Blokaden af Venedig 1849.* Ed. Joost Dahlerup. Copenhagen 1911

Dalla Pozza, Antonio M.: *Nostro Risorgimento: lettere dal carteggio dei marchesi Gonzati su Vicenza nel Quarantotto.* Florence 1941

Dallolio, Alberto: *La difesa di Venezia nel 1848 nei carteggi di Carlo Berti Pichat e di Augusto Aglebert.* Biblioteca dell'Archiginnasio II XVII Bologna 1920

Dall'Ongaro, Francesco: *Venezia l'11 Agosto 1848. Memorie storiche.* Capolago 1850

Damerini, Gino: *Tommaseo amico e nemico di Carrer. Nuova Antologia* 1933

D'Azeglio, Costanza: *Souvenirs historiques de la marquise Constance D'Azeglio.* Rome 1884

D'Azeglio, Massimo: *Massimo D'Azeglio alla Guerra d'indipendenza.* Documenti inediti. Modena 1911

D'Azeglio, Massimo: *Relazione succinte delle operazioni del Generale Durando nello Stato Veneto.* Milan 1848

D'Azeglio, Massimo: *Things I Remember* (tr. E.R. Vincent) Oxford 1966

Debrunner, Jean (Johann): *Venise en 1848–49.* Turin 1850

De Chiara, Stanislao: *I martiri cosentini del 1844: documenti inediti.* Rome-Milan 1904

De Laugier, Cesare: *Le milizie toscane nella Guerra di Lombardia del 1848, narrazione storica. Documenti della Guerra Santa d'Italia* 12 Capolago 1850

Dell'Agostino, Erminia: *Cenni sulla poesia patriotica, popolare e popolareggiante nel Lombardo-Veneto (1847–1866).* Sondrio 1921

Della Peruta, Franco: *Democrazia e socialismo nel Risorgimento.* Rome 1973

Della Peruta, Franco: 'Problemi sociali dell'Italia della Restaurazione'. *Studi Storici* 17 1976

Del Lungo, I. & Prunas, P. eds.: *Niccolo Tommaseo e Gino Capponi, carteggio inedito, dal 1833 al 1874.* 2 vols. Bologna 1914

Demarco, Domenico: *Le rivoluzioni italiane del 1848.* Studi in onore di Gino Luzzatto, vol. 3. Milan 1950

Depoli, Attilio: *La missione Rebizzo a Venezia nel 1848.* Rassegna storica del Risorgimento XLIV 1957

Derosas, Renzo: 'Strutture di classe e lotte sociali nel Polesine preunitario'. *Studi Storici* 1977

Dizionario biografico degli italiani. Rome 1960 - (ongoing)

Durando, Giovanni: *Schiarimenti sulla Condotta del Generale Durando.* Bologna 1848

Errera, Alberto: *Daniele Manin e Venezia (1804–1853.)* Florence 1875

Errera, Alberto & Finzi, Cesare: *La vita e i tempi di Daniele Manin,* Venice 1872

Fabris, Cecilio: *Gli avvenimenti militari del 1848 e 1849.* Turin 1898

Faleschini, Antonio: *I tentative di offesa aerea contro Venezia nel 1849 (documenti inediti)* Rassegna storica del Risorgimento XLII 1955

Fantoni, Gabriele: *Biografie di dieci patrioti veneziani del 1848–49. Rivista storica del Risorgimento italiano* 3 1898

Fantoni, Gabriele: *Angelo Toffoli, ministro degli artieri in Venezia nel 1848–49. Il Risorgimento Italiano* I no. 2 1908

Fantoni, Gabriele: *Fanciulli eroi del 1848. Rivista storica del Risorgimento italiano* 3 1898

Fantoni, Gabriele: *I fasti della Guardia Nazionale del Veneto.* Venice 1869

Fasanari, Raffaele: *Il Risorgimento a Verona.* Verona 1958

Federigo, Federico: *Il processo criminale-politico di Daniele Manin.* Venice 1866

Ferrari Bravo, Umberto & Marconi, Arturo: *Un auto-difesa inedita di Daniele Manin.* Nuovo Archivio Veneto 1906 Ferrazzi, Giuseppe: *Elogio storico di Monsignor Zaccaria Bricito bassanese.* Bassano 1852.

Fiorentini, Lucio: *Le dieci giornate di Brescia.* Rome 1899

Flagg, Edmund: *Venice, City Of The Sea.* 2 vols. London 1853

Fontana, Giacopo: *Estratto dal Discorso che pronunziava Antonio da Venezia, al secolo Tornielli, nel campo di SS Gio.e Paolo la mattina 30 Aprile 1848.* Venice 1848

Fulin, R.: *Venezia e Daniele Manin: ricordi.* Archivio Veneto 9 1875

Fusinato, Arnaldo: *Poesie complete.* Milan 1909

Gambarin, Giovanni: *Daniele Manin in esilio e Venezia.* Archivio Veneto 88 1958

Gambarin, Giovanni: *Il Mazzini, il Tommaseo, il Manin e la difesa di Venezia,* Archivio Veneto 9 1929

Gerlin, Giovanni: *Daniele Manin, cenni biografici.* Venice 1867

Giacomelli, Angelo: *Reminiscenze della mia vita politica* Florence 1893

Ginsborg, Paul: *Daniele Manin and the Venetian Revolution of 1848–49.* Cambridge 1979

Giordani, Carlo: *Giovanni Prati, studio biografico.* Turin 1907

Girardi, L.A.: *Dell'assedio di Venezia e Marghera.* Capolago 1850

Giuriati, Domenico: *Memorie d'emigrazione.* Milan 1897

Grande Accademia vocale ed istrumentale che per argomento di patria e cittadina carita sara data nel Gran Teatro la Fenice. Venice 1848

Grandi, Terenzio: *Gustavo Modena, attore patriota (1803–1861)* Pisa 1968

Greenfield, Kent Roberts: 'Commerce and New Enterprise at Venice 1830–48'. *Journal of Modern History* 11 1939

Greenfield, Kent Roberts: *Economics and Liberalism in the Risorgimento.* Baltimore 1965

Guest, Ivor: *Fanny Cerrito, the Life of a Romantic Ballerina.* London 1956

Guiccioli, Alessandro: *Del diario inedito.* Nuova Antologia 1932

Hearder, Harry: *Italy in the Age of the Risorgimento, 1790 - 1870.* London 1994

Hearder, Harry: *La rivoluzione veneziana del 1848 vista dal Console generale ingles.* Rassegna storica del Risorgimento XLIV 1957

Horner, Susan: *The Tuscan Poet Giuseppe Giusti and his Times.* London 1864

Imbriani, Vittorio: *Alessandro Poerio a Venezia.* Naples 1884

Imbriani, Vittorio: *Fame usurpate.* 3rd edn. Bari 1912

Incisa, L. & Trivulzio, A.: *Cristina di Belgiojoso.* Milan 1984

Ingegneria e politica nell'Italia dell'Ottocento: Pietro Paleocapa. Venice 1990

In occasione della solenne esposizione della reliquario del prezioso sangue di N.S. G.C. &c Venice 1848

Jäger, Edoardo: *Storia documentata dei corpi militari veneti e di alcuni alleati (milizie di terra) negli anni 1848–1849.* Venice 1880

Jennings, Laurence C.: 'Lamartine's Italian Policy in 1848, a Re-examination'. *Journal of Modern History* 42 1970

La Forge, Anatole de: *Histoire de la République de Venise sous Manin.* 2 vols. Paris 1849

La Marmora (Della Marmora) Alberto, ed. M. Degli Alberti: *Alcuni episodi della Guerra nel Veneto.* Milan 1915

Laven, David: *Venice and Venetia under the Habsburgs, 1815–1835.* London 2002

Lecomte, Jules: *Venise, déscription littéraire, historique et artistique.* Paris 1845

Le Masson, Alexandre: *Venise en 1848 et 1849.* Paris 1851

Leonardi, Maria ed.: *La chiesa veneziana dal tramonto della Serenissima al 1848.* Venice 1986

Leoni, Carlo: *Epigrafi e Prose.* Florence 1879

Leys, M.D.R.: *Between Two Empires.* London 1955

Lizier, Augusto: *Il caso Cavedalis.* Archivio Veneto 1949

Lizier Augusto: *Prodromi e primi momenti del '48 a Treviso.* Archivio Veneto 1949

Lorenzetti, Giulio: *Venice and its Lagoon.* Translated by John Guthrie. Trieste 1975

Lucchini, Angela: *Memoriale del Maresciallo Radetzky sulle condizioni d'Italia al principio del 1848. Nuova Rivista Storica* XIV 1930

Lutyens, Mary: *Effie in Venice.* London 1965

Luzio, Alessandro: *Profili biografici e bozzetti storici.* 2 vols. Milan 1927

Luzio, Alessandro: *Radetzky.* Bergamo 1901

Macartney, C.A.: *The Habsburg Empire 1790 -1918.* London 1968

Macfarlane, Charles: *A Glance at Revolutionized Italy.* 2 vols. London 1849

Mack Smith, Denis, ed.: *The Making of Italy 1796 - 1870.* New York 1968

Mack Smith, Denis: *Mazzini.* London 1994

Maineri, B.E. ed.: *Daniele Manin e Giorgio Pallavicino, epistolario politico 1855 - 1857.* Milan 1878

Malamani, Vittorio: *La censura austriaca delle stampe nelle provincie venete 1815–1848. Rivista storica del Risorgimento italiano* 1 (1896) 2 (1897)

Mangini, Nicola: *I teatri di Venezia.* Milan 1974

Mangini, Nicola: *La politica scolastica dell'Austria nel Veneto dal 1814 al 1848.* Rassegna storica del Risorgimento XLIV 1957

Marcello, Alessandro: *La rivoluzione del 1848–49 vista da un contemporaneo.* Ed. Rodolfo Gallo. Venice 1950

Marchesan, Antonio: *La cronaca di Mestre degli anni 1848 e 1849 e saggio di altri scritti inediti di Giovanni Renier.* Treviso 1896

Marchesi, Vittorio: *Storia documentata della rivoluzione e della difesa di Venezia negli anni 1848–9*. Venice 1916

Marescotti, Angelo: *Guerre recenti del Veneto*. Venice 1848

Marshall, Ronald: *Massimo D'Azeglio, an artist in politics*. London 1966

Martin, Henri, tr. Charles Martel: *Daniel Manin and Venice in 1848–49*. London 1862

Martina, Giacomo: *Pio IX (1846–1850)* Rome 1974

Martinengo Cesaresco, Evelyn, Countess: *Italian Characters in the Epoch of Unification*. London 1911

Memorie istoriche dell'Artiglieria Bandiera-Moro, Assedio di Marghera e fatti del ponte a Venezia 1848–9

Meneghello, Vittorio: *Il quarantotto a Vicenza, storia documentata*. 3rd edn. Vicenza 1898.

Menghini, Mario: *Lodovico Frapolli e le sue missioni diplomatiche a Parigi (1848–1849)* Florence 1930

Meriggi, Marco: *Amministrazione e classe sociali nel Lombardo-Veneto (1814–1848)*. Bologna 1938

Meriggi, Marco: *Il Regno Lombardo-Veneto*. Turin 1987

Metternich, Karl von: *Memoires, documents et ecrits divers laisses par le prince de Metternich*. 8 vols. Paris 1880–4

Michel, Ersilio: *Esuli italiani nelle Isole Ionie* (1849) Rassegna Storica del Risorgimento XXXVII. 1950

Michelini, Alessandro: *Storia della marina militare del cessato Regno di Sardegna*. Turin 1863

Military Events In Italy (tr. Earl of Ellesmere) London 1851

Minghetti, Marco: *Miei ricordi* .3 vols. Turin 1888

Miscellanea Veneziana (1848–49) Regio Istituto per la storia del Risorgimento 2nd series, vol. 5. Rome 1936

Modena, Gustavo: *Epistolario* ed. Terenzio Grandi. Rome 1955

Modena, Gustavo: *Epistolario con biografia (1836–1861)* Rome 1888

Montecchi, Mattia: *Fatti e documenti risguardanti la divisione civica e volontare mobilizzata sotti gli ordini del Generale Ferrari dalla partenza da Roma fino alla capitolazione di Vicenza*. Capolago 1850

Monteleone, Giulio: *La carestia del 1816–1817 nelle provincie venete*. Archivio Veneto 1969

Monterossi, P.A.: *Memorie storico-biografiche di Daniele Manin*. Venice 1848

Monti, Gennaro Maria: *La difesa di Venezia nel 1848–1849 e Guglielmo Pepe*. Rome 1933

Monypenny, W.F. & Buckle, G.E.: *The Life of Benjamin Disraeli, Earl of Beaconsfield*. London 1907

Morandi, Antonio: *Il mio giornale dal 1848 al 1850.* Modena 1867

Morley, John: *The Life of Richard Cobden.* 12th edn. 1905

Moscati, Ruggero: Austria, *Napoli e gli stati conservatori italiani (1849–1852)* Naples 1942

Moscati, Ruggero: *La diplomazia europea e il problema italiano nel 1848.* Naples 1947

Mutinelli: *Annali delle provincie venete dall'anno 1801 al 1840.* Venice 1843

Noaro, Agostino: *Dei volontari in Lombardia e nel Tirolo e della difesa di Venezia nel 1848 - 49.* Turin 1850

Nobili, Mario: *Corrispondenza tra Emanuele e Carlo Fenzi nel 1849.* Rassegna storica del Risorgimento XXVI 1936

Norwich, John Julius: *Venice, The Greatness and the Fall.* London 1981

Norwich, John Julius: *Venice, Paradise Of Cities.* London 2004

Nugent, Laval, Graf: *Erinnerungen an meinen Vater.* Florence 1897

Odorici, Federico: *Cessione di Venezia ai regi Commissari Cibrario e Colli nel Agosto del 1848 . Ateneo Veneto* vol.3 1872

Olivo, Tebaldo: *Venezia e il 22 marzo 1848.* Venice 1889

Omodeo, Adolfo: *Difesa del Risorgimento* Turin 1951

Onori funebri renduti al generale Guglielmo Pepe. Turin 1855

Orsini, Felice: *Memorie Politiche.* Milan 1962

Oxilia, Giuseppe Ugo: *La campagna toscana del 1848 in Lombardia.* Florence 1904

Palmer, Alan: *Metternich, Councillor of Europe.* London 1972

Pascolato, Alessandro: *Manin e Venezia nel 1848 -49, pagine postume.* Milan 1916

Pecorari, Paolo: *Motivi d'intransigentismo nel pensiero del Patriarca di Venezia Jacopo Monico durante il biennio 1848–49.* Archivio Veneto 134 1971

Pecorari, Paolo: *Spunti e documenti inediti per una storia religiosa del Quarantotto veneziano.* Archivio Veneto 137 1974

Pepe, Guglielmo: *Narrative Of Scenes and Events in Italy from 1847 to 1849, including the Siege of Venice.* 2 vols. London 1850

Perini, Federico Augusto: *Giornalismo ed opinione pubblica nella rivoluzione di Venezia.* Padua 1938

Pesci, Ugo: *Il Generale Carlo Mezzacapo e il suo tempo.* Bologna 1908

Pierantoni, Riccardo: *Storia dei Fratelli Bandiera e loro compagni in Calabria.* Milan 1909

Pilot, Antonio: *L'assalto al Palazzo del Patriarca Card. Monico a Venezia nell' agosto del 1849.* Rassegna storica del Risorgimento. XI 1924

Pilot, Antonio: *Palloni austriaci su Venezia nel 1849.* Rassegna storica del Risorgimento XIV 1927

Pimodan, Georges de: *Souvenirs de la guerre d'Italie sous le Marechal Radetzky. Revue des Deux Mondes* 1850

Pino-Branca, Alfredo: *La finanza di Guerra del Governo provvisorio veneto. Studi in onore di Gino Luzzatto* vol. 3. Milan 1950

Pirri, Pietro: *La missione di Mons. Corboli Bussi in Lombardia e la crisi della politica italiana di Pio IX (aprile 1848) Rivista di Storia della Chiesa in Italia* 1 1947

Pisacane, Carlo: *La guerra d'Italia del 1848–49.* Milan 1946

Piva, Edoardo: *La cacciata degli Austriaci da Rovigo nel marzo del 1848.* Nuovo Archivio Veneto 32. 1916

Planat de La Faye, F.: *Documents et pièces authentiques laissés par Daniel Manin.* 2 vols. Paris 1860

Poeti Minori dell'Ottocento, ed. Ettore Janni. 2 vols. Milan 1955

Polver, Gaetano: *Radetzky a Verona nel 1848.* Verona 1913

Ponteil, F.: *1848.* Paris 1966

Quadri, A: *Prospetto statistico delle provincie venete.* Venice 1826

Quarterly Review, The. Vol. 86 no. CLXXI December 1849

Quazza, Guido: *La missione Martini a Venezia e il problema della fusione. Il Risorgimento,* 1951, part 2.

Radaelli, Carlo Alberto: *Cenni biografici di Daniele Manin.* Florence 1889

Radaelli, Carlo Alberto: *Storia dell'assedio di Venezia.* Naples 1865

Radetzky von Radetz, Karl Anton: *Briefe des Feldmarschalls Radetzky an seine Tochter Friederike 1847–1857* ed.Bernhard Duhr. Vienna 1892

Randaccio, Carlo: *Storia delle marine militari italiane dal 1750 al 1860.* 2 vols. Rome 1886

Rath, R.J.: 'L'amministrazione austriaca nel Lombardo-Veneto (1814–1821)', *Archivio Economico dell'Unificazione Italiana* Series 1 vol. 9 Rome 1959

Reato, Danilo: *Il Caffè Florian.* Venice 1984

Regele, Oskar: *Feldmarschall Radetzky.* Munich 1957

Reiset, Gustave, Comte de: *Mes souvenirs: les debuts de l'independence italienne.* Paris 1901

Ricciardi, Giuseppe: *Storia dei Fratelli Bandiera e consorti.* Florence 1863

Robertson, Priscilla: *Revolutions of 1848, a social history.* Princeton 1972

Rothenberg, Gunther E.: 'The Austrian Army in the Age of Metternich'. *Journal of Modern History* 40 1968

Rovani, G.V.: *Di Daniele Manin, Presidente e Dittatore della Repubblica Veneta,Memoria Storica.* Capolago 1850

Salata, Francesco: *Venezia nel 1848–49 e la politica austriaca.* Archivio Veneto 58 1928

Santalena, Antonio: *I Trevigiani alla sortita di Mestre del 27 ottobre 1848.*

Treviso 1886

Santalena, Antonio: *Treviso dal 19 marzo al 13 giugno 1848, ricordi storici*. Treviso 1885

Santini, Luigi: *Alessandro Gavazzi: aspetti del problema religioso del Risorgimento*. Modena 1955

Sanzin, Luciano Giulio: *Federico Seismit-Doda nel Risorgimento*. Bologna 1950

Scarpa, G.: *L'agricoltura del Veneto nella prima meta del XIX secolo. L'utilizzazione del suolo. Archivio economico dell'unificazione italiana* vol. 8. Turin 1963

Schönhals, Karl von: *Biografie des k.k. Feldzeugmeisters Julius Freiherr von Haynau*. Vienna 1875

Schönhals, Karl von: *Campagnes d'Italie de 1848 et 1849*. Tr. Theophile Gautier fils. Paris 1859

Schwarzenberg, Adolph: *Prince Felix zu Schwarzenberg, Prime Minister of Austria*. New York 1946

Scritti di Daniele Manin e Niccolò Tommaseo che furono causa della loro prigionia. Venice 1848

Settembrini, Luigi: *Ricordanze della mia vita*. Milan 1961

Sinclair, J.D.: *An Autumn in Italy*. Edinburgh 1829

Sior Antonio Rioba, giornale buffo, politico e pittoresco. Venice 1849

Sked, Alan: *The Decline & Fall of the Habsburg Empire 1815 - 1918*. London 1989

Sked, Alan: *The Survival of the Habsburg Empire: Radetzky, the Imperial Army and the Class War 1848*. London 1974

Smyth, Howard McGaw: 'Austria at the Crossroads, the Italian Crisis of June 1848', in *Essays in the History of Modern Europe* (ed. McKay) New York 1936

Spinola, Marchese Ippolito: *Ricordi di un vecchio marinaro*. Rome 1884

Stiles, William H.: *Austria in 1848–49*. New York 1850

Storino, Giuseppe: *La sommossa cosentina del 15 marzo '44*. Cosenza 1898

Talleyrand-Périgord, Duc de Dino, Alexandre de: *Souvenirs de la Guerre de Lombardie pendant les années 1848–1849*. Paris 1851

Taylor, A.J.P.: *The Habsburg Monarchy 1809–1918*. London 1948

Taylor, A.J.P.: *The Italian Problem in European Diplomacy*. Manchester 1934

Tenhulle, Comte de: *Le Feld-Zeugmeister Baron d'Aspre* . Paris 1895

The Last Awful Tragedy or Conspiracy of the Crowned Heads Exposed. New York 1845

Tommaseo, Niccolò: *All'Assemblea di Venezia, Discorsi due*. Venice 1848

Tommaseo, Niccolò: *Diario intimo* ed. Raffaele Ciampini. Turin 1938

Tommaseo, Niccolò: *Venezia negli anni 1848 e 1849* ed. P.Prunas. 2 vols. Florence 1931,1950.

Tonetti, Eurigio: *Governo Austriaco e notabili sudditi: congregazioni e municipi nel Veneto della Restaurazione (1816 - 1848).* Venice 1997

Tosoni, Attilio: *Storia della rivoluzione di Brescia dell'anno 1849.* Brescia 1882

Tramontin, Silvio: *Cappellani militari e assistenza religiosa alle truppe a Venezia durante il governo provvisorio (1848–1849) Risorgimento Veneto* 2 Venice 1976

Tramontin, Silvio: *Pio IX e il Veneto. Risorgimento Veneto* 3. Venice 1978

Trevelyan, G.M.: *Garibaldi's Defence of the Roman Republic.* London 1907

Trevelan, G.M.: *Manin and the Venetian Revolution of 1848.* London 1923

Ulloa, Gerolamo: *Guerre de l'independence Italienne en 1848 et en 1849.* Paris 1859

Valussi, Pacifico: *Dalla memoria d'un vecchio giornalista dell'epoca del Risorgimento italiano.* Udine 1967

Valsecchi, Franco & Wandruszka, Adam: 'Austria e province italiane 1815–1918', in *Potere centrale e amministrazione locale.* Bologna 1981

Vannucci, Atto: *I martiri della liberta italiana.* 2 vols. Turin 1850

Van Nuffel, Robert O.J.: *Intorno alla perdita della flotta all'inizio della rivoluzione veneziana.* Rassegna storica del Risorgimento XLIV 1957

Vanzetti, Carlo: *Due secoli di storia dell'agricoltura veronese.* Verona 1965

Varenne, Charles de la: *Les Autrichiens et l'Italie.* Paris 1858

Venezia e le Sue Lagune. 3 vols. Venice 1847

Ventura, Angelo: *Lineamenti costituzionali del governo provisorio di Venezia nel 1848–49.* Padua 1955

Ventura, Angelo: *Verbali del Consiglio dei Ministri della Repubblica Veneta 27 Marzo - 30 Giugno 1848.* Venice 1957

Vera storia dei fatti di Padova dei giorni XII e XIII del giugno 1848 corporate con documenti. 2nd edn. Padua 1848

Victoria, Queen of Great Britain: *The Letters of Queen Victoria 1837 - 1861.* 3 vols. ed. AC Benson & Viscount Esher. London 1908

Visconti Venosta, G.: *Memoirs of Youth.* Tr.William Prall. London 1914

Vollo, Giuseppe: *Daniele Manin.* Turin 1860

Welden, Ludwig, *Freiherr von: Episoden aus meinem Leben.* Graz 1855

Zorzi, Alvise: *La repubblica del Leone.* Venice 1979

Zorzi, Alvise: *Venezia austriaca.* Rome-Bari 1985

Zorzi, Alvise: *Venezia scomparsa* 2 vols. 2nd ed. Milan 1977

Zucchi, Carlo: *Memoriale del Generale Carlo Zucchi* , ed. Nicomede Bianchi. Milan 1861

NOTES

Prologue: Who Dies For The Motherland?

p.3 Bragora] Lorenzetti pp.300–1

p.4. Admiral Bandiera] Cappello: *Le famiglie Bandiera* pp.100–1
Tipaldo] Radaelli p.3
'Italy was our mother'] Ibid p.4

p.5 L'Esperia] Barbiera: *I fratelli Bandiera* p.22 Pierantoni pp.89–98
Carlyle on Mazzini] quoted in *The Last Awful Tragedy* p.26

p.6 Mazzini and the Bandieras] Barbiera op.cit. p.39 Causa pp.21–4,
63. For Melanie Metternich's belief that they were under Mazzini's
orders, see Pierantoni p.154
'Our choice'] Causa pp.48–9

p.7 'When he shook my hand'] Cappello op.cit. p.119

p.8 Baroness Bandiera in Corfu] Barbiera pp.32–3, Pierantoni
pp.213–4 'a scapegrace'] Barbiera pp.32–3
'I lack the strength'] Ibid p.33

p.9 The Italian revolution] Pierantoni p.318
The whole operation] Causa p.64
Bandieras' co-conspirators] Carci pp.1–20

p.10 Journey to Calabria] Details in Caputi: *Esposizione*
'You have given us life'] Ricciardi p.60
Uniform] Battaglini p.1, quoting Bonafede

p.11 Boccheciampe] Carci pp.28–35 tries to exonerate Boccheciampe
from the charge of premeditated betrayal. See also Bonafede p.15,
Caputi p.18

p.12 Charges] Barbiera p.53

p.13   Flores's exchange with Emilio] Ibid p.54
        Domenico Moro] Settembrini p.161 says that Flores was so
        charmed by Moro's appearance that he later offered him a pardon,
        but the latter refused it as dishonourable.
        Citizens of Cosenza] Pierantoni p.405, Ricciardi p.66
        Judgment] Carci p.51
p.14   Nardi to Stumpo] Carci p.19
        Lupatelli's joke] Ricciardi p.96
p.15   'Chi per la patria muor'] *Donna Caritea*'s librettist was Paolo
        Pola. The original chorus, sung by the Portuguese army, appears
        in Act 1 scene 9: the opening line, altered by the Cosenza martyrs,
        is 'Chi per la gloria muor'.
        Execution] Ricciardi p.100, Barbiera p.61
p.16   Pacchione's sculpture] Carci p.20
        Boccheciampe's fate] Ricciardi p.137. According to Carci p.35,
        Boccheciampe continued to live in Corfu, shunned by everybody
        and dying poor and blind in 1887
        'the Italians'] Bonafede p.20
        Medals distributed] Details in Vannucci p.202
p.17   Bandiera martyrology] Ricciardi pp.315–20
        'They wished to die'] Mazzini quoted in *The Last Awful Tragedy*
        p.29
p.18   Betrayal by the British] Causa p.63, Pierantoni pp.336–41 and
        Ricciardi p.50 all maintain that some intelligence-sharing took place.
        Melanie Metternich's comments in her diary for 20–23 March and
        20–23 June 1844 would seem to support this. See also Aberdeen
        Papers XC p.139 for indications that the Tory Foreign Secretary Lord
        Aberdeen was well aware of Italian revolutionary cells in the Ionian
        Islands. Aberdeen recommends to the Prime Minister, Sir Robert
        Peel, 6 May, 1844, 'that Austrian agents be authorized to go to Corfu'.

Chapter 1. The Peace of The Tomb

p.20   Fall of the Venetian Republic] Good accounts in Norwich: *The
        Greatness & The Fall* pp.234–9, Zorzi: *Repubblica* pp.533–77
p.21   Jacobinized community] For a study of this, see Giovanni
        Pillinini, *Venezia giacobina*, Venice 1997
p.22   First Austrian occupation] See Michele Gottardi, *L'Austria a
        Venezia*, Milan 1993
        Destruction of churches] Norwich: *Paradise of* Cities pp.21–22,
        Zorzi: *Venezia scomparsa*

p.24   Monti's sonnet] Poem is entitled 'Il Congresso di Vienna'

p.25   Full of good sense] Hübner p.34

p.26. 'Power's foremost parasite'] Byron: 'The Age of Bronze' line 72
       Palmerston on Metternich] See also his comments in a letter to
       King Leopold of the Belgians 15 June 1848, quoted in Ashley vol.
       1, p.97
       Metternich's political system] Interesting observations in Stiles vol.
       1 p.61

p.27   Bellegarde's proclamations] La Varenne p.33, Bianchi Giovini vol.
       2 pp.150–1
       Austrian bureaucrats] Summary of requirements in Mozzarelli

p.28   The letter of the law] Details here are from Codice Penale
       Universale Austriaco

p.29   Secret societies] On the growth of these in the Veneto, see Angela
       Mariutti: *Organismo ed azione delle societa segrete del Veneto durante
       la seconda dominazione austriaca (1814–1847)* in '*Miscellanea di
       storia Veneziana*' vol. 3. Venice 1930. Her points are not reliably
       supported by the available evidence, but the details she includes
       make interesting reading
       Byron and the Austrian police] Carte Segrete vol. 2 pp.205–8,
       Docs 87–9

p.30   Rossini, Vernet, Dumas] Ibid pp.301 Docs 309, 323, 333, 379,
       461
       Austrian censorship] Extensive treatment in Bianchi Giovini vol.
       1 pp.105–126. Malamani offers a less detailed account

p.31   Suspect books] Carte Segrete vol. 3 pp.35–40

p.32   Mailath on Study of history] Quoted in Bianchi Giovini 1 p.110.
       Austrian schools] Mangini: *Politica scolastica*. Della Peruta:
       Problemi sociali p.60 points out that illiteracy in Lombardy-
       Venetia was the lowest in Italy during this period
       Secular catechism] Bianchi Giovini 1 pp.1–5

p.33   Administrative system] Stiles pp.280–1, Bianchi Giovini 2
       pp.200–4, Rath, Vanzetti, Tonetti
       Archduke Rainer] For a sympathetic view see Meriggi: *Regno
       Lombardo-Veneto*. Polver p.68 adopts a more negative approach

p.34   Life in the Polesine] Derosas: *Strutture di classe*

p.35   Famine in the Veneto] Monteleone: *Carestia*

p.36   Metternich in Venice] Palmer pp.156–7

p.37   Wordsworth sonnet] 'On the Extinction of the Venetian Republic'

p.38   Austrian demolition of churches] Broglio Solari p.133, Zorzi:
       Venezia scomparsa

p.39 Cicognara] Zorzi: *Venezia austriaca* pp.335–7, Fernando Mazzocca: *La promozione delle arti da Leopoldo Cicognara a Pietro Selvatico, in 'Venezia e l'Austria'* pp.21–31

p.39 Leggenda Nera] See, for example, Stiles p.287. Mario Infelise: *Intorno alla leggenda nera di Venezia nella prima meta dell'Ottocento, in 'Venezia e l'Austria'* pp.309–323

p.40 'The people here'] Sinclair p.48
'The change to Venice'] Stiles p.287
'Working soberly'] *Quarterly Review* CLXXI p.187

p.41 Emperor Ferdinand] Robertson pp.189–91, Palmer pp.268–9
'Do not alter'] Palmer p.269

p.43 Societa Veneta Commerciale] Greenfield: *Commerce and Ne Enterprise* p.320

p.45 Florian versus Quadri] Lecomte p.64 notes Florian as a meeting place for 'elderly Venetians with long memories and younger ones with hopes for the future'

p.46 'How can anyone stop me'] Sand: *Lettres d'un voyageur*, tr. Rabinovitch & Thomson, London 1987, p.85

p.47 'The moon, like a torch'] Lecomte pp.44–5
'Hotfoot from Marseilles'] 'Il touriste', Poeti Minori vol. 2 p.164

p.48 'Those whom Venice'] Lecomte p.45
'The tender-hearted'] Broglio Solari pp.328–9
Venetian theatres] Mangini: Teatri pp.182–235

p.50 Railway project] Detailed account in Bernardello: *La prima ferrovia*

Chapter 2. A Little Man in Spectacles

p.54 'What people'] Leoni p.383
'While the clandestine press'] Belgiojoso pp.118–124

p.55 Famine and commercial crisis] Ginsborg pp.58–64, Brunello p.156

p.56 'The times were unfavourable'] Corboli Bussi quoted in Martina p.52
'This holy man'] Ibid p.52

p.59 'Being at all times'] Berkeley vol. 2 p.302
'The catastrophe'] Ibid p.199
'The conduct of Austria'] Curato: *Gran Bretagna e Italia* vol. 1 pp.39–41, 52

p.60 'roving mission'] Monypenny & Buckle vol. 3 p.183
'a private agitating tour'] Morley p.408
Banquet for Cobden] Codemo Gerstenbrand: *Pagine* p.437

p.61   'music and gay liveries'] Morley p.440
        Scientific conference] Soppelsa pp.99–118, Pascolato pp.1–20

p.62   'Venezia e le sue lagune'] The volumes were edited by Niccolo
        Priuli, a socially-conscious nobleman who pioneered the foun-
        dation of infant schools in the Veneto
        'we look poorly'] Venezia e le sue lagune vol. 1 p.165
        Potato jokes] Trevelyan: *Manin* p.55, Guiccioli p.367
        Footnote quotation] Carte Segrete 3 p.351

p.63   Cantù's speech] Quoted in *Atti della societa italiana per il progresso
        delle scienze* 1922 pp.152–8
        'It is ungenerous'] Bertolini: *Tempesta* p.129

p.64   Jews in Venice] Calimani: *Ebrei*

p.66   Manin's baptismal name] Vollo p.7
        Manin's publications] Aricò: *Censura*

p.67   'his philosophical creed'] Quoted in Ginsborg p.54
        'At first'] Brunetti: *Manin intimo* p.44

p.69   ' We don't wish'] Ibid. p.199

p.71   Nazari's petition] Bianchi Giovini 1 pp.250–1
        Manin's instance] Scritti di Manin e Tommaseo pp.33–6

p.72   'The Dalmatian'] Tommaseo is frequently referred to as 'il
        dalmata' (the stress is on the first syllable) by Italian writers

p.74   Tommaseo's address] Scritti p.21
        Second instance] Ibid pp.33–6

p.75   Confidential report] Federigo pp.5–9
        Disturbances at Treviso] Full account in Lizier: *Prodromi*

p.76   'any sort of allusion'] Carte Segrete 3 p.128
        Tommaseo to Bishop of Treviso] Pascolato p.23–4

p.77   Milan tobacco riots] Ginsborg p.72, Sked: *Survival* pp.106–112

Chapter 3. 22 March 1848

p.80   'All is well'] La Forge p.165
        'During the whole period'] Ciampini p.386
        Call's reports] Federigo pp.1–9

p.81   'I shall protest'] Errera & Finzi p.XCII
        Manin's address to the tribunal] Federigo pp.14–24

p.83   Zennari's cross-examination] Errera & Finzi pp.130–3 La Forge
        p.183 says that Zennari's brief was to uncover a supposed network
        of conspiracy underlying Manin's legal struggle
        Manin's reply] Ibid pp.133–9
        Tommaseo's fear] Ibid p.161

p.84   'I cannot know'] Ibid p.224

p.85   Call's charge to the court] Ibid pp.259–61
        Home comforts] Manin intimo p.207
        Teresa Manin to Call] Errera & Finzi pp.119–27

p.87   Maria Gozzadini] Fasanari pp.126–8
        Padua demonstrations] Cusani pp.14–16, Piva pp.485–7

p.88   Patriotic protests] Pascolato p.25, Perini pp.4–7
        'Do you think I am stupid'] Guiccioli p.368, Carte Segrete 3,
        Doc 574 p.172

p.89   'Among the very earliest'] Guiccioli p.213

p.90   Police informer at La Fenice] Carte Segrete 3 Doc 571 p.129
        Closure of La Fenice] Degli Antoni p.313
        'There is hardly a Venetian house'] Dawkins p.17

p.91   'Three days of blood'] Leoni p.376
        Manin's second interrogation] Federigo pp.68–89

p.92   Zennari's summing-up] Errera & Finzi pp.288–311

p.94   De Tocqueville] quoted in Leys p.246
        Fall of the July Monarchy] Ibid pp.247–55, Ponteil pp.25–31,
        Robertson pp.24–42
        Revolution in Vienna] Robertson pp.206–215

p.95   'If the hour of reconstruction'] Lamartine quoted in Jennings
        p.333

p.96   Zichy to Radetzky] Sked: Survival pp.125–6

p.98   Liberation of Manin & Tommaseo] Contarini p.9, Flagg p.349,
        La Forge p.211

p.99   Death of Ernesta Viezzoli] La Forge p.185

p.100   Riot in the Piazza] Morandi p.290, Contarini p.8, Dawkins,
        quoted in Planat de La Faye i. p.93

p.101   'Do not forget'] Planat de La Faye i. pp.90–1

p.102   Manin's ideas for a republic] Cessi: Come nacque la repubblica,
        Ciampini p.402
        Palffy meets the deputation] Cessi: Capitolazione pp.23–40

p.103   Manin's petition to Palffy] Ibid p.23
        Palffy's response] Ibid p.25

p.104   'I am here'] Planat de La Faye i. p.125
        Cinque Giornate] Visconti Venosta pp.45–81

p.105   Revolution in Verona] Schönhals p.69 claims that Rainer had simply
        moved from Milan to Verona according to his custom at this time
        of year
        Ludwig to Ernst] Planat de La Faye i. pp.95–102 See Costanza
        d'Azeglio p.207 on political divisions within Rainer's family

p.106   'Indeed I have a plan'] Planat de La Faye i. p.131

p.107   Marinovich] Flagg ii. p.360, Stiles i. p.299, La Forge i. p.282

p.108   Murder of Marinovich] Barbiera: *Voci e volti* pp.164–173.
        According to La Forge, Marinovich's last words were 'After all the
        good I did for you !'

p.109   'You may be killed'] Monterossi p.12
        Manin at the Arsenal] Degli Antoni's narrative is in Planat de
        La Faye i. pp.129–37

p.110   Cap-badges in the canals] Olivo p.27, Morandi p.298

p.111   Avesani versus Palffy] Cessi: *Capitolazione* pp.27–9 Terms of capit-
        ulation in Flagg i. pp.379–80, Stiles i.p.303

p.112   Manin's speech] Planat de La Faye i. p.106

p.113   'I know that you love me'] Ibid p.142

p.114   'like a dream'] Ibid pp.143–5
        'All of a sudden'] Trevelyan: *Manin* p.114
        Pulling down the eagle] Stiles i. p.304

Chapter 4. Springtime in Utopia

p.115   Palffy and Zichy] Flagg pp.59,370,380, Stiles i.pp.303,306

p.116   'shameful capitulation'] Sked: *Survival* p.242
        Palffy saves the navy] Full account in Van Nuffel: *Perdita*

p.117   'I saw a little man'] Pimodan p.628

p.118   'The young man saw'] Ibid p.630

p.119   Ronda della Guardia Civica] Text & music in Carnesecchi
        pp.40–41

p.120   Tommaseo's diplomatic letters] Ciampini p.408

p.121   Castelli] For background and early career see E.Castelli pp.1–30
        Paleocapa] Biographical details in *Ingegneria e politica*

p.122   'unimpeachable moral conduct'] Ibid p.480
        Manin's cabinet] For the most scathing analysis of its composi-
        tion, see *Quarterly Review* CLXXI p.201. Manin acknowledges
        tokenism in the note quoted in *Daniele Manin intimo* p.219

p.123   'amiable creature'] Fantoni: *Toffoli* p.236

p.124   'So I'm still'] Ibid p.234
        Departure of the Italian troops] On the subsequent effect of this,
        see Pisacane pp.46–51

p.125   'No communism'] Modena quoted in Ginsborg p.115
        Changes in the law] Pascolato p.40

p.126   Santa Caterina high school] Raccolta Andreola 1.i,pp.86–8
        Morandi on the Venetians] Morandi p.286

p.127 'Venice arose'] Ibid p.310

Revolution at Bassano] Detailed account in Brentari: *Storia di Bassano*

p.128 Revolution at Rovigo] Account compiled from Biscaccia and Piva

p.129 'Generous, splendid'] Tonetti p.158

p.130 Paduan patriotism] Leoni pp.387,411

Pasini and the revolt at Vicenza] Details from Bonghi pp.213-7

p.132 'Our Manin'] Ibid p.223

p.133 Communal declarations] These are all in *Adesioni delle provincie Sette Communi*] See Broglio Solari pp.324-337

p.135 Effect of the Cinque Giornate] Berkeley ii pp.78-96

Disunity in Milan] Cattaneo, chs 8 & 9, deals with this in detail. See also Belgiojoso pp.92-100

p.136 'more ideal than England'] Ciampini p.434

Modern historian] Guido Bezzolla in *Storia dell cultura veneta 6*

p.137 'In those provinces'] Costanza d'Azeglio pp.215, 219-20

'any French government'] Lamartine quoted in Jennings p.334

p.140 Radetzky and the rural militia] Lucchini: *Memoriali*. A more extensive treatment of the whole issue in Sked: *Survival* ch.10

Chapter 5. Stripping the Artichoke

p.143 'During the Terror'] Metternich to Aberdeen, 7 May 1849, Stanmore Papers LXXVII p.91

p.144 Boyhood of Charles Albert] 'Carlo Alberto' in *Dizionario Biografico*

p.145 'He talks too glibly'] Metternich's memoir of this meeting is in Stanmore Papers op.cit. LXXVII pp.80-81

Charles Albert's character] See, among many other comments, Reiset pp.259-60, Baillie Cochrane pp.28-9, Schönhals p.123, Talleyrand-Perigord p.132, Luzio: *Profili* p.67

'He is not wholly bad'] Omodeo p.186

p.146 'If God ever vouchsafes us'] Berkeley i. Pp.260, 292

'Make way for the King of Italy'] Talleyrand-Perigord p.133

p.147 D'Azeglio's interview] D'Azeglio: *Things I Remember* pp.338-342

Statuto] Mack Smith: *Making of Italy* pp.136-9

'He did not act'] Omodeo p.182

'Lies to others'] Stanmore Papers LXXVII p.84

p.148 Artichoke metaphor] Stiles i.p.204

p.149 Austrian army training] Sked: *Survival* pp.3-11

p.150 Croats] Flagg i.pp.330 describes them as 'tall, bony, all muscle and sinew, with sharp faces and long moustaches – patient, enduring, frugal, disciplined and, at eight paces, dead shots.'

Radetzky] Details here from Regele, Luzio: *Radetzky*, and Blaze de Bury

p.151   Dissident officer] Freiherr Fenner von Fenneberg, quoted in Sked: *Survival* p.87

p.152   'little old man'] Blaze de Bury pp.624–5
      'seating himself beside me'] Hubner pp.34–6

p.153   Radetzky at Verona] Details from Polver and Fasanari
      'Without money or provisions'] Radetzky: *Briefe* p.76

p.154   Attitude of the peasantry] Polver p.336 notes deliberate Austrian effort to stir up peasants against their landlords. For more on this see Sked: *Survival* pp.185–7. For general attitudes see Marchesi pp.162,385–6, Schonhals p.127, Bava p.115 and Della Peruta: *Democrazia e socialismo*
      First battle of Goito] Berkeley ii pp.121–5

p.156   Sorio action] Giacomelli pp.82–7

p.157   Female civic guard brigade] Cappello: *Famiglie Bandiera* pp.77–8, Raccolta Andreola 1.ii p.523
      'All vagabonds'] Stiles i. p.311

p.158   Modena] Details from Grandi: *Gustavo Modena*
      Giulia Modena] Mazzini (quoted in ibid p.82) called her 'very beautiful but imposing, matronly and classical in an Amazonian style'
      'We ran to catch'] *Gustavo Modena, politica ed arte* Letter LIV
      'from the boxes'] Ibid LIV

p.159   'I cannot express my sorrow'] La Marmora pp.14–16, Jäger pp.66–7 Laval Nugent] Berkeley p.244. Nugent is, so far as I can ascertain, the only Austrian general of the 1848–9 wars to find inclusion in the *Oxford Dictionary Of National Biography*.

p.160   'Assembled in haste'] Radaelli p.98 gives the strength of Nugent's army as 18,000. For its composition see Morandi p.313
      'disastrous and inexplicable loss'] Salata p.37
      Surrender of Palmanova] D'Agostini pp.17–18
      Carlo Zucchi] Ibid p.124

p.161   Caterina Percoto] Ibid pp.403–408. On Percoto herself, see Bruno Maier's introduction to his selection of her *Novelle*, Bologna 1974

p.162   'Christ at the column'] Details from Caffi: *La mia prigionia*

p.163   'the immortal pontiff'] D'Agostini p.17

p.164   Nugent's attack on Udine] Ibid pp.48–53, Fabris pp.263–4
      Hartig mission] Sked: *Survival* pp.134–44

p.165   Failure of resistance in Friuli] D'Agostini pp.63–8

p.165   Zucchi's supposed vow] Fabris p.262
         'Your national guards'] Ginsborg pp.182–3

p.166   Casati versus Cattaneo] See Cattaneo's harsh verdict on Casati
         (to whom he later applies his favourite pejorative, 'Jesuitical') in
         Insurrezione pp.26–7
         New Venetian republic] Worth noting here Manin's letter to
         Palmerston, 20 August 1848, quoted in Planat de La Faye i. p.431,
         underlining the democratic nature of the provisional government
         Rebizzo mission] Details from Depoli: *Missione Rebizzo*
         'such material assistance'] Planat de La Faye i. p.182

p.167   'speaking in German'] Depoli p.665
         'a limping Genoese'] Tommaseo, quoted by Depoli p.671
         Mission to Piedmontese headquarters] Fully dealt with by Cessi:
         Repubblica Veneta i.

p.169   Attack on Castelnuovo] Polver pp.215–226. Further details in
         Fasanari. That this was not an isolated instance is shown by, for
         example, Marescotti p.12

Chapter 6. 'Vengo correndo!'

p.172   One of his brothers] Giacomo, whose *Della nazionalità italiana*
         was published in 1842
         Giovanni Durando] Details of his military career from Aspesi:
         Ombre e luci, though this concentrates mainly on Giacomo Durando

p.173   D'Azeglio's proclamation] Marshall pp.116–9

p.174   'If Pius IX wishes it'] D'Azeglio: *L'Italie* p.33

p.175   'He suggested Birmingham'] Planat de La Faye i. p.194
         'we should cause all Europe'] Ibid p.194

p.176   'In the name of Italy'] Ibid p.196
         'Fill them with courage'] D'Agostini p.73. La Marmora's reply in
         ibid p.74

p.177   Troops in Treviso] By the end of April 1848 the number of men
         stationed in the city was approximately 17,000

p.179   Cornuda] D'Agostini pp.83–9, Fabris pp.308–12, Giacomelli
         pp.118–133

p.180   'The terrified horses'] Barnaba p.73
         'Vengo correndo'] Montecchi p.22

p.181   Durando's apologia] Details from *Schiarimenti*. D'Azeglio's
         Relazione succinct portrays Durando as the victim of intrigue and
         indiscipline. See Pisacane p.87 for a more critical view
         'I expected you to support me'] Montecchi p.109

p.182   Giuseppe Olivi] Giacomelli pp.57, 63
         'We realized'] Santalena p.40
         'Cinque soldati'] Macfarlane i p.315
         Attack on Duke of Modena's servants] Santalena p.50

p.183   11 May] Ibid pp.52–3, Giacomelli pp.140–3, Fabris p.323
         Guidotti's suicide] Giacomelli p.146

p.184   Allocution] Martina pp.237–253, Marshall pp.119–121
         'he seemed to accept'] Minto to Palmerston, quoted by Martina
         op.cit. p.229

p.186   Neapolitan volunteers] For a reactionary view, see Macfarlane i
         p.157.
         Minghetti ii p.10 notes their unreliability: this is not borne out
         by available evidence
         'I want to pay my debt'] Imbriani: *Poerio* p.3

p.187   'The Neapolitans'] Santalena p.59

p.188   'I cannot describe to you'] Imbriani: *Poerio* p.41. Although already
         in the Veneto, the poet seems to have entered Venice aboard one
         of the ships
         'to free you from your oppressors'] Turotti p.4

p.189   Cardinal Monico] Tommaseo: *Venezia 1848–9* i p.91, ii pp.80, 351,
         Pecorari: *Motivi d'intransigenza* pp.41–2, *Spunti e documenti* p.80
         'We must all conquer'] Pecorari: *Spunti e documenti* pp.85–6
         'I beg you in God's name'] Ibid p.94

p.190   Comments on priests] See Tramontin: *Patriarca e clero*. For patri-
         otic clergy see Jager pp.35–7
         Ugo Bassi] Good short account in Martinengo Cesaresco
         pp.265–300. On his foppishness see Marchesan p.69

p.191   Alessandro Gavazzi] Details from Santini: *Gavazzi*
         'Instead of listening'] Ibid p.21

p.192   'Wretched sailors'] Dallolio p.22
         'Ladies resigned'] Flagg i. p.426
         'So magical an effect'] Leoni p.399

p.193   Working-class discontents] Bernardello: *Paura del Communismo*
         offers detailed analysis of these

p.194   'A hatred of the present state'] Pisacane pp.329–30

Chapter 7. The Cat-Eaters' Last Stand

p.196   'Inaction'] Costanza d'Azeglio p.249
         'Officers and soldiers'] Ibid pp.223, 244–5. Supported by Bava, p.72

p.197   'l'orgasme'] Costanza d'Azeglio p.215

p.198   Santa Lucia] Blaze de Bury p.661
         'At every point'] Pimodan p.642

p.200   'Italy has never loved us'] Luzio: *Radetzky* p.34
         'Since the creation'] Barbieri pp.684–5

p.201   'I doubt you will ever'] Ibid p.690
         Oudinot's proclamation] Ibid p.691

p.202   Hummelauer mission] Ibid pp.695–700

p.203   'a true republican'] Frederico Seismit-Doda, quoted in Giacomelli
         p.74
         Antonini's arm] Giacomelli p.74, Fantoni: *Fanciulli eroi*
         pp.479–488, Leoni p.442

p.205   'Lights at all the windows'] Meneghello p.97, Barnaba p.80

p.206   'Decorum and the sense of duty'] Oxilia p.89
         'Still a pleasure'] Ibid p.92

p.207   uniforms to be ordered] De Laugier pp.54–5

p.208   'courage heroique'] Pimodan p.654
         'stubbornness and valour'] Schönhals p.197
         'Twice the gunpowder'] De Laugier quoted in Berkeley ii
         p.299

p.211   D'Azeglio at Vicenza] Codemo Gerstenbrand: *Pagine* p.460
         'I can assure you'] Dalla Pozza pp.91–2

p.212   'falling in their hundreds'] Barnaba p.82

p.213   'Le Waterloo de la Venetie'] La Forge i p.90
         'Never have I seen'] Pimodan p.663
         Surrender of Vicenza] Meneghello pp.127–130

p.214   'Between brave soldiers'] Alberi p.90
         'The soldiers were almost'] Pimodan p.666

p.215   'numerous Amazons'] Schönhals p.217
         'The Municipality'] Alberi p.80
         'One of the finest'] Schönhals p.206
         Charles Albert at Verona] Bava p.47

p.216   'It was a sight'] Biscaccia p.118

p.217   Bombardment of Treviso] Santalena pp.65–85, Codemo
         Gerstenbrand: *Pagine* p.463
         'a strong, compact army'] Santalena p.85

p.218   Surrender of Palmanova] D'Agostini p.139. Zucchi's own account
         is in *Memorie* pp.123–134
         'That imbecile'] Modena: *Epistolario* LXVII, Grandi: *Modena*
         p.III
         'very considerable arsenal'] Welden p.247

p.219   'Osoppo now relies'] Barbarich p.29

p.220   'a 36–pound cannon ball'] Schönhals p.225. Smyth p.73 maintains
        that this account is largely imaginary
        'I seriously believe'] Charles Albert to Franzini, quoted in Bianchi
        p.62
        'duped by revolutionary intrigue'] Blaze de Bury pp.629–30
p.221   Schwarzenberg vs. Wessenberg] Smyth pp.70–77
        Parisian counter revolution] Leys pp.263–6
p.222   'The revolutionists of Paris'] Smyth pp.77–78

Chapter 8. 'What About Us?'

p.224   'the last citizen'] Bezzolla, in *Storia della cultura veneta 6* p.156
        'the moment had arrived'] Ibid p.159
        'Just as your gospel'] *A Venezia* in *Poeti minori* ii p.173
        'Venice alone'] Planat de La Faye i. p.281–2
p.225   Venetian naval capacity] Randaccio p.125, Spinola p.99
p.226   'causeless instances'] Berkeley ii. p 282
        Neapolitan refusal to return home] Radaelli pp.135–6, Ulloa ii
        pp.130–3, Monti p.52
        'I assure you'] Imbriani: *Poerio* p.110
p.227   'I prefer rather'] Randaccio pp.129–31
p.228   'a great quantity'] Curato: *Gran Bretagna e Sardegna* p.204–7
        'Non intendo ben'] Perini p.146
p.229   'Before Charles Albert'] Ventura: *Avesani* p.111
p.231   Enrico Martini] Quazza p.126, Cessi: *Missione* p.139
        Civic Guard demonstration] Ginsborg p.249
p.232   Rivalry between cities] Caluci pp.339–40, Ventura: *Verbali* p.58
        Young Veronese] Ibid p.85
p.233   Valussi at Trieste] Valussi p.72
        'I take it as understood'] Planat de La Faye i. p.289
        'Let us hurry'] Dall'Ongaro p.26
        'A Venice revived'] Planat de La Faye i. p.291
p.234   'Ponder your deliberations'] Ibid p.295
        Tommaseo's speech] Ibid p.306
p.235   Paleocapa's reply] Ibid p.308, Raccolta Andreola 2 pp.472–6
p.236   'Let us give the lie'] Planat de La Faye i. p.310
        'a fine orator'] Ciampini p.445. The pen portrait ends with a typi-
        cally Tommasean flourish of malice: 'He died in exile of a heart-
        attack – cruelly but not undeservedly punished'.
        'this woman'] Dall'Ongaro p.46. On the Comello family see
        Zorzi: *Venezia austriaca* p.257

p.237 'I beg my fellow citizens'] Planat de La Faye i. p.315
Cicogna on fusion vote] Marchesi p.255

p.238 'tended to destroy'] Valussi quoted in ibid p.259

p.239 Pepe's attack on Cavanella] Morandi pp.545–8

p.240 'a remarkably handsome man'] Hearder pp.136–7. For a more
admiring testimony, see Ulloa ii pp.136–7. On Pepe's popularity
with women see Monti p.8

p.241 'physical handicaps'] Raccolta Andreola 3 pp.82–3
'Wearing clean uniforms'] Morandi p.336
'with few exceptions'] Imbriani: *Poerio* p.150

p.242 'the theatrical intrigues'] La Marmora p.87
'The army embarked'] Anfossi p.216
'Our troops suffer'] Costanza d'Azeglio pp.254–5

p.244 'loved by all'] Agrati p.79

p.245 Circolo Italiano] Ginsborg p.262
'Lies and calumny'] Marchesi p.263

p.247 Charles Albert at Milan] Good accounts in Belgiojoso pp.106–117
and Cattaneo ch.12
Paleocapa on Salasco armistice] Cessi Drudi p.140

p.248 Events of 11 August] Ginsborg pp.264–6, Ventura: *Lineamenti*
pp.91–6, Agrati pp.76–9, Marchesi pp.272–5

p.251 'O shining night'] Marchesi, p.275

Chapter 9. Waiting for the French

p.252 Toyshop dolls] Contarini pp.78–9
'Our forlorn Iliad'] Costanza d'Azeglio pp.279–84

p.253 We shall always remember'] Schönhals p.275

p.254 'magic lantern slides'] Ibid p.276

p.255 Clough poems] Texts from *Poems of Clough* ed.H.S. Milford,
London 1910, pp.64, 66

p.256 Albini's refusal to leave] Randaccio p.48
The shame of Campoformio] Radaelli p.216
'The existence of a people'] Planat de La Faye i. p.343

p.257 Tommaseo's Paris mission] Ciampini pp.459–60
'il nostro Manin'] The expression is more often given in its
Venetian dialect form, 'el nostro Manin'

p.258 'we must tell France'] Planat de La Faye i. p.345
'To destroy the monarchs'] Raccolta Andreola 4 pp.199–204
'the moral assistance'] Gambarin: *Mazzini, Tommaseo* p.320

p.259 Mickiewicz's Polish legion] Ibid p.341

p.260 'a floating idea'] *The Times* 4 August 1848

p.261 'the friends of peace and order'] Ginsborg p.283

p.262 Metternich and Disraeli] Palmer p.316

'that boaster'] Cessi Drudi p.151. On Tommaseo's unsuitability for his post, see Valentino Pasini's comments in MCV Doc.Manin 2436

'Poor Toffoli'] Leone Serena, quoted in Ciampini p.462

'that boring eccentric'] Incisa & Trivulzio p.295

p.263 'Now we belong'] Quoted in Ginsborg p.285

p.264 Appeal to France] Reprinted in La Forge i. pp.410–22

p.265 'aspires only to confer'] Barié p.176

Austria's right to Lombardy-Venetia] Ibid p.180

p.268 Revolution in Vienna] Robertson pp.237–250

Austrian re-occupation of the Veneto] Raccolta Andreola 4 pp.217, 400. A graffito on a Paduan wall read 'Welden, parti/ O ti faremo in quarti !' – 'Welden, get out or we'll chop you into quarters'.

p.269 'the flower of courtesy'] Ibid p.495

'a veritable herd'] Marchesan p.114

'I did not order'] Ibid p.114

'Machiavellian hair-splitting'] The phrase sounds better in the original German – 'Machiavellischer Spitzfindigkeit'

p.270 Dall'Ongaro's article] Marchesi p.290

p.271 Mortgaging works of art] Relevant documents in Fulin CXVI-CXXXI

p.272 'What sort of a nation'] Raccolta Andreola 4 p.100

p.273 'Spare a coin for Venice'] Mameli's poem is attached to a pamphlet collection of Fusinato's poems published in Genoa to raise money for the cause

'The beggar queen'] Quoted in La Varenne p.225

p.274 Charitable initiatives] See, for example, Raccolta Andreola 4 pp.112, 502, 5 pp.300, 531

'Venice needs three million'] Marchesi p.294

Chapter 10. The Making of Heroes

p.275 Siege of Osoppo] Details taken from Barbarich: *Memorie storiche*

p.276 Prohaska and the Barnaba family] Barnaba pp.106–8

p.277 'This response'] Barbarich p.120

'I greet you today'] Barnaba p.192

p.278 'uniforms in rags'] Jäger p.79

p.279   Torniello brigade] Ibid pp.111–15
p.280   Cavalry regiment] Ibid pp.150–2
        Arrival of Swiss] Debrunner p.53
        'magnificent attire'] Ibid pp.115–6
        British volunteers] Names in Jäger op.cit., Santalena: *Trevigiani*
p.280   Bandiera e Moro regiment] Jäger pp.209–10
        'a dish of rice'] Morandi p.375
        Marinelli's report] Tramonti: *Capellani militari* pp.67–8
p.282   Sickness among Austrian troops] Welden pp.41–2
p.283   Treporti operation] Radaelli pp.245–7
p.285   Mestre expedition] Ibid pp.247–55, Monti pp.127–33, Pepe
        pp.189–97
        'Thanks to sound discipline'] Dallolio pp.229, 234
        Renier on Bassi] Marchesan p.69
p.287   Ladies' Nursing Committee] Carrano p.78, Raccolta Andreola 5
        pp.106–8
        'Brothers, brothers !'] Dallolio p.238
        'Venice, obedient'] Imbriani: *Poerio* p.215
p.288   Poerio's poem] Poeti Minori ii. p.149
p.289   'Yes, I am at peace'] Imbriani: *Poerio* pp.327–333, Dallolio p.244
        Zucchi versus Garibaldi] Trevelyan: *Garibaldi* pp.84–5
p.290   Murder of Pellegrino Rossi] Ibid pp.86–7, Cessi: *Mito di Pio IX*
        pp.75–6
p.292   Bassi to Manin] Planat de La Faye ii p.39
p.293   Sior Antonio Rioba affair] Ginsborg p.310
        Ferdinand's abdication] Beller p.49
        Schwarzenberg] Sked: *Habsburg Empire* pp.137–141, Beller
        pp.49–50
p.297   Gondoliers sing Tasso] Cavedalis ii pp.51–2

Chapter 11. Only a Man

p.298   Dawkins to Palmerston] Planat de La Faye i. p.477
        Palmerston's reply] Ibid ii. pp.36–7
p.299   'the real fact'] Ashley p.107
p.300   Victoria to Leopold] Benson & Esher ii p.199
        'made over to Austria'] Ibid p.198
        'enraged woman of the town'] Ashley i. p.442
p.301   'Darling, if you only knew'] *Daniele Manin intimo* p.224
        Winter in Venice] Valussi p.98, Debrunner p.119, Ginsborg
        pp.307–8

p.302　'a growing resentment'] Bernardello: *Paura* p.91
　　　　Gala at La Fenice] Mangini: *Teatri* pp.195–6

p.303　Marco Antonio Canini] Details given in Bernardello: *Paura* pp.97–107

p.305　Manin to Gavazzi] Planat de La Faye ii.pp.74–5

p.307　'he appropriated'] Canini p.67

p.308　'The great citizen'] Planat de La Faye ii.pp.79–80

p.309　Tommaseo's accounts] Ciampini pp.474–5

p.310　Manin's reply to Ozanam] Planat de La Faye ii.pp.85–6

p.311　'The Costituente'] Marchesi p.366

p.313　Leopold's flight] Leopold: *Governo* pp.374–386
　　　　'I Lombardi'] Contarini, 27 January 1849

p.314　Modena's letter] Ms is in ASV Gov.Prov. Busta 388 fasc VII

p.315　'Our assembly'] Valussi p.100
　　　　'because Venice'] Marchesi p.381

p.316　Sirtori's demands] Raccolta Andreola 6 p.306
　　　　'ensure the enjoyment'] Marchesi p.377

p.317　'Citizens, my honour'] Ibid pp.377–9

p.318　'We are forced to admit'] Ginsborg p.329

p.319　Mazzini's arrival in Rome] Trevelyan: *Garibaldi* pp.98–110

p.320　Emergency adjournment] Planat de La Faye ii p.154

Chapter 12. Whatever the Cost

p.321　Aberdeen to Metternich] Stanmore Papers LXXVII p.285
　　　　'the real policy'] Abercromby quoted in Taylor: *Italian Problem* p.199

p.322　'Whatever happens'] Metternich to Aberdeen] Stanmore Papers op.cit.p.54

p.324　'memory of his defeats'] Schönhals p.316

p.325　Hess's proclamation] Raccolta Andreola 6 pp.464–7

p.326　On the parade ground] Schönhals p.324

p.327　Austrian manoeuvres] Ellesmere pp.246–53
　　　　Attack on Conche] Radaelli pp.294–8

p.328　'stout-hearted resolve'] Oskar, Freiherr von Wolf-Schneider von Arno, quoted in Regele pp.293–4

p.329　Novara] Detailed accounts in Ellesmere pp.262–74, Schonhals pp.353–65

p.330　'Let me die'] Reiset p.305
　　　　'I am no longer'] Ibid p.309

p.331　'Imagine, my dear boy'] Costanza d'Azeglio pp.341, 344
　　　　'God has guided me'] Radetzky p.94

p.332 'justice of the Austrian cause'] Stanmore Papers op.cit. p.287
       Disraeli to Metternich] Moneymen & Buckle iii pp.173, 180
       'Austrian soldiers'] Ibid p.189
       French policy after Novara] Taylor: *Italian Problem* pp.223–233
p.333 'It was noteworthy'] Schönhals: *Haynau* p.21. Radetzky, quoted
       in Schwarzenberg p.57, said of him 'Haynau is like a razor; after
       it has been used, it should be put back in its case'
p.334 Haynau's note to Manin] Planat de La Faye ii p.165
p.335 Manin to Pasini] Ibid p.167
       Tecchio to Manin] Ibid p.170
p.337 Assembly of 1 April] Ibid pp.171–3
p.338 'can scarcely open his mouth'] Fenzi p.286
p.339 Haynau at Brescia] Account based on Fiorentini and Tosoni
p.340 'Should we understand'] Cicogna quoted in Marchesi p.393
       'Venice must resist'] Carrano p.117

Chapter 13. These Dear Italian Youths

p.342 'In the Italian drama'] Moscati: *Diplomazia* pp.115–7
p.343 'Among all the tears'] Codemo: *Pagine* pp.471–2
p.344 Austrian siege preparations] Cavedalis ii pp.232, 235, 238,
       Schönhals pp.402–8, Ulloa ii pp.216, 226
       Paolucci's command] Debrunner p.181, Ulloa ii pp.150–1
p.345 Plan of attack] Schönhals p.408
       'Ready to let fall'] Planat de La Faye ii pp.224–5
p.346 Ulloa to Haynau] Ibid p.225
       Manin to Radetzky] Ibid p.227
       Radetzky to Manin] Ibid p.228
p.347 Cavedalis's withdrawal plan] Ulloa ii.p.232
       'In a few moments'] Fenzi p.301
p.348 'You cannot imagine'] Ibid pp.303–4. See also Debrunner
       pp.271–2
p.349 Giusti on the Tuscans] Horner pp.258–60, 268
       'awaiting illumination'] Leopold p.388
       'Austria's thousands'] Elizabeth Barrett Browning: *Casa Guidi
       Windows* II
p.350 French expedition] Ponteil p.204–7, Trevelyan: *Garibaldi*
       pp.110–18
p.351 Dawn raid] Radaelli pp.336–7
       Bravery of the wounded] Fulin CXLIII, Fantoni: *Dieci patrioti*
       pp.19–47

p.351   Giuseppe Finzi] Calimani p.740

p.352   'No sooner had he breathed'] Debrunner pp.132–6

p.353   Ancona agreement] Planat de La Faye ii p.261

p.354   Hungarian legion] Debrunner pp.141–3
        Brondolo raid] Marchesi p.410, Debrunner p.190, Ulloa ii p.248

p.355   'A moving spectacle'] Cavedalis ii p.261
        'most beautiful moonlight'] Debrunner p.185
        'What a scene !'] Bertuch p.70
        'Cracked heads'] Girardi pp.122–3, 131

p.356   Evacuation of Marghera] Ulloa ii p.234, Planat de La Faye ii
        p.243, Memorie istoriche p.56

p.357   Mining the viaduct] Ulloa ii p.273 Sirtori's booby trap] Ibid p.271,
        Memorie istoriche p.57

p.358   Praise for the defenders] Bianchi p.301, Cavedalis ii pp.135–9,
        Dawkins p.128, Debrunner p.214

p.359   'You young men'] Raccolta Andreola 7, pp.298, 333

p.360   'Radetzky's sabre-rattling'] Vasseur's diary, 7 June 1849 MCV
        Manin papers 'Life is in God's hands'] Planat de La Faye ii
        p.245

Chapter 14. Austria Plays for Time

p.363   'a greater set of rascals'] Dahlerup p.49
        Austrian navy reforms] Ibid pp.52–3, 119

p.364   Kissing Radetzky] Ibid p.89
        Venetian navy] Zorzi: Venezia austriaca p.236, Cavedalis ii. p.260
        Stefani affair] Ulloa ii. p.278

p.366   Bruck to Manin] Planat de La Faye ii p.246

p.367   'My impression'] Moscati: Diplomazia pp.127–9
        'To all my representations'] Dawkins pp.94, 124, 126

p.368   Transfer of Piedmontese funds] Caluci pp.388–93. C. had been
        the Provisional Government's ambassador to Milan in the spring
        of 1848

p.370   'a convenient political condition'] Planat de La Faye ii pp.366–9.
        Further details of negotiations in Cavedalis ii pp.302–7

p.372   Military commission] Ginsborg p.339

p.373   'I opposed'] Cavedalis ii p.310. See also Ginsborg pp.339–41
        Carlo Mezzacapo] The brother of Luigi Mezzacapo (see p.335)
        'They are better'] Monti p.95
        'So many virtues'] Radaelli p.384

p.374   Puttimato affair] Radaelli places this in the summer of 1849. For the sake of narrative convenience I have accepted his dating, but Document b3979 in MCV Manin papers, a letter from De Capitani about a libellous poem against him, suggests that the episode may have happened as early as December 1848

p.375   Prostitutes] Flagg ii. p.461, Stiles i. p.312, *Quarterly Review* op.cit. p.207

Food controls] Fenzi p.318, Marchesi p.445, Carrano p.275

p.376   'Venetians'] Marchesi p.430

p.377   Hospital deliberately targeted] Ulloa ii p.385

p.378   'persons in power'] Dawkins p.154. See also Ulloa ii pp.286–7, Planat de La Faye ii p.271

p.379   'mixed wonder'] Ciampini p.550. Other details from *Miscellanea veneta*, pp.140, 144, 147

p.380   Austrian cholera] Marchesi p.450

Bruck to Venetian envoys] Planat de La Faye ii pp.282–3

p.381   'infinitely agreeable'] Ibid p.295

p.382   Assembly vote] Ibid pp.299–302

'In the end'] Ibid p.305

Manin to De Tocqueville] Ibid p.307

'his red shirt'] Trevelyan: *Garibaldi* p.219

Chapter 15. 'All'ultima polenta!'

p.384   'The great majority'] Dawkins p.98

'The veil is now torn'] Ibid p.126

p.385   Manin's leadership] Ginsborg pp.334–6

Balloons] Debrunner p.264, Flagg ii p.313, Pilot: *Palloni*

p.386   Austrian bombardment] Radaelli pp.409–10, Ulloa ii pp.516–7

p.388   Resistance vote] Planat de La Faye ii p.339

p.389   Range of bomb damage] MCV Manin papers Doc 3819, Ginsborg p.351, Fulin CLI

'the people, surprised'] Ibid CL

p.390   Refugees] Valussi p.104, Pesci p.353

'ruin, destruction and death'] Details from Cattonari

p.391   'Whoever, walking here'] MCV Manin papers Doc 967, Fenzi p.318, Cavedalis p.318, Carrano p.375

p.392   Dawkins to Manin] Dawkins p.184

Sirtori's raid] Debrunner p.278

p.393   'the cannibal party'] Ibid pp.290–1

Cholera epidemics] Zorzi: *Venezia austriaca* p.46. See also Giuseppe Giusti's ghoulishly funny 'dance of death' poem *Il colera*,

written during a Tuscan outbreak of the disease in the 1830s
Cholera statistics] MCV Manin papers, Docs 783,797, Brunetti:
Opera del Comune pp.9–10

p.394   'an odd fish'] Zorzi: *Venezia austriaca* p.323

p.395   Attack on Palazzo Querini Stampalia] Pilot: *L'assalto*

p.396   Surrender debate] Planat de La Faye ii pp.358–74, Marchesi
pp.456–7, Ginsborg pp.356–7

p.397   Belvèze] Name always given as 'Paul-Henry', not 'Paul-Henri'
'What characterizes him'] Belvèze p.99

p.398   'The calm, the patience'] ibid p.107
Meeting with Manin] Ibid pp.107–9
Manin at the Frari] MCV Manin papers Doc 3819

p.399   'Pompeii'] Fulin CLIX-X
Dawkins cannon ball] Vasseur, 17 August

p.400   'You wish to fight'] Marchesi p.480
Bogus Garibaldino] Ginsborg pp.357–8, Debrunner pp.499–500,
Marchesi pp.480–1, Cavedalis ii p.490

p.402   'To be forced to yield'] Marchesi p.482

p.403   Dahlerup to Schwarzenberg] Quoted in ibid p.500
Venetian navy] Ibid pp.461–77

p.404   'In truth it seemed'] Radaelli pp. 441–2
Radetzky's proclamation] Planat de La Faye ii p.388

p.405   Suppression of the Hungarian revolution] Macartney pp.430–2,
Robertson pp.299–304
Bruck to Manin] Planat de La Faye ii p.387

p.406   Peace negotiations] Ibid pp.389–90, Schönhals p.422

p.407   Carlo Fenzi] Fenzi p.322
'Sora la tore'] Dell'Agostino p.418

p.408   Surrender document] Ginsborg p.362, Zorzi:*Venezia austriaca*
p.101, Marchesi p.487, Planat de La Faye ii pp.391–3

p.409   Guns fall silent] Cosenz p.528
Paying the troops] Ulloa ii p.350, Radaelli p.449

p.410   Surrender announcement] Planat de La Faye ii p.397

p.411   'A Venezia'] Poeti minori ii. pp.99–101

Epilogue: 'Only a Tear for Venice?'

p.412   'La ville est calme'] Belvèze p.115

p.413   'Here's our dear master'] Errera p.387
Collection for Manin] Martin ii p.243
'pangs of exile'] Planat de La Faye ii p.399

p.414   'republican trash'] Brunetti; *Opera del Comune* p.99

p.415   Radetzky's return] Dawkins p.371, Regele p.307, Marchesi p.494,
        Quarterly Review op.cit. p.226
        'I must always'] Cicogna quoted in Marchesi p.494

p.416   slaps in the face] Giuriati pp.9–12
        'Not only'] Ciampini p.575
        Seaton's warning] Ibid p.580

p.417   Tommaseo's vow] Ibid pp.581–2
        'that cry'] Michiel p.336

p.418   'Let him stay'] Ciampini p.583
        'pretentious failures'] Mack Smith p.170

p.419   'all finished'] *Manin intimo* p.242

p.420   Emilia's last illness & death] Martin ii pp.262–3

p.422   'Nobody loved me'] Gerlin p.244
        'the exile Manin'] Gambarin: *Manin in esilio* pp.172–3
        'the greatest sacrifice'] Pepe p.112

p.422   'Yours was a talent'] *Onori funebri* pp.33–5

p.425   Fate of Ippolito Caffi] See G.Avon Caffi's article in *Miscellanea
        Veneta* pp.17–41
        'Since 1849'] Ciampini p.577

p.427   Venice becomes Italian] Zorzi: *Venezia austriaca* pp.150–4

p.430   Return of Baroness Bandiera] Barbiera: *Bandiera* p.1

p.431   'a mini-republic'] Imbriani: *Fame usurpate* pp.340, 364–5

INDEX